T4-ALF-575

Money, Banking, and Monetary Policy

The Irwin Series in Economics
Consulting Editor **Lloyd G. Reynolds** *Yale University*

DOUGLAS FISHER

Department of Economics and Business
North Carolina State University

Money, Banking, and Monetary Policy

1980

RICHARD D. IRWIN, INC. Homewood, Illinois 60430
Irwin-Dorsey Limited Georgetown, Ontario L7G 4B3

ISBN 0-256-02365-4
Library of Congress Catalog Card No. 79–90544

Printed in the United States of America

1 2 3 4 5 6 7 8 9 0 MP 7 6 5 4 3 2 1 0

TO MY WIFE

Preface

The main objective of this text is that of bringing a complete and unified treatment of modern monetary economics to the undergraduate student. While the material included in the text is carefully described in a long introduction placed just before Chapter 1, there are a few points of general principle which should be stated at this stage. Most importantly, this book is not deliberately slanted in either the Monetarist or the Keynesian direction, but rather it attempts to provide a synthesis of these positions as they bear on money and financial markets and on the conduct of monetary policy. Indeed, it is my view that this controversy is overdone in both the technical and the popular literatures and that the "controversial" style of discourse seriously impedes the novice's attempt to come to grips with the important issues in these areas. I will not forbear to identify the polar positions, of course, but I hope the broad area of consensus becomes clear as the story unfolds.

I have chosen to present my material on the nature of the financial system in Parts I, III, and IV of the book, with monetary policy discussed in Part II. The traditional money and banking course—that is, a course with an interest in the problems of macroeconomic policy—could then be constructed around Chapters 1 to 13, with all of the advantages of a continuous treatment. If, on the other hand, one were more interested in financial markets themselves, Part II could be skipped and Parts I, III and IV made the basis of the course. Of course, one cannot easily serve two masters at once, and the careful reader will note that the policy themes are echoed in Parts III and IV of the book.

The user of the text will notice that there is a considerable amount of illustrative material, culled from the journals occasionally but generally taken directly from either the *Federal Reserve Bulletin* or *International Financial Statistics*. It is my belief that this abundant store of data provides a unique opportunity for the monetary and financial economist both to illustrate the nature of financial markets—domestic and international—and (when possible) to confirm or reject his theoretical propositions. In a nutshell, the "real" world for the monetary and financial economist is this sort of data (and, of course, *The Wall Street Journal*), and the teacher and student should achieve considerable gains if they explore this rich vein. Furthermore, this material is readily updated if current observations are needed, and that is the way I handle my course.

There is, at the end of each chapter, a section of references either to material which elaborates the issues in the text or to new material not covered in detail; thus the instructor desiring term paper topics may make use of these references for that purpose. There are also two sets of questions to each chapter, the first being a conventional set of essay questions (which generally raise new issues) and the second a set of true-false discussion questions for which there are not always clear-cut answers. I find the latter very useful in class, particularly if one is not too dogmatic about the answers, both in permitting a large variety of topics to be covered and in exposing the student to the kind of problems one actually encounters in monetary and financial economics (especially as they are discussed in the press).

Finally, I would like to offer my thanks to Thomas Grennes (of North Carolina State University) and Andrew Policano (of the University of Iowa) for their valuable comments on a significant part of the text. Kathy Buelin typed most of two drafts of the text and carefully constructed the tables; she was helped by Pat Banadyga and Patricia Gay. My thanks also go to my wife, Lois, who carefully edited the second draft of the manuscript.

February 1980 Douglas Fisher

Contents

Introduction

The general subject of this book is the role of money and of banks in economic activity. This is a multifaceted subject that involves the government (as a creator of money, a borrower, and a macroeconomic policy maker), the banks, financial intermediaries (such as savings and loan institutions), industrial corporations, and, of course, individuals; it also involves foreign financial markets. Much of the generality of our subject arises because we live and work in a "monetary economy"; indeed, it is hard to imagine an economy without money. Thus, practically all of our daily transactions are exchanges of money for goods and services of all sorts, and all of our quoted commodity prices are *money prices*—that is, so many dollars per unit of each commodity. The prices of much of the stock of personal wealth are quoted in money terms—for example, those of common stocks, bonds, and houses—and we receive our income in the form of money. Not only are things this way now, but they have been so for a very long time; some form of money undoubtedly was invented about the time the first large-scale exchanges of commodities occurred. And, whether or not it can be proved, it is true that since we have had economic data, we have had money, for having money around and therefore having the prices of everything quoted in terms of money makes data collection both easier and likelier.

Money as a general commodity is clearly of such considerable use that a large "industry" has developed to "produce" it. As economists we are interested in this industry; we are interested in how prices and quantities are determined in this industry; we are interested in the competitive structure of this industry; and, indeed, we are interested in the history of this industry. In addition, money can confer social benefits and costs beyond those perceived by the users (the public) or the creators (for example, the banks and the government); indeed, whether or not we have much money in our bank account, we share in the advantages (better information) and disadvantages (inflation) of living in a monetary economy. In this event we may wish to control (or at least regulate) the industry in the social interest. The most obvious control of this sort is in somehow discouraging customers from suddenly withdrawing their funds from a commercial bank when they come to doubt its solvency; on several occasions these panics (when on a broad scale) have brought a broad-based financial collapse to the American economy and adversely affected industries far removed from the banking industry proper.[1]

The foregoing is a very general statement of the material contained in Part I of this book. More specifically, we begin in Chapter 1 with a discussion of the nature of money—its uses and its economic properties—and with the definition of what we call the "price level." These basic concepts, and many variations, are presented in the context of recent American data. In Chapter 2 we begin a set of three chapters on the institutional structure of American banking; here the workings of American banks (Chapter 2) and the Federal Reserve System (Chapter 4) are described through their balance sheets and income statements. The emphasis throughout is on commercial banks as profit-maximizing institutions, on the one hand, and the Federal Reserve as a regulator and supervisor, on the other. In the course of the discussion, especially in Chapter 3 and toward the end of Chapter 4, we consider both the nature of the competitive forces in the industry (that is, we consider whether we have a monopoly problem in banking) and the regulatory climate that has arisen. We will argue that, as it turns out, many of the regulations—such as the ceiling interest rates on certain bank deposits—may be overdone and, in any event, are frequently justified on grounds that no longer seem relevant (if they ever were).

Chapter 5, at the end of Part I of the book, proposes to tie up the first four chapters by producing an analysis of what is essentially the *aggregate supply of money*. To a certain extent, indeed, it is a bridge chapter to the

[1] The most serious financial crashes in U.S. history, when the banks were forced to halt some or all of their operations because their customers turned away from them, were in 1837, 1857, 1873, 1907, and 1929–33. Generally there was also a depression following or during these monetary contractions.

macroeconomic Part II of the book—but in any event it is much less institutional in nature. Thus, in Chapter 5 we look at the supply of money as it is influenced by banks, the government, and the public, and in this context we consider several basic measures of the quantity of "base money" in the economy. This base money is explained in terms of the traditional *banking multiplier* as well as in several more general ways before the discussion turns to historical and current examples of how "money supply theory" helps to isolate the influence of money on the (American) economy.

The other side of the coin, of course, is the demand for money, and we (arbitrarily) make this the first topic in Part II of the book. The theme for Part II is to emphasize the role of money as a key variable in modern macroeconomic policy. That is, the possibility of control of the quantity of money—and thereby the control of any other variables that money may influence—has generated a good deal of professional and official interest in *monetary policy*. To appreciate this subject fully it is necessary to construct a simple macroeconomic model, however, in Chapters 6 through 9, where the model is the familiar *IS-LM* one; here we also augment the model to deal explicitly with the rate of inflation in Chapter 9.[2] With the model in hand we turn to a discussion of the problems and potential of monetary control. In the first instance, this involves a consideration of the multiple *objectives* (such as price stability or full employment) and multiple techniques (such as open market operations or changes in reserve requirements) of policy as well as a view of the links between the monetary variables and the other variables in the system. We should underscore here three aspects of the presentation in Part II: we will be compelled to integrate the discussion of monetary policy with that of fiscal policy (partly because both aim at the same objectives); we will be compelled to deal with the international aspects of monetary control (if only because the problem of inflation now seems to be a worldwide one); and we will be compelled to present considerable historical material (including some recent history) in order to explain fully how the policy has been implemented.

The discussion of the objectives and instruments of monetary policy is contained in Chapter 10; in Chapter 11, before we complete the design of American monetary policy, we take up the Phillips curve (a once-popular device that has lately proved to be unreliable) and the modern "accelerationist" and "rational expectations" hypotheses. These variations on some traditional themes are interesting in their own right, as it turns out, but they are also interesting in that they underscore a fundamental problem in the design of monetary policy: we literally do not know which

---

[2] Note that Chapter 8, which utilizes the aggregate demand–aggregate supply approach, can be omitted without serious harm to understanding the later sections of the book.

model (for example, a Keynesian or a Monetarist) or which variation of a model should be used to determine the optimal role for monetary policy. This problem, indeed, sets the stage for Chapter 12, in which it is argued that under these conditions—that is, when our knowledge of the economic system and its linkages is as imperfect as it seems to be—we may be able to conduct a policy only if we use what is known as the "targets-indicators" approach. This method, which emphasizes control mainly through the financial markets, is probably what the Federal Reserve actually uses, but, as our actual policy discussion in Chapter 12 of recent policy suggests, it is far from clear, regardless of whether one looks at their statements or their results, that the authorities use the policy correctly. Indeed, as we dissect recent policy, we will draw on the material in Chapters 5 through 11 to interpret the recent (unsuccessful) policy stance.

In Part III of the book we will take aim at American financial markets. Generally speaking, we do this because both Parts I and II are seriously incomplete in omitting this material. Initially, we will point out that the broadest definitions of money actually include the liabilities of institutions other than commercial banks. That is, the "intermediaries" such as mutual savings banks and savings and loan associations offer a liability (regular shares or deposits) that may well be increasingly competitive with the liabilities of commercial banks (i.e., with demand deposits and bank savings and time deposits). Under a broad definition of money, that is to say, the intermediaries are also "creators" of money. In addition, the existence and the growth of intermediaries may pose serious threats to our ability to conduct an effective monetary policy; that is, it is widely believed that we should attempt to control not just the liabilities of banks (plus the quantity of currency in circulation) but also those of the principal financial intermediaries. If we do not, and their liabilities are close substitutes for bank liabilities in the eyes of their customers, then any attempt to control lending (for example) by controlling only the banks, might be frustrated as customers switch to the uncontrolled intermediaries.

Another theme in Part III, again of relevance to the earlier parts of the book, concerns the development of some formal "portfolio" material. If we visualize money as one of a number of potential forms in which an individual can hold his financial wealth—with others being bonds and equities (i.e., common and preferred stocks)—then it is possible to generalize our understanding of the role of money by using this theory. The payoff comes in being able to derive more general statements about the determinants of money holding; thus, we will find that more than one interest rate is relevant to money holding and that, therefore, the problem of monetary control is considerably more complicated than one might have thought. We will also see that a distinction between long- and short-term securities (i.e., a distinction concerning the date of the maturity of bonds) helps to clear up some of the problems concerning the elusive concept of "liquidity," a property that money is often said to possess; this, too, will be seen to have direct macroeconomic policy implications. Finally, in Part III, we will flip the coin over and observe some of the effects of monetary regulations and policies on the capital markets; here we will consider bond (Chapter 15) and stock (Chapter 16) markets. This material will considerably broaden our understanding of how money affects the economy, and will generalize the discussion of the "transmission mechanism" that was first brought up in Chapters 9 and 11 of Part II.

In Part IV of the book we will turn to a rapidly changing area of monetary economics—that of "international money"—in order to generalize still further the findings of the earlier chapters of the book. The idea is to ask ourselves how our earlier conclusions might be altered if we broaden our framework to that of the *open economy*—that is, an economy that has substantial financial and commodity dealings with other nations. We will begin with fundamentals again, and so Chapter 17 discusses the determination of exchange rates between the currencies of nations and analyzes the chief device we have for measuring the financial and trade flows between the nations of the world; this device is the *balance of payments* account.

While the early part of Chapter 17 is essentially noncontroversial, this is certainly not the case for the last part of that chapter and Chapter 18. In Chapter 17 we discuss the "international payments arena" as it has evolved from the 19th-century gold standard to the present system of the controlled (or "dirty") float of exchange rates. The basic issue concerns the choice between "dirty floats," free floats, or perfectly fixed-rate regimes, and those issues serve to bring us into Chapter 18, where many of the formal results we have in these areas are discussed. Here we will see that under competitive conditions, when goods and capital are free to flow internationally, a fixed-exchange-rate standard encounters some considerable problems and that, in any event, the government of a country that attempts to control its exchange rate often has to use domestic policy tools (for example, interest-rate policy) to help in the stabilization. Finally, and by no means of least importance because it is left to the last chapter, we draw together the discussion of the "international inflation" of recent years (which we first discussed in Chapter 9) when we consider what we might call "international monetarism." This subject brings up the "world" rate of inflation and, with typical monetarist enthusiasm, the "world" money supply. Along with these rather provocative ideas we will consider the more basic "monetary approach to the balance of payments"; this latter is the latest in the Classical-Neoclassical-Monetarist tradition and has considerable value in showing how inflation can be transmitted across national boundaries.

Part I

Domestic money and banking

1

The nature and uses of money

1.1 INTRODUCTION

The logical place to begin a discussion of the role of money is by trying to define the subject carefully. This may seem unnecessary, for we all have a pretty good idea of what money is, but, as it turns out, considerable clarity can be gained by going over some of the issues. To begin with, one has a choice of approaches, even with regard to the process of definition itself. Thus, one may attach labels to real-world objects, taking what is called a nominalist approach; alternatively, one can define various characteristics (for example, the "liquidity" of money) and then search for the real-world entity that has these characteristics, taking what we often term the a priori approach.[1] In the case of the nominalist a clear procedure exists: one begins with a real-world entity (for example, currency plus the demand deposits of commercial banks), gives it a name (money), and then gets on with his work (on, for example, the supply and demand for this "money"). In the case of the a priori approach, however, one introduces a list of economic characteristics and then searches among all of the

[1] We mean here that money possesses certain properties, such as liquidity, portability, storability.

possible types of financial instruments to find those that fit best. A considerable empirical effort might well be required here, for invariably there will be more than one characteristic and more than one candidate for the honors. As we will see, there are elements of both approaches in the modern treatment of money.

The problem of the definition of money is also tied up with the problem of *aggregation,* as we shall see later in this chapter. An aggregation is a *sum,* formally, and we are here thinking of the aggregation of various types of money. We might decide, for example, that our money is the total of currency plus commercial bank deposits; this we arbitrarily call *narrow money*. When we sum two such entities as currency and deposits we automatically assume the two are alike in the eyes of money holders; this may well be correct in the sense that demanders are in the habit of holding (for example) one dollar of currency for every four dollars of demand deposits, but in some cases such an assumption may not do. The best example we have of an exception to this is the "currency panic," already referred to in the Introduction, when the public "goes off" bank deposits and tries to switch large quantities of its deposits into currency. In this event the "definition" would not be very reliable, since bank deposits no longer would be considered a close substitute for currency under panic conditions (conditions in which deposits seem very unsafe).

Aggregation problems also arise specifically in the a priori approach to the definition of money. That is, since it is impossible (in practice) to think of a product with a single characteristic and many products will have (monetary) characteristics in common, we will have to measure the relative proportion of the various characteristics which each financial asset contributes, and add these proportions together in order to get the total value of that characteristic. Furthermore, and this is a good reason for not taking an a priori approach, we usually have more than one characteristic, so that we open the door to a host of problems of aggregation, as we consider all of the possibilities that seem relevant.

We will keep all of these general issues in mind as we continue our discussion of the nature and uses of money, but we will see that a broad agreement actually does exist over some of the problems, so that we shall not end up in as muddled a state as we are in at the start. We will begin with a discussion of the characteristics, turn to a historical fable of how the use of money has developed, consider the main forms of money in a historical context and, finally, take a look at some specific aggregation problems in the context of the U.S. money supply. There will also be space for some final reflections on the important theoretical and policy issues that have arisen in the course of the discussion as well as for some material on the *price level.* We are interested in the latter because it measures the average *purchasing power* of money.

1.2 THE ROLE OF MONEY IN THE ECONOMY

1.2.1 Two approaches to defining money

The most frequently cited services performed by money are those of (1) a medium of exchange, (2) a store of value, (3) a unit of account, and (4) a measure of value. These properties are generally associated with the Classical and Neoclassical (and even Monetarist) economists—and, as we shall see, an alternative Keynesian scheme exists—but they are not thereby outmoded (although there are some problems with them). When we emphasize the function of money as a *medium of exchange,* on the one hand, we focus attention on the property that causes it to be used in most markets—its general *acceptability* as payment for commodities, for services, or for other financial entities. Thus currency, especially in small denominations, is a medium of exchange because it can be used to buy almost anything practically anywhere (at least within the borders of the country whose government issued it). Demand deposits, drawn on by check, are also widely accepted, although these days they are being replaced (as is currency) by credit cards. When we emphasize money's function as a *store of value,* on the other hand, we stress a different property: namely, its usefulness as a store of our wealth. That is, if it is easily portable, fairly or even completely indestructible, and constant in value, it will make a better store of value than otherwise. Clearly, currency or bank deposits work well here, although a person's house may be a better store of value (although it is immovable), particularly if its market value increases with inflation, while that of currency and bank deposits does not (as, indeed, it does not).

The other two Classical properties of money in our list are really properties of a "monetary economy." Thus, if all prices are quoted in money terms—in dollars per unit—then it is possible to conceive of an average of all of these prices. This average is similar in concept to the *price level* that is so much in use in modern discussions of the influence of money.[2] The average price would then be useful as a measure or *standard of value* of a unit of money; that is, one's financial position—or the purchasing power of a person's income—can be assessed against the average purchasing power of money (of, that is to say, the dollar). One can also, with some reservations, compare price averages at different points in time or at different points in space. In this sense a monetary economy has a ready standard of (average) monetary values. In addition, in a monetary economy—that is, in an economy in which all (or most) market prices are

[2] The price level we are familiar with is the Consumer Price Index. It is discussed in Section 1.6.

quoted in money terms—it is convenient, as well, to keep records of money prices (although it is not strictly necessary to do so); this activity relies on the property of money as a *unit of account*. As is true of the concept of a standard of value, the gains here are largely of a social nature in that everyone can make use of the accounting system or the standard of value whether or not he or she uses and holds money (although, to be sure, the use of money would normally be widespread in the economy if this system is to be useful). Indeed, money itself quite probably confers some general social benefits because of its wide acceptability; there are potential social costs, too.[3]

We must face, though, the problem of joint properties we mentioned earlier because there are two criteria (if we stick to the medium-of-exchange and store-of-value functions), and most potential financial commodities will not only possess both of these characteristics, but possess them in unequal degree. It may be, in certain circumstances, that a personal check is more useful for a small purchase than is a $100 bill, whereas a $1 bill is more useful than a personal check. Then, we might recall, a house may be a better store of value than a savings account although the latter is much more easily used (is more liquid). Along the same lines the $100 bill may be better as a store of value than its equivalent in $1 bills, particularly if a lot of money is being hidden away (stored). Thus, the classical a priori approach does present one with some interesting problems because of its multi-dimensionality.

An alternative a priori scheme for classifying financial assets—associated with John Maynard Keynes[4]—might well be thought of as avoiding these problems. In particular, Keynes suggested that we ask not *what* services money performs but *why* people hold it. Keynes, that is to say, suggested that people hold money for (1) transactions purposes, (2) precautionary purposes, or (3) speculative purposes. This arrangement, actually, inquires into the reasons for a *demand* for money and will be discussed in more detail in Chapter 6. Here we are interested in the characteristics that Keynesian money might have and in the possibility that a particular dollar in a holder's possession may be labelled a "transactions dollar," another a "speculative dollar," and so forth.

With regard to the *transactions motive,* we find an almost perfect overlap with the medium of exchange concept. Individuals will, at any point in time, be holding balances that they are planning to spend presently or in the near future (before they have to replenish their money balances); these

[3] As we will see in Chapters 2–4, concern about potential undesirable "externalities"—that is, effects outside the "money industry" itself, has motivated much of the extensive banking legislation in the United States. Consider, for example, the general credit collapse that might follow the collapse of part of the banking system.

[4] John Maynard Keynes, *The General Theory of Employment, Interest, and Money* (New York: Harcourt, Brace, 1936).

are their transactions balances. As well, we may either underestimate our needs for future purchases or overestimate future revenues. In such cases, if we are sensible, we will tend to keep sums of money tucked away to satisfy our *precautionary motive*. Finally, we may be speculators in a broad sense; we may have funds on hand, or wealth stored in very short-term securities, in anticipation of a fall in the price of some commodity or financial asset. The size of this stock of funds held for the *speculative motive* would then rise or fall depending on whether the assets we tend to speculate in are expected to have falling or rising prices.

This Keynesian arrangement is clearly not like the more conventional one described earlier in this section, but it, too, fails to provide any unique set of money assets to be distinguished from nonmoney assets. We can, for example, store our wealth in the form of overpayments on our family car; then, if an emergency arises, a relatively inexpensive renegotiation of our car loan will produce funds useful in the same way a savings account would be, although possibly at a somewhat greater cost. In addition, for known transactions, or, more usually, for unexpected transactions, we may well use our bank credit card rather than attempting to store liquid funds; that is, we may deliberately set our cash holding at a minimum, to "keep the pressure on" or to earn the maximum amount of interest, and deal with the overflow by using our credit cards. Finally, with regard to the speculative motive, it is arguable that cash is only incidentally piled up just before a purchase and just after a sale and that the optimizing wealth holder gets rid of this cash as quickly as he can, to earn the interest. Finally, and most discouragingly, we should note that any money *actually* held by an individual can be used for any one of the three purposes; this means that an analyst cannot generally earmark a particular item as, for example, the transactions balance unless one knows the *intention* of the money holder. This we generally cannot tell just by looking at the data.[5]

1.2.2 The development of a monetary economy: A pseudo-historical fable

Let us attempt a sketch of how money might have come into existence, in order to develop a feeling for its properties and for the important dynamic aspects of our definitional problem. We shall begin, somewhat archly, with a nonmoney—or barter—economy. For this economy, let us

[5] Economists once tried to argue that demand deposits were transactions balances and that time and savings balances were precautionary and speculative balances. This may well be the case for some of us, but many of us, particularly these days, use our savings accounts much more aggressively, so that such a division may well not work. This approach, anyway, is no longer in fashion, especially in view of the provisions adopted in November 1978, permitting banks automatically to cover checks drawn on checking accounts by using savings account balances.

assume that individuals are in possession of fixed amounts of physical commodities and that they wish to exchange these commodities because they are not satisfied, individually, with the arrangement they have inherited. There certainly can be production of goods, and there may be all manner of modern techniques; but expositional convenience suggests it is better if we think in terms of a simple society, perhaps an island economy, that is sufficiently small so that people come into frequent contact with one another. We are assuming that each individual, in some unspecified fashion, has come to possess certain amounts of consumer goods; then we can argue that each individual will be presumed to want to get the most satisfaction he can from his limited—and arbitrary—initial supplies of commodities. He will do this by going out in the market and bartering his stock of commodities for others that he prefers.

As the individual progresses in the market he comes into contact with an enormous amount of relevant information. In the absence of any agreed-upon medium of exchange, commodities will tend to be exchanged directly at what we might call relative prices—that is, the number of coconuts per grass skirt and the number of ears of corn per sea shell (ad infinitum)—and there will be a considerable number of these. Even if the trader has only one commodity to sell, he may well need to know all of the relative prices of all the other commodities in order to get the most out of his own stock of commodities. Indeed *information* on prices may well become a valuable "commodity" in its own right and may even command a price of its own—for example, in the form of lists of prices—in such a market.[6] Furthermore, if the information is accurate, it will reduce the many uncertainties that traders face in any market; indeed, any device that reduces uncertainties—if it is not too costly—will provide a real gain.

In the situation we are posing here, for the time being, there is only a private sector—that is, there is no government to impose some sort of arbitrary order on it—so the development of a monetary economy has to take place in response to expected *profits* of some sort. To begin with, it may readily occur to the natives on the island economy that one tactic that may reduce their costs of transactions is to accumulate their transactions into bigger lots. In this case, the transactions are still direct (that is, still barter), but clearly by bunching their dealings, they could reduce *transactions costs* for any period of time, so long as it does not simultaneously become more difficult to locate a (big-lot) trader. In addition, another kind of cost, *waiting costs,* will be increased, for while one is accumulating stores of consumer's goods, he is obviously unable to consume them and

[6] Below we will discuss a time in American history (just before the Civil War) when as many as 8,000 kinds of currency circulated in the United States. There were those who made their living publishing lists of the market values of these currencies, many of which were not worth their face value.

he has to incur the direct costs of storage.[7] This is important and worth emphasizing. There are, as things are laid out in our simple world so far, two kinds of costs connected with the exchange of commodities—transactions costs and waiting costs—and these two, together, make up *exchange costs*. Furthermore, an economic problem arises because waiting costs *rise* from the effort to lower transaction costs, so that there must be a trade-off between these two. That is to say, up to a point, the lumping of transactions into bigger lots can be expected to lower exchange costs by reducing transactions costs more than it will increase waiting costs. The consumers in our system can be expected to juggle the size of their transactions lots until the optimum-sized lot is obtained.

The system just described has no medium of exchange, as such. We can now complicate our system a little more by assuming that individuals begin to accumulate quantities of certain commodities that they have no intention of actually consuming themselves. In the previous case, we permitted individuals to accumulate balances of their own commodities in order to reduce exchange costs; but it is only a short step to trading their own commodities for more universally acceptable and nonperishable commodities, such as gold and silver, holding the latter, and then trading these for the items they wish to consume, *at the time* they wish to consume them. The use of certain commodities in this sense, as some kind of intermediaries in exchange, represents the introduction of *commodity money* into the economic system.

Commodity money, which has appeared in response to the need for it, at least as we have set up our simple economic system, will certainly end up reducing transactions costs (hence improving the efficiency of the market system). As well, it will probably reduce waiting costs, compared to storing one's commodities directly, if only because the average consumer is likely to hold smaller balances of the more useful, more flexible, "hard" money, than of any consumable commodity. Let us be clear on another point, in case it seems as if we have strayed onto the topic of the demand for money: if the medium of exchange (commodity money) is introduced into the barter system, it will have been because individuals have gained on net, in some way. If individuals gain, in turn, it is simply that their exchange costs, as we have defined them, have fallen. Furthermore, and this is an important point in the economic analysis of the role of money, the use of a commodity money has probably speeded up exchange for each individual. This gain in time, that is the time saved, can then be used for other purposes (leisure, work, or, for that matter, more consumption activity). A *monetized* economy is a natural extension of any economy in

[7] The main items would be space and deterioration (we neglect interest foregone, although, in principle, our island economy does have an interest-producing capital stock).

which trading is an important activity, and the historical record confirms that this is so.[8]

To continue with the pseudo-history, though, we might suppose that particular traders of great reputation begin to offer promissory notes, or issue and accept interest-paying *bills of exchange,* based on commodities or, even, based on commodity money, with the notes themselves serving as media of exchange.[9] In comparison to commodity money, the paper "money" thus introduced represents a significant improvement in the technique of exchange. The issuers of this form of money will profit in some way (possibly in connection with the interest earned on a money-lending operation) and the issue of this money will continue up to the point that profits disappear. While the issuer of this kind of money seems to be profiting on the basis of the spread in the interest earned on the two forms of financial instrument—that is, on the funds lent out and on the funds taken in—the issuer has to employ his or her own resources as well. Indeed, in the final analysis, he or she commits energy and skills, and it is the value of these in alternative uses that has to be set against the returns on the financial operations.

We have not commented at each stage on the advantages that money has brought in comparison to the barter economy, but it is appropriate to do so now. The most obvious gains accrue to the users of money: the paper money and commodity money have greater use in exchange and are much better stores of value, especially since they do not deteriorate as readily as (other) commodities. As well, and there are those who think these are especially critical roles, the use of money has dramatically loosened the information constraints in the economy. When all prices are quoted in money terms, *and the value of money is not itself subject to great fluctuation,* it is considerably easier for a trader to acquire accurate price information and to keep books. Furthermore, nontraders may take advantage of this information, so that *externalities* have developed; these externalities might be social benefits that exist above the private benefits (there also might be social *costs* on net). There is another gain, and that is that the *uncertainties* of economic trading have been reduced. That is, the

[8] J. R. Hicks, in his *Theory of Economic History* (Oxford: Oxford University Press, 1969) argues that a necessary aspect of modern development—leading to the Industrial Revolution—is effective penetration of all economic activity by the *market*. Hicks argues that this penetration is much more rapid and is generally irreversible if it occurs through the development of monetary institutions. In a word, banks preceded the Industrial Revolution and this precedence was necessary.

[9] A promissory note is a *promise* to pay a fixed sum at some future date (presumably after the funds have been earned); a bill of exchange is an *order* to pay a sum (again in the future) usually to a *third party*. The ordinary check, then is a kind of a bill (or *draft*), payable on demand rather than at some future (usually specified) date. The bill arises out of the needs of business traders, who need, in effect, to borrow before their funds come in.

information of a monetary economy is easily communicated and most likely to be more accurate than that available in a barter economy; furthermore, money itself can be transmitted more safely and easily. These are considerable advantages, and they would tend to increase as "money" spreads through the economy and, especially, as it improves in quality over time.

At this point, clouds appear on the horizon, for money also attracts the interest of the government. Indeed, among the reasons for implementing a monetary reorganization of an economy that was previously based upon barter (or commodity money), quite possibly the political may dominate. That is, in order to exercise power more effectively or to make the tax system more efficient, or both, the use of money might be promoted so that all values will have a common (*taxable*) denominator. One of the most important features of such a scheme will be the designation of what is *legal tender*—that is, what must be accepted for all debts, public or private. At an early stage, the government may well be satisfied simply to promote the development of the private money-creating industry, perhaps by selling monopolies for certain monetary services (such as controlling the official mint). Thus, a private money industry may become well established and may be able to purchase government favor by offering various important services. No doubt the chief of these services—in recent history at any rate—is the ability to help the government balance its books, either by aiding in the collection of taxes, or, these days, by absorbing in some way some of the ever-increasing deficits of modern government.

Pseudo-history continues to march on, though, and the authorities may now decide to issue a money of their own, designating it as a "legal tender"; this might be done for various reasons, and stability of the system, steadiness of tax revenues, efficiency of bond sales, and the prospect of profiting directly in some way from money creation will probably be the dominant motives. The government's money can actually exist comfortably along with that of other financial institutions, of course, but one suspects that the authorities, with the taxing system at their disposal, will quickly succumb to the temptation to drive out their competitors, either by subsidizing their own money-producing operation or by explicitly increasing the cost of production of their rivals, perhaps through an excise tax. Both the paper money and deposit money of the government's rivals could be eliminated in this way, but if the development of a modern economy was achieved with a good measure of private initiative, it is likely that a credit network, itself useful to the government, will also exist. In this event, it is also likely that bank deposits would be preserved, possibly through a fractional reserve banking system (one in which commercial banks hold reserves on deposit at some central depository), in which the government might retain the right of determining the total quantity of circulating media in the economy. This part of the fable, as it stands, follows American experience pretty closely, as we will see below and in Chapters 2 and 4.

With the tax machinery and money-creating machinery in its hands, with a modern monetized economy at its feet, and with an additional and general instruction from the populace to correct any problems (such as inflation, unemployment, or a disorderly financial sector) that might emerge, our modern government is now in a position to *interfere* directly with monetary exchanges. Thus *monetary policy*—the deliberate alteration of monetary quantities or (indirectly) prices in order to achieve (even) nonmonetary objectives—may well become another of the facts of life in our historical fable, although the inevitability of this development could be disputed. We will, without a doubt, have to say a good deal more about the uneasy and changing relations between the government, the (private) financial sector, and the public in the remainder of this book; for now, though, we have achieved our purpose and may return to actual events.

1.3 THE DEVELOPMENT OF MONEY: SOME REFLECTIONS ON A DIVERSE TOPIC AS IT APPLIES TO THE UNITED STATES

The pseudo-historical fable of the previous section was unrealistic in that a modern economy was seen to evolve out of a primitive economy without any ebb and flow. In reality modern monetary systems evolved in a very uneven manner—and with quite a rush in modern times—so that it is necessary to adjust the previous story in order to bring it into line with what really happened. It is necessary because the cycles in the evolution of the monetary economy are bound up, perhaps in a cause-and-effect relationship, with the general business cycles in the economy.

This is a book about the role of money in the United States, so it is a little inefficient to begin our story with the forms of money in ancient times. It is enough to note that in early times there were often in use forms of money that would not perform all of the functions of money well—for example shells, stones, or even cattle—and that systematic use of coined money appeared rather late in the ancient world (as near as we can presently tell) by, let us say, the 6th century B.C. In ancient Greece, by 400 B.C., record keeping and the coinage were quite sophisticated, and, certainly, the Romans understood and operated a monetary economy complete with credit and, no doubt, business cycles.[10] The immediate post-Roman period, up to the 11th century, was not one of rapid growth in the

[10] Wars and events in the Mediterranean agricultural sector seem to have been leading causes here, although, no doubt, there were also disturbances in money and credit markets going on at the same time.

Western world, and, one suspects, monetary practices quite possibly deteriorated somewhat. At any rate, by the mid-13th century, trade and commerce were extensive in Europe, with the Italians and French, particularly the former, leading the way, and modern practices can fairly be said to date from that time, although most modern forms of financial instrument (most notably the check) were unknown then.

Much of Europe was unified into nation-states by the late 15th and early 16th centuries, and with the passing of the pressing religious issues of the Reformation, merchant interests and national interests became merged into "mercantilism"—an all-embracing approach to the development of the nation-state—which emphasized gold, foreign trade, and colonies (and, later, industry) as areas to concentrate on in building a nation's wealth. It was in the early stages of this period that the English, French, and Dutch invaded the primitive North America, bringing with them what was portable from their sophisticated financial system; this, of course, contrasted sharply with the barter-and-shell economy of the American Indians. Indeed, England, by 1607, had the Royal Exchange (a general commodity and stock exchange), merchant bankers, money lenders (by this time the Italian and German merchant bankers had been driven from England), and a strong commercial fleet. From this beginning, until the American Revolution, no independent financial system grew up in the United States; thus, in 1776, the United States was part of the richest conglomerate nation in the world, with a kind of central bank (the Bank of England began operations in 1694), with possibly the world's leading capital market at its disposal (the Dutch and French markets were very large as well), and with the English navy virtually unassailable, after its victories over France in the Seven Years War (1756–63).

After the American Revolution, the monetary history of the two countries diverged considerably, although the two shared most of the business cycles in the Western world pretty equally. England continued with its central-style bank, but the Americans, until 1914, tried a central-style bank in two experiments (in the period 1791–1836), tried "free" banking (from 1836 to 1864) and, finally, tried a regulated currency with a national banking system (from 1864 to 1914); the modern central bank, the Federal Reserve, began operations in 1914. During the years from 1776 to 1914 the monetary system often seemed chaotic—there were severe crashes, with attendant bank and business failures, in 1837, 1857, 1873, 1893, 1907, (and in 1929–33)—and we had, even at the best of times, an apparently unruly system. Indeed, in the days of free banking (1836–64) a large number of banks actually issued their own currency (probably as many as 8,000 different types of bill), and these actually traded at prices that varied with respect to each other and, of course, with gold, depending on the market view of their value. This partial reversion to the complexity of a barter economy was not emulated in England; as well, the use of checks as a form of payment was considerably delayed in the United States, not really becoming generally used until after the Civil War, although they existed in the United States from the 18th century (their use in England predates even this). Yet with all of this dissimilarity, the business cycles in England and the United States have coincided to this day, although the United States has grown more rapidly, at least after 1850.

We will not further elaborate the history of American money here, since historical surveys are part of our later chapters on banking and on the role of central banking. But we should make two important generalizations now about the role of money in American development. One, perhaps the most important, is that the American economy in 1776 was part of what was no doubt the most sophisticated and probably the most stable financial system in the world (and, no doubt, the richest). It has often been said that the British Industrial Revolution, which also dates from this time, could not have occurred at anything like the pace it did without its complex and competent financial system. The same may be said of the United States; in 1776 the financial techniques were known, the capital was there, and broad European (and American) markets for American products existed; the rapid growth of a peculiarly American financial system that began then has certainly been a *necessary* part of American growth, no doubt to this day. The second generalization concerns the safety of the system, in the sense of safeguards against the failure of commercial banks. As near as one can tell, there is no solid American evidence—whatever we might think reasonable—that a safer system is *inevitably* better for growth. In particular, the period of free banking brought many bank failures, but it also brought rapid economic growth. In contrast, the period of currency control, from 1864 to 1914, featured a long depression (1873 to 1878 or even 1884, by some estimates) and, at least, a long deflation—that is, fall in the price level—from 1873 to 1896. Finally, and most alarmingly, the period of a modern central bank (from 1914) includes the most severe depression in American history (1929–35) and the most rapid non-war-related inflation (after 1971) in our modern history. Evidently, the complete dissection of the monetary beast is going to be a complicated matter, if such simple truths as "regulation and control bring stability" cannot be proved.

1.4 THE MONETARY AGGREGATES: DEFINING MONEY IN PRACTICE

To this point we have avoided putting labels on actual "monies" and have preferred to establish some broad economic and historical aspects of "moneyness." What has emerged, one hopes, is a rather broad view of financial markets, in which a reasonably steady evolution is the order of the day. Even so, we must freeze the discussion at the present time, and discuss the principles of the definition of money as it applies to the American economy. This involves a consideration of the various monetary "aggregates"—M_1, $M_1{}^+$, M_2, M_3, M_4, and M_5—as measures of (or "definitions of") the total money stock in the United States.

The five main aggregates—ignoring $M_1{}^+$ for the moment—currently kept track of by the Federal Reserve, and the prime contenders for the title of "money," are the following.

> M_1 consists of demand (that is, checking) deposits at commercial banks,[11] foreign demand balances at the Federal Reserve Banks (that is, at the 12 branches of our central bank), and currency *outside* the Treasury, Federal Reserve Banks, and vaults of the commercial banks.

This total stood at $361.5 billion at the end of December 1978 and consisted of $97.5 billion of currency and $264.0 billion of demand deposits. To put this total into perspective, consider that this amounts to $1,643 for *every* man, woman, and child in the United States (assuming a population of 220 million persons). Note further, in anticipation of some further comments, that this total has tended to grow steadily, in *per capita* terms.

A second widely used measure of the money stock is

> M_2, consisting of M_1 plus the savings deposits, time deposits open account,[12] and time certificates of deposit (CDs)—other than large (over $100,000) negotiable CDs of large banks—of American commercial banks.

The total of M_2, at the end of December 1978, was $876.3 billion; thus, deducting $361.5 for M_1, the time and savings deposits in American commercial banks were $514.8 billion; more revealing of liquid savings, though, is a third measure,

> M_3, consisting of M_2 plus the deposits of mutual savings banks, savings and loan shares, and credit union shares.

M_3, at the end of December 1978, was $1,500.9 billion, whereof savings in savings banks, S&Ls, and credit unions was $624.6 billion (making a total for short-term savings of $624.6 billion + $514.8 billion = $1,139.4 billion). More revealingly, perhaps, the total of $1,500.9 billion represents $6,822 for every man, woman, and child in the United States or, to gain another perspective, the typical (average) family of four had $27,289 in

---

[11] We exclude "domestic interbank," United States government demand deposits, and cash items in the process of collection (*float*).

[12] The savings deposit is the passbook account; a time deposit contains an explicit maturity, usually from 30 days upward. The CD, thus, is merely a time deposit with a certificate. Most time deposits, other than the very large CDs, are not exchanged in credit markets. Note that the passbook account carries the restriction that a 30-day notice of withdrawal may be required of customers, if the bank so desires. This has not been common practice, though, for a long time.

cash and readily liquid assets, a total that may surprise many readers of this book.

Finally, and somewhat parenthetically at this point, the Federal Reserve publishes two other measures of the money stock, M_4 and M_5 (not to mention M_1^+, to be discussed below). These are

M_4, consisting of M_2 plus the large negotiable CDs excluded from M_2;

M_5, consisting of M_3 plus the large negotiable CDs excluded from (M_4).

Most of the discussion of CDs will occur in Chapter 2, when we consider how banks have expanded their activities energetically in recent years, but for now it is enough to note that the CD represents an arrangement undertaken between a bank and (usually) a large corporate customer. The interest rate on these securities is negotiated and they are marketable, and so on four accounts, their size, their variable interest rate, their marketability, and their corporate character, they are unlike the items included in M_1, M_2, and M_3. Indeed, scant use is made of M_4 and M_5 in policy discussions and we will have no further discussion of them in this book.

There are two principal characteristics of these items that propel us, immediately, into the theoretical and policy issues of monetary economics: the measures of the money stock vary differently—in trend, over the business cycle, and over the seasons of the year. Thus several problems are forced upon us, if we wish to practice monetary control (that is, monetary policy). Which measures are most appropriate for monetary control (in a theoretical sense) and, accordingly, are they the ones actually employed by the Federal Reserve? On the other hand, how have these measures been affected by institutional changes in the economy, and what is the prognosis? (For example, what effect might NOW accounts have?) We will deal with the technical questions here and in Chapter 6, saving the final policy issues until Chapter 12.

Table 1.1 provides data on the five measures of the money stock over the years from 1959 through 1978. While the broad trends in all series are generally upward, a closer examination of these data provides some insight into how these aggregates vary *both* over time *and* with respect to each other. The latter becomes a policy problem almost immediately, because each of these measures has some claim to being considered the best measure of "moneyness" in the economy. To see some of the differences we get in these five measures, consider first the trends in the data. Thus, while all items have grown in every year of the sample, their rates of growth have been different overall and, worse, have varied for certain subperiods of the sample. Thus, for example, M_3 has grown 352 percent over the period, while M_1 has grown by 134 percent—average annual rates of 35.2 percent and 13.4 percent respectively (a ratio of 2.63 to 1)—while in the period 1959–68, these changes were 100 percent and 45 percent respectively—or average annual rates of 15.7 percent and 5.6 percent,

Table 1.1: Annual data for five measures of the money stock; 1959–1978 ($ billions; seasonally adjusted)

	M_1	M_2	M_3	M_4	M_5
1959	143.4	210.9	303.8	210.9	303.8
1960	144.2	217.1	319.3	217.1	319.3
1961*	148.7	228.6	342.1	231.4	344.8
1962	150.9	242.9	369.2	248.5	374.9
1963	156.5	258.9	400.3	268.5	410.0
1964	163.7	277.1	434.4	289.9	447.2
1965	171.3	301.3	471.7	317.7	488.1
1966	175.7	318.1	495.4	333.6	510.9
1967	187.3	349.9	543.9	370.5	564.5
1968	202.2	382.9	589.6	406.4	613.1
1969	208.8	392.3	607.3	403.3	618.2
1970	219.6	423.5	656.2	448.8	681.5
1971	233.8	471.7	742.8	505.0	776.1
1972	255.3	525.3	844.5	568.8	888.0
1973	270.5	571.4	919.6	634.4	982.5
1974	283.1	612.4	981.5	701.4	1,070.5
1975	294.8	664.3	1,092.9	746.5	1,175.1
1976	312.2	739.7	1,236.9	803.0	1,300.2
1977	335.4	806.5	1,374.0	881.2	1,448.8
1978	361.5	876.3	1,500.9	973.0	1,597.5

* Note that the large CDs appear in the data first in 1961.
Source: Board of Governors of the Federal Reserve System and *Federal Reserve Bulletin*.

respectively (a ratio of 2.80 to 1). To see a cyclical difference, compare the pattern for M_1 and M_3 over the troubled years between 1971 and 1975, a time when rapidly increasing inflation was followed by a recession and, eventually, a decrease in the rate of inflation. Figure 1.1 illustrates the behavior of M_1 and M_3, as drawn from Table 1.1. There one can clearly see that M_1 and M_3 both had peaks in their growth in 1972, although M_3 was up only a little, while M_1 increased much more rapidly. More seriously, M_3 showed a large increase in its rate of growth in 1975, while the rate of growth of M_1 continued downward. Seasonal factors also produce different effects on M_1 and M_3.[13]

The main problem the foregoing presents is one of knowing just how to interpret an actual change in a monetary aggregate. If a trend effect, cyclical effect, or seasonal effect is different from those observed before—and those mentioned here were—then a given change may be of

[13] The data that the Federal Reserve uses are available in seasonally adjusted and unadjusted form. The seasonal adjustment factor in the monetary data changes from year to year and, in any event, depends on such things as federal government expenditure/receipt patterns. The changes are not small and depend on past policy decisions, the effect of which is not always possible to estimate. See Wallace H. Duncan, "Seasonally Adjusted Numbers: Are They Any Good?" *Voice, Federal Reserve Bank of Dallas* (August 1978).

Figure 1.1: Percent changes in M_1 and M_3, 1971–1975

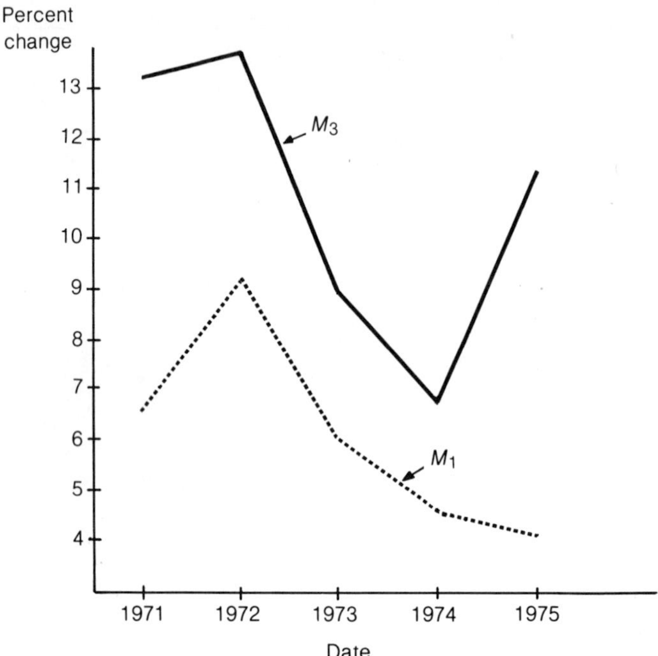

policy concern or it may not. Consider, for example, the behavior of M_1, M_2, and M_3 in 1978, as described in Table 1.2. Here we list their rates of change (at annual rates). What is noticeable there is the startling increase in M_1 in April, matched by *some* expansion in M_2 and M_3 (coming mainly from the fact that M_1 is contained in M_2 and M_3). This was unprecedented and largely ignored by the Federal Reserve, apparently on the grounds that it represented a recovery in the demand for money from the harsh winter.[14] To see a different sort of effect, note that the total of M_1 remained almost constant for the last three months of the year while M_2 and especially M_3 rose. How much of the relative constancy of M_1 was due to the *announced* policy of tight money and how much to the institutional changes in the American money market in June and November, is anybody's guess at this stage.[15] But to have a sensible policy we have to know which it is and, it is clear, we are far from that objective.

[14] The rate of growth of M_1 in May was 7.2 percent; this was down from the total in April, to be sure, but was *above* the announced long term target rate of growth of M_1, which was 6.5 percent. We will return to this aspect of the problem in Chapter 12.

[15] In June 1978, financial institutions began offering CDs that were tied to the Treasury bill rate; by the end of the year savings banks had over $60 billion of these outstanding. On

Table 1.2: Percent changes in the money stock in the United States in 1978 (annual rates)

	M_1	M_2	M_3	M_1^+
January	10.3	9.5	9.1	—
February	−.7	4.7	5.7	—
March	3.5	5.6	6.5	—
April	19.0	11.5	9.8	—
May	7.2	7.1	7.2	—
June	7.5	7.8	8.4	—
July	4.8	8.0	9.3	1.5
August	8.5	10.4	11.8	7.2
September	14.1	12.5	13.9	12.1
October	1.7	6.5	8.9	.8
November	−2.0	4.7	6.7	−4.9
December	1.7	2.7	5.6	−1.4

Source: *Federal Reserve Bulletin*. The data are seasonally adjusted.

In Table 1.2 there is also included a fourth column for M_1^+, yet another measure of the money stock. M_1^+ is an expanded version of narrow money (M_1), which the Federal Reserve feels is somewhat more representative of the total quantity of the "medium of exchange" in the American economy:[16]

> M_1^+: M_1 plus savings deposits at commercial banks, NOW accounts at banks and thrift institutions, credit union share draft accounts, and demand deposits at mutual savings banks.

The total of M_1^+ was $586.7 billion in December 1978, and this compares with $361.5 billion for M_1 and $876.3 billion for M_2, at the same time. The idea behind this new measure is to include along with narrow money the potentially more mobile "interest-bearing checking accounts" (NOW accounts) of commercial banks and the intermediaries and to account for the recent (as of November 1, 1978) ability of banks to offer automatic conversion from passbook accounts (*savings* as opposed to *time* deposits) to checking accounts.[17] Indeed, it has been argued that M_1^+ will, after Americans adjust to it, be a much more representative measure of the stock of

---

November 1, commercial banks were able to offer a new service to their customers—this was the ability to use the checking account solely as a conduit between payments and their savings accounts, in effect permitting the payment of interest on what were formerly demand deposits. Banks, in general, imposed charges on their customers when they took this option. Of course, what this does, as its use gradually expands, is reduce M_1 compared to M_2 and M_3. See Chapters 6 and 12 for a further discussion of the issues involved.

[16] "A Proposal for Redefining the Monetary Aggregates," *Federal Reserve Bulletin* (January 1979).

[17] NOW (Negotiable Order of Withdrawal) accounts are directly checkable savings accounts; their use is spreading rapidly, and federal legislation pending in early 1980 undoubtedly will extend NOW accounts across the country.

"immediate purchasing power" in the economy and, as such, will be widely employed in the execution of monetary policy. Whether this is to be the case remains to be seen, of course, but we could note, with reference to Table 1.2, that M_1^+ shows a sharper response to the tight money policy of November–December 1978 than does any of the other measures. We will return to some of these issues in Chapter 12, but for now we should note that this policy seems not to have been as tight as the M_1^+ figures suggest.

1.5 THEORETICAL ISSUES IN THE DEFINITION OF MONEY, ONCE AGAIN

We have had both Keynesian and Neoclassical definitions of money and it is instructive, now that we have passed through the data once, to see which measures fit into these schemes most readily. Beginning with the medium of exchange function, we note that only M_1—currency and demand deposits—and NOW accounts presently can be directly exchanged, at least by means of checks. Then if we insist on this characteristic, and ignore the automatic transfers from savings to checking accounts now possible, we need look no further for our definition of money. But even the modern Neoclassical economists—the Monetarists—do not leave it at this. Thus, if M_1 is an "abode of purchasing power," perhaps one can say that savings and time deposits are *temporary* abodes of purchasing power as Milton Friedman has argued.[18] Therefore, while one normally can spend only M_1, if he can and does easily shift back and forth between M_1 and M_2 (and even M_3) in practice, the two are almost perfect substitutes with respect to the medium of exchange function of money, and on that account these two ought to be lumped together. Apparently the government also sees things this way, since its policy is clearly to facilitate this transfer further.

All financial assets are stores of value, but there is one fundamental distinction between M_1 (or currency) and the other measures of the money stock and that is that the items in M_1 itself do not pay interest, while the additional items that make up the other measures all do. This raises several questions, the most important of which is: what is it that M_1 does that causes people to hold it when an interest-paying alternative is available? The answer, if you are a Neoclassicist, is that it is useful in exchanges and stores value in a more flexible way and, if you are a Keynesian, is that it is held for transactions, precautionary, and/or speculative purposes. To a certain extent, though—especially in a perfectly competi-

[18] Milton Friedman, "Post-War Trends in Monetary Theory and Policy," *National Banking Review* (September 1964).

tive market—we can take the interest payment foregone by holding M_1 as a measure of the intrinsic services provided by M_1.[19] Even so, while the interest rate paid on close alternatives to non-interest-paying assets may well be a good measure of the market value of the "characteristics" of these assets, it is still not clear that we should call these assets "money." Mainly it is the ease of transfer from M_1 to M_2 and the fact that all financial assets seem useful as *stores of value* that cause the problems here.

A problem recognized is sometimes a problem solved, and we may approach the store-of-value property that financial assets have in common by trying to distinguish between assets on the basis of their *liquidity,* with the most liquid being money and the least liquid being nonmoney. If such an idea is to have any merit, though, we must be able to draw a distinct line between a liquid and a nonliquid asset; clearly, to do this, liquidity itself must be defined, and, as it turns out, there are three candidates for this elusive concept. The one most widely used is the "ready availability of the asset at a *well-defined* market price." If a single price exists, the price would be well-defined; but for most items there is a spread between "bid and ask" prices. Thus we might test for liquidity by looking at the differences between the "asking" and "bidding" prices for assets; in this case M_1 is perfectly liquid—since you can always get a dollar bill for a dollar check (although you have to write a check for it)—while M_2, with savings and time deposits in it, is less so, since an interest penalty is generally paid for early withdrawal of these deposits. Indeed, the gap between bid and ask prices seems to widen as one goes on to consider the non-negotiable CDs, which are also in M_2. For large negotiable CDs, which enter in M_4 and M_5, the ready market is perhaps not always there for certificates of such a size ($100,000) so a gap may well exist here, although its size, relative to that of the small nonnegotiable CD, is not clearly larger.

A second scheme for measuring liquidity, suggested by the problem just raised of selling a large CD is the "ability to sell an asset on demand . . . for a nominal sum fixed in advance." All of the items in M_1 to M_5 seem to meet this criterion—since you can bail out of any of them when *you* want to (that is the meaning of "on demand") and one generally knows the penalty costs in advance, but there are actually two separate characteristics in this definition that may differ from time to time and from asset to asset.[20] On the whole, though, M_1 seems more "liquid" than, say,

---

[19] Some attempt has been made to identify the "implicit" rate of return on deposits (we cannot do this for currency). For a summary see Michael A. Klein, "The Implicit Deposit Rate Concept: Issues and Applications," *Economic Review, Federal Reserve Bank of Richmond* (September/October 1978).

[20] The two are "on demand" and "nominal sum fixed in advance." The nominal sum is the interest penalty in the case of the items discussed here, and it may well be larger for a savings deposit (M_2) than a savings and loan deposit (M_3).

M_5, although the difference might not be so large as to matter for some purposes.[21]

Basically, economists settle issues of the degree of similarity between "commodities" by measuring the substitutability that demanders of the products have given them. That is, if, in practice, the public sees M_1 and time and savings deposits as perfect substitutes for all possible uses to which they might put them, then they *are* the same thing for all practical purposes, and we look to M_2 as our measure of money, disregarding all the apparent differences we have noted. But there is bad news here, for recent studies have indicated that so far as we are able to *prove*—that is, as a result of careful empirical estimation of the degree of substitution between financial assets—we cannot even claim that currency and demand deposits (that is, the components of narrow money) are close enough substitutes at all times to be considered a single product. And the problem gets worse as you broaden the measure to M_2, M_3, M_4, and M_5.[22] We also have found out, incidentally, that different types of customers use their funds differently: for example, individuals put their temporarily accumulated funds into time or savings deposits, while business firms (especially the large ones) put them into Treasury bills (although recently, individuals have shown more interest in Treasury bills). These results, while provisional, certainly imply that the supply and demand for several "monies" may have to be analyzed simultaneously, even in tranquil times.

One final approach—the Monetarist—has been proposed that attempts to cut the knot rather than to untie it. Consider the following two quotations from a book by Milton Friedman and Anna J. Schwartz:

> Strictly speaking, the "best" way to define money depends on the conclusions that we reach about how various monetary assets are related to one another and to other economic variables; yet we need to define "money" to proceed with our research. The solution, also common in scientific work, is successive approximations.
>
> The selection is to be regarded as an empirical hypothesis asserting that a particular definition will be most convenient for a particular purpose because the magnitude based on that definition bears a more consistent and regular relation to other variables relevant for this purpose than do alternative magnitudes of the same general class.[23]

[21] A third measure of liquidity often used is the "term to maturity" of the asset. Thus cash "matures" instantly, while many Treasury bills have a life of 90 days, maturing 90 days after they are issued. Some securities mature in over 30 years. By this measure longer maturities, for which you must wait a long time, are less liquid. We will return to problems of the term to maturity in Chapter 15.

[22] See the discussion in Douglas Fisher, *Monetary Theory and the Demand for Money* (New York: Wiley, 1978).

[23] Milton Friedman and Anna J. Schwartz, *Monetary Statistics of the United States* (New York: National Bureau of Economic Research, 1970), p. 91.

This approach, which imparts much of the flavor of Monetarism, can be paraphrased as follows. We seek *no* theoretical definition of money; instead, if our policy problem is the control of the level of national income, then, if a particular measure is related closely to national income over time, it is that measure in which we are interested. By "successive approximations" we compare M_1 to the successively broader M_2, M_3, M_4, and M_5. If, say, M_3 is closely and stably related to national income (one of the final variables we might be interested in) then it is M_3 that we "define"—pragmatically—to be money. Of course, if M_3 is closely related to income *and,* in turn, we can also control M_3 somehow, then the complete policy design is clear. Of course, what we are saying is that there is no separate issue of the definition of money in this Monetarist case; we set up our "control of the economy" problem and work with whatever variable works best. If it is M_1 one time and M_3 another we do not care, so long as we can recognize it, and so long as our policy seems to work. Naturally, whether or not such a simplistic approach works better than one based on, say, a more close adherence to one or another of the "characteristics" approaches is the real issue. We will have considerably more to say about these policy issues in succeeding chapters, although we will not return to the definition of money again.

1.6 POSTSCRIPT: THE PRICE LEVEL

In the previous sections of this chapter we have discussed the definitions of the quantity of an economic good—money—but we have not discussed its price. Economists are interested in both quantity and price, so we will, in this final section, consider the sense in which the *price level* may serve as the price of money. Recall, to begin with, our concern with the "standard of value" in a monetary economy in Section 1.2. There we noted that when we have a monetary economy, and all prices are quoted in money terms, it may be useful to calculate an *average* value of all money prices; this, indeed, is our price level.

Immediately, though, we run into a problem, because the commodity we are most interested in (money) will not have a price of its own in this sense. That is, the rate of exchange between money and itself—or, for example, between currency and time deposits—is always fixed, so long as the money prices of the items in the definition of money are also fixed.[24] The natural thing to do under these conditions is to find some commodity that is widely exchanged for money and to use it as the basis of estimating

[24] Note that if we include *marketable* securities, such as United States Treasury bills, in our definition of money, then our money total will vary with the market price of Treasury bills. This would be a disadvantage to having too broad a definition of money unless, of course, Treasury bills are in fact perfect substitutes for the other items in the measure of money, as discussed earlier in this chapter.

the market value of money. Indeed, since money is exchanged in all markets, it is natural to use the average of the money prices of *all* the commodities that can be exchanged for money as the basis of this calculation. This, then, is the rationale for using the price level in order to determine "what the dollar is worth," especially for making comparisons at different points in time or space.

What we have said amounts to the view that if we calculate an average of all money prices, this average will represent the "purchasing power of money." The most obvious average is a *weighted* average of all of the individual prices; Equation (1.1) represents this idea:

$$\bar{P} = W_1P_1 + W_2P_2 + \cdots + W_nP_n = \sum_{i=1}^{n} W_iP_i. \tag{1.1}$$

Here the weights reflect the percentage of total funds spent on each commodity (so they sum to unity: $\sum_{i=1}^{n} W_i = 1$) and the P's are the individual money prices; notice, especially, the summation notation, which will be used at several points in this book, and is explained in Chapter 6 more completely.[25]

This type of weighted average clearly includes the information required for a "price of money." Thus, we could compare the average price level for 1978 ($\bar{P}_{1978}$) with that of 1979($\bar{P}_{1979}$), *assuming fixed weights* over that period. Table 1.3 contains some sample data for such a comparison. To calculate the index for January 1, 1978, we merely apply Equation (1.1); the result is that $\bar{P}_{1978} = \$1.80$. When the same thing is done for January 1, 1979, the result is $\bar{P}_{1979} = \$1.85$. We may, then, compare these two prices by calculating $P_I = \bar{P}_{1979}/\bar{P}_{1978} = 1.028$.[26] This tells us that in a year, the average price of the four commodities rose 2.8 percent. P_I, indeed, is an important concept in monetary analysis; it is a price index (i.e., it is, formally, an index number) of the type that is so widely employed in the discussion of inflation. Indeed, 2.8 percent is the rate of inflation in this example.

We will take a look at some actual price index data in a moment, but let us, first, tackle some problems. First, let us emphasize that it is not $\bar{P}$ (or

[25] See Footnote 7 in Chapter 6.

[26] Formally,

$$P_I = \frac{\sum_{i=1}^{n} W_iP_{2i}}{\sum_{i=1}^{n} W_iP_{1i}}$$

represents the index number, where the sum is taken over the four commodities, and the W_i represent the unchanged weights. The actual index calculated by the government uses *quantities* as weights. For a discussion of the problems inherent in the price indexes used in the United States, see William H. Wallace and William E. Cullison, *Measuring Price Changes,* 3d ed. (Richmond, Va.: Federal Reserve Bank of Richmond, 1976).

P_I) that is the value of money, but $1/\bar{P}$, the inverse of the price level. That is, we wish to know how much a dollar will purchase of some standard commodity (like that defined in Table 1.3). If $\bar{P}$ falls, then the dollar will increase in value; that is, when the price level declines, money is worth

Table 1.3: The calculation of a price index (fixed weights)

	Money price		
Item	*January 1, 1978*	*January 1, 1979*	*Weight**
Apples	$3.00	$3.10	.25
Pears	2.50	2.70	.30
Plums	.50	.55	.15
Cherries	.75	.60	.30

* Note that a "units" problem is avoided by using weights that sum to unity. That is, if apples and pears were calculated in bushels, and plums and cherries in pounds and ounces, we may not wish to form a *direct* index, even of money prices, since a change in units would appear to change prices, on average.

more (will buy more). Second, we should underscore the fact that we made our calculations from Table 1.3 on the basis of *fixed* percentage weights. This actually sidesteps an important problem that arises because in normal circumstances the weights will not remain fixed over time. Indeed, when you stop to think about it, any price change will produce changes in consumer expenditures, which will change both quantities purchased and weights. Thus, in the example of Table 1.3, we assumed that even when apples rose in price and cherries fell in price our consumer did not shift the percentage of his funds in these two (or any other) items. This seems unreasonable and could, for example, lead to an overestimate of the rate of inflation when the price of a single important product rises significantly.

Finally, we should note a related and even more important point: while a rise in a single price will, other things unchanged, cause a rise in the price level, only in the case when other things *are actually unchanged* (in this case the most important other things are the weights) can we be certain that a single price rise will have this effect in practice. This is important in the analysis of "single cause" theories of inflation: since a rise in the price of oil is likely to bring about substantial changes in both the weights and prices of any general index, we cannot argue directly from the event (a rise in the price of oil) to the price level, although there may well be *some* effect (see Chapter 9). The reason we cannot is that the weights will change away from oil and oil-intensive products and, no doubt, some other prices may well fall or, at least, rise less rapidly than the general average.[27] It seems, indeed, that the public has an exaggerated idea of the potential of single-cause theories of inflation and, further, it seems that the fundamental misunderstanding relates to the calculation of the price index. So this is an especially important issue.

It is, finally, instructive to look at the behavior of various price indexes for the United States in recent years. Thus, Table 1.4 contains index

Table 1.4: Price indexes for the United States (annual averages, 1965–1977; 1967 = 100)

	Consumer	*Wholesale*	*Producer**
1965	94.5	96.6	—
1966	97.2	99.8	—
1967	100.0	100.0	—
1968	104.2	102.5	—
1969	109.8	106.5	—
1970	116.3	110.4	—
1971	121.2	113.9	—
1972	125.3	119.8	—
1973	133.1	134.7	—
1974	147.7	160.1	—
1975	161.2	174.9	—
1976	170.5	183.0	170.3
1977	181.6	194.2	180.6
1978	195.4	209.0	194.6

* Since November 1978 a new index has appeared, for producer prices, in place of the wholesale index. It is for producer *finished* goods rather than for producer prices for *all* commodities.

Source: *Federal Reserve Bulletin*.

numbers for consumer and wholesale prices since 1965; the base year is 1967 (that is, 1967 = 100) and the weights are quantities (numbers of cars, etc.). Here we can see that the period of most rapid inflation in consumer (retail) prices and wholesale prices was from 1973 to 1975 (when the former rose by 21 percent and the latter by 30 percent). It is, *a propos* of the comments just made about the potential disruption to indexes caused by uneven price changes, appropriate to note several subsector price changes. First of all we note a difference between consumer and wholesale prices, arising in the 1974 data, that has persisted, once it got established, as the period wore on (implying that wholesale price rises do not necessarily get passed on). Then, for another example, from 1967 to 1975, food prices rose 75 percent and total housing prices rose 66.8 percent (both

[27] You probably will have observed that during the "great inflation" of the early 1970s, most prices did rise with oil prices. We shall see in Chapter 9 that this can be explained satisfactorily in several other ways without reference to the overly simple view that "a price rise in an important industry" will lead to a general price rise directly. We will refer to some empirical work on this problem in that chapter, as well.

above the average of all consumer prices of 61.2 percent in Table 1.4), while apparel (42.3 percent), transportation (50.6 percent), health and recreation (53 percent),[28] and other goods and services (47.4 percent) all increased more slowly than the general rate. These changes, certainly, must have brought major changes in the composition of individual budgets that should turn up in the aggregate weights of the price index for the economy as a whole, however these weights are calculated. Thus, while the price of money fell (that is, its purchasing power fell), it certainly did not fall the same for everyone. Our "standard of value" is evidently only an approximate one.

1.7 STUDY QUESTIONS

Essay questions

1. Historians tell us that such things as cows and even large rocks have served as money in the past. Is it conceivable that such could again be the case? What functions of money are not well served by these items? Does it make any difference to your answer if average prices are rising very rapidly?

2. We have pointed out that a fall in the price of money causes the real quantity of money to fall. Why is this so? Is this fact of any economic importance? That is, is the economic system any worse off for the loss of the quantity of money caused by a rise of prices?

3. Why can we unashamedly assert that an individual is poorer when the price level rises? Does this simple truth extend to the aggregate of individuals? Do we have to know how the gains and losses are distributed before we conclude that a change in the price level is undesirable?

True-false discussion questions

These statements are meant to be somewhat ambiguous, and to provoke discussion thereby.

1. If it took no time to clear markets (that is, if they cleared instantly), then money could serve no useful (economic) purpose.

2. The *fiat* money (currency) issued by the government does facilitate exchange, although it is worthless in the sense of not having solid backing. This implies that it is not very useful as a store of value for private wealth holders.

---

[28] The medical care component of this average actually rose by 68.6 percent, which is faster than the average rate of inflation.

3. The problem of the definition of money is essentially a practical one in that whatever is most closely related to the price level is probably "money" for all practical purposes.

4. When we "define" money to be M_3 compared to M_1, we do so on store-of-value grounds as well as medium-of-exchange grounds, since M_3 contains items that are not direct media of exchange.

5. The new measure of money (M_1^+) has recently (1978–79) shown a decrease relative to M_1 even though it contains the same interest-bearing accounts to which money holders are redirecting their funds. This suggests that money was extremely "tight" during that period.

6. It is impossible for *both* the price level and the interest rate to serve as the price of money at the same time; these are *alternatives.*

7. People do not hold money primarily as a store of value these days because its value is deteriorating at the rate of inflation in the economy.

8. We could expect M_3 to behave differently from M_1 over the year because the size of M_3 balances reflects the efforts of individuals to balance their consumption over the year, while M_1 does not (to the same extent).

9. When an individual price in an important industry rises (for example, automobiles), then the overall price index rises *and* the pace of inflation accelerates.

10. The interest rate is the price of money when money is thought of as a capital good, while the price level is its price if it is thought of as a consumer good.

1.8 FURTHER READING

Articles in the *Economic Review, Federal Reserve Bank of Richmond* (November/December 1977) on the definition of money.

Brunner, Karl, and Allan H. Meltzer. "The Uses of Money: Money in the Theory of an Exchange Economy," *American Economic Review* (December 1971).

Fisher, Douglas. *Monetary Theory and the Demand for Money.* New York: John Wiley & Sons, 1978, Chapter 1.

Friedman, Milton, and Anna J. Schwartz. *Monetary Statistics of the United States.* New York: Columbia University Press, 1970, pp. 89–146.

Gambs, Carl M. "Money—A Changing Concept in a Changing World." *Monthly Review, Federal Reserve Bank of Kansas City* (January 1977).

Wallace, William H., and William E. Cullison. *Measuring Price Changes.* Richmond, Va.: Federal Reserve Bank of Richmond, 1976.

Yeager, Leland B. "Essential Properties of the Medium of Exchange." *Kyklos,* vol. 7., no. 1 (1968).

2

The commercial bank

2.1 INTRODUCTION

The modern American commercial bank is a complex organization whose functions range from the servicing of individual customers' deposit accounts to the high-speed transmission of large sums of money on behalf of large firms and even governments (including, of course, foreign governments). Banks, as it turns out, are in many ways the centerpieces of our monetary system, and much depends, ultimately, on having a coherent and correct theory of banking at the core of one's financial analysis. In that spirit, we will use this chapter to describe the detailed operations of commercial banks in terms of their income statements and their balance sheets with a view toward revealing both the nature of, and the trends in, their business operations. This, then, is an individual-bank-oriented discussion; in Chapter 3, in turn, we will look at how banking markets actually operate—at the competitive structure of banking markets—in order to complete the characterization of banking institutions. In this chapter we will look at banks especially as profit-maximizing firms engaged in the business of banking, rather than as some kind of quasi-public service institutions whose everyday operations should be regulated in the public interest. The latter view will appear toward the end of Chapter 2, although many of the matters of general concern will be taken up in Chapter 3; the ones appearing in this chapter concern the restrictions on interest rates in the banking sector.

We begin Chapter 2 with a historical sketch of American banking, from about 1776. The reason we do this is a simple one: modern American banks grew, or rather evolved, from fairly simple activities involved in purely commercial operations and short-term lending to become the giant financial conglomerates we now know. The story of this evolution tells us quite a lot about our present system and its peculiarities and, perhaps of greater importance, it helps us in projecting future developments. We should keep both of these objectives in mind as we unravel the historical thread.

2.2 AMERICAN COMMERCIAL BANKING FROM THE REVOLUTION TO THE FIRST WORLD WAR

The principal characteristic that stands out with reference to the American banking system from 1776 to 1914 is the absence of a central bank in the modern sense of the term. That the country evolved from a rich and populous, but technically backward, colony to a "super power" in those 138 years, without the guidance of a central bank is not remarkable when you consider the vast resources, both physical and human, upon which it was able to draw. Furthermore, as we can argue, the same resources could be said to have as much to do with the rapid development of the United States *after* the advent of the Federal Reserve System (after 1914, that is to say). What is also remarkable about the history of American growth is that the commercial banking system grew in a very dispersed way, with variations in practices and regulations between communities so considerable as to defy any simple statistical description. Again we note that the disparity among regions continues into modern times; for example, some states will insist that banks have no branches, while others permit statewide branching. And again we could argue that the diversity may well have had no obvious effect on the American growth rate, positive or negative.

What we can say, though, and it is the theme of this section, is that, centrally directed or not and overly diverse or not, it was a *necessary* condition for rapid American growth that the commercial banking system grow in quantity and quality as rapidly as it did. Indeed, the parallel growth of both the economy and the banking system continued through thick and thin, and it is this more humble story, rather than the high drama of the many disorders in the financial system, that one should mark down as important to the development of the American economy in modern times. The high drama—the crashes and booms and the political battles over the control and manner of operation of the system—is not irrelevant however, for at least in part the behavior of the system under extreme pressure may well illustrate the degree of flexibility it possesses. We will have many illustrations of these points, as we proceed.

2.2.1 The first banks, 1780–1836

The first American bank after the Revolution was the Pennsylvania Bank, which opened its office in Philadelphia in July 1780. At that time the United States was in a difficult situation financially, and the bank was primarily designed to aid in the financing of the war effort.[1] The Pennsylvania Bank did not survive for long, although it was chartered in two other states (New York and Massachusetts); while it was probably the first bank, the first bank in the modern sense was the Bank of North America, which began its operations in 1782, after the British surrender at Yorktown; this bank issued "notes"—that is, currency—and dealt primarily in government obligations and short-term (maximum of 45 days) private securities. The federally chartered Bank of North America was located in the nation's capital (Philadelphia) and, as such, inspired competition in New York (The Bank of New York, 1784), Boston (The Massachusetts Bank, 1784), and Baltimore (The Bank of Maryland, 1790). Their names suggest their origin (they were state-chartered banks); as well, some of their capital came from the same state governments. Whatever the form, though, the United States quickly obtained banking in its four main commercial centers, although the various governmental units were, probably, the chief beneficiaries of these early efforts in the sense that their fiscal efforts were eased by having explicit connections with the financial community.

By 1800 there were 29 commercial banks in the United States; these banks were mostly involved in foreign and domestic commerce, with the financing of the federal government's debt having been taken over by the (first) Bank of the United States (1791–1811), an institution that was federally chartered and that performed some of the functions of a central bank.[2] Growth of these first banks continued steadily and fairly evenly

[1] We will note, in the pages that follow and in our survey of the development of central banking, that wars seem to have had a remarkably positive effect on American "financial ingenuity." Other countries have had the same experience, going back at least to the Middle Ages.

[2] The First Bank of the United States (called the Bank of the United States, formally) was created by Congress mainly in response to the fiscal needs of the government. It was inspired by Alexander Hamilton. The bank was authorized to have a capitalization of $10 million (the next largest bank was the Bank of Pennsylvania, capitalized at $3 million), of which the public took $8 million; it had eight branches. It was a highly visible bank, being the largest corporation in the country, and was thought to be overly representative of Eastern and, even, European moneyed interests; its original charter of 20 years failed to receive Senate renewal (by one vote), and agricultural interests (and banks in other cities) were instrumental in its demise. The various branches and the head office became commercial banks with state charters, in general, after the dissolution. We will refer again to its role as a central bank in Chapter 4.

(there were no general panics in the period) with a period of especially rapid growth in numbers following the demise, in 1811, of the First Bank of the United States and following the War of 1812.[3] Thus, by 1820 the United States had some 200 commercial banks of about as wide a commercial application as one could imagine, with the broad categories being "money banks" (founded on merchant capital), "agrarian banks" (often government sponsored), and a large variety of other banks, some of them founded on unusual principles.[4] These banks lent money for fairly short terms, held deposits (although checking was not common), and issued notes (currency) of their own. The notes were not always seen as money by the public, but often were considered as liabilities of the banks that issued them; this feature, coupled with an often casual system of inspection, frequent territorial wars between banks, and fairly low holdings of gold and silver reserves, made the system especially vulnerable to individual failure and to crises of a more general sort. Indeed, our first big financial panic came in 1814 (when the British burned Washington) and the second in 1818, when the postwar boom (and inflation) came to an abrupt end.

From 1816 until 1836 the United States again had a federally chartered bank (The Second Bank of the United States); the banking industry, still buttressed by the note-issuing privilege, expanded rapidly during this period, reaching both west- and southward and developing greater size and number in the traditional centers. There was a minor financial crisis in 1825, but the greatest financial troubles of the period begin with the famous Bank War of the 1830s. We will discuss this event, which involved a gigantic power struggle between President Andrew Jackson and the largest corporation of any sort in the United States (the Second Bank of the United States), in Chapter 4, but a fact of considerable interest here is that when the Bank War was over and the Second Bank was no more, commercial banks once again handled the finances of the federal and state governments. In addition, and possibly of more significance, variety, which had certainly never been absent from the American banking scene, returned with a vengeance (until the Civil War, at least) as the United States entered an era of "free banking."

2.2.2 Banking from the panic of 1837 to the National Banking System

In 1833, just before the Bank War, there were around 400 commercial banks in the United States; in 1836, only three years later, there were 600, a 50 percent increase; furthermore, bank liabilities (notes and deposits)

[3] The bank charter was not renewed by Congress, and the bank branches became private banks (in general) with state charters.

[4] For example, the Manhattan Company—later to become the Chase Manhattan Bank—was founded in 1799 to fund a waterworks. On the whole, politics and banking were much more closely related then than is the custom today in the United States.

grew at about the same rate. Some of this growth was due no doubt to the decline of the Second Bank of the United States (after 1834), which had operated somewhat like a central bank in that it had branches all over the country, but of more significance, perhaps, the Western world was in one its periodic boom periods, with the United States in the take-off stage on its move toward an industrialized economy. At the base of the American boom was a railroad-and-cotton prosperity coupled with strong immigration and a vigorous westward movement. A fact of more immediate monetary consequence at this time, though, was that there was a rapid gold inflow into the United States, an inflow that was caused partly by an increase in cotton exports and that, whatever its cause, brought both higher prices (up 31 percent from early 1835 to their peak in early 1837) and more liquidity (commercial banks' holdings of gold doubled between 1832 and 1836, while that for the country as a whole went up 150 percent). This boom collapsed in the spring of 1837 (as the cotton industry turned down), and gold (and silver) was rapidly drained out of the banks (but not out of the country). Indeed, on May 10, 1837, all American banks suspended their gold and silver payments, not resuming this aspect of their business (they were glad to issue their notes, of course) until May 10, 1838. The first really general financial crash in the United States had occurred with, as we have just sketched out, multiple causes.

The period of "free banking" that began at this time has been much misunderstood in both contemporary and, for that matter, recent commentary. By "free banking" we mean that commercial banks, instead of having to get specific and unique charters passed by an act of a state legislature, could set up shop more or less automatically, so long as they met the requirements of the state (which set up a blanket method of charter for this purpose). These requirements were generally administered by a state agency, itself created by an act of the state legislature; we may refer to these banks as "state banks," but we should certainly not leap to the conclusion that they were thereby unsafe (although some were) compared to either later banks or earlier banks in American history.[5] For one thing, it must be emphasized that the individuals who set up banks contributed their capital to the banking firm, and it stands to reason that they judged their risks as carefully as they could. For another, the bad banking practices that did exist were probably not widespread; these practices include most notably "wildcat banking," which is often (erroneously) said to have been a widespread practice that imposed large costs on the development of the American economy.[6] This belief has arisen partly from the

[5] Note that the states of the United States still have "free banking" in this sense; what is different about the 1836–64 period is that there was no central bank and there were no federally chartered banks.

[6] The term "wildcat banking" actually specifically refers to the practice (also not widespread) of stashing the bank's hard cash assets or its books at a remote branch (out in the wildcat country) where one could not easily arrange an inspection of their adequacy.

(usually legal) practice of permitting banks to issue notes (currency) on the basis of a security (usually some sort of government bond) that had a market value less than that of the bank notes. Clearly, the unscrupulous could make a quick profit in this way (and skip out of town), and some certainly did, but only a few.

As a system, free banking spread from Michigan in 1837, and New York, in 1838, to be the general practice in the states that had any banking at all.[7] It was accompanied by state regulation and, sometimes, by state or private insurance schemes. One of the state plans was the Safety Fund in the state of New York, which passed into law when Martin Van Buren was governor (January–March 1829) and was used frequently until the 1860s; another was the system of control exerted by the large Suffolk Bank in Boston, which, at its peak in 1850, held part of the reserves of some 500 New England banks (in the form of deposits).[8] In general, one might argue, banks in the East, the Midwest to Chicago, and the South to New Orleans, probably showed no special signs of instability or malpractice. Thus, since American development to 1860 occurred mostly in this area, one can readily argue that the flexible form of entry into banking just described gave the United States what it needed—a money supply that responded to the demand for money, at the cost, though, of a certain amount of chaos and inefficiency and, as both earlier and later, at the cost of some inflation.

There were, to be sure, some financial disturbances in this period, the most notable being the crash of 1857. In this case we hardly need to go into detail, for the story is exactly the same as in 1837, although there is no Bank War to blame it on. That is, the United States again had a cotton-and-railroad boom, and there was a steady inflow of gold (some of it Californian and some of it the result of an inflow of British capital) that enabled the gold-based financial system to expand rapidly. In 1857 there

---

[7] Diversity there was. In 1852, seven states had no banks; indeed, Texas had none until 1904 (except in the period 1869–76) and California had no banks from 1849 to 1879. Bank runs were common and sometimes violent in the Midwest, and nowhere on the frontier did farmers show much enthusiasm for banks. But, again, very little of the rapidly growing American GNP was generated in these areas. Note that much of this early variety has survived to the present and is visible, for example, in the design of the Federal Reserve System (see Chapter 4) or in the laws on bank branching (see Chapter 3).

[8] The Suffolk bank actually often forced other banks in the region to enter into these "correspondence" relations. It was able to do so because funds (bank notes) tended to gravitate toward Boston; since the Suffolk Bank could press for settlement in gold, the note-issuing bank would have to curtail its other business as its hard cash was paid out. It was then agreed that the Suffolk bank would forego this claim and reissue the notes, if the other banks would do business with them. It did provide a somewhat safer New England currency—since the Suffolk Bank was careful—in return for some monopoly revenues for the Suffolk Bank.

may have been around 1,600 American commercial banks that dealt in notes and drafts,[9] transferred funds for their customers, dealt in stocks and bonds directly and for their customers, lent money for short- and (less frequently) for long-term loans, and discounted the bills of exchange brought to them by their customers. In addition, to facilitate exchange, *clearing houses* for bank notes and drafts were developed, the first in New York City in 1853. The crash of 1857 started with the failure of the Ohio Life Insurance and Trust Company (a bank) in the autumn; this bank was involved with banks all over the country. Earlier, the railroad industry had shown signs of collapse, and as news of the Ohio failure reached the financial heart of the country, the New York banks began to liquidate. New York bank customers began to panic on October 13th, and on the 14th these banks had to suspend their gold and silver payments. The suspension was short-lived, however, and was lifted in December (in New York) of the same year. A steady gold inflow into the banking system (and into the country) seems to have provided the cure in this case.

Before considering the last long period before the Federal Reserve arrived, we should comment on one other aspect of the banking system in this period and that is the occasional general *suspension* of gold and silver payments by banks that we have already noted (in 1837 and 1857). This suspension meant, technically, merely the revoking by a bank of its obligation to redeem its notes and deposits in metal money; no other banking functions were stopped unless customers so desired it. Thus, if customers were willing, notes could still circulate and banks could lend money (providing notes or deposits for the customers). This is important to an understanding of how the system worked in this period since it is very clear that many writers consider suspension identical to failure, when, in fact, it was not. Indeed, suspension "cleared the air" for, it has been argued, the worst part of a panic is the fear; that is, it is the worst part if the banks do not *also* fail. To put it another way, while clearly not ideal in many respects, the banking system up to 1860 (up to 1914, as we shall see) had a fairly simple method of dealing with adverse pressures brought about by (often) unusual circumstances: the banks suspended. We will see that it is not clear that the Federal Reserve System, at least until just after the worst part of the Great Depression of the 1930s, was as flexible in dealing with its strains.

---

[9] By 1860 there may well have been 8,000 different types of currency in circulation, with another 5,000 types of forged notes. This profusion, which clearly was costly, was dealt with by the banks, generally, which carefully researched the problem of a note's worth on the open market. It is perhaps remarkable that the notes of failed banks circulated so long after the failure, if they were acceptable in exchange, as they often were. This was especially the case in frontier areas, where alternative means of payment were not always available.

2.2.3 The National Banking System

The Civil War brought enormous changes to the American economy, not the least of which were its effects on banking and finance. The principal financial realities of the period were:

a. The need of the federal government for extraordinarily large revenues for its war effort.

b. A rapid inflation, which helped force the United States off the gold standard.[10]

c. Not independently, a new banking arrangement, the National Banking System.

Massive war expenditures, along with their method of finance (largely through bond issue and money creation) were responsible for much of the inflation, of course, so that part of the problem is easily dealt with. With regard to the government's role, the most significant fact was the dramatic increase in the scale of the government, at least for the time being. In the period of large deficits during the Mexican War, the largest federal government deficit was $31.4 million (in 1846) while, at the same time, the Treasury note issue was at a peak of $15.5 million (in 1858, during the short depression that followed the panic of 1857, the note issue reached $19.8 million). The Civil War, on the other hand, cost the federal government $4,171 million more than its normal revenues. While the new income tax and, especially, excise taxes, raised some of this money (the income tax netted $194 million), the biggest source of funds was the war loans. These started with an item of $250 million in 1861, which was sold mostly to the commercial banks. Sandwiched between this loan and a massive issue of $500 million in February 1862 (which was sold directly to the public) Congress created the Treasury currency known as Greenbacks; the issue of this currency quickly reached $449 million and provided much of the ready money needed to smooth the war effort. Bond issues of $300 million and $600 million followed in 1863 and 1864.

As the war progressed it became apparent that the banking system was too dispersed to handle government fiscal operations smoothly; this problem, and a rising concern with the safety of the commercial banks, prompted the National Currency Act of February 20, 1863. This was a proposal for a uniform note issue by commercial banks. The act stated that state-chartered banks could accept a national charter—or new banks could accept a national charter—in return for the right to issue their share of a standardized currency. The initial act did not make these notes legal ten-

---

[10] The immediate cause was a bond issue, which the Treasury insisted be paid for in gold; the United States' banks were forced to suspend in December 1861, and the country went off gold, officially, at that time.

der (there were, at the time, prejudices against legal tender, as if it implied a weak currency), and no banks joined the system; a new act, which did make the currency legal tender, was passed in 1864, and by the end of 1864 there were 638 new national banks (no state banks switched, though) operating under the National Banking System.[11] State banks did not come over until 1865, when Congress imposed a tax on state bank notes; those that needed the note issue to make profits switched, and by the end of 1865 there were more than 1,500 national banks. By 1870 the size of the national bank currency issue stood at $354, but a notable fact of this entire period, to 1914, is that the use of currency relative to the use of deposits actually declined fairly sharply, as the country developed (the use of checks increased rapidly in this period). Finally, one should note that state banks continued to thrive, their share of the total deposits falling below 50 percent only in the late 1870s.

But the National Banking System had two features that subsequent opinion has branded as undesirable. First, the currency issue was not "elastic" and second, the reserves of commercial banks were "pyramided" in the sense that a few large banks held much of the effective reserves of the system. An elastic currency, roughly, can be defined as one that can expand or contract to meet changes in the public's taste for currency (versus demand deposits). Indeed, it was the failure to provide elasticity in this sense—and in particular the failure to provide currency (or hard money) when there were general runs on commercial banks—that was one of the principal defects of the pre-1914 banking system. It is important to realize that the actions of the public were not really irrational in such cases: the public was instructed that it had a right to substitute currency for deposits at any time (it had *demand* deposits). In fact, Congress had actually made it impossible for the promise to be honored for everyone at once, since the quantity of currency could not readily expand without congressional action; further, such action was rarely adequate. Of course the system prior to the National Banking System also did not have an elastic currency (as just defined) so this is not a unique characteristic of that arrangement.

With regard to the pyramided reserves in the National Banking System we can actually note a parallel (but not a pyramid) in the Federal Reserve Act. The National Banking System consisted of *Central Reserve City* (CRC) banks, which held as their reserves Treasury currency, specie, and coin; *Reserve City* (RC) banks, which could do the same, but which also held a sizeable part of their actual reserves as balances in the CRC banks;

---

[11] Popular belief was that if a currency needed to be made legal tender it was a weak currency (recall gold was "real" money at that time); this accounts for not making it legal tender. Bankers apparently preferred the protection of legal tender status, however, as the results of the legislation seem to indicate.

and *Country Banks,* which could hold a sizable proportion of their reserves in RC banks.[12] The upshot was that a dollar of gold supported (at times) a large volume of bank deposits, possibly to the extent of $15 of deposits to $1 of gold at the peaks of prosperity; that is more than our present system has, with only $10 billion of gold left, but we are no longer on the gold standard, either.

There was another unfortunate aspect of the arrangement of reserves in the National Banking System: there was no provision for either drawing on or increasing reserves in an emergency. A commercial bank, since it could not cash in reserves (a call for reserves merely ran down some other bank's reserves), had basically two main options open to it:

a. It could hold substantial idle (cash) excess reserves at all times, thus avoiding the suspension.

b. It could, as it did before the National Banking System was adopted, suspend whenever there was a panic, reopening after the panic was over.

The advantage of the second alternative to commercial banks was that interest earnings on the cash were not foregone; and, not surprisingly, a significant number of banks actually apparently did prefer to keep their cash balances low and to suspend when the pressure was applied, as it was in the panics of 1873, 1884, 1893, and 1907. Clearly, the new order had not dealt with this recurring problem, although it did provide a less heterogeneous currency and, no doubt, a somewhat better inspection of banks, on average.

2.3 THE FEDERAL RESERVE SYSTEM

Following the 1907 panic, the government of the United States turned to the problems of bank regulation and control of the money supply, with some fresh ideas. State banks were again rising in number and importance compared to national banks, and the "elastic currency" problem had evoked some *ad hoc* central bank policy from the United States Treasury and, worse, from groups of private citizens (such as the consortium led by J. P. Morgan, which provided cash during the 1907 panic). The Federal Reserve Act of 1913, itself an outgrowth of earlier legislation,[13] aimed (1) to provide an elastic currency, (2) to afford a means of "rediscounting"

[12] As we will see in Chapter 4, the Federal Reserve System has such a distinction, although in recent years the terminology has changed; the original Federal Reserve Act had terminology very similar to that in the National Banking Act.

[13] The Aldrich-Vreeland Act of 1908 actually created a mechanism for an elastic currency; as well, it had a deposit-insurance scheme. Most importantly, though, it created a National Monetary Commission, which, after a thorough study, reported to Congress in 1912. The result was the Federal Reserve Act.

commercial and government paper in order to provide a lender of last resort,[14] (3) to establish more effective supervision of commercial banks, and (4) to provide a required reserve in the form of balances held at the Federal Reserve Banks, rather than at other commercial banks. National banks were required to join the system or lose their national charters, and the Federal Reserve took over the (by then) minor note issue, requiring that national banks deposit a U.S. government bond of equal value for any note issue they desired. In effect, the currency issue was nationalized. This left the United States with the present system of state banks and national banks, with the latter subject to the regulation of both the Federal Reserve and the Comptroller of the Currency (on behalf of the National Banking System); state banks, of course, were invited to join the system, and some did.

We are going to emphasize the monetary control aspects of the Federal Reserve System later in this book (and this is what was really new about the System, compared to the National Banking System), but for now we should anticipate a few later topics with regard to the effect of the Act on the institutional structure of banking. Most importantly, probably, the Federal Reserve Act provided a lender of last resort by permitting the member banks of the system to rediscount their good commercial or federal paper (bills of exchange or Treasury bills) at the official rediscount rate. In effect, banks under pressure could now borrow reserves. In fact, this system has evolved into something much less flexible than it sounds, mostly because commercial banks tend to discount more than the Federal Reserve would like (because the banks find that the discount rate is low enough to permit additional profits to be earned). In any event, the principal safeguards to the banking system that we now have are

a. The flexible supply of currency and coin (it is supplied on demand).
b. The presence of officially regulated and centralized reserves (the *federal* reserve).
c. The public's confidence in the regulatory restraint of the Federal Reserve System.
d. Federal deposit insurance.

This last actually grew out of the monetary chaos of the 1930s (although we have mentioned several precursors in our survey), when the financial system, still not as flexible as one might wish in the face of panic, once again collapsed. We shall return to these topics below, but for now we should note that there is some controversy over whether (*b*) and (*c*) are really true, in the sense (taking up the Monetarist view for the moment)

[14] That is, member banks of the system were permitted to borrow reserves (especially in a panic) if they had suitable (short-term) collateral.

that the use of unwise policy invalidates (*b*) and reduces (*c*). We will see that there are numerous allegations of policy mistakes in the course of our study of U.S. monetary policy.

From the mid-1930s until fairly recent times a tightly regulated and extremely safe commercial banking system has grown rapidly, along with the American economy. While we have seen that a more diverse banking system also can be associated with rapid economic growth (from 1837 to 1864, for example), we must note that Americans seem almost pathologically concerned with the stability of their banks. While bank failure is not impossible, as we shall see, the number of failing banks in the United States is very small indeed, and the unpleasant consequences to bank customers have generally been minimal (generally restricted to the temporary interruption of ordinary business arrangements), so that failure is not really a major issue, as such. Banks have also grown extremely large, though, especially in the great urban centers (through mergers, through holding companies, through expansion, and through branching); and their functions have broadened considerably, the latest being a variety of "nonbank" activities, as well as extensive foreign operations. We will return to the Federal Reserve System in detail in Chapter 4, but for now we have enough historical background to tackle the problem of the description of a modern commercial bank, as we shall do in the remainder of this chapter.

2.4 THE BANKING BUSINESS

A typical firm can be visualized as trying to maximize profits in its product market, subject to the constraints imposed by the real world in which it operates. In economic analysis, this real world is normally represented by cost and production conditions on the one hand, and demand conditions on the other, although institutional constraints (and regulations) also play a role. Let us, accordingly, assume that the typical banking firm attempts to maximize profits; this may not be true for some banks, but it will certainly do, as a matter of fact, for the general sort of analysis we shall conduct here. Profits, then, can be defined as equal to total revenues (TR) less total costs (TC), as in Equation (2.1).

$$\text{Profits} = \text{TR} - \text{TC}. \qquad (2.1)$$

Our analysis, clearly, breaks down into the discussion of, first, TR and then TC, with the former flowing from a consideration of the demand side of the "product" market. A commercial bank, for the most part, is in business because it is the depository for the funds of individuals, businesses, the government, and other commercial banks. Thus, in June 1978, as Table 2.1 illustrates, *all* commercial banks in the United States had total deposits of $965.8 billion, of which ordinary demand deposits (at $317.5

Table 2.1

The Banking Sector: All Commercial Banks
Last Wednesday of June, 1978
($ billions)

Assets			*Liabilities*		
Cash assets		$ 166.8	Demand deposits		$ 374.8
Currency and coin	$ 12.0		Interbank	$ 49.3	
Reserves with Federal Reserve banks	29.6		U.S. government	8.0	
			Other	317.5	
Cash items in the process of collection	69.3		Time deposits		591.0
			Interbank	10.2	
			Other	580.8	
Loans and Investments		985.0	Borrowings		106.8
Loans, gross	722.1		Other liabilities		52.5
U.S. Treasury securities	97.9				
Other investments	165.1				
Other assets		63.2	Capital accounts		89.9
Total Assets		$1,215.0	Total liabilities		$1,215.0

Source: *Federal Reserve Bulletin.*

billion) and ordinary time deposits (at $591.0 billion) represented the bulk. Note that government and interbank deposits are small, but that borrowings (either from other banks or corporations, as we shall see) and accumulated capital are surprisingly high. We will return to these items in a moment.

The *liabilities,* except for the balancing item of course, contribute costs to the commercial bank. That is, savings and time deposits must be paid interest (at a rate that varies by the length of maturity of the deposit, in general), and so must borrowings (most of which are done at or near the federal funds rate). The federal funds rate stood at 7.28 percent at the end of June 1978. Of course, for all of these accounts "services" (for example, personnel costs) must be provided. These days banks seek to manage their liabilities in various ways. For one thing, they advertise vigorously for customers and they offer a wide variety of plans for checking and savings account customers. But there are other aspects to this management, buried in the figures in Table 2.1. For one thing, the borrowings refer really to activities in the federal funds market, which is a market in very short-term funds (often available within one day) not usually subject to reserve requirements. Originally this market dealt in excess reserves (called federal funds)—banks with excess reserves lending them overnight at the federal funds rate to banks that were short—but lately, as the market has expanded, nonmember banks, foreign banks, and even nonbanks (such as security dealers) have become involved in this rapidly growing (possibly 20 percent per year) and competitive market. As the market has changed and broadened, indeed, banks have tended to use these funds as semipermanent sources of funds rather than just for temporary shortages.

In the same total—borrowings—in Table 2.1 there are a significant number of repurchase agreements (RPs) in U.S. government securities (mostly Treasury bills). The repurchase market originated in the government securities market, where the collateral security (the Treasury bill) was sold to the public (usually not a commercial bank) with the formal understanding that the dealer would repurchase the security later at a price that included the interest charge. Banks now also use the RP extensively as a device for borrowing funds from the nonbank public and, as things presently stand, these borrowings provide them with funds that are not subject to reserve requirements.[15] In October 1979, though, many of these items were subjected to an 8 percent reserve requirement, as part of the tight money policy in that month.

But probably the most important item not separately broken out in Table 2.1 is one actually included in our broader measures of the money stock (M_4 and M_5); this is the large (over $100,000) negotiable certificate of deposit (the CD). A CD is a time deposit for which a certificate is given; the certificate is desired because it is useful as collateral and, for purposes of this section, because it can be sold. It, like all other deposits, cannot be "discounted," so it pays interest explicitly. The CDs are hidden in "other time deposits" in Table 2.1; they must (by Regulation D of the Federal Reserve) have a minimum maturity of 30 days (as such they are insured up to $40,000 by the FDIC). Where the management comes in, especially, is that the interest rate as well as the length of maturity can be negotiated under present conditions, so that the commercial bank has a chance to compete for liquid funds. Large negotiable CDs, of which there were more than $100 billion at American commercial banks at the end of 1978, are highly favored by large business corporations.[16] They are, though, a volatile component of the bank's liabilities, showing a sharp cyclical pattern; thus, for all banks, CDs turned down in 1966 and were sharply down (over 50 percent) in the 1969–70 recession, and in the recession after 1974 they were down more than 33 percent.[17] On net, though, their rise, along

[15] Clearly, this device could interfere with monetary policy, at least if that policy is designed to interfere with a bank's lending power. The federal government securities market (including agencies as well as the Treasury) is a very volatile one, with frequent large, partly indigestible, dealings to contend with. The RP helps the market absorb the securities (although, to be sure, these are now also semipermanent forms of lending, and many RPs have no fixed maturity). Note, also, that there are some interbank RPs, for roughly the same reasons that the federal funds market itself exists between banks.

[16] The first CD was offered by the First National City Bank of New York in 1961; by 1968 there were over $20 billion of them, and by December 1979 there were over $97 billion.

[17] Originally the CDs were given interest ceilings under the Federal Reserve's Regulation Q. In the tight money periods of 1966 and 1969 (see Chapter 13) banks faced a run-off of these deposits when other short-term rates (especially those on Treasury bills) exceeded the legal maximum CD rate. In 1970, after the data on the 1969 "crunch" were evaluated, the

with Federal Funds dealings and repurchase agreements, has allowed banks a little more elbow-room in the increasingly competitive market for the swelling quantity of liquid assets.

Finally, with reference to some recent institutional changes, we note that commercial banks are permitted to offer the new Treasury bill "money market instruments" and to offer customers automatic transfer of funds between checking and savings accounts. The former have been available since June 1978, and are evidenced by certificates issued in amounts of $10,000 or more (the smallest Treasury bill has a face value of $10,000) at the current Treasury bill rate (for six months' maturity).[18] The purpose is primarily to enable banks to avoid the run-off of their time deposits into Treasury bills that generally occurs when interest rates hit cyclical peaks. Indeed, the timing of this legislation was reasonably good in that late in 1978 many interest rates reached their post–World War II peaks in the United States. The automatic-transfer privilege is just the latest step in an evolutionary process that is currently cutting away the restrictions on interest rates in the American financial sector. The reasons for the existence of these restrictions will be discussed later in this chapter, but for now we note that since NOW accounts (interest-bearing accounts upon which negotiable orders of withdrawal may be drawn) appeared in Massachusetts in 1972, the American system has been on the road toward paying interest on all demand deposits. Thus, while originally the NOW accounts were offered only by mutual savings banks in New England, they are now offered by S&Ls and commercial banks, and their use has extended out of New England. With the automatic transfer (at a cost) between savings and checking accounts, customers may now, in effect, earn interest on their checking accounts. Indeed, since the system was adopted on November 1, 1978, the change has been rapid and, as we saw in Chapter 1, has provoked a new definition of money, $M_1{}^+$, from the Federal Reserve.

But these important institutional matters aside, commercial banks are businesses, just like any other; as such they provide staff and facilities to handle the multiplicity of activities that their customers expect. These activities range from the "retail" outlets—the convenient branches that most of us use—to the often sophisticated financial management services provided by the trust departments of banks. Table 2.2 presents some summary data on bank costs gleaned from the annual survey published in the *Federal Reserve Bulletin;* the series starts in 1969. What is most notable about these figures is the absolute regularity of the noninterest expenses in

---

ceiling was abandoned. The 1974 experience is clearly due to other factors. They have also been subject to reserve requirements from time to time, the most notable instance being the 8 percent requirement imposed after October 6, 1979.

[18] Federally insured savings and loan associations and mutual savings banks can pay an extra .25 percent interest; see the discussion in Chapter 13.

Table 2.2: The operating expenses of all insured commercial banks ($ millions)

	1969	1970	1971	1972	1973	1974	1975	1976	1977	1978
Salaries, wages, and employee benefits	6,758	7,683	8,355	9,040	10,076	11,526	12,624	14,686	16,276	18,654
Interest on time and savings deposits*	9,758	10,444	12,168	13,781	19,747	27,777	26,147	34,896	38,701*	50,054
Interest on federal funds purchased and other comparable securities	1,203	1,396	1,093	1,425	3,883	5,970	3,313	3,306	4,536	7,247
Other interest expenses	532	568	281	327	752	1,192	666	1,009	1,207	1,897
Net occupancy expense	1,069	1,249	1,403	1,575	1,774	2,041	2,312	2,753	3,036	5,559
Furniture and equipment	770	905	1,014	1,083	1,196	1,355	1,525	1,713	1,923	
Provision for loan losses	519	695	860	964	1,253	2,271	3,578	3,644	3,244	3,499
Other operating expenses	3,382	4,525	4,337	4,640	5,432	6,514	7,149	8,452	9,537	11,194
Total expenses	23,992	27,465	29,511	32,836	44,113	58,645	57,313	70,458	78,484	98,104

Note: Some of the banks reported in Table 2.1 are "uninsured" and hence are not reported in this table; these uninsured (mostly foreign) banks had deposits of around $14 billion in 1978.

* In 1977, the second year the figures were available, this total consisted of $6,732 for large CDs issued in the United States, $10,216 for interest on deposits in foreign offices, and $21,753 for regular time and savings deposits.

Source: *Federal Reserve Bulletin.*

comparison with the interest costs. The former all seem to grow steadily, but the interest expenses fluctuate, in this period rising sharply in 1973–74, during a period of rapid inflation, and actually falling in 1975, and then rising sharply again in 1976, 1977, and 1978, as the American economy expanded. This behavior reflects, of course, the behavior of interest rates in the economy, in general.

On the other side of the balance sheet, of course, one finds the earning assets of the commercial banks; the figures are also included in Table 2.1. Here, looking at the broad aggregates, we find the cash items that make up bank reserves; these consist of currency and coin as well as (for member banks of the Federal Reserve System) balances with the Federal Reserve and balances with other banks (which comprise much of the reserves of nonmember banks).[19] The last entry, cash items in the process of collection, is also known as *float*. It is surprisingly large. The loans and investments of commercial banks, as the main earnings generators, should also be described more completely, although we will stop well short of the infinite detail possible. In Table 2.3 we illustrate a more detailed break-

Table 2.3: A comparison of some of the earning assets of member and nonmember banks (June 30, 1978; $ millions)

	Member banks		*Nonmember banks*	
Total securities at book value		178,753		82,519
U.S. Treasury	67,406		30,466	
Other U.S. government agencies	25,193		14,654	
State and political subdivisions	82,541		34,716	
Others	3,603		2,682	
Loans, gross		485,054		188,560
Real estate loans	131,891		60,986	
To financial institutions	33,355		11,071	
To security brokers and dealers	11,043		673	
To farmers (not real estate)	14,813		12,205	
Commercial and industrial loans	170,678		50,913	
To individuals	105,611		47,971	
Other loans	17,663		4,741	
Other assets		224,744		55,422
Total assets		888,551		326,501

Source: *Federal Reserve Bulletin* (December 1978).

[19] We should note, for later reference, that the member banks of the Federal Reserve System were 5,611 in number at the end of June 1978, of a total number of American banks of 14,701. They had deposits of almost 72 percent of the $926.2 billion for all banks at that date; the percentage of the total of both items, and particularly the percentage for all banks, has been falling steadily in recent years. This problem is discussed in Chapter 4.

down of some of the asset items of both member and nonmember banks, for June 28, 1978. Here we note that both types of banks hold large portfolios of government securities, although the percentages differ somewhat; thus government securities make up 19.7 percent of the total assets of member banks and 24.4 percent of the total assets of nonmember banks (mainly because the latter can hold them as part of their official reserves, depending on state laws). More noticeably, perhaps, one sees that member banks are more involved with security brokers (that is, 1.2 percent versus .02 percent) and financial institutions (3.8 percent versus 3.4 percent) and less involved with loans to farmers (1.7 percent versus 3.7 percent). These results reflect the fact that nonmember banks are smaller than member banks on average and are, on average, located in communities of a smaller size (away from the financial centers).[20] We will discuss the reasons that so many banks do not belong to the Federal Reserve System in Chapter 4.

Turning to the revenue from commercial bank operations, let us look at a table comparable to that for costs (which were illustrated in Table 2.2); here (in Table 2.4) we consider the operating income of all commercial banks. Clearly, interest income on loans dominates the earnings of American commercial banks (it is some two-thirds of the total), while that on other securities, which are mostly government issues of one sort or another, makes up the bulk of the remainder (it produced 14.5 percent of commercial banks' income in 1978). In Table 2.2 we noted that interest payments on time and savings deposits were the largest item in bank operating expenses; put the two together and a simple picture emerges: the commercial bank is a lender in one market (to individuals or the government) and a borrower in another (borrowing the demand and time deposits of its customers).

Let us, then, see how the net profits of insured American banks behaved over the 1969–78 period; the figures are carried in Table 2.5. A number of interesting things about commercial banks emerge from these figures. In the first place, it is readily apparent that the net interest earnings of banks fluctuate considerably. Thus, Line (3) shows that the balance of the interest payments and the loan interest receipts of commercial banks was only a little higher (at $11,717 million) in 1972 then it was in 1969; indeed, these "net interest earnings" actually fell in 1971. More significantly, by far, commercial banks' net interest earnings rose sharply

[20] In the total "other assets" are commercial paper and bankers' acceptances held by other banks. Commercial paper is short-term notes issued by a large corporation (usually) and bought by commercial banks (and others). The financial lending firms (credit corporations) are the main issuers of bills of exchange that have been accepted (endorsed, in effect) by commercial banks. The banks, in accepting the bills, increase their creditworthiness. Banks, in June 1978, themselves held about $7.5 billion of the total of $28.3 billion of bankers' acceptances outstanding.

Table 2.4: The operating income of all insured commercial banks in the United States ($ millions)

	1969	1970	1971	1972	1973	1974	1975	1976	1977	1978
Loans										
Interest and fees on loans	20,645	22,859	22,954	25,498	35,213	46,942	43,197	51,472	58,811	75,948
Federal funds and repurchase securities	811	1,004	870	1,023	2,474	3,695	2,283	1,980	2,471	3,664
Securities										
U.S. Treasury	2,837	3,069	3,384	3,376	3,436	3,414	4,415	5,953	6,369	9,335 (U.S. Treasury and U.S. government agencies combined)
U.S. government agencies and corporations	549	686	914	1,144	1,469	2,014	2,343	2,410	2,466	
States and political subdivisions	2,213	2,617	3,124	3,490	3,861	4,449	4,911	5,116	5,338	6,003
Other	134	151	238	319	372	467	532	855	967	1,094
Trust department	1,035	1,132	1,258	1,366	1,460	1,506	1,600	1,795	1,980	2,138
Service charges on deposits	1,117	1,174	1,226	1,256	1,320	1,450	1,547	1,629	1,797	2,039
Other operating income	1,369	1,882	2,236	2,593	3,189	3,935	5,457	9,180	9,870	12,949
Total operating income	30,710	34,574	36,204	40,065	52,794	67,872	66,285	80,390	90,069	113,170

Source: *Federal Reserve Bulletin.*

Table 2.5: The net revenues of insured American banks: 1969–1977 ($ millions)

	1969	*1970*	*1971*	*1972*	*1973*	*1974*	*1975*	*1976*	*1977*	*1978*
1. Interest payments on time and savings deposits	9,758	10,444	12,168	13,781	19,747	27,777	26,147	34,896	38,801	50,054
2. Interest and fees earned on loans	20,645	22,859	22,954	25,498	35,213	46,942	43,197	51,472	58,811	75,948
3. Balance (item 2 minus item 1)	10,887	12,415	10,786	11,717	15,466	19,165	17,050	16,576	20,110	25,894
4. Gross operating profits (last row in Table 2.4 minus last row in Table 2.2)	6,718	7,109	6,693	7,229	8,681	9,227	8,973	9,932	11,585	15,066
5. Income taxes	2,166	2,173	1,688	1,708	2,120	2,084	1,790	2,289	2,829	4,155
6. Net income (some capital gains and losses are included)	4,321	4,818	5,213	5,630	6,555	7,068	7,249	7,861	8,898	10,731
7. Cash dividends declared	1,768	2,036	2,227	2,191	2,423	2,760	3,025	3,031	3,299	3,714
8. Time and savings interest rate	—	—	—	4.76	5.91	7.21	6.09	5.74	5.72	—
9. Loans (gross) interest rate	—	—	—	7.43	8.73	10.30	9.03	8.89	9.15	—
10. Prime commercial paper rate	7.83	7.72	5.11	4.69	8.15	9.87	6.33	5.35	5.60	7.99
11. Implicit deposit rate	4.73	5.38	5.28	5.31	5.65	6.55	7.45	8.14	—	—
12. Consumer Price Index (1967 = 100)	109.8	116.3	121.2	125.3	133.1	147.7	161.2	170.5	181.8	195.4

Sources: Items 1 to 10, 12—*Federal Reserve Bulletin* (July 1977, June 1978); item 11—William E. Becker, Jr., "Determinants of the United States Currency-Demand Deposits Ratio," *Journal of Finance* (March 1975) (as amended and corrected).

in 1973 and 1974, only to decline again in 1975 and 1976; 1977 and 1978 are the strongest years in the table. There is, clearly, a cyclical pattern in the net interest earnings of banks.

In Lines (8)–(11) in the table, data have been collected on the behavior of the various interest rates that are relevant to commercial banks. Line (8) has an average time and savings rate and Line (11) has an implicit deposit rate (on demand deposits) that represents the costs, to banks, of taking deposit accounts. This implicit rate, that is to say, represents the cost to the bank of providing services to their deposit customers (on a *pro rata* basis). In Line (9) we have the banks' loan rate and in Line (10) the rate on prime commercial paper (the four- to six-month obligations of the most important corporations); these two rates represent banks' earning assets. The hypothesis at hand, roughly, is that during periods of rising interest rates banks will tend to show extra interest earnings since the interest rates they receive are likely to stay up with market rates, while the interest rates they pay are either less responsive or subject to interest rate ceilings (Regulation Q). Thus, net interest earnings shot up by 32 percent and 24 percent—in 1973 and 1974—the gap between the time and savings rate and the loan rate rose moderately, and the gaps between the time and savings rate and the implicit demand deposit rate and the loan and commercial paper rates both rose sharply. These are the hypothesized results. Furthermore, in 1975, when profits slid back somewhat, these gaps narrowed, particularly those between the prime commercial paper rate and the two cost rates, the implicit deposit rate and the time and savings rate. Evidently, the behavior of the various relevant interest rates tells us a lot about bank profits, particularly in view of the use of rate ceilings on various bank deposits.[21]

Turning to the net profits of commercial banks in these years, we can look at Lines (4)–(7) of Table 2.5. Here we see that increases in the other expenses in Table 2.2 have actually eaten into American bank operating profits, although the rapid gains in 1973 and 1974 and the decline in 1976 still show up on the final figures. We note, as well, that while commercial banks clearly seem to have prospered in this period, with net income growing 148.3 percent over the nine years, income taxes paid grew by only 91.8 percent in the same period. Indeed, the stockholders of insured American banks seem to have done pretty well, as Line (7) of the table indicates, with dividends rising 110.0 percent over the period. Furthermore, after a comparison with Line (10), in which the consumer price index is given, we see that commercial banks' net income (up 148.3 per-

[21] Under the institutional conditions prevailing since 1978, with automatic transfers between savings and demand deposits and with (especially) the use of the "money market instruments"—the time deposits in $10,000 lots geared to the Treasury bill rate—some of this cyclical sensitivity of bank profits may well moderate in the future.

cent) and dividends (up 110.0 percent) also compare well with the inflation rate, since the consumer price index rose during the period from 109.8 to 195.4, a gain of 78.0 percent.[22] Evidently bank stocks were a decent hedge against inflation during this period.

There is a little more to the inflation problem than that just mentioned which one can see in Table 2.5; this is that the years of the most rapid profit inflation for banks (1973 and 1978) were also years of rapid price inflation.[23] This relation is not a coincidence, in all likelihood, and its explanation is easily given with reference to the behavior of interest rates. Thus, inflation seems to have raised "earnings" interest rates more than it did "cost" rates, for commercial banks (the prime rate shot up especially sharply in 1973, 1974, and again in 1978). We will defer the detailed discussion of this phenomenon until Chapter 6 (on the demand for money) and Chapter 9 (on inflation), but for now it is enough to note that lenders, who expect to receive dollars worth less (in purchasing power) at some future date, will require some additional interest payment in compensation, while borrowers, who expect to pay back in depreciated dollars, will be happy to let them have it. This will produce higher interest rates in periods of actual inflation, when it is reasonable to suppose that lenders and borrowers will expect inflation to continue, and will plan accordingly. The result, higher interest rates in periods of inflation, should affect market-determined interest rates. Thus, since the earnings rates of commercial banks fluctuate, while the payout rates do not (as much) largely because of the interest ceilings on time and savings rates set by the Federal Reserve, rapid inflation tends to transfer resources from the public to the banking sector, at least for a time.

We will take up the question of the interest ceilings immediately, but for now we should also note that removal of the interest ceilings (5 percent on time and savings deposits and zero on demand deposits) will not necessarily imply that these kinds of deposits will then have rates equal to lending rates, or any such thing. Indeed, given the high costs of bank operations (see Table 2.2) and the vulnerability of the items in that table to inflation, it may be that only a modest additional change would come to demand and time deposit interest rates if the ceiling were lifted. But, at least, the accidental redistributive effects, which occur as individuals shift their funds to take advantage of marginal differences in yields, may well be eliminated.

---

[22] Note that the size of bank capital also grew in this period so that we cannot directly compare these figures. Even so, bank profits clearly kept up with inflation.

[23] The point is stated in this way because prices also rose rapidly in 1975, although the net effect of the recession in the United States seems to have been to hurt bank profits in that year. Note the resurgence of inflation and higher bank profits in 1977 and 1978.

2.5 RESTRICTIONS ON INTEREST RATES

The years have seen the development of governmental controls over three basic interest rates involving American commercial banks; these rates apply to demand deposits, time and savings deposits, and the reserves of member banks held by the Federal Reserve Banks. With regard to demand deposits, since the passage of the Banking Act of 1933, all insured commercial banks insured by the FDIC have been prohibited from paying interest on demand deposits (although automatic transfers are now permitted). With regard to time and savings deposits, since the passage of the same act, the Federal Reserve and the Federal Deposit Insurance Corporation are empowered to set legal maxima, covering all federally insured commercial banks, member and nonmember alike. The maximum rates are given in Table 2.6. Finally, since the Federal Reserve Act (1913), the Federal Reserve does not pay interest on the deposits it holds, which are counted as the reserves of member banks. We will discuss the first two of these regulations in this chapter, leaving the question of interest payments on reserves to Chapter 4.

Considering first the regulations on time and savings deposits, we note that the situation is quite complicated, as Table 2.6 indicates. Thus passbook accounts—Line (1)—in commercial banks currently pay a maximum of 5.25 percent, while the rate at mutual savings banks and savings and loan banks is 5.50 percent; these rates have been adjusted recently, as the table also indicates (currently, most of these institutions pay the maximum). To get more than 5.25 percent from a bank, a saver must lock his money up; thus, in a six-year time deposit, described in Line (9), he can get 7.50 percent; he can get the same from a savings and loan association or a mutual savings bank with a four-year time deposit. The new money market instruments, described in Line (13) and the footnote, continue this pattern.

The fact that these rates are so similar reflects an underlying problem that the American financial system has occasionally had with its liquid savings; this is the *runoff problem* caused by the behavior of (mainly) small savers who shift their funds among the commercial banks and savings institutions or, even, entirely out of this sector into Treasury bills. The reason that the runoff is a serious problem is that when commercial banks find their time and savings deposits falling as a percentage of their total deposits (or, of course, in absolute terms) they may well have to curtail their operations in loans and investments somewhat. The reason they are affected even if the total of deposits does not change (for example, it would not change if the savings and loan bank redeposits the funds into the commercial banking system) is that savings and time deposits have lower reserve requirements than do demand deposits (see Table 4.4).

Table 2.6: Maximum interest rates payable on time and savings deposits at federally insured institutions (percent per annum)

	Commercial banks				Savings and loan associations and mutual savings banks			
	In effect Sept. 30, 1979		Previous maximum		In effect Sept. 30, 1979		Previous maximum	
Type and maturity of deposit	Percent	Effective date	Percent	Effective date	Percent	Effective date	Percent	Effective date
1. Savings	5.25	7/1/79	5.00	7/1/73	5.50	7/1/79	5.25	‡
2. Negotiable order of withdrawal (NOW) accounts*	5.00	1/1/74	—	—	5.00	1/1/74	—	—
Time								
3. 30–89 days	5.25	9/1/79	5.00	7/1/73	—	—	—	—
4. 90 days to 1 year	5.50	7/1/73	5.00	9/26/66	5.75	—	5.25	1/21/70
5. 1 to 2 years	6.00 (5 and 6)	7/1/73 (5 and 6)	5.50	1/21/70	6.50 (5 and 6)	‡ (5 and 6)	5.75	1/21/70
6. 2 to 2½ years			5.75	1/21/70			6.00	1/21/70
7. 2½ to 4 years	6.50	7/1/73	5.75	1/21/70	6.75	‡	6.00	1/21/70
8. 4 to 6 years	7.25	11/1/73	—	—	7.50	11/1/73	—	—
9. 6 to 8 years	7.50	12/23/74	7.25	11/1/73	7.75	12/23/74	7.50	11/1/73
10. 8 years or more	7.75	6/1/78	—	—	8.00	6/1/78	—	—
11. Governmental units (all maturities)	8.00	6/1/78	7.75	12/23/74	8.00	6/1/78	7.75	12/23/74
12. Individual Retirement Accounts and Keogh (H.R. 10) plans†	8.00	6/1/67	7.75	7/6/77	8.00	6/1/78	7.75	7/6/77
13. Money market time deposits§	—	—	—	—	—	—	—	—

Note: Maximum rates that can be paid by federally insured commercial banks, mutual savings banks, and savings and loan associations are established by the Board of Governors of the Federal Reserve System, the Board of Directors of the Federal Deposit Insurance Corporation, and the Federal Home Loan Bank Board under the provisions of 12 CFR 217, 329, and 526, respectively. The maximum rates on time deposits in denominations of $100,000 or more were suspended in mid-1973.

* For authorized states only. Federally insured commercial banks, savings and loan associations, cooperative banks, and mutual savings banks were first permitted to offer NOW accounts on Jan. 1, 1974. Authorization to issue NOW accounts was extended to similar institutions throughout New England on Feb. 27, 1976.

† 3-year minimum maturity.

‡ July 1, 1973, for mutual savings banks; July 6, 1973, for savings and loan associations.

§ Must have a maturity of exactly 26 weeks and a minimum denomination of $10,000, and must be nonnegotiable. The ceiling rate for commercial banks is the discount rate on most recently issued six-month U.S. Treasury bills. The ceiling rate for savings and loan associations and mutual savings banks is .25 percent higher than for commercial banks.

Source: *Federal Reserve Bulletin.*

Indeed, drastic changes here could actually produce drastic changes in the money stock, as we shall discuss in Chapters 5 and 13. So our concern is with the behavior of the money stock.

When we turn to the annual data, though, things seem less exciting than we might have expected, considering the possibilities. Consider Table 2.7.

Table 2.7: The time and savings deposits of commercial banks and savings institutions ($ billions)

	Commercial bank savings and time deposits	*Savings and loan, mutual savings bank, and credit union deposits*
1959	67.5	92.9
1960	72.9	102.2
1961	79.9	113.5
1962	92.0	126.3
1963	102.4	141.4
1964	113.4	157.3
1965	130.0	170.4
1966	142.4	177.3
1967	162.6	194.0
1968	180.7	206.7
1969	183.5	215.0
1970	203.9	232.7
1971	237.9	271.1
1972	270.0	319.2
1973	300.9	348.2
1974	329.3	369.1
1975	369.5	428.6
1976	427.5	497.2
1977	471.1	567.5
1978	514.8	624.6

Source: Table 1.1; M_2 minus M_1 and M_3 minus M_2 from figures provided by the Board of Governors of the Federal Reserve System.

Only in 1966, when the savings institutions had a slightly slower growth in their deposits (during the credit crunch of 1966) and 1969, when the same happened to commercial banks (during the credit crunch of 1969) are there any significant deviations; in both cases, though, no sign of a large runoff (or a "reverse" runoff) is apparent. Evidently, the flow of liquid savings into our major financial institutions is a very well-behaved phenomenon, at least insofar as the annual data show.[24] On the other hand, it does not seem likely that the controls on maximum interest rates have much to do with this, although a certain "equity" within the liquid savings sectors is

[24] In Chapter 13 we will discover that during the earlier of the two "credit crunches" just mentioned, there were actually some severe effects on the nonbank intermediaries; indeed, the housing industry was extremely disturbed at that time. The controls over *all* rates—and the Federal Home Loan Bank—are results, partly, of these experiences.

achieved in this way. Note that in 1978, when short-term interest rates rose rapidly, commercial banks and savings banks do not seem to have suffered any appreciable runoff, perhaps because of the availability of the interest-sensitive "money market instruments" (available in June 1978) or, coincidentally, because of the introduction of the more attractive automatic transfers between demand and savings accounts in November 1978.

Whether it is an interest ceiling of zero, 5 percent, 5.25 percent, or, even, an automatic transfer between items with a zero and a 5 percent ceiling, the ceiling, when effective, automatically implies that a nonoptimal solution to the determination of quantities in the market will occur; consider Figure 2.1. Here we see that when the interest ceiling is effective,

Figure 2.1: The market for bank savings and time deposits

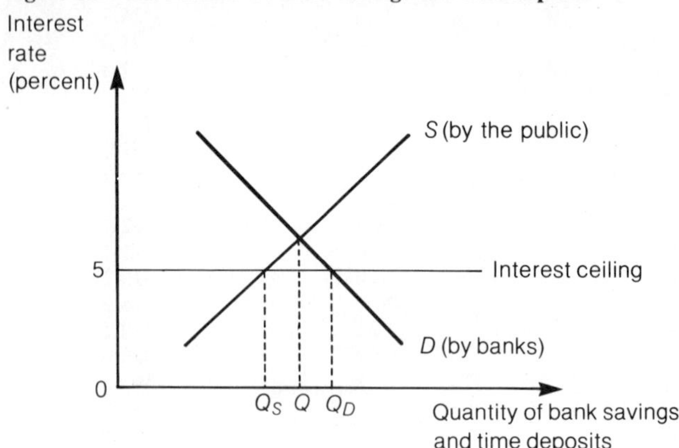

there are two quantities in the market; Q_S, then, is the quantity of such deposits desired by the public and Q_D is the amount of deposits banks would like to hold, both at an interest rate of 5 percent. Of course only the smaller of these two will be actually held and this is Q_S; the optimal amount, in the sense of the first sentence in this paragraph, is Q, the quantity that clears the market described there. As drawn, the optimal interest rate is higher than 5 percent.

Now whether or not interfering with a competitive market can be justified depends mostly on what might happen without those controls. In the case of the rate ceilings on time and savings deposits, it is unlikely that much would happen although, to be sure, interest payments to customers would certainly be higher (as well, no doubt, interest charges would be higher). The biggest dispute, over the years, has been over the interest ceiling on demand deposits, which, while set at zero currently, can be avoided by using the automatic transfer mechanism. As it stands, a number of reasons have been advanced for having such a limit and, while not all of these factors seem relevant today, one should recall that the thinking behind this still supports the Regulation Q controls on savings and time deposit rates. There are three main arguments in favor of controls.

1. The practice of paying interest on demand deposits once drew funds from country banks (or banks in agricultural sectors) to the big city banks. This (*a*) drained funds from the agricultural sector and (*b*) resulted in such funds being used to make short-term loans to investors in the stock or commodities markets. With regard to (*b*), then, in a general liquidity crisis, especially one involving rapidly falling stock market prices, country banks' funds tended to be tied up, so that when the country banks called in their deposits (reserves), they were not readily available (and big city banks often had to suspend, in the worst crises). A number of the banking panics during the period 1837 to 1933 may well have got going in just this way. Note that if big banks do not pay an interest rate, they do not attract funds, so this justified a rate of zero. This argument is all but dead, today.

2. Prohibiting interest payments on demand deposits, helps prevent "excessive competition" and "unsound banking practices." In particular, if interest rates were variable banks would be led, by higher costs, to take on riskier assets (since, as we shall see in Chapter 14, riskier assets tend to have higher expected yields); when they do so, they would increase their vulnerability to financial panics. Thus, if banks pay nothing on deposits, we would eliminate this cost-determined item that, incidentally, would otherwise tend to fluctuate with the business cycle. That is, banks may overextend themselves in exactly the circumstances one would not want them to, at the peak of a (speculative?) boom. One suspects that this argument is still widely accepted.

3. Finally, it was argued (in the 1930s) that since bank earnings would be depressed by the high insurance charges paid to the Federal Deposit Insurance Corporation, this restriction would help to restore their profits. Note, especially, that both the restriction and the FDIC were the result of the same act, the Banking Act of 1933. This argument, too, seems less relevant, although we have observed, in Table 2.5 especially, the effect of the interest restrictions on bank profits.

The main argument running the other way, for the moment ignoring the specific items just described, is that the social benefits from the restrictions on interest rates (mainly having to do with the stability of the American banking system) are not larger than the social costs. Economists, in particular, argue that there are two significant wastes from the present system, aside from the general allocative inefficiency that results from fixing prices in a competitive economy.

1. Banks have tended to offer a variety of services to their customers in place of interest payments. These services are elements of barter in the

monetary system that are, no doubt, more expensive to the economic system than letting a price system operate. One of these services, in particular, is free checking, a practice that has caused customers to overuse check writing (it is, after all, a free good). If customers paid the cost of these services—and were paid an interest rate on their deposits—there would be much less check writing (and resources could be directed to other sectors of the economy). The number of checks written is, indeed, astronomical. Most of the new plans offered by banks under the automatic transfer from savings to checking accounts since November 1978 have restored (or raised) charges on checking accounts, but the effect this will have on check writing remains to be seen.

2. Individual savers tend to work very hard trying to keep their demand deposits at a minimum. This has cost them time and it has also cost the banking sector, in the sense that the volume of business has required, in recent years, special electronic techniques so that quick transfers can be made. Indeed, the appearance of such devices has made it a lot easier for banks to offer the new automatic transfers. That is, the restriction has stimulated technological change in payments techniques which, in turn, has tended to undermine the old system by lowering the cost of adjusting to the new system. The force of competition, in a word, has undermined the restriction, proving its lack of validity.

Finally, we might well consider what might happen if Congress, as it may well do in time, decides to end the practice of not paying interest on demand deposits, merging demand and savings deposits. In the short run, no doubt, banks would pay a positive interest rate and, no doubt, their profits would fall, since curtailing services might not be very easy at first. But whether or not banks would go into higher-yielding, and riskier, assets is not at all clear. For one thing, their owners (the stockholders of the bank) might well prefer that this not happen and instead opt for a realignment of services. For another thing, bank profits might well recover quickly, and demand-deposit interest rates might well go very low, after a short period of adjustment. Then, too, when a depositor receives a cash payment he must pay income taxes on it; conversely, a service provided in lieu of cash is not taxed. Finally, it is not clear, if it ever was, that banks actually take on riskier assets when their payout interest rates are market rates. Indeed, in the 1920s, banks did not engage in such practices to anything like the extent popular opinion attributed to them. Thus, for one thing, only a small percentage of their deposits were interest-paying at that time. Then, for another, the many failures of the 1930–33 period were due more to the general scramble for liquidity and to the inflexibility of the Federal Reserve System in the face of a liquidity squeeze, than to unwise bank behavior, so far as anyone has been able to demonstrate.[25] On net,

[25] We will return to the 1920–30 period in Chapters 4 and 5 in our historical discussions.

the case against the restriction seems to have a slight edge, although there are enough issues here to keep the debate going for awhile.

2.6 STUDY QUESTIONS

Essay questions

1. Discuss the ways that commercial banks have to attract more funds for lending even though there is no expansion in the total of reserves in the banking system. Divide your answer into the categories of "asset management" and "liability management," and consider some specific ways they might operate. Can they increase the "power" of a fixed reserve base, then? Explain.

2. How might the Federal Reserve, using its lending rate to commercial banks (the discount rate) tax bank profits? At what stage of the business cycle would this be most justified? Can banks pass on any increase in costs here to their customers, in order to avoid the tax?

3. It has been suggested elsewhere that commercial banks actually are manufacturing deposits for their customers, rather than "accepting" deposits. If this is correct, then a bank is just like any other business firm in this respect. How might one, then, deal with the liability we usually think goes with the deposit? That is, consider and discuss senses in which the deposit may not be a liability of the bank at all, but a product with an implied guarantee (of instant repurchase). Reference: Boris Pesek and Thomas Saving, *Money, Wealth, and Economic Theory* (New York: Macmillan, 1969).

True-false discussion questions

These statements are meant to be somewhat ambiguous, and to provoke discussion thereby.

1. The capital account of a commercial bank has no economic significance because it is merely a balancing item, like the "net worth" of the business firm.

2. In the 19th century, the notes of failed commercial banks circulated; this cannot be explained except in terms of the ignorance of the people using this money (ignorance of the true state of the failed bank).

3. Commercial bank profits would not fluctuate with the inflation rate if banks paid interest on demand deposits.

4. A financial system with controls over interest rates is likely to be a more stable financial system.

5. From the point of view of economic analysis, the failure of a commercial bank is no more important than the failure of any business firm.

6. While commercial banks can and do compete vigorously in loan markets, as *borrowers* they are essentially passive, since most of their liabilities (e.g., demand deposits) are brought to them by their lenders (or customers).

7. The main reason that inflation seems to stimulate bank profits is that inflation is produced by increases in the money supply and commercial banks are the main producers of money.

8. There is no real inconsistency in treating the commercial bank as both a profit-maximizing and a public-service institution, since by better serving the public's interests it also maximizes its profits.

9. Commercial banks face competitive markets in terms of their assets and noncompetitive markets in terms of their liabilities. This puts them in much the same position as farmers.

2.7 FURTHER READING

Federal Reserve Bank of Richmond. *Instruments of the Money Market*. 4th ed., 1977, Chapters 5–9.

Friedman, Milton, and Anna J. Schwartz. *A Monetary History of the United States*. Princeton, N.J.: Princeton University Press, 1963.

Hammond, Bray. *Banks and Politics in America*. Princeton, N.J.: Princeton University Press, 1957.

Higgins, Bryon. "Interest Payments on Demand Deposits: Historical Evolution and the Current Controversy." *Monthly Review, Federal Reserve Bank of Kansas City* (July/August 1976).

Homan, Paul T. "Changes in the Composition of Bank Assets and Liabilities." In Havrilesky, Thomas N., and John T. Boorman, eds., *Current Perspectives in Banking*. Arlington Heights, Ill.: AHM Publishing Company, 1976. See also papers in the same source by Edward E. Veazey (No. 3), on federal funds; Ronald D. Watson (No. 5), on bank bond management; Randall C. Merris (No. 7), on the prime rate; Stuart A. Schweitzer (No. 10), on bank liability management; Arnold A. Dill (No. 12), on member bank borrowing; George J. Vojta (No. 15), on bank capital adequacy; Stuart Greenbaum (No. 18), on correspondent banking; Margaret E. Bedford (No. 22), on the taxation of commercial banks; and Robert E. Knight (No. 24), on electronic funds transfers.

3

Banking markets: Problems and policies

3.1 INTRODUCTION

The subject matter of this chapter, what economists call the "market structure" of the American commercial banking industry, is the nature of monopoly and competition in American banking, as these have developed in the course of the 20th century. The most pressing issues concern the degree of competition in the industry and its relation to the allocation of our monetary resources; the following questions arise. Do we have too much or too little banking? Should we encourage mergers and branching to eliminate redundancy, or will more result anyway? Have we gone too far—or not far enough—in the regulation and supervision of commercial banks? Finally, should more competition and even more bank failure be encouraged in order to stimulate better prices for both borrowers and lenders?

Throughout this discussion there is a constant theme that runs as follows. For a variety of reasons we have turned away from the freely competitive form of behavior in the banking industry that was common in the 19th century and have evolved a web of controls and regulations that seem largely to insulate American commercial banks from the full force of competition. We will want to inquire as to the *extent* of this control and, as well, into the reasons for it. We will discover that many of the controls date from the 1930s, when American banking surely reached its lowest point; we will also discover that bankers have a way of getting what they want, and that internal competition has a way of undermining nonmarket solutions in spite of our fairly carefully administered regulations. For example, when mergers are blocked, banks branch; in turn, when branching is blocked, bankers form "holding companies" that may have controlling interests in several banks, thus sidestepping the regulations. As a result, therefore, there has been considerable institutional change in American banking, and while some of it is in line with experiences in other industries, some is unique to banking.

3.2 CONCENTRATION IN AMERICAN BANKING

The overriding fact about American banks is that while many of them are big—enormous, really—many are also quite small. When an industry—and banking is an industry—is dominated by a few large firms, we describe it as *concentrated*. Concentration is a relative concept, with a single-firm monopoly being a totally concentrated industry, while an industry with many small units, none of them big enough to use its market power to earn monopoly profits, is unconcentrated. When there are monopoly profits, furthermore, there are economic problems, for monopolists distort the allocation of resources (in their favor). We have some difficulty determining to what extent actual profits are monopoly revenues (in practice) but, at least, we are able to measure concentration, and to infer that an economic problem *may* exist (especially if we detect a trend toward greater concentration). One way we might measure the degree of concentration in an industry is to calculate the percentage of an industry's sales or assets that is "concentrated" in the top (say) 10 per-

Table 3.1: Share of total commercial bank deposits of 100 largest U.S. banking organizations (1934–1968)

Date	*Percentage*
December 1934	56.7
December 1940	59.4
December 1958	49.1
December 1962	49.5
December 1964	48.0
June 1968	49.0

Source: Benjamin F. Klebaner, "Recent Changes in the Structure of Banking," in *Bank Structure and Competition*, (Chicago: Federal Reserve Bank of Chicago, 1970).

cent of the firms in the industry; another, the one used here, is to calculate the share of total assets or deposits owned by a few (for example, ten) of the largest banks. For banking, one could use *either* total assets or total deposits as the measure of size; when this is done for deposits, we find that up to 1968, at least, *concentration* may not have been increasing in American banking, although the size of the typical banking firm certainly was. In this connection, consider Table 3.1, in which is listed the share of total deposits held by the 100 largest banks in the United States over the 1934–68 period. Here we see, rather clearly, that after reaching a peak somewhere just before 1940, the share of the largest 100 seemed to have stabilized at about 50 percent of the total by 1968.

The reason we are interested in concentration is that it provides an index of market power, although it is not a perfect one, to be sure.[1] If an industry is heavily concentrated—if a small number of firms have most of the business in the industry—then these firms may collude on price, or on other matters, and obtain monopoly profits. Indeed, if they were able, somehow, to keep out competition, then these monopoly profits might well be even greater. Thus the broad evidence up to 1968, at least, does not indicate an increasing ability to control the market in American banking, in that smaller banks (and bank number 101 on that list is very small compared to bank number 1 in 1968—the Bank of America) seem to have grown at the same rate as larger banks. But we may also look at some more recent data, in Table 3.2, collected from the *Fortune* magazine annual table of the 50 largest banking corporations. I have tabulated the results for the end of 1956, 1966, and 1976 and added some calculations of my own on ratios and some calculations based on figures in the *Federal Reserve Bulletin;* the text continues the series to 1978. Surprisingly, these figures show a mild upward trend in concentration over the 1956 to 1966 period (and thus are comparable enough to those in Table 3.1) and then a *very sharp* increase, no matter which figures one looks at, between 1966 and 1976. Thus, the mushrooming size of some of the world's largest banks seems finally to have brought to them a disproportionate share of American banking resources, with the top ten banks in 1976 controlling 34 percent of total banking assets and 34 percent of total deposits and the top 50 now controlling well over 50 percent of the total. Furthermore, the two largest banks, the Bank of America and the Citibank, are on a path that will have netted each of them $100 billion in assets by early 1980.

As any student of banking knows, though, comparing banks in Chicago (in a state with single-unit banking) with banks in California (which has statewide branching) may not be a valid approach. One reason that is so is that most banks do business primarily in their limited and local geographic

[1] A small number of large firms (i.e., an industry that is oligopolistic) may well be highly competitive in practice although, to be sure, collusion is certainly easier in this case.

Table 3.2: The top ten commercial banking companies ranked by total assets ($ millions—end of year)

		1976		*1966*		*1956*	
Holding company	*Bank*	*Rank*	*Assets*	*Rank*	*Assets*	*Rank*	*Assets*
BankAmerica Corp., San Francisco	Bank of America	1	73,913	1	18,213	1	9,992
Citicorp, New York	Citibank N.A.	2	64,282	3	15,066	3	7,588
Chase Manhattan Corp., New York	Chase Manhattan Bank, N.A.	3	45,638	2	15,776	2	7,757
Manufacturers Hanover Corp., New York	Manufacturers Hanover Trust Co.	4	31,483	5	7,729	4	3,137*
J. P. Morgan & Co., Inc., New York	Morgan Guaranty Trust Co. of New York	5	28,766	4	7,864	6	3,055†
Chemical New York Corp., New York	Chemical Bank	6	26,614	6	7,277	5	3,070
Bankers Trust New York Corp., New York	Bankers Trust Co.	7	22,249	7	5,945	8	2,821
Continental Illinois Corp., Chicago	Continental Illinois National Bank & Trust Co. of Chicago	8	21,975	8	5,609	9	2,769
First Chicago Corp., Chicago	First National Bank of Chicago	9	19,834	10	4,941	7	2,922
Western Bancorporation, Los Angeles	United California Bank (Los Angeles) and about 25 other banks	10	19,672		—		—
Security Pacific Corp., Los Angeles	Security Pacific National Bank		—	9	5,088	10	2,546

	1976	*1966*	*1956*
Total assets of 50 largest	581,738	163,415	83,718
Top 10, % of top 50 (total assets)	60.92	57.22	54.54
Top 50, % of total assets, all banks	56.40	36.96	33.39
Top 10, % of of total assets, all banks	34.39	21.15	18.21
Top 10, % of top 50 (deposits)	60.98	57.26	54.32
Top 10, % of all banks (deposits)	33.94	20.30	18.39
Top 50, % of all banks (deposits)	55.65	35.46	33.87

* Manufacturers Bank (before the merger with the Hanover Bank).
† Guaranty Trust (which merged with Morgan).
Source: *Fortune; Federal Reserve Bulletin*.

areas; indeed, the giant Bank of America in San Francisco comes into contact with the giant Citicorp of New York as much in foreign markets as in domestic, although in the domestic market such areas as wholesale banking, dealings in credit cards, and dealings in government securities are all important areas of conflict.[2] Thus the question of competition is clearly more complicated than the examination of nationwide ratios can reveal. The top ten banks have not changed their identity much, over the period studied. For 1978, to add a note to the table, Continental Illinois did rise to the number 7 position, Bankers Trust fell to number 9, and First Chicago fell to number 10. At that time, the Bank of America had $94.9 billion of assets, a gain of 28 percent over the figures in Table 3.2. The share of the top 10 in total bank assets declined slightly in the two years from December 1976 to December 1978, being 33.9 percent at the later date. The top 50 banks, though, grew from 56.4 percent to 60.4 percent in the same period.

Even though a rise in the *overall* concentration index may well suggest an increasingly monopolistic (and unresponsive) banking structure, it is probably the extent of *local* competition, where the typical bank does its business, with which we should concern ourselves. Table 3.2 actually does contain some information of a qualitative sort on local concentration; in particular, *six* of the top ten banks are "concentrated" in New York City. More revealingly, of the top 50 banks in the 1976 list in *Fortune,* 20 were located in just seven cities: New York (9), Chicago (4), Detroit (3), Los Angeles (3), San Francisco (3), Philadelphia (3), and Pittsburgh (2). It is arguable that of these cities, all but New York have highly concentrated banking sectors in the sense of being dominated by a very small number of firms. Thus, in 1968, the three largest banks in Pittsburgh had 81.1 percent of total deposits, while in Los Angeles, the five largest banks had 84.3 percent of total deposits.[3] On the other hand, around the country one finds a very mixed pattern with, in some cases, very concentrated banking sectors in very small towns ("one-bank towns"); as well, of course, one finds communities with increasing and communities with decreasing concentration, no matter how concentration is measured.

Probably the most interesting source of variation in the concentration figures comes from statewide figures on this measure (after all, we do not have branching across state lines, just yet). Looking at some Federal Reserve figures by state in Table 3.3, we see, formally, the extent of the variety that exists. We distinguish three types of states in this table: those which in 1973 had unit banking (U), limited branching (L), or statewide

[2] Note that these banks differ markedly in terms of their typical business, too. Indeed, recently, Bankers Trust sold many of its retail outlets in order to concentrate on wholesale banking. Others specialize in overnight lending, etc.

[3] Benjamin F. Klebaner, "Recent Changes in the Structure of Banking," in *Bank Structure and Competition* (Chicago: Federal Reserve Bank of Chicago, 1970).

Table 3.3: Percentage of statewide deposits held by five largest banking organizations

State	*1957*	*1961*	*1968*	*1973*
Alabama (L)	41.5	39.2	33.5	45.1
Alaska (S)	81.5	85.2	84.1	87.9
Arizona (S)	98.6	98.1	95.4	94.7
Arkansas (U)	24.2	23.9	21.1	21.0
California (S)	76.5	81.9	77.9	75.6
Colorado (U)	41.0	48.0	45.6	47.6
Connecticut (S)	49.3	56.4	56.6	61.3
Delaware (S)	86.6	91.7	92.0	92.0
District of Columbia (S)	73.4	88.7	91.4	88.8
Florida (U)	21.0	21.7	25.2	31.7
Georgia (L)	50.7	56.9	52.4	47.7
Hawaii (S)	N.A.	96.6	91.0	89.2
Idaho (S)	85.2	84.5	86.5	87.9
Illinois (U)	42.5	42.5	40.6	41.3
Indiana (L)	27.4	29.8	28.1	25.1
Iowa (U)	20.8	19.2	17.4	18.5
Kansas (U)	19.8	19.3	16.7	13.2
Kentucky (L)	32.3	33.9	33.5	29.7
Louisiana (L)	40.3	40.1	31.1	28.1
Maine (S)	38.8	47.7	48.4	69.9
Maryland (S)	51.9	57.6	62.7	61.3
Massachusetts (L)	57.3	64.2	65.4	62.9
Michigan (L)	52.9	50.0	48.4	46.9
Minnesota (U)	63.7	63.1	59.9	57.4
Mississippi (L)	25.7	28.4	32.4	33.4
Missouri (U)	38.8	35.4	29.4	32.8
Montana (U)	58.4	57.3	58.5	52.8
Nebraska (U)	40.3	41.2	37.7	31.8
Nevada (S)	100.0	98.6	95.6	97.0
New Hampshire (L)	34.7	34.9	37.8	40.1
New Jersey (L)	22.5	22.9	22.4	29.3
New Mexico (L)	56.6	55.7	50.3	63.6
New York (L)	52.3	54.9	58.5	55.4
North Carolina (S)	42.4	57.3	66.5	68.1
North Dakota (U)	53.1	54.3	49.2	49.8
Ohio (L)	35.3	33.4	32.5	33.3
Oklahoma (U)	41.1	37.4	34.5	28.7
Oregon (S)	91.4	89.2	87.4	83.1
Pennsylvania (L)	36.3	38.7	37.8	33.4
Rhode Island (S)	98.2	98.2	96.5	92.7
South Carolina (S)	50.6	53.0	55.4	56.1
South Dakota (S)	42.9	43.4	45.5	49.3
Tennessee (L)	40.1	40.9	39.9	42.1
Texas (U)	26.4	27.0	23.5	25.3
Utah (S)	78.8	76.6	72.2	72.0
Vermont (S)	29.1	36.0	47.4	54.9
Virginia (S)	28.0	27.1	46.4	50.7
Washington (S)	74.4	73.5	72.9	76.2
West Virginia (U)	24.6	22.1	19.3	17.5
Wisconsin (L)	31.5	33.3	31.9	32.9
Wyoming (U)	48.1	46.0	37.7	45.0

Note: U = Unit banking state; L = Limited branching state; S = Statewide branching state.

Source: Samuel H. Talley, "The Impact of Holding Company Acquisitions on Aggregate Concentration in Banking," *Board of Governors of the Federal Reserve System, Staff Economic Studies* (1974).

branching (S). Of the nine states with concentration ratios greater than 80 percent, *all* had statewide branching in 1973; of the ten states that had concentration ratios of less than 30.0 percent, *all* had either limited branching or unit banking in 1973. Of even more interest are the figures on the changes in concentration: 13 of the 15 states that had unit banking in 1973 had *decreases* in their concentration ratios from 1957 to 1973, and 13 of the 20 states that had statewide branching in 1973 had *increases* in their concentration ratios. Thus, clearly, concentration increases with branching, no matter how you slice it.

Our index of concentration, though, is far from a perfect measure of monopoly power (whatever that elusive concept might mean) and, in addition, is even further removed from the more general concept of the "economic efficiency" of the industry. If the *natural* size of a representative bank is much *larger* than presently has been attained—and it may well be—then we are basically being denied the optimal size of banking firm by a system of state and federal laws that are supposed to be increasing economic efficiency. Indeed, the optimal size just referred to may be much more efficient—may provide services to customers (borrowers and depositors) much more cheaply—than our present system. Furthermore, we may still have an "effective competition" in the industry, even if it should shrink from over 15,000 units to, say, 10 if the surviving giant banks were to engage in a stiff competition in terms of services *and* prices. In any event, bank concentration, aided by branching and, as we shall see, by mergers and possibly by the formation of holding companies, is probably on the increase in the United States (perhaps *even in local markets*).

3.3 MERGERS IN AMERICAN BANKING

One of the main ways a business firm can grow is in merging its operations with a competitor, thereby creating a larger firm. Mergers have been very common in American business (and in banking), and we are presently living in one of those periods in which a broad "merger movement" is afoot, although in the banking industry, at least, there seems to be a pause in this activity. The main reason for a merger, of course, is that the individual firms involved *expect* to gain additional profits thereby. The expected extra profits could come from a variety of sources; among these are:

a. The new combination may provide the opportunity of eliminating (now) redundant items in the capital equipment or in the labor force of the merging firms.

b. The new combination may have additional market power.

c. There may be tax advantages, such as tax write-offs of certain losses, not available to the individual firms.

d. There may be "economies of scale" in the new operation in any of its product activities, in management, in advertising, and in research.[4]

Whatever the source of the expected gains, commercial banks have been exerting a steady pressure on the authorities (mostly the Federal Reserve) to permit more mergers. And, we should note, banks are especially easy to merge in view of the uniformity brought to their financial structure by government regulation (and, no doubt, by banking practices, which differ very little from community to community).

While all of the factors just mentioned—and no doubt some others—are relevant in particular cases of merger, we should underscore the point that the pressure on the authorities to permit more mergers is greater the greater the economic advantages expected from expanding the scale of the commercial bank. In particular, if on net (taking into account all their operations) large banks show a steady tendency to have a greater "profit rate" than do small banks (where the profit rate is defined as the rate of return on capital), then banks will try to grow as fast as they can—by retained earnings, by new equity, by borrowing, by branching, and by merger—in order to gain these anticipated revenues. Furthermore, the facts suggest that such an opportunity exists in American banking, at least among the smaller banks; for example, the data in Table 3.4 show considerably higher rates of return for larger, insured commercial banks in the 1954–74 period,[5] with the difference very consistent over time, although not for every time period. It seems, then, from Table 3.4, that smaller banks were able to economize on their capital (that is, did not have to issue much new equity) as they grew large, so that they earned more, per dollar of invested capital, than did small banks. So the pressure to grow large in any way possible has been considerable and, perhaps, is increasing (compare 1954–59 to 1970–74, for example). Note, though, that the rate of return on capital has declined in all but the $5–10 million size grouping; mergers (etc.), thus, may have been the best way to avoid declining profit rates in this industry. Note, as well, as Table 3.5 illustrates, that when we look at the very largest banks versus all others, and calculate the rate of return on assets *and* rate of return on equity, there is no obvious difference. Thus, by the asset measure of capital, the big money market banks have considerably lower rates of return, while using equity as a base, the differences are not strong (although all rates show declining profits). Thus, while the decline in earnings rates is real enough (it appears in both tables), the advantages of larger size are not (at least on *actual* profit rates). The empirical record is clearly somewhat ambiguous.

[4] By "economies of scale" we mean that an x percent increase in the size of the firm (or in an activity of the firm) will result in a less than x percent increase in costs (and presumably a more than x percent increase in profits).

[5] The insurer is the Federal Deposit Insurance Corporation (FDIC).

Table 3.4: Rate of return on capital, all insured commercial banks, by bank size

	Bank size ($ millions)					
Year	*Less than 5*	*5–10*	*10–25*	*25–50*	*50–100*	*More than 100*
1954	13.546%	15.553%	17.169%	18.494%	18.652%	17.833%
1955	12.495	13.868	14.374	14.721	14.854	14.757
1956	12.168	13.238	13.943	14.471	15.001	15.055
1957	11.996	13.239	14.277	14.699	15.450	16.409
1958	12.304	14.659	16.618	18.934	18.752	20.705
1959	11.983	12.486	12.973	12.581	12.678	13.128
1960	13.027	14.583	16.191	17.488	17.568	19.280
1961	11.900	13.864	15.179	16.577	16.996	19.535
1962	11.416	13.057	13.997	14.339	15.307	16.578
1963	10.686	12.528	13.211	13.473	14.294	15.625
1964	10.984	13.051	13.576	13.849	13.622	14.639
1965	10.233	12.371	13.044	13.534	13.268	13.845
1966	11.038	12.550	13.028	13.257	13.005	13.019
1967	11.508	12.808	13.387	13.968	13.599	14.449
1968	11.826	13.751	14.414	14.703	14.075	14.463
1969	11.719	15.243	16.380	16.256	16.033	15.910
1970	12.276	15.770	16.599	16.162	15.980	15.488
1971	11.046	14.986	16.216	15.560	15.470	14.486
1972	8.766	13.966	15.797	15.719	15.267	14.439
1973	9.713	16.118	17.265	16.839	15.281	15.069
1974	9.302	15.674	16.871	14.944	14.098	15.234
1954–59	12.415	13.841	14.892	15.650	15.898	16.315
1960–64	11.603	13.417	14.431	15.145	15.557	17.131
1965–69	11.265	13.345	14.051	14.344	13.996	14.337
1970–74	10.221	15.303	16.550	15.845	15.219	14.943
1954–74	11.425	13.970	14.977	15.265	15.202	15.712

Note: Rate of return on capital is defined as net income before taxes divided by total capital account. This is not synonymous with "rate of return on equity," a preferable measure (see the text). Denominators for the 1969–74 period were calculated from all commercial banks. Ratios were computed from aggregate dollar amounts and expressed as percentages. Post-1968 figures are not strictly comparable because changes in reporting procedures were introduced in 1969. The remaining discrepancies, however, are minimal.

Source: Annual Reports of the Federal Deposit Insurance Corporation; Assets and Liabilities: Commercial and Mutual Savings Banks, FDIC; and report(s) of income and of condition submitted to the Federal Reserve System as published in Edward C. Gallick, "Bank Profitability and Bank Size" *Monthly Review, Federal Reserve Bank of Kansas City* (January 1976).

Mergers, for some time, have been especially numerous, and, no doubt, will certainly go on. It has been estimated that during the 1950 to 1962 period, nearly 2,000 banks, with resources of over $40 billion, were acquired by other banks.[6] Indeed, since 1950, well over 4,000 commercial banks have merged, many, no doubt, as the result of a "takeover" of a

[6] Kalman J. Cohen and Samuel R. Reid, "The Benefits and Costs of Bank Mergers," *Journal of Financial and Quantitative Analysis* (December 1966).

Table 3.5: Profit and dividend rates of insured banks of different sizes

	1973	1974	1975	1976	1977
I. Return on Average Assets					
All banks	.75	.72	.69	.70	.71
Banks less than $1 billion	.92	.91	.83	.86	.90
Banks over $1 billion	.61	.57	.57	.57	.56
Money center banks	.60	.56	.56	.54	.50
II. Return on Average Equity					
All banks	12.9	12.6	11.8	11.6	11.8
Banks less than $1 billion	13.2	12.5	11.3	11.6	12.2
Banks over $1 billion	12.5	12.8	12.5	11.6	11.3
Money center banks	13.2	14.2	13.8	12.3	11.4
III. Cash Dividends (% of net income)					
All banks	—	39	42	39	37
Banks of less than $100 million assets	—	28	30	27	26
Banks of $100 million–$1 billion	—	46	46	45	37
Banks over $1 billion					
Not money center	—	48	53	47	46
Money center	—	43	44	43	45

Source: *Federal Reserve Bulletin* (June 1978).

small bank and its branches by a substantially larger bank. Mergers are surely undertaken in the expectation of increased profitability for the investors, and they probably increase concentration in banking markets, but the latter depends on the growth of the total banking industry in the area and cannot be decided in its own light. For example, a study of mergers in the 1961–68 period in three states that had considerable merger activity reveals that banking concentration did not necessarily rise in these circumstances; this is documented in Table 3.6.

In Table 3.6 concentration is measured by the percentage of deposits held by the five largest banks. Thus, in California, a vigorous growth of the entire banking community has modified somewhat the effect of mergers on concentration, although California is clearly a state with considerable concentration (see Table 3.3 for a further decline to 1973). North

Table 3.6: Mergers and concentration in banking for three states, 1961–1968

	Number of mergers, 1961–68	Number of banks		Concentration*	
		1961	1968	1961	1968
California	69	122	162	81.4	77.9
New Jersey	60	247	229	22.5	22.4
North Carolina	67	171	121	60.9	66.5

* Percentage of deposits in five largest banks.
Source: Alexander J. Yeats, "An Analysis of the Effect of Mergers on Banking Market Structures," *Journal of Money, Credit and Banking* (1973), p. 624.

Carolina, on the other hand, had a sharp decline in the number of banks and a rapid rise in its concentration; indeed of all the states in the country, only Virginia and Vermont had a more rapid increase of concentration in this period (and North Carolina's concentration increased straight up to 1973, as Table 2.3 shows).[7]

In the face of the possibility that profit rates are helped by the extremely intense recent merger activity in the industry, what sort of legal climate do we have? In a nutshell, American policy seems to be generally permissive, with some backsliding; the proposals of only the largest banks are subjected to severe scrutiny (and some are, of course, turned down). The general rules that have been laid down follow the general prescription in the Clayton Act of 1914, which prohibits the acquisition of the stock of another company when "the effect of such acquisition may be substantially to lessen competition, or to tend to create a monopoly;" in addition, interlocking directorates are prohibited in banking.[8] The regulations are administered by the Board of Governors of the Federal Reserve System for banks that are members of the Federal Reserve System, although the Justice Department can attack mergers even after the Board has approved them. Note that mergers between state-chartered banks are approved by their respective state banking commissions (under these general guidelines).

The next question concerns the manner in which the Federal Reserve determines whether a merger is or is not in the public interest, in view of the problem that the legal definition is not entirely clear. For this purpose, Congress has attempted to lay down some guidelines in the Bank Merger Act (1960), as amended (1966), and the Bank Holding Company Act (1956) as amended (1970). In addition there have been some court cases, the most notable being the Philadelphia National Bank case (1963) and the First National Bank of Lexington, Kentucky, case (1964).[9] In practice the authorities look at measures of concentration in the various banking activities and at the form of the merger (they do not seem to like mergers in

[7] Note that these states did not have any holding company activity during this period, to confuse the issue. We will discuss the bank holding company in the next section. Note as well, that Virginia went from limited to statewide branching in 1962.

[8] "No private banker or director, officer, or employee of any member bank of the Federal Reserve System or any branch thereof shall be at the same time a director, officer, or employee of any other bank, banking association, savings bank, or trust company . . . except . . . [by permission of] . . . the Board. . . ."

[9] The Bank Merger Act divided the responsibility for ruling on mergers between the Federal Deposit Insurance Corporation (insured nonmember banks), the Federal Reserve (member banks), and the Comptroller of the Currency (national banks). In the amendment (1966) it was decided that the Justice Department could attack a merger (presumably passed by one or more of the three agencies) in the courts; this had already happened in the Philadelphia case (1963), in which the Clayton Act (1914) was invoked and the Lexington, Kentucky, case, in which the Sherman Antitrust Act (1890) was invoked. We will discuss the holding company legislation mentioned in the text in Section 3.4.

which equity is replaced by debt—that is, in which the old stockholders are bought out by funds raised through a bond issue) and make a judgment. The opinions are routinely published in the pages of the *Federal Reserve Bulletin,* when the Federal Reserve is the agency involved. The weight given to "substantially lessen competition" in the Clayton Act clearly varies from situation to situation, but the general impression one gets reading these reports is that of a vague "public interest criterion" in terms of whether local concentration will increase significantly or not. Indeed, one could argue that so long as the Federal Reserve operates under its present rules, the merger movement in banking will continue, although if the pages of the *Federal Reserve Bulletin* are any indication, the merger activity is presently declining somewhat (either because of stricter surveillance *or* because the good opportunities have been used up, for the moment).

3.4 BANK HOLDING COMPANIES

Actually, the same pages of the *Federal Reserve Bulletin* that reflect the current decline in merger activity among banks are also recording a large volume of applications to form bank holding companies. Bank holding companies—companies formed to hold the stock of one or more banks—have long existed as a practice in the industry (they were in existence after the arrival of the National Banking System). The modern growth of this form, which at first might seem somewhat unrelated to the day-to-day management of the banking firm, seems related to two main factors:

a. Multibank holding companies have been formed—or have expanded—in order to sidestep state regulations on branching (or merger).

b. Both multibank and one-bank holding companies have emerged to enable commercial banks to branch into nonbanking activities.

In addition, as implied in (*a*), there is the possibility of gaining some advantages similar to the "economies of scale" that seem to have motivated much of the American merger and (as we shall see) branching activity in the banking industry. These, in particular, include offering more services (that is, expanding into new product lines), strengthening the capital structure of the firm, and improving the mobility of capital over the relevant area (that is, expanding their market geographically), as well as, simply, profiting from a more efficient operation.

The typical bank holding company of the 1920s, when this business form really started to develop, was a state-chartered corporation empowered to do business—often any business—within the state. What their owners—usually bankers—did was to acquire the majority interest in a number of financial institutions in order to gain the advantages listed above; at the time the United States was in a general merger movement, and this device was much favored since the holding company can create a de facto merger of banks that the authorities find hard to deal with since it retains the (apparent) autonomy of the separate institutions. Probably, in the 1920s, the two most important reasons for the many mergers were the relative weakness of the many small banks—the rate of bank failure was very high then (see Section 3.6)—and the existence of the great bull market in securities, which put pressure on financial institutions (as it did on everyone) to try to accumulate more funds to get a piece of the action. The latter was almost certainly the dominant motive.

In the Banking Act of 1933, the Board of Governors of the Federal Reserve System gained some control over bank holding companies, so long as one of the banks controlled was a member of the Federal Reserve System. This, however, was a regulatory power of little practical use, and the Federal Reserve could not even prevent the expansion of holding companies across state lines. In 1956, when a new merger movement was in progress, Congress passed the Bank Holding Company Act. This act provides our formal definition of a *bank holding company:* any company that directly or indirectly holds 25 percent or more of each of two or more banks or one that controls the election of a majority of the directors of two or more banks. (In addition, an operation is a holding company if it has 25 percent interest in two or more banks held "in trust.") The Act of 1956 also required that all multibank holding companies—whether member banks of the Federal Reserve System or not—must register with the Board of Governors of the Federal Reserve System and must submit to an examination by the Federal Reserve System. The purpose of the law, clearly, was to control the formation and expansion of the *multibank* holding company and to limit the range of its activities to those traditional in banking. In addition, the act instructed the Federal Reserve to take an interest in both the solvency of the banking operation that resulted and in its general effect on competition in the area which it served.[10] The act was amended in 1966 to bring its language on what constituted a monopoly into line with that of the Bank Merger Act of 1960 (itself consistent with the Clayton and Sherman Acts).

The Act of 1956 seems to have produced (or coincided with) a slowdown in the rate of formation of bank holding companies until around 1965, as the data in Table 3.7 indicate. But after 1965 there was another takeoff of the holding-company form as more than a third of the American banking system came under the control of *multibank holding empires*. One cannot help but think that this is another manifestation of the general

[10] The act also prohibited expansion across state lines unless the states concerned should permit it (none does). But the nonbank activities can and do cross state lines.

Table 3.7: Multibank holding companies in the United States, 1956–1973

End of	*Number of companies*	*Number of banks*	*Percentage of United States banking offices*	*Percentage of total deposits in United States*
1956	49	428	5.8	7.5
1960	42	426	6.2	8.0
1965	48	468	6.7	8.3
1970	111	895	11.8	16.2
1973	218	1726	22.4	34.2

Source: Gregory F. Boczar, "The Growth of Multibank Holding Companies: 1956–1973," *Federal Reserve Staff Study* (1976), p. 5.

merger movement in banking, undertaken for the same reasons but taking this particular form because (*a*) one obtains branches in unit-banking states,[11] (*b*) the chances of success were greater than attempting a merger, and (*c*) the opportunity was present to engage in nonbanking activities.

The first is an important factor, clearly, while the second is hard to evaluate. The third, though, probably accounts for the interest of the superpowers in the banking industry; and it is these superpowers that were mainly involved in the dramatic growth after 1965. This factor also stimulated growth in the *one-bank holding company,* as we shall now see.

Between June 1, 1968, and December 31, 1970, 690 new one-bank holding companies were formed in the United States; they represented more than 50 percent of the total of 1,318 one-bank holding companies in existence at the end of that period. While some concern over this activity had been expressed in the debates over earlier banking legislation, this rapid development seems to have caught everyone by surprise. As already noted, the principal reason for this sudden spurt was probably the fact that one-bank holding companies were not restricted in the scope of their nonbank activities—depending on state laws—and so a loophole in the law was exploited. Of course the existing law (the Act of 1956) was aimed primarily at banking monopolies, so this omission is understandable. In fact, one-bank holding companies are obviously not going to bring a direct banking monopoly, although, to be sure, considerable financial power could be generated in some communities by, for example, tying together finance companies and mortgage companies into the one-bank holding company; in addition, such financial conglomerates could obtain the advantage of the risk-spreading that comes with diversification (see Chapter 14). At any rate, for almost purely regulatory reasons, the Board of Gov-

[11] At the end of 1974, the 15 unit-banking states had 2,143 banks controlled by holding companies, while the 21 full-branching states had 423 banks so controlled. But, one should note, many of the banks in the unit states were controlled by one-bank holding companies.

ernors now has to decide (usually favorably) on a large number of applications for the registration of one-bank holding companies.[12]

Finally, let us attempt to visualize how the development of holding companies might have contributed to the concentration of American banking; obviously, this topic involves primarily the multibank holding company. As it stands, with concentration probably increasing, this may well be an important issue in the years to come. For the moment, we only have data, based on the results in Table 2.3, that generally did not show an increase in concentration (except in some states). For those results, which showed the overall concentration declining by 2 percent from 1968 to 1973, the same author estimated that if there had been no holding company activity, concentration would have fallen by 4 percent; in other words, holding company activity, overall, contributed to a 2 percent *increase* in concentration. (The increase is limited, of course, to some states, so that in some cases it is more than the average of 2%.) On the other hand, other data suggest that the top 20 banking firms in the country did not rely on holding company acquisitions for their phenomenal growth.[13] Thus, while these results underscore the potential effect of this type of

---

[12] The following list of permitted and nonpermitted activities for bank holding companies, as determined by the Board of Governors, appeared in *Business Conditions, Federal Reserve Bank of Chicago* (August 1973), p. 6.

Activities APPROVED by the Board

1. Dealer in bankers' acceptances
2. Mortgage company
3. Finance company
4. Credit card company
5. Factoring company
6. Operating an industrial bank
7. Servicing loans
8. Trust company
9. Investment adviser to real estate investment trusts and to investment companies under the Investment Company Act of 1940
10. Furnishing general economic information and advice
11. Providing portfolio investment advice
12. Full pay-out leasing of personal property
13. Investments in community welfare projects
14. Providing bookkeeping or data processing services
15. Acting as insurance agent or broker, primarily in connection with credit extensions
16. Underwriting credit life insurance

Activities DENIED by the Board

1. Equity funding (the combined sale of mutual funds and insurance)
2. Underwriting general life insurance
3. Real estate brokerage
4. Land development
5. Real estate syndication
6. Management consulting
7. Property management

Activities UNDER CONSIDERATION by the Board

1. Leasing real property
2. Armored car and courier services
3. Mortgage guarantee insurance
4. Management consulting for nonaffiliated banks
5. Savings and loan associations

[13] Samuel H. Talley, "The Impact of Holding Company Acquisitions on Aggregate Concentration in Banking," *Staff Economic Study, Board of Governors of the Federal Reserve System* (1974).

reorganization on the measured concentration in the banking industry, it is still possible that other, more direct, estimates of the benefits of monopoly—such as excess profits or higher interest rates in locally concentrated markets—may give results more suggestive of increasing monopoly power.

Another way of looking at the economic role of the multibank holding company is to consider the effects on a bank that has been acquired in this fashion. Actually, the differences are not striking, and a number of studies have shown that multibank holding companies do not differ from other banks in terms of their prices, their capital structure, or the composition of their liabilities, but *more fundamentally,* they do not differ in terms of their profitability (or their rates of growth).[14] These results, particularly that on profits, are somewhat perplexing in view of the enthusiastic adoption of the multibank holding company by the private-enterprise banking industry. There are, though, some less essential differences, such as the finding that holding-company banks

a. Tend to acquire more state and local debt and move away from cash and U.S. government securities.

b. Tend to increase the proportion of their loans that are installment loans.

c. Have both greater costs and greater revenues (so that profits remain constant).

Items (*a*) and (*b*), at least, suggest a slightly higher risk taken up by these banks (presumably this is possible because of the broader capital structure) but (*c*) also shows that this extra risk is not compensated for by higher profits. On this evidence, at least, the holding company movement has produced no solid *ex post* evidence in its favor; presumably *ex ante* the banks saw some potential gains in profitability or they would not have entered into the holding companies. These results certainly do not suggest that the movement will continue at the same rate as in the immediate past, although other factors may emerge (or have affected the situation in the past even though researchers failed to identify them).

More recently, the Board of Governors has released the results of a comprehensive study of the holding company movement.[15] The above points were corroborated, although the board did not feel that the addi-

[14] See Samuel H. Talley, "Bank Holding Companies: Their Growth and Performance," *Staff Economic Study, Board of Governors of the Federal Reserve System* (1972); apparently this pattern is confirmed even at the micro level; see Stuart G. Hoffman, *The Impact of Holding Company Affiliations on Bank Performance: A Case Study of Two Florida Multibank Holding Companies,* (Atlanta: Federal Reserve Bank of Atlanta, 1976).

[15] *The Bank Holding Company Movement to 1978: A Compendium* (Washington, D.C.: Board of Governors of the Federal Reserve System, 1978).

tional risk was necessarily socially desirable. In addition, they noted several other broad conclusions about the movement.

a. There was no general evidence that there were gains due to economies of scale in multibank holding companies.[16]

b. There has been little general change in concentration in the banking industry due to holding companies and (therefore) little effect on competition in the industry (pro or con).

This study, too, finds no reason for Americans to worry about holding companies, at least at this juncture.

3.5 THE BRANCH BANK CONTROVERSY

Around 1900, virtually all banks were unit banks, that is, banks with one office, and even up to the end of World War II, fewer than 10 percent of American banks operated branches. But since then branching has become more and more widespread, and state laws have relaxed in this respect, so that now the majority of American banking units are branches, although not in all states. Indeed, branch banking, on a nationwide basis, has expanded over the years, and as Table 3.8 illustrates for the 1969–74 period, has expanded rapidly at times. Here one sees that actually a large

Table 3.8: Branch banking in the United States, 1969 and 1974

	Total banks		*Federal Reserve member banks*	
	Number	*Branches*	*Number*	*Branches*
U.S. 1969	13,622	19,985	5,871	15,015
U.S. 1974	14,457	28,244	5,782	19,787
Statewide branching				
California 1969	155	2,857	77	2,557
California 1974	198	3,459	63	2,964
Limited branching				
New York 1969	320	2,294	283	2,167
New York 1974	304	3,084	224	2,907
Pennsylvania 1969	492	1,611	342	1,211
Pennsylvania 1974	406	2,188	265	1,511
Unit banking				
Illinois 1969	1,088	68	501	50
Illinois 1974	1,203	186	491	105

Source: *Federal Reserve Bulletin* (April 1975; April 1970).

[16] But note that electronic funds transfers (which are gaining ground quickly) may provide extra gains of the nature of economics of scale to banking firms that are multibank holding companies or financial conglomerates.

part of the recent growth in the American banking system (especially in terms of numbers of banking units) has been in branching activity; this has been about evenly divided between member and nonmember banks of the Federal Reserve System, although the number of banks in the system has tended to decline (this decline, continuing even now, is discussed in Section 4.5).

But the most interesting thing about branching in the United States is the diversity among the various states, primarily as a result of state laws. Roughly speaking, we can divide states into three categories: states with unit banking, states with limited branching, and states with statewide branching. Table 3.6 actually contained some data for four large states that illustrate some of this diversity. Thus in the two limited branching states, New York and Pennsylvania,[17] the number of banks actually declined while the number of offices rose during the period covered; in California, with statewide branching, both actually *increased*. In the unit bank state, Illinois, there was an increase in both banks and branches; these branches were limited by law to drive-in facilities no more than 1,500 feet from the main building.

The situation, around 1976, for the entire United States, is shown in Figure 3.1. Here one sees that the (predominantly) agricultural midwest

Figure 3.1: Branch banking in the United States

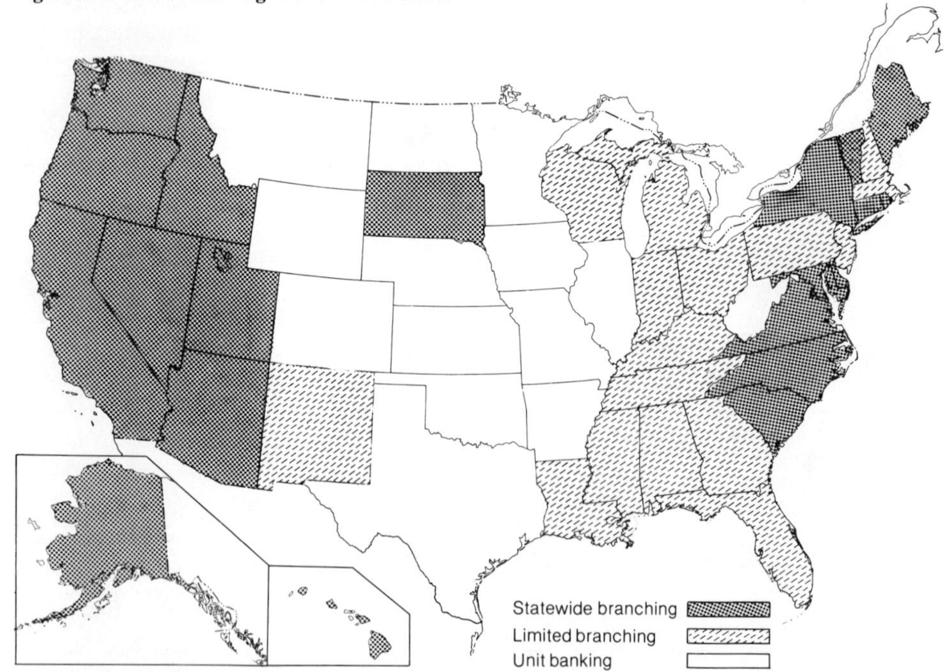

[17] New York got statewide branching in 1976 and Florida got limited branching in 1978.

favors unit banking, while in the rest of the country either limited or statewide branching is the rule, with the states along the edges of the country tending to favor statewide branching. One is tempted to try to explain this pattern, which is gradually changing, in historical terms. Probably many of the state laws on banking were laid down soon after the states entered the union; if these laws were developed during a period of recurrent bank failures, or if the state had the usual agricultural mistrust of banking monopolies, a unit banking structure would have been adopted. These, though, are merely conjectures.

The present legal climate was established by the McFadden Act (1927), which permitted national banks to operate branches in their home office city,[18] and the Banking Act of 1933, which permitted national banks to branch to the extent permitted to state banks. At the time of the act there were 2,780 branches of banks in the United States. These acts simulated a number of state acts in the same period, going one way or the other, depending on the aforementioned state "tastes." But, in any event, state laws are presently relaxing gradually, particularly in the limited branching states, and branching is on the increase geographically as well as numerically.[19]

The numbers on branching are interesting, to be sure, but the most interesting aspect of branching is the long-standing debate over its effects. We have seen some apparent consequences of branching in earlier sections of this chapter. Most importantly, in Section 3.2 we noted that in recent years states with unit banking showed declines in statewide concentration compared to states with unlimited branching. In addition, in Section 3.3 we noted that states with limited or statewide branching have showed a strong merger movement; in many cases this, too, has increased concentration. Finally, in Section 3.4 we noted that the formation of multibank holding companies has occurred in response, at least partly, to the desire to branch (in effect) where branching is either limited or forbidden by state law. Of course, as we have also noted, the ability to enter into nonbank activities may have been the most important incentive to form multibank holding companies.

The clearest charge against branching is that it leads to higher concentration of ownership of the banking units, and that higher concentration, in turn, leads to the distortions brought by monopoly power to the allocation of our financial resources. We have seen some figures on the degree of

[18] The members of the National Banking System, until 1927, were not permitted to branch at all, although there was no provision in the National Banking Act to that effect.

[19] New York, in 1971, passed an act permitting statewide branching as of 1976, and Virginia went over to statewide branching in 1962; other states have liberalized their laws in recent years. Until 1978 foreign banks could operate branches across state lines. One notices, in the discussions in Congress in 1979, that the sentiment behind the McFadden Act is gradually weakening, and one can anticipate that banks will soon be branching over state lines in some functions (wholesale banking being one) and, eventually, even in terms of their retail outlets.

concentration suggesting, at least, that the premise may be true, but those either were on a statewide basis or compared large banks to small banks. In local markets, where population and incomes are expanding rapidly—and branching is certainly popular in such situations—a vigorous "branching competition" may exist to counteract any increase in overall *firm* size. Along the same lines, a vigorous debate over whether branching is subject to "economies" or "diseconomies" of scale has erupted. By an "economy of scale," to repeat, we mean that a 10 percent increase in, say, loan activity, is achieved with a less than 10 percent increase in costs. It appears, then, that there actually are economies of scale for many banking operations (e.g., lending, deposit-taking, etc.), considering the banking operation as a whole, but whether branching itself leads to such economies has certainly not been verified, although the evidence seems slightly in favor of mild economies of scale.[20] On net, then, bank customers may have benefited from the extension of branches in recent years, but, in turn, the industry will tend to grow more concentrated at the same time, as firms try to take advantage of the economies that they perceive to be there.

The preceding, which raised an issue concerning the economies of branches versus banks as a whole gets us into another area, the pros and cons of "full-service" versus "partial-service" banking units. In fact, bank branches actually differ depending on their location and depending on the services that they provide (for example, one often finds very small branches located on or near university campuses). Indeed, many branches do not offer all of the services available from the bank as a whole; the omissions range from certain retail operations, like providing foreign currencies on demand, to specialized investment or trust operations. In addition, the research operation (an increasingly important aspect of a commercial bank's activities) and the management function are generally centralized. This is, in many ways, an advantage of branching from an economic point of view, since resources are likely to be saved in this way. But there are some disadvantages. In particular, the customer at the branch may want a service not available there; furthermore, some decisions may have to be referred to the central office, where the "local interest" may not survive. Indeed, the branch may be less responsive to all sorts of local community needs—most especially the local community need for capital—than a unit bank on the same location would be. On the other hand, it is just as well to point out that one may not even get a unit bank on the same location, if the branch's economies of scale come partly from being able to use the centralized facilities more efficiently. Many small towns, after all, do not have a bank.

---

[20] "The Perennial Issue: Branch Banking," *Business Conditions, Federal Reserve Bank of Chicago* (February 1974).

By far the biggest advantage of the branch, though, is the flexibility this form has brought to the banking industry. As it stands, small banking operations can be dotted around the landscape, following trade and permitting customers to sample some pretty sophisticated financial and electronic technology at much less cost to themselves. That is, transactions costs are lowered, to the customer, and net costs may be too, if the branch can offer the service at the same rate as the head office. Finally, to close the subject of branch banking, we note that branching may eliminate some of the risks of the banking firm, by permitting banks to shift with population and other trends, as the situation requires. At the extreme, unit banks caught in an expanding urban ghetto may well find it advantageous to close their doors rather than to attempt to follow their customers, assuming they cannot come to terms with the requirements of their new clientele. This directly brings us to the last topic in this chapter, the multifaceted problem of bank failure.

3.6 BANK FAILURE

Prior to the 1930s, it seems, an inevitable accompaniment to every financial and business depression in the United States was widespread bank failure (and/or bank suspension). Thus, as Figure 3.2 shows, bank failures showed peaks in the 1871–79, 1893, 1903–08, and 1913–15 periods, indicating that there was a cyclical pattern to the problem, since each of these periods showed a significant depression of economic activity as well. By far the most intriguing aspect of Figure 3.2 is the rising tide of bank failures that emerged after the First World War under the aegis of the newly created Federal Reserve System. This reached a peak in 1931, when approximately 2,000 banks, with deposits of around $1.7 billion, failed. Under the Federal Reserve System either something had gone wrong technically or capitalism itself was on the ropes; the lawmakers opted for the former, and the 1930s saw a period of reform of the system, which seems to have brought the problem under control, but not without an early relapse in 1933, as Table 3.8 shows. Indeed, from 1929 to 1933, the number of banks in operation fell by more than one-third.

As Table 3.9 also reveals, a sudden drop in bank failures/suspensions occurred from 1934 onwards, returning the system in the 1930s to something like the state it was in prior to the advent of the Federal Reserve. This was achieved through the legislation of the early 1930s; the areas in which regulation was adopted, mostly in the Banking Act of 1933, concerned bank interest rates paid on deposits (as discussed in Chapter 2), bank behavior, the periodic examination of bank records, and most importantly, the creation of the Federal Deposit Insurance Corporation (FDIC). It was widely believed then (as now) that bank failures could be prevented by careful supervision and control—hence the regulatory provisions—but

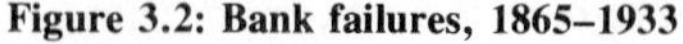

Figure 3.2: Bank failures, 1865–1933

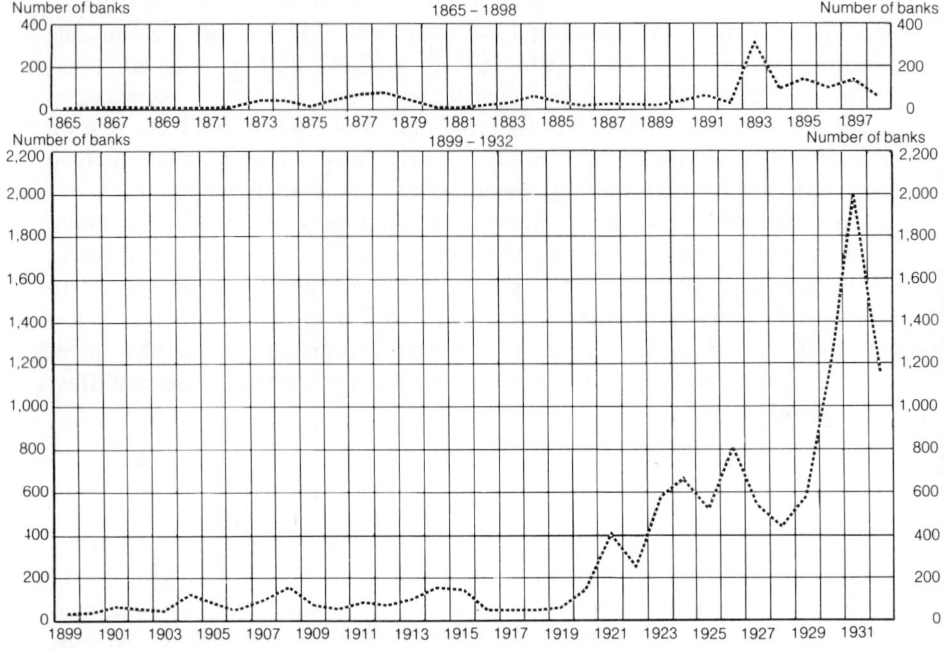

Source: *Review, Federal Reserve Bank of St. Louis* (November 1975).

it was probably the insurance scheme, the FDIC, that, because it ensured that customer's deposits were safe even if the bank failed, brought an end to the recurrent "runs" on American commercial banks. The run, after all, was directly responsible for the sudden contraction of the banking system that was the special feature of the typical financial panic.[21]

The Federal Deposit Insurance Corporation exacts a premium from all insured banks (a small number of commercial banks, mostly foreign in origin, are not insured) in return for insuring demand and savings accounts up to $40,000 (at present); the amount insured was $2,500 in the original act. The powers available to the FDIC in the case of failed banks, are

a. Direct payment to insured depositors.

b. The replacement of management or the encouragement of mergers to protect the depositors.

c. Direct loans (since 1950).

[21] In Chapter 5 we will examine this matter in more detail, using a model of money stock determination.

Table 3.9: Commercial bank suspensions in the United States, 1926–1940

	Number of suspensions	*Deposits ($ million)*
1926	975	260
1927	669	199
1928	498	142
1929	659	231
1930	1,350	837
1931	2,293	1,690
1932	1,453	706
1933	4,000	3,597
1934	61	37
1935	31	14
1936	72	28
1937	82	34
1938	80	58
1939	71	159
1940	48	143

Note: Suspensions were more numerous than failures, as a comparison of Figure 3.2 and Table 3.8 should suggest; that is, some (but in 1931 not many) suspended banks do reopen (2,000 of the 4,000 banks suspended in 1933 did *not* reopen).

Source: Milton Friedman and Anna J. Schwartz, *A Monetary History of the United States: 1867–1960* (Princeton, N.J.: Princeton University Press for the National Bureau of Economic Research, 1963), p. 438.

d. Transferring the deposits to an insured bank—especially created for the purpose—for a period of no more than two years. This bank may then be sold (by stock subscription) to the public.

These powers, clearly, provide considerable protection to depositors, to the system, and even to bank owners, and are not much in debate as desirable methods of control (although [*c*] and [*d*] are rarely employed).[22]

In fact, bank failures continued to decline after 1940; by 1960 virtually no banks in the country failed at all (there were two failures that year). This seems to have happened because, over the years, the FDIC has broadened its powers and has been able actually to aid a distressed bank and thus to *prevent* the failure of individual banks. Now the issue of prevention of bank failure is presently a hot one, since there might well be an optimal rate of failure in the industry, not necessarily zero, at which the country gets just enough competitive pressure to keep banks in the indus-

[22] When a bank is taken over by the FDIC, frequently that regulatory agency ends up with a collection of assets to dispose of (if the FDIC has to pay off any depositors, it obtains a claim on the assets). These assets are not necessarily conventional business enterprises (see *The Wall Street Journal,* September 20, 1978).

try from obtaining significant monopoly revenues. The proponents of strict bank regulation argue that the costs of a bank failure go far beyond the individual bank itself, even involving a potential threat to the system as a whole. Certainly, historically, bank runs were usually triggered by the collapse of a key bank although, since the failure of the Franklin National Bank of New York (a bank with $1.7 billion in deposits at the time) in October 1974 did not produce a general panic, this might be an overrated factor.[23] Of course the direct effect on the community, in terms of upsetting the finances of loan and deposit customers, is another matter. We must remember, as well, that deposit money may well be a "public good" in that there are social benefits to a smoothly working monetary system that go far beyond the direct benefits to the customers, employees, and owners of the banks. In this connection we should recall that capitalism in the United States was clearly threatened by the upturn in the failure rate of banks in the 1920s, and the advantages of a monetary economy were not so obvious by 1933.

All of this public interest notwithstanding, a case actually can be made in favor of bank failure or, more exactly, in favor of permitting competitive forces to operate more freely in the banking and financial markets. We have discussed (in Chapter 2) how permitting banks to pay interest on all their deposits and removing interest ceilings might eliminate some of the runoff and portfolio problems that increase the costs of operating our financial system; as well, we doubted the effectiveness of such controls in preventing unsound competition among commercial banks, in any event. In addition, regulations such as those discussed in this chapter may tend to reduce banks' incentives to compete and to innovate, bringing less progress to an industry many feel has tended to become increasingly conservative behind its protective shield. Last, and by no means least, we should note that "failure" in any industry is merely the "orderly" exit of

[23] The Franklin Bank failure was the largest in U.S. history, topping that of the U.S. National Bank of San Diego a year earlier (the deposits of the latter were $934 million). The FDIC was trying to save the San Diego bank before it collapsed from managerial errors; when the collapse became certain, the FDIC arranged that the Crocker National Bank would operate the offices of the San Diego Bank as branches of the Crocker Bank (the Crocker actually "won" in a sealed-bid contest). The main reason for special concern in this case was that insured deposits totaled $700 million (a big bill for the FDIC) and uninsured totaled $230 million (a big shock to the public's confidence). The Franklin Bank's failure was the result of poor management also, with its foreign exchange losses being most important, since after the public announcement of those losses, depositors withdrew 53 percent of their deposits in a very short time. This time the Federal Reserve was initially involved in lending reserves; when the bank was suspended, its liabilities and certain assets were sold to the European-American Bank and Trust Company (a consortium of banks). In both cases no business days were lost in the switchover to a new owner. See Walter A. Varvel, "FDIC Policy Toward Bank Failures," *Economic Review, Federal Reserve Branch of Richmond* (October 1976). In December 1977 the European American Bancorporation was the 28th largest U.S. bank with deposits of $4.5 billion and the Crocker bank was the 13th largest, with deposits of $10.5 billion.

firms that are no longer competitive.[24] Thus, if the government legislates effectively against failure, it may well impose the costs of an inefficient allocation of resources on the economy, costs that may be greater than the gains to the system as a whole through the externalities and internal economies of scale. On the other hand, recent events suggest that bank regulations has slackened somewhat (How else could two such large banks as the U.S. National Bank of San Diego and the Franklin National Bank of New York have failed?) and that banks are apparently competing more energetically in their traditional activities as well as in offering new services, in branching, and in getting into activities not traditional for the industry.[25]

There is some evidence on these matters. First of all, we note in Table 3.10 that there has been a marked increase in failures and possibly in competitive pressures in recent years, although the absolute numbers remain small compared to the number of banks (roughly 15,000) in the system. A failure, of course, is no reason to cheer, and so it is just as well to consider firstly *why* these banks failed. The same study that produced the data in Table 3.10 showed that in recent years,

Table 3.10: Number of bank failures in the United States, 1960–1976

Year	*Failures*	*Year*	*Failures*
1960	2	1969	9*
1961	9	1970	7*
1962	2	1971	6*
1963	2*	1972	3
1964	8	1973	6*
1965	9	1974	4*
1966	8	1975	12*
1967	4*	1976	16*
1968	3*		

* These were all insured banks in these years. The average annual number of bank failures, 1946 to 1959, was 4.4.

Source: Peter S. Rose and William L. Scott, "Risk in Commercial Banking: Evidence from Postwar Failures," *Southern Economic Journal* (July 1978).

[24] We have not underscored the fact, but entry into the banking industry is by no means automatic either; in particular, the insistence on a demonstrated need for more banking services and on a large capital base provides a barrier to would-be banking firms and a cushion to those firms already in the industry. A perfectly competitive industry has "free" exit and entry, and the banking industry, on this account, is clearly not perfectly competitive. Regulations differ widely from state to state, however, and it is generally pretty easy to get a state charter.

[25] There is evidence on bank service charges, though, that suggests that banks do find ways to use the price mechanism to compete; see Dale Osborne and Jeanne Wendel, "The Surprising Variety of Checking Account Prices," *The Voice, Federal Reserve Bank of Dallas* (May 1978).

a. Unit banking states had more failures (55 percent in the 1946–76 period were in unit banking states).
b. Failing banks were generally small (70 percent had deposits of less than $4 million).

In the Franklin and San Diego cases, the principal *cause* of failure mentioned was the inability to diversify. Looking even further into the details of the failed banks (compared to successful banks in the same community) the authors noted that failed banks, in the years prior to failure,

a. Were less liquid (had a higher loans/assets ratio).
b. Had smaller holdings of government securities (10.5 percent compared to 16.2 percent *one year* prior to closing).
c. Had a higher percentage of time and savings deposits (which are more expensive to manage, apparently).
d. Charged higher loan rates and paid higher rates on time and savings deposits.
e. Generated lower profits up to *seven years* prior to closing.

These factors are not especially surprising, on net, and they certainly suggest that there are risks in banking (some of which would be eliminated by permitting branching and growth by merger). They also suggest that failing banks can be spotted some time in advance (up to seven years in effect), by a routine examination of balance sheet data.[26] Indeed, bank regulators do just that, although the general issue, whether we should continue to control to such an extent that failure is almost impossible, is not resolved to this point.

3.7 STUDY QUESTIONS

Essay questions

1. In this chapter we should have given the impression that commercial banks appear fairly adept at avoiding restraints on their growth. Can you think of ways they can grow across state lines, then? How about their growth across national borders, especially in the future?

[26] But not by the behavior of their dividends. Apparently banks, unlike business firms in general, are *especially* reluctant to trim their dividends in the face of adversity. This practice, which certainly helps contribute to undermining the bank's assets, may have been changing a little in recent years. In any event, there is evidence that not only the bank, but the financial community, regards a cut in bank dividends as an especially bad sign; there is also evidence that cutting banks do better than comparable noncutting banks, almost as if cutting in the first step to facing up to the reality that the business can fail. See Howard Keen, Jr., "Bank Dividend Cuts: Recent Experience and the Traditional View," *Business Review, Federal Reserve Bank of Philadelphia* (November/December 1978).

2. Discuss the shortcomings of the practical measures of concentration used to describe the banking industry. What differences can you see between using bank assets rather than bank deposits as the base? Is the situation the same for business firms? Would profits make a good base? Would employment?

True-false discussion questions

These statements are meant to be somewhat ambiguous, and to provoke discussion thereby.

1. The increasing size of the largest commercial banks does not necessarily suggest increasing monopoly power by these banks (in financial markets).

2. A bank holding company is not, unless it is a multibank holding company, a device leading to more concentration in financial markets.

3. The net effect of the excessive regulation in the American banking system has been to produce the observed tendency toward greater concentration of the banking system.

4. Branching may be the best way for commercial banks to grow in view of the greater economies of scale in central operations (such as management) than in retail operations (such as checking accounts).

5. The one-bank holding company is regulated because of the danger that commercial banks will get into (risky) activities not related to banking rather than on account of any concern over excessive monopoly power.

6. In the absence of economies of scale in branching, commercial banks would generally not be expected to open up new branches.

7. While individual failure in any industry is clearly undesirable from the individual firm's point of view, it is generally beneficial to society as a whole. This argument does not apply to banking, though, because the *direct* repercussions of a failure go beyond the individual firm and its customers.

8. One advantage of the bank holding company to society as a whole derives directly from its ability to permit the bank to lower the costs of banking by, in effect, diversifying the bank's portfolio.

9. Banks generally branch when they cannot merge and form multibank holding companies when they can do neither. This implies that these are alternative courses that are pursued for the same reasons (differing from area to area *primarily* on account of differences in state laws).

3.8 FURTHER READING

Articles in Havrilesky, Thomas M., and John T. Boorman, eds., *Current Perspectives in Banking*. Arlington Heights, Ill.: AHM Publishing Co., 1976. Alfred Broaddus (No. 27), on the meaning of bank structure; George J. Benston (No. 29), on optimal banking structure; Samuel B. Chase, Jr., and John J. Mingo (No. 30), on bank holding companies; Donald I. Baker (No. 31), on chartering and branching; Jack M. Guttentag (No. 40), on bank structure and bank failure; and Thomas Mayer (No. 41), on preventing bank failure.

Black, Fischer, Merton H. Miller, and Richard A. Posner. "An Approach to the Regulation of Bank Holding Companies." *Journal of Business* (July 1978).

Bowsher, Norman N. "Have Multibank Holding Companies Affected Commercial Bank Performance?" *Review, Federal Reserve Bank of St. Louis* (April 1978).

Scott, John Troy. *Price and Nonprice Competition in Banking Markets*. Boston: Federal Reserve Bank of Boston, 1977.

Talley, Samuel H. "The Impact of Holding Company Acquisitions on Aggregate Concentration in Banking." *Staff Economic Studies, Board of Governors of the Federal Reserve System* (1974).

Tussing, A. Dale. "The Case for Bank Failure." *Journal of Law and Economics* (October 1967).

Varvel, Walter A. "FDIC Policy Toward Bank Failures." *Economic Review, Federal Reserve Bank of Richmond* (October 1976).

Yeats, Alexander J. "An Analysis of the Effects of Mergers on Banking Market Structure." *Journal of Money, Credit and Banking* (May 1973).

4

The Federal Reserve System

4.1 INTRODUCTION

The Federal Reserve Act of December 23, 1913, created the Federal Reserve System, which began operation in 1914. Considering the economic climate at the time—frequent financial panics, impending war, and an economy just then in a recession—it is small wonder that such an institution, a system of "federalized reserves," was deemed necessary. Actually, it is hard to understand why it did not come earlier (after all, the Bank of England dates to 1694, and many of the major international trading partners of the United States had central banks by 1914). Be that as it may, the principal monetary problems were then seen as the inelastic nature of the supply of currency (especially in the face of panics) and the nature of the reserve system, in which commercial banks' reserves were like an inverted pyramid resting on a small quantity of gold and silver; indeed, a considerable portion of the country's commercial bank "reserves" were held as balances in other commercial banks.

To deal with these problems, the Federal Reserve Act proposed to centralize the reserves of commercial banks in a federal depository, to lend reserves to banks in trouble, and to supervise and provide the elastic currency that now was to include a Federal Reserve note. It was empowered to conduct open market operations—that is, to buy and sell securities on its own account—and to accept short-term government and private securities (bills) as collateral for borrowed reserves. In addition, it determined the composition and percentage (of deposits) of the reserves of the commercial banks that became members of the system and imposed a prohibitive tax on the note issue of those national banks that did not use government bonds as collateral for their notes. Finally, it required that all national banks join the system or lose their charters (they could, of course, apply for a state charter if they did not wish to join the system); from the start state-chartered banks had the option to join or not and many did.

We will not discuss in detail the many changes in the Federal Reserve Act from its inception to the present, although in passing in this chapter and the next, some of the more important changes will be mentioned. Instead, the subject material of this chapter will be a description of the structure of the Federal Reserve System as it now stands, partly through the income and balance sheets of the Federal Reserve Banks and the member banks and partly through a discussion of the legal situation. We will, in addition, consider some of the problems the system has—notably that of its declining membership in recent years (which we have already remarked upon)—although we will not discuss the interesting problems of monetary policy (as conducted by the Federal Reserve) until Part II of the book. Nevertheless, we are left with a considerable body of material.

4.2 THE OVERALL STRUCTURE OF THE FEDERAL RESERVE SYSTEM

The Federal Reserve System is a collection of commercial banks (called member banks) supervised by 12 Federal Reserve Banks, themselves regional "central" banks. It is, at present, overseen by a Board of Governors whose duty it is to administer all of the provisions of the Federal Reserve Act of 1913, as amended (frequently). The structure of the American banking system is laid out in Figure 4.1. In Figure 4.1 the boxes in the center represent the Federal Reserve System; note that all but the state nonmember banks are subject to two supervisory agencies (and this count does not include the role of the FDIC, of which all but a handful of America's banks are members). Complexity is the order of the day in American banking.

4.2.1 The Board of Governors

Let us begin at the top, at the Board of Governors of the Federal Reserve System; here is where the power to regulate much of the Amer-

Figure 4.1: The supervisory structure of the American banking system

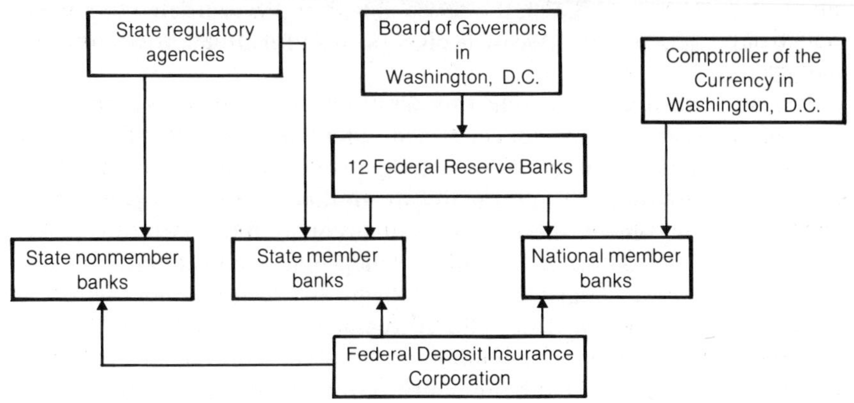

ican banking system and to control monetary policy is vested. The board consists of seven members, appointed by the president of the United States (with the consent of the Senate) for nonrenewable terms of 14 years (unless they fill the unexpired part of a previous member's term); one of these members is the Chairman, as determined by the president every four years (unless the position becomes vacant).[1] Indeed, it is the chairman around whom most of the controversy over monetary policy swirls (the present chairman is Paul Volcker, who was appointed by President Carter; he replaced G. William Miller in 1979, who in turn replaced Arthur Burns in 1978,[2] and it is the chairman who seems to exercise the most influence on monetary matters.

The powers and responsibilities of the Board of Governors are quite broad. They are to examine the books of the (12) Federal Reserve Banks and the member banks and to administer (or to delegate the administration of) the complex regulations that have grown up in law and in practice in our banking system. To assist them in their policy operations, Congress has also created a Federal Advisory Council (which has 12 members, one from each Federal Reserve district), which meets periodically and considers and makes recommendations on matters of monetary policy; as well,

[1] The seven members of the board must come from seven different Federal Reserve districts. They need not be bankers and, indeed, they often are not.

[2] There have been only 12 chairmen since 1914. The earlier ones are Charles S. Hamlin (1914–16), W. P. G. Harding (1916–22), Daniel R. Crissinger (1923–27), Roy A. Young (1927–30), Eugene Meyer (1930–33), Eugene R. Black (1933–34), Marriner S. Eccles (1934–48), Thomas B. McCabe (1948–51), William McChesney Martin (1951–70), Arthur Burns (1970–78), G. William Miller (1978–79). See the *Federal Reserve Bulletin* (November 1978) for a complete tabulation of the board members from the beginning.

in the Banking Act of 1933, the Federal Open Market Committee (consisting of 12 members, including the seven governors) was created to conduct actual monetary policy.[3] We will discuss their functions in Chapters 10 and 11.

The principal issue in connection with the Board of Governors of the Federal Reserve System concerns the autonomy, or lack of it, of the Federal Reserve within the Washington power structure. Insulated by 14-year terms (and often by personality) from the day-to-day operations of the federal government, the Board of Governors of the Federal Reserve is able *in theory* to conduct a monetary policy that is considerably at variance with what the Treasury, the president, or Congress might wish it to follow. Indeed, the law (the Federal Reserve Act, as amended) specifically designed a degree of autonomy for the American central bank that is not necessarily the rule in other countries (for example, the British and the Canadian central banks—the Bank of England and the Bank of Canada—seem much more directly responsive to the needs of the ruling political party). Indeed, the Board of Governors is actually independent of the member banks. Finally, the Federal Reserve (the Federal Reserve Banks in this case) runs at a large "profit" (we shall see how this arises in the next section) so it is also not even dependent on a Congressional appropriation for its operating expenses, although in the final analysis Congress disposes of the surplus funds (after the bills are paid).

This "independence" is not as real as might at first seem to be the case, however, both because of the central position of the chairman of the board (who can be replaced, as things now stand, by a new president of the United States in the second year of his term) and because of the realities of running a large-scale modern government with a persistent deficit (see Chapter 12).[4] On the former we noted that in recent times the appointment of the chairman has become a hot political issue; indeed it was clear, when Arthur F. Burns was replaced by G. William Miller (by President Carter) in early 1978, that Burns's influence on (or, if you wish, conduct of) monetary policy was an issue in this change.

With regard to the realities of life in Washington, it is hard to say too much, since so much of the story of American monetary policy is in-

[3] The five other members are presidents or vice presidents of Federal Reserve Banks; they are elected regionally (e.g., the boards of directors of the Federal Reserve Banks of Boston, Philadelphia, and Richmond jointly elect one member).

[4] In the original Federal Reserve Act the Chairman of the Board of Governors was the Secretary of the Treasury, who was an ex-officio member of the Board (as was the Comptroller of the Currency). In the Banking Act of 1935 both the Secretary of the Treasury and the Comptroller of the Currency were removed from the board entirely (effective February 1, 1936) and the modern "independence" dates from that act. Note, though, that monetary policy until 1935 reflected the strength of individual persons as much as explicit power; see Friedman and Schwartz, *A Monetary History*.

tertwined with the story of the federal government's needs, particularly as these needs run toward the financing of persistent federal budgetary deficits. We will reserve much of this discussion for Chapters 5 through 15, but for now we should indicate that, given the size of the deficit and given the tendency to want to attempt sizable fiscal policies from time to time, the Federal Reserve is often faced with the choice of letting interest rates clear the market (and thus fluctuate considerably) or of using its control over the money stock via open-market operations (etc.) to stabilize the interest rate (so that the money stock fluctuates considerably). By and large, one suspects, the latter has been the policy, and this has often led to a smooth adjustment to the Treasury's needs and a minimum interest burden on the American national debt, at the cost of some considerable fluctuations in the American money stock, however measured. We will have some specific examples of this type of policy in Chapters 9 through 15. And we will consider the consequences of this model of operation at several points, but for now the important point is that Federal Reserve independence, while clearly a technical possibility, is not always a reality, particularly when the Federal Reserve agrees with the Treasury that a stable interest rate is good for the country.

4.2.2 The Federal Reserve Banks

As already described, there are, in the Federal Reserve System, 12 regional Federal Reserve Banks, each essentially autonomous with respect to its day-to-day business operations (as we shall see). The best way to start, again, is to look at a picture (Figure 4.2) of the situation, as published in the *Federal Reserve Bulletin*. Here we see that the districts are numbered from east to west (and north to south) with the more populous (in 1913) areas of the East having a greater concentration of Federal Reserve Banks.

The first question anyone asks about the Federal Reserve, after noticing that Missouri has two of the twelve branches, is "Why are there twelve units of a *central* bank?" The answer is rooted in American banking and financial history. In particular, it seems, Americans have always had some special fears concerning centralized financial power and those in the mostly midwestern agricultural states have been especially fearful of Eastern money powers, so a "regionally representative" concept was designed in 1913 and has survived to the present. This has taken the form of establishing regional units (which are instructed to keep an eye on regional developments and are often staffed with members of the region's financial community in the higher positions), of ensuring that the members of the Board of Governors, the Federal Advisory Committee, and the Federal Open Market Committee are distributed evenly around the 12

Figure 4.2: The Federal Reserve System

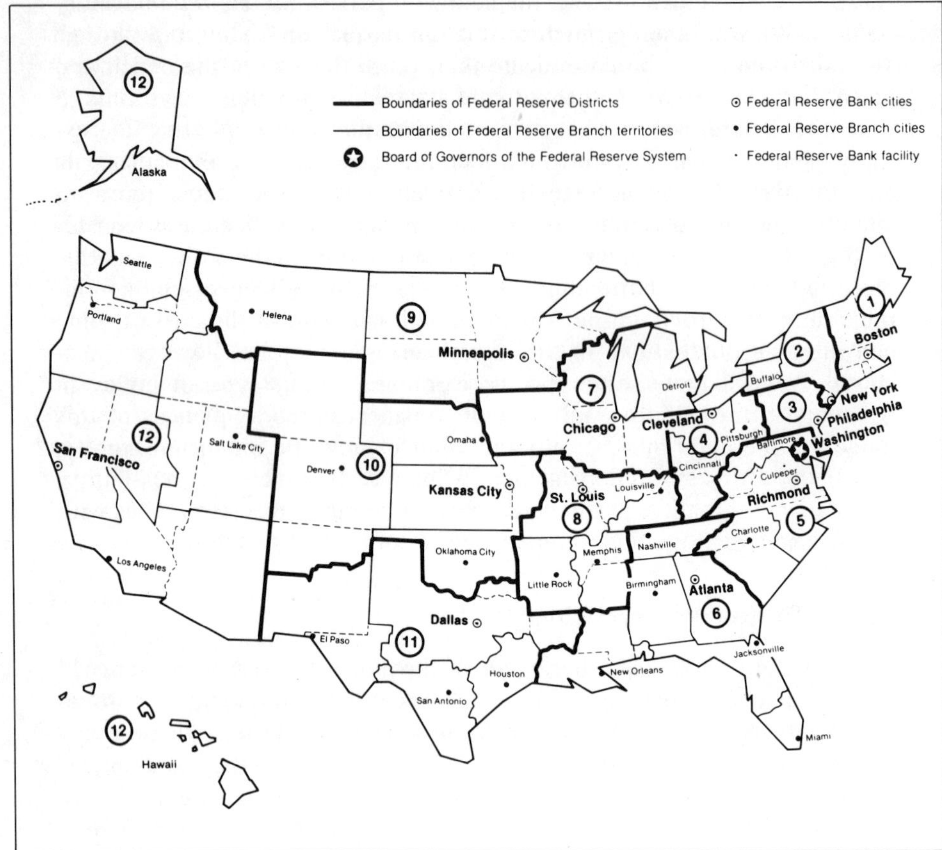

Source: *Federal Reserve Bulletin.*

districts, and of putting the discount function (the "lender of last resort" function) under the control of the regional banks (this includes the setting of the discount rate). But this decentralization is more official than real, we should emphasize, and these days, at least with respect to monetary policy, the direction to the system comes from the top—from the Board of Governors (and the Chairman of the Board of Governors, in particular) and the Federal Open Market Committee.

When the Federal Reserve System was established, it was decided that the member banks would actually "own" the Federal Reserve Bank in their district and would provide their capital. This ownership, which persists to this day, confers no rights, except that of earning a small dividend on their stock (see Table 4.3), and the control of each regional bank is vested in a nine-member Board of Directors, six elected by the member banks and three appointed by the Board of Governors.[5] This control concerns the running of the establishment more than anything else, including primarily its regulatory and research functions.

In their business operations each of the Federal Reserve Banks is representative of the System as a whole in that many items are allocated to the separate branches on a *pro rata* basis. Table 4.1 contains a summary statement of the "condition" of the 12 Federal Reserve Banks at the end

Table 4.1

The Condition of the Federal Reserve Banks
December 31, 1978
($ millions)

Assets		*Liabilities*	
Gold certificate account	$ 11,671	Federal reserve notes	$103,325
SDR certificate account	1,300	Member bank reserves	31,152
Coin	274	U.S. Treasury deposits	4,196
Member bank borrowings	1,174	Other deposits	1,624
Acceptances held under repurchase agreements	587	Deferred availability cash items	6,494
Federal agency obligations	8,029	Other liabilities	2,119
U.S. government securities	110,562	Total liabilities	$148,910
Cash items in process of collection	12,926	Capital paid in	1,078
Bank premises	394	Surplus	1,078
Other assets	4,149		
Total assets	$151,066	Total liabilities and capital accounts	$151,066

Source: *Federal Reserve Bulletin*.

of December, 1978. Thus, as their assets, the Federal Reserve Banks hold the United States gold stock (or, rather, they hold the certificates, to the same value) and federal government securities, the latter in an amount of $110 billion. Our ultimate monetary reserve, then, consists primarily of the debt of the federal government, acquired by the Federal Reserve either as agent for the Treasury or in the open market.[6] The Federal

[5] The six elected by the member banks consist of three who are "chosen by and representative of the member banks" (are in fact bankers) and three who are "actively engaged in their district in commerce, agriculture, or some industrial pursuit" (are in fact nonbankers). These (approximate) quotations are from the Federal Reserve Act.

[6] In Chapter 5 we will discuss the *monetary base,* a measure of one of the determinants of the American money stock. As we will see, by far the most important component of the monetary base is the Treasury security account of the twelve Federal Reserve Banks. We will point out that the act of purchasing a Treasury security creates reserves (bank reserves and currency); these reserves are the base of our fractional reserve banking system.

Reserve System supported, at the end of 1978, some $876.3 billion of M_2 (currency, demand deposits, and savings and time deposits). Note that at the end of 1969 gold certificates were valued at $10,036 million and the Federal Reserve Banks held $55,709 million of government securities; clearly, we are very far removed from the old gold standard.[7]

On the liabilities side of the Federal Reserve's balance sheet there are three main items: Federal Reserve notes (the stock of currency), the reserves of member banks, and U.S. Treasury deposits. The first two of these make up the total of what we call *high-powered money* (H); it is the base of the monetary system in the sense that it represents the cash and ultimate reserves of both the commercial banks and the public. In the days when the gold stock was linked automatically to this item, the American money stock had a tendency to fluctuate with the American gold stock (which, in turn, had a tendency to fluctuate with the state of the American balance of payments). There is still some tendency for this to occur in modern times, but it is no longer an automatic relationship. Finally, note that the direct role of the Federal Reserve as the monetary agent of the U.S. Treasury is shown by the $4 billion the U.S. Treasury has on deposit with the Federal Reserve Banks.[8]

The description in this section of the consolidated Federal Reserve Banks conceals some interesting variations that the individual banks show, particularly in the size and in the type of operations of the Federal Reserve Banks. Table 4.2 presents the assets and liabilities of the Federal Reserve Bank of Minneapolis; while it has the same general profile as the Federal Reserve System as a whole, it is readily apparent that it is not one-twelfth of the System. Thus, its "gold certificate allocation" is but 2 percent of the total in Table 4.1. This compares with an allocation of some 30 percent that the New York Federal Reserve Bank (which conducts the bulk of the foreign operations for the System) receives; other items are similarly scaled down.

But in some ways the most interesting aspects of the operation of a typical Federal Reserve Bank are in its earnings accounts rather than in its

---

[7] Note, as well, that at the end of 1978 commercial banks held $63.6 billion worth of government securities; since other government agencies possibly held another $13 billion of a marketable debt in the neighborhood of $488 billion, a little less than half of the U.S. marketable debt is held as some official or monetary institution's interest-earning liquid assets. See Chapter 15 for a continuation of this discussion.

[8] The complete discussion of the issues with regard to the gold stock are deferred to Part IV of the book. Recently (1978) it was decided to return to the system operated before 1974, which had Treasury deposits in commercial banks rather than in the Federal Reserve Banks. The disadvantage thereby eliminated was that the Federal Reserve was involved in numerous large-scale dealings in Treasury securities—necessary because commercial banks' *reserves* were altered each time the Treasury used its account—which made it difficult to conduct open-market operations. Indeed, Federal Reserve "tidying up" operations were cut in half, in 1979, when the Treasury balances were partly shifted away from the Federal Reserve.

Table 4.2

Federal Reserve Bank of Minneapolis
Statement of Condition
December 31, 1978
($ thousands)

Assets		*Liabilities*	
Gold certificate account	$ 231,177	Federal Reserve Notes	$1,854,810
Interdistrict settlement fund	−435,146	Deposits	
SDR certificate account	28,000	Member bank reserve accounts	866,328
Coin	11,182	U.S. Treasury—General Account	182,605
Loans to member banks	10,250	Foreign	6,081
Securities		Other deposits	7,638
Federal agency obligations	189,477	Total deposits	$1,062,652
U.S. government securities	2,627,263	Deferred availability cash items	559,983
Total securities	$2,816,740	Other liabilities	51,384
Cash items in process of collection	802,060	Total liabilities	3,528,829
Premises and equipment (less depreciation of $8,217)	30,992	Capital paid in	34,040
Other assets	101,654	Surplus	34,040
Total assets	$3,596,909	Total capital accounts	68,080
		Total liabilities and capital accounts	$3,596,909

Source: Federal Reserve Bank of Minneapolis, *Annual Report* (1978).

balance sheets. Table 4.3 illustrates the situation for the Federal Reserve Bank of Minneapolis for the year 1978; the second column gives some figures on what it actually does to earn its income. Here we see that the Federal Reserve Bank of Minneapolis obtains the greatest part of its earnings as interest upon its large holdings ($2,627,263,000) of U.S. government securities; furthermore, much of this is *paid right back* to the Treasury ($151 million of the $200 million), so that the whole business is somewhat of a bookkeeping operation. For the system as a whole, some $7 billion is switched back to the Treasury in this fashion, at present.

The expenses of a Federal Reserve Bank are very much like those of the commercial banks, except that they arise in the performance of the services listed under "Volume of operations" in Table 4.3. That is, in 1977, the Federal Reserve Bank of Minneapolis lent on 987 occasions to the member banks in the Ninth Federal Reserve district; in addition, it processed the currency and coin supply (for example, replacing the worn-out currency with new), handled (that is, *cleared*) 718 million checks with an aggregate value of $263 billion (can you imagine how much the system as a whole cleared?), and transferred funds for commercial banks amounting to $941 billion. Furthermore, it performed a research function; the Federal Reserve Bank of Minneapolis, like all of the Federal Reserve Banks, maintains a research department that produces statistics of vari-

Table 4.3

The Federal Reserve Bank of Minneapolis
For the Year 1977

Earnings and expenses ($ thousands)	
Current earnings	
Interest on loans to member banks	$ 2,379
Interest on U.S. government securities and federal agency obligations	200,243
All other earnings	377
Total current earnings	$202,999
Current expenses	
Salaries and other benefits	16,299
Postage and expressage	3,135
Telephone and telegraph	585
Printing and supplies	944
Real estate taxes	1,521
Furniture and operating equipment (Rentals, depreciation, maintenance)	1,505
Depreciation, bank premises	873
Utilities	489
Other operating expenses	1,815
Federal Reserve currency	992
Total current expenses	$ 28,158
Expenses reimbursed or recovered	1,942
Net expenses	$ 26,126
Current net earnings	176,783
Net profit (or loss)	(18,252)
Assessment for expenses of Board of Governors	1,596
Dividends paid	1,921
Payments to U.S. Treasury	151,704
Transferred to surplus	$ 3,310
Surplus account	
Surplus, January 1	30,730
Transferred to surplus (as above)	3,310
Surplus, December 31	$ 34,040

Volume of operations	*Number*	*Dollar amount*
Loans to member banks	987	$1.4 billion
Currency received and verified	148 million	1.3 billion
Coin received and counted	637 million	87 million
Checks handled	718 million	263 billion
Collection items handled	.3 million	2.2 billion
Issues, redemptions, exchanges of U.S. government securities	9.2 million	81.1 billion
Securities held in safekeeping	523,772	2.5 billion
Transfer of funds	1,001,192	941 billion

Source: Federal Reserve Bank of Minneapolis, *Annual Report* (1978).

ous sorts (for the public and for the System) and publishes the results of original research either in its journal or as separate studies.[9] But its business is that of handling the U.S. currency and coinage, of transferring funds and clearing checks for commercial banks and the Treasury, and of operating the "lender of last resort" function in the Ninth Federal Reserve District.

4.2.3 The member banks of the Federal Reserve System

We have discussed, in previous chapters, the nature of American commercial banks—and the member banks of the Federal Reserve System are not unique, so far as American banks go—so here we will concentrate on these banks as members of the System; this is a preface to the important policy questions of this and the next chapter concerning the control of the American money stock. To begin with, as already noted, banks that join the Federal Reserve System do so by buying into the Federal Reserve Bank in their district; thus the member banks "own" the Federal Reserve Banks, an ownership that brings them dividends (see Table 4.3), but very little influence over any important decisions (other than to elect the members of the local Board of Directors). In return for submitting to regulation, inspection, and control—and for holding their reserves (which do not pay interest) in the Federal Reserve Bank—they receive discount privileges, check clearing, and fund transferring, and get currency and coin service (and some other services to be discussed in Section 4.4).

Of the regulations that they face, the most important are the regulations on interest rates, which, however, apply to all commercial banks (and were discussed and listed in Chapter 3) and those on the percentage of each type of deposit that they must hold as reserves (and which apply only to member banks, as things now stand). This latter is illustrated in Table 4.4, as of November 30, 1978. Here we see that large banks must hold 16.25 percent of their net demand deposits as vault cash or reserves at the Federal Reserve Bank, while small banks hold but 7 percent; the reserves on savings and time deposits are 3 percent or less, although for time deposits of 30 to 179 days, for banks having over $5 million of deposits, these must be 6 percent. These reserve requirements, which have drifted downward over the years, are set by the Board of Governors within the limits as defined by Congress; the limits are described at the bottom part of the table.[10]

---

[9] The original work is published subject to the approval of the Board of Governors (which can remove any officer of the regional bank, for cause). It is not always approved.

[10] The average reserve ratio of member banks fell from 9.7 percent in early 1970 to 6.4 percent in February 1977. According to a Federal Reserve study the sources of this fall are (*a*) a shift from demand deposits to time deposits (which have a lower reserve requirement), and (*b*) the lowering of reserve requirements. These two influences were about equal in their effect. See Thomas D. Simpson, "The Behavior of Member Bank Required Reserve Ratios Since 1968," *Staff Economic Studies, Board of Governors of the Federal Reserve System* (July 1978).

Table 4.4: Member bank reserve requirements (percent of deposits)

Deposit type and size ($ millions)	*Requirements in effect Nov. 30, 1978*		*Previous requirements*	
	Percent	*Effective date*	*Percent*	*Effective date*
Net demand*				
0–2	7	12/30/76	7.5	2/13/75
2–10	9.5	12/30/76	10	2/13/75
10–100	11.75	12/30/76	12	2/13/75
100–400	12.75	12/30/76	13	2/13/75
Over 400	16.25	12/30/76	16.5	2/13/75
Time				
Savings	3	3/16/67	3.5	3/2/67
Other time				
0–5, maturing in				
30–179 days	3	3/16/67	3.5	3/2/67
180 days–4 years	2.5	1/8/76	3	3/16/67
4 years or more	1	10/30/75	3	3/16/67
Over 5, maturing in				
30–179 days	6	12/12/74	5	10/1/70
180 days–4 years	2.5	1/8/76	3	12/12/74
4 years or more	1	10/30/75	3	12/12/74

	Legal limits, Oct. 31, 1979	
	Minimum	*Maximum*
Net demand		
Reserve city banks	10	22
Other banks	7	14
Time	3	10
Borrowings from foreign banks	0	22

Note: Required reserves must be held in the form of deposits with Federal Reserve Banks or vault cash.

* Demand deposits subject to reserve requirements are gross demand deposits minus cash items in process of collection and demand balances due from domestic banks. The Federal Reserve Act specifies different ranges of requirements for reserve city banks and for other banks. Reserve cities are designated under a criterion adopted effective Nov. 9, 1972, by which a bank having net demand deposits of more than $400 million is considered to have the character of business of a reserve city bank. The presence of the head office of such a bank constitutes designation of that place as a reserve city. Cities in which there are Federal Reserve Banks or branches are also reserve cities. Any banks having net demand deposits of $400 million or less are considered to have the character of business of banks outside of reserve cities and are permitted to maintain reserves at ratios set for banks not in reserve cities.

† Negotiable order of withdrawal (NOW) accounts and time deposits such as Christmas and vacation club accounts are subject to the same requirements as savings deposits.

Member banks may also borrow reserves from the Federal Reserve Bank in their district. Until 1919, this was done at the request of the member banks and, since the discount rate was often below the rate at which a member bank could itself lend the funds, a substantial volume of borrowed reserves existed (during and just after World War I, borrowed reserves were the largest component of total member bank reserves). Since 1919, however, borrowing from the Federal Reserve has been a privilege rather than a right of member banks, and pressure has been exerted on commercial banks by the Federal Reserve to keep this item at a minimum. Four reasons for borrowing seem to dominate, though:

a. To deal with a very temporary shortage of reserves on the day on which the account must be balanced.[11]

Table 4.5: Reserves and borrowings of member banks ($ millions)

	1976	*1977*	*1978*
All member banks			
Reserves			
At Federal Reserve Banks	26,430	27,057	31,158
Currency and coin	8,548	9,351	10,330
Total held	35,136	36,471	41,572
Required	34,964	36,297	41,447
Excess	172	174	125
Borrowings at Federal Reserve Banks	62	558	874
Large banks in New York City			
Reserves			
Held	6,520	6,244	7,120
Required	6,602	6,279	7,243
Excess	−82	−35	−123
Borrowings	15	48	99
Large banks in Chicago			
Reserves			
Held	1,632	1,593	1,907
Required	1,641	1,613	1,900
Excess	−9	−20	7
Borrowings	4	26	10
Other large banks			
Reserves			
Held	13,117	13,993	16,446
Required	13,053	13,931	16,342
Excess	64	62	104
Borrowings	14	243	276
All other banks			
Reserves			
Held	13,867	14,641	16,099
Required	13,668	14,474	15,962
Excess	199	167	137
Borrowings	29	241	489

Source: *Federal Reserve Bulletin*.

[11] Banks can and do borrow from other member banks with excess reserves (federal funds) at the federal funds rate; the federal funds rate has been the principal target rate (i.e., rate to control) for the Federal Reserve in its conduct of monetary policy. See the discussion in Chapter 12.

b. To meet a seasonal need.[12]
c. For profit.
d. To bail out a troubled bank (see Chapter 3).

Since the borrowing for profit is explicitly frowned on by the Federal Reserve, the federal funds market (especially that part of it in excess reserves) has met this latter motive in recent years.

Table 4.5 shows the situation for December 1976 to December 1978 for member banks of the Federal Reserve System. Here we see that total system borrowing consistently increased over the period, with the borrowings pretty evenly divided over the system, by bank classification. The borrowings by member banks described in Table 4.5 are carried out at the discount rate of the Federal Reserve Bank in the same district as the member bank. These rates are centrally determined, by the Board of Governors, but their acceptance by the district Federal Reserve Bank is often delayed.[13] This is not an important matter, since there is probably no significant economic principle involved, but it is certainly a nuisance factor, and it is somewhat typical of our (probably) over-regulated and overly complex banking system that such vestiges of provincialism exist.

4.3 SHOULD THE FEDERAL RESERVE PAY INTEREST ON MEMBER BANK RESERVES?

As we have pointed out already, since passage of the Federal Reserve Act of 1913, member banks of the Federal Reserve System have received no interest on their deposits with the Federal Reserve Banks; in addition, if they fail to keep the required reserve, which is checked weekly, they must pay an interest penalty on the shortage. This situation has been widely discussed in recent years for two reasons:

a. "Pegged"—that is, fixed—interest rates would tend to bring about a misallocation of resources in an otherwise competitive economy.
b. Member banks may be leaving the Federal Reserve System because of the relative burden of this provision.

In addition, of course, there is a potential issue over whether the system is "fair" to the member banks in comparison to the nonmember banks. We will not discuss the "opting out" problem here, since it is the subject of

---

[12] Banks in areas that are largely agricultural are permitted to borrow on a seasonal basis since farmers, in general, have a decidedly seasonal need for funds (especially during and after the spring planting).

[13] On January 9, 1978, the discount rate was raised to 6.50 percent at the New York and Chicago Federal Reserve Banks; this change reached Boston, Minneapolis, and Kansas City on the 10th, but was not enacted in Philadelphia or Cleveland until the 20th. This is about as long as the lags get, these days.

Section 4.4; instead, we will concentrate on the facts and on the allocative and equity issues involved in having a fixed-interest-rate system of this sort.

The figures in Table 4.5 report that the total reserves of member banks at the end of 1978 were $41,572 million, consisting of $31,158 million of reserve deposits and $10,330 million of currency and coin. Both of these items are liabilities of the Federal Reserve; thus, for example, if the Federal Reserve paid 7.5 percent on *all* of its liabilities, something like $2.9 billion would be transferred to the member banks and would, therefore, not be transferred to the U.S. Treasury as things stand. Put this way, the simple mechanics of the operation are compelling: the Treasury would have to find another source for its $2.9 billion and member commercial banks, other things being equal, would enjoy greater profits.

Perhaps the chief argument against the "zero interest regulation" is that nonmember banks and nonbank intermediaries are not themselves required to "lend" assets free of an interest charge to the government (although, as we will see, not all can profit, depending on state laws). This should give them a competitive edge. In addition, we could argue, since some of the revenues would otherwise be passed on to bank customers or, alternatively, since some of the costs are passed on to bank customers, bank customers tend to suffer from the regulation. An argument running in the other direction holds that commercial banks should not be paid interest since they receive the benefits of the stable financial system provided by the Federal Reserve; conversely, so does the public, which is let out of this "tax" (although some of the tax is shifted onto the customers of banks who, after all, receive no interest on their deposits). In addition, it can be argued, the "zero interest" provision is justified since the Federal Reserve provides free services (for example, the clearing of checks and the transferring of funds) that member banks would otherwise have to pay for. This is certainly true, as things stand, but it might be better for banks to pay for their services as they use them, rather than merely on the basis of their reserve balances.[14] Finally, we should note that "no-interest" reserves have become ingrained in the system and that any such major change will hurt some and help others (the nonmember banks, for example, which may now be undercut), so that the change itself may be undesirable.

An argument against changing the present rules that seems to stick a little better than some of the above is that member banks are actually *not entitled* to earn interest on their reserves. That is, one way of looking at the relation between member banks and the Government is to emphasize

[14] In addition, since large banks seem to make proportionately more use of these services (see Section 4.5), we find a reason (an "unfair" tax) that smaller banks, especially, might be opting out of the system, as they are.

that member bank reserves, as *liabilities* of the Federal Reserve, are actually *issued* (in effect) by the Federal Reserve. That is, when the Federal Reserve decides to increase the money stock, it *produces* more reserves by buying bonds either in the open market or directly from the Treasury. Indeed, whether or not the Federal Reserve held bank reserves, insofar as it bought Treasury securities *and created deposits or currency,* the Federal Reserve's books would look the same (and it would not need to pay interest on the deposits). So the banks' *right* to these interest payments is certainly not a clear one. Then to add a little spice to the argument, since the production is for the common good anyway—because a controlled monetary system with a *federalized* reserve may be better than an uncontrolled one—member banks, as *one* group of the beneficiaries of the more stable system, are not entitled to yet further unearned compensation.[15]

The converse—and it is also a reasonable one—is that our money supply would in any event tend to expand at a rate that corresponds to increases in the demand for money. Thus, whether the Federal Reserve provided a managed component of a larger total, or whether the larger total was entirely supplied by a competitive private banking system, the total would be about the same in either case, other things being equal. Thus there is nothing special about the reserves of member banks, issues of the instability of the banking system aside. In addition, having "no-interest reserves" creates certain allocative inefficiencies in the sense just noted, especially in that such a large portion of our money supply is backed by a "free good" (to the government); the result is that we probably do not have as much of it as an "ideal" allocation might suggest. Of course, whether these are important issues is not easy to determine; neither is the way in which the balance of the argument should run. We should note, though, that the decline in Federal Reserve membership (which may be weakening our monetary control) could easily force the issue, in that the Federal Reserve may have to pay interest to hold on to its membership; alternatively, they could tax member banks' rivals in a similar way (by requiring *all* banks, even savings banks, to hold their reserves at the Federal Reserve), although this would certainly not be very popular. Such proposals are currently being considered by Congress.

---

[15] Actually, we did not point out above, when we discussed the payment of interest on demand deposits, that the commercial bank could be thought of as the *producer* of demand deposits, which it *sells* to the public, giving them, however, the right to *repurchase* them on demand. This idea, which implies that demand deposits are not a liability of the bank (which therefore need not, or would not, pay interest), is advanced by Boris Pesek and Thomas Saving in *Money, Wealth, and Economic Theory* (New York: Macmillan, 1968). Applied to the Federal Reserve in this case, the view might be that reserves are *produced* by the Federal Reserve when it decides how large the money stock should be. It produces them in effect, by buying (and holding) a Treasury security. Indeed, the argument seems more germane to the Federal Reserve than to a commercial bank (since the latter simply cannot ignore its liability as things stand).

Bankers, of course, would prefer to have the income, and they are pretty vocal on this topic.

4.4 THE DECLINING MEMBERSHIP IN THE FEDERAL RESERVE SYSTEM

One of the many reasons that the Federal Reserve System was erected was that, at the time, growth outside of the National Banking System was faster than growth within. This was a source of worry primarily because it implied a looser regulation of the system at a time when loose regulation was thought to have been responsible for many of the recurrent financial disorders in the country. By analogy, if nothing else, the declining membership in the Federal Reserve System, which we have already remarked on at several points in this book, implies a loosening of control, and possibly, a more variable effect of monetary policy, at least if that is conducted solely in terms of the control of member bank reserve accounts (it need not be, of course). We will come to these issues and some others, in due course, but first, we should take a look at the data. Table 4.6 presents the data for the number of banks and Table 4.7 does the same for the volume of deposits affected.

The figures in Table 4.6 indicate that from 1960 to 1967 the number of national banks (Column 7) increased;[16] otherwise, the attrition is pretty steady, especially for state member banks; over the period 1960–77, 763 banks left the System while 235 joined it, leaving the System smaller by 528 banks. Of course, many new banks did not join the System either, and many banks disappeared through merger; the net figures for the same period are −507 for the System and +1,831 for non-member banks. Turning to deposits in Table 4.7, we see that the System has lost about $15 billion of deposits; on this basis, which reflects the fact that the leaving banks are generally quite small, the problem is not as serious (note in Table 3.2 that the Bank of America, a System member, alone gained assets in the 1966 to 1976 period of more than $55 billion). Put in this light, things sound not quite so serious, although one still can worry about the future if the trend goes on. In addition, we should emphasize that new banks are not joining the System, so that the System's share of total deposits has fallen over the years (from around 90 percent in 1941 to around 75 percent at present (see Table 2.3). Finally, as Table 4.8 indicates, there has been a tendency for the average size of a withdrawing bank to increase over time. So we must, it seems, take the problem seriously, and Congress is currently considering legislation in this area.

We are not planning to make much of the monetary control problem of

[16] This, apparently, was the result of a relaxation in the severity of national bank regulation during the period. This attrition has been going on since the 1940s.

Table 4.6: Changes in the number of member banks of the Federal Reserve System

Year	Joining			Withdrawing			Net change		
	National members	*State members*	*Total*	*National members*	*State members*	*Total*	*National members*	*State members*	*Total*
1960	6	7	13	−9	−25	−34	−3	−18	−21
1961	5	4	9	−1	−16	−17	4	−12	−8
1962	8	5	13	−6	−26	−32	2	−21	−19
1963	18	3	21	−13	−22	−35	5	−19	−14
1964	19	4	23	−5	−19	−24	14	−15	−1
1965	12	1	13	−7	−22	−29	5	−21	−16
1966	10	4	14	−7	−32	−39	3	−28	−25
1967	7	1	8	−5	−21	−26	2	−20	−18
1968	6	3	9	−12	−40	−52	−6	−37	−43
1969	9	1	10	−28	−41	−69	−19	−40	−59
1970	5	0	5	−39	−38	−77	−34	−38	−72
1971	7	4	11	−21	−20	−41	−14	−16	−30
1972	12	6	18	−22	−36	−58	−10	−30	−40
1973	8	4	12	−21	−28	−49	−13	−24	−37
1974	8	9	17	−20	−28	−48	−12	−19	−31
1975	8	4	12	−10	−32	−42	−2	−28	−30
1976	8	10	18	−23	−23	−46	−15	−13	−28
1977*	4	5	9	−29	−16	−45	−25	−11	−36
Total	160	75	235	−278	−485	−763	−118	−410	−528

* Through June.

Source: John T. Rose, "An Analysis of Federal Reserve System Attrition Since 1960," *Staff Economic Study, Board of Governors of the Federal Reserve System* (1977).

Table 4.7: Deposits acquired by the member sector as a result of changes in membership of the Federal Reserve System, 1961–1977 ($ millions)

Year	Joining			Withdrawing			Net change		
	National members	State members	Total	National members	State members	Total	National members	State members	Total
1961	56.6	10.7	67.3	−1.7	−98.6	−100.3	54.9	−87.9	−33.0
1962	168.8	49.9	218.7	−30.9	−357.7	−388.6	137.9	−307.8	−169.9
1963	97.3	19.8	117.1	−143.8	−138.1	−281.9	−46.5	−118.3	−164.8
1964	181.7	84.7	266.4	−34.0	−232.7	−266.7	147.7	−148.0	−.3
1965	59.2	35.6	94.8	−61.4	−320.3	−381.7	−2.2	−284.7	−286.9
1966	225.2	56.5	281.7	−67.5	−432.9	−500.4	157.7	−376.4	−218.7
1967	72.4	16.3	88.7	−15.7	−380.1	−395.8	56.7	−363.8	−307.1
1968	83.2	64.7	147.9	−65.6	−399.2	−464.8	17.6	−334.5	−316.9
1969	49.3	1.6	50.9	−1,046.7	−616.2	−1,662.9	−997.4	−614.6	−1,612.0
1970	103.3	0	103.3	−558.7	−393.7	−952.4	−455.4	−393.7	−849.1
1971	52.4	139.5	191.9	−400.0	−263.2	−663.2	−347.6	−123.7	−471.3
1972	132.2	406.8	539.0	−563.1	−1,302.9	−1,866.0	−430.9	−896.1	−1,327.0
1973	117.7	106.0	223.7	−498.6	−1,392.1	−1,890.7	−380.9	−1,286.1	−1,667.0
1974	125.6	627.0	752.6	−1,640.5	−1,349.1	−2,989.6	−1,514.9	−722.1	−2,237.0
1975	140.5	191.4	331.9	−239.9	−728.1	−968.0	−99.4	−536.7	−636.1
1976	254.4	439.7	694.1	−1,100.0	−953.2	−2,053.2	−845.6	−513.5	−1,359.1
1977*	66.0	202.8	268.8	−2,004.0	−1,741.0	−3,745.0	−1,938.0	−1,538.2	−3,476.2
Total	1,985.8	2,453.0	4,438.8	−8,472.1	−11,099.1	−19,571.2	−6,486.3	−8,646,1	−15,132.4

* Through June.
Source: John T. Rose, "An Analysis of Federal Reserve System Attrition Since 1960," *Staff Economic Study, Board of Governors of the Federal Reserve System* (1977).

Table 4.8: Number of insured commercial banks withdrawing from the Federal Reserve System

Deposits (*$ millions*)	*1968*	*1970*	*1972*	*1974*	*1976*	*1977**
0–2	5	7	3	1	0	1
2–5	18	27	11	2	1	3
5–10	17	15	11	5	9	6
10–25	8	16	21	18	13	13
25–50	3	10	5	9	13	6
50–100	1	2	2	3	5	3
100–500	—	—	5	10	5	13
Average size of bank ($ millions on deposit)	8.9	12.4	32.2	62.3	44.6	83.2

* Through June.

Source: John T. Rose, "An Analysis of Federal Reserve System Attrition Since 1960," *Staff Economic Study, Board of Governors of the Federal Reserve System* (1977).

declining membership, but in view of the Congressional interest in the problem and the fact that the Hunt Commission (1971) has recommended that in the interest of monetary control, reserve requirements should be extended to nonmember banks,[17] some further discussion may be appended here. It is clear that shifts of funds between member and nonmember banks do occur and that such shifts could be greater at times of (for example) monetary tightness. On the other hand there is not a lot of evidence that this has happened, whatever its potential; indeed, a number of studies have indicated that monetary policy would not be much improved if reserve requirements were extended to nonmember banks.[18] This is true even for smaller banks and these are the very banks that are leaving the System, for the most part. But there are several issues here: one is fairness across the entire banking sector, and another involves the question of this section—the erosion of the Federal Reserve System. Both of these issues are part of the general debate that has produced bills in Congress, but at this writing no final law has been passed, although all proposals move in the direction of more uniform requirements. In one such bill all large banks, member or not, would be required to hold reserves of 11 percent of their demand deposits while all small banks would have no reserve requirements at all. All banks, then, would be required to purchase the check clearing and other services from the Federal Reserve.

[17] *Report of the President's Commission on Financial Structure and Regulation* (Washington, D.C.: U.S. Government Printing Office, 1971).

[18] William N. Cox, III, "Small Banks and Monetary Control: Is Fed Membership Important?" *Working Paper, Federal Reserve Bank of Atlanta* (January 1977). The reasons it is not likely to be improved much are that such funds shifts are relatively rare, apparently, *and* the Federal Reserve can still conduct open-market operations whether or not it has any bank reserves to hold, merely draining off bank liquid assets instead of reserves when it conducts a "tight" money policy.

It remains to be seen, of course, what effect such a system might have on the membership problem.

But we are able to be a little more precise on these questions, because of the numerous studies that have been made. It is a question, quite simply, of the costs and benefits of membership in the System. Among the benefits to the members are the safety implied by a careful examination (the stockholders may prefer this as a check on management); in addition, the Federal Reserve provides wire transfer, check clearing, collateral safekeeping, and coin and currency shipping for its members. On the debit side, three factors are most often mentioned: the paperwork associated with membership is especially burdensome, member banks are more restricted in their portfolio flexibility, and member bank reserves impose costs because they pay no interest (compared to nonmember banks). This last item seems to be the principal factor and it is a sizable item, as we saw in Section 4.4.

We will consider the "bank reserve problem" again in a moment, but first it is instructive to consider how state regulations on reserves affect the story; it is a diverse one, as one might expect. To begin with, as Table 4.4 indicated, in the Federal Reserve System bank reserves are graduated in favor of smaller member banks, with the smaller ones required to hold a 7 percent reserve against deposits and the larger, 16.25 percent. States are marvelously varied in this respect, with half of them permitting government securities (which earn interest) to be held as reserves. Most states also permit items in the process of collection and correspondent balances to count as reserves.[19] The latter are usually demand deposits, but they do come with "services" attached, so they are valuable to the depositing bank. To get an idea of how varied the state requirements are, consider a summary of a table that appeared in a recent *Review* of the Federal Reserve Bank of St. Louis; it is presented as Table 4.9.

The story is an interesting one. State reserve requirements vary from nothing (in Illinois) to 27 percent (in Vermont), although all but Vermont and South Dakota have requirements lower than or equal to those of the Federal Reserve. All permit demand balances to be counted and, as noted, more than half permit banks to earn interest on their deposits. But the most fascinating thing is the diversity: for example, a considerable number of the "unit banking" states (which are concentrated in the agricultural Midwest) do not permit securities to count as reserves.[20] This diversity carries over into the enforcement of the regulations, the penal-

[19] The Federal Reserve permits only items actually "collected" to be counted as reserves.

[20] In a companion study to the one that provided Table 4.9 it was noted that state banks generally hold reserves *in excess* of those required; thus if the Federal Reserve lowered requirements to gain members, states would not be able to fight back by lowering theirs. See R. Alton Gilbert, "Effectiveness of State Reserve Requirements," *Review, Federal Reserve Bank of St. Louis* (September 1978).

Table 4.9: State reserve requirements on demand deposits in 1978

State	*Reserve requirement*	*Vault cash*	*Demand balances due from banks*	*Securities*
Alabama	10%	Yes	Yes	No
Alaska	20%	Yes	Yes	No
Arizona	10%	Yes	Yes*	Yes†
Arkansas	(FR)	Yes	Yes*	No
California	(FR)	Yes	Yes*	Up to 80%†
Colorado	15%	Yes	Yes*	Yes†
Connecticut	12% 1st $5 million; 12.5% thereafter	At least 1/6	Yes*	Up to 1/6
Delaware	7% 1st $100 million; 9% thereafter	—At least 50%*—		Up to 50%‡
Florida	20%	Yes	Yes	Yes†
Georgia	15%	—At least 50%*—		Up to 50%†§
Hawaii	12%	At least 25%	Up to 75%*	No
Idaho	15%	Yes	Yes*	No
Illinois	None	—	—	—
Indiana	10%	Yes	Yes	No
Iowa	7%	Yes	Yes*	No
Kansas	(FR)	Yes	Yes	No
Kentucky	7%	—At least 75%—		Up to 25%†§
Louisiana	(FR)	—At least 50%—		Up to 50%‡
Maine	10%	Yes	Yes*	Yes†‖
Maryland	15%	—At least 2/3—		Up to 1/3‡
Massachusetts	Boston 20%; Other 15%	At least 15%	Up to 80%	Up to 80%‡
Michigan	11%	Yes	Yes*	No
Minnesota	(FR)	—At least 70%—		Up to 30%†
Mississippi	(FR)	—At least 70%—		Up to 30%‡§
Missouri	(FR)	—At least 50%—		Up to 50%‡‖
Montana	7.5% first $2 million; 10% thereafter	Yes	Yes*	No
Nebraska	15%	—At least 50%—		Up to 50%†

ties for noncompliance, and the frequency of inspections at the state level; thus, for example, Colorado has no periodic reports and no penalties, while California has biweekly reports and a sizable penalty. Along the same lines, Maryland has no periodic reports, but if on repeated examinations the bank is in violation, the directors and the officers of the bank can be removed; similarly, Minnesota, which has no periodic report, assessed a 12 percent (per annum) penalty on violators, and 54 of 547 nonmember banks in 1976 paid this penalty. But the general impression one gets is that the pressure is much less of a burden than it is in the Federal Reserve System, and the ability to profit on one's reserves is greater in the sense that state banks are usually permitted to count as reserves items that are interest-earning.

Table 4.9 ***(continued)***

State	*Reserve requirement*	*Vault cash*	*Demand balances due from banks*	*Securities*
Nevada	(FR)	Yes	Yes*	No
New Hampshire	12%	—At least 60%—		Up to 40%†
New Jersey...........	(FR)	Yes	Yes*	No
New Mexico..........	12%	—At least 50%—		Up to 50%†
New York	(FR less 1%)	Yes	Yes*	No
North Carolina........	(FR)	Yes	Yes*	No
North Dakota.........	8%	Yes	Yes*	No
Ohio	7%	Yes	Yes	No
Oklahoma	(FR)	Yes	Yes*	No
Oregon...............	12%	Yes	Yes*	No
Pennsylvania	12%	—At least 50%*—		Up to 50%‡#
Rhode Island	15%	Yes	Up to 60%*	Yes†
South Carolina........	7%	Yes	Yes	No
South Dakota.........	17.5%	—At least 40%*—		Up to 60%†
Tennessee	10%	Yes	Yes	No
Texas	15%	Yes	Yes*	No
Utah.................	(FR)	Yes	Yes	No
Vermont	27%	Yes	Yes	Yes‡
Virginia..............	10%	Yes	Yes	No
Washington...........	(FR)	Yes	Yes	No
West Virginia	7%	At least 20%	Yes	No
Wisconsin	20%	—At least 2/3—		Up to 1/3‡
Wyoming.............	20%	—At least 50%*—		Up to 50%†

(FR) Same or approximately the same as the Federal Reserve System.
* Restricted to certain "depository banks."
† Mainly unpledged U.S. government securities.
‡ Mainly unpledged debt obligations of the state or of the United States.
§ Permits CDs.
‖ Includes federal funds.
Includes other marketable securities.
Source: R. Alton Gilbert and Jean M. Lovati, "Bank Reserve Requirements and Their Enforcement: A Comparison Across States," *Review, Federal Reserve Bank of St. Louis* (March 1978).

Turning to the specific items already mentioned in connection with the Federal Reserve System itself, let us first consider the value of the service received by member banks and then look at some figures on the net losses incurred by not receiving interest on their reserve balances with the Federal Reserve Banks. The first thing to recall is that it is small banks that tend to withdraw from the System and that the new banks that also decided not to enter are of small size, too. Then, let us look at the actual amount spent by the Federal Reserve System in providing its services; Table 4.10 carries the summary. Evidently, then, a discussion of check and cash handling will be sufficient to tell the story, since 92 percent of the costs are involved there (and the benefits to the member banks are probably proportional to the costs incurred by the Federal Reserve Banks). To

Table 4.10: Costs of providing services to member banks in 1976

Service	*Cost ($ thousand)*	*Percent of total*
Check collection	124,567	65.6
Coin and currency service	50,221	26.4
Wire transfers	5,673	3.0
Safekeeping of securities	7,225	3.9
Discounts and credits	2,303	1.2
Total	189,989	100.0

Source: R. Alton Gilbert, "Utilization of Federal Reserve Bank Services by Member Banks: Implications for the Costs and Benefits of Membership," *Review, Federal Reserve Bank of St. Louis* (August 1977).

see how size is involved in this story, that is, to see one important reason that small banks are not as interested in Federal Reserve membership as are large banks, consider Table 4.11. Here we see that larger banks make

Table 4.11: Use by member banks of Federal Reserve services in 1976–1977 (a survey of 233 banks in Illinois and Missouri)

Size of banks (average assets in group)	*Percentage of banks clearing checks through System*	*Average number of checks cleared per bank*	*Average annual implicit subsidy to member banks from money service*	*Percentage of banks initiating wire transfers*	*Average annual number of wire transfers*
3,891.6	5	21,816	664.42	15	68
7,179.8	0	0	838.11	10	102
9,592.3	15	215,740	830.95	5	102
11,706.4	25	837,271	813.56	30	134
15,051.6	10	232,416	1,046.53	20	92
17,723.6	30	383,042	2,230.80	50	95
21,790.2	10	365,472	1,799.80	35	94
25,991.2	40	360,959	2,036.80	65	191
30,952.0	40	1,172,649	2,087.80	65	312
40,961.1	35	950,337	3,376.00	70	176
69,106.8	70	1,778,203	5,392.80	75	704
425,173.8	92	16,355,889	12,990.77	85	19,649

Source: R. Alton Gilbert, "Utilization of Federal Reserve Bank Services by Member Banks: Implications for the Costs and Benefits of Membership," *Review, Federal Reserve Bank of St. Louis* (August 1977).

considerably greater use (on a percentage basis) of check clearing and wire transfers and that the per-bank (but not per dollar of assets) implicit subsidy for cash services is greater for a larger bank. In a nutshell, then, the large banks seem to get more from the Federal Reserve than do the small banks in the sense that they use the free services more frequently.

With regard to the explicit cost of having reserves that pay no interest, we find it hard to generalize in view of the diversity of the alternative (the alternatives are shown in Table 4.9 for each state). That is, in Chapter 3 we merely paid each bank on its reserves according to the federal funds rate; this sidesteps the issue in this section, which is this: What happens to a bank's earnings on its reserves when it drops out of the System? Presumably, they would go up in the states with lower reserve requirements or in the states that permit interest-bearing securities to be counted as reserves. So it depends on the state. Indeed, in some states large banks would find it especially attractive to drop out, given the big differences they would get in their requirements.[21] Finally, we should note that there is another small bank–large bank issue involved here; this is that small banks are generally less efficient than large at avoiding the tax by keeping their excess reserves at a minimum. Thus, small banks may opt out to avoid paying the tax, rather than stay in and pay for their inefficiency. And, as well, we should recall that, in many of the states, the inspections are less frequent and the penalties are less severe.

4.5 STUDY QUESTIONS

Essay questions

1. We have pointed out in passing that the Federal Reserve System is neither technically nor politically independent of the Treasury or of Congress. Should this independence be strengthened or weakened (and why)? Why might Congress be unhappy if the Federal Reserve suddenly decided to pay interest on commercial bank reserves? Is the independence of the Federal Reserve one of the issues likely to come up?

2. Explain, in detail, how an increase in the quantity of currency in circulation comes about. Do this realistically, starting with the initiator of the action (the public) and consider how things work through the various sectors (the public, the banks, and the Federal Reserve), assuming no change in reserve requirements.

True-false discussion questions

These statements are meant to be somewhat ambiguous and to provoke discussion thereby.

[21] A recent study of Sixth District (six southern states) banks (all those states had *lower* reserve requirements) showed that large banks paid a much larger *net* "subsidy" than did smaller banks. On this sort of evidence we may well yet see a spurt of withdrawals by large banks unless Congress evens out requirements. See Stuart G. Hoffman, "The Burden of Fed Membership for Sixth District Banks," *Economic Review, Federal Reserve Bank of Atlanta* (November/December 1978).

1. Since the quantity of gold backing our money supply is only around $10 billion, any severe run on commercial banks would quickly close down the American banking system.

2. Commercial banks are leaving the Federal Reserve System primarily because they do not like the excessive regulation they are subject to as members.

3. Federal Reserve Bank profits rise with inflation rates for much the same reasons that commercial bank profits do.

4. If all commercial bank reserves were held in the Bank of America, and the federal government took a one-fifth ownership of the Bank of America, our banking system would be potentially more unstable than it presently is.

5. If the Treasury were to sell bonds directly to the public rather than to the commercial banks and the Federal Reserve, then the Federal Reserve would find it easier to operate independently of the Treasury.

6. The regional variations in the construction of the Federal Reserve System are important in the regulation of banks but not in the control of the American money supply.

7. Federal Reserve control over the money stock is at present more hampered by the aggressive "liability management" of commercial banks than by the shrinkage of the relative importance of the Federal Reserve System.

8. Commercial banks generally borrow from the Federal Reserve in order to take advantage of the extra profits that tight money brings.

9. A careful comparison of pre- and post-1914 U.S. financial history strongly suggests that nonmonetary factors have been responsible for the depressions (and, indirectly, the panics) in the United States. This is clear since the arrival of the Federal Reserve has stabilized the monetary aspects while the panics and depressions continued.

10. The fact that the principal asset of the Federal Reserve System is U.S. government securities and not gold *directly* explains why we currently have too much money and, certainly, too much inflation.

4.6 FURTHER READING

Articles in Havrilesky, Thomas M., and John T. Boorman, eds., *Current Perspectives in Banking*. Arlington Heights, Ill.: AHM Publishing Company, 1976. Edward G. Boehme (No. 43), on falling Fed membership; Ira Kaminow (No. 44), on interest on reserves; and W. Lee Hoskins (No. 45), on selling Fed services.

Board of Governors of the Federal Reserve System. *The Federal Reserve System: Purposes and Functions*. 6th ed., 1974.

Gilbert, R. Alton, and Jean M. Lovati. "Bank Reserve Requirements and Their Enforcement: A Comparison Across States." *Review, Federal Reserve Bank of St. Louis* (March 1978).

Gilbert, R. Alton. "Utilization of Federal Reserve Bank Services by Member Banks: Implications for the Costs and Benefits of Membership." *Review, Federal Reserve Bank of St. Louis* (August 1977).

Rose, John T. "An Analysis of Federal Reserve System Attrition Since 1960." *Staff Economic Study, Board of Governors of the Federal Reserve System* (1977).

Watson, Ronald D., Donald A. Leonard, and Nariman Behravesh. "The Decision to Withdraw: A Study of Why Banks Leave the Federal Reserve System." *Research Papers, Federal Reserve Bank of Philadelphia,* No. 30 (September 1977).

5

The determinants of the stock of money

5.1 INTRODUCTION

If we define money as currency (and coin) plus demand deposits (and sometimes commercial bank time and savings deposits), then at present the supply of these items is provided by commercial banks and the Federal Reserve, with the latter providing the currency and coin and the former providing the deposits. Indeed, we will concentrate for the most part, on narrow money (currency plus demand deposits) in this chapter and the next, leaving the broader measures, which normally involve the payment of interest, for other chapters. Here, then, we will take a look at the important underlying factors in the determination of the American money stock (M_1), with a view toward determining the principal causal factors behind the sometimes dramatic changes in that stock.

We will begin with the traditional "banking multipliers" argument; this involves the demonstration that an increase in "base money" in a fractional-reserve banking system implies a multiple expansion of deposits if the funds are passed from bank to bank by means of (for example) lending activity. We will find that this analysis can be generalized by means of some simple identities in the banking structure, and, when this is done, certain (past) monetary disturbances can be analyzed as to whether (or to what extent) the *public*, the *commercial banks*, or the *central bank* (or some foreign source) might be the chief influence on the situation. With regard to the central bank's contribution, the apparatus just mentioned works the problem of monetary influence in terms of a concept known as *high-powered money* (reserves plus currency in circulation); recently, another concept, the *monetary base,* which analyzes all "reserve-creating" influences on the money stock, has come into use. We will consider its contribution and then in a final section of the chapter compare the two measures on some recent U.S. data.

To illustrate the potential of our basic money supply theory, we will use the approach to analyze two important periods in American monetary history. One of these is the period from 1831 to 1839, a period in which there was a large gold inflow into the United States as well as some considerable domestic disturbances (such as the "Bank War," which pitted President Andrew Jackson against the (second) Bank of the United States, and the crash of 1837). The second period is that from 1929 to 1939, in which our most severe financial and business collapse occurred. We will find, in both instances, that our money stock theory does help to tell the story in a more revealing way; this is, to repeat the point, because it divides the influences on the money stock into the three categories—the public, the banks, and outside (government or foreign) sources—and these sectors almost certainly were the chief actors in the drama. But for now we return to the basic task of showing how the "banking multiplier" itself works.

5.2 THE BANKING MULTIPLIER

We will begin by assuming that the banking system consists of two commercial banks and that the stock of currency is issued by the Treasury;[1] in terms of balance sheets the initial situation for commercial banks might look like Table 5.1, which is the balance sheet for each of the two commercial banks. In this table we see that each bank has issued deposits of $50, which are liabilities to them in the sense of a representation of a liquid "debt" to the deposit owner. Each bank also has, as assets (i.e., "behind" the deposits) $10 of currency and $40 of loans; the former are *liquid* assets and the latter are (presumably) less liquid. Finally, each bank has a capital account, matched arbitrarily by an investment of an equal amount; the capital account represents accumulated profits held (one might imagine) as "investments." The student should look back to the actual balance sheets of Chapter 2 to verify these items.[2]

[1] The system we begin with corresponds, in outline at least, with that existing in the United States from the 1830s until 1914, although there were then many different types of banks (the banks of our illustration in this chapter do not issue currency).

[2] The profits arise, as we have pointed out, mainly because the bank pays lower interest (and possibly incurs lower expense) on its deposit liabilities than it earns on its loan assets.

What we now want to do is show how a $10 injection of new currency into the system produces a multiplied expansion of the banking system (i.e., a multiplication of money, loans, and deposits). Assume, thus, that a new Treasury issue of $10 (to finance some government spending) enters the system; let it first appear in the hands of an individual, who deposits it in Bank A. The initial situation for Bank A is as follows:

Assets		*Liabilities*	
Currency	$20	Deposits	$60
Loans	40		
Investments	10	Capital accounts	10
Total assets	$70	Total liabilities	$70

The money supply now consists of the original $200 plus the $10 of new money. Bank A, if it wishes to retain the 1 : 5 ratio of reserves (currency) to deposits that it has in Table 5.1 will (let us assume) lend out $8 of the $10. Let us suppose this money (it is in the form of cash) is spent by the customer and that the receiver of the funds deposits them into Bank B; under the circumstances, our new version of Table 5.1 is Table 5.2.

The money stock, defined to be currency in circulation ($100) plus deposits in commercial banks ($60 + $58) is now $218. However, we are not done because Bank B in the new situation in Table 5.2 is not in equilibrium, since it is holding $8 of excess reserves (if it wishes to maintain the 1 : 5 ratio of currency to deposits). Suppose, then, that it decides to lend out 80 percent of its new deposits; its balance sheet would look like this:

Assets		*Liabilities*	
Currency	$11.60	Deposits	$58.00
Loans	46.40		
Investments	5.00	Capital accounts	5.00
Total assets	$63.00	Total liabilities	$63.00

Finally, suppose that the proceeds of the loan by Bank B went to a customer who deposited them back in Bank A; this situation is depicted in Table 5.3. Bank A now has "excess reserves" of $6.40 and the money supply has expanded (by $6.40, the deposit in Bank A) from $218 to $224.60. The process would tend to continue along the same lines, so long as the public continues to try to hold the same *absolute* amount of currency and the two banks continue to try to keep their reserves-deposits ratios at 1 : 5.

The example just given provides us with the information needed to

Table 5.1: A two-bank economy

Bank A				Bank B			
Assets		*Liabilities*		*Assets*		*Liabilities*	
Currency	$10	Deposits	$50	Currency	$10	Deposits	$50
Loans	40	Capital accounts	10	Loans	40	Capital accounts	5
Investments	10			Investments	5		
Total assets	$60	Total liabilities	$60	Total assets	$55	Total liabilities	$55

Table 5.2: The two-bank economy after one round

Bank A				Bank B			
Assets		*Liabilities*		*Assets*		*Liabilities*	
Currency	$12	Deposits	$60	Currency	$18	Deposits	$58
Loans	48			Loans	40		
Investments	10	Capital accounts	10	Investments	5	Capital accounts	5
Total assets	$70	Total liabilities	$70	Total assets	$63	Total liabilities	$63

Table 5.3: The two-bank economy after two rounds

Bank A				Bank B			
Assets		*Liabilities*		*Assets*		*Liabilities*	
Currency	$18.40	Deposits	$66.40	Currency	$11.60	Deposits	$58.00
Loans	48.00			Loans	46.40		
Investments	10.00	Capital accounts	10.00	Investments	5.00	Capital accounts	5.00
Total assets	$76.40	Total liabilities	$76.40	Total assets	$63.00	Total liabilities	$63.00

derive the traditional banking multiplier. In particular, we seek an answer to the question of how far a sum of new base money (currency in this simple example) expands in a fully-lent-up banking system, such as the one just described. We started with \$10, and then in succeeding rounds we obtained \$8 and \$6.40; this was obtained, in effect, as follows:

$$\text{Change in money stock} = \Delta M = \$10 + {}^4/_5(\$10) + {}^4/_5(\$8) + \cdots$$

This can further be formalized, where ΔB represents the new currency and r represents the reserve ratio ($^1/_5$ in our example), as

$$\Delta M = \Delta B + (1 - r)\Delta B + (1 - r)^2\Delta B + \cdots \tag{5.1}$$

and the process goes on until the addition to the sum gets close to zero (it does this because $r < 1$). Note that we need the fact that $^4/_5(\$8) = (^4/_5)(^4/_5)(\$10)$ since $^4/_5(\$10) = \$8$. To get a more general expression, we need merely *sum* the Equation (5.1), in which case we get

$$\Delta M = \frac{1}{r}\,\Delta B. \tag{5.2}$$

The number $1/r$, then, where r is the reserve ratio, is the banking multiplier in this example;[3] its value is 5 for our example, which implies that for every \$1 increase in B there is a \$5 increase in M. In terms of our example, which we stopped in Table 5.3 before it ended, the result is thus shown to be \$50 of new money created by the expansionary process, from an original "injection" of currency of \$10 (so that M_1 would go to \$250).

There are, however, several things about the simple analysis just concluded that are not really satisfactory. Most notably, we assumed that banks made no other adjustments in their portfolios, that they held no excess reserves, and, perhaps least realistically, that the public did not change the quantity of currency it held, being satisfied to keep redepositing the new currency every time it came into its hands until the new currency ended up in bank reserves (at the end of the process, when the money supply reached \$250, bank reserves, held in the form of currency, would be \$30). A second way of approaching the same problem provides us with considerably more flexibility than Equation (5.2) for interpreting the monetary data.

Let us define the money supply (M) of our example as consisting of

$$M = C_p + D, \text{ or } \$200 = \$100 + \$100, \tag{5.3}$$

where C_p is currency in the hands of individuals and D represents the

---

[3] To sum an infinite series, such as $S = 1 + x + x^2 + x^3 + \cdots$ when the terms approach zero ($x < 1$), we can multiply S by x, to get $xS = x + x^2 + x^3 + \cdots$ and then subtract xS from S, as just defined, to get $S - xS = 1$, since all the terms to infinity in the two expressions cancel each other out. The result, then, is $S(1 - x) = 1$ or $S = 1/(1 - x)$, which is what we used to get Equation (5.2) from Equation (5.1), where $x = 1 - r$.

deposits of banks; we do not count currency in the banks as part of the money supply, for it is not held in order to be spent but is held only as bank reserves against deposit money. Then, let us define the base of the system, which we will call *high-powered money* (H) as

$$H = C_b + C_p, \text{ or } \$120 = \$20 + \$100. \tag{5.4}$$

Here C_b is currency in the banks (held as reserves) and C_p is, again, currency in the hands of individuals. As our next step, we can divide Equation (5.4) by Equation (5.3), in which case we get Equation (5.5):

$$\frac{M}{H} = \frac{C_p + D}{C_b + C_p}. \tag{5.5}$$

Finally, we may rearrange the terms on the right side by dividing each separate term by D, in order to obtain our final equation; this equation explains the relation between M and H in terms of the items in the square brackets:

$$M = H\left[\frac{\frac{C_p}{D} + 1}{\frac{C_b}{D} + \frac{C_p}{D}}\right], \text{ or } \$200 = \$120\left[\frac{1 + 1}{.2 + 1}\right] = \$120\left[\frac{2}{1.2}\right]. \tag{5.6}$$

Most importantly, this equation, in which C_p/D and C_b/D are given sample values of 1 and 0.2, permits us to analyze the effect on the quantity of money of changes in bank preferences (changes in C_b/D), changes in the public's preferences (changes in C_p/D), and changes in the central bank's contribution (changes in H).[4]

Now assume that individuals—merely altering the form in which they hold wealth as far as they can tell—decide to switch \$50 from demand deposits to currency, perhaps in response to a doubt about the safety of commercial banks. If you want something historical to fix on, think of the financial panics in 1837, 1857, or 1873, etc., in which just that happened on a broad scale. It is clear from the figures of our earlier tables that the banks do not have the cash needed in their reserves, and it should also be clear that bankers will not want to run down all their cash anyway, since cash is their reserve in this problem. Let us assume that bankers wish to keep \$1 of currency for every \$5 of demand deposits, whatever the actual size of their demand deposit accounts (below, we will discuss an instance, in 1937–38, when they seemed to have changed their preference after a

[4] For this equation to be used successfully in the manner suggested here, it is necessary that the three "determinants" be independent of each other; this is not obvious, as the rest of this chapter makes clear. *One* of the problems comes from interest-rate influences on C_p/D and C_b/D; this problem may be more pronounced, it would seem, to the extent that some of the components of M_1 pay interest. In Chapter 13 we consider monetary multipliers with an M_2 or an M_3 rationale, but at the cost of considerable complexity.

series of panics and actually desired *more* than the minimum). Let us ignore the interactions between the three "sectors" here—that is, let us assume that the public, the banks and the government are independent of each other—in which case we can see a dilemma directly, because individuals seem to wish to obtain more currency than the system possesses (they want \$150 when the system has only \$120). Therefore, if they continue to try to convert their deposits to cash they will eliminate the banks completely; thus, they will dry up all their loans and deposits and all of the bank's investments *and still only get \$120.* This, clearly, is a system with an inflexible (or inelastic) currency, but with a vengeance. This situation, which clearly could impose tremendous social costs, especially in that loans and investments would also dry up, only comes about because the system is not flexible in permitting some amount of convertibility between the two kinds of money in it.

If we take the point of view, alternatively, that individuals change their taste for currency and now want three-fourths rather than one-half of their liquid wealth in the form of currency—and make that a sudden change—then there is a numerical solution to the problem short of the complete collapse of the system (assuming also, that the preference of the banks for a reserve deposit ratio of 1 : 5 is not changed).[5] In our case we said that individuals decided to hold smaller deposits and more cash, and we can now interpret this to mean that C_p/D has risen to 3.0. If we put this new result into Equation (5.6), we get

$$M = \$120 \left(\frac{3 + 1}{0.2 + 3}\right) = \$120 \left(\frac{4}{3.2}\right) = \$150, \tag{5.7}$$

which represents a considerable reduction in the supply of money to the system as a result of the increased desire to hold currency. Let us emphasize this result, for it is fundamental to the understanding of the behavior of the American financial system until the end of the depression of the 1930s: changes in the tastes of individuals, represented by shifts in their preferences for cash, were often responsible for significant destruction of the money stock, depending on whether or not changes in H and in banks' preferences for reserves offset the "currency panic."

Furthermore, the consequences are not limited merely to the banking system, for along with the contraction of money one customarily finds a contraction of credit. Indeed, in our example, as Table 5.4 makes clear, loans by the banking system have fallen from \$80 to \$30. This is another of the consequences of a financial panic, because so long as the stock of

[5] This is a fairly strong assumption, actually. It is known that as a panic progresses, bankers' attitudes toward liquidity change, and they, themselves, require more liquidity (see the discussion of both the 1830s and the 1930s below, where it seems to happen this way, following a customers' panic). If the banks start to hold greater reserves, then the money stock would be further reduced, on this account (see Equation 5.6).

Table 5.4: The two-bank system after the currency drain (consolidated)

Assets		*Liabilities*	
Currency	$ 7.50	Deposits	$37.50
Loans	30.00	Capital accounts	15.00
Investments	15.00		
Total assets	$52.50	Total liabilities	$52.50

currency is not expanded in response to the increased demand, banks must call in loans, since the currency preferences of the public have to be met.[6] The destruction of credit, which financed business spending, consumer spending, and even stock market speculation,[7] forces on all sectors of the economy a readjustment that is serious in proportion to the extent of the currency panic.

5.3 AN ILLUSTRATION: THE BANK WAR AND ITS AFTERMATH (1831–1839)

One thing should be pointed out about the more general analysis just laid out before we move on. This is that we may immediately connect up our analysis with any banking system that is built on "reserves," whatever their nature, merely by relabelling our "currency" concept as reserves; thus, for the member banks of the Federal Reserve System, as we shall see, at present the reserves would be the reserves held at the Federal Reserve plus vault cash (currency in the bank) instead of merely the "currency" of our example. During the 1830s, then, commercial banks held deposits in other banks and gold and silver coins and bullion (which items we can refer to as "specie"); the latter represented the equivalent of the currency reserves in our example, there being no central bank money at the time.

The story of the events of the 1830s begins with the presidential election of 1828, in which Andrew Jackson defeated John Quincy Adams (the incumbent); Jackson was the first U.S. "frontier" president, and as such, was a hard-money man who had special appeal to the farmers and to the other nonbusiness elements in the country. Jackson felt that "eastern money forces" had opposed his election and, in particular, that the gigantic ($35 million) Bank of the United States (which was federally chartered

[6] If there were financial intermediaries also offering credit (that is, if there were nonbank lenders), things might not work out this way, as Chapter 13 illustrates.

[7] As in 1929.

in 1816 for a period of 20 years) was lined up with the opposition.[8] Jackson's view on money, that the overuse of paper money brought financial crises, was, of course, popular with some elements at the time; as well, his hostility toward the (Second) Bank of the United States extended to its director Nicholas Biddle, an Eastern aristocrat who was acutely aware of the potential of his bank (which had branches all over the country) as a device for conducting a centralized monetary policy.

The Bank War—the struggle between Jackson and the bank—was initially over the recharter of the bank. You will recall, from Chapter 2, that the First Bank (1791–1811) failed by one vote to be rechartered in Congress; to avoid this problem, the directors of the Second Bank sought an early passage of the recharter bill in the summer of 1832 (four years before the expiration of the charter) on the grounds that Jackson would not stand against the bank in an election year. Their strategy did not prevail, however, and while the bill to recharter passed Congress handily, Jackson vetoed it on July 10, 1832; since the majority was insufficient to override his veto and since Jackson won the election anyway, the bank was finished (although the Bank War was not). Jackson's reasons for finishing off the bank were the following:

a. It was unconstitutional, having crossed state lines in its activities.

b. It was operated illegally.[9]

c. It represented mainly the financial powers of the East and abroad (and as such it was a danger to American democracy).

These arguments had sufficient appeal to carry the day, although they were not especially accurate with regard to the facts (for example, the federal government itself was the largest single owner of the bank).

After 1832 the Bank War continued since the bank's charter was to run until 1836. In the fall of 1833, Jackson, ever thorough, wished to remove the federal government's deposits from the bank and to redistribute them among other banks; these deposits were in the amount of almost $10 million (the Bank had "discounted" bills of nearly $63 million); Table 5.5 carries the figures for this and some of the following discussion.

[8] The Second Bank was capitalized at $35 million, of which the federal government took $7 million. It was set up with 18 branches, although there were ultimately 25. Foreigners owned stock, but the total probably never exceeded one-fifth of the paid-in capital; it was a very popular stock among American investors.

[9] Bank notes, at the time, had to be signed by the president of the bank. The Second Bank actually issued notes at its regional offices signed by the director there, rather than by Biddle; this (certainly trivial) action was in violation of its charter. In addition, no doubt, the bank, as a private profit-making corporation, did contribute to political campaigns. This was not illegal at the time and no one went to jail for it, but it was in dubious taste (and was the source of some of Jackson's hostility).

Table 5.5: The Second Bank of the United States, 1833–1834 ($ millions)

	Bills held	*Public deposits*	*Private deposits plus notes*	*Specie*	*Reserve ratio**
July 1833	61.63	6.51	28.11	10.10	.359
Aug.	63.58	7.60	28.36	10.02	.353
Sept.	63.22	9.18	28.91	10.21	.359
Oct.	62.97	9.87	27.86	10.66	.383
Nov.	61.11	8.23	27.31	10.34	.379
Dec.	58.12	5.16	27.43	9.82	.358
Jan. 1834	56.50	4.23	27.00	10.03	.371
Feb.	54.24	3.07	25.52	10.52	.412
Mar.	54.15	2.60	25.14	10.39	.413
Apr.	52.27	2.93	23.81	10.18	.428
May	51.18	3.25	23.07	11.18	.485
June	50.35	2.73	22.36	12.30	.550
July	49.49	2.68	22.05	12.82	.581
Aug.	48.20	2.61	22.66	13.63	.602
Sept.	47.98	2.15	22.63	13.86	.612
Oct.	47.71	2.04	23.22	15.56	.670

* Specie divided by the sum of private deposits and notes.

Source: Jacob Meerman, "The Climax of the Bank War: Biddle's Contraction, 1833–34," *Journal of Political Economy* (August 1963), p. 381.

Jackson actually did not have an easy time getting his secretary of the treasury to do the job for him and it was not until the appointment of Roger B. Taney, in September 1833, that he got what he wanted. Taney announced a list of seven banks (later much expanded) into which the federal deposits would be diverted;[10] in a short time federal deposits at the Second Bank were cut in half. Jackson's actions here were far from exemplary, no doubt, and they provoked Nicholas Biddle to precipitate what is now known as Biddle's Panic. That is, Biddle made some pronouncements following what he felt was a Treasury-inspired run on the Savannah, Georgia, branch of the Bank of the United States, and he ordered the Bank to curtail its operations. Thus from September 1833 to June 1834, the period of the panic, lending by the bank (bills held) declined by $12.87 million, while the bank's reserve ratio (specie against private deposits and notes) rose to the astronomical figure of 55 percent; this, surely, was overinsurance and, no doubt, was an overreaction on Biddle's part.

[10] The banks have been called the "pet" banks; indeed Taney himself held stock in one of them (the Union Bank of Maryland, in Baltimore). Note that the deposits were not pulled out, as such, but that no new deposits were made; that is, the government's balance was allowed to run down, as it was used. Note also that the U.S. Senate censured the president (and refused to confirm Taney), mainly over the firing of his predecessor (Duane); Taney, though, became Chief Justice of the United States and survived in that post long enough to issue the famous Dred Scott decision in 1858.

During many of the numerous panics in the American banking system (the first of these was just after the War of 1812), a generalized contraction of the financial system occurred. Generally banks suspended gold payments (and some even failed), and both short and long term credit became hard to get (and interest rates rose). The "panic" that occurred in the fall of 1833 did produce this sort of side effect; indeed, prices fell and some short-term interest rates (on bills) reached as much as 24 percent (those were the days when prices and interest rates were fully flexible). But, as Table 5.6 illustrates for the annual data, the effect of all this on the American money supply was not especially great, mainly because of an inflow of gold and silver (specie). Thus, Table 5.6 shows that the rate of

Table 5.6: Money, gold, and prices, 1830–1840 ($ million)

	Money stock	*Specie*	*Price index**
1830	114	32	88
1831	155	30	91
1832	150	31	93
1833	168	41	98
1834	172	51	97
1835	246	65	116
1836	276	73	127
1837	232	88	108
1838	240	87	117
1839	215	83	101
1840	186	80	89
1841	174	80	—
1842	158	90	—

* March 1835 = 100; last month of year.
Source: Peter Temin, *The Jacksonian Economy* (New York: W. W. Norton and Company, 1969).

growth of the money stock decreased in 1834, but that any overall effect of Biddle's Panic was overcome by the liquidity which was arriving from abroad in the form of specie. Indeed, the end of the contraction and the specie inflow produced a strong upward effect on the money stock in 1835, an effect that continued until 1837.

We may gain another perspective on this period and employ our model of the determinants of the money stock, which we developed in Section 5.2, by looking at the various ratios that are relevant to that model, as laid out in Table 5.7. The model, in this context, is given by

$$M = H\left[\frac{\frac{S_p}{D} + 1}{\frac{S_p}{D} + \frac{S_b}{D}}\right], \tag{5.8}$$

Table 5.7: The determinants of the U.S. money supply, 1832–1842

	M (*$ millions*)	$\frac{S_p}{D}$	$\frac{S_b}{D}$	H (*$ millions*)
1832	150	.05	.16	31
1833	168	.08	.18	41
1834	172	.04	.27	51
1835	246	.10	.18	65
1836	276	.13	.16	73
1837	232	.23	.20	88
1838	240	.18	.23	87
1839	215	.23	.20	83
1840	186	.24	.25	80
1841	174	.30	.23	80
1842	158	.35	.33	90

Note: M = money supply; S_p = specie in the hands of the public; D = bank deposits and bank notes; S_b = specie in the bank; H = total U.S. specie supply.
Source: Temin, *The Jacksonian Economy*.

where S_p stands for the specie in the hands of the public and S_b for specie in the banks. D represents bank deposits and bank notes, both assumed to be the liabilities of the commercial banks. The notes, of course, were currency issued by the banks. H denotes the total of specie (the main form of high-powered money in a gold-standard world) in the United States. This, to be perfectly explicit, is a gold-standard approach to the analysis of the period, but we were on the gold standard then. It appears that in 1834 banks *considerably* increased their preference for specie, an act that would ordinarily have reduced the money supply if it had not been for the gold inflow (ΔH = $10 million); the public actually reduced their reserves compared to 1833. Biddle's Panic was evidently a fizzle.

But possibly what is most interesting about Table 5.7 is the story it tells about the rest of the decade, particularly about the Crash of May 1837, which, you will recall from Chapter 2, produced a bank suspension (of specie payments) for a year. Thus, the figures tell us, the money stock peaked in 1836, falling steadily after that right to the end of the period; in 1837 another large inflow of gold ($15 million) was not enough to offset the negative effect of a 25 percent rise in bank liquidity and 77 percent rise in the public's relative cash holdings (S_p/D). The crash of 1837 was a reality that did survive beyond the immediate period.[11] Banks, after the Crash of

[11] It has been hypothesized that the events of 1834 left a permanent scar on both the public and the banks, and thus the events of 1837 were indirectly part of the payoff for the troubles in 1833–34 ("Once bitten, twice shy"); see M. Sushka, "The Antebellum Money Market and the Economic Impact of the Bank War," *Journal of Economic History* (December 1976). We will use this argument in our discussion of the 1930s (as put forward by Milton Friedman), and it clearly has some applicability here. The ratios in Table 5.7 do not tell us this, especially since the figures return to their pre-War totals in 1836. That, though, is not a direct test of the hypothesis.

1837, continued to add to their specie reserves, as Jackson's hard-money policy was continued by his successors and the United States went through recurrent financial crises (there was a cotton market collapse in 1839 and the Bank of the United States, by then a state-chartered bank, failed in 1841 as two waves of failures hit the country). Thus, by 1842 banks held reserves of 33 percent against their note and deposit liabilities. The public, similarly, continued to increase its cash holdings, with the highest ratio (.35) occurring in 1842 (a year in which a significant number of commercial banks failed). Indeed, the banking multiplier, which stood at 5.00 in 1832, had fallen to 1.98 by 1842. On net, then, the combination of the Bank War, the Crash of 1837, and the collapse of the cotton boom in 1839 seem to have produced a remarkable effect on the American financial community.[12] It is small wonder that many have concluded that if we had had a central bank at the time, the troubles would have been considerably smaller than they were.

5.4 THE FEDERAL RESERVE AND THE MONEY STOCK IN THE GREAT DEPRESSION: A FURTHER APPLICATION OF MONEY SUPPLY THEORY

During the years between the two World Wars, the United States (and the rest of the world) experienced a series of economic disasters unparalleled in history, the most notable of which was the Great Depression of 1929–35. During the period from 1929 to 1933, as Table 5.8 shows, Gross National Product (in *constant* dollars) fell by 29 percent, unemployment rose from 3.2 percent to 24.9 percent of the work force, and consumer prices fell by 24.5 percent. The effect of four consecutive years with unemployment over 20 percent was monumental; there is no wonder that many Americans have a pathological fear of "it" returning. The hypotheses concerning the causes of these events are numerous; and they range from the "Great Crash" hypothesis (that the stock market crash brought everything else down with it) to the Marxist view that this was just one more dying paroxysm of the capitalist beast. We will, more conservatively, consider a range of monetary and real hypotheses.

First of all, there is the view that it was the behavior of the money supply, particularly the banks' R/D, and the Federal Reserve H, that

[12] The Secretary of the Treasury (Woodbury) declared on July 11, 1836, that all public land sales were henceforth to be in specie. This "hard-money act" is known as the Specie Circular; it seems that a certain amount of chaos ensued, since specie normally drained away from the areas in which land sales occurred (on the frontier), but in this instance it was forced to circulate back in that direction (tying it up "in transit"). The Specie Circular, by further returning the United States to a barter (gold and silver for land) basis did create a situation in which reserves were tied up, although it is not known how much was tied up. The act was seen, at the time, as a contributor to the panic of 1837; it was repealed in 1838.

Table 5.8: Aggregate data for the U.S., 1919–1939

	Gross National Product (\$ billions)*	*Consumer Price Index (1947–49 = 100)*	*Unemployment (percent)*
1919	74.2	74.0	2.3
1920	73.3	85.7	4.0
1921	71.6	76.4	11.9
1922	75.8	71.6	7.6
1923	85.8	72.9	3.2
1924	88.4	73.1	5.5
1925	90.5	75.0	4.0
1926	96.4	75.6	1.9
1927	97.3	74.2	4.1
1928	98.5	73.3	4.4
1929	104.4	73.3	3.2
1930	95.1	71.4	8.9
1931	89.5	65.0	15.9
1932	76.4	58.4	23.6
1933	74.2	55.3	24.9
1934	80.8	57.2	21.7
1935	91.4	58.7	20.1
1936	100.9	59.3	17.0
1937	109.1	61.4	14.3
1938	103.2	60.3	19.0
1939	111.0	59.4	17.2

* 1929 dollars.

Sources: Peter Temin, *Did Monetary Forces Cause the Great Depression?* (New York: W. W. Norton, 1976); Stanley Lebergott, "Annual Estimates of Unemployment in the United States, 1900–1954," *The Measurement and Behavior of Unemployment* (National Bureau of Economic Research) (Princeton, N.J.: Princeton University Press, 1957), pp. 215–16.

turned a severe contraction into a disaster. Figures on the determinants of the money stock as required in the model of Section 5.2 are contained in Table 5.9. Here we see that banks' reserve ratio (consisting of cash plus actual reserves) turned up after September 1930 and turned up sharply after September 1931, reaching a total of 16.42 percent by June 1934 compared to the 7.68 percent in March 1929. We also see a familiar pattern for C/D, representing the "liquidity preference" of the public, which rose from 9.22 to 22.52 percent by March 1933, although at the later date it began to recover for reasons we shall discuss. Returning to our money supply formula, we now write it as Equation (5.9), reflecting the institutional changes brought about by the arrival of the Federal Reserve System; the important difference from our earlier discussions is that R here represents the actual total reserves of commercial banks held as balances at the Federal Reserve Banks:

$$M = H\left[\frac{\frac{C}{D} + 1}{\frac{C}{D} + \frac{R}{D}}\right]. \tag{5.9}$$

Table 5.9: The determinants of the money stock, 1929–1934

	M_1 ($ billions)	H ($ billions)	R/D	C/D	M_2 ($ billions)
1929					
March	26.3	7.15	7.68%	9.22%	46.2
June	26.2	7.10	7.60	9.31	45.9
September	26.4	7.08	7.65	8.99	46.3
December	26.4	6.98	7.55	9.03	45.9
1930					
March	26.3	6.96	7.65	8.76	46.2
June	25.3	6.91	7.75	8.84	45.3
September	25.0	6.83	7.71	8.76	45.1
December	24.9	7.12	8.24	9.46	44.0
1931					
March	24.8	7.09	8.07	9.64	43.9
June	23.9	7.30	8.57	10.35	42.6
September	23.4	7.50	8.76	11.71	40.9
December	21.9	7.74	9.56	14.06	37.3
1932					
March	21.1	7.54	9.02	15.29	35.8
June	20.4	7.79	9.58	16.81	34.5
September	20.2	7.90	10.18	17.04	34.0
December	20.3	8.03	10.95	16.53	34.0
1933					
March	19.0	8.41	11.88	22.52	30.0
June	19.2	7.94	11.92	19.68	30.1
September	19.2	8.09	12.82	18.98	30.3
December	19.8	8.30	13.33	18.62	30.8
1934					
March	20.7	9.00	16.05	16.42	32.2
June	21.1	9.26	16.42	16.10	33.1

Note: C = currency in the hands of the public; D = deposits in banks; H = high-powered money (= $C + R$); R = total reserves of commercial banks held as vault cash and balances at Federal Reserve Banks. The reserves are total reserves and include vault cash. Thus they are held against time deposits as well as the demand deposits included in the M_1 figures; figures on M_2 are also included in the last column.

Source: Friedman and Schwartz, *A Monetary History of the United States, 1867–1960* (Princeton, N.J.: Princeton University Press, 1963).

The bracketed expression of our new version of the "banking multiplier"; this number stood at 6.55 in September 1929, indicating, *if it were a constant,* that, a dollar of high-powered money ($H = C + R$) would generate $6.55 of broad money (since C/D and R/D are figured on the basis of M_2); in March 1933, the value of this multiplier stood at only 3.56 and in June 1934, at the end of the series, it was only 3.57, the latter reflecting the further rise in the bank reserve ratio (by this time including substantial excess reserves).

The first question concerns which of the three determinants most influenced the fall in the money stock: C/D, R/D, or H? The middle three columns in Table 5.9 show the values for these ratios. We see that from March 1929 to March 1931, C/D did not rise appreciably, a reflection of the fact that the public was not panicked but that banks were requiring more reserves per dollar of deposits than before and that the Federal Reserve was apparently not offsetting this change in banks' liquidity preference by increasing the stock of high-powered money. The last can be concluded because H, an indicator of the Federal Reserve policy, remained fairly constant (it actually declined in the middle of the period).

One might wonder why the Federal Reserve allowed the stock of high-powered money to fall in the year and a half after the crash of 1929. Several explanations have been offered. One view is that there was considerable conflict within the system over what to do, with the result that the most that could be agreed upon was a mild tendency toward "cheap money" (lower interest rates) without any explicit policy toward the quantity of money by means of open-market operations or changes in reserve requirements.

> As the recession in business took hold, considerable disagreement developed within the system as to the usefulness of cheap money in stemming the decline. In general, the New York Bank under Harrison pressed for cheaper money, and the Board rather reluctantly went along . . . Despite these reasons for hesitation, the System's reaction to declining business was to cheapen money, and the cheapening, as measured by rediscount rates, was considerable.[13]

Cheaper money, in this context, meant a fall in interest rates. Cheaper money, induced by increasing the money stock, should do the job, but we are probably not too far off the mark when we conjecture that the Federal Reserve probably actually *followed* market interest rates downward, so that the interest rate they set was always too high, although falling, in the sense of being above rather than below the equilibrium rate. It is important here to realize that whether monetary conditions are tight or not cannot be judged from the actual fall in interest rates alone but must be supplemented with information on the relation between the supply and demand for funds. There seems to have been little recognition of this fact at the time.

There has been a serious attempt to explain this apparent inaction of the Federal Reserve as part of a systematic policy followed from 1922 until 1933, when it became untenable. Elmus R. Wicker argues both (*a*) that the Federal Reserve used the discount rate either to push gold toward Britain (1927) or to attract it toward the United States (1931) depending on international circumstances and (*b*) that in this period the authorities were never actually aiming at internal objectives.[14] Thus, prior to modern times, it can be argued, the typical central bank saw its main task as that

---

[13] Harold Barger, *The Management of Money* (Chicago: Rand McNally & Company, 1964), pp. 97–98. Friedman and Schwartz also discuss this point (*A Monetary History*, p. 375).

[14] Elmus R. Wicker, "Federal Reserve Policy 1922–1933: A Reinterpretation," *Journal of Political Economy*, vol. 73, no. 4 (August 1965).

of helping to stabilize the exchange rate (in this case between the dollar and foreign currencies). When the exchange rate worsened, one way to help the situation was to raise domestic interest rates, thus drawing funds from abroad (and increasing the demand for the dollar). This, Wicker claims, was the dominant policy in this period as it was for most countries that had active central banks prior to the Great Depression of the 1930s. We will return to those issues in Part IV of the book. It turns out that the fall in interest rates in the early 1930s is consistent with this position because interest rates were falling in Britain too; all that had to happen in order to attract gold to the United States was for U.S. rates to fall more slowly, and this, indeed, happened. But what we are most interested in here are the sharp breaks in *C/D* and *R/D* in Table 5.9. Indeed, from October 1930 until early 1933 the United States went through the most protracted and severe monetary and financial crisis in its history. Three great waves of bank failures spread throughout the country. The first began in October 1930, and in November and December of that year 608 banks closed their doors; in March 1931, partly precipitated by bank failures in Europe, a second wave of failures hit the system. This wave, in contrast to the first, severely affected bankers and depositors; and, as Table 5.9 suggests, the sharp rises in both *R/D* and *C/D*, in the former case continuing until the late 1930s and in the latter case until June 1933, began at this point. As Friedman and Schwartz note, "once bitten, twice shy, both depositors and bankers were bound to react more vigorously to any new eruption of bank failures or banking difficulties than they did in the final months of 1930."[15]

Large-scale open market purchases begin in April 1932, a year and a half after the first banking panic, but by then we were deep into the depression; at that point the figure for unemployment stood at 23.6 percent of the labor force (for the year). In fact, another wave of bank failures, beginning late in 1932, resulted in a series of state bank holidays, beginning in October 1932; these, in turn, culminated in the nationwide bank holiday of 1933. In that case, beginning on March 6 and lasting until March 13, 14, or 15, depending on the location of the bank, all banks were closed and none was permitted to reopen without federal or state licenses to do so. Needless to say, this eliminated, for reasons that are far from convincing, a large amount of the money stock. Further, and of more lasting seriousness, there was a permanent fall in the number of banks as a result of the holiday: "More than 5,000 banks still in operation when the holiday was declared did not reopen their doors when it ended, and of these, over 2,000 never did thereafter . . . The 'cure' came close to being

[15] Friedman and Schwartz, *A Monetary History,* p. 314. Recall our mention of this proposition in connection with the Bank War of the 1830s (and the crash of 1837) in Section 5.3.

worse than the disease."[16] For this case, we find our leaders *purging* the system of its *alleged* weaknesses, rather than directly reconstructing it, although as reference to Table 3.7 indicates, the *combined* effect of all the government's actions in this period was effectively to eliminate bank failure.

When we return to the figures of Table 5.9, we see that panic is indeed writ in the behavior of depositors (the severe rise in C/D) and in the increasing desire of commercial banks to hold excess reserves. The latter are not explicitly identified in the table; but it is obvious as a matter of arithmetic that with reserve requirements unchanged, a rise in the *actual* ratio of deposits to reserves held by commercial banks will result in excess reserves. The increases in the stock of high-powered money, while in the correct direction, are woefully inadequate to the task at hand; further, there is the year-and-a-half delay in the beginning of large-scale open market operations that needs to be justified.

We already have one explanation: the personal disagreements of the early years. But there are other factors, as well, this time centering on the authorities' apparent disregard of the rising tide of bank failures; these failures were shown in Table 3.7. Friedman and Schwartz adduce three reasons for the Federal Reserve's lack of concern for the failures.

a. Federal Reserve officials felt no responsibility for nonmember banks, more of which failed than member banks.
b. The failures were concentrated among smaller banks, which were not influential in policy matters.
c. The few large banks that failed were thought to have done so because of poor management.

Now the first two factors, if valid, establish some myopia, but the third raises some fundamental issues. Since banks were business firms that could fail, failure was always part of banking history; and when times were bad in general, so that other firms were failing, banks suffered their share of the load (as we demonstrated in Chapter 3). If business in general collapses, business firms and individuals will become insolvent, and the holders of their liabilities will suffer real losses. Banks, for example, as lenders to business firms, would certainly tend to feel the same cycles that business firms feel.

It seems that banks, like business firms, need not be accused of mismanagement if they do not anticipate business cycles correctly. We do have, and did have at the time, agencies empowered to deal with cycles; and it is at their door that bank failure is to be laid insofar as the rate of failure of banks was abnormal. We do not know whether bank managers

[16] Friedman and Schwartz, *A Monetary History*, p. 330.

did make especially foolish loans in the overly enthusiastic 1920s, for no student of banking has yet separated the cyclical effect from the mismanagement effect. But, with hindsight, we do know that a lot of *viable* banks were lost to the American economy through the cyclical effect, through the rigidity of the reserve system, and through the holiday in 1933.

But there are alternatives to the "money supply" theory (which puts much of the blame for the severity of the Depression on the Federal Reserve and the banks), and they deserve an airing, too; these are the "money demand" and the "real causes" views. To be a really convincing theory of the story of the 1929 to 1933 period, the "money supply" theory ought to be able to show some "causes" that occur visibly before the events; this it does not do. Thus, over the years 1929 to 1931, the money stock fell 11.4 percent while GNP, in constant dollars, fell 14.3 percent, prices fell 11.3 percent, and unemployment rose from 3.2 percent to 15.9 percent of the labor force. These figures can, though, illustrate the "money demand" hypothesis, for what we find is that *nominal* income fell by 25.7 percent during this period (11.4 plus 14.3) while money holding fell by *only* 11.4 percent. That is to say, people were holding more money, per dollar of GNP, in 1931 than they were in 1929; this may have reflected a significant change in the taste for money.[17] This hypothesis, thus, asserts that money was drained from the banking system, in effect, by an increase in the demand for money. Corresponding to this increase in money demand, households decreased their demand for commodities and other assets. Consequently, by this view, the contractionary effects on aggregate demand emanated from the public rather than from the banking system or the Federal Reserve.[18]

With regard to the "real causes hypothesis," which is, certainly, the one most widely believed, an even more persuasive case can be made. The argument is the Keynesian one that real events—the declines in farm prices, the coal industry, construction, and especially, investment—that preceded the market crash of 1929 actually brought about the Depression. Furthermore, once started, the economic system continued down because once a *severe* downturn is started in an unstable economy like the American, it goes ever downward, propelled as it were by "accelerator-

[17] In Chapter 6 we will show that *usually* a dollar's increase or decrease in nominal GNP produces between $.90 and $1.00 change in the demand for (nominal) money balances. This was clearly not the case in 1929–31.

[18] Peter Temin, in *Did Monetary Forces Cause the Great Depression?* (New York: W. W. Norton, 1976), argues that this shows up in the effect of interest rates on the demand for money (as interest rates fell, they caused people to hold more and more money); see the discussion in Chapter 6. This can be interpreted in terms of Equation (5.9), as well; here we would argue that the term in brackets is variable and, indeed, depends on interest rates. In particular, because of the effect of the interest rate on C/D (and, maybe, on R/D) it makes the multiplier *fall* when interest rates fall.

multiplier" effects.[19] Consider the figures in Table 5.10. Recalling Table 5.9, we note that the money stock had stopped growing by 1929; this suggests (or causes?) a decline in the economy prior to September 1929. Even more convincing, though, is the behavior of gross investment, which was lower in 1929 than it was in 1926 (although on an uptrend) and, especially, *construction* (including housing), which reached its peak in 1926 and was declining steadily in the late 1920s. That is, the Keynesians argue that the boom in real goods and services came to an end in 1926 or 1927, but was artificially kept going by consumer spending (Column 1) and by the stock market boom; the latter was speculative in character and was not based on real activity, as the figures in Table 5.10 indicate. The stock market got so far out of hand that an enormous crash occurred, and it was this crash, which wiped out much of the collateral of financial and business firms, that led to the waves of bank (and business) failures in the early 1930s. Sound private banking practices, it is argued, would have

Table 5.10: Real factors in the inter-war period, 1919–1939 ($ billions, 1929 dollars)

	Total consumption expenditures	*Gross investment*	*Construction*	*Gross National Product*
1919	50.2	10.7	4.8	74.2
1920	52.7	12.8	5.0	73.3
1921	56.1	7.4	4.9	71.6
1922	58.1	10.6	7.1	75.8
1923	63.4	15.6	8.2	85.8
1924	68.1	12.4	9.0	88.4
1925	66.1	16.4	10.0	90.5
1926	71.5	17.1	10.7	96.4
1927	73.2	15.6	10.4	97.3
1928	74.8	14.5	9.8	98.5
1929	79.0	16.2	8.7	104.4
1930	74.7	10.5	6.4	95.1
1031	72.2	6.8	4.5	89.5
1932	66.0	.8	2.4	76.4
1933	64.6	.3	1.9	74.2
1934	68.0	1.8	2.0	80.8
1935	72.3	8.8	2.8	91.4
1936	79.7	9.3	3.9	100.9
1937	82.6	14.6	4.6	109.1
1938	81.3	6.8	4.1	103.2
1939	85.9	9.9	4.9	111.0

Source: Peter Temin, *Did Monetary Forces Cause the Great Depression?*, p. 4.

[19] In Chapters 7, 8, and 11 we will consider some of the details of this. The idea is that of a "vicious circle"; as incomes decline, so does spending on both consumer and investment goods. Then at the next stage, as spending declines, so do incomes. The process does not have any necessary stopping point (some feel) so that drastic action (e.g., fiscal policy) must intervene. This we did not do in 1929–33, although there was some fiscal policy thereafter.

helped stave off the derivative problems of the financial sector of the economy, but no more.

5.5 THE RECESSION IN 1937: ANOTHER GREAT DEBATE

The preceding discussion is the classic case of a confrontation, over the facts, between the Keynesians and the Monetarists; it seems that both views encompass enough of the facts to ensure their survival. This was not always the case, though; there was a time, not too long ago, when practically no one put any faith in the "money supply hypothesis." To see how this is relevant, let us consider a second period, the recession in 1937–38 (see the figures in Tables 5.8 and 5.9) for which a "money supply" cause is, as we will see, even more apparent. In particular, there is one aspect of the previous discussion that ties in with the events of the later 1930s; and that is that banks, which started to acquire excess reserves in 1931, actually continued to hold substantial amounts until the 1940s. In fact, the reserve-deposit ratio for banks, which stood at 11.92 in June 1933, was up to 31.85 in June 1940 and only then began to move gradually downwards, reaching 9.92 *by 1960.* But from 1931 onwards, there were substantial excess reserves, and that is the principal fact of interest in the late 1930s; some figures are given for 1935 to 1938 in Table 5.11.

Table 5.11: Excess reserves and required reserves for United States commercial banks, 1935–1938

	Reserve Ratios	
Date	*Required*	*Usable (excess)*
June 1935	8.9	9.4
December 1935	8.6	11.4
June 1936	8.7	9.4
December 1936	13.0	7.9
June 1937	17.5	3.5
December 1937	16.9	5.9
June 1938	15.3	9.9
December 1938	14.9	11.2

Source: Phillip Cagan, *Determinants and Effects of Changes in the Money Stock: 1875–1960* (New York: National Bureau of Economic Research, 1965), p. 192.

If you believed that the Federal Reserve had done all it could to make money plentiful prior to 1936, then you, like the Federal Reserve, would worry, as the economy began to pull out of the depression, about banks having a reservoir of lending power that could frustrate anti-inflationary policy. It seems a little premature, in the early stages of recovery, to be concerned about the other extreme, but so it was in the 1930s. The figures that guided officials are contained in Table 5.11; the table distinguishes between the *required* reserve ratio and the *usable* reserve ratio, rather than the excess reserve ratio. For the record, the usable reserve ratio is a somewhat broader concept, along the lines of the *monetary base* (see below), of the lending ability of commercial banks.

As can be seen in the figures, the required reserve ratio was almost doubled by the Federal Reserve over a very short period. The changes came in three steps, in August 1936 and in March and May 1937. The timing of these changes was most unfortunate, for the peak of the business cycle expansion was also reached in May 1937. This coincidence is probably not an accident, and thus it is that the Federal Reserve is accused by many of killing the emerging boom in its attempt to solve a problem that may not even have existed. But things are even worse than that, for the short recession of 1937–38 was quite deep, with unemployment averaging 19 percent of the labor force in 1938. Further, as Table 5.11 shows, excess reserves were not eliminated by the action; indeed, by December 1938, with the Federal Reserve still firmly maintaining its new reserve requirements, excess reserves were almost exactly restored to the December 1935 figures. The result was that the money stock, which fell from March 1937 to May 1938, only reached the level of December 1936 by October 1938.[20]

But things are never as simple as they seem, even if it is obvious that the Federal Reserve's timing was uninspired, and we must recognize that the swing in the money stock might have been caused by a recession (in real terms) rather than the other way around as was the case with the 1929–33 period.[21] Further, it is difficult to understand why banks held excess reserves even after the public had regained confidence in the banks themselves. That is, we see from Table 5.9 that the currency-deposit ratio began to fall almost immediately after the banking holiday, which had the virtue, at least, of helping to restore the public's confidence in the system. We could, though, argue that commercial bankers were "thrice bitten" and (much as state banks do now) simply decided to set their own reserve requirements, much in excess of those officially set. This, as just noted, was not so obviously necessary, since it was the public's loss of confidence that (most often) brought down commercial banks, but it is understandable and it has happened before in U.S. history (recall the 1837–41 period).

[20] A fall in the money stock is an unusual event.

[21] George Horwich, "Effective Reserves, Credit, and Causality in the Banking System of the Thirties," in Deane Carson, ed., *Banking and Monetary Studies* (Homewood, Ill.: Richard D. Irwin, Inc., 1963) © 1963 by Richard D. Irwin, Inc. The explanation is a Keynesian one.

And there is a further fact: the Federal Deposit Insurance Corporation (FDIC) began operating on January 1, 1934, and within six months, nearly 14,000 of the nation's 15,348 commercial banks, accounting for some 97 percent of all commercial bank deposits, were covered by insurance. If, as seems likely, commercial bankers were aware of the significance of this insurance with regard to its effect on individual's attitudes toward the safety of their accounts, then the excess reserves were not held for protection by the banks, but rather were simply unusable because of slow business conditions. As things stand, we must conclude that this important issue is not yet resolved. But there is one aspect worthy of special note: in spite of the complicated and sometimes excessive legislation of the 1930s aimed at making commercial banking safe from failure, the single piece of legislation that stands out as having significantly altered the economic climate in favor of stability is the Banking Act of 1933, which created the FDIC. The main reason for the importance of the FDIC is that the Federal Reserve System actually has a *locked-up* reserve that is not available to meet a deposit drain (rather, banks must borrow for that purpose). Individual depositors, then, were perfectly reasonable when they doubted the safety of their deposits; these doubts were stilled by the FDIC, which the public perceived, correctly as it turns out, as at last bringing safety to the system.

5.6 EXCESS RESERVES, FREE RESERVES, AND THE MONETARY BASE

There are several qualifications and extensions we must append to the discussion of this chapter involving the actions of the banks and of the Federal Reserve. As it stands, we have characterized banks either in terms of their actual reserves or (in our historical discussion) in terms of "excess" reserves, but we have not offered any formal analysis of the latter. It turns out that another concept, *free reserves,* is often considered even more critical in this context (especially by the Federal Reserve in its conduct of monetary policy), so we will turn to the task of describing the nature of these important concepts here. Along the same lines, but with regard to the contribution of the Federal Reserve to the determination of the money stock (via H), we can also construct a measure of *all* "exogenous" (or "outside") influences on the money stock;[22] this measure is the *monetary base,* and it includes all manner of outside and policy controllable influences on the money stock, as we shall see.

[22] To a Monetarist (and sometimes to a Keynesian) money is arbitrarily produced by the Federal Reserve; if not, they argue, outside (e.g., foreign) or random influences dominate. All together, these make up the category of *exogenous* influences. The opposite are *endogenous* influences (such as the case in which the quantity of money is determined by the *demand* for money).

Table 5.12 contains the basic data for much of this section. In the table, we find, first of all, actual *total reserves* (consisting of vault cash, which is presumably held by banks in order to service the needs of their customers, and reserves that are held with the Federal Reserve banks); in addition, we find *excess reserves,* defined as the difference between total reserves and *required reserves:*

$$\begin{array}{ccccc} \text{Total reserves} & - & \text{Required reserves} & = & \text{Excess reserves.} \\ TR & - & RR & = & ER. \end{array} \tag{5.10}$$

It is possible that excess reserves are a good *indicator* of the tightness of the financial system; presumably when commercial banks are under pressure, they will allow their excess reserves to run down before actually denying funds to their customers. We have seen that the Federal Reserve thought so in 1935, and acted accordingly, possibly to the detriment of monetary stability. In any event, as Column (7) of the table indicates, excess reserves do seem to fluctuate with the cycle, (looking only at end-of-year totals), with the quantity at its lowest in 1971 and in 1976–78, all years of vigorous expansion, and at its highest in 1965, 1968, and 1974. The latter, of course, was a year in which all four quarters showed negative real growth for the United States (a full recession year).

One aspect that is not picked up by the level of excess reserves is that member banks, using the rediscount privilege, can and do borrow from the Federal Reserve; in fact, borrowing often exceeds excess reserves, so that banks have *net borrowed reserves*. One thing they can do when pressed by the need for funds, rather than letting their excess reserves fall, is actually to borrow reserves; to the extent that they do this, we will find that the excess reserves indicator will not give us the correct signals. On the other hand, if we calculate the difference between banks' excess reserves and their borrowings, we have some idea of the *net* borrowings of the banks; we define *free reserves*—that is to say, excess reserves that are free to be lent rather than held to back borowings at the Federal Reserve—to be excess reserves minus borrowed reserves:

$$\begin{array}{ccccc} \text{Free reserves} & = & \text{Excess reserves} & - & \text{Borrowed reserves} \\ FR & = & ER & - & BR. \end{array} \tag{5.11}$$

The Federal Reserve claims all manner of virtues for the level of free reserves or the ratio of free reserves to deposits as a measure of net tightness or ease in the money market.[23] The reason they take this position is that they firmly believe that a commercial bank's attitude toward its debts is the same as your attitude toward your debts: you want to repay

[23] We would use the ratio of free reserves to deposits—or of excess reserves to deposits, for that matter—to remove the (largely irrelevant) effects of changes in the size of the system from the data.

Table 5.12: The reserves of member banks and the monetary base, 1965–1978

	Currency	*Demand deposits*	M_1	M_2	*Total reserves*	*Required reserves*	*Excess reserves*	*Borrowings at the Federal Reserve*	*Free reserves*	H	*Monetary base (B)*	$\frac{M_1}{B}$
1965	36.4	135.1	171.3	301.3	22.72	22.27	.45	.45	.00	59.1	57.5	2.98
1966	38.5	136.8	175.7	318.1	23.80	23.41	.39	.56	−.17	62.3	60.0	2.93
1967	40.6	146.7	187.3	349.9	25.26	24.92	.34	.24	.10	65.9	63.8	2.94
1968	43.6	158.8	202.2	382.9	27.22	26.77	.46	.76	−.30	70.8	68.3	2.96
1969	46.1	163.2	208.8	392.3	28.03	27.77	.26	1.09	−.83	74.1	71.1	2.94
1970	49.2	170.7	219.6	423.5	29.26	28.99	.27	.32	−.05	78.5	75.9	2.89
1971	52.6	181.3	233.8	471.7	31.33	31.16	.16	.11	.05	83.9	81.2	2.88
1972	57.0	199.2	255.3	525.5	31.35	31.13	.22	1.05	−.83	88.4	88.5	2.88
1973	61.6	209.5	270.5	571.4	35.07	34.81	.26	1.30	−1.04	96.7	95.5	2.83
1974	67.8	215.0	283.1	612.4	36.94	36.60	.34	.70	−.36	104.7	104.2	2.72
1975	73.8	221.4	294.8	664.3	34.99	34.78	.26	.13	.13	108.8	112.3	2.62
1976	81.0	232.9	312.2	739.7	34.96	34.66	.17	.62	−.45	116.0	117.3	2.66
1977	88.6	249.9	338.5	806.5	36.15	35.96	.17	.56	−.39	124.6	129.9	2.60
1978	97.5	263.3	360.8	871.6	41.57	41.45	.12	.87	−.75	139.1	142.1	2.54

Note: Year-end figures.
Sources: *Federal Reserve Bulletin; Review, Federal Reserve Bank of St. Louis.*

them. Indeed, the Federal Reserve encourages this attitude by being severe toward "chronic" borrowers. Before 1921, in the early days of the Federal Reserve System, this was not the case; then, in fact, borrowed reserves exceeded required reserves. Under free market conditions, if the Federal Reserve merely supplied whatever the banks wanted, this situation would tend to arise whenever the discount rate (the interest rate charged by the Federal Reserve on borrowed reserves) is less than the interest rate earned by the bank. In recent years, when many interest rates were well above the discount rate, banks have not taken advantage of this situation, and this is the result of the sternness of the authorities; indeed, banks are generally reminded that their borrowing is only a privilege, and a very short-term one at that. Policing the system this way has proved easier than any attempt to keep the Federal Reserve's discount rate in line with market rates.

Turning to the figures in Table 5.12 we see that "free reserves" do fluctuate; indeed, if a negative value indicates "net borrowing" from the Federal Reserve, then both 1969 (recession) and 1972–73 (rapid inflation) indicate periods of "tightness" in the money market, and 1967, 1971, and 1975 (while the inflation was raging, but the economy was in recession) indicate "ease." But we should be careful here, because the level of free reserves is actually determined by the commercial banks themselves, and they, no doubt, compare the official discount rate with their own earnings rate so that free resources may actually depend on the "demand" for them by commercial banks. To get an idea of whether or not there might be anything to this proposition, we present a graph in Figure 5.1 of the situation for the 1965–78 period, using the data from Table 5.12 and some other data on the difference between the prime rate of commercial banks and the Federal Reserve's discount rate. The hypothesis, then, is that if the bank profit motive is at work, when the net profits $(i_p - i_D)$ go *up,* banks will work to *reduce* their free reserves; as the figure shows, this is *very* clearly the case in the 1965–78 period. Thus the level of free reserves may well be a *demand*-determined measure (by banks) and not a *supply* (i.e., monetary policy-determined) phenomenon. This brings us to *high-powered money* (currency plus reserves) and the *monetary base,* both of which may well be dominated by supply (policy) responses and so able to serve as *indicators* of the influence of monetary policy.

We have seen that free reserves and excess reserves may reflect important feedback from the economy and so give ambiguous signals as to the intentions of the monetary authorities. In contrast, high-powered money (H), which consists of currency *plus* member bank reserves at the Federal Reserve, can be determined completely by the Federal Reserve (look back at Chapter 4 if you are unable to recall how this can be worked); so, too, can the monetary base (B), a number calculated by the Federal Reserve Bank of St. Louis; the latter is really an adjusted form of H, so in the

Figure 5.1: The demand for free reserves—Illustration of the hypothesis

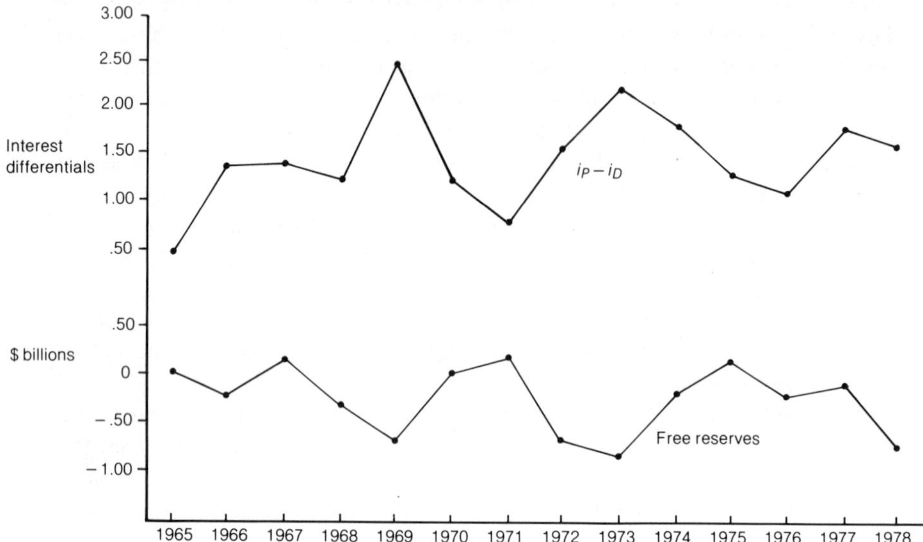

following we will limit our discussion to the monetary base. There are two methods of computing the base, which is derived from the balance sheet figures for the Federal Reserve System. One method emphasizes the *determinants* of the base (*sources*), and the other emphasizes the *uses* of the base; the latter is similar to the total of high-powered money, but with a "reserve adjustment." The method of calculation is described in Table 5.13 as it was done for February 1975. The simplest definition is, clearly, the "uses" approach; in effect, the Monetary Base is H (i.e., high-powered money) plus an adjustment for changes in reserve requirements (this latter is an *accumulated total* reflecting the general easing of reserve requirements over the years).[24] The *sources* identify the main influences on the base, the most important of which are the securities held by the Federal Reserve Banks (the total of which can be changed by open market operations, that is, by monetary policy). Finally, changes in the gold stock *can* directly affect the monetary base (and hence the money stock), but, if

[24] When reserve requirements are lowered, the amount of deposits that the amount of total reserves in the system can support is increased; these are reserves "liberated" by the easing of requirements. The adjustment accounts for shifts of reserves between banks with different reserve requirements but does not reflect shifts between time and savings deposits. The latter are probably pretty strong at present and so the base, like many of our measures, may be providing ambiguous signals to the authorities; this concern reflects, of course, the recent automatic transfer and NOW account activity of commercial banks, as well as the imposition of an 8 percent reserve requirement on CDs, etc., in late 1979.

Table 5.13: Computation of the monetary base, February 1975 ($ millions)

Sources		*Uses*	
Federal Reserve Credit		Member bank deposits at the Federal Reserve	28,342
U.S. government securities	85,523	Currency held by banks	9,179
Loans	147	Currency held by the public	67,800
Float plus other Federal Reserve assets	5,337		
Other factors			
Gold stock plus special drawing rights	12,026		
Treasury currency outstanding	9,284		
Treasury deposits at the Federal Reserve*	−2,374		
Foreign deposits with the Federal Reserve*	−317		
Treasury cash holdings, other liabilities and other Federal Reserve deposits*	−4,305		
Source base (total)	105,321	Source base (total)	105,321
Reserve adjustment	6,782	Reserve adjustment	6,782
Monetary base (total)	112,103	Monetary base	112,103

* These factors absorb funds and therefore they are deductions from the base.
Source: Albert E. Burger, "Revision of the Monetary Base," *Review, Federal Reserve Bank of St. Louis* (April 1975).

undesired, can readily be neutralized by offsetting actions in the security accounts.

There are actually two reasons that we have an alternative measure of monetary influence (either H or B). They are measures of the direction of policy (as we have said) *and* they may well be better measures of monetary (M_1, M_2) influence on the economy especially in view of recent institutional changes affecting M_1 and M_2. Generally, both H and B tend to predict the money stock (M_1, M_2) pretty well, especially on annual data. Thus, in Table 5.12 we have put down both H and B (the latter for the monetary base); then, clearly, the issue is a marginal one, since the two move so closely together (the reserve adjustment is fairly small and not very volatile); indeed, both measures seem to follow the two measures of the money stock (M_1, M_2) pretty closely, as well, although the coincident trends in the series make it hard to see what is going on. An alternative, in the last column in the table, is to look at the value of the multiplier (if $M_1 = hB$, then h is the "monetary base multiplier"); these values indicate that the multiplier has fallen steadily in recent years, with a big drop in 1974 and 1975, two years in which there was rapid inflation (*and recession*). Most importantly, though, if we could predict the base in 1974 (or make it what we wish by means of open-market operations), and, if we had used the monetary multiplier in 1973 to *predict* M_1 in 1974, we would have *over-predicted* by more than \$11 billion (i.e., predicted a \$24 billion increase when the *actual* change was only \$13 billion).[25] If the authorities had used the monetary base in this fashion, they may well have decided that the money supply was going to grow too rapidly *and hence they might have tried to cut back.* If they had cut back by \$11 billion we would have gotten only a \$2 billion increase in M_1. This would have been too great a slowdown, in all probability.[26]

The figures in Table 5.12 are on an annual basis, though, while monetary policy is really conducted on a month-by-month basis. To get some idea of how variable the data can be and to show explicitly how the recent innovations in policy may have altered the environment *while* a tight money policy was in progress, consider the data for 1978 in Table 5.14.

Table 5.14: The monetary base during the tight money policy of 1978

	Monetary base		M_1		M_2		*Consumer price index*	
	\$ billions	*Percent change*	*\$ billions*	*Percent change*	*\$ billions*	*Percent change*	*\$ billions*	*Percent change*
January	131.3	—	341.7	—	815.9	—	187.2	—
February	132.6	11.9	341.8	.4	819.1	4.7	188.4	7.7
March	132.9	2.7	342.9	3.9	822.6	5.1	189.8	8.9
April	133.6	6.3	348.5	19.6	830.3	11.2*	191.5	10.7
May	134.8	10.8	350.6	7.2	835.2	7.1	193.3	11.3
June	136.1	11.6	352.8	7.5	840.6	7.8	195.3	12.4
July	137.1	8.8	354.2	4.8	846.2	8.0	196.7	8.6
August	138.0	7.9	356.7	8.5	853.5	10.4	197.8	6.7
September	139.3	11.3	360.9	14.1	862.4	12.5	199.3	9.1
October	140.8	12.9	362.0	3.6	867.4	7.0	200.9	9.6
November	141.4	5.1	360.6	−4.6†	870.5	4.3	202.0	6.6
December	142.1	5.9	360.8	.6	871.6	1.5	202.9	5.3

Note: All percentage changes expressed as annual rates.
* The time deposit component of this figure increased at 5.2 percent.
† The demand deposit component of this figure fell at 9.9 percent.

Here we see that the narrow money stock has fluctuated quite a bit, increasing at a 19.6 percent rate in April and decreasing at a 4.6 percent rate in November (remember automatic transfers?), while M_2, the monetary base, *and consumer prices* show no such fluctuations. Indeed, *if* the monetary

[25] That is, we would have predicted an M_1 of \$294.9 billion (I used the 1974 *base* of \$104.2 billion on the grounds that the authorities *can* make the base anything they want). By now, of course, the downtrend in h is well established so such a sizable mistake is not likely. Even so, a \$6 billion error would have been made if the change in h from 1972 to 1973 (from 2.88 to 2.83) were projected.

[26] Note that this is all in terms of M_1; perhaps, after all, M_2, M_3, M_4, or M_5 is the appropriate measure of "moneyness," as discussed in Chapter 1.

measure is to indicate government policy *and* to predict the inflation rate (Column 8), then the monetary base (with about a six-month lag) looks to be by far the best bet, at least for 1978. As a consequence of these realities and the confusion emanating from the frequent institutional changes in the financial markets the monetary base has come into greater use in recent years and is, in fact, published weekly in *The Wall Street Journal.*

5.7 STUDY QUESTIONS

Essay questions

1. The theory of money stock determination which we have discussed (in terms of C/D, R/D, and H) works best if there are no direct interactions between the three determinants. How might such interactions arise? (Be specific.) Would it help if the interaction were a stable (that is, regular and predictable) one? Why or why not?

2. Why do we refer to the stock of currency and member bank reserves as high-powered money? Does currency have the same high power as reserves? How would open market operations in currency differ from those in Treasury securities? Be specific and consider both expansionary and contractionary monetary policy.

3. Consider a system in which reserve requirements were 100 percent. How would a bank acquire its earnings in such a system? Would banks and banking disappear then? How would we go about transforming our system to a 100 percent reserve system? Would the quantity of credit (loans, especially) be smaller under such a system? See Milton Friedman, *A Program for Monetary Stability* (New York: Fordham University Press, 1960).

4. What difficulties might the Federal Reserve have in providing currency for a currency panic? How, exactly, would they go about doing this in order to avoid making things worse? Does one still run up against the problem that commercial banks need to dispose of earning assets in order to liquidate (to meet the currency drain)?

True-false discussion questions

These statements are meant to be ambiguous, and to provoke discussion, thereby.

1. It is highly unlikely that a banking panic would occur if banks were required to hold one dollar of reserves for every dollar of deposits.

2. An increase in the required reserve ratio will not have any effect on the quantity of money if commercial banks are holding sufficient excess reserves.

3. Banks do not create money but only lend out the deposits that are entrusted to them.

4. The 1830s and 1930s had in common the experience that cumulative banking failures were the result of the rigidity of the system.

5. By the standard multiplier analysis we can show that commercial banks will exert more influence on the money stock by varying their excess reserves than will the public by varying its currency holdings, under present conditions.

6. If commercial banks were permitted to vary the interest rate on time deposits, the money stock would probably be harder to predict than it is at present.

7. More bank failure may indicate the presence of more competition in the banking industry, but since it is cut-throat competition, clearly, it is undesirable (and increases risk in the banking system).

8. One reason that the monetary base does not predict M_1 accurately is that the base responds to changes in the currency-deposit ratio (and M_1 = currency *plus* deposits).

9. Excess reserves move in the same direction as free reserves primarily because commercial banks try to keep their borrowing at the Federal Reserve at a minimum.

5.8 FURTHER READING

Cagan, Philip. "Interest Rates and Bank Reserves—A Reinterpretation of the Statistical Association," in Guttentag, J., and Philip Cagan, eds., *Essays on Interest Rates.* New York: National Bureau of Economic Research, 1969.

Friedman, Milton, and Anna J. Schwartz. *A Monetary History of the United States.* Princeton, N.J.: Princeton University Press, 1963.

Galbraith, John Kenneth. *Money: Whence it came, where it went.* Boston: Houghton Mifflin, 1975.

Temin, Peter. *Did Monetary Forces Cause the Great Depression?* New York: W. W. Norton, 1976.

Temin, Peter. *The Jacksonian Economy.* New York: W. W. Norton, 1969.

Tobin, James. "Commercial Banks as Creators of 'Money'," in Carson, Deane, ed., *Banking and Monetary Studies.* Homewood, Ill.: Richard D. Irwin, Inc., 1963.

Part II

Monetary policy

6 The demand for money

6.1 INTRODUCTION

We have spent the first five chapters of this book developing a picture of the supply of money as it operates through banking markets; it is time to drop the other shoe and consider the demand for money. While we do this, we will also gradually broaden the scope of our study to consider some of the macroeconomic and policy questions of the influence of money on the economy. Our main task in this chapter, of course, is a discussion of the subject of the demand for money in a generally *macroeconomic* context, but in an introductory section on "microfoundations" we will also discuss the "choice" problems facing individuals and businesses. The reason we prefer macroeconomics here is simply that we wish to appraise the role of a type of *macroeconomic* policy—monetary policy—on the American economic system. A detailed microeconomic analysis, while offering some insights into how money fits into the system, is of less use in dealing with the policy question; even so, we will frequently refer to "microfoundations" in our discussion.

Before beginning, it is necessary to point out again that we have noticed a potential distinction between interest-bearing and non-interest-bearing money both in a definitional and in a supply sense. In Chapter 1 we pointed out that non-interest-bearing money is held because it is expected to be used in future exchanges and is an especially effective store of value; on the other hand, in Chapters 2 and 3, we discovered that it is easily conceivable that removal of the interest ceiling (of zero) on demand deposits might bring about a positive rate of interest on this liability of commercial banks; indeed, just such a phenomenon is occurring. In Chapter 1 we also pointed out that the interest payment on some forms of "especially liquid" assets may well be accepted by the user in lieu of the services of currency and demand deposits, since he must *hold* the liquid asset in his savings account to gain the interest payment. Along the same lines, in Chapter 2 we found that much, but not all, of a commercial bank's activity is that of "intermediation" between its deposits (its liabilities) and its loan and investment portfolio (its assets). That is, we noticed that the better part of a bank's activity could be characterized by the difference between two interest rates (see Table 2.5). Finally, in a completely different context, we noted in Chapter 1 that when one turns to macroeconomic policy questions, then "money" may be defined in a very practical way, for example as a financial entity closely related to the price level, in which case the interest-rate factors just mentioned may well be of less practical concern in general.

To avoid this theoretical thicket, it seems best, for the better part of this chapter, to stay with the demand for *narrow money* (currency plus demand deposits) rather than to discuss, in detail, the more conglomerate concepts of M_2 to M_5, or to consider what happens when part of M_1 pays interest. We will, though, want to look at *currency* vis-à-vis *demand* deposits, and, when we discuss the empirical results briefly, we will return to some of the questions related to the *broader* measures of money. As well, in our policy discussion and in Part III of the book, when financial intermediaries enter the picture, we will return to the questions raised by the presence of interest-bearing substitutes for narrow money.

6.2 SOME MICROECONOMIC ASPECTS OF MONEY HOLDING

Fundamental to the demand for any economic good, and we certainly are asserting that money is such a good, is that it provide economic services. Some goods are pure services, such as shoeshines, and are essentially used up at the time of their creation; but many goods can be reused, and most consumer goods have some durability. Those goods that do possess durability offer the chance of a rearrangement of one's using-up pattern; that is, one can store durable goods against future needs. In this sense, money is a durable good and, like all durable goods, provides continuing services to its users—services that are, no doubt, also available from other durable goods, although in the end the acquiring of a unit of money is a tacit confession that it was expected to be the best good in providing those services, at that time. Money, because of its low physical perishability, is especially useful in permitting the rearrangement of one's expenditure pattern; and if one has money, his options into other goods are generally open.

Most products provide both direct and indirect services, but this is a distinction that is not going to be entirely clear in practice. For some products the direct services dominate, as for example, an apple, which provides an obvious gustatory satisfaction. There is a range of products that provide substantial amounts of both direct and indirect services, such as a refrigerator, which chills our white wine (a direct service) and enables us to stockpile consumer goods for later consumption (an indirect service, since we save shopping time rather than directly satisfying one of the senses). Money, as a provider of services, is no less a consumer product because it provides mostly indirect services, and, like the storage capacity of the refrigerator, the service provided is partly that of saving time by allowing the consumer to arrange expenditures more efficiently over time. Money *also* permits exchange to occur at well-known prices, in a generally acceptable and portable medium, and its widespread use certainly cuts down considerably on the uncertainty in the economic system, provided, of course, that the quantity of money itself is not subject to unpredictable changes.

If we restrict our analysis to the demand for money by an individual consumer, then a standard microeconomic analysis is possible. Here a consumer is assumed to be a price-taker and is limited to (that is, constrained by) his or her current income, wealth (which is based on future income), and by what might be called the *consumer technology* (which we will not discuss to any great extent). Generally speaking, then, any change in wealth or income will tend to produce a change in the same direction in an individual's money holding;[1] this effect need not be exactly proportional, but it is most likely to be positive. With regard to prices, we can argue that since money is "just like" any other commodity to an individual consumer, any effect on money holding of a change in other commodity prices will be either positive or negative, depending on whether the other commodity is a substitute (i.e., alike in its economic characteristics) or a complement (like left shoes and right shoes to the consumer). Finally, if the price of money itself changes, one would expect a change in the individual's demand for money as well as in the individual's demand for other commodities. This price, or value of money as we pointed out in Section 1.6, is $1/\bar{P}$, the inverse of the price level.

Actually, introduction of the "price of money" in this way raises some

[1] Of course an individual *may* actually hold less money as his or her income rises, but this is unlikely to be a general result and so we can ignore it, at least in the aggregate.

interesting problems—problems that are at the heart of a monetary economy—concerning the distinction between *real* and *nominal* values. In our discussion of money in Chapter 1 we described two components of the American narrow money stock—currency and demand deposits—and gave their sum a name (M_1). This M_1 is really a *nominal* quantity of money in the sense that it is valued at *face* value (a dollar is a dollar is a dollar . . .) no matter what happens to its purchasing power. To find the *real* value of money we need to calculate the "purchasing power" of money: its *value in exchange* for other commodities. The calculation is very simple, since the price level, our standard of value, gives precisely that information. Thus, if the average of all money prices in the economy (a simple economy and a simple average) is \$1.50 (P = \$1.50), and if we have \$200 (M = \$200), then the \$200 will purchase 133.3 standardized units of commodities. If, then, the price level rises for some reason to, say \$2.00 on average, our \$200 will buy only 100 units of the "standard" commodity. In this event our purchasing power has clearly declined. Finally, let us give this an algebraic expression. Let M stand for the \$200; M is the *nominal* quantity of money. Then M/P, which is how we got 133.3 and 100 units, respectively, is the *real* quantity of money; we call it "real money balances" or "real balances."[2]

There are three important reasons that we went into the detail of the last few paragraphs. One, the most obvious, is that we wished to justify the use of $1/\bar{P}$ as the price of money in the sense of its exchange value; when you have defined a commodity and identified its price, you can conduct an economic analysis of it. A second important reason for our interest concerns the "consumer choice" problem we have been discussing in this section. Clearly, we have two concepts, nominal money (M) and real money (M/P), and the demand for these items can be expected to differ. In particular, it is most logical to argue that the individual's demand for *nominal* money balances will depend on *nominal* income and *nominal* wealth, and the demand for *real* money balances will depend on *real* income and *real* wealth. So we have to be careful, in our discussion, as to which concept we have in mind. The third reason for going into this long discussion of real and nominal values concerns a concept known as the "real balance effect." You probably noticed, in the example just given, that as the price level rose, the value of the individual's money balances fell. This is a general proposition: financial entities that are written (denominated) in nominal form—bonds and money, particularly—without

[2] Note that whether we use $\bar{P}$ (the average of money prices) or P_I (the price index), M/P will refer to the "real quantity of money." Note, as well, that we get the *real* quantity of other goods—like consumer goods (C)—by dividing the actual expenditures on consumer goods by the price level (the price index). The expression C/P, then, is "deflated" or "real" consumption expenditures. We will go over these matters again in Chapter 7, when we employ these concepts in a macroeconomic model.

purchasing power clauses, will deteriorate in value with inflation (rises in the price level). Thus, the part of an individual's personal *wealth* in the form of bonds and money actually falls in value when there is inflation, and it falls at the rate of inflation. Since consumers probably consume more when their wealth increases, they may well consume less when the value of their real balances falls, that is, if they notice the decline. This is known as the *real balance effect* (it is an *effect* on consumption), and it is thought by some economists to be an important phenomenon, at least in the event that price level changes are large and unpredictable.

Consider the following situation. During the first part of the great inflation of 1973–75, the value (purchasing power) of individual savings accounts was falling at the rate of inflation, which reached a rate of around 16 percent a year. Indeed, the interest payments were often less than the rate of inflation so that savings accounts, were, in effect, paying a *negative* rate of interest. If consumers were caught by surprise by the force of the inflation, then they may have not responded immediately. But when it dawned on them that the real value of their liquid savings had fallen drastically, they may have responded (in this case) by cutting their consumption expenditures in order to replenish the value in their savings accounts, even though a more sensible hedge against further inflation would have been consumer durables or housing (etc.). Indeed, one notices in Table 1.1 (in the difference between M_1 and M_2, which is time and savings deposits) that the figures for savings steadily increased, right through the recession, with a large jump from 1975 to 1976 in percentage terms. The recession itself *may* well have been induced (or at least helped along) by a drop in consumer expenditures that was *itself* the result of previous changes in the rate of inflation. In this way the "real balance effect" can provide a link between largely "monetary" events, such as changes in the price level, and "real" events, such as recessions. We must, though, caution the reader that this is more an illustration than a completely documented explanation of what actually happened in that period. There were plenty of *real* (i.e., nonnominal) causes—remember the energy crisis?—of the events in that period to keep the debate going for years over what caused that recession to be so deep (both consumption and investment declined, for one thing).

6.3 THE INTEREST RATE AND THE DEMAND FOR MONEY

Everyone is familiar with interest rates, of course, but when one sets down his thoughts, particularly with regard to the relation between interest rates and money holding, a certain amount of care is necessary. The idea of interest as a payment on a capital sum saved is the place to begin. Thus, if you have $200 in your savings account and you leave it there for a year, then, if the bank pays a simple interest rate of 5 percent, you will have $210 after the year is up. Algebraically we have said that the initial sum (call it S_1) is equal to the following expression (S_2) after a year:

$$S_2 = S_1 + .05S_1 = (1 + .05)S_1. \tag{6.1}$$

You should verify it. Now if you leave the sum of money you have accumulated in the account for a second year, you will have

$$S_3 = (1 + .05)S_2 = (1 + .05)(1 + .05)S_1 = (1 + .05)^2S_1, \tag{6.2}$$

which, if you work it out, is $220.50. Notice the extra $.50, which is the result of "compounding" the interest rate. This expression generalizes, so that we can write

$$S_n = (1 + i)^{n-1}S_1 \tag{6.3}$$

for a sum of money left to pay interest for n (any number of) years.

Suppose, as a second example, you are to receive a payment of $210 in a year's time. Suppose, as well, that you know for *certain* that you will receive that payment and that you wish to have the funds *now;* how much will you get if you can *sell* the right to receive the sum to someone else who is willing to wait the full year? If that person considered putting his funds in a savings account as his alternative, and the savings account earns 5 percent, he would tend to charge you 5 percent as well (if he thinks the risks are the same). Thus you will *not* get $210 but .05 × $210 less than that from him. Expressed algebraically, where S_2 represents your sum, the sum you can get is

$$S_1 = \frac{S_2}{1 + .05} = \frac{S_2}{(1 + i)}. \tag{6.4}$$

Notice the similarity between Equations (6.4) and (6.1); indeed, if you multiply Equation (6.4) through by $(1 + i)$ you get Equation (6.1). The difference, then, is a matter of interpretation: Equation (6.1) shows how a sum of money lent at interest grows while Equation (6.4) shows what a future sum of money is worth to a lender when he can lend his money elsewhere, at the same rate of interest. In Equation (6.4), S_1 is referred to as the "present value" of the sum of money S_2. We may generalize for a series of different sums of money received over any number (n) of future years:

$$\text{Present value} = \frac{S_2}{1 + i} + \frac{S_3}{(1 + i)^2} + \cdots + \frac{S_n}{(1 + i)^{n-1}}. \tag{6.5}$$

Thus the expression $S_2/(1 + i)$ represents, formally, a "discounted" future sum and the expression

$$\frac{S_3}{(1 + i)(1 + i)} = \frac{S_3}{(1 + i)^2}$$

represents a second "discounting" because the sum is expected to be received in *two* years' time (and the lender loses the *compound* interest on the alternative).

We will have no particular use for the more general expression of Equation (6.5) just yet, but we need to clarify the relation between the interest rate and money holding, and some grasp of the essentials just outlined is necessary. If our "money" includes the time deposit (is M_2, for example), then we see immediately that there is a complication, because the time deposit pays an interest rate, but that interest rate is not the same, for example, as the interest rate on a savings and loan deposit or as the yield on a government bond.[3] Thus when the time-deposit rate goes up, we might normally want to hold more of the time deposit; we may, that is to say, switch our funds from other assets (if their interest rates do not go up at the same time) to broad money (M_2). On the other hand, if the time-deposit rate does not change and the savings and loan rate goes up, we may well switch our liquid wealth from M_2 to the savings and loan account, since the *alternative* place for our funds is more attractive. We call this second role of the interest rate an *alternative* (or opportunity) *cost* role. Note that the effect on the demand for time deposits is opposite in its sign (a negative effect) in the alternative cost case from the "own rate" effect (which was positive). Note, also, that the savings and loan deposit was assumed to be a *substitute* for the time deposit. If it had been a *complement,* then it would have had a *positive* effect.[4] Even more importantly note that all interest rates tend to move together, although not to the same extent (see Table 2.5 and Chapter 15), so that no easy generalization will fit all circumstances when our measure of "money" also pays interest, as do M_2 to M_5 in the Federal Reserve's accounts and as does some of M_1, in effect, as a result of the recent innovations of automatic withdrawals and NOW accounts.

---

[3] The *yield* is defined as follows. We can formally relate the market price of the bond (P_b) to the stream of fixed future "interest" payments ($C_1, \ldots, C_n$) by the following relation:

$$P_b = \frac{C_1}{1+i} + \frac{C_2}{(1+i)^2} + \cdots + \frac{C_n}{(1+i)^n} + \frac{\text{Face value}}{(1+i)^n}.$$

This is a more complicated formula; it is the formula from which a yield, such as those appearing in standardized bond tables, is calculated. Here the C's (defined as coupons) are the stream of bond-interest payments (one for each year); the face value is the issue price of the bond, which is paid back in n years and i is the yield, calculated as a residual after all the other information has been obtained from, for example, the daily newspaper.

Notice that the yield in this equation moves in the opposite direction from the price of the bond: as bond prices rise, their yields fall; and conversely.

[4] Formally, we say that two goods (X_1,X_2) are substitutes if (for example) a price rise in X_1 induces a switch to X_2 and are complements if the converse holds. Here the interest rate paid is being used as the price although it really represents the flow of services (that is, the yield) on the asset. Of course we abstract from any elements of speculation or uncertainty.

We see, then, one practical reason for considering money to be only M_1: the items included do not actually pay interest. In this event only the *alternative cost* explanation is required, assuming that we are correct in our measure of money, and it might generally be expected to be a negative effect: a rise in the opportunity cost of holding money—that is, a rise in the interest rate paid by some alternative available asset—would increase the "cost" (in this sense) of holding money.[5] We would, in this event, reduce our money holding, switching some of our funds over to other, more profitable, assets. Figure 6.1 provides the illustration, where we consider the demand for *real* money balances.

Figure 6.1: The relationship between the quantity of money demanded and the interest rate—an opportunity cost rationale

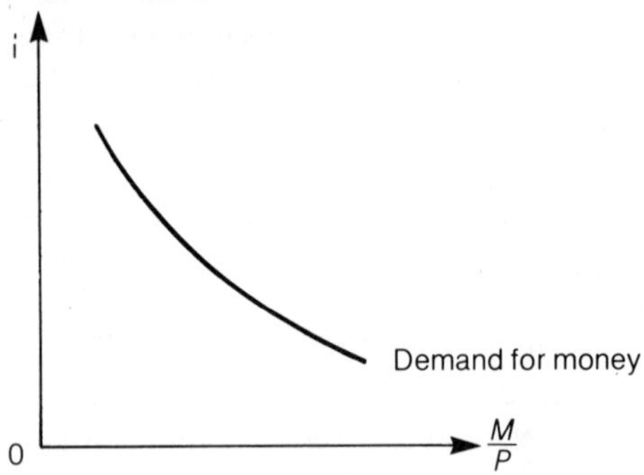

6.4 THE NEOCLASSICAL DEMAND FOR MONEY

What we have said so far about the demand for money is quite straightforward. We have discussed three variables in connection with money holding: the level of income or wealth, the price level, and the interest rate. The results for income and the interest rate were that

a. An increase in income (Y) or wealth (W) could be expected to increase the quantity of money demanded (M_d); similarly, an increase in *real* income (Y/P) or *real* wealth (W/P) will increase the *real* demand for money $(M/P)_d$.

b. An increase in the interest rate (i) can be expected to decrease the quantity of money demanded.

---

[5] We are saying, in effect, that money is a substitute, but not too close a substitute, for the interest assets represented by i. Note that M_1 provides direct services rather than a direct interest yield. As discussed in Chapter 1, these services can certainly be described in general—mediating in exchanges, saving time in exchange, etc.—but are hard to measure.

Further, both results would occur, approximately, whether we were talking about the demand for nominal balances (M_d) or the demand for real balances, $(M/P)_d$. To put the matter formally, Equation (6.6) represents a general "demand for money" function, of an unspecified form,[6] which would be generally accepted by most economists as representative of the influences just discussed:

$$\left(\frac{M}{P}\right)_d = f\left(\frac{Y}{P}, i\right). \tag{6.6}$$

Note again that Y/P is real income.

We did not actually deal with the price level explicitly in our former discussion; in the sense of saying that a 10 percent rise in the price level produces an x percent *change* in the quantity of money demanded, but we did point out that the ratio $1/P$, the inverse of the price level, does represent the price (or exchange value) of money. Our "price theory" tells us that for most commodities an increase in the price brings a decrease in the quantity demanded; this "law of demand" implies that the price-quantity relation known as the "demand curve" has a negative slope. Thus if money, too, were a normal good the relation between $1/P$ and M_d would be expected to be like that drawn in Figure 6.2. Note, especially, that we are talking about M_d, the demand for nominal money balances, here.

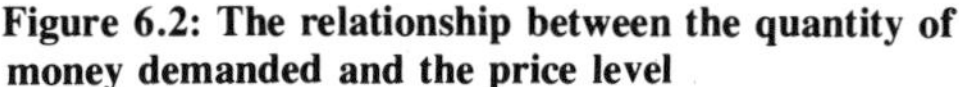

Figure 6.2: The relationship between the quantity of money demanded and the price level

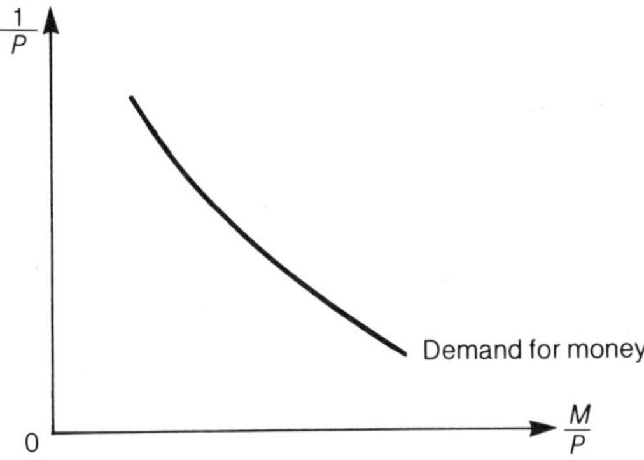

[6] Equation (6.6) says merely that there is a dependence. A *specific* functional form might be the *linear* case,

$$\left(\frac{M}{P}\right)_d = a + b\frac{Y}{P} + ci,$$

in which a is a constant (intercept) and b and c are the slopes.

Actually, in the previous paragraph, we have argued by analogy with standard demand theory, and that is not the only way we can relate the quantity of money demanded and the price level. In particular, let us consider the *quantity theory of money*—a proposition associated with Classical (e.g., John Stuart Mill) and Neoclassical (e.g., Irving Fisher) economists—which links changes in the price level to changes in the quantity of money in a causal sense. To begin with, let us write down the sum of expenditures on all goods and services in the economy, which we used to calculate the price level in Chapter 1, as in Equation (6.7):

$$S = P_1Q_1 + P_2Q_2 + \cdots + P_nQ_n = \sum_{i=1}^{n} P_iQ_i. \tag{6.7}$$

Here instead of the weights we used in Equation (1.1), we use the actual quantities of goods exchanged.[7] This expression gives the total expenditures on all goods and services purchased in the economy over a period of time; it is all quantities purchased times their prices in this (arbitrary) period. We can conceive of an average price for the commodities—call it P—that would be calculated by the rules of Equation (1.1); this can then be factored out from the expression in Equation (6.7). This is the *price level,* and Equation (6.8) shows it factored out from the sum on the right:

$$S = P \sum_{i=1}^{n} Q_i. \tag{6.8}$$

[7] We are going to find it very convenient to use the more compact summation notation, so we should develop some rules here. First of all, let us shorten Equation (6.7) to

$$S = \sum_{i=1}^{n} P_iQ_i.$$

We can, if we wish to generalize, merely change the limit on the index (i) to fit the size of the problem; in this case n is "everything" we wish to include in our summations (such as the expenditures that make up GNP). Σ is an algebraic symbol signifying the sum obtained by addition of any number of similar terms; let us establish a few things about these sums that we will use later in this and other chapters; these can be verified by putting in numbers:

$$\sum_{i=1}^{n} a_i = a_1 + a_2 + a_3 + \cdots + a_n \text{ (a a variable);} \tag{i}$$

$$\sum_{i=1}^{n} b = nb \text{ (b a constant);} \tag{ii}$$

$$\sum_{i=1}^{n} ab_i = a \sum_{i=1}^{n} b_i \text{ (a a constant, b a variable);} \tag{iii}$$

$$\sum_{i=1}^{n} (a_i + b_i) = \sum_{i=1}^{n} a_i + \sum_{i=1}^{n} b_i; \tag{iv}$$

$$\sum_{i=1}^{n} (a_i + b_i)^2 = \sum_{i=1}^{n} a_i^2 + \sum_{i=1}^{n} b_i^2 + 2 \sum_{i=1}^{n} a_ib_i. \tag{v}$$

The expression $\sum_{i=1}^{n} Q_i$ represents the sum of all commodities purchased, in *real* terms. Specifically, this sum aggregates pounds of potatoes, numbers of automobiles, bottles of wine, etc. We may also calculate an average quantity, using the same approach we adopted in Equation (1.1); let us call the resulting expression $\bar{Q}$. Then, when we replace *each* of the items in Equation (6.8) with $\bar{Q}$ we get

$$S = P \sum_{i=1}^{n} \overline{Q} = Pn\overline{Q} = PQ. \tag{6.9}$$

$\bar{Q}$, then, is a constant, and when this is summed n times, we get n of the $\bar{Q}$'s; this is $n\bar{Q}$ (see Footnote 5). We will refer to $n\bar{Q}$ as Q, for simplicity, so our final equation, *still representing the total expenditure on goods and services over a period of time,* is given by equating the first and last expressions of Equation (6.9).

Suppose, for purposes of illustration, that the period of time over which the expenditures are measured is a year. In a monetary economy we could argue that one *must* use money for all the exchanges that lie behind Equation (6.9). Furthermore, money normally circulates, so that it can be used more than once during the year. On average, then, if M represents the actual quantity (the average) of money being used in the United States *over the same period of time* represented by the total expenditures in Equation (6.9), and V represents the number of times it was spent in the year (on average), then

$$MV = PQ \tag{6.10}$$

is a *necessary* relationship for a fully monetary economy. Consider a simple illustration of this truism (or identity)—called the *equation of exchange*—on recent U.S. data. For the fourth quarter of 1977, Gross National Product was \$1,963.7 billion; this was total expenditure on goods and services, which, in our notation, is PQ. The total stock of M_1 in the United States—the average for the same quarter—was \$334.1 billion. Thus the money stock (M_1) was spent on average 5.88 times; that is, V, the velocity of money, was 5.88.

The expression just obtained is, as we stated, a truism, and it is an accurate representation of the process of exchange so long as all exchanges of goods and services are accompanied by the transfer of money. (That is, it would not be valid if a large percentage of transactions were barter, in which case goods are directly exchanged for goods, as is not the case in the United States).[8] It is, on the other hand, the basis of several

[8] During war periods or in periods of rapid and rapidly changing rates of inflation, the incidence of barter may increase. Such may have been the case for the confederate states during the later stages of the American Civil War; see E. Lerner, "Inflation in the Confeder-

interesting "monetary-oriented" theories of economic behavior—the overlapping Classical, Neoclassical, and Monetarist theories—and it even can be used to illustrate how Keynesian theories differ; thus it is a key concept in the study of money. Consider the crudest version of the *Quantity Theory of Money*. When, *in fact,* in any economy, V and Q are constant, or approximately so, a doubling of M, however that is achieved, must lead to a doubling of prices, on average (and conversely). Thus *if* velocity is constant, and *if* we are at full employment so that Q is constant, then *if* the quantity of money rises—because of a gold discovery or a monetary policy or whatever seems likely—prices will inevitably rise (and if V and Q actually stay perfectly constant) this rise will be essentially instantaneous.

Actually, no economy has ever been at "full" employment (however defined) for very long, and, further, "full employment" itself is probably a variable; indeed, as we shall see, velocity cannot be taken as a constant in any event, so the crude quantity theory does not take us very far, although, no doubt, a positive *association* between the quantity of money and prices seems a reasonable enough proposition to retain. In the hands of Milton Friedman and the Chicago school, though, the quantity theory has become (or maybe always was) a theory of the demand for money.[9] Friedman says that the well-known classical proposition, that establishes a firm link between money and prices, will hold *if* the demand for real money balances depends only on the two variables Y/P and i and *if* this dependence is a regular and complete one.[10] There are several ways to illustrate this proposition.

For one, return to our demand for real money balances, Equation (6.6):

$$\left(\frac{M}{P}\right)_d = f\left(\frac{Y}{P},i\right).$$

If we can multiply through by P, the price level, we get $\left(\text{if } P \text{ factors out of } \left(\frac{M}{P}\right)_d\right)$

$$M_d = Pf\left(\frac{Y}{P},i\right), \tag{6.11}$$

the "nominal demand" for money. This expression says that whenever prices double, given $f(Y/P,i)$, then the quantity of money demanded (M_d) will double. The key, of course, is the assumed constancy of the function

---

acy, 1861–5" in M. Friedman, ed., *Studies in the Quantity Theory of Money* (Chicago: University of Chicago Press, 1956). Note that to the extent purchases are made on credit (e.g., on a bank credit card), M should be suitably defined to include these credit balances.

[9] Milton Friedman (ed.), "The Quantity Theory of Money: A Restatement" *Studies in the Quantity Theory of Money* (Chicago: University of Chicago Press, 1956).

[10] Friedman actually advances a somewhat more complicated theory in some of his works, but this seems to be the central message. See, for example, "A Monetary Theory of Nominal Income," *Journal of Political Economy* (April 1970). We also use the term "stable" (i.e., not shifting over time) as a synonym for "regular"; we mean, when we call it "complete," that there are no other important variables omitted.

$f(Y/P,i)$; in particular, the "regular and complete" assumption would guarantee that people would want to hold twice the quantity of money if the price level doubled. This result would not follow, of course, if the rise of prices in some way changes *real* income (Y/P) or interest rates, especially if this effect is irregular. We have already discussed the possibility of an alteration of private wealth as the price level changes (the real balance effect) and this is one such factor; indeed, as we proceed in this chapter and the next two we will also link interest rates and prices.

A second and more revealing way of looking at the same problem is to look further at Equation (6.10), the equation of exchange. First of all, notice that we can use Y/P, total expenditures on goods and services, in *real* terms, for Q (which had approximately the same meaning) in that equation; as well, we can put velocity on the other side of the equation:

$$M = \frac{1}{V} P \left(\frac{Y}{P}\right). \tag{6.12}$$

To avoid confusion, since $P(Y/P) = Y$, let us write $y = Y/P$ for real income so that we have

$$M = \frac{1}{V} Py. \tag{6.13}$$

Now M is the *actual* quantity of money, and Equation (6.13) should still be interpreted as a truism, with V defined as the *income* velocity of money. We could, though, argue that the actual quantity of money is fixed (for example, by the Federal Reserve), in which case something like Figure 6.3 would hold. Point a, then, represents equilibrium in the monetary sector; it is the point at which $M_d = \bar{M}$ and so the money market is cleared. Thus *at equilibrium,* we may substitute M_d for M in Equation (6.13); furthermore, since M is arbitrarily fixed, for any other $\bar{M}$ (rep-

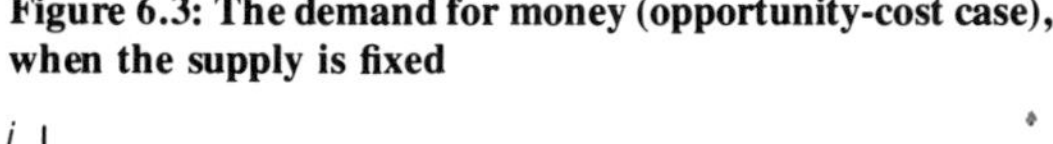
Figure 6.3: The demand for money (opportunity-cost case), when the supply is fixed

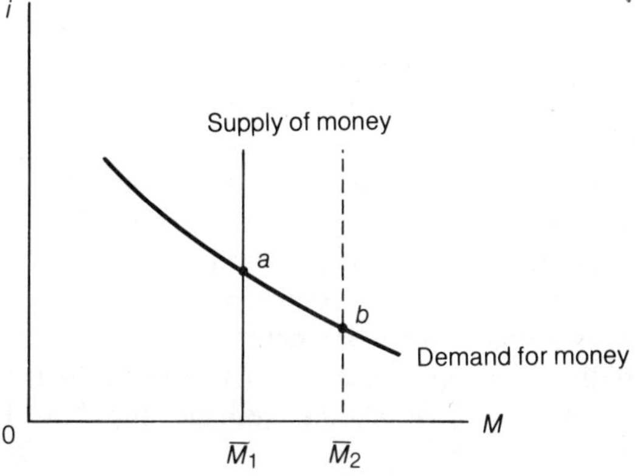

resented by a shift of the vertical $\bar{M}$ line) we can look at Equation (6.13) at a new point of equilibrium. Note, again, that $\bar{M}$ is the actual quantity of money; note, also, that when we write $M_d = (1/V)Py$ or $M_d = (1/V)Y$ we also have a realistic demand *function* for money if V is itself a function of something. Clearly, that something is the rate of interest, since y—real income—is already in the problem; we are, of course, referring to our earlier discussion of the determinants of the demand for money.

This formulation of the Neoclassical demand for money is a little complicated, perhaps, but it does bring out an important aspect of that theory; this concerns the behavior of velocity. In particular, Equation (6.13) would be a useful form of the demand for money and it would link *directly* into the doubled money–doubled prices proposition of the Neoclassical economists *if* V were constant and y were *full-employment* real income. In this case it is a *full* equilibrium theory because it is worked through the money market, as represented by Figure (6.3). Thus, for a doubling of $\bar{M}$, from $\bar{M}_1$ to $\bar{M}_2$, we will not be able to equate M_d and $\bar{M}$ until prices have doubled; equilibrium, that is to say, requires that prices double. This holds so long as velocity is constant, of course. More generally this is now a causal sequence that says, in effect, that if "too much" money (for the demand for money as represented by y and V) is produced, then prices will tend to rise. This is the "too much money chasing too few goods" argument. Note another important implication of our equilibrium approach here: *if* the quantity of money doubles (so that equilibrium requires a doubled price level), and *if* price controls prevent a rise in the price level (as they did in 1971–73 in the United States), then the removal of price controls (as in 1973) will be associated with a rise in prices (which occurred after 1973) so long as y and V have not changed (y up and V down) in the meantime.

In truth, of course, V is not a constant, and, in fact, it depends on interest rates. Indeed we may manipulate our equation of exchange one more time, in the equilibrium context, to get

$$V = \frac{Y}{M_d},$$

in which case we realize that *if* M_d depends on the interest rate, as we argued it did, then so must V. Furthermore, there is a direct reason for arguing that there is a connection between velocity and the interest rate. The reason is that when the interest rate rises, money holders may well try to *economize* on their money balances by "turning them over" more frequently per unit of time. In this manner individuals hold each dollar for a shorter period of time and the average money balance held decreases. This, in effect, is a change in "payments habits," prompted by the fact that money holding becomes more expensive when the interest rate rises. Under these conditions we should replace the hard-line "constant-velocity'' statement of the crude Quantity Theory of Money with the following more reasonable proposition: *If velocity is a stable function of the interest rate, then an increase in the quantity of money will tend to induce a rise in the price level in the same direction, especially in an economy that is near or at full employment.*[11] The mechanism by which this is brought about is very simple: if people acquire unwanted money balances in some way, they will spend them on goods and services or on ''earning'' assets; this will tend to drive up the prices of these goods, services, and assets especially in the event that the *production* of goods, services, and assets does not respond.[12] Indeed, since money is involved in every market it is reasonable to argue that all prices are affected to some extent.

The key to an exactly proportional change between money and prices in this theory is clearly the behavior of velocity, so long as income does not also respond. We have, so far, thought of velocity as a number—the average number of times the money stock is ''turned over'' in a year—but there is more to it than that. For one thing, velocity is the only number in this equation that can represent payments habits; these might not be particularly stable at times and, in any event they will have long-run, cyclical, and seasonal movements pretty much as M_1 to M_5 had. More importantly, velocity itself (as a function of interest rates) may not be stable. Let us consider some actual data. For the United States, for the years 1915–54, Figure 6.4 shows the long-run pattern for income velocity (Y/M) and compares it to a long-term interest rate. Clearly the relation is a positive one—an increase in V is generally associated with an increase in the interest rate—and it is fairly regular, in the sense that the gap is fairly constant, especially since 1935. But not always, as the 1920 figure shows, so there is some reason to look further. Thus, we may compute a comparable relation for the 1969–1977 data, taking the annual average long-term rate and the level of real Gross National Product from the *Federal Reserve Bulletin,* and M_1 from Table 1.1; the results appear in Table 6.1.

These figures, actually, give us evidence on several matters. For one thing, the relation between M_1, which represents real narrow money balances (M_1/P), and real GNP (Y/P) seems to be a positive one: only in 1973,

[11] As we will discuss in Chapters 9–12, a change in the money stock may well affect real economic activity (and hence employment) as well as prices. Recent evidence suggests that the real effects are short-run and the price level effects are long-run. If this is true, as it probably is, we see why monetary policy may be (and has been?) used to try to control the American unemployment problem (even though in the long run it has no such effect).

[12] This statement is also not invariant with respect to the method by which the change in the money stock is achieved. Thus the government may purchase securities or simply spend money (currency, for example) on goods and services and the channels of influence are different in these two cases (as we shall see in Chapter 11). In formal Neoclassical monetary economics it is traditional to have a helicopter hover over the countryside and sprinkle it with money; this is certainly in the spirit of Figure 6.3, but it has brought some derision to the approach that is distracting to the real issues involved.

Table 6.1: A comparison of aggregate data for the United States, 1969–1977

	Real GNP (y) ($ billions)*	*M_1 ($ billions)*	*Consumer Price Index*	*Real money stock† ($ billions)*	*Velocity*	*Long-term interest rate (percent)*
1969	1,085.7	208.8	.876	238.4	4.55	6.10
1970	1,080.5	219.6	.928	236.6−	4.57	6.59+
1971	1,190.8	233.8	.967	241.1+	4.92	5.74−
1972	1,181.3	255.3	1.000	255.3+	4.63	5.63−
1973	1,245.7	270.5	1.062	254.7−	4.89	6.30+
1974	1,224.6	283.1	1.179	240.1−	5.10	6.99+
1975	1,202.1	294.8	1.286	229.2−	5.24	6.98−
1976	1,274.7	312.2	1.361	229.4+	5.56	6.78−
1977	1,337.5	335.4	1.449	231.5+	5.78	7.06+

* 1972 dollars.
† M_1 divided by the Consumer Price Index.
Source: *Federal Reserve Bulletin*.

Figure 6.4: Velocity and the interest rate, the United States, 1915–1954*

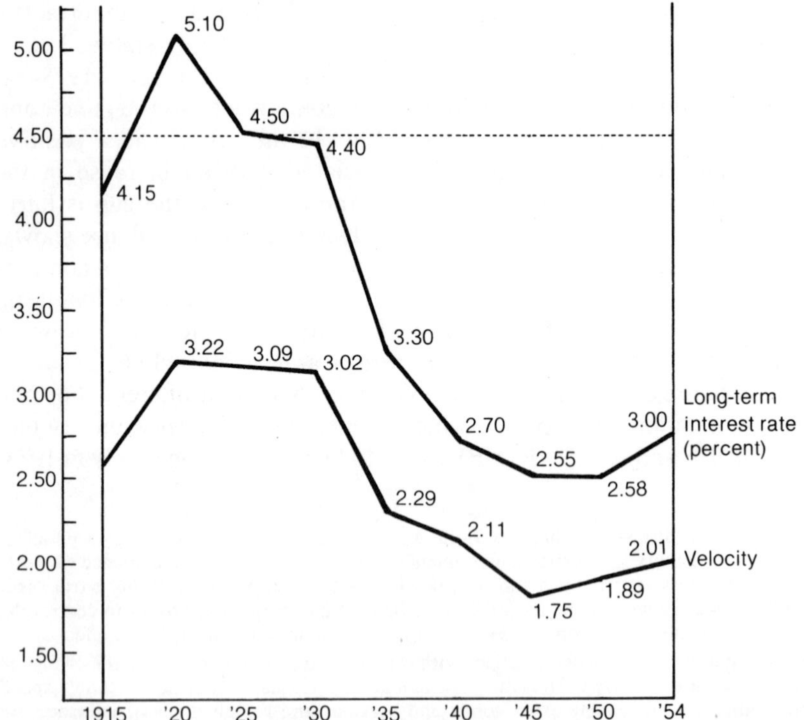

* The interest rate is the 30-year yield reported by David Meiselman, *The Term Structure of Interest Rates* (Englewood Cliffs, N.J.: Prentice-Hall, 1962). Velocity is that for currency and demand deposits (M_1) appearing in Friedman and Schwartz, *A Monetary History of the United States, 1867–1960* (Princeton, N.J.: Princeton University Press, 1963).

when a tight money policy was applied by the Federal Reserve *and* prices were rising rapidly, did they fail to move together. The year 1976, when real GNP rose sharply while real money balances rose only a very small amount, is also clearly a significant deviation from a precise relationship. The relationship between M_1 and the price index is also a very strong one: both increased steadily over the entire period; this clearly implies that M_1 and *nominal* income (Y) would also tend to move together. With regard to the interest rate, we note that in six of the eight cases (only 1975 and 1977 did not show this effect) a *rise* in the interest rate was associated with a *fall* in the stock of real nominal money balances actually held by the public. This, indeed, is the *negative* effect that our alternative cost theory postulated. But note that the peculiarity in 1976, in the real income–real M_1 relationship, is *not* explained by an offsetting peculiarity in the interest rate.[13]

Turning to velocity, finally, we consider in Figure 6.5 a graph analogous to that in Figure 6.4; here we simply graph the numbers in the last two

Figure 6.5: Velocity and the interest rate, 1969–1977

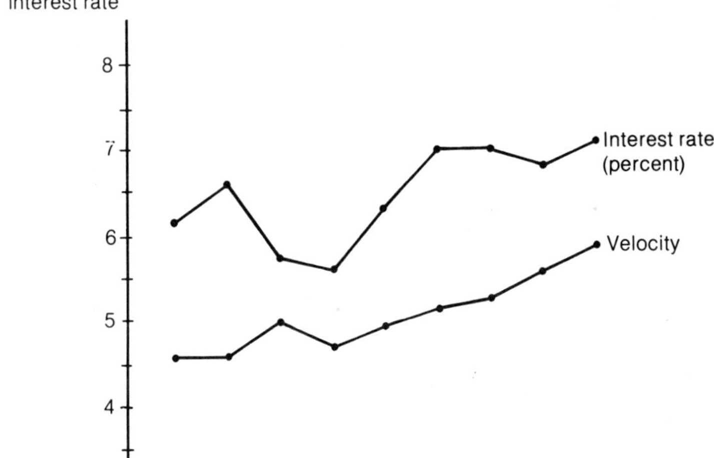

[13] Recall that this paragraph can be taken as evidence on the demand for money in the event that $M_d = M$ (i.e., that the money market is in equilibrium) *or,* if not, in the event that M, the actual stock of money, is determined solely by the demanders. The latter is discussed further in Chapters 7 to 11.

columns of Table 6.1. In place of the steady relation we found in Figure 6.4 we actually see three cases, in 1971, 1975, and 1976, when the two moved in opposite directions; indeed, the opposite moves in 1971 and 1976 are quite sharp. Now of course these are annual data while the data in Figure 6.4 were taken every five years, so some within-period variations were probably covered over in the earlier comparison, but an inescapable conclusion, nevertheless, is that the relations among the relevant data in the monetary part of the economy—that is, the broad relations between money, prices, and interest rates (and real income)—seem subject to more variation than the simple Neoclassical theory, as amended here, can handle. We will see how the Keynesian analysis deals with some of these questions before turning, in Section 6.6, to a discussion of how the variables discussed here have actually affected the demand for money in the United States.

6.5 THE KEYNESIAN DEMAND FOR MONEY

Much of what was discussed in Section 6.3 is consistent with the demand for money of either Keynesians or Monetarists, at least with regard to which variables belong in the demand for money. Where the two theoretical positions seem to differ most is in their estimates of how strongly income and interest rates affect the demand for money. But there are several other approaches associated with the "Keynesian Revolution" in monetary and macroeconomic thought that do not fit neatly here. One of these emanates from Keynes himself and has been widely employed, especially in the textbooks, as a representative Keynesian model.

In Keynes's *General Theory* there appear two separate views of the demand for money. On the one hand, he distinguishes three purposes for which money is demanded: (*a*) transactions, (*b*) precautionary, and (*c*) speculative. We discussed these in Chapter 1 as a possible definitional scheme. On the other hand Keynes actually wrote down the famous "separable" demand-for-money equation in terms of the two dominant variables that influence that function:[14]

$$M = M_T + M_S = L_T(Y) + L_S(i). \tag{6.14}$$

Here we have, *loosely*, transactions balances (M_T) and speculative balances (M_S), the one depending on income and the other on the interest rate.

We have said that the relation between the demand for money and the interest rate can be described, in one way, by means of the opportunity-cost criterion. In this case *any* non-interest-bearing money held would

[14] John Maynard Keynes, *The General Theory of Employment, Interest, and Prices* (New York: Harcourt, Brace, 1936).

tend to respond in the opposite direction to changes in the interest rate; this applies to both M_T and M_S here, so clearly an opportunity-cost rationale is *not* part of this particular separable arrangement (at least if $M_T = L_T(Y)$ and $M_S = L_S(i)$ is what is intended). Then, too, there is the problem of the precautionary balances, which seem to have vanished from the problem, at least as Equation (6.14) is specified.

Perhaps, initially, it would be just as well to clarify Keynes's three kinds of money demand somewhat, in order to see what is involved. The *transactions demand,* of course, does not refer just to payments made on the day on which we acquire our money balance. Indeed, an important aspect of the transactions demand for money concerns the *timing* of receipts and expenditures over the foreseeable future for the individual. We might know *for certain* what this pattern will be, and yet need to carry money (or have money in the checking account); indeed, we will need to hold some average balance because our expected expenditures will not coincide in time with our expected receipts. Further, there is the possibility that we will not know exactly when, in the planning period ahead of us, we will have to pay our bills. That is, many of our payment dates are not known with certainty; the expenditure is planned, and all that is missing is the date of the expenditure. This, strictly speaking, is still a part of the transactions demand for money; the funds are ready, but we do not know precisely at what date we will have to pay up. Note that one may indeed, hold these funds in a savings account, earning the interest, while awaiting the bill. These balances would presumably not show much response to interest rate variations.

A shade removed from this last sort of transactions demand is the case in which the *size* of the future expenditure also is unknown. After all, who knows precisely how much the electric bill is going to be, particularly in the heating season or, these days, in the cooling season? In these cases it is really not important whether the date of the future purchase is known (we usually know *when* the electric bill is coming) for one must still, at least around that date, hold money balances that may turn out to be excessive; Keynes called these *precautionary balances.* These balances would tend to be larger if the wealth-holding unit had considerable uncertainty in income and payment patterns; this uncertainty may be related to income, in the sense that individuals with larger incomes may have more unpredictable payments (and income, for that matter). We may well, in this event, ignore the foregone interest.

The foregoing does not explicitly deal with the idea that non-interest-bearing money is a stock of wealth and, as such, is an alternative to holding an interest-bearing asset such as a savings account. An important determinant of the transactions demand for cash is the transactions *cost* between M_1 (narrow money) and other earning assets. Prior to the electronic funds transfer system (EFTS), the transactions cost associated with moving funds between savings accounts and M_1 may have been sufficiently large in terms of time and energy (and penalties) to induce the typical money holder simply to hold M_1 and make relatively infrequent transfers between M_1 and his savings account. Thus, for everyday transactions, the money holder would simply hold M_1 and, in effect, ignore the interest foregone. At present, though, with EFTS it is certainly more difficult to argue that the transactions balance is not sensitive to the interest rate and, further, we may also find precautionary balances equally sensitive *and,* in the long run, equally small.

What has just been said amounts to the argument that if we downgrade the opportunity cost role for the interest rate, then it might be that we could *combine* transactions and precautionary balances into M_T in Equation (6.14); we would expect income to affect this total positively, generally. This leaves Keynes's *speculative demand* for money, M_S. Here the fundamental idea is to take money holding as the alternative to bond holding. Thinking first of bonds, we note that a fundamental fact is that bond yields fluctuate—or, if you prefer, bond prices fluctuate—so that there is some risk associated with bond holding. Actually, for most bonds there are two sorts of risk: a risk that the company will default and the risk that the individual will require his funds before the bond matures. If bond prices did not change over the time period—that is, if there were some law prohibiting bond price changes—this latter risk would not be a problem; but we do not live in that kind of world. Some bond prices are subject to wide swings; and even if they were not, the individual still could make a small swing a wide swing for himself by buying bonds with borrowed money (on margin). When one buys on margin, whether it be a stock or a bond, then in effect one is borrowing in order to increase his *leverage* for potential capital gains. If a bond costs $900, and the margin is 10 percent, then the investor need only put $90 down to obtain the bond. If, then, the bond quickly rose to $990, the investor could sell, ending up with a $90 capital gain, which doubles his money. Since bond margins can be as low as 10 percent a "wide" swing in the bond market is 10 or even 5 percent. Wide swings, which are as a rule unpredictable, necessarily imply risk, and risk brings out the speculators. In fact, there are speculators in the bond market—that is, persons who believe they know what is going to happen in the market—and sizable gains have been made dealing in corporate and government bonds; sizable losses, too.

Take a specific example. If bond prices have risen for a while, so that people in the market begin to expect bond prices to fall, it is only sensible that they will take some action. As things stand (simplifying the problem to a certain extent), individuals can escape the expected fall in bond prices in only three ways: one escape route is into money, where there is no direct interest sensitivity; the second is into common stocks, where prices might also fall; and the third is into real property, which is, among other disadvantages, quite illiquid (hard to dispose of). It is easy to see that money may be particularly suitable for this purpose; indeed, at any time individuals as a group can be expected to be holding such balances, which we may now define as *speculative balances*. Finally, what we have said implies that the amount of these balances held will depend on the current level of interest rates relative to the level *expected* to rule. This dependence is such that when interest rates rise a significant distance above the recent average of rates, speculators may well expect them to fall in the future. As we have said earlier in this chapter, by the definition of a bond yield, if the interest rate (the yield) is expected to fall, then the price is necessarily expected to rise. Logically, then, speculators will move out of money into bonds if they believe bond prices will rise.

Now what gives this Keynesian theory its peculiar flavor is not so much the foregoing—which is, after all, consistent with the opportunity cost argument in that a *negative* relation between the interest rate and the demand for money results in both cases—but two ideas that buttress the theory: the "differences-of-opinion rationale" and the "liquidity trap"; let us begin with the former. The theory we have just sketched out concerns a single individual: if the *individual* expects the bond price to fall so far as the theory is specified, he would tend to put *all* his wealth into money; he will do the opposite if he expects the price to rise. In any event, so far as we have specified his choices, he is a *plunger* in market terminology. This is actually how Keynes put it. To get to the overall (aggregate) demand for money we might argue, for example, that each individual has a different opinion about whether or not bond prices are going to fall; then, as bond prices gradually rise (as the interest rate falls) more and more people change their view and switch out of bonds into money; this produces the curve in Figure 6.6, which is the same as that in Figure 6.3 except for the flat part. Thus the "differences-of-opinion" rationale is

Figure 6.6: The Keynesian prediction of the effect on the demand for money of the interest rate

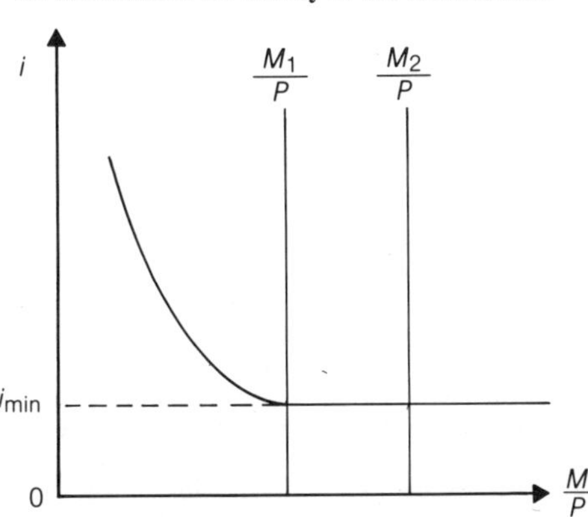

sufficient to provide an explanation of the smooth negative slope of Figure 6.6, even with individuals acting as if they were plungers, having no doubts about their predictions.[15]

It may be, though, that the interest rate falls so low—that is, bond prices rise so far—that *no one* expects it to fall any further. In this event the demand for money would become perfectly flat and a "liquidity trap" would occur. It is termed a liquidity trap because all additional real money balances supplied to the system—represented here by rightward shifts of the M/P curve—would be added to liquid (money) balances and no one would want to buy bonds. The direct implication, and too much is made of this in the textbook literature, is that monetary policy, if it depends on lowering the interest rate for its effect, will not be operative beyond i_{min}. Specifically, monetary policy can increase aggregate demand for products by causing a decrease in the interest rate, which may, in turn, increase investment and consumption. Additions to the money stock beyond that point will merely be added to *idle* money balances (M_s) and will not lower the interest rate.[16] This proposition, though, rests on two assumptions that have been thoroughly discredited by a large number of empirical studies over the last two decades:

a. There is a liquidity trap *in practice.*

b. The influence of monetary policy is exerted solely by means of interest-rate effects.[17]

In addition, we might as well note that an opportunity-cost rationale for the demand for money would not produce anything like Figure 6.6; the interest rate would just go on falling, at least until it reached zero. On the other hand, whether or not sudden shifts in the supply of money would produce only small changes in the interest rate—the real sense of Keynes's argument—is another matter that we must postpone until we have broadened our discussion of monetary policy over the next few chapters.

---

[15] The differences of opinion may apply to what the interest rate *normally* is. That is, for some time economists tried to test this theory in terms of a normal interest rate (for example, 3 percent) or a normal *band* of interest rates (3–5 percent). The idea for the latter is that within the band there may well be no negative relation, while outside, the Keynesian proposition may well work. We can also introduce *uncertainty* into the problem, as we shall see in Chapter 14. This enables us to dispense with the differences-of-opinion formulation.

[16] This is discussed in detail in Chapters 7, 8, and 11.

[17] See David Laidler, *The Demand for Money: Theories and Evidence* (New York: Dun-Donnelly, 1976) and Douglas Fisher, *Monetary Theory and the Demand for Money* (New York: John Wiley, 1978) for surveys of this evidence. While some evidence for a liquidity trap in the sense of a limit to the *expected* fall in interest rates has been found, no *actual* traps have been discovered, on the basis of United States data that include the very low interest rates of the 1930s. The limit works like this: when the interest rate is, say 5 percent, it seems that no one expects it to fall below 2 percent, so far as we can tell from the data. As we approach 2 percent (actually, we do not get there), this limit seems to bump down a little; indeed, over more recent data, it seems to be sliding up. The concept, evidently, is an elusive one.

6.6 A BRIEF SURVEY OF THE EVIDENCE ON THE DEMAND FOR MONEY

Economists have put a considerable effort into the testing of the aggregate demand for money for the United States as well as for a large number of other developed and underdeveloped countries. We will not look at all of the evidence here, reserving some items for the discussion of inflation in Chapter 9 and some for the discussion of uncertainty and related matters in Chapters 13 to 16. Even so, a considerable amount of material exists (see Footnote 17 for two surveys). The questions raised are the following:

a. Is the rate of interest an important variable, and if so, is the relation an elastic or an inelastic one?

b. Is it preferable to use income or wealth in the demand for money?

c. Is the price-level effect on the demand for money a proportional one?

d. Which definition of money, from currency to M_5, is the most appropriate?

e. Is the demand for money stable over time?

We will discuss these, in turn.

***a.* The interest rate.** It seems safe to say that there is almost total agreement that at least one interest rate belongs in the demand for money. Indeed, there is also widespread agreement that the demand for money is normally "interest-inelastic" in that a one percent rise in the rate of interest produces less than a one percent drop in money holding (perhaps *much* less). The liquidity trap (when the demand for money approaches perfect elasticity) does not appear to be a case of any special interest.[18]

***b.* Income or wealth.** Either income or wealth appears to be an important variable in the demand for money, with wealth possibly slightly stronger. The reason for the better performance of wealth, quite possibly, is that *both* money holding *and* consumption may be guided by *long-run* considerations (such as wealth measures) rather than short-run situations (such as *current* income measures). The effect, of course, is a positive one and the estimates of the elasticity (in each case) seem to have varied from the inelastic to the elastic, with the inelastic probably dominating slightly.[19] Again by inelastic, we mean that a 1 percent change in wealth produces a less than 1 percent change in money holding.

***c.* The price level effect.** Apparently, so far as we can say, a change in the price level produces an equi-proportionate change in the quantity of nominal balances demanded (a case of unitary elasticity). Thus, this part

---

[18] As we shall discuss in Chapter 15, there seems to be some disagreement over whether a long-term rate, a short-term rate, or both, should be used in the demand for money.

[19] We will discuss, in Chapter 16 under the heading of the Inventory Model, one reason why this might be so. This is referred to as "economies of scale" in the literature.

of the Neoclassical theory seems valid. On the other hand, variations in the *rate of inflation* (the rate of *change* of prices) have been having an unusual effect on the demand for money—and to some other equations in our macroeconomic models—so we shall want to continue this discussion (in Chapter 9).

d. **The definition of money.** There does not seem to be a consensus on this issue, with some scholars finding M_1 a reasonably well-determined relation and some favoring M_2 or even M_3. The Federal Reserve resolves the issue by issuing its policy directives (see Chapter 12) with reference to both M_1 and M_2. Lately, of course, with the automatic transfers between demand deposits and savings deposits, M_2 has become more relevant in the policy discussions.

e. **The stability of the demand for money.** Generally speaking, the demand for money—especially the demand for M_1 as a function of the short-term interest rate and income—has been stable (that is, unshifting) since 1951.[20] Only during the recent rapid inflation did signs of shift turn up, but these may have gone away, at least for the time being. The demand for M_1 has not been stable, though, since the introduction of automatic transfers in November 1978.

6.7 THE DEMAND FOR CURRENCY

These days, with the rapidly increasing substitutability between the demand deposits and time deposits of commercial banks, a natural question arises as to the possibility that currency will take the place of M_1 as a guide to the public's demand for a medium of exchange. Indeed, under current Federal Reserve practice, the public is permitted any quantity of currency it wishes, and the Federal Reserve usually attempts to eliminate the effects on the monetary base of switches by the public between currency and deposits. The important question for our discussion of the demand for money, then, is a simple one: Is currency sufficiently unlike demand deposits in the eyes of money holders to be separately treated?

When one looks at the actual data on currency holdings in the United States, two things stand out: (1) There is a different time pattern in the behavior of currency compared to demand and time deposits on seasonally adjusted data; and (2) Currency holdings *per capita* are astonishingly large. In Table 6.2 we consider the recent monthly behavior of the three components of M_2; this is a measure that the Federal Reserve has been making increasing use of. There we can see a steady rise in all three components, with the only unusual event being a large jump in the total of demand deposits in April 1978, when the money supply took off (see

[20] S. Goldfeld, "The Demand for Money Revisited," *Brookings Papers on Economic Activity*, no. 3 (1973).

Table 6.2: The components of M_2 in the United States, 1976–1978 (seasonally adjusted, $ billions)

	1976			*1977*			*1978*		
	Currency	*Demand deposits*	*Time deposits*	*Currency*	*Demand deposits*	*Time deposits*	*Currency*	*Demand deposits*	*Time deposits*
January	74.2	220.8	454.4	81.3	233.0	493.8	89.3	250.1	550.5
February	75.1	221.5	457.3	82.0	232.5	497.8	90.0	249.1	556.8
March	75.7	222.3	458.5	82.4	233.7	500.2	90.6	249.5	562.1
April	76.7	225.0	461.6	83.1	237.4	505.7	91.2	257.3	565.2
May	77.4	226.0	462.0	83.6	237.1	509.2	92.1	258.5	571.6
June	77.6	225.6	465.9	84.0	238.0	514.8	92.8	259.9	574.5
July	78.1	226.8	470.0	85.1	241.6	519.5	93.3	260.9	579.4
August	78.6	227.8	468.7	85.5	242.8	522.5	94.0	262.8	583.0
September	79.1	227.2	472.5	86.4	244.0	525.8	94.0	262.8	583.0
October	79.8	230.7	477.5	87.1	246.6	532.2	95.2	265.7	589.7
November	80.3	230.3	483.4	87.7	247.0	540.0	96.6	264.4	608.8
December	80.6	232.1	489.8	88.5	248.2	544.9	97.5	264.1	611.4

Source: *Federal Reserve Bulletin.*

Chapter 12). Dominated as they are by the trend, these data are hard to visualize, but when we graph them in the ratio form recommended in Chapter 5 we can see several patterns (Figure 6.7). Most importantly,

a. C/D, the ratio of currency to demand deposits, and particularly C/T, the ratio of currency to time deposits, do not appear to fluctuate appreciably from month to month.

b. C/D is on a pretty strong upward trend, while C/T is on a mild downward trend.

Figure 6.7: Currency ratios in the American economy, 1976–1978

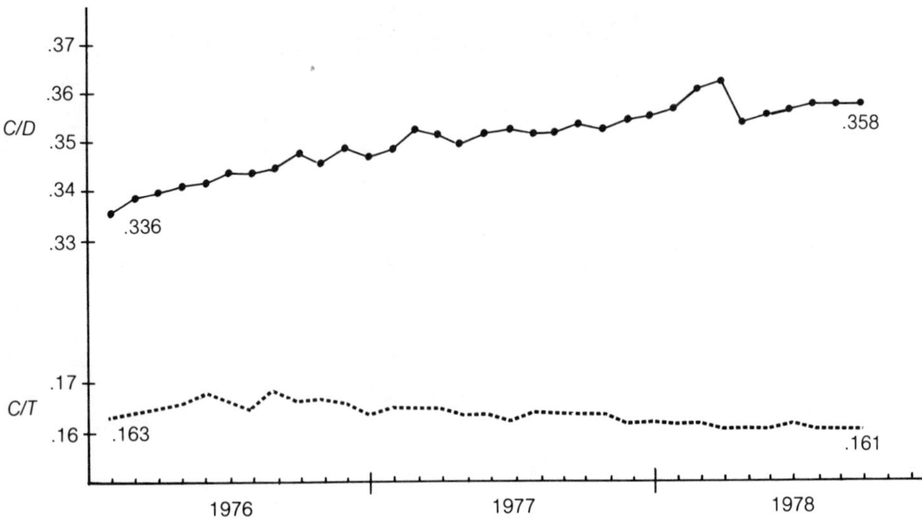

By implication, then, even before the innovation of November 1978 (as discussed in Chapters 2 and 3), the importance of demand deposits in the basic money supply was steadily deteriorating. Lest this be thought to be in some way unique to this short period, we should note that in December 1968, C/D was .282 and C/T was .212. Since these trends go in opposite directions, the effects of what is apparently a change in the taste for deposits can be essentially accounted for by looking at M_2.[21]

The other fact of interest about currency is its quantity. Using a popula-

[21] In a recent study made at the Federal Reserve Bank of Philadelphia by D. Mullineaux ("The Stability of the Demand for Money: Some Adaptive Regression Tests on Monthly Data," mimeo) it is argued that a disaggregation down to currency is necessary to find a satisfactorily stable function. Mullineaux finds the demand for demand deposits *unstable;* the demand for M_2, then, was more stable than the demand for M_1, as the data here suggest might be the case.

tion of 220 million as a deflator, the *per capita* holdings of the components of M_2 were the following, in September 1978:

Currency:	$ 427
Demand deposits:	1,194
Time deposits:	2,650.

While the last is a little surprising (it suggests that the average family of four has savings accounts *in banks* of $10,600), the figures on currency (and less so, perhaps, deposits) are really amazing (a family of four, in effect, holds or has held for it, $1,708 of currency). Currency, of course, does serve as a medium of exchange and a store of value; in the latter capacity it seems a riskier store than the demand deposit (which is insured up to $40,000 per account). As a medium of exchange, it is uniquely useful (at least the small bills are) but demand deposits:

a. Are safer to hold.

b. Enable the individual to pay through the mail more safely.

c. Provide a receipt.[22]

d. Provide a method of keeping track of expenditures.

e. Provide access to loan facilities.

Of course, the figure of $1,708 just given refers to business cash as well as individual cash; while the business cash is not directly estimated by anyone, an occasional study of the payment habits of firms does surface; these imply that an upper limit of one-third of the $1,708 would suffice here.[23] This phenomenon is not confined to the United States, as Table 6.3 indicates. Since the total remaining after deducting business cash is far greater than the amount needed for transactions, we can legitimately ask why people hold so much, and who holds it. The following have been proposed:

a. For black market, tax evasion, and criminal activity (notice the Swiss figure).

b. For currency speculation.

Neither choice is very convincing (for the latter we note that the total of cash held does not fluctuate as speculation would suggest). *Apparently,* people hoard it, particularly in the larger denominations; indeed, it is

---

[22] Checks in the near future may well not serve as receipts; thus in a number of European countries, banks have abandoned the practice of returning cancelled checks to their customers, and U.S. banks are currently studying this possibility.

[23] In a study of the Dutch data, for which the same problem of an apparent excess quantity of cash exists, pretty good *sample* data put firms' holdings at around 15 percent. See J. S. Cramer and G. M. Reekers, "Money Demand by Sector: A Survey for the Netherlands in 1971," *Journal of Monetary Economics* (1976).

Table 6.3: Per capita currency holdings in various countries in 1970 (in U.S. dollars)

United Kingdom	$123
West Germany	169
Italy	180
Netherlands	213
United States	242
France	260
Sweden	262
Belgium	381
Switzerland	537

Source: J. S. Cramer and G. M. Reekers, "Money Demand by Sector. A Survey for the Netherlands in 1971," *Journal of Monetary Economics* (1976), p. 106.

probably not everyone who holds it but a disproportionate number of elderly people and people who are self-employed. If this is accurate it does not seem to represent a policy problem and, at least, it is comforting to know that this source of the demand for currency is stable.

6.8 ELECTRONIC FUNDS TRANSFERS AND THE DEMAND FOR MONEY: A NOTE

As the 1970s draw to a close, the move toward computerized banking and computerized payment, even at the retail level, is clearly accelerating. It seems highly likely that payment by both cash and check will shrink in favor of payment by plastic and in this event the continuing trend away from demand deposits and even currency (compared to time deposits) may accelerate. Of course, we should recall that the recent development of automatic transfers between savings and demand deposits in banks (customers were doing it anyway) and the development of checking privileges in savings and loan associations and mutual savings banks implies that there may well be close enough substitution between all of the components of money up to M_3 that apparent instabilities in the components will disappear in aggregation. These effects are likely to occur, it would seem, but little else needs to be said with regard to the demand for money. We have discussed these matters as they affect banking practice and we will also discuss the policy issues (particularly in Chapter 12) and the effects on financial intermediaries (in Chapter 13). But with regard to the demand for money there is no solid evidence, at present, that either the list of variables or the stability is in danger, so we can leave this topic at this point, for the time being.

6.9 STUDY QUESTIONS

Essay questions

1. In a certain sense the critical element—for the demand for money in a market economy—is the time it takes to clear a market. Indeed, we save time when goods are exchanged more rapidly. Does this way of putting things help to make clear the role of the interest rate as a determinant of the demand for money? Explain.

2. When the quantity of money increases, velocity will change if none of the other variables changes. Can you explain what is happening to cause money to be absorbed into the system? Does your answer depend in any way on what causes the quantity of money to change?

3. We have made a distinction between transactions motives, precautionary motives, and speculative motives for holding money. Why do we use a bond yield as our basis of comparison for the speculative demand? Will an individual speculator ever hold money and bonds at the same time? Is the consistency of the speculator involved?

4. The "liquidity trap" of Keynes is a possibility even though its existence has never been convincingly demonstrated. Why does it pose a threat to the effectiveness of monetary policy? Can you think of any other effect an increase in the quantity of money might have even if it could not result in a lower interest rate?

True-false discussion questions

These statements are meant to be somewhat ambiguous and to provoke discussion, thereby.

1. The interest rate on a time deposit represents the opportunity cost of holding money while at the same time representing the direct yield on money.

2. The main reason individuals hold more money when prices rise is to replace the real value of this item of wealth.

3. The velocity of money could vary considerably even if the demand for money did not.

4. If velocity goes up when the interest rate declines, then monetary policy will be likely to be fairly ineffective.

5. We can associate the influence of income with the Classical theory of the demand for money and the influence of the interest rate with the Keynesian theory of the demand for money.

6. The reason the equation of exchange holds is that we live in a monetary economy; conversely, it would not hold to the extent that we had a barter economy.

7. A doubling of the price level and a doubling of the interest rate would tend to leave the quantity of money demanded unchanged.

8. The Keynesian explanation of how interest rates influence the demand for money is an opportunity-cost rationale, essentially.

9. Velocity responds to changes in the interest rate, but would not respond to changes in income since such changes usually produce a proportionate change in money holding.

6.10 FURTHER READING

Laidler, David. *The Demand for Money: Theories and Evidence*. 2d ed. New York: Dun-Donnelley, 1977.

Boorman, John T. "The Evidence on the Demand for Money: Theoretical Formulations and Empirical Results." In Havrilesky, Thomas N., and John T. Boorman, eds., *Current Issues in Monetary Theory and Policy*. Arlington Heights, Ill.: AHM Publishing Corp., 1976.

Saunders, P. G., and D. J. Taylor. "The Demand for Money." In Heathfield, David, ed., *Topics in Applied Macroeconomics*. London: Macmillan, 1976.

7

A basic macroeconomic model (Part I: The *IS* and *LM* curves)

7.1 INTRODUCTION

In this chapter we will lay out a standard macroeconomic model of economic activity that leads ultimately to an explanation of how employment and the price level are determined. Our main purpose for advancing in this direction is that there are a number of general (that is, macroeconomic) aspects of the monetary policy debate that are especially important, and there is no obvious alternative to constructing a *simple* macroeconomic model in order to spell out the problems and (where they exist) the solutions. Indeed, we will make considerable use of the model in the explicit policy chapters that follow in the remainder of Part II, so the reader should be especially careful to master the details of the model as it is developed here and in Chapter 8.

Table 7.1 presents a brief sketch of the model as it will appear in Chapters 7 and 8.[1] We will first consider three major sectors (a goods market, the money market, and the labor market) and then we will construct a model that links them together. Omitted, mainly for ease of expos-

[1] The presentation of these and later chapters is on the same level as that in Robert J. Gordon's *Macroeconomics* (Boston: Little, Brown and Company, 1978) although it is hoped that the compactness of the material here makes it a little easier to follow the argument.

Table 7.1: An outline of a standard macro model

Market	*Chapter 7*	*Other chapters*
1.	Real goods	
	Consumption	
	Investment	Government (Part II and III)
		Net foreign spending (Part IV)
2.	Inputs	
	Capital	
	Labor	
3.	Nominal goods	
	Money	
		Bonds (Part III)
		Equities (Part III)
		Foreign exchange (Part IV)

ition in this chapter, are the bond market (and other financial markets) and foreign markets; these will be discussed (and included at least loosely in the model) in Parts III and IV of this book. Note, too, that fiscal policy is only tacked on to the discussion in this and succeeding chapters.

7.2 THE *IS* CURVE

In what follows we will first construct an analysis in terms of the often-used *IS-LM* model, where the *IS* curve describes the situation in the "real goods" or commodities sector, and the *LM* curve describes the situation in the "nominal goods" or money sector. We will also at a later stage include the input (factor) markets in our analysis, and to do so, two approaches will be taken: one will take the view that factor markets are always in equilibrium (a Classical approach), and the other, in Chapter 8, will work in terms of "aggregate demand" and "aggregate supply" (a Keynesian approach). The latter will enable us to provide an explanation of the price level that is more nearly in accord with the way economists think of the problem these days. With suitable adjustments, we will be able to link up our study of prices with that of inflation (itself the *rate of change* of prices) as discussed in Chapters 8, 9, and 11. But first we begin with the consumption and investment functions representing the two main sectors involved with private (i.e., nongovernmental) spending.

7.2.1 The consumption function

An individual consumer will tend to increase his or her consumption of a particular good if his or her income increases (*given* that all other variables are constant) and if the price of that commodity falls (given the constancy of all other variables). An *aggregate* consumer will tend to increase the consumption of *all* consumer goods if *aggregate* income (Y) increases (and if the prices (P) of *all* consumer goods fall). This statement, or rather the income component of it, is represented by the equation

$$C = f(Y),$$

where the general functional notation $f(Y)$ is adopted, since no particular form is assumed (as yet). Let us take these variables (Y, P) in turn.[2]

John Maynard Keynes is generally credited with the first formulation of what is now known as the *Absolute Income Hypothesis*.[3] This view holds that a simple, and possibly *linear*, relation may exist between consumption and income whether consumption is measured in *nominal* or in *real* (i.e., deflated by prices) form; one version is illustrated in Figure 7.1. Here a

Figure 7.1: Consumption as a function of income

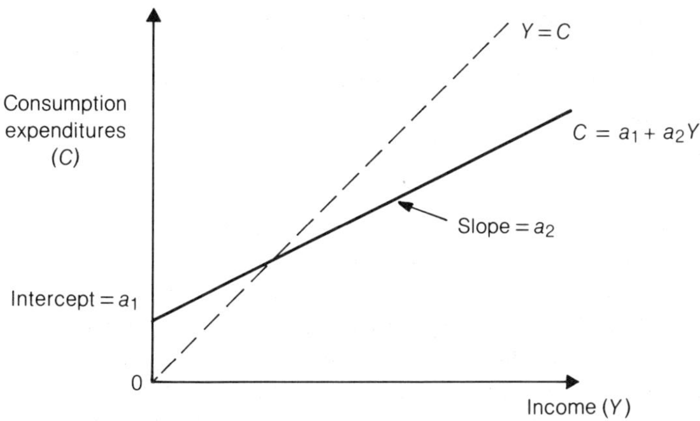

linear relation ($C = a_1 + a_2Y$ is the equation of a straight line) between nominal consumption and nominal income is assumed; as income rises, consumption rises, but not by as much ($a_2 < 1$). Let us write this consumption function as Equation (7.1) and consider its properties:

$$C = a_1 + a_2Y. \tag{7.1}$$

First of all, let us put in some numbers, not necessarily realistic, to show what is meant. Thus if a_1 = \$10 billion, and a_2 = .9, then when Y is equal to \$800 billion (that is, when current national income—if that is what Y stands for—is equal to \$800 billion), aggregate consumption will be ex-

[2] We will ignore the effect of the interest rate on consumption, an effect that may well be negative but that in any event is in some dispute in both theoretical and empirical studies. The general drift of what follows is not affected by this omission.

[3] John Maynard Keynes, *The General Theory of Employment, Interest and Money* (London: Harcourt, Brace, 1936).

pected to be \$730 billion (\$10 billion plus \$720 billion). a_1 and a_2 are the *parameters* of this relation: a_1 is the "intercept" and a_2 the "slope" of the straight line, as marked on Figure 7.1.[4] a_2 is also referred to as the *marginal propensity to consume* in the sense that it describes the additional consumer spending (90 cents) that results from an addition to income of \$1.

Just before we introduced Equation (7.1) we also mentioned the price level as a possible variable for the consumption function, on the grounds that a general rise in prices might discourage consumption in general.[5] What one observes, in fact, is that *nominal* consumer spending (C) and nominal income (Y) tend to rise together in such a way that price level effects do not seem to matter (much). That is, it is *probable* (under normal conditions) that if consumers receive a 10 percent increase in their income, and at the same time all prices rise by 10 percent, that consumers will consume the same amount in *real* terms after the price rise as before. In effect, we may write Equation (7.1) as Equation (7.2); this is frequently referred to as the assumption of the *absence-of-money illusion* in the consumption function.

$$\frac{C}{P} = a_1 + a_2 \frac{Y}{P}. \tag{7.2}$$

This equation may not, however, be totally correct in that several other price-level-related effects might also matter. That is, as the price level rises consumers may actually cut back on their expenditures, *even in real terms*. The first of these factors, as we noted briefly in Chapter 6, comes under the heading of the "real balance effect." This was that consumers may cut back on their expenditures because the real value of some of their wealth is less after an inflation. After all, as we reported in Chapter 1, at the end of 1978, there was \$6,822 of M_3 for every man, woman, and child in the United States, and all of this vast accumulation of liquid wealth was undermined by the inflation going on then, which had reached an annual rate of 13 percent by early 1979. In Chapter 6 we were, however, discussing the situation in 1974, when the inflation, which reached 16 percent, may actually have surprised consumers. Thus at the end of 1974 consumers may have discovered that the purchasing power of their savings had gone down (it certainly had); they may have then reacted by "oversaving" in the next year in order to try to catch up. This is the sort of

[4] In this book we will usually employ linear relations since most of the points that need to be made can be done in this way. In addition, when we combine equations, it is very easy to do so with linear equations. Graphs get very messy (although they are equivalent) when several arguments are conducted at once, as we will often want to do.

[5] We saw, in Chapter 1, that during the recent "great inflation" in 1974–75, saving (i.e., non-consumption) may well have risen, at least if the rise of M_2, etc. is an indication of this. Apparently other countries experienced this phenomenon at the same time, as we shall discuss in Part IV of this book.

effect we have in mind here. There is, also, a second reason for a general effect of the price level on consumption, and this concerns the *expectations* of consumers. If consumers see a rise in current prices, they may *postpone* consumption if they think that prices will settle down again (optimists); conversely, if consumers observe a rapid rise in prices, they may buy now, in anticipation of a *future* rise in prices (pessimists). By and large, one suspects the optimists have it, on the recent data, but in any event this factor, too, suggests that another variable, the *expected* price level, might be an additional influence on real consumption.[6]

We should digress briefly, here, because our basing of the consumption function on the *Absolute Income Hypothesis* actually runs counter to some considerable professional opinion that favors either the *Permanent Income Hypothesis* or the *Life Cycle Hypothesis*. The first of these propositions has been attributed to Milton Friedman;[7] the argument is that consumers tend to try to stick to a long-run consumption plan and generally ignore short-run (transitory) changes in their income and wealth, unless and until the changes are perceived to have become regular (that is, "permanent"). Approximately, then, this theory argues that consumption depends on the stable components of *wealth* rather than on *current* income; indeed, there is some evidence in favor of this view. The foregoing is not just an academic dispute, actually, and may be relevant for the macroeconomic policy debate. Suppose, for example, that government macroeconomic policy is aimed at consumer spending, through an income tax cut; in this case such a cut may well not affect consumer spending if consumers perceive the cut to be a temporary one. This position, indeed, applies to any temporary change in consumer income or wealth.

The second of these theories—the *Life Cycle Hypothesis*—also emphasizes the future plans of consumers, but in a more explicit way. Here it is suggested that consumers go through cycles (or stages) in their lives, living off others' (wealth) in their early years (dissaving), saving in their most productive days, and living off their own savings (accumulated wealth) after retirement. This theory, clearly, also emphasizes consumers' wealth, but it differs from the Permanent Income Hypothesis in focusing attention on the age of the spending unit (or the average age of the population). But for our purposes *in this chapter*, it is not especially important whether we write Y, Y_P (for *permanent* income), or W in our consumption function, as long as all equations have the same variable, so we will not pursue the distinctions raised in this paragraph further; on the other hand, when we come to discuss the actual transmission of

---

[6] If the *expected* price level is a factor, then so too is the *actual* price level, since (almost certainly) price expectations are based on actual price level changes.

[7] Milton Friedman, *A Theory of the Consumption Function* (Princeton, N.J.: Princeton University Press, 1957).

monetary and fiscal policy in Chapter 11 we will have to return to these problems, and that is why they were introduced in this section.

7.2.2 The investment function

We will not be able to construct an aggregate investment function quite as easily as we did the consumption function because of a problem that we have pretty much ignored in the book to this point: the result of a *net* investment—a construction or purchase of a new capital good—is an addition to the country's capital *stock* and, as such, the investment has a *durability* that extends its life well beyond the period of its purchase.[8] To begin with, investment is undertaken by business firms whose *raison d'etre* is the making of profits. Business firms can be conceived, in a general way, as operations that employ factors of production—labor (L) and capital (K)—producing goods and services—or outputs (X)—by means of a production relation (or function). A production function, to begin at the end, can be written in a functional form as in Equation (7.3), where only a general dependence between the inputs (K, L) and the outputs (X) is stated.[9] Ordinarily, increases in either factor would tend to increase production, *ceteris paribus*.

$$X = \phi(L, K). \tag{7.3}$$

Output (X), of course, is what consumers (and other investors) buy, although we are here writing it in real terms (X), and L and K should also be viewed as real quantities of the factors of production.

Investment, we have said, is the addition to the firm's (or nation's) *net* capital stock, where the capital stock is broadly defined to include buildings, machines, materials, and inventories of goods. This we may write as

$$I \equiv \text{Net change in } K \text{ per unit of time} \equiv \Delta K. \tag{7.4}$$

Now investment spending, in a general macroeconimic model, also depends on income (or wealth) and the interest rate, but neither of these relationships is as simple as one might wish.

With regard to the effect of the interest rate on aggregate investment, we will begin with a relation such as Equation (6.5), which defined the "present value" of a stream of returns. We generally think of a business firm as an entity that is maximizing profits and is currently considering an

---

[8] Actually, many consumer goods are durables, and money, also is highly durable. We can deal with the former by arguing that the theory of Section 7.2.1 was expressed in terms of the flows of services (i.e., current uses) of all consumer goods. We can deal with the latter by working our monetary theory in terms of the *holding* of quantities (i.e., stocks) of money, much as is recommended by the Keynesians. Indeed, we will generally take that approach in what follows.

[9] ϕ in Equation (7.3) represents the general functional notation as f did in Equation (7.2).

investment project to that effect. The investment project will have a present cost (C) and is expected, let us say, to bring in a stream of future net returns ($R_1, \ldots, R_n$) for the expected life (n years) of the project. *By analogy* with Equation (6.5), the net expected *present value* of this project will be

$$\text{P.V.} = \frac{R_1}{(1+i)} + \frac{R_2}{(1+i)^2} + \ldots + \frac{R_n}{(1+i)^n} - C, \qquad (7.5)$$

where i represents the market rate of interest (that is, i represents the cost of the funds that must be borrowed in order to finance the project).[10] The aggregate firm, here, will continue to borrow (and purchase capital equipment at the cost C) until all profits have disappeared (until P.V. = 0); it does this because it is here assumed to have a fixed equity.[11]

The effect of a change in the interest rate—here representing the cost of borrowed funds to the firm—is then a straightforward one in Equation (7.5). That is, a rise in the cost of borrowing, by reducing the *present value* of the stream of revenues, will tend to make projects unprofitable that had previously been considered to be profitable. In a nutshell, a *rise* in the interest rate will *reduce* investment, and a graph such as Figure 7.2—which represented the demand for money—could be drawn up. We may represent this idea by a linear equation comparable to Equation (7.2), again written in *real* terms because of the (additional) assumption of the absence-of-money illusion in investment spending; the result is

$$\frac{I}{P} = b_1 - b_3 i. \qquad (7.6)$$

This will be our investment function in what follows, and we will, *for convenience only*, ignore income.[12]

---

[10] Note that the interest rate represents either the opportunity cost of funds or the direct cost. That is, borrowed funds will have to pay an explicit interest rate, while retained earnings will have to *forego* an implicit interest rate (they could be lent out at i). The two rates here are assumed to be identical on the assumption of perfect competition in all product and capital markets. The firm borrows, as we will discuss in Chapter 16, by either issuing bonds or by issuing new stock (equity).

[11] In Chapter 16 we will discuss, briefly, the firm's "leverage"—that is, the debt/equity ratio. The firm here, as it acquires capital equipment by means of bond financing, is building in a considerable volume of *fixed* interest payments. This may prompt it to stop building new projects before P.V. hits zero. In an industry that has economies of scale (such as banking?) such considerations may put a damper on expansion that would otherwise not exist. Of course, if bank "failure" is impossible—and failure results when you cannot meet your fixed payments—then banking firms may perceive no limit to their expansion possibilities: R, in effect, is rising in Equation (7.5); consider Table 3.2 to be evidence on this point.

[12] With regard to income, the effect operates through Equation (7.4). If firms expect, or observe, a rise in their sales, they will attempt to produce more output; they can do this—says Equation (7.4)—by taking on more labor and increasing their capital stock. Now if the sales of the aggregate firm are directly dependent on income (Y), and they are, then income and the capital stock are directly related; each higher level of income will require a higher

Figure 7.2: The investment function

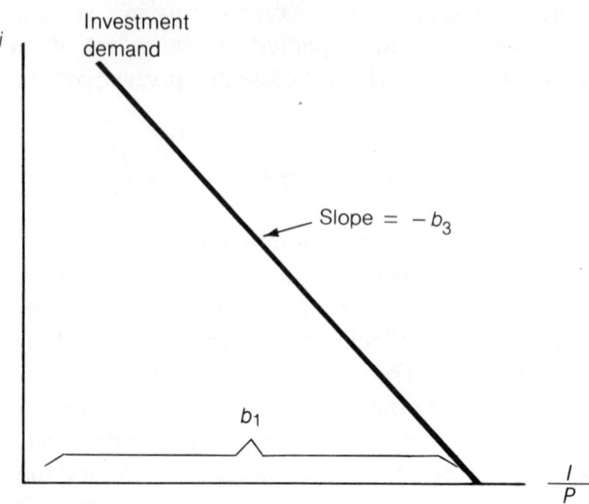

Finally, let us add a note on the government although we will, for simplicity, ignore it in much of the following discussion. Let us suppose that the government has a fixed level of expenditure and that it finances this expenditure by either income taxes, so that (Y/P) is *after-tax income*, or, whenever the income tax revenue is insufficient, by new bond issues (that is to say, by *deficit financing*). We need not concentrate on the financing of its expenditures here, although in Chapter 11 we will report that it makes a big difference in the design of fiscal policy. Instead, here, we will merely write out a government spending function similar to Equations (7.2) and (7.6):

$$\frac{G}{P} = t_1. \tag{7.7}$$

We will use this later in the Chapter, but for now we will return to the simpler model, with C/P and I/P as we consider the derivation of the *IS* curve.

7.2.3 The derivation of the *IS* curve

We have, now, written down a system of three equations representing the two sets of behavioral hypotheses on consumption and investment, in

level of the capital stock. Equation (7.5), then, defines investment to be the *change* in the capital stock; thus, clearly, if the desired capital stock *depends* on income, and investment is equal to the *change* in the capital stock, then investment will depend on the *change* in income. This idea, which is known as the *accelerator* because it implies large percentage changes in investment for small percentage changes in income, can be written as $I = b(\Delta Y)$. This is probably the correct way to define investment, but it is a mathematically complicated way (we would have to solve a differential equation), and so we will not pursue the role of income further here.

four variables—(C/P), (I/P), (Y/P), and i—and in four parameters—a_1, a_2, b_1, and b_3. We may *close* our model by assuming equilibrium in the goods market, in the sense that all spending, $(C/P) + (I/P)$, is equal to all of the income generated by spending activity, (Y/P). Let us consider what is involved. If individuals do not consume, then they must save. Thus, returning to the nominal dimension for the moment, every dollar of income (Y) received can be partitioned between consumption (C) and saving (S), this justifies the equation

$$Y = C + S. \tag{7.8}$$

Now savings are funds that are available to be invested; indeed the financial system (broadly defined to include equity markets) serves to match up savers and investors. So long as there are saved funds that are not desired for investment, or so long as there are investment projects that cannot obtain the funds they need at the going interest rate, then *disequilibrium* exists between savings and investment, and further adjustments in the economic system are indicated. These adjustments would be in income, the interest rate, and even in the price level, and these adjustments would continue as long as the funds saved were not invested. To see this, let us rework our analysis in real terms.

Let us, when we return to the real dimension, define total spending to be equal to

$$\frac{C}{P} + \frac{I}{P} = \frac{X}{P} \tag{7.9}$$

and total income to be equal to

$$\frac{Y}{P} = \frac{S}{P} + \frac{C}{P}. \tag{7.10}$$

Then, if all of the income generated by productive activity, (Y/P), is spent so that $(Y/P) = (X/P)$, then it follows that

$$\frac{I}{P} = \frac{S}{P}.$$

If, instead of being equal, total spending is greater than the total income generated by productive activity, then the sellers of products will find their shelves emptying of goods; they will respond by raising prices and they will borrow more for expansion (so that interest rates may rise). They will also order more goods so that production, (X/P), rises. The net effect is a rise in incomes that could bring (Y/P) into equality with (X/P).

We refer to the condition that $(X/P) = (Y/P)$ as an equilibrium condition because it is true only at equilibrium (in the spending sector). In terms of graphs, we have the situation depicted in Figure 7.3. Note that we could add government spending, (G/P), here directly, if we wished to give fiscal

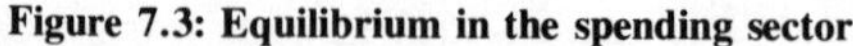
Figure 7.3: Equilibrium in the spending sector

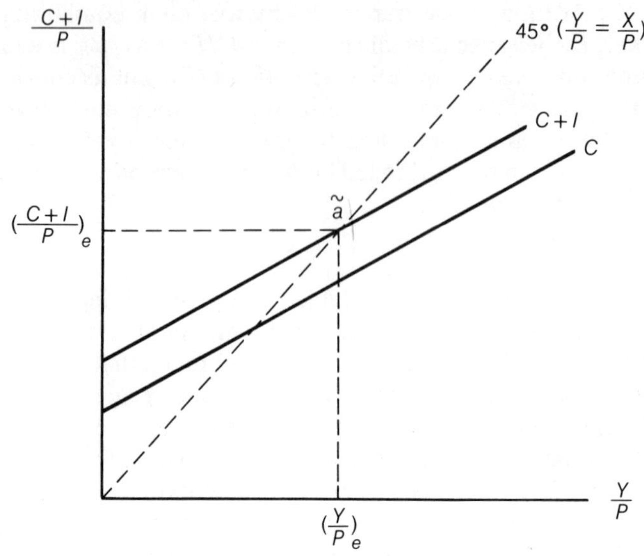

policy a role to play. Then we show, at point *a*, the single point that represents equilibrium in the spending sector. Note that investment was merely added to consumption (since investment did not depend on income). There is an alternative approach here, though, that can be worked out in simple algebraic terms. That is, we can use our basic equations

$$\frac{C}{P} = a_1 + a_2 \frac{Y}{P} \tag{7.2}$$

$$\frac{I}{P} = b_1 - b_3 i \tag{7.6}$$

and the *equilibrium* condition that

$$\frac{Y}{P} = \frac{X}{P} = \frac{C}{P} + \frac{I}{P}$$

to obtain a *solution* in a mathematical form. This solution is

$$\frac{Y}{P} = a_1 + a_2 \frac{Y}{P} + b_1 - b_3 i,$$

which, solved for i, is

$$i = \left(\frac{a_2 - 1}{b_3} \right) \frac{Y}{P} + \frac{a_1 + b_1}{b_3}. \tag{7.11}$$

This, clearly, is the equation of a straight line in the i, (Y/P) dimensions.

To visualize the *IS* curve (or $I = S$ curve, to explain its meaning), we can graph the relation in Equation (7.11) directly.[13] We can actually locate this function quite specifically since $(a_1 + b_1)/b_3$, the intercept, is positive, and generally $(a_2 - 1)/b_3$, the slope, is negative (so long as a_2 is less than 1). The situation is depicted in Figure 7.4. Note again that the *IS*

Figure 7.4: The *IS* curve

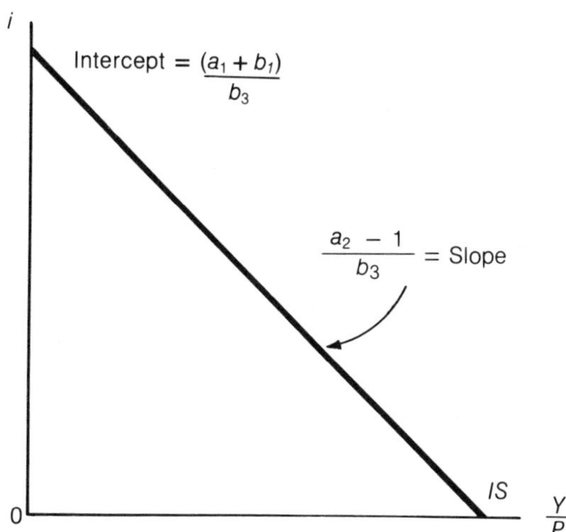

relation is one that gives various pairs of i and (Y/P) at which the goods market is in equilibrium; pairs of i and (Y/P) that lie to the right or left of the *IS* curve represent points at which the goods market is in *disequilibrium*. Here we clearly see that the *IS-LM* framework does not restrict us to equilibrium situations and we must count this an advantage since we will want, later, to consider situations such as stagflation—periods when inflation and unemployment are both increasing—in which a general disequilibrium may be in effect.

We cannot illustrate monetary policy here, but we can impose a very simple sort of fiscal policy. The coefficiants, a_1 and b_1, represent the influence of whatever other variables cause shifts in the position of consumption and investment functions. The kinds of effects that could shift these functions are changes in tastes *or*, more importantly, changes in expectations. Thus if, for example, a_1 increased by one unit, Equation (7.11) shows that i would rise by $(1/b_3)$. Now a simple sort of fiscal policy would be to put real government spending into the model in a fashion

[13] An alternative is to do a visual summation of Figures 7.3 and 7.2; the latter is standard in intermediate macroeconomic books and the interested reader should have no trouble in verifying Figure 7.4.

parallel to the *shifts* of the consumption and investment functions; that is, if we add the equation $(G/P) = t_1$ tō our model *and* solve for (Y/P) using Equations (7.3), (7.8), and (7.10), ignoring the method which the government uses to finance its expenditure, we obtain the standard Keynesian multiplier equation:[14]

$$\frac{Y}{P} = \frac{a_1 + b_1 + t_1}{1 - a_2} - \left(\frac{b_3}{1 - a_2}\right) i. \tag{7.12}$$

This function, then, is the same as the one graphed in Figure 7.3, although the intercept is now calculated along the horizontal axis, in view of our change of focus. The government spending (and investment) multiplier, then, is given as

$$\Delta\left(\frac{Y}{P}\right) = \frac{1}{1 - a_2}\Delta\left(\frac{G}{P}\right) = \frac{1}{1 - a_2}\Delta b_1, \tag{7.13}$$

which is, of course, the standard result. If, then, $a_2 = .9$, a \$1 billion dollar government (or investment) expenditure will create \$10 billion of new income (and spending). But we should note, in anticipation of some later results, that this is an extreme and unrealistic magnitude.[15]

7.3 THE *LM* CURVE

Let us, to begin with, reproduce Equation (6.11), expressing the general demand for money, in a linear form comparable to the equations we have used for the consumption and investment functions in this chapter; this appears as

$$\left(\frac{M}{P}\right)_d = f_1 + f_2\left(\frac{Y}{P}\right) - f_3 i. \tag{7.14}$$

We may imagine, after our discussion in Chapter 5, that the supply of money, via the Federal Reserve and the banking system, *also* depends on the interest rate and *may* depend on real income; let us, though, ignore the latter effect, and write our supply function, also in a linear form, as

$$M_s = g_1 + g_3 i. \tag{7.15}$$

---

[14] Note that we have turned Equation (7.11) around to obtain a solution for (Y/P) in terms of i rather than the converse. Also note that government spending is financed by deficit financing *unless* we redefine all of the income variables in terms of after-tax income.

[15] One reason—and not the only one by any means—is that we have introduced another market—the bond market in which the deficit is financed—and not described how it is cleared when a new government expenditure is made. In fact, the new expenditure is going to put upward pressure on interest rates (as the bond market adjusts to the new expenditures) and this, in turn, will *adversely* affect investment. This effect would tend to reverse the thrust of the original fiscal policy. But this is only one of the reasons that economists think fiscal (and, as we shall see, monetary) policy tends to be blunted in practice.

Here we are assuming that an *increase* in the interest rate will cause an *increase* in that amount of nominal money supplied by the banks or the government; in justification, as our discussion of Chapter 2 should clearly imply, banks, for their part, will naturally want to hold more deposits if the interest rate rises since (as we noticed) their profits tend to rise with the interest rate ($g_3 > 0$). On the other hand, whether the government tends to increase high-powered money (H) or the monetary base (B) when the interest rate rises, depends on whether it tries to *stabilize* the interest rate. If it does, then when the interest rate *rises*—as if it were on account of "tightness" in the money market—the government would tend to increase H (or B) and, hence, the money supply would tend to rise. This too, would lead to a *positive* value for g_3.

The money market is in equilibrium, of course, when the supply of money is equal to the demand. This can be expressed in *nominal* terms, as

$$M_d = M_s$$

or in real terms, as in

$$\left(\frac{M}{P}\right)_d = \frac{M_s}{P},$$

where Equation (7.15) is divided through by the price level to put it into conformity with Equation (7.14). Let us use the real approach, though, and see what an *equilibrium* relation comparable to the *IS* curve looks like in the (Y/P) and i dimensions; Equation (7.16) is the result, where we simply divided Equation (7.15) by P to obtain the right-hand side:

$$f_1 + f_2\left(\frac{Y}{P}\right) - f_3 i = \frac{g_1}{P} + \frac{g_3}{P}\,i. \tag{7.16}$$

As before, we may solve this equation for the interest rate to obtain the equation of a straight line; this is the *LM* curve (*L* for liquidity—i.e., money demand—and *M* for money supply). This is

$$i = \frac{f_1 - \dfrac{g_1}{P}}{f_3 + \dfrac{g_3}{P}} + \frac{f_2}{f_3 + \dfrac{g_3}{P}}\,\frac{Y}{P}, \tag{7.17}$$

which is graphed in Figure 7.5. In the figure the sign of the intercept,

$$\frac{f_1 - \dfrac{g_1}{P}}{f_3 + \dfrac{g_3}{P}},$$

depends on whether f_1 is less than, equal to, or greater than (g_1/P). Since f_1 is the intercept (on the M/P axis) of the money demand

Figure 7.5: The *LM* curve

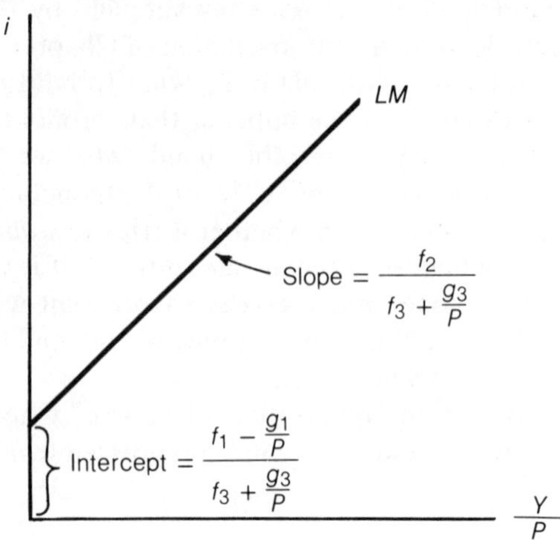

curve, and g_1/P is the intercept of the money supply curve (which will lie to the left of f_1), we can certainly assert that the intercept in Equation (7.17) is positive. Further, the slope of the *LM* function

$$\frac{f_2}{f_3 + \frac{g_3}{P}}$$

is clearly positive.

Now there is one important thing about our treatment of the *LM* curve that is different from our treatment of the *IS* curve, and that is that there is another variable, *P*, the price level, in the equation. This inclusion is the result of our writing the money supply equation with a type of "money illusion" in it.[16] This formulation has two important and immediate consequences:

a. Our system has three variables—*i*, (Y/P), and *P*—and hence, generally, has no simple solution for just two of them (except with the third held constant).

b. For this reason, the *LM* curve shifts with changes in the price level.

We will resolve these problems in the remainder of this chapter, but for now, let us consider in which direction the *LM* curve shifts when the price level changes. To ascertain this influence, let us graph the underlying

[16] As discussed in Chapter 2, banks supply *nominal* money balances and are, in effect, indifferent to the price level; similarly, in Chapter 5, we discussed, in terms of the determinants of the *nominal* money stock, both the commercial banks and the Federal Reserve as suppliers of money.

money market functions, Equations (7.14) and (7.15), the former expressing the demand for money in real terms and the latter, the supply of money, in nominal terms, *but deflated* by the price level. The graph appears as Figure 7.6. When the price level rises the demand for money does not alter, since it responds (by assumption) only to changes in real income.[17] But the nominal quantity of money supplied is reduced in value by a rise in the price level (look back to the discussion in Chapter 1) and the M_s curve shifts *to the left*, as noted in Figure 7.6.

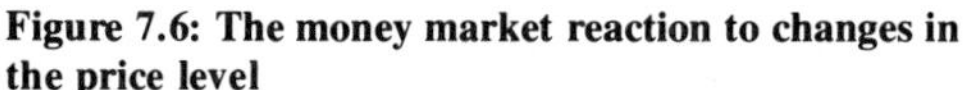

Figure 7.6: The money market reaction to changes in the price level

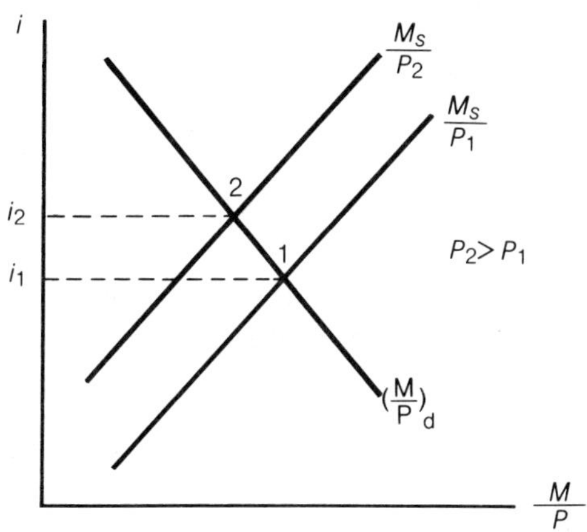

We may directly translate this effect into an effect on the *LM* curve by noting that points 1 and 2 have different interest rates ($i_2 > i_1$) but unchanged real income (look at Footnote 17). This is depicted in Figure 7.7, which shows that the *LM* curve has shifted unambiguously to the left (or upward, really) as a result of the price level increase. This explains the influence of P in Equation (7.17) in a fairly direct manner.

Let us reflect on this result for a moment. Equation (7.11) or Figure 7.4 presents a solution for a spending equilibrium curve in terms of two variables, real income, (Y/P), and the interest rate, i; similarly, Equation (7.17) presents a solution for the money equilibrium curve in terms of the same two variables *and the price level.* We can begin our analysis, then by graphing a solution to this economic "system," for a fixed price level, as

[17] Real income, you may recall, is nominal income divided by the price level. The following equivalent expressions explain the comment in the text and show why the price level effect does not affect M_d:

$$\frac{Y}{P} = \frac{PY}{P} = y.$$

Figure 7.7: The effect of a rise of the price level on the *LM* curve

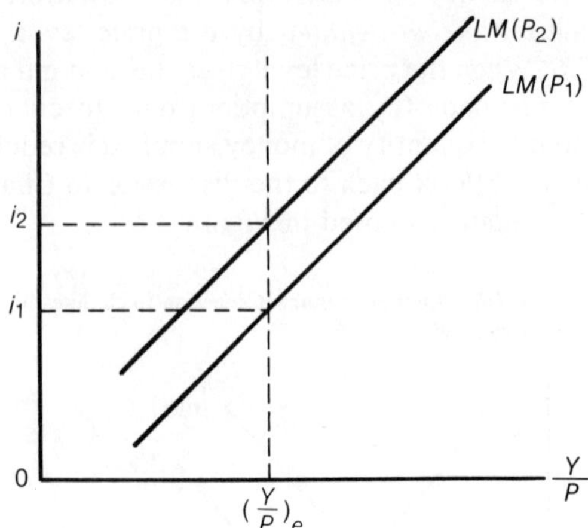

in Figure 7.8. Here the overall equilibrium is shown as the intersection of an *IS* and an *LM* curve and it produces equilibrium values of i_e and $(Y/P)_e$.[18]

Figure 7.8: Overall equilibrium (for a fixed price level)

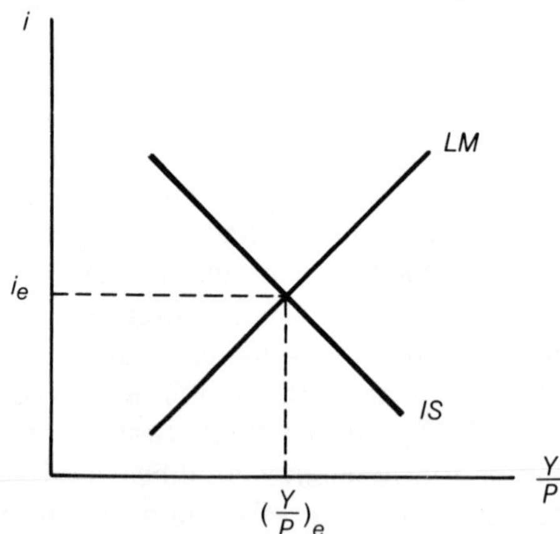

[18] We are not going to produce mathematical solutions to our model from this point on, but we will carry this material along in the footnotes for the convenience of those who wish to calculate exact results. Thus Equations (7.11) and (7.17) are, respectively (using $y = Y/P$ for clarity),

$$i = \frac{a_2 - 1}{b_3} y + \frac{a_1 + b_1}{b_3} \qquad (7.11)$$

7.4 POLICY EXPERIMENTS WITH THE *IS-LM* MODEL

Now if you were a Keynesian using this model, and believed that the price level is relatively rigid (or fixed), then you might find the model just laid out an adequate one for explaining the determination of real income (and nominal income for that matter, since in (Y/P), for P fixed, a theory explaining the determination of (Y/P) also simultaneously explains Y). Instead, if you were a Monetarist and believed (*a*) that the money supply function was like Equation (7.16) and (*b*) that the price level is an important variable, then the system as drawn here is not yet complete.[19] You might even complete it by assuming that (Y/P) is fixed, for example at the "full employment" level, in which case a diagram like Figure 7.8—but with *nominal* rather than real income on the horizontal axis—would be appropriate. It would also be complete, in the sense that a solution for Y and i would contain no other variables.[20] But since neither P nor (Y/P) is fixed in the real world that we seek to understand through our modelling, it is better to go on and try to find an explicit solution for the price level by expanding the model; this we will do in Chapter 8 after we have first

---

$$i = \frac{f_2}{f_3 + \frac{g_3}{P}} y + \frac{f_1 - \frac{g_1}{P}}{f_3 + \frac{g_3}{P}} \tag{7.17}$$

Eliminating the interest rate between these two expressions yields

$$\frac{a_2 - 1}{b_3} y + \frac{a_1 + b_1}{b_3} = \frac{f_2}{f_3 + \frac{g_3}{P}} y + \frac{f_1 - \frac{g_1}{P}}{f_3 + \frac{g_3}{P}},$$

whence, for our overall solution,

$$y_e = \frac{\dfrac{f_1 - \frac{g_1}{P}}{f_3 + \frac{g_3}{P}} - \dfrac{a_1 + b_1}{b_3}}{\dfrac{a_2 - 1}{b_3} - \dfrac{f_2}{f_3 + \frac{g_3}{P}}}.$$

To obtain the equilibrium interest rate we can then substitute this value of y back into Equation (7.11) or (7.17).

[19] Note that in the Keynesian analysis, so long as P is constant, the fact that the money supply function is in nominal terms is not important—"money doesn't matter." For the Monetarist case, it does.

[20] Note that if (Y/P) is fixed, then either P or Y (but not both) becomes the variable to determine. It might be useful, to check your understanding of what is going on here, to try to develop the equations just described in terms of the model in this chapter.

considered some applications of the *IS-LM* model directly. It is also better to avoid excessive reference to Keynesians versus Monetarists, since what has just been described represents only the simplest versions of these theories (and, no doubt, represents ideas currently not held by any economists).

Our *IS-LM* model—with *P* given—has both a fiscal and a monetary policy in it now, with the former policy modified with reference to the money market. To visualize the effect of an increase in government spending let us shift the *IS* curve to the right, as we noted would happen in Equation (7.13). To visualize what happens, consider Figure 7.9, where there is an

Figure 7.9: The government spending multiplier with an *LM* curve

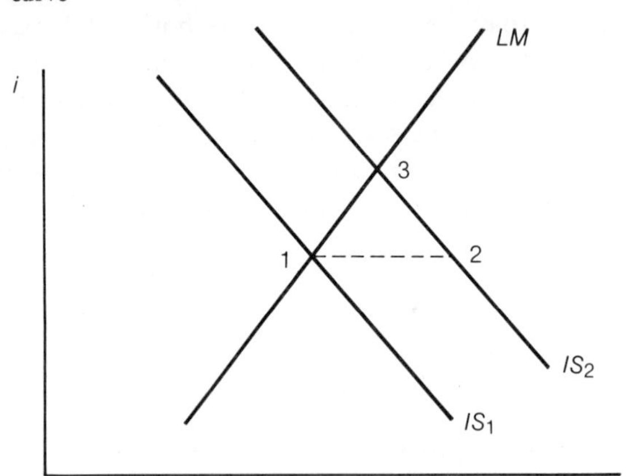

increase in government spending, which shifts the *IS* curve to the right. The simple multiplier of Equation (7.13) would take us from point 1 to point 2, but at point 2 the money market is not in equilibrium. To restore equilibrium in the money market, as the graph indicates, we must move up the new *IS* curve (IS_2) to point 3, in which case the interest rate *rises* and real income *falls* in order to bring the money market into equilibrium. Thus point 3 represents an "adjusted" government spending multiplier and, no doubt, also represents a more realistic solution to the question of the effect of fiscal policy (however that may be financed).

But we have ignored one further aspect of our model in this chapter: we have held the price level fixed and have not considered what might happen if it, too, could take up some of the slack created by the fiscal policy. To see how this might operate and to anticipate some of the discussion of Chapter 8, let us *assume* that there is a full-employment level of real income (call it y_f) and let us represent it as the vertical line in Figure 7.10. Let us suppose we start with IS_1 and LM_1 and overall equilibrium at point

Figure 7.10: Fiscal policy with flexible prices

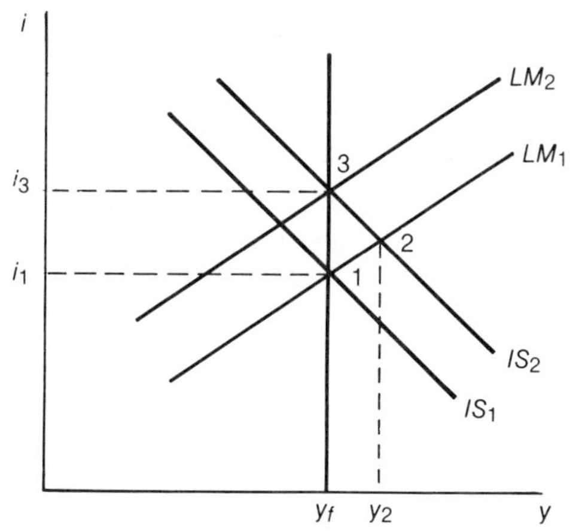

1. Then assume that an expansionary fiscal policy shifts the *IS* curve to IS_2 so that point 2, as in Figure 7.9, represents a solution for both the *IS* and *LM* curves. At point 2, though we are trying to generate a real income (y_2) greater than full employment real income (y_f). We cannot do this, of course, and so the net effect of the fiscal effort—financed by the expansion of the money supply represented by point 2 *on the LM curve*[21]—is inflationary, as attempts to bribe resources away from alternative uses in a fully employed economy can only result in inflation. The effect of a rise in prices, as we saw earlier, is to shift the *LM* curve to the left, and this movement is also shown in Figure 7.10. Indeed, overall equilibrium, so far as our model is specified, requires that we return to y_f, at a higher interest rate *and higher price level.* The fiscal policy, in this case, produced only inflation and higher interest rates as one might have expected under the working assumption of full employment.

Lest this be thought to be an attack on the usefulness of fiscal policy, let us hasten to add that monetary policy is subject to the same qualifications; consider Figure 7.11. Begin again at point 1 with both the spending and monetary sectors in equilibrium and let an increase in the money supply shift the *LM* curve to LM_2. But at point 2, just as with its counterpart in Figure 7.10, we are attempting to produce more than our resources will permit. *Again* the price level will rise, and again the *LM* curve will shift to the left, until (we can assume) we return to point 1, the original equilibrium position. Expansionary monetary policy, too, resulted in inflation, with the only difference between fiscal and monetary policy being that fiscal policy tended to produce a higher interest rate.

[21] Look back at Figure 7.6 or Equation (7.17) to see that this statement is, indeed, correct.

Figure 7.11: Monetary policy when prices are flexible

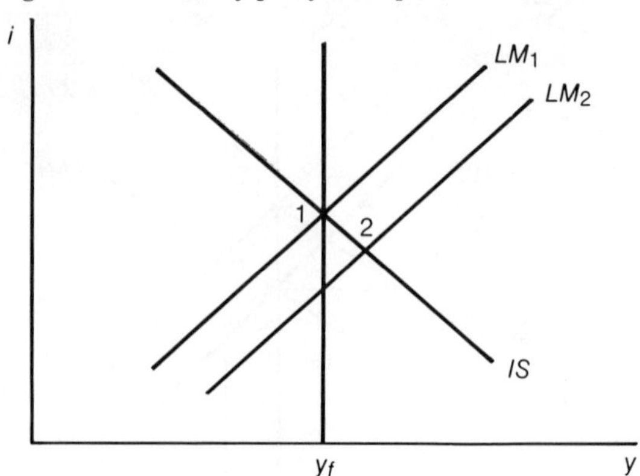

These examples illustrate the potential of the *IS-LM* apparatus to illuminate policy choices, especially in the event that y_f lies to the right of point 2 in Figures 7.10 and 7.11, but they also illustrate that some effort ought to be made to solve the problem of the determination of the third variable—the price level—which we have been handling in a rather casual fashion to this point. The model appropriate to that task—and of more general use on questions of inflation and unemployment—is the aggregate demand–aggregate supply model and we turn (in Chapter 8) to a consideration of its properties, as well as to some illustrations of our monetary and fiscal policy problems.

7.5 STUDY QUESTIONS

Essay questions

1. Consider, again, your answer to Question 4 in Section 6.6.

2. Consider, in the *IS-LM* Model, the net effect on the equilibrium values of income and the interest rate of

a. An increase in consumption coupled with a decrease in the supply of money.

b. A decrease of investment coupled with an increase in the demand for money.

3. Look at some recent national income data for consumption, investment, the money stock, interest rate and income and plot the relationships suggested in this chapter. How do the theories work out? Do things get better or worse when all of the nominal quantities are calculated in real terms?

4. Complete the *IS-LM* model of this chapter with investment *also* depending on real income and consumption also depending on the interest rate. Are any of the *qualitative* conclusions of this chapter altered? Why or why not?

True-false discussion questions

These statements are meant to be somewhat ambiguous and to provoke discussion, thereby.

1. Investment must equal saving for equilibrium to occur in the goods (spending) sector; this clearly implies that the supply and demand for money must also be equal if $I = S$, since one of the forms in which savings can be held is in money.

2. An increase in consumer spending implies an ambiguous change in real income and employment because it implies a rightward shift of the *IS* curve and a leftward shift of the *LM* curve (because of the reduction in the demand for money).

3. An increase in the supply of money leads to a rise in the price level but to no change in real income in two cases: when we are in Classical full employment or when we are in the "liquidity trap."

4. Since investment is only accidentally equal to saving, the *IS* curve is really only accidentally relevant; it is merely a borderline (in effect) between the realistic positions of the economy.

5. A reduction of the demand for money combined with a reduction of the supply of money will tend to have an ambiguous effect on income and the interest rate.

6. Both investment and the demand for money are negatively related to the interest rate, but only the former is along the lines of the "opportunity-cost" rationale.

7. If the government spends, then, at the very least, it must either tax or create money, since the spending has to be paid for in some way.

8. The main reason that an expansion of the money supply stimulates a growth in real income is that it lowers interest rates, and this, in turn, stimulates consumption and investment.

9. While the Federal Reserve can control the nominal stock of money (M), any attempt to control the real stock (M/P) runs into the problem that the demanders of money make their calculations in real terms.

7.6 FURTHER READING

The best approach to further reading for Chapters 7 and 8 is to work with any of the large number of intermediate macroeconomic theory textbooks. There is no need to list them. Two recent books that take a largely nonquantitative approach and that are written on many of the same topics covered here are the following:

Gordon, Robert J. *Macroeconomics*. Boston: Little, Brown and Company, 1978.

Dornbusch, Rudiger, and Stanley Fischer. *Macroeconomics*. New York: McGraw-Hill, 1978.

Two other books, at a higher level than this text, may also be useful:

Motley, Brian. *Money, Income and Wealth*. Lexington, Mass: D.C. Heath, 1977.

Crouch, Robert L. *Macroeconomics*. New York: Harcourt, Brace, Jovanovich, 1972.

The standard graduate level work, for those students already having completed an intermediate macroeconomics course, is

Branson, William H. *Macroeconomic Theory and Policy*. 2d ed. New York: Harper and Row, 1979.

8

A basic macroeconomic model (Part II: Aggregate demand and aggregate supply)

8.1 INTRODUCTION

Chapter 7 dealt with the familiar and useful *IS-LM* model, which was built up from the basic macroeconomic behavioral relations concerning consumption, investment, money demand, and money supply. What these sectors provide, *when combined,* is the aggregate demand for commodities (adjusted for the determination of money market equilibrium), but what they do not do is give us a firm hold on the major problems of macroeconomic policy, which concern excessive *inflation* and unemployment. Indeed, neither variable is even in the model to this point (although inflation is a positive rate of change of the price level, which itself is in the model) and so it is necessary to consider the counterpart to aggregate demand—aggregate supply—if we are to complete our formal discussion satisfactorily.

What we will do in Chapter 8 is outline the basic aggregate demand–aggregate supply model, using mainly graphical techniques (with a small amount of mathematics buried in the footnotes), beginning with aggregate demand (since it is basically a summary of work done in Chapter 7). When we come to consider aggregate supply, we will concentrate on the labor market—on labor supply and demand—and we will introduce, once again, the concept of money illusion, but this time we will place it in the labor supply function. The aggregate business firm will appear here, in addition, represented by a production relation (function), but its role will not be central to the policy material, and so we will only sketch out its function. We will, at the end, have a satisfactory model of inflation and unemployment and we will, in a final section, consider several policy situations, by way of illustration. Many other illustrations of the material in both Chapters 7 and 8 will appear in later chapters, especially up to Chapter 12.

8.2 THE DERIVATION OF AGGREGATE DEMAND

In Figure 7.8 we presented an overall solution to the *IS-LM* system in which an equilibrium interest rate and level of real income were shown to exist (at i_e, y_e). This was constructed for a fixed price level and, in the accompanying discussion, we showed that the effect of a rise in the price level is to shift the *LM* curve to the left, just as it shifts the M_s curve to the left in the money market (which is the only market underlying Figure 7.8 in which the price level enters). We may use these facts to generate an aggregate demand curve, as follows. Suppose, for example, that we repeat our experiments in Figures 7.10 and 7.11 and represent this as in Figure 8.1, where we are now interested in what happens to real

Figure 8.1: The effect of a change in the price level on real income

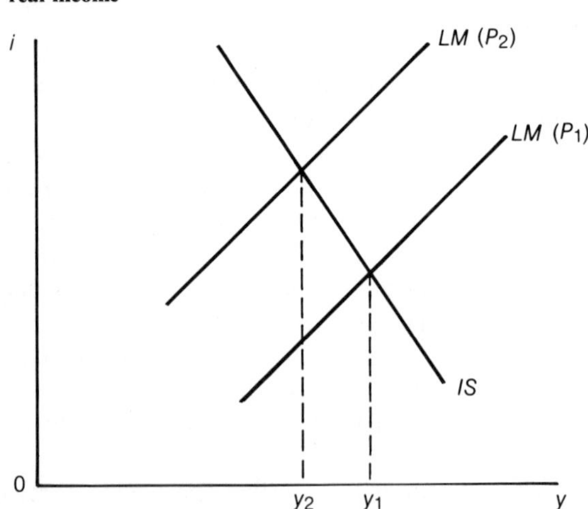

income, as measured along the horizontal axis, and are uninterested in what causes the price rise. As can readily be seen in the diagram, a *rise* in the price level from P_1 to P_2 is associated with a *fall* in real income in the *IS-LM* sector.

Now this result, which is perfectly clear analytically, also has a perfectly clear representation in a graph of P and y, as we can see from Figure 8.2. Here the pairs (P_1, y_1) and (P_2, y_2) are simply carried over from Figure 8.1. What this result says formally is that if the price level falls, real

Figure 8.2: Aggregate demand

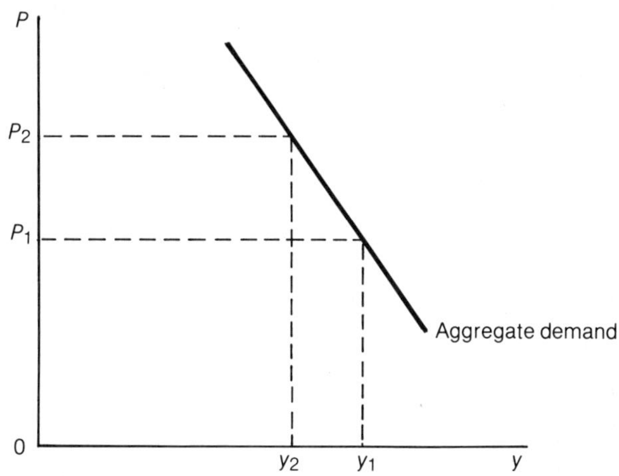

money balances will be destroyed (M^s/P shifts to the left) and as they are destroyed, the existing money stock can only be reallocated among the demanders if interest rates rise. The *LM* curve shifts left to absorb this effect and, since the *IS* curve is negatively sloped (since, in effect, investment will decline as the interest rate rises), real income also declines. This result should be clear at this point although an algebraic version of the curve can also be deduced by examining the equation in Footnote 18, Chapter 7.[1]

[1] We repeat that equation here:

$$y = \frac{\dfrac{f_1 - \dfrac{g_1}{P}}{f_3 + \dfrac{g_3}{P}} - \dfrac{a_1 + b_1}{b_3}}{\dfrac{a_2 - 1}{b_3} - \dfrac{f_2}{f_3 + \dfrac{g_3}{P}}}.$$

This equation, where P is now interpreted as a variable, is for aggregate demand. To see the slope clearly, if your calculus fails you, just substitute $M_s = g_1$ for $M_s = g_1 + g_3 i$, and a simpler form results. The role of g_3 is to provide a change in the slope, which complicates the calculation here.

8.3 THE DERIVATION OF AGGREGATE SUPPLY

To find a comparable relation for supply—that is, to find an *aggregate supply* curve—we must investigate how goods are supplied; this involves bringing in the labor market (and some explicit Keynesian analysis), as well as specifying more precisely how goods are produced. Let us begin with the aggregate firm. We might start by supposing that a typical (aggregate) profit-maximizing firm uses two inputs, capital and labor, in its production process; let us suppose that a linear "production function" describes how a firm combines inputs (L, K) to produce real outputs (X):

$$X = \phi(L, \bar{K}) = \phi_1 L + \phi_2 \bar{K}. \tag{8.1}$$

We will for convenience, also assume that the capital stock (K) is fixed ($K = \bar{K}$).[2] Here we will argue that an increase in the stock of labor induces an *increase* in production (X); indeed, the only way one can produce an increase in output is to take on more labor in view of the assumption we just made that the capital stock is fixed.

Equation (8.1) can directly provide a rationale for a simple demand-for-labor function for the aggregate firm. That is, *given a desired output* (X) and given the capital stock ($K = \bar{K}$), then under competitive conditions, the demand for labor would be a function only of the real wage (the interest rate is irrelevant since the capital stock is fixed).[3] This idea is represented by Equation (8.2),

$$L_d = h_1 - h_2 \left(\frac{W}{P}\right) \tag{8.2}$$

and is graphed in Figure 8.3. This relation is essentially based on (Neoclassical) microanalysis and, aside from the assumption of competitive markets, is not much challenged in the literature. Indeed, relaxation of most of our assumptions would not cause a different slope for this relation—after all, it is only the reasonable proposition that if the real cost of labor increases (other things held constant), firms will tend to hire a smaller number of workers—and the linear forms used in this chapter are arbitrary (and adopted for simplicity) and harmless enough. But the lack of controversy just referred to does not carry over to the *labor supply* function, which we will write here in a Keynesian form that nicely com-

[2] Since investment is not equal to zero in our spending equations (if they are to mean anything), the assumption of a fixed capital stock has to be regarded as a provisional one. Like the writing of investment in terms of changes in income rather than in terms of the level of income, the result of letting the capital stock vary is mathematically too complicated for the level of analysis of this book.

[3] To be more general, we would not take output as constant, in which case we would write $L_d = h(W/P, X)$. Below, we will achieve the same effect (approximately) by combining our equilibrium quantity of labor with Equation (8.1).

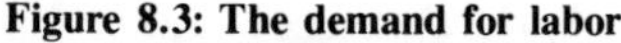

Figure 8.3: The demand for labor

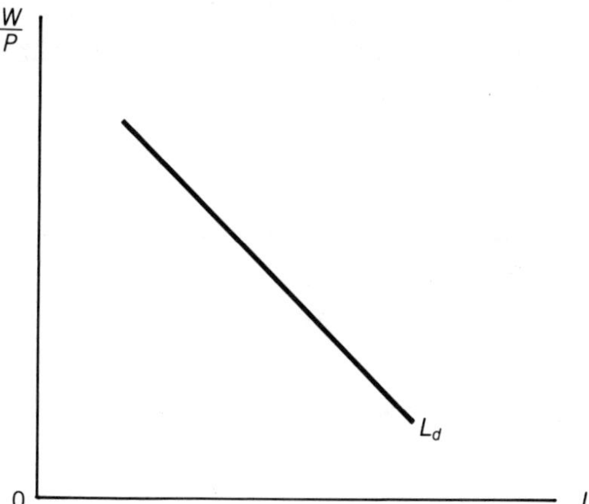

plements the Monetarist approach to this point; but first we need to consider how labor markets might function.

Workers, needless to say, are consumers, and, as such, they need income; they can get this, as things are set up here, only by offering their labor services. Furthermore, since work is generally unpleasant and, whether it is unpleasant or not, uses up *time* that could be used in other activities, workers will be willing to work *more* only if they are paid more. Many of us work on a contractual basis, in which a union of some sort or a governmental unit represents our individual interests in the labor market. These contracts often run for years, although they frequently contain the potential for revision. As well, no doubt, prior training and our tastes tend to lock us into certain occupations and, of course, into certain regions of the country (depending, partly, on the occupation). More important, at least to the Keynesians, is that many workers or their representatives probably will respond not to actual *real* wages, but to their *anticipated* real wages and may make mistakes in the calculation of their real wages and, accordingly, make offers of services that they later come to regret. This idea, that workers either through the technique of bargaining or by explicit error in their calculation of real wages, may imply that workers will actually respond to a rise in *money* wages, believing real wages to have risen, and actually offer more services in response *even when real wages have actually fallen*. This notion, that workers can be surprised by a rapid inflation, then, is a significant aspect of the Keynesian approach to the problem of the determination of income. In addition, it is a focal point in the discussion of the effect of monetary policy on the economy (although we will defer the complete discussion of that aspect until Chapter 11). Finally, and most relevantly for this section, it leads to an explicit aggregate supply function (in the Y/P, P space) and a last (and more general) solution to our determination-of-income problem.

The preceding comments imply that our labor supply function ought to be written in the form

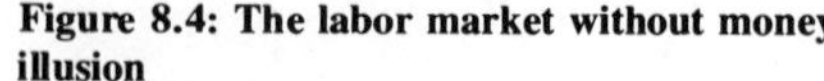

$$L_s = j_1 + j_2 \frac{W}{P_e}, \tag{8.3}$$

where P_e is the price level workers expect to rule over the period of the contract. If $P = P_e$, then both workers and bosses have the same (correct) real wage and a labor market solution, as in Figure 8.4, would result in which

Figure 8.4: The labor market without money illusion

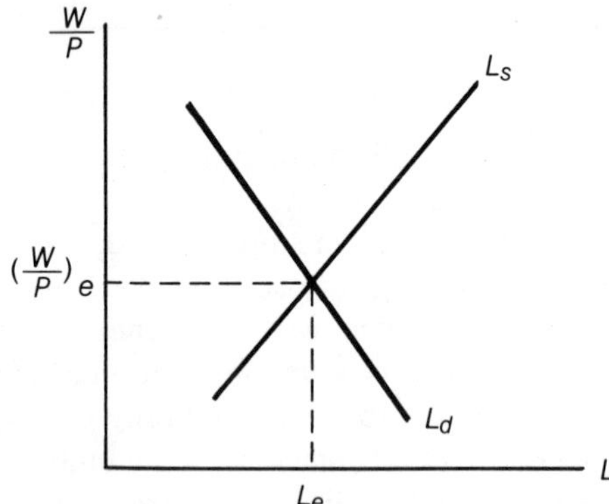

pairs of L and W/P would be determined. The quantity L would be carried to Equation (8.1), where it would, in effect, be converted to real output (X). Since the price level is not a factor in this solution ($W/P = Pw/P$, where w is the real wage), the "aggregate supply" which results would be represented by a vertical line as in Figure 8.5, and we could legitimately refer to this solution as a "full-employment" one in that all workers willing to work at $(W/P)_e$ in Figure 8.4 are, in fact, doing so. We may refer to this solution as the "classical full-employment case."

But suppose, instead, that P does not equal P_e and workers either over-anticipate ($P_e > P$) or, more likely, under-anticipate ($P_e < P$) the price level in their calculations. To make matters more concrete, suppose workers are faced with an inflationary surprise and they agree to a two-year contract on the basis of P_1, only to find later that in fact the price level is P_2, which is higher. In terms of Equation (8.3), what we are saying is that if workers expect the real wage to be (for example) \$3 an hour, and offer labor-hours in exchange for that, then if the real wage is *actually* only

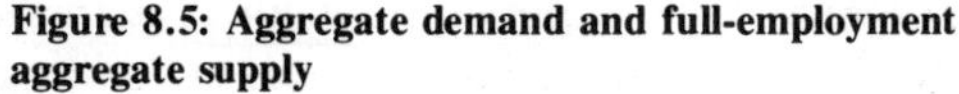

Figure 8.5: Aggregate demand and full-employment aggregate supply

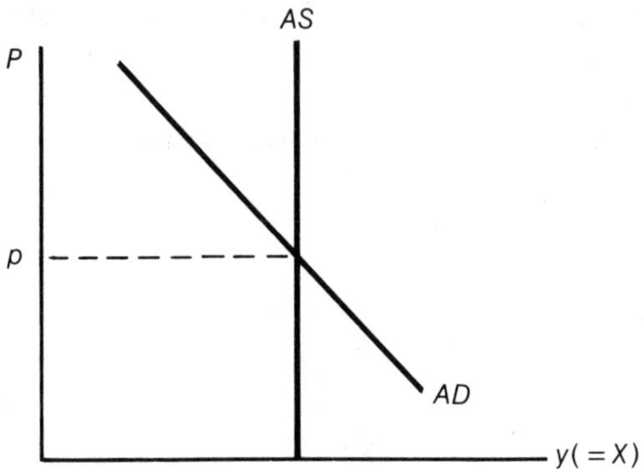

$2.50 an hour, the 4,000 hours offered is more than they would be willing to offer (for $j_1 > 0$) for the lower real wage (it isn't "worth it"). In terms of our labor-market equilibrium, what this suggest is that the labor supply curve will shift to the right if an *unanticipated* inflation catches workers by surprise (as well it might). The situation is graphed in Figure 8.6, where

Figure 8.6: The effect of an unanticipated inflation on the labor market

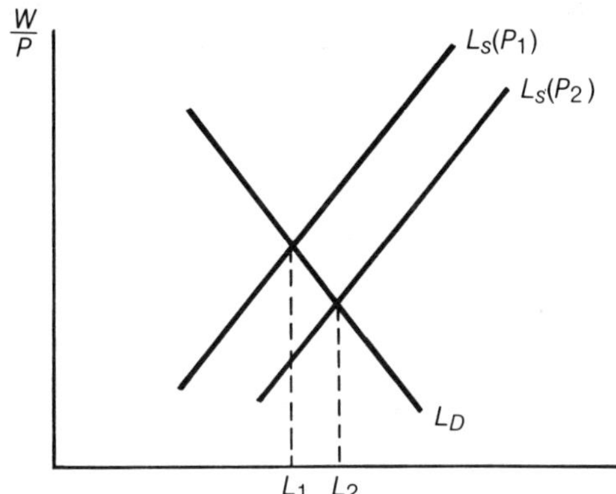

the result is a higher quantity of labor employed than would have been the case if no (unanticipated) inflation had occurred.

To see how the aggregate supply of commodities responds to the price level, we need merely repeat the experiment that underlay the construction of Figure 8.5. Thus, suppose that prices rise (and are not correctly anticipated) so that the actual number of workers hired is larger. By

Equation (8.1) this means that aggregate output is increased (it is more profitable to hire the extra workers who are, after all, willing to work more for less). Clearly, then, a positively sloped relation between P and X (=y) has been developed, as illustrated in Figure 8.7. This relationship is then

Figure 8.7: Aggregate demand and aggregate supply—the short-run solution

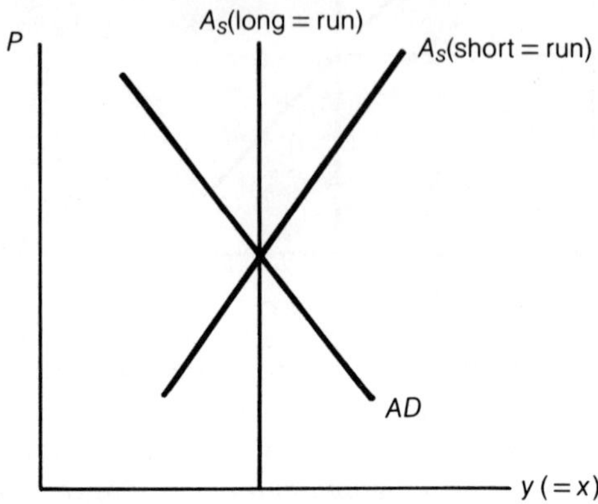

described as a "short-run" one for reasons that we will make clear immediately.[4]

The positive slope to the aggregate supply curve resulted from what we often refer to as a "trick" played (by the "creator" of the inflation) on

---

[4] To provide a more exact solution, in the manner of our previous footnotes, make the *extreme* assumption that $P_e = 1$, in which case

$$L_s = j_1 + j_2 W.$$

Combining this equation with that for the labor demand,

$$L_d = h_1 - h_2 \frac{W}{P},$$

we obtain, after eliminating W, the relation

$$\frac{L_d}{h_2} - \frac{h_1}{h_2} = -\frac{L_s}{j_2 P} + \frac{j_1}{j_2 P}$$

at equilibrium. For $L = L_d = L_s$, this produces

$$L = \frac{\left(\frac{j_1}{j_2 P} + \frac{h_1}{h_2}\right)}{\left(\frac{1}{j_2 P} + \frac{1}{h_2}\right)},$$

which, when combined with Equation (8.1), yields an aggregate supply of workers. This trick, which works because workers made a miscalculation, cannot be sustained in the long run because workers' self-interest dictates that they recalculate their work offers as soon as possible. In the long run, then, the aggregate supply curve will tend to swing back to the vertical position shown in Figure 8.5 and again in 8.7 as workers catch on to the nature of the "game" and *reduce* their offer of services in accordance with a *correct* real-wage calculation. Any macroeconomic policy, we may surmise, whose principal pressure is on the price level, has the potential of providing a reduction of *unemployment* (an increase of employment) in so far as it falsifies projections made by workers (and union leaders) as to what the true rate of inflation is going to be. To some economists (notably the Monetarists) this mechanism describes the main thrust of macroeconomic policy.

8.4 POLICY EXPERIMENTS IN THE AGGREGATE SUPPLY—AGGREGATE DEMAND FRAMEWORK

For our first experiment let us consider a type of deliberate policy such as that just suggested; that is, let us suppose the Federal Reserve initiates an easy money policy in order to reduce unemployment. By our model, we can link employment (and therefore unemployment) directly to aggregate output ($X = y$) and so the aggregate demand–aggregate supply model is the appropriate framework. In Figure 8.8 we illustrate the short-run

Figure 8.8: An inflationary monetary policy

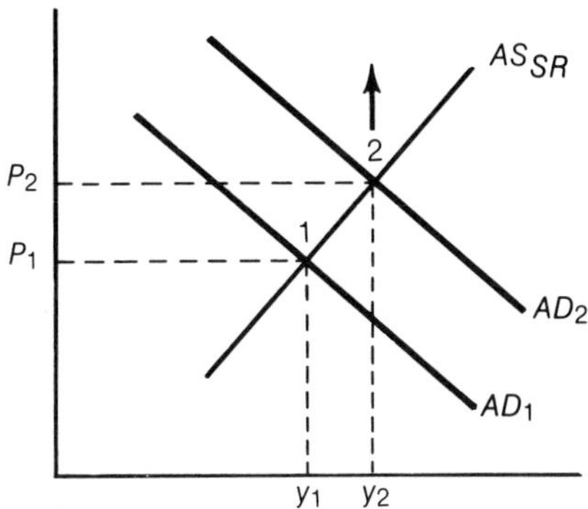

$$y = \phi_1 \left[\frac{\left(\frac{j_1}{j_2 P} + \frac{h_1}{h_2} \right)}{\left(\frac{1}{j_2 P} + \frac{1}{h_2} \right)} \right] + \phi_2 \bar{K}.$$

The assumption that the labor supply depends only on the nominal wage is not defensible, of course, but it is that of *extreme* money illusion. The text case, which is in the same direction, is more reasonable.

effect of the policy, which is to raise real income to y_2 and prices to P_2 (note that $(P_2 - P_1)/P_1$ is the rate of inflation—start with $P_1 = 1$. Now if y_1 is the long-run level of (full-employment) real income because the long-run aggregate supply is vertical at that level, then real income will tend to drift down (and unemployment up) unless further increases in aggregate demand (further injections of money) are made to prevent it. The economy *can* continue on the path marked by the arrow, at "overfull" employment, but the managers of the policy now run the risk that the short-run aggregate supply curve could start shifting backward more rapidly (as the rules of the game are made more clear) and y_2 can be maintained only at the cost of *accelerating* inflation. Perhaps, one might further conjecture, the few cases of runaway inflation in world history (to be discussed in Chapter 9) can be explained in this way.

As a second application of the aggregate demand–aggregate supply framework to recent policy consider the potential of a cost-push cause of inflation. Suppose, in particular, that labor unions press for higher wages, so that we get the result shown in Figure 8.9 for the labor market. This left-

Figure 8.9: Cost-push in the labor market

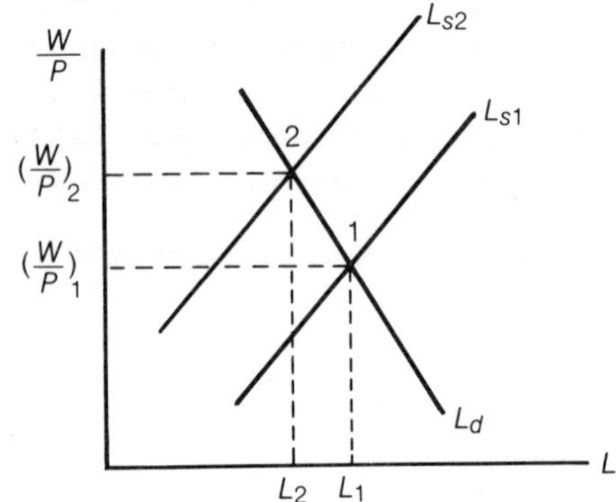

ward shift of the labor supply curve does, indeed, produce a rise in an important cost since the real wage then rises to $(W/P)_2$. *But* employment is less at point 2 (the new equilibrium in the labor market) and, via our production function, output must decline (and so unemployment, *ceteris paribus*, must rise). In turn, in terms of our aggregate demand and aggregate supply analysis, this leftward shift of the labor supply function produces (by itself) a fall in real income at (let us say) no change in the price level; aggregate supply must shift to the left, as illustrated in Figure 8.10. This shows a fall in real income and a rise in the price level at the new overall equilibrium point (point 2). Note that the movement back up the aggregate demand curve is effected by a reduction of the real money supply (M_s/P) so far as our aggregate demand "sector" is concerned.

Figure 8.10: Cost-push in terms of aggregate supply and aggregate demand

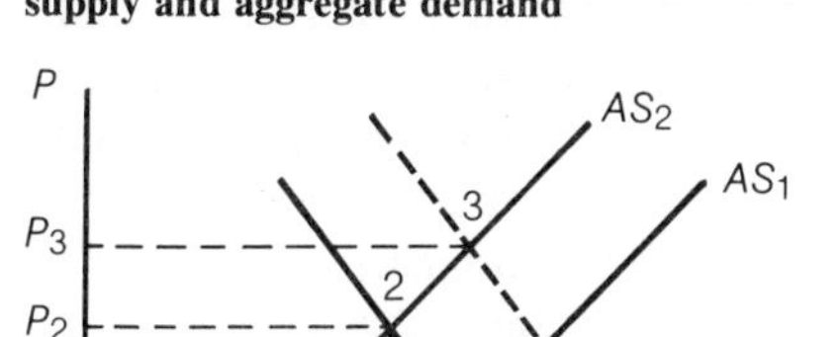

Now we come to an interesting result that is at the heart of the modern macroecnomic policy dilemma. Point 2 represents less employment (more unemployment) than a modern democracy might be able to tolerate. If left to itself, the situation might correct itself, for the unemployed workers created by the original cost-push force will now offer their services for less, creating downward pressure on wages and suggesting that a rightward shift of aggregate supply, which *increases* output and lowers unemployment, might soon ensue after the original change. This self-correcting mechanism would *certainly tend to* operate if point 2 in Figure 8.9 represents disequilibrium in the labor market. But of more interest is the fact that if significant unemployment crops up, whatever its source, the monetary (and fiscal) authorities may move to eliminate it, in an obvious way, by increasing the money supply and, thereby, shifting the aggregate demand curve to the right. This further shift aborts the effort of the labor market to return to equilibrium at the old price level; instead, we may move to point 3, where the labor market is back at the old level of employment (L_1 in Figure 8.9) and the price level is permanently higher, at P_3. This process is referred to as the "monetary accommodation" of a nonmonetary pressure (such as cost-push) and is an important ingredient of the *non*-monetarist explanation of the *causes* of inflation in modern times.

We may, in conclusion, doubt that the ever-weakening labor unions have had much to do with the rapidly accelerating (and sometimes decelerating) inflations that Western industrialized nations have had in recent years, but we do have other popular nonmonetary causes to consider, the most notable being OPEC. It is conceivable (and arguable) that the net effect of OPEC price increases in the early 1970s was to shift both the aggregate demand and aggregate supply schedules to the left, creating an intense pressure on Western governments to respond with monetary and fiscal stimuli, to avoid deep recession. If they did, and later chapters in this book will argue that there is a lot of evidence for this view, then increases in unemployment may have been "successfully" avoided until inflation became too severe to ignore. The move against inflation (look at Chapter 10 for the American version) may then have produced the recession (in 1974) that the earlier stimulus evaded. While the cause of the situation was nonmonetary, the extent *and severity* of the inflation, and the extent and severity of the contraction needed to restore inflation rates to resonable levels, was quite possibly *monetary*. In a nutshell, acceptance of the "OPEC recession" in (say) 1972 may well have produced a lower unemployment figure than acceptance in 1974. But we are now considering actual American experiences for which not all the data have been provided, so we turn, in Chapter 9, to a detailed discussion of inflation itself.

8.5 STUDY QUESTIONS

Essay questions

1. Consider what happens to the price level and real income, in the aggregate demand/supply model when

a. Consumption shifts upward and the supply of labor also increases.

b. Investment increases and the demand for labor also increases.

Discuss, in addition, the possible reasons why these pairs of events might actually come together.

2. Work out diagrammatically how a sudden lowering of the price for oil charged by OPEC might affect prices, interest rates, and real income. Be sure to justify carefully any monetary or fiscal policy you include in your analysis.

True-false discussion questions

These statements are meant to be somewhat ambiguous and to provoke discussion, thereby.

1. If aggregate supply is greater than aggregate demand, then a price level fall must occur, as the unwanted goods are disposed of; this process holds whether or not there is money illusion in the labor market.

2. The aggregate demand curve slopes negatively because any increase in real income necessarily implies an increase in both consumption and investment.

3. Our aggregate-supply theory concentrates on the labor market—especially on the supply of labor—and basically eliminates the aggregate firm by holding its contribution—the supply of capital—constant.

4. Cost-push inflation is a logical possibility, of course, but the conditions that it requires are unthinkable; this is especially true of the condition that the Federal Reserve accomodate the inflation with an increase in the money supply.

5. If there were money illusion in the commodity market (in, for example, the consumption function) and nowhere else in the sectors relevant to the aggregate demand curve, then the aggregate demand curve would tend to have a positive slope.

6. When we say that aggregate demand is a negative function of the price level, and that the price level is an important component of national income ($Y = Py$) then we are saying that a fall in national income inspires a rise in aggregate demand, *along* the aggregate demand curve.

7. The main reason economists now doubt the effectiveness of cost-push factors as a major force behind inflation is that such pressures tend to be self-defeating, in the absence of some sort of monetary accommodation (validation).

8.6 FURTHER READING

Look back to the references in Chapter 7 for the further reading appropriate to Chapter 8.

9

Inflation: Facts and theories

9.1 INTRODUCTION

In recent years "double-digit" inflation has become all too familiar a fact of life in practically every country in the world; at the same time, in many cases unemployment rates have also been unusually high for what most people consider to be relatively prosperous times, creating, jointly, a pretty dismal record for these same economies. In all likelihood, part of the problem is worldwide in that the recent timing of these events in all of these countries seems to have been approximately the same, so it is clear that we will not have achieved a full explanation until we have passed through Part IV of this book, where we take up the international aspects of our subject; there is, however, considerable material available on the national level to provide for a preliminary discussion. In addition, there are a considerable number of theoretical issues to consider.

Before turning to some data on inflation, we should attempt a definition of the concept itself. Basically, we understand by *inflation* that some price index is rising: the rate of change of this price index (or level) is positive; the opposite, then, is *deflation*. But we should note other definitions and other problems that emerge almost immediately. For one thing, as we noted in Chapter 1, a single price could rise and thus cause the average (level or index) to rise because of the fixed weights in the typical formula: is that inflation? For another, the items in the index could have improved in quality over the time period measured, and thereby fetched higher prices: is that also inflation? On the subject of alternative definitions we should note that the most popular of these is "too much money chasing too few goods." This is actually almost a theory of what *causes* inflation, in that if too much money chases too few goods, prices may well tend to (or actually) rise, other things being equal.[1] But we are clearly best off with the most straightforward approach to definition, in which any significant increase in the consumer price level is "price" inflation.[2]

Let us, before we plunge into the theoretical discussion, document the situation in recent years for a sample of countries; the calculations presented here were derived from figures collected by the International Monetary Fund (IMF). To read Table 9.1, consider the figures for the United States: in the eight years between 1953 and 1961, American consumer prices rose only 12 percent; in the next eight years they rose 22 percent; and from 1969 to 1977 they rose 65 percent. In 1977 they rose 6.5 percent and in 1978 they rose 7.5 percent. Most of the world's advanced countries had the same experience, and most recorded double-digit inflation in the 1970s, but the actual rates vary considerably between the countries, with a number of countries still remaining in double digits in 1977 and 1978 (Spain and Israel have the worst records in the top part of Table 9.1. These results suggest at least two problems, which we should try to resolve.

a. Why did practically all of the major industrial countries have gradually—and then suddenly—worse figures over the 24 years?

b. Why are the rates so different from country to country, particularly in recent years?

The answers to these questions will go a long way toward clearing up the question of what the main causes of inflation are, almost certainly, although the final answers must await the discussion in Part IV of this book, when we tackle what is now known as the "world inflation rate."[3] Note

---

[1] Because $MV = Py$, as discussed in Chapter 6; see Section 9.5 for a further discussion of this proposition. The "other things being equal" refers, for example, to V and y being held constant.

[2] It is put in this way because there is a popular concept known as "wage" inflation, which seems to mean either a rise in average money wages (which seems a useful concept) or a rise in consumer prices that is *caused by* a rise in wages. Indeed, there is no difference to some, since they believe that most price increases are wage-induced (the cost-push theories of inflation, for example). We will discuss these views further, below.

[3] Note that centrally planned economies (e.g., the Soviet Union) also have inflation problems. Thus from 1970 to 1975, Hungarian prices rose 15 percent, Polish prices rose 13 percent, and Yugoslavian prices rose 143 percent. In the Soviet Union, while consumer prices did not rise, nominal wages rose 20 percent and disposable per capita income rose 27 percent over the same period; there was, evidently, a problem of suppressed inflation (although possibly not a severe one). See R. Portes, "The Control of Inflation: Lessons from East European Experience," *Economica* (May 1977).

Table 9.1: Eight-year inflation rate in selected countries, 1953–1978

	1953–1961	*1961–1969*	*1969–1977*	*1977*	*1978*
Advanced					
and European					
United States	.12	.22	.65	.065	.075
Canada	.12	.25	.71	.080	.090
Australia	.23	.20	1.16	.125	.079
Sweden	.27	.36	.93	.114	.072
West Germany	.14	.22	.51	.039	.022
France	.37	.37	.94	.095	.092
Italy	.18	.38	1.45	.170	.117
Japan	.20	.54	1.19	.080	.038
Denmark	.23	.60	1.01	.111	.101
Israel	.60	.53	—	.346	.506
United Kingdom	.22	.35	1.65	.158	.081
Spain	.56	.68	1.67	.245	.197
Switzerland	.10	.32	.54	.013	.010
Underdeveloped					
Advanced					
Latin America					
Mexico	.65	.22	1.73	.264	.175
Argentina	5.57	4.32	203.31	1.761	1.755
Colombia	.82	1.49	2.90	.300	.174
Venezuela	.09	.10	.57	.077	.072
Chile	—	—	2216.59	.920	.320
Brazil	4.59*	21.65	5.48	.437	.387
Other underdeveloped					
Honduras	—	.19	.59	.087	.062
Malaysia	−.08	.08	.56	.048	.049
India	.22	.68	.81	.084	.025
Peru	.75	1.18	—	.380	.578
Turkey	1.38	.60	2.76	.261	.453
Guatemala	.03	.06	.91	.126	.079

* Wholesale prices.
Source: *International Financial Statistics* (IMF).

that an "oil-induced" inflation will be hard to prove on the basis of 1977 and 1978 inflation rates for the industrialized countries, many of which had more dependence on oil than the United States, *and less inflation.*

Table 9.1 also contains some figures for relatively less developed countries. These figures are much more variable than those for the advanced countries, with some underdeveloped countries enduring incredibly high inflation rates. Chile, for example, had over a 200,000 percent increase in prices in the 1969 to 1977 period and had almost a doubling of prices in 1977 (which, as things stand, was one of their better years).[4] Argentina, also, did not do very well in that period, (oil-rich Venezuela did do extremely well) and had a 176 percent increase in prices in 1977.

[4] Note that a figure of 1.00 in this table is a 100 percent increase in prices.

We will not discuss underdeveloped countries in this book in much detail, but we should at least offer an explanation of the figures we provided in Table 9.1. The main explanation of the variation among the underdeveloped countries is probably political, and among the political events most conducive to price disturbances is the revolution, although a revolution does not have to result in (or be produced by) a rapid inflation. More normally, many lesser developed countries have sought to tax their residents by increasing the money supply steadily (that is, by spending government-created money on goods and services) rather than by using the more direct methods of taxation available to the governments of advanced countries. Since the currency issue confers earnings on the central bank, and the central bank normally transfers its earnings to the treasury, this is a workable scheme, although the result is inflation (and, sometimes, excessively rapid inflation if things get out of hand). Brazil is one country that has been known to take this approach to its revenue needs (although as Table 9.1 shows, matters apparently got out of hand in the 1960s, when prices rose more than 2,000 percent); indeed, the rapid Brazilian inflation for 1977 and 1978 reflects the likelihood that the Brazilian government still uses this method of finance. At any rate, whatever the cause, hyperinflation (runaway or overly rapid inflation) is rare and has not been observed among the major industrial countries in recent years, so that problem does not seem to be an especially pressing one.[5] But for now let us turn to some

[5] In the table only Brazil (1961–69), Argentina, and Chile had any in recent years. Philip Cagan, in an important study in the 1950s, looked at seven European hyperinflations; the figures are as follows:

	Date	*Number of times price level rose*	*Number of times currency expanded*
Austria	1921–22	69.9	19.3
Germany	1922–23	1.02×10^{10}	7.32×10^{9}
Greece	1943–44	4.70×10^{8}	3.62×10^{6}
Hungary	1923–24	44.0	17.0
Hungary	1945–46	3.81×10^{27}	1.19×10^{25}
Poland	1923–24	699.0	395.0
Russia	1921–24	1.24×10^{5}	3.38×10^{4}

These are generally war- or revolution-related hyperinflations, although, one notes, the supply of currency was expanded by the government at almost the same pace that inflation was proceeding, in each case. These results, actually, imply a Monetarist cause of the hyperinflation in that if the rise of currency had been stopped, so too would have been the inflation, although, no doubt, once rapid inflation got going a collapse of the economy may well have resulted if such an action were undertaken. The general collapse generally came anyway, though, once the inflation really got out of hand. Reprinted from Philip Cagan, "The Monetary Dynamics of Hyperinflation," in Friedman, Milton, ed., *Studies in the Quantity Theory of Money* (Chicago: University of Chicago Press, 1956) by permission of the University of Chicago Press. © 1956 by The University of Chicago.

theoretical problems, before considering the contrasting theories of the causes of inflation.

9.2 THE REAL RATE OF INTEREST

One of the serious omissions in our discussion of the basic *IS-LM* model is that we have actually done our analysis in terms of the nominal rate of interest (which we designated as i). On the other hand, we emphasized the difference between nominal and real values in all our other variables (in particular the nominal versus the real values of consumption, investment, and money balances demanded). In the case of the spending totals we found that we could distinguish a nominal from a real value by *deflating* the nominal value with the price level (or index); what this deflation did was to remove from the variable the effect of changes in the value of money (or, if you prefer, changes in the average price of "everything"). Now interest rates, because they are, in effect, the ratio of money in the future to money at the present time (see Chapter 6), are already deflated in the sense just described; the new element—that is, the variable distinguishing the nominal from the real interest rate—is the rate of inflation. Consider the following example.

Suppose that the underlying interest rate for money to be paid back next year is 5 percent and that over the same time average prices are *expected* to rise by 2 percent; this underlying rate of interest, let us say, represents the real rate of productivity in the economy. Clearly, a person repaying a loan in a year's time will, other things being equal, pay back in dollars worth 2 percent less than they were at the start of the lending period; the purchasing power of the returned funds is, we are saying, expected to fall. If both lenders and borrowers have the same expectation about the inflation rate and if both act on their expectations, then, since the borrowers gain and the lenders lose an equal amount, the 5 percent interest rate will be marked up in the market by 2 percent to reflect inflation. In this event, we have

$$\begin{array}{ccccc} \text{Nominal or money rate of interest} & = & \text{Real interest rate} & + & \text{Expected rate of inflation} \\ 7\% & = & 5\% & + & 2\% \end{array} \tag{9.1a}$$

or, formally,

$$i = r + \left(\frac{\Delta P}{P}\right)_e . \tag{9.1b}$$

This is an interesting and important proposition: given a real rate of interest (r) that reflects the underlying "reality" in investment and consumption decisions, nominal interest rates (which are those actually observed in the market) will tend to fluctuate with the *expected* rate of inflation.

Furthermore, if the expected rate of inflation is related to the actual rate of inflation, as well it might be, then the nominal rate of interest will also tend to be related to the actual rate of inflation.[6]

What we have just described is a relation between the nominal interest rate and the expected rate of inflation; it was the expected rate because a loan contract automatically reaches into the future and necessarily involves expectations about changes in the price level (since the funds that are paid back must be spent or reloaned at future prices). We may, alternatively, look at actual data, and try to calculate the extent to which the actual rate of inflation has been mirrored in nominal interest rates. This provides us with a different type of real rate of interest that in this case tells us how much a lender actually got on his loan, in real terms, *after* an inflation actually took place. Let us illustrate this concept with a separate equation:

$$r_x = i - \left(\frac{\Delta P}{P}\right). \tag{9.2}$$

The x in Equation (9.2) indicates *ex post* (after the fact) and this r should not be confused with that of Equation (9.1), which involved the expected (*ex ante*) rate of change of prices; note, though, that the nominal interest rate (i) is the same in either equation (it is still the actually observed interest rate).

At this point we should look at some data, in order to fix the ideas. To begin with, Table 9.2 shows some sample real rates (r_x) for 1977 and 1978 for the United States. Here we see that there are many negative figures in the real rates (especially for the prime rate and the savings rate), possibly suggesting that the inflation that did occur in those two years was greater than that that had been anticipated (under the assumption that all borrowing and lending contracts had a term of one year). Indeed, for all but the fourth quarter of 1977, holders of savings deposits (passbook accounts) paid a substantial "tax" for the privilege of holding these deposits. Indeed, in 1978, some astronomically negative real rates were earned on passbook accounts. Here we see one of the undesirable effects of inflation: real interest charges become variable, upsetting the allocation of resources over time (compared to a stable price level), and some sectors (especially the small-saving and fixed-income sectors) have to pay a disproportionate share of the cost of adjustment to the new price level. It is no wonder that after a period of rapid (and no doubt partly unanticipated) inflation individuals sometimes seek to restore their savings at a more

[6] We can go one step further, if the actual rate of inflation is related to the actual rate of change of the nominal money stock (see Section 9.4), then the nominal rate of interest will be related to the rate of production of money. This, of course, brings us back to the monetary authorities, who have some control over the latter.

Table 9.2: A sample of nominal and real interest rates, 1977–1978 (averages for quarters)

Year and quarter	*3-Month inflation rate**	*Nominal prime rate*	*Real prime rate*	*Nominal savings rate*	*Real savings rate*	*Nominal bond yield*	*Real bond yield*
1977							
I	7.1%	6.25%	− .85%	5.00%	−2.10%	8.47%	1.37%
II	8.9	6.47	−2.43	5.00	−3.90	8.45	− .45
III	6.1	6.90	.80	5.00	−1.10	8.33	2.23
IV	4.7	7.67	2.97	5.00	.30	8.48	3.78
1978							
I	8.0	7.98	− .02	5.00	−3.00	8.77	.77
II	11.6	8.30	−3.30	5.00	−6.60	9.01	−2.59
III	8.2	9.14	.94	5.00	−3.20	9.13	.93
IV	8.5	10.81	2.31	5.00	−3.50	9.36	.86

* Expressed as an annual rate.
Source: *Federal Reserve Bulletin*.

rapid pace than usual (as we noted might have happened in the United States in 1974 (see Table 1.1).[7]

One obvious conclusion to be drawn from the preceding is that certain interest rates—those that are market-determined—will tend to reflect the actual rate of inflation (although, of course, not perfectly since it is the expectation of inflation that is built into the interest rate, not an actual rate of inflation). Thus if we seek an answer to why nominal (market) interest rates have been so high in recent years—and this includes private and government bond rates as well as mortgage rates—we need look no further than the rate of inflation to explain a considerable part of this phenomenon. In some ways this is not a serious matter, if one's income is equally flexible, since a market rate can take care of itself, but because of all of the "pegged" interest rates in the financial sector, it is clear that someone is bearing the real burden of inflation. And this burden is not necessarily on those most able to pay, of course.

Lest it be thought that this is a situation unique to the United States, consider some data for 1977, for the world's major industrialized countries, as shown in Table 9.3. There we find that 6 of the 14 industrialized countries (and 6 of the 8 with the highest inflation rates) showed negative real interest rates for the entire year—so the phenomenon is not limited to

[7] Why do individuals hold savings accounts that have a negative payoff? Ask yourself what advantages you get by retaining such accounts even when they deteriorate. You are likely to emphasize safety and liquidity as well as the (related) possibility that you may use the funds in the near future. These are obviously the sort of reasons people have for submitting to this form of "taxation." Of course it is also costly, in terms of time, brokerage fees, and information-gathering, to deal in better hedges against inflation, and these factors probably also contribute to the reluctance of wealth holders to reduce their liquid savings when they are being taxed so heavily by inflation.

Table 9.3: Nominal interest rates and inflation rates (14 industrial countries, 1977)

	Inflation rate	*Government bond yield*	*Real bond yield*
High inflation			
Italy	17.0%	14.62%	−2.38%
United Kingdom	15.9	12.73	−3.17
Sweden	11.4	9.74	−1.66
Denmark*	11.1	13.11	2.01
Medium inflation			
France	9.5	9.61	.11
Norway	9.2	7.39	−1.81
Japan	8.0	7.33	− .67
United States	7.8	7.67	− .13
Belgium	7.1	8.80	1.70
Canada	6.5	8.70	2.20
Netherlands	6.4	7.54	1.14
Austria	5.5	8.74	3.24
Low inflation			
West Germany†	3.9	6.60	2.70
Switzerland	1.3	4.05	2.75

* Average of first three quarters of year.
† Mortgage bond yield used for interest rate.
Source: *International Financial Statistics* (IMF).

the United States. Note, finally, that the countries with the highest inflation rates tend to have the highest nominal interest rates. This is in accord with the theory we have sketched in this section, which states that if actual inflation is rapid, then capital markets will tend to build in a premium on nominal interest rates to reflect the general expectation that the inflation will continue. We do not see (or expect to see) a perfect relation, as we have pointed out, because Table 9.3 reflects r_x and not r (and the two need not coincide). Active monetary policy also might be involved in these results, further obscuring the picture by controlling the short-term or even long-term interest rate, as we will discuss further in Chapters 11 and 12.

9.3 THE *IS-LM* MODEL WITH EXPECTED INFLATION

The basic model of Chapters 7 and 8 was built entirely on the nominal interest rate (i); in order to see how *expected* inflation itself can be a cause of inflation and in order to describe a process known as the monetary *validation* of nonmonetary influences, we need to extend the model. In the earlier model, the *IS* curve, now in a simple linear form, was written in the general form

$$i = n_1 - n_2 y \tag{9.3}$$

and the *LM* curve as

$$i = k_1 + k_2 y, \tag{9.4}$$

where y $(= Y/P)$ defines real income. Here, for example,

$$k_2 = \frac{f_2}{f_3 + \frac{g_3}{P}} \tag{7.17}$$

in the original formulation in Equation (7.17). Note that we are retaining the feature that the graph of Equation (9.4) shifts with changes in the price level.

When we introduce expected inflation into the model we immediately discover that the two sectors (*IS* versus *LM*) are probably not affected in the same way by inflation: in particular, we can argue that the spending sector ought to be written in r, the real rate, and the money sector in i, the nominal rate.[8] With regard to the consumption decision, for example, we could assert that since individuals might well expect both to spend and to earn future dollars that are equally inflated, they will look just at the real rate of interest and ignore (as consumers) their expectations about the rate of inflation. Consider your own situation: if you preferred present consumption to future consumption to the tune of 5 percent—and thus had to earn a 5 percent interest rate in order to bribe you to save anything—then, even if you expected all prices to rise by a further 2 percent, you would ignore this latter development, since (we are assuming) you fully expect your income to go up by 2 percent as well. You suffer no penalty, in this event, and you continue to calculate in real terms and will consume, in real terms, the same amount in both present and the future as you originally planned, no matter what the rate of inflation. Producers, too, will receive inflated product prices to match their inflated costs, and they, too, will tend to make their temporal allocation decisions in terms of the real interest rate. Thus, in these circumstances, Equation (9.3) should be written as

$$r = n_1 - n_2 y. \tag{9.5}$$

With regard to the monetary sector, though, things are quite different. First of all, we should note that we already have the price level effect included in Equation (9.4); that is, Equation (9.4) is partly based on the demand for real balances insofar as they depend on real income. Further, whether you have real or nominal money balances behind Equation (9.4), the nominal interest rate represents the income foregone by holding (non-interest-bearing) money balances (M_1). When the inflation rate goes up,

[8] Note that these concepts are as defined in Equation (9.1), not (9.2).

since your money balance is a final asset (you must forego real consumption to get any more real balances), you are taxed on your nominal balances and you get no gain anywhere else (the government or the banks will probably get it); thus you would require further compensation. To put it another way, if bond interest rates go up with the rate of inflation, the opportunity cost of holding non-interest-bearing (or fixed interest) money assets goes up, no matter whether you deflate the assets by the price level, or not; Equation (9.4), thus, is the correct way to write the *LM* curve when inflation is expected.

What we have, then, is a system with three equations, (9.1), (9.4), and (9.5), with three variables (i,r,y) and one "parameter" (the expected rate of inflation). To obtain a solution, we can go either of two ways; that is, we can substitute Equation (9.1) into (9.4) or into (9.5). We will, in our example, take the latter route and in the process eliminate the real interest rate.[9] This gives us an *IS* curve, after substituting $r = i - (\Delta P/P)_e$ into (9.5), of

$$i = n_1 + \left(\frac{\Delta P}{P}\right)_e - n_2 y. \tag{9.6}$$

We will continue with Equation (9.4) as our *LM* curve.

To see what happens to the workings of our system in this event, let us return to a picture of the basic *IS-LM* model; Figure 9.1 is the result. Now suppose that for some reason the expectation of a more rapid inflation becomes widespread in the economy, because economic agents have

Figure 9.1: The influence of expected inflation on the economy

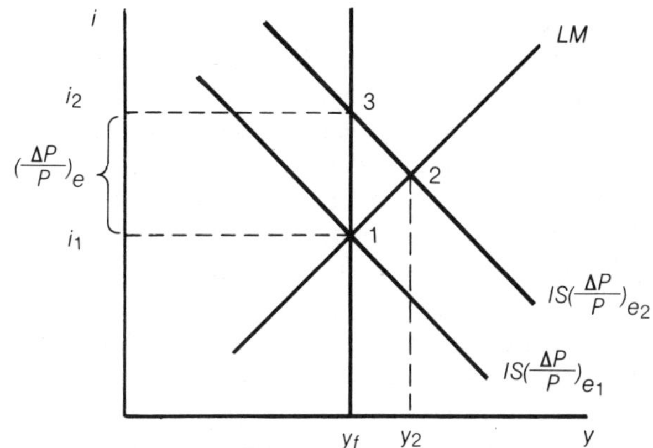

[9] The "real" interest rate refers to the marginal productivity of aggregate investment in this model, in *real* terms. It is not easy to measure this concept directly and this is the main reason for returning to the nominal interest rate here.

picked up information on, for example, a sudden increase in the monetary base.[10] As Equation (9.6) is written, this will shift the *IS* curve to the right, as drawn in Figure 9.1. Again, as in Chapter 7, we have an untenable situation in that equilibrium requires that the nominal interest rate rise to clear the market, and when it does, we are off the *LM* curve. Note that we are arbitrarily holding to the assumption of full employment—hence the vertical y_f curve—in order to simplify things. But we are not off the *LM* curve at point 2, and it is the contemplation of what happens there that provides the answer to how we get to point 3 in Figure 9.1. Let us look back at a picture of the money market, in Figure 9.2, to see what is going on behind our analysis. In Figure 9.2, then, point 1 represents the solution

Figure 9.2: The money market after an increase in spending

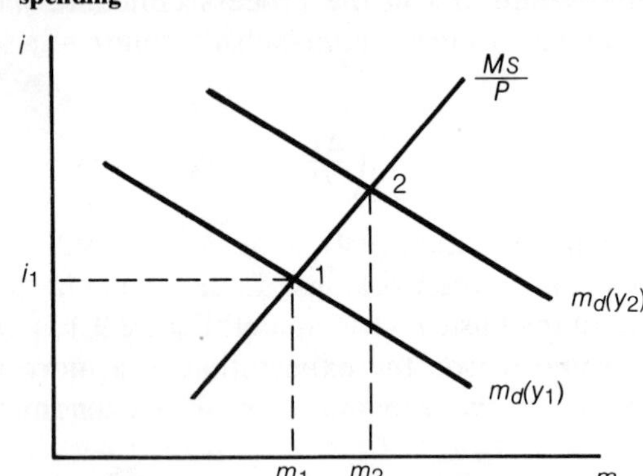

carried over from point 1 in Figure 9.1; further, if spending in real terms increases (recall that we put the inflationary effect on the *IS* curve arbitrarily) so that the *IS* curve shifts to the right, then real income will increase. In turn, in Figure 9.2, spenders will demand more money for transactions purposes (and the demand for money will shift to the right) and the authorities will supply more, so that the quantity m_2 results (recall $m = M/P$). This last explains what happens as we move out the *LM* curve in Figure 9.1.

At point 2, in Figure 9.1, then, we have an effective aggregate demand for a quantity of output of y_2; on the other hand, y_f is all the economy can

---

[10] We are going to say more, in Chapter 11 especially, on how price expectations might be formed, but for now we should note that the current view is that economic agents form their estimates on the basis of the past behavior of the money stock. In our example here we used the monetary base because a change in that may well *precede* the change in the money stock, as discussed in Chapter 5. Clearly, if this is how economic agents do form their expectations, then it is clear that they are accepting a Monetarist interpretation of what causes inflation, in effect (monetary validation aside).

produce. The resolution, clearly, is a rise in the price level in this "demand-pull" type of inflation although, to be sure, the demand-pull factor was merely the expectation of inflation in this example. What is interesting here, though, is that as a result of the rise in the price level, the *LM* curve will now start to shift to the left (look back to the discussion in Chapter 7 on this same point). In this event, so long as point 2 lies to the right of y_f, prices will rise; as they rise, the *LM* curve shifts to the left. The resolution is at point 3, where the pressure has come to an end and the rise in the price level has stopped, but, of course, at a higher price level. Notice, once again (as in Chapter 7), that if the authorities attempt to resist the rise in the nominal interest rate, and steadily increase the nominal supply of money so that the *LM* curve does not shift to the left, then we can have a permanent rate of inflation equal to the rate of expected inflation. We will have, in such a case, permanent disequilibrium in the economy in the sense that points 1, 2, and 3 are all necessary to characterize the "solution" of the system under this kind of pressure.

We have, once again, illustrated the process of the validation of a nonmonetary cause of inflation—in this case it was the sudden (and irrational?) increase in expected inflation—as it works through our simplified model of the economy. Notice, further, that the validation was of two types: one of these was perfectly natural and arose from the restoration of equilibrium in the money market at a higher interest rate; the other, the more virulent form, arose when the government (it is assumed) tried to hold to a particular nominal interest rate (i_1, in this case). In the first of these, when the interest rate was permitted to rise all the way to i_2, the inflation (price rise) eventually stopped; the process was self-defeating in that the rate of inflation (probably) would tend to decline as we approach point 3 in Figure 9.1. In the second instance, though, the expectation of a particular rate of inflation is rewarded with an actual rate of inflation of a quite possibly comparable magnitude. Indeed, in the second case it is just barely conceivable that an unstable (or runaway) inflation could occur. But note that we generally need the second stage type of policy—the increase of the supply of money to prevent the nominal interest rate from rising—in order to produce the rapid inflation here. To put the matter more forcefully, it is generally inconceivable that a rapid inflation can take hold of an economy for any considerable period of time without a helping hand from the producers of money (usually, that is to say, from the government). This does not mean that money uniquely causes inflation, but it does suggest a specific policy—nonvalidation—to deal with inflationary pressures; the technique, because it deals with the source of the inflation, is simpler and more obvious than controlling unions or directly attempting to fix prices. The latter are "causes," but only of disequilibrium (or change) and not necessarily of inflation. Of course, controlling unions might well be useful as an additional device, since a potential "causal" factor is removed in that way.[11] But validation is still necessary to make big inflations out of small inflations. Note that this applies to energy crises and all manner of important one-shot causes that would tend to shift the curves in Figure 9.1.

9.4 THE NONMONETARY CAUSES OF INFLATION

Roughly speaking, we can divide our analysis of the causes of inflation into two sets for purposes of classification: these are monetary and non-monetary. We have, to this point, considered an increase in the quantity of money as a causal factor (although not in much detail) and we have proposed that when nonmonetary forces are validated, inflation (even steady inflation) can be produced. But there is a considerable body of opinion, ranging from the professional economist to the man in the street, which holds that money production is merely a by-product of the inflationary process and that the causes lie elsewhere, in the real (that is, nonfinancial) sectors of the economy. Here, indeed, is where most of those who think of themselves as Keynesians take up their position.

We will take up some of these views here—although this is a book about money and financial markets—because many of these views are so widespread and, more relevantly, because many of these views are incomplete without careful reference to what is happening to the money stock. Before we go on, though, we should note that the evidence is actually in favor of many competing theories, at least the way things stand now, so we should not expect a resolution of these issues at this stage. Furthermore, while the traditional disputes—the cost-push versus demand-pull argument or the Keynesian versus the Monetarist dispute—have some value, we will downplay these confrontations here. The reason, mainly, is that inflationary pressures can arise anywhere and can be validated in quite an innocent way so that in practice the lines between these positions are actually quite fuzzy. Note, in addition, that our method of approach may not be neutral with respect to such things as the Keynes-versus-the-Classics debate.[12]

---

[11] If unions managed, somehow, to have a considerable effect it could be analyzed as a leftward shift of the y_f curve in Figure 9.1; this would be analyzed, then, in exactly the same way that the expected inflation was.

[12] In the analysis of Section 9.3 we chose to have inflationary expectations shift the *IS* curve and to work in (i,y) space. We could just as well have substituted Equation (9.1) into (9.4) instead of (9.3) and worked in (r,y) space, in which case inflationary expectations would have been seen to shift the *LM* curve, to the same effect (in the end). The point, really, is that consumers and producers are both money holders, and it is clearly incidental which way we go. A Keynesian might express a preference for the approach taken in Section 9.3 and a Monetarist the opposite, although, since the result is the same, there is no issue involved in that choice.

The first, and recently most commonly espoused nonmonetary view, is that of wage- and price-setting behavior as a primary cause of inflation. In particular, most frequently mentioned are increases in monopoly market power (which leads to higher product prices), increased trade union activity (which leads to higher wage costs and, by means of conventional mark-up price procedures, to higher product prices), and labor unrest (which leads to a reduction in the supply of labor and, in a normal labor market, to a higher wage). Behind these views one finds the idea that a change in the structure (or price) of a particular market leads to a change in prices in general. To begin with, we should note that both a rise of union power and a rise of monopoly power have to occur in those theories, since the mere existence of such power leads to no obvious effect even on the price of the product, unless you assume the firms involved were not maximizing profits in the initial situation (that is, that they had a lower-than-profit-maximizing price). This assumption of nonoptimal behavior seems far-fetched. Indeed, put this way, when you have to explain variable rates of inflation such as those we have exhibited (both over time and across countries) in Table 9.1, it seems clear that this sort of effect could at best be only a small part of a general collection of nonmonetary hypotheses. Furthermore, it is arguable that monopoly and union power is not even increasing (or varying) sufficiently to explain much of our recent actual inflation experience; this seems especially obvious when you compare different countries. Note that union power, as measured by the percentage of workers unionized in the American economy, is actually declining.

But the cost-push theory also relies on the method of transmission of a cost-push force as it works its way through the economy, and in this event it is on firmer ground. In particular, if most prices and wages are rigid downward (as Keynes thought) and if price changes in general are artifically "administered," then general price rises could occur by a kind of ratchet effect. What we are saying here, in effect, is that the economy is not in competitive equilibrium, or anything like it, and that average money prices respond when individual prices change. This is, of course, especially clear in the cases when (*a*) the price index, because of its fixed weights, simply rises (as it did when the oil crisis came) or (*b*) when the unemployment that results from a cost-push pressure is attacked by the government with fiscal and monetary policy. To repeat, rigidities and the cost of resource reallocation could bring some inflation, although, to be sure, one may be permitted to doubt its staying power once the force has spent itself, without some sort of extra monetary accomodation (validation).

The other major nonmonetary theory is that of the "demand-pull" force, and it essentially involves the role of big government. Actually, we referred to one form of this force in the last paragraph when we said that a cost-push force that produced unemployment, for example, could be turned into an inflation by fiscal and monetary policy directed toward unemployment. More generally, a government that is steadily increasing in size could bring about a number of pressures on prices, and all of these sources have their advocates:

a. The pressure of increasing government expenditures on an economy near full employment.
b. The pressure of higher rates of taxation or higher interest rates on the costs of business firms (this is a popular cost-push hypothesis).
c. The general erosion of the forces of competition by the encroachment of the government (at fictitious prices) in decisions previously made by the more efficient market.
d. The political need to finance government expenditures by bond issues (and money creation) at fixed interest rates (the latter to keep the burden of the national debt down).

We have already discussed the last, in effect, and must consider it a valid nonmonetary candidate, along with the "validated unemployment" theory. Of course, money is "involved" here, as it probably must be since when we discuss inflation we are discussing the rate of change of the exchange value of money (the price level).

9.5 THE MONETARY HYPOTHESIS

Basically, the Monetarists argue that the principal influence on money income, or on the price level, is the quantity of money; indeed, to put it baldly, a really convinced Monetarist would say that there has not been a persistent inflation without an accompanying or preceding increase in the quantity of money. Formally, he might argue that an increase in the stock of money is both necessary and sufficient to explain a general rise in average prices.[13] We will have to consider in more detail, in Chapters 11 and 12, exactly how a monetary impulse works its way through the economy (and contrast this approach with some alternatives), but for now let us lay out some cases in which the monetary hypothesis is clearly true and then look at some recent evidence. This should convey the flavor of the Monetarist view reasonably well, in much the same way we illustrated the non-Monetarist position.

Consider, first, a situation (often assumed by the Monetarists) in which the monetary authorities can and do determine the quantity of money, possibly even for policy reasons (that is, deliberately); we will use the

---

[13] He might not even add the proviso "other things being equal," which certainly would enable him to lean on the equation of exchange as "proof."

Federal Reserve as the straw man here. In Chapter 6, in order to illustrate one of our propositions about the demand for money, we used the equation of exchange, $MV = Py$, both as a relation that must hold and as a statement about the demand for money in a Classical-Monetarist model. This equation can also be written in a dynamic form—that is, can also refer to percentage changes in its components—in which case we have

$$\frac{\Delta M}{M} + \frac{\Delta V}{V} = \frac{\Delta P}{P} + \frac{\Delta y}{y} = \frac{\Delta Y}{Y}. \tag{9.7}$$

Here we are saying that the percentage change in nominal income ($\Delta Y/Y$) consists of the percentage change in real income ($\Delta y/y$) and the percentage change in the price level ($\Delta P/P$, which is, of course the rate of inflation). By the assumption that goods must be purchased with money, these changes in purchases must equal the actual percentage change in the quantity of money ($\Delta M/M$) plus the percentage change in the number of times money is spent ($\Delta V/V$) in the time period in which the changed expenditures occurred.

Immediately, we can move to a full-employment interpretation of Equation (9.7). If we are at full employment ($\Delta y/y = 0$) and if payments habits are fixed ($\Delta V/V = 0$), then any increase in the rate of production of money must be accompanied by inflation (and conversely). To take a more realistic situation, if the rate of production of money is greater than the rate of increase of real income minus the rate of increase of velocity, then inflation must result; that is, Equation (9.7) implies that

$$\text{if } \frac{\Delta M}{M} > \left(\frac{\Delta y}{y} - \frac{\Delta V}{V}\right), \text{ then } \frac{\Delta P}{P} > 0.$$

This can be directly verified, with numbers, of course. Thus, whether or not all inflations have been caused by or triggered by monetary injections (that is, whether or not a monetary injection is necessary for sustained inflation), it is clear that our monetary authorities can produce any reasonable rate of inflation by a suitable monetary policy (provided, as seems likely, $\Delta V/V$ does not totally frustrate their efforts). The money hypothesis is certainly a *sufficient* explanation of inflation. We can, though, produce inflation in another way here; thus, if $\Delta M/M$ and $\Delta V/V$ are fixed, then a slowdown of the rate of growth of real income (y) could itself produce inflation according to Equation (9.7). While this case may not have been of much empirical interest in recent times, given that money is usually running ahead of everything else, we will discuss, in Chapter 17, an instance in American history (over the entire period from 1873 to 1896) when prices actually fell steadily. This was a period of rapid growth in real income but of relatively slow growth in the quantity of money ($\Delta y/y > \Delta M/M$). So such things can happen, although by far the most volatile component of Equation (9.7) is the quantity of money, under "normal" conditions.

Now there is something in modern monetary control that we will discuss in more detail in the next three chapters that leads one in the direction of the Monetarist interpretation of events; this has to do with the "real" versus "nominal" interest rate problem. In Equation (9.2), above, the actual rate of inflation appeared; in Equation (9.1), the expected rate of inflation appeared.[14] What these equations together tell us is that the nominal rate of interest normally will respond to the rate of inflation and that this response is not the usual "tightness" or "ease" that the layperson (and the newspaper) attribute to all changes in the nominal rate of interest. In effect, it is a money illusion to think that a rise in the interest rate that was actually caused by a rise of $(\Delta P/P)_e$ was caused by a rise in r. It would seem, further, that this simple relation has not penetrated very far in official thinking or, for that matter, in popular discussion, even though it is a 19th century discovery, in its formal version. Let us consider an example.

Suppose we begin with a stable-prices set of values for Equation (8.7) of 4 percent for $\Delta y/y$, 4 percent for $\Delta M/M$ and no change in V or P. Indeed, it would be plausible also to assume that the nominal interest rate is constant, too, at 6 percent. We will want to return to causes from time to time, but, for the moment, let us suppose that $\Delta y/y$ suddenly decreases, say to 2 percent, perhaps as a result of an oil crisis or the approach of full employment (real income is growing, but its rate of change has fallen to 2 percent). Under these circumstances, with the rate of change of the money stock assumed to be unchanged, real money balances will rise by 2 percent, in line with the expansion of real output; this is illustrated in Equation (9.8), in which the consequence is that the price level must rise by 2 percent, under our assumptions:

$$\frac{\Delta M}{M} + \frac{\Delta V}{V} = \frac{\Delta P}{P} + \frac{\Delta y}{y} \quad ; 4\% + 0\% = 2\% + 2\%. \tag{9.8}$$

The Federal Reserve, in this situation, might consider adopting either of two policies, for, after all, they cannot control P or y directly: either they might hold interest rates steady (for the time being) or they could

[14] Note that Equations (9.2) and (9.7) can be solved simultaneously to yield

$$\frac{\Delta M}{M} + \frac{\Delta V}{V} = (i - r) + \frac{\Delta y}{y}.$$

This can be used to demonstrate a very Neoclassical model of inflation. If $\Delta V/V$ and $\Delta y/y$ are constant, then one can make the nominal rate different from the real rate by a suitable injection of money. The result, by Equation (9.2), is inflation. Why would one want to (say) raise the interest rate? Perhaps because the economy is experiencing a balance-of-payments problem and it is desired to attract short-term capital from abroad. Incidentally, this analysis is very similar to the one that continues in the text, which is descriptive of Monetarism. The Neoclassical analysis I have in mind is that of Knut Wicksell, *Interest and Prices* (New York: Kelly and Millman, 1965).

consider holding the rate of growth of the quantity of money at 4 percent. We will refer to stabilizing M or i as their alternative targets, where their goal is overall "stability," loosely.[15] First of all, then, let us suppose that the Federal Reserve has decided to stabilize the interest rate.[16]

When the Federal Reserve stabilizes the interest rate, the interest rate they work on is the nominal rate of interest; but, as we have seen, when there is an increase in the rate of inflation, the nominal rate of interest will tend to rise. Let us suppose that the increased inflation, in our example, leads to an increase in the nominal rate of interest to 8 percent, up 2 percent because of an expected (future) increase in the rate of inflation. Now if the Federal Reserve is controlling nominal interest rates through open market operations—that is, by buying securities in order to push up their prices and push down their yields—it will tend to push the nominal interest rate downward. But this action will tend to increase the money stock by, let us say, an additional 2 percent per year. This expansion will throw Equation (9.8) out of balance; if we argue that real income cannot expand any further and that velocity remains constant (it might in the short run), then the rate of change of prices would tend to rise to 4 percent per year. Obviously, things can go on like this forever, for nominal interest rates *again* would tend to go up, and so would the rate of inflation if the Federal Reserve continued to try to restrict the money interest rate to 6 percent by increasing the money supply. The economy might now be described as "overheated" because the rate of inflation is increasing, and money might be described as "tight" because interest rates are higher (and rising, if we press on); but these words do not describe the situation correctly for the money supply is plentiful in relation to the demand for it. Even nominal Gross National Product would be rising—by 6 percent—mostly on account of the increasing rate of inflation, which the Federal Reserve, by this time, is really directly causing.

In this case the opposite policy—that of controlling the rate of growth of the money stock—would not have produced this result. This is easy to appreciate because, clearly, the worst we would have experienced in that case was the original 2 percent inflation if the monetary authorities did nothing. Further, if the authorities had reacted to a rise in the rate of inflation by reducing the rate of growth of the money stock to 2 percent, there would have been no ultimate increase in the rate of inflation at all.

---

[15] We are not, of course, claiming the actual Federal Reserve policy is this simple-minded. Nevertheless, (especially in Chapter 12) we will point out that there has been more than a touch of this myopia in their behavior in recent years *and,* we should add, there is *no* clear evidence that they concern themselves with the nominal/real distinction.

[16] We will also allow that there are perfectly good reasons for doing so, the most important of which is simply that they think that stabilizing the interest rate means stabilizing the economy. They might also think that stability in the financial markets, in the sense of unchanging prices, is more important than anything else.

Control of the money stock rather than control of interest rates is essential if we are to have stability of the price level under these conditions. The limit to this process in our example is, of course, some reversing action, based on the realization that the policy is misguided. Most likely, of course, is the possibility that the Federal Reserve will suddenly decide to let interest rates go higher and slow down the rate of growth of the money stock. But, as you can see, an important potential cause of the observable instability of prices comes from (or could come from) an official policy of stabilizing the nominal interest rate. This process is an important part of the Monetarist version of the causes of inflation if only because modern governments (not only the American) are known to prefer stable nominal interest rates, for various reasons.

Finally, let us consider two sets of evidence of the relative importance of the monetary view—mostly to illustrate what is going on—in addition to the evidence that was scattered around in our earlier historical surveys. For one, consider the data on hyperinflations in Footnote 5 of this chapter. We showed that a monetary injection was part of the story. Thus, in Hungary, prices rose by a factor of 3.81×10^{27} while the quantity of money became multiplied by 1.19×10^{25}. Let us be clear on this: while the quantity of money did not rise as much as prices (either because of a change in velocity, a change in real income, or because people "over-reacted" to the existing inflation), it had to be increased more or less equally for prices to go that far. That is, somebody actually had to issue new bills, in new units presumably, and banks had to lend, in the new units, right up to the number 1.19×10^{25}. It must have taken a lot of paper. Why, then, did the governments involved actually issue so much new money? The answer seems related to two factors:

a. These were war-torn economies in which the traditional tax-collecting machinery had broken down, so a "tax" on money was deemed a useful way to get real resources for the governmental sector, in efforts to reconstruct the economy.

b. The effectiveness of the tax eroded quickly, as people caught on to the nature of the game and revised their expectations accordingly. In this event, since the government still wanted its real resources, it felt it had no choice but to step up the rate of production of nominal money balances.

Indeed, in all seven cases illustrated in Footnote 5, calculated real tax revenues were pretty steady in the early months of the inflation but declined in the middle; this decline was followed, near the end of the hyperinflation, by a spurt of money creation, which was followed by a spurt of inflation and then, almost immediately, by a collapse of the inflation (and, in general, by a collapse of the economy). Whether or not one thinks a "money-tax" policy was the cause of these inflations, one has to agree that a runaway inflation is undesirable on the record (because it ends in a general collapse of the monetary system).

Turning to a case when inflation did not run away, let us look at American data in the period of the "great inflation" of the early 1970s.[17] The broad facts are the following: the United States emerged from a time of recession and fairly low growth (and high unemployment) in the 1969–71 period into a prosperity that was slowed down, but not halted, by

a. Widespread crop failures.
b. An increase in the price of oil by some 400 percent.
c. A generalized and probably negative effect of environmental and safety control measures on productivity.
d. A system of wage and price controls (in several phases), which may have reduced efficiency but, at least, probably reduced the ability of the system to respond to the shocks from items (*a*), (*b*), and (*c*).

These factors, especially the first two, are widely believed (by non-Monetarists, especially) to have (*a*) produced the rapid inflation in the period, and (*b*) ultimately produced the recession of 1974–75 in the United States (and in all other countries in which people either eat or drive cars).

Let us, first, document the "real" downturn in the United States, in the figures in Table 9.4; note that there is no dispute by the Monetarists over the factual accuracy of points (1), (2), and (3) above, so we will not present figures on these aspects of the situation. Here we see that real GNP (y) began to decline in the first quarter of 1974 and did so, at quite a rapid rate, until the second quarter of 1975; the unemployment rate also began to rise at the same time, peaking one quarter later than the low point in GNP; the total of 8.7 percent was the largest since the 1930s.[18] Again, these facts are not in dispute, although, as we shall see, what caused the downturn and, indeed, what caused the inflation, is.

Turning to the monetary and price story, let us consider the figures in Table 9.5; we include figures on the federal budgetary deficit, expressed as a percentage of nominal GNP. The monetary hypothesis emerges pretty clearly from these figures. In particular, the rate of growth of the money supply—perhaps designed to ward off unemployment (if it was, it was pretty successful), perhaps designed to stabilize the nominal rate of interest—rose sharply in 1972, reaching an annual rate of growth of almost

[17] For later reference we should note that this inflation was experienced by all countries (see Table 9.1); we will return to a more specific discussion of some of these other countries in Part IV of this book.

[18] Note that we have not come close to the 4.8 percent rate of unemployment since then, even though a very long period of prosperity has ensued. The reasons are complex, of course, but two factors seem most important: (*a*) the *natural* (or equilibrium) level of unemployment may well be *higher* than 5–5.5 percent and (*b*) the earlier levels were too low in the sense that they could be maintained only at a high (*and rising*) rate of inflation.

Table 9.4: Real activity in the United States, 1973–1976

Year and quarter	*Real GNP (compounded annual rate of change)*	*Industrial production index (compounded annual rate of change)*	*Unemployment*	*Total civilian employment (compounded annual rate of change)*
1973				
I	9.5%	—	4.9%	—
II	0.4	5.8%	4.8	4.8%
III	1.7	4.1	4.8	2.1
IV	2.1	2.5	4.8	3.8
1974				
I	−3.9	−4.8	5.0	2.5
II	−3.1	3.7	5.1	0.7
III	−2.6	2.5	5.6	0.5
IV	−6.8	−20.1	6.7	−3.1
1975				
I	−9.9	−31.9	8.1	−5.6
II	5.6	3.6	8.7	0.6
III	11.4	24.0	8.6	3.3
IV	3.3	10.0	8.5	0.5
1976				
I	9.2	12.2	7.6	5.6
II	4.3	7.4	7.4	5.3

Source: Donald S. Kemp, "Economic Activity in Ten Major Industrial Countries: Late 1973 through Mid-1976," *Review, Federal Reserve Bank of St. Louis* (October 1976).

9 percent by the end of the year. A confirmed Monetarist at this point would then have asserted that within 6 to 18 months, a comparable rate of inflation would appear, other things being equal. Thus, the sudden spurt of inflation (the rate of inflation for the entire year of 1972 was 3.4 percent) in early 1973—notice how close the figures for the inflation rate are to those for the money supply, *one year earlier*—would be explained, by the Monetarists, as the by-product of the excessive monetary expansion. As we have seen earlier, the non-Monetarists would also have an explanation, involving rigid prices in the downward direction (and the like).

The last question we might try to answer here concerns what brought about the recession, which showed up in the first quarter of 1974, at the same time that the inflation rate was approaching its peak (remember *stagflation?*). No doubt the real events mentioned above—postponed by the aggressive monetary and fiscal policy[19]—were largely responsible for the recession, but one should notice that by the first quarter of 1974, the rate of monetary expansion was only half the rate of inflation, suggesting tight money by a Monetarist's definition, so that it could be that an exces-

[19] Although Column (3) of Table 8.5 hardly shows any aggressive fiscal policy (if that is the correct way to measure fiscal influence anyway).

Table 9.5: Money, prices, and the budgetary deficit in the United States, 1973–1976

Year and quarter	*The money supply (2-quarter moving average of compounded annual rates of change)*	*Rate of inflation (2-quarter moving average of compounded annual rates of change of consumer price index)*	*Net federal budget position as a percent of nominal GNP (annual rates) (+ = surplus, − = deficit)*
1972			
I	5.0%	—	—
II	7.9	—	—
III	8.5	—	—
IV	8.9	—	—
1973			
I	8.4	4.9%	−2.99%
II	7.1	7.5	2.38
III	6.1	8.7	−0.32
IV	5.4	9.2	−1.49
1974			
I	5.7	11.2	−2.06
II	5.9	12.0	2.78
III	5.0	11.8	−0.44
IV	4.2	12.3	−3.30
1975			
I	2.3*	10.3	−4.99
II	4.1	7.2	−3.14
III	7.4	7.3	−4.78
IV	4.8	7.5	−6.69
1976			
I	2.5	5.6	−5.55
II	5.6	4.6†	—

* Low point in the money supply.
† Low point in the inflation rate.
Source: Donald S. Kemp, "Economic Activity in Ten Major Industrial Countries: Late 1973 through Mid-1976," *Review, Federal Reserve Bank of St. Louis* (October 1976).

sive decrease of the rate of growth of money tipped the economy into recession (interest rates were very high then), which began in early 1974. Note, finally, that the low point in the inflation (marked †) follows the low point in the rate of growth of the money stock (marked *) by some months as well, so that the Monetarist hypothesis has some merit on the way up, too, at least in interpreting the events.[20] Finally, note that fiscal policy, after a considerable delay, may have gotten the economy going in early

[20] The way a Monetarist would explain the persistence of inflation during 1974, even though the money series had turned down after 1972, is through the negative figures for the growth in GNP. That is, recall from Equation (9.8) that a slowdown of economic activity, given a smaller slowdown in $\Delta M/M$, would, given $\Delta V/V$, produce a rise in $\Delta P/P$. We were still overproducing money, that is to say, in the 1973 to early 1974 period, compared to the falling demand for it. And velocity may not have been rising in response to the rising interest rates, further exacerbating the situation.

1975, since this figure picks up at the end of 1974. We have yet, though, to consider the interaction between fiscal and monetary policy (see Chapter 11, especially).

9.6 STUDY QUESTIONS

Essay questions

1. Analyze the effectiveness of the following methods of measuring price expectations.

a. A sample questionnaire to businessmen. The questions bear upon expectations of real income, employment, the behavior of the money stock, and the interest rate.

b. A random house-to-house canvass of Americans. One question is asked: How much inflation will we have in the next six months?

2. Do expectations of the inflation rate get built into the actual inflation rate directly? How might this actually work out? (I.e., what actual behavior of the people doing the expecting might actually bring about the inflation?) Be specific in your answer, since vagueness here is particularly unrewarding.

3. Compare the likely causes of inflation in developed countries with those in underdeveloped countries. Are there any common causes that you can think of? What role do national governments play in each case?

4. Why might the Federal Reserve try to stabilize the nominal (money) rate of interest? Could they stabilize the real rate of interest (as defined in this chapter)? What effect does perfectly anticipated monetary policy have on the relation between the real and the money rate of interest?

True-false discussion questions

These statements are meant to be somewhat ambiguous and to provoke discussion, thereby.

1. An economy that is rapidly growing will tend to produce a falling and not a rising price level, so long as the money stock does not grow rapidly as well; this proposition implies that the popular "bidding away resources" explanation of inflation would be hard to demonstrate.

2. The interest rate and the inflation rate cannot simultaneously be "the" opportunity cost for holding money unless there is very rapid inflation.

3. While price controls repress inflation, they are essentially incapable of controlling it.

4. The "validation" of nonmonetary events is both necessary and sufficient to deal with the causes of modern inflation.

5. When interest rates rise, money has become "tighter," generally speaking.

6. Inflation is worse in underdeveloped countries than it is in advanced countries because the financial system is less developed and, hence, less able to absorb the impact of changes in the money supply.

7. If the nominal rate of interest is 10 percent, with actual inflation running at 13 percent, then, since money is being given away (in real terms), one might expect heavy investment and consumption demand, and even more pressure on prices.

8. Generally speaking, U.S. inflation rates tend to run ahead of those in the other industrialized powers because the U.S. economy tends to run closer to full employment.

9. Since investment depends on the *real* interest rate and since an increase in the rate of inflation will reduce the real interest rate, we can argue that accelerating inflation will tend to be associated with increased investment, at least in the short run.

10. The importance of the distinction between nominal and real interest rates is that it shows clearly that higher interest rates must generally be considered a result of inflation rather than a cause.

9.7 FURTHER READING

Curwen, Peter Jeremy. *Inflation*. London: Macmillan, 1976.

Foster, Edward. "Costs and Benefits of Inflation." *Studies in Monetary Economics, Federal Reserve Bank of Minneapolis,* no. 1 (1972).

Helbing, Hans H., and James E. Turley. "A Primer on Inflation: Its Conception, Its Costs, Its Consequences." *Review, Federal Reserve Bank of St. Louis* (January 1975).

Laidler, David, and Michael Parkin. "Inflation: A Survey." *Economic Journal* (December 1975).

Vogel, Robert C. "The Dynamics of Inflation in Latin America, 1950–1969." *American Economic Review* (March 1974).

Wiles, Peter. "Cost Inflation and the State of Economic Theory." *Economic Journal* (June 1973).

10

The objectives and instruments of American monetary policy

10.1 INTRODUCTION

In this chapter we will take a break from the theoretical material we have been discussing and take a preliminary look at some of the inner workings of American monetary policy. We will generalize a good deal, but we will take it as our principal purpose to clear up as much as possible concerning the mechanics of monetary policy. In this book the material on the conduct of monetary policy is divided into two main parts: a discussion of *objectives* and *instruments* in Chapter 10 and a discussion of *targets* and *indicators* in Chapter 12. In particular, we start with the goals (objectives) as they have evolved over time and then we look at the techniques (or instruments) that the legislators have given to the monetary authorities in order to enable them to achieve the objectives. These are the two ends of the policy structure and, no doubt, correspond to most views of what constitutes a description of monetary policy, but we will also show that in fact, the monetary authorities do not work directly on the goals (such as "price stability") but on other variables (interest rates, free reserves, and the monetary quantities M_1 and M_2) as approximate objectives. They use these other variables, called targets and indicators, for various reasons, the most valid of which is that they feel they can do a better job of monetary control in this way. But in this chapter we will limit our discussion to the objectives and instruments, leaving the targets and indicators and the discussion of recent monetary policy in the United States, to Chapters 12 and 13.

Before we begin, it is just as well to set out a sketch of the overall monetary policy framework as it will be developed in the next few chapters; this will help both to clarify the issues and to set up the more intricate arguments of later chapters. First of all, we should state that by the *monetary authorities* we normally mean the managers of the Federal Reserve System (the Board of Governors or the Federal Open Market Committee), the Secretary of the Treasury, and the President of the United States, although we will often talk as if the Board of Governors is the actual authority.[1] These officials are involved in the decisions about the money supply, etc., in various ways, although the involvement is not always direct, except for the Board of Governors. The lower part of Figure 10.1, thus, illustrates the material of this chapter, with the decision makers, the monetary authorities, in the central position; in the upper part of the figure, to complete the design, we have included the subject matter

Figure 10.1: A schematic representation of American monetary policy

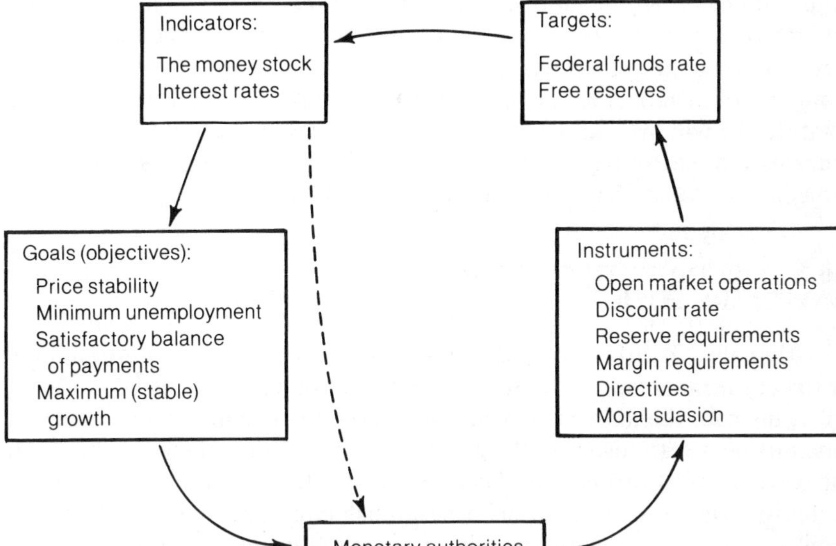

[1] The members of the board are appointed by the president and confirmed by Congress. Recently, one notices a closer relation between the chairman of the Board of Governors and the White House.

of Chapter 12, as well. The arrows indicate the direction in which policy "flows" normally.

We should begin with the objectives; in response to political pressure, and through either legislation or administrative decision, the American government has decided that it wants a reasonable (or even zero) rate of inflation, minimum unemployment, minimal difficulty with the balance of payments or the exchange rate, and a rapid and even (no business cycles) rate of growth of the economy in real terms. The monetary authorities—notably the Federal Reserve—bear part of this load and, for their part, have been instructed by Congress to monitor the money and capital markets and, when necessary, to conduct monetary policy to help achieve the above-stated objectives. To enable them to carry out this assignment, they are given tools (*instruments*) in the form of the ability to set the discount rate, the reserve requirements of member banks, and the minimum down payment that stockbrokers must ask of their customers when they buy stocks, as well as the ability to buy and sell (mostly government) securities in the open market. When these instruments are employed, they affect, after a lag, the objective variables. To judge their progress, the authorities do not wait for the final variables to change since they may, after all, change in the meantime from other causes; instead, they aim at and watch certain intermediate financial variables—primarily interest rates and monetary quantities—to see what effect their actions are having *as the policy is unfolding*. This intermediate reading accounts for the broken arrow in Figure 10.1 and, incidentally, accounts for much of the complexity of monetary policy as it is presently practiced in the United States. We will lay out all of the design, and try to clear up some of the puzzles that surround it, but for now, let us go back to the start—to the objectives—to see how those are currently defined.

10.2 THE OBJECTIVES OF AMERICAN MONETARY POLICY

Originally, in 1913, Congress through the Federal Reserve Act did not instruct the monetary authorities to deal with the variables listed in Figure 10.1; instead, the authorities were instructed to accommodate commerce and business with regard to the general credit situation of the country and, in particular, to furnish an elastic currency, to furnish means of rediscounting commercial paper, and to establish more effective supervision of banking in the United States. These modest aims arose, as was pointed out in Chapter 4, from a perception of what was missing at that time in the American system of monetary control. Of course, the post–World War I inflation and the Great Depression of the 1930s arrived and a whole new perspective emerged, taking, to a certain extent, a legal form. Indeed, as a direct outgrowth of the turbulent '20s and '30s, the Employment Act of

1946 instructed the Federal Reserve, as an arm of the government, to take the responsibility for

> maintaining, in a manner calculated to foster and promote free competitive enterprise and the general welfare, conditions under which there will be afforded useful employment opportunities, including selfemployment, for those able, willing, and seeking to work, and to promote maximum employment, production, and purchasing power.

All that is missing, in this prescription, is any reference to the balance of payments (or to gold), although, as we have already seen, this had been part of the policy scenario often enough in earlier years to warrant some mention even then.[2] In any event, at present, our objective variables are the price level (P) or the rate of inflation ($\dot{P}$), unemployment (U), the balance of payments (B) or the exchange rate (E), and the rate of growth of GNP in real terms ($\dot{y}$).

The foregoing are the variables in which the policy makers are interested; the next question concerns the actual values that we desire these objective variables to take (these are the *specific* objectives). Consider, first, the price level. If prices are growing steadily at, say, 2 percent per year, then an economy can accommodate itself to the situation by using escalator clauses in wage contracts, in social security payments, and the like, so that pay scales and income receipts will reflect the inflation rate; in this event practically no one would suffer. Of course there are many ways to slice the economic pie, and someone is bound to suffer (and someone to gain), but in principle one could index a steady inflation quite accurately. Furthermore, as we have already pointed out, since interest rates will tend to reflect the expected rate of inflation, with a steady 2 percent inflation, expected inflation will tend to equal actual inflation, and money interest rates will simply be marked up 2 percent so that capital markets also will not be unduly disturbed. Thus the frustration of expectations and some of the undesirable distributional effects of a variable inflation will not occur to concern the authorities. These remarks establish that the appropriate variable to measure price effects is the *rate of change* of prices rather than the level of prices; furthermore, it is important because changes in the rate of inflation may well affect expectations (and hence

[2] No doubt, one could argue, these were new objectives and the balance of payments objective was already enshrined in policy and did not need to be restated formally. Furthermore, stable purchasing power (stable prices) would certainly help with balance of payments problems. In contrast, there is evidence that the Federal Reserve itself did not begin to get interested in the balance of payments until after 1961 (some ten years after the U.S. gold outflow started); this evidence is on page 2 of a document published by the Federal Reserve in 1963 (*The Federal Reserve System: Purposes and Functions*), which says: "Today it is generally understood that the primary purpose of the System is to foster growth at high levels of employment, with a stable dollar in the domestic economy and with over-all balance in our international payments." In previous editions of the same publication (1947, 1954, 1961), there was no mention of the balance of payments.

even investment spending) and may also create undesirable distributional or allocative effects (especially in financial markets). As a consequence, in the United States, the preference is for a low rate of inflation, possibly in the 1 to 2 percent per year range, which the economy enjoyed in the 1950s (although at that time it was considered to be unduly rapid).

With regard to the full-employment variable, the question that first arises concerns whether or not the usual variable, *unemployment* as a percentage of the labor force, is the appropriate objective variable. For one thing, the monetary authorities themselves may be instructed (or may take it upon themselves) to watch the level of employment rather than the rate of unemployment, leaving the latter to social rather than to macroeconomic policy. For another, the rate of unemployment will not reflect (*a*) the underemployment that results from workers taking jobs that do not fully utilize their skills or (*b*) the fact that the size of the labor force itself will vary with the condition of the economy or with the season of the year. In hard times, for example, workers retire early, as they did in the 1930s; furthermore, when jobs are plentiful and the chances good, workers may join the ranks of the unemployed in order to conduct a more efficient job search. On the other hand, there are problems of "labor force participation" to worry about; thus, in recent years women appear to have squeezed men out of the labor force so that while total employment has risen, visible male unemployment has also risen to historically high levels, for such a prosperous economy. On net, though, we can suppose that there is some desired rate of unemployment, not necessarily zero, which the authorities keep in mind, in their conduct of policy. Perhaps a long-run objective of 3–4 percent would do, although at present getting anything like 5–6 percent for a long period of time is cause for a celebration.

With regard to the "international objectives," any discussion of macro-policy objectives must reflect the rapid changes in that area in recent years. In the days when the International Monetary Fund (IMF) helped to operate a system of (relatively) fixed exchange rates between national currencies, one often saw a very real conflict develop between a country's internal objectives and those of the group of nations in the IMF. In this period, countries used their stocks of gold, IMF balances, Special Drawing Rights (after 1968), and convertible currencies for the front-line battle in defense of the value of their currencies; they often fought behind the lines as well, controlling their domestic economies by means of fiscal and monetary policy, to the same end.[3] But the IMF system has come crashing down on its own inconsistencies, and now the world stock of

[3] This is not to say, as we will see below, that use of fiscal or, especially, monetary policy in order to control foreign reserves directly (via interest rate effects) was not common; in this paragraph I am merely dividing up the issues for expositional ease. The concepts in this sentence are explained in detail in Chapter 17; for now these items can be thought of, collectively, as "international liquidity."

liquid reserves is dominated by a single convertible currency, the U.S. dollar, and most countries seem to be attempting to hold to a relatively stable exchange rate in a half-hearted way (the so-called dirty float). Thus, while it is hard to be precise over what is being done in particular cases (the United States, for example, usually conducts no firm policy at all toward its persistent and growing balance-of-payments deficit, although in late 1978 a somewhat aggressive policy was adopted); it is important to point out here that certain policy choices over what to do about the balance of payments may have a great deal to do with how successful the fight against inflation is going to be. We will not further anticipate the subject matter of Part IV of the book, but for now, let us note, we cannot find any *consistent* interest in the balance of payments in American monetary policy since World War II. So we will move on.

Also since World War II, there has been a vigorous discussion, much of it in a popular form, over the validity of having a growth objective in the United States. In all likelihood, the authorities of most countries have not used monetary policy aggressively to achieve a desired rate of growth of the economy and have used fiscal policy only sparingly in this context. These facts notwithstanding, nothing is more widely debated these days, and one suspects that if clearly understood trade-offs between the rate of growth and the depletion of resources are eventually established, a considerably broader set of objectives will then become relevant in the discussion of monetary policy (since trade-offs between the rate of growth and the rate of inflation, for example, are already pretty well defined). That is, faster growth means more pollution, so, in a nutshell, we can limit our pollution by limiting the rate of growth of the money stock—that is to say, by tight money; this policy would also hold back "monetary pollution" (inflation). A more relevant, and also growth-related, objective that we have often touched on in this book also comes under this heading; this is stability of the capital markets or, more usually, stability of the interest rate. While we will discuss the role of the interest rate as a target variable in Chapter 12, we should note here that an orderly capital market—however this is to be judged—may well be thought to be the best background for a successful growth policy. Indeed, one could go so far as to say that monetary orderliness in general may well be helpful to growth and even to the achievement of the other objectives we have described in this section.

This leaves us with a rather important theoretical question concerning the objectives—namely, the *interactions* between the objectives—that we must take up before we look at the data. Think of the variables: $\dot{P}$, B, U, and $\dot{y}$ as the final variables in an *IS-LM* type macroeconomic model. Then, any sudden change in an underlying factor—a bad harvest, a sudden gold outflow, or a monetary (or policy) disaster—will generally change *all* of the variables (eventually). To categorize the effects, we could argue that some objective variables will move in a *complementary* fashion (so that two objectives are simultaneously improved) and that some variables will be *substitutes* (such that improvement in one area is matched by deterioration in the other). For an example of substitutability, consider the Phillips curve, a concept we will discuss more fully in Chapter 11, which postulates a trade-off (a substitution) between inflation and unemployment on the grounds of an observed statistical regularity. The Phillips curve has actually not stood up particularly well, particularly in its long-run form, but there does appear to be a short-run trade-off between unemployment and the rate of inflation, such that if we decide to reduce unemployment quickly by means of monetary or fiscal policy we may well have to pay for it by an increased (in the short run) rate of inflation. We will return to this particular problem in Chapter 11.

An example of the complementarity of the objective variables occurs when the implementation of a policy of more rapid growth actually reduces unemployment as well.[4] Since we cannot always say whether the final variables are substitutes or complements in practice (and, indeed, there may well be changes over time depending on what policy approach is taken), we probably can leave it that the variables are "mutually" interacting and that we should construct our basic model accordingly. But the fundamental fact of life here is that the authorities must grapple with the problem of the interaction between objectives because the authorities have been instructed to try to improve *all* of the objective variables at once. Note, further, that we are discussing the interactions that may *actually* exist among the objective variables; the authorities, though, may well not perceive these differences or, rather, have a different idea as to what they are. We must remember, after all, that both the model and the policy are the property of the authorities and that both may be seriously in error.

Before we catalogue the arsenal of weapons that Congress has handed over to the monetary authorities, in order to permit a little reality to creep into this discussion we ought to take a look at how the objective variables have done in recent years. Table 10.1 contains some figures (we omit the interest rate). Thus, if we believe we ought to have a rate of inflation of 2 percent or so, an unemployment rate of 4 percent, along with a stable balance of payments and a rapid and even rate of growth, then Table 10.1 is not full of cheer. In particular, in the 14 years covered there we have had two recessions and three booms (although overall the rate of growth has been impressive); we have seen large fluctuations in the balance of

[4] A more rapid inflation may result from too high a growth rate (especially if it is induced by monetary policy); this will reduce unemployment but also, probably, worsen the balance of payments (since American goods have become more expensive and because American consumers are spending more abroad on account of their higher incomes). Two up and two down on that one, accepting the external objective as reasonable (see Chapter 18).

Table 10.1: The objective variables in the United States, 1965–1978

	Rate of inflation (consumer prices)	*Unemployment*	*Employment change*	*Real GNP (annual rate of growth in 1975 prices)*	*Balance of payments on goods and services ($ billions)*	*SDR/$ rate*
1965	1.7%	4.5%	4.2%	5.9%	8.4	1.00
1966	2.8	3.8	5.2	6.0	6.0	1.00
1967	2.9	3.8	3.0	2.7	5.7	1.00
1968	4.2	3.6	3.2	4.4	3.4	1.00
1969	5.4	3.5	3.7	2.6	3.3	1.00
1970	5.9	4.9	.6	−.3	5.8	1.00
1971	4.2	5.9	.3	3.0	2.4	1.00
1972	3.4	5.6	3.5	5.4	−1.9	.92
1973	6.2	4.9	4.4	5.4	11.0	.84
1974	11.0	5.6	2.0	−1.4	8.6	.83
1975	9.1	8.5	−1.8	−1.3	22.6	.82
1976	5.8	7.7	3.1	6.0	10.0	.87
1977	6.5	7.0	3.4	4.9	−9.4	.86
1978	7.5	6.0	4.2	4.4	−8.8	.80

Sources: *Federal Reserve Bulletin; International Financial Statistics* (May 1978).

goods and services and a 14 percent depreciation of the U.S. dollar against the International Monetary Fund currency (SDR stands for Special Drawing Rights); and, worst of all, 2 percent inflation and 4 percent unemployment seem gone forever. Thus, in 1976, 1977, and 1978, good years in terms of real growth and employment, the rate of unemployment did not get below the 1965–74 rate, the balance of payments seemed to become a disaster area (as did the SDR/$ exchange rate), and the inflation rate only dropped to just under 6 percent, only to rise again to near double-digit figures. The record, thus, is not very impressive, unless one believes that the principal concern has been growth (and possibly employment)[5] and that these have been generally accepted substitutes, in fact, for poor achievement elsewhere.

10.3 THE INSTRUMENTS OF MONETARY POLICY

10.3.1 Open market operations

Informally, in much of the preceding discussion, we have attributed "monetary" or "interest rate" control to the monetary authorities or to the Federal Reserve but we have never set down precisely how this is achieved (if it is); it is time to turn to that task. Actually, it is a long story, and we will have to go clear to the end of Chapter 12 before we have it all, but here, at least, we can lay out formally how control of the *instruments* of monetary policy (themselves) might influence the economy.

Let us start with an instrument that is not an instrument. We have been saying, loosely, that the Federal Reserve can control the stock of money by means of open market operations;[6] indeed, we explained the expansion of deposits in terms of such an example. All of this seems to imply that the quantity of money is an instrument and that if one could work out the relationship between money and the economy, including the feedback, then one has a good idea of how money affects the economy. In fact, a lot of hands get involved in the creation of money; and, of more importance, we must remember that money (real money balances) is a product whose value depends on the behavior of the price level. It is best, under these circumstances, to say that the Federal Reserve can, *if it wishes,* control the

[5] Employment rises, even when unemployment does not drop very much when, in effect, workers are squeezed out by technological change. In other words, technological change does lead to more rapid growth, but it does not lead to a proportional rate of growth of employment if the technological change is *labor saving*. This is probably an underlying factor behind the substitution of growth for unemployment one can observe in Table 10.1.

[6] Specifically, an open market operation is the buying or selling (by the Federal Reserve) of Treasury securities in the open market. The open market in the United States consists of a small number of commercial banks and nonbank brokers located mainly in New York City.

nominal stock of money (M), with the *instrument* of open market operations. This is no small statement, as we shall see.[7]

In practice, most references in economic analysis to instruments of monetary policy are references to open market operations. When we assert that the Federal Reserve can control the quantity of money, we mean that it can always buy and sell government securities in exchange for money and can thereby achieve any reserve position for commercial banks that it desires. The procedure works as follows: if the Federal Reserve wishes to increase the quantity of money, it can put in an order to buy government securities from the New York commercial banks; the order goes out from the trading desk of the New York Federal Reserve Bank following (presumably) the guide lines in a directive from the Federal Open Market Committee. What happens, so far as the Federal Reserve is concerned, is that it acquires an asset (Treasury securities) equal to a liability (member bank reserves) in the amount of the open market operation. What happens so far as the commercial bank is concerned is that it has given up an asset (the Treasury security) in exchange for *excess* reserves equal to the amount of the open market operation. Since banks are then in "disequilibrium" from a profit-maximizing point of view, what happens next could easily follow the line of argument laid down in Chapter 5, when it was merely new currency that entered the system. What ultimately happens to interest rates, prices, real income, and unemployment depends on a number of things, although taken one at a time, interest rates would tend to fall, prices would tend to rise, real income would tend to rise, and unemployment would tend to fall. Finally, an open market purchase is (or tends to be) expansionary and an open market sale is contractionary.

We can look at some recent data, as published by the Federal Reserve, to try to spot some significant open market operations, but when we do so, we should realize that the day-to-day operations of the Federal Reserve banks are often so complicated that such detection is a little ambiguous. The item we should look at is published in the *Federal Reserve Bulletin* on a monthly basis. Looking first at annual figures in Table 10.2 we note that there has been a steady increase in gross System purchases of government securities over the years, an increase that largely reflects the fact that the Federal Reserve provides both the currency and the member bank reserves, which are the main components of the monetary base. In a growing economy, of course, the monetary base will also tend to grow. One also notices annual fluctuations in the figures, but the most revealing item in the table in this sense is the bottom line, which shows the *net* changes in

---

[7] For one thing, in the case of a totally open economy, as we shall see in Chapter 18, a capital inflow, due to tighter money at home, can wipe out the effectiveness of the domestic monetary contraction by providing the capital the domestic authorities are rationing.

Table 10.2: Annual open market transactions, 1970–1978 ($ billions)

	1970	*1971*	*1972*	*1973*	*1974*	*1975*	*1976*	*1977*	*1978*
All maturities									
Gross purchases	12.4	12.5	10.1	18.1	13.5	21.3	19.0	20.9	24.6
Gross sales	5.2	3.6	6.5	4.9	5.8	5.6	8.6	7.2	13.7
Redemptions...............	2.2	2.0	2.9	4.6	4.7	10.0	5.0	4.6	2.0
Treasury Bills									
Gross purchases	11.1	8.9	8.5	15.5	11.7	11.6	14.3	13.7	16.6
Gross sales	5.2	3.6	6.5	4.9	5.8	5.6	8.5	7.2	13.7
Redemptions...............	2.2	1.1	2.5	3.4	4.6	6.4	5.0	2.1	2.0
Net change in U.S. government securities	5.0	8.1	−0.3	8.6	2.0	7.4	9.1	5.8	7.7
Other items (net)	—	—	—	—	—	1.1	.7	1.3	.7
Net change in total system account	5.0	8.9	0.3	9.2	6.1	8.5	9.8	7.1	7.0

Source: *Federal Reserve Bulletin.*

the System account. This, too, is generally positive (it reflects the net effect on the base), but at least once, in 1972, it was nearly zero, almost certainly reflecting the attempt by the Federal Reserve to tighten money that year. But, we should recall, the money supply did not tighten up in 1972 (see below), as it turns out,[8] and this fact suggests that there may well be a lag between the open market operation and its effect on the money stock. Indeed, there is also a lag between the change in the money stock and changes in prices and employment. This slippage is an important part of the policy problem and will be one of the subjects taken up in Chapter 11 when we discuss the transmission of monetary pressures onto the economy.

But open market operations have probably been more in the nature of "fine tuning" than they have been of strong anti-cyclical pressures. To see how they might actually be operated we can look at monthly net System operations in 1971–73 and 1977–78 to see what turns up; Table 10.3 carries the figures. Very clearly, in the early period, monetary contraction, so far as the Federal Reserve is involved, actually started in June 1972, although the money stock did not start to decline until January 1973 (as we saw in

[8] The figures on the money stock are, in $ billions, seasonally adjusted:

1972		*1973*	
June	248.1	January	255.4
July	247.7	February	256.7
August	248.6	March	256.6
September	250.1	April	258.2
October	251.6		
November	252.7		
December	255.5		

Table 10.3: Open market operations and money supply, 1971–1978, various years

	Open market operations ($ millions)					Money supply ($ billions)		
	1971	*1972*	*1973*	*1977*	*1978*	M_1(*1977*)*	M_1(*1978*)*	M_2(*1978*)*
January	—	−787	2,197	−3,969	−7,220	314.3	340.1	814.8
February	—	−1,789	644	1,886	1,425	314.5	339.9	818.0
March	—	2,408	1,636	50	4,107	316.1	340.9	821.8
April	−707	472	1,106	4,998	1,315	320.5	346.3	829.7
May	1,099	1,386	−1,470	−3,461	−834	320.7	348.6	835.1
June	705	−221	1,085	6,305	8,783	321.9	352.8	840.6
July	316	−570	2,416	−4,020	−2,305	326.8	354.2	846.2
August	1,148	22	−915	−801	2,744	328.4	356.7	853.5
September	634	−1,009	7	6,764	4,460	331.6	360.9	862.4
October	−326	206	2,440	−10,900	−969	334.6	362.0	867.4
November	862	−442	−1,307	2,260	−2,419	334.7	360.6	870.5
December	2,850	596	1,386	8,042	—	336.7	361.2	875.8

* Seasonally adjusted.
Source: *Federal Reserve Bulletin*.

Footnote 8, above). By January 1973, the Fed was expanding again, but the money stock did not move up significantly until April 1973. So much for the idea that the money stock can be taken as an instrument of monetary policy (or, for that matter, can be taken as an exogenous variable). In 1977, as we shall discuss further in Chapter 12, the money supply once again grew rapidly, but this time during the summer months. While the totals for the year in Table 10.2 do not indicate any severe restraint, a kind of off-and-on policy is discernible beginning with May; July, August, and October were also repressive months. As Column (5) of the table indicates, the money stock did slow down in May, after the sharp increase in April (so open market operations can work quickly, if that was what was going on). On the other hand, the efforts of the summer were largely ignored and it took a record swing in the open market account in October to hold the growth of the money stock constant; then, in November and December the money stock (and the open market account) started up again.

The year 1978 was characterized by considerable monetary disturbance, as we have already noted at several points in earlier chapters. We noted that M_1 expanded rapidly in April and again in June through October, and it is certainly no coincidence that the net system open market account grew by $5.4 billion in March and April *and* by $13.7 billion from June through September.[9] Monetary expansion was particularly rapid in August and September, when the net system balance was up $7.2 billion, M_1 was up $6.7 billion, and M_2 was up $16.2 billion (the increase in M_1 was 11.3 percent and that in M_2 was 11.5 percent, expressed as annual rates). The monetary base also increased by 9.6 percent. As the figures for October–December indicate, a modest tight money policy ensued (see Chapter 12, also), at least partly inspired by the American balance of payments difficulties. While M_1 declined (perhaps because of the innovations with regard to interest-paying checking accounts), both M_2 and the monetary base expanded. A Monetarist, at any rate, would not be surprised that the inflation problem continued into 1979 (and was not better dealt with in 1978).

10.3.2 The discount rate

Actually, the Federal Reserve has a considerable number of instruments at its disposal; indeed, it seems to have many more instruments

[9] As we will see in our detailed discussion of the 1978 Federal Reserve policy decisions (in Chapter 12) the Federal Reserve's Open Market Committee gives the impression, in its minutes, that it was pursuing a tight money policy all through the year. The figures of Table 10.3 do not corroborate this story. The financial columns of American newspapers also gave the impression that a tight money policy was being pursued; no doubt both opinions were based on the behavior of the interest rate rather than on the behavior of the monetary base.

than it has objectives, as things stand. Furthermore, all of these have been used, sometimes more than one at a time, to exert influence over the monetary sector at one time or another. One of these tools was planted in the list of original purposes of the Federal Reserve System in Chapter 4 and this was to "furnish a means of rediscounting" for commercial banks. In particular, the Federal Reserve can lend reserves to commercial banks, accepting Treasury bills as collateral; indeed, it has made wide use of this device. What is involved, quite simply, is that commercial banks borrow reserves with acceptable collateral at a rate specified by the Federal Reserve, in a fashion analogous to an individual's personal loan. Now the process of borrowing reserves (or rediscounting, if you prefer to emphasize the collateral side) gives the Federal Reserve a policy instrument in three senses: it can agree or refuse to lend; it can set the rate at which loans are negotiated; and it can determine the quality of the collateral that it accepts. In practice, it sets the lending rate (the discount rate) as one of its instruments of monetary policy.

The discount rate is varied by the Federal Reserve in order to affect the price of the credit that member banks might seek to arrange with the Federal Reserve Banks (borrowed reserves, in December 1978, were $.87 billion, a very small item). Furthermore, a change in the discount rate is expected to have some influence over interest rates in general, and this has to be taken as the purpose of discount rate policy, that is, in the cases in which it is aggressively applied. Let us look at the *total* set of all changes in the discount rate since 1950, in Table 10.4. The general impression the table gives is that there are bursts of activity in the discount rate instrument, followed by periods when there are no changes; the longest such period lasted from August 12, 1960, to July 17, 1963, but even recently, for example throughout 1972, there were substantial periods when no changes were made in the discount rate.

Let us, though, concentrate on the recent periods we considered in Section 10.3.1, in which an active monetary policy involving open market operations was identified. In 1972, open market operations to reduce the money supply began in June (the money supply did not really respond until early 1973); we see from Table 10.4 that the Federal Reserve did not raise the discount rate until January 1973. So discount policy and open market policy do not seem to have been in harmony, at least in the early stages of that operation. From August 14, 1973, to January 10, 1975, throughout the recession for all practical purposes, the Federal Reserve actually raised the discount rate, not getting below the May 1973 figure until after the recession was over. Then, as the economy expanded, and inflation gradually subsided, it lowered the discount rate until in November 1976 the rate was down to 5.25 percent.

In 1977, 1978, and 1979 there was a noticeable coincidence of discount policy and open market policy, at times, especially in the three periods

Table 10.4: The discount rate since 1950 (The New York Federal Reserve Bank)

Effective date	*Discount rate*	*Effective date*	*Discount rate*
1950 August 21	1.75%	1971 January 8	5.25%
1953 January 16	2.00	January 22	5.00
1954 February 5	1.75	February 19	4.75
April 16	1.50	July 16	5.00
1955 April 15	1.75	November 19	4.75
August 5	2.00	December 17	4.50
September 9	2.25	1973 January 15	5.00
November 18	2.50	February 26	5.50
1956 April 13	2.75	May 4	5.75
August 24	3.00	May 11	6.00
1957 August 23	3.50	June 11	6.50
November 15	3.00	July 2	7.00
1958 January 22	3.00	August 14	7.50
January 24	2.75	1974 April 8	8.00
March 7	2.25	December 9	7.75
April 18	1.75	1975 January 10	7.25
September 12	2.00	February 5	6.75
November 7	2.50	March 10	6.25
1959 March 6	3.00	May 16	6.00
May 29	3.50	1976 January 19	5.50
September 11	4.00	November 22	5.25
1960 June 10	3.50	1977 August 31	5.75
August 12	3.00	October 26	6.00
1963 July 17	3.50	1978 January 9	6.50
1964 November 24	4.00	May 11	7.00
1965 December 6	4.50	July 3	7.25
1967 April 7	4.00	August 21	7.75
November 20	4.50	September 22	8.00
1968 March 22	5.00	October 16	8.50
April 19	5.50	November 1	9.50
August 30	5.25	1979 July 20	10.00
December 18	5.50	August 17	10.50
1969 April 4	6.00	September 19	11.00
1970 November 13	5.75	October 8	12.00
December 4	5.50		

Source: *Federal Reserve Bulletin.*

when a particularly firm policy was adopted. In the first of these, October 1977, the discount rate was bumped up to 6 percent while the net system open market account drained $10.9 billion from the economy; in this case the chief weapon was clearly the open market operation (but see Section 10.3.3). On November 1, 1978, the same day that the government announced that it was undertaking a massive "save the dollar" campaign, the discount rate was jumped a full point (1 percent) to 9.5 percent. This was the largest change since World War II—and the highest discount rate, as well. What inspired this severity was no doubt the international "problem" (see Chapters 17 and 18) and the hope that short-term capital would be lured to the United States in response to the higher interest rates. Open market policy was, apparently, only mildly restrictive, and the monetary base and M_2 grew steadily over the last three months (as they did over the last three months of 1977). The lesson is clear: a higher discount rate is not necessarily an indication of tighter money, at least in the sense of rationing the quantity of money.

But what is actually fundamental in the above is not the level of the discount rate, but the relationship between this rate and other interest rates in the economy. It is possible, but not very likely, that if other rates are geared to the discount rate, they will go up. More likely, though, if there is an open market operation and a change in the discount rate (as in late October 1977) we should see a strong effect on the money stock (we did, on M_1, in November 1977 and perhaps in late 1978 and again in late 1979) and on interest rates. But what we need, for the three periods we are looking at, are some comparative interest rates, and these are provided in Table 10.5. Thus, in 1971, the rise of .25 in the discount rate (DR) in July was accompanied by a rise in the prime rate (PR) of .50; the next fall in the DR of .25 (in November) was also accompanied by a fall of .50 in the PR; in December the DR was cut another .25. In 1972 the discount rate was not changed, and the reason is now apparent (it actually seemed inconsistent before): the prime rate had not risen above 5.7 percent (which was below the rate in much of 1971). That is, the system managers may have judged that money was "easy" based on the prime rate; at any rate, they did not want to start a panic. By the time the DR was raised, in early 1973, the PR was on its way up; for the first seven months of 1973 the discount rate stayed about 1 percent behind the prime rate, but when the latter took off, the Federal Reserve simply stopped conducting any discount rate policy, for all practical purposes, for reasons that are far from clear (they *may,* of course, have decided to go for an open market policy at that point and simply put the discount policy aside as irrelevant, given its small *actual* effect).

In 1977 we note that changes in the discount rate seem to have lagged well behind the prime rate. Thus, in the ninth column of Table 10.5 a measure of the net pressure in 1977 (PR − DR) suggests that the interest pressure was gradually lessening: market interest rates were running well ahead of the official lending rate of the Federal Reserve. Carrying this over into 1978, we again note that the prime rate stayed well ahead of the discount rate, although the "tight money" month of November did show a reversal of the upward trend in the difference. In December, though, the largest gap in the period could be observed (just over 2 percent) and that, at least, indicates that the discount rate was not putting pressure on the prime rate. The conclusion, inescapably, is that discount policy may be used as an instrument of monetary policy, but that it probably is not (very often). Rather, one can say, the discount rate is moved to keep the Federal Reserve's lending rate roughly in line with market rates, possibly

Table 10.5: The discount rate and the prime rate compared

	1971		*1972*		*1973*		*1977*			*1978*		
	Prime	*Discount*	*Prime*	*Discount*	*Prime*	*Discount*	*Prime*	*Discount*	*Prime – Discount*	*Prime*	*Discount*	*Prime – Discount*
January	6.25	5.25	5.25	4.50	6.00	5.00	6.25	5.25	1.00	7.93	6.50	1.43
February	5.75	4.75	4.75	4.50	6.00	5.00	6.25	5.25	1.00	8.00	6.50	1.50
March	5.25	4.75	4.75	4.50	6.25	5.50	6.25	5.25	1.00	8.00	6.50	1.50
April	5.25	4.75	5.00	4.50	6.75	5.50	6.25	5.25	1.00	8.00	6.50	1.50
May	5.50	4.75	5.00	4.50	7.00	6.00	6.41	5.25	1.16	8.27	7.00	1.27
June	5.50	4.75	5.00	4.50	7.50	6.50	6.75	5.25	1.50	8.63	7.00	1.63
July	6.00	5.00	5.25	4.50	8.25	7.00	6.75	5.25	1.50	9.00	7.25	1.75
August	6.00	5.00	5.25	4.50	9.25	7.50	6.83	5.25	1.58	9.01	7.25	1.76
September	6.00	5.00	5.50	4.50	10.00	7.50	7.13	5.75	1.38	9.41	7.75	1.66
October	6.00	5.00	5.75	4.50	10.00	7.50	7.52	5.75	1.77	9.94	8.00	1.94
November	5.50	4.75	5.75	4.50	9.75	7.50	7.75	6.00	1.75	10.94	9.50	1.44
December	5.50	4.50	5.75	4.50	9.75	7.50	7.75	6.00	1.75	11.55	9.50	2.05

Source: *Federal Reserve Bulletin.*

to ensure that borrowing by the member banks is not a source of excessive profits to banks and possibly to reassure Americans that the Federal Reserve is on the job. Note that in November 1979 the gap between the prime rate and the discount rate grew to over 3 percent as the Federal Reserve once again (as in 1973) stopped using the discount rate as a policy tool. In this case, though, there was a shift in policy toward letting interest rates (such as the prime rate and the federal funds rate) find their own level, while at the same time focussing attention on the control of monetary quantities. We will return to this policy switch, if such it was, in Chapter 12.

10.3.3 Reserve requirements

We noted in Chapter 4 that minimum reserve requirements for commercial banks are set by the Federal Reserve. In fact, if banks are not holding excess reserves, then a rise in the minimum reserve requirement can force banks to call in reserves and a fall can provide them with funds that were previously labeled "required reserves" and are now labeled "excess reserves" and that would be available for further lending. This obviously is about as direct a technique as a monetary manager could wish for, but this technique has not been employed aggressively in recent years, quite possibly because the Federal Reserve can make the quantity of bank reserves anything it likes by using open market operations. All of the changes since 1949 are listed in Table 10.6.

There are, then, three "systems" (labeled I, II, and III) in reserve requirement history: (I) the Central Reserve City–Reserve City–Country Division system, a vestige of the National Banking System based on the location of a bank; (II) a modified system adopted in 1966, based on both size and location; and (III) the present system, which is based solely on bank size, as measured by deposits. Whatever the system, though, only in 1951 (Korean inflation), 1969, and July 1973 have we ever had an increase in reserve requirements (since World War II). The last of these occurred at the same time the discount rate was raised from 6.50 to 7.00 percent and accompanied a large open market operation designed, of course, to reduce the money stock. As Table 10.3 indicated, all of this only slowed the money stock down (although a recession started later that year). In the tight money episodes of 1977 and 1978, no use was made of this weapon, although in late 1979 reserve requirements of 8 percent were required to be held against certain commercial bank liabilities (e.g., CDs, etc.) that theretofore had not been subject to reserve requirements. But in any event, changes in reserve requirements are generally on a downward trend, and this policy is much favored by the member banks who (*a*) have to provide this interest-free "loan" to the government, and (*b*) do not like to be forced explicitly to undertake expensive portfolio adjustments, especially

Table 10.6: Reserve requirements of member banks

I.	*Net demand deposits*			
	Central reserve cit banks	*Reserve city banks*	*Country banks*	*Savings deposits*
In effect Dec. 31, 1949	22.0%	18.0%	12.0%	5.0%
1951 January 11	23.0	19.0	13.0	6.0
January 25	24.0	20.0	14.0	—
1953 July 9	22.0	19.0	13.0	—
1954 June 24............	21.0	—	—	5.0
July 29	20.0	18.0	12.0	—
1958 February 27	19.5	17.5	11.5	—
March 20	19.0	17.0	11.0	—
April 17	18.5	—	—	—
April 24	18.0	16.5	—	—
1960 September 1	17.5	—	—	—
November 24	—	—	12.0	—
December 1........	16.5	—	—	—
1962 October 25	—	—	—	4.0

II.	*Net demand deposits*				
	Reserve city banks		*Country banks*		
	Under $5 million	*Over $5 million*	*Under $5 million*	*Over $5 million*	*Savings deposits*
1966 July 14	16.5	16.5	12.0	12.0	4.0
September 8	—	—	—	—	—
1967 March 2	—	—	—	—	3.5
March 16	—	—	—	—	3.0
1968 January 11.........	—	17.0	—	12.5	—
1969 April 17	17.0	17.5	12.5	13.0	—

III.	*Net demand deposits ($ millions)*					
	0–2	*2–10*	*10–100*	*100–400*	*Over 400*	*Savings deposits*
1972 November 9	8.0	10.0	12.00	16.50	17.50	3
November 16	—	—	—	13.00	—	—
1973 July 19	—	10.5	12.50	13.50	18.00	—
1974 December 12.......	—	—	—	—	17.50	—
1975 February 13	7.5	10.0	12.00	13.00	16.50	—
1976 December 30.......	7.0	9.5	11.75	12.75	16.25	—

Source: *Federal Reserve Bulletin*.

when the reserve requirements are raised. The last factor seems to flow from the severity of the adjustment needed when changes of even .25 percent (the minimum change) are made. One suspects that this instrument will continue to be used sparingly, in the years to come, barring a financial disaster, but then one also notes that the Germans (and lately the

Japanese) have made much use of the reserve requirement weapon, and one also notes that their track record (on inflation, especially) is a little better than that of the United States.

10.3.4 The other instruments

The three instruments just described constitute the major weapons in the Federal Reserve's arsenal; furthermore, they are enough to get the job done, especially if one wants a change in interest rates or a change in the quantity of money, although with regard to the latter, the instruments may have to be applied vigorously and, even so, the effect may take some time to show itself. But Congress, also, has provided the Federal Reserve with other instruments, some of which are not actively employed in their stabilization policy, but could be. These are margin requirements, controls over maximum interest rates, and something called "moral suasion."

Moral suasion, as a specific monetary device, refers to the attempt to direct or exhort banks—maybe even nonmember banks—to follow some policy line (such as to "cut down on their loan activity" in the interest of restraint) that is being set but not necessarily enforced by (for example) open market operations. At one time, for example, the fight against (the much more modest) inflation was felt to be a moral battle in which we all would have to participate by some sort of self-restraint. Banks, too, were to join in (by not lending) and so were business firms (by not marking up prices), unions (by not going on strike for higher wages) and the federal government (by not incurring such a huge deficit). This sort of policy (also called a "jawbone" policy for obvious reasons) is certainly popular, but the effect, if any, is hard to evaluate; perhaps it is popular because it need not be adhered to, in general, unless it suits each of the economic agents in the sectors just mentioned.

The controls over *maximum interest rates* are not used as direct policy tools, other than to try to stabilize the flow of funds between financial institutions, as things stand. We will discuss this problem in Chapter 13, so we will forbear for now. This leaves the *margin requirement.* The Federal Reserve, indeed, has control over margin requirements, which are specified not only for banks, under Regulation U, but for brokers and dealers in the stock markets themselves, under Regulation T, and for everybody else under Regulation G (dating from March 11, 1968). The general idea behind margin requirements is that minimum down payments on the loans to stock market investors—in particular anyone who borrows the funds that he uses to buy or sell stocks—decreases the investors' leverage factor; in fact, since the leverage is the direct result of using someone else's money, and the margin reflects the amount of the initial loan that is to be covered by the market value of the securities, raising the margin reduces this leverage. Thus, one could obtain, in 1979, a loan of

Table 10.7: Margin requirements (percent)

Type of security	*Mar. 11, 1968*	*June 8, 1968*	*May 6, 1970*	*Dec. 6, 1971*	*Nov. 24, 1972*	*Jan. 3, 1974*
Margin stocks	70	80	65	55	65	50
Convertible bonds	50	60	50	50	50	50
Short sales	70	80	65	55	65	50

Note: Regulations G, T, and U of the Federal Reserve Board of Governors, prescribed in accordance with the Securities Exchange Act of 1934, limit the amount of credit to purchase and carry margin stocks that may be extended on securities as collateral by prescribing a maximum loan value, which is a specified percentage of the market value of the collateral at the time the credit is extended. Margin requirements are the difference between the market value (100 percent) and the maximum loan value. The term "margin stocks" is defined in the corresponding regulation. Regulation G and special margin requirements for bonds convertible into stocks were adopted by the Board of Governors, effective Mar. 11, 1968. Regulation U refers to banks and Regulation T to stock brokers and dealers.

$50 for a $100 common stock purchase and has, as a result, a margin of paid-in money of $50 to absorb a fall in the price of the stock, an amount that seems enough, under present conditions, for most potential fluctuations in most stocks.

Table 10.7 contains all of the adjustments in margin requirements since 1968. The margins have not been changed often, and one of the reasons might be a fairly widespread feeling that this sort of control is not really part of the Federal Reserve's responsibility.[10] In fact, this technique was adopted as an outgrowth of the stock market crash of 1929 and the attendant belief that the speculation of 1929 had something to do with the banking crises of the early 1930s. It is not easy to prove that this particular instrument operates on the economy through the monetary mechanism, to say the least, so it is not easy to prove that it is the Federal Reserve's responsibility. But, of course, one reason the Federal Reserve might have a legitimate interest in controlling stock market margins is that it has taken on much of the general responsibility for stabilizing the economy, under the Employment Act of 1946; furthermore, credit (and, under Regulation U, bank credit) is involved in any margin deal, so the Federal Reserve has some interest, although other agencies of the federal government could have been instructed to do so under the same act, for all that the Federal Reserve uses it. In any event, the amounts involved are not particularly large.[11] We might note, finally, that whatever else it has done, manipulation of the margin requirement has had a strong effect on stock market lending and, for short periods at any rate, a strong effect on stock market prices (the averages, that is to say). This, indeed, may itself be a destabilizing influence, as we will discuss in Chapter 16.

10.4 CONCLUSION

While we do not need a lengthy conclusion to this chapter, it is just as well that we attempt to draw the discussion together just a little before we consider precisely how the policy variables might affect the economy. The main impression one carries away from a complete discussion of objectives and instruments is that *complexity* is the order of the day. There are multiple and interacting goals, there are multiple and interacting instruments and, worse, the instruments do not clearly reach the objectives. Indeed, our discussion of the instruments made no mention of unemployment, the balance of payments, or the rate of growth, and only scant mention of prices. Furthermore, as we have seen, it is not even clear that

[10] The Securities Exchange Act of 1934 gave this authority to the Federal Reserve.

[11] At the end of June 1978, commercial banks' loans to security brokers and dealers—primarily for the margin operations of their customers—were $11.1 billion, and other loans by commercial banks to purchase or carry securities were $4.4 billion. The total of these two items was only 2 percent of "other gross loans" of commercial banks.

monetary policy can reach the quantity of money itself—unless a decisive move is made—and this seems especially disconcerting for the "fine tuning" type of operations we seem to want to conduct in this area.

We will discover, in Chapter 11, that things are even worse than this, expecially because we do not know as much as we would like to about the links between money and the economy (as discussed only in general terms in the model of Chapters 7 and 8)—or, indeed, enough about the model itself—to run the simple-minded models we are used to talking about. But there is a way out, and it is available to the Federal Reserve, and that will be the topic of discussion in Chapter 12.

10.5 STUDY QUESTIONS

Essay questions

1. Suppose the Treasury were to raise new funds simply by printing currency instead of selling bonds. Would the ultimate consequences (on income and the interest rate) be the same in each case? How would each operation work its way through the economy? Why doesn't the Treasury actually print money now?

2. How do you think the Federal Reserve ought to reconcile the conflicts between the objectives of macroeconomic policy? Would having more instruments help? In this connection, are the discount rate and control over reserve requirements separate and distinct instruments from open market operations?

3. By being strict in its discounting policy, the Federal Reserve keeps discount dealings to a minimum and prevents banks from taking advantage of the marginal differences in short-term rates. What is their objection to unrestricted borrowing by the member banks? How might they prevent excessive use of the discount privilege? Does the present system pose any threat to the lender-of-the-last-resort function of the Federal Reserve?

4. Bankers object to the use of variable reserve requirements. Why? Why don't member banks just adjust their interest rates and pass on any additional costs (or gains) to their customers when reserve requirements are changed?

5. We observe that a change in stock market margin requirements affects stock prices, at least in the short run. Does this also affect the total volume of credit in the economy? Do you see this as an effective way of aiding in the overall control of credit in the U.S. economy? Do you see this as an effective way of aiding in the overall control of credit in the U.S. economy? Explain carefully.

True-false discussion questions

These statements are meant to be somewhat ambiguous, and to provoke discussion thereby.

1. It is not likely that unemployment will rise at the same time as prices because an increase in unemployment implies falling demand and falling demand, in its turn, implies falling prices.

2. The quantity of money is itself not an effective instrument of monetary policy largely because its quantity is determined jointly by banks, the public, and the authorities.

3. The Federal Reserve is limited in its conduct of antidepressionary monetary policy by the quantity of securities it has in its portfolio.

4. When the minimum reserve requirement is raised, it is conceivable that the direct fall in the money stock would be offset by the public's holding more of the now safer demand deposits.

5. Banks can more readily avoid the effects of open market operations than they can avoid the effects of changes in reserve requirements.

6. If the nominal interest rate becomes a final goal (or objective) of the monetary authorities, rather than unemployment or the rate of inflation, then stability of the capital markets will tend to be bought at the expense of instability in the product markets.

7. Open market operations and the discount rate—as policy tools—tend to work in approximately the same way on the economy, since both involve adjustments in the reserve component of the monetary base (if they work at all).

8. A rise in the Federal Reserve's discount rate brings tighter money to the economy primarily because it directly produces rising market interest rates (such as the prime rate).

9. It is possible, but not likely, that the growth, balance of payments, unemployment, and inflation variables will all get worse at the same time, in the United States.

10.6 FURTHER READING

Articles on reserve requirements in *Business Conditions, Federal Reserve Bank of Chicago* (June 1972 and March 1974); *Monthly Review, Federal Reserve Bank of Kansas City* (April 1974 and May 1976); *Business Review, Federal Reserve Bank of Philadelphia* (June 1974); and *Business Review,* Federal Reserve Bank of Dallas (December 1976).

Board of Governors of the Federal Reserve System. *The Federal Reserve System: Purposes and Functions.* 6th ed. Washington D.C., 1975.

Fisher, Douglas. *Monetary Policy*. London: Macmillan, 1976.

Guttentag, Jack M. "The Strategy of Open Market Operations." *Quarterly Journal of Economics* (February 1966).

Holbik, Karil, ed. *Monetary Policy in Twelve Industrial Countries*. Boston: Federal Reserve Bank of Boston, 1973.

O'Brien, James M. "Federal Regulation of Stock Market Credit: A Need for Reconsideration." *Business Review, Federal Reserve Bank of Philadelphia* (July/August 1974).

Poole, William. "Interest Rate Stability as a Monetary Policy Goal." *New England Economic Review* (May/June 1976).

Romans, J. T. "Moral Suasion as an Instrument of Monetary Policy." *American Economic Review* (December 1966).

11

The transmission mechanism of monetary policy and the debate over the Phillips curve

11.1 INTRODUCTION

This chapter is going to extend considerably the discussion of monetary (and occasionally fiscal) policy; in particular, a variety of topics on what economists now call the "transmission mechanism" of monetary and fiscal policy will come under discussion here. Because the issues are actually very diverse, the shape of this chapter may seem a little uneven, but, as we shall see, the issues are also very important, involving as they do the very plausibility of trying to control economic activity by means of monetary policy. Basically, our concerns in this chapter are the lines of influence between the pulling of the lever (the open market operation) and the final effect on the system when all of the wheels have stopped turning. This involves primarily the consideration of a monetary influence as it works its way through the economy (*specifically*), splitting its influences into real and nominal effects, somewhat arbitrarily. As we will see, matters of expectations (about inflation rates) and the related Phillips curve come into this discussion (toward the end of the chapter), but we will also want to discuss the "lags-in-effect" of policy formally and to undertake some simple comparisons between fiscal and monetary policy.

In Section 11.2 we will begin the story with a general discussion of how monetary (and fiscal) policy affect the economy. This will include, in

Section 11.2.1, a discussion of the lags in the effect of policy (as well as a general discussion of monetary and fiscal influences); then in Section 11.2.2 we will undertake a discussion of the "crowding out" of macroeconomic policy, as well as an analysis of what we need to add to the general model of monetary influence when we include the government's "budget constraint" in the problem.[1] That done, we will turn in Section 11.3 to the Phillips curve. This is a device (which is still used to a certain extent) that explains the relation between inflation and unemployment (two of the objectives of Chapter 10) in a very simple fashion. As such, it has a key role to play in our efforts to construct a stabilization policy, that is, *if* there is such a stable relationship. As it turns out, the data do not support its existence, over a wide variety of experiences, so that we are led to consider why it has failed to be confirmed; this leads us into a discussion of the "expectations-augmented Phillips curve" of the Monetarists and, more provocatively, into a discussion of the nihilistic "rational expectations" hypothesis, a neo-Monetarist proposition that denies that monetary policy has any substantial effect on real variables.

11.2 THE EFFECTS OF FISCAL AND MONETARY POLICY

11.2.1 The general picture

It was the fashion, not too long ago, to present a story of the effects of fiscal and monetary policy that emphasized the directness and strength of the former and the indirectness and subtlety of the latter. Thus fiscal policy was to deal with depressions and recessions, and monetary policy with the *fine tuning* of the economy and, in particular, with the rate of inflation. This picture, though, was too simple; thus, we have already pointed out that we seem to have trouble even getting monetary policy going (Section 10.3) and for that matter, as we shall see, fiscal policy is not easy to start up. When the two types of policy get going, as well, they are subject to a lot of negative effects that tend to reverse their basic thrust; in addition, they actually work through the economy in a slow and somewhat indetectable way. Indeed, monetary policy may well produce no important real effects at all (except for imperfections in the system), but let us consider the traditional argument before we consider some of the variations.

Fiscal policy, generally, can be interpreted either as a change in a basic tax rate or a policy-induced change in government spending. If it is an expansionary fiscal policy, then the government will tend to run a deficit;

[1] This refers to the fact that if the government has to spend, it must raise the funds somewhere (tax, bond issue, etc.), and when it does, there are (different) monetary implications.

this deficit, we will assume, is *bond financed,* but we will not, for the moment, consider how the method of finance affects the outcome of the policy. Fiscal policy will act like a shift in investment spending and affect the economy by the same multiplier, as expressed in Equations (7.11) and (7.12). Product markets, then, will tend to be directly stimulated (let us assume the government actually spends the funds it raises in the product markets) and as incomes increase, employment increases. Very straightforward.

Monetary policy—let us say an expansionary open market operation—begins with the trading desk of the New York Federal Reserve Bank from which an order goes forth to buy a quantity of Treasury bills from the large New York banks. The banks, then, acquire excess reserves, and as they search about for loan and investment customers, they depress interest rates; as they *lend,* the money supply expands.[2] To a Monetarist, the lending activity itself generates spending; as well, the upward pressure on security prices (bond prices in the first instance) provides capital gains to be spent or invested. To a Keynesian, whatever effects we get from the monetary policy depend on how responsive consumption and investment are, *in real terms,* to changes in interest rates. If investment is "interest-elastic"—that is, responds quickly—then the effects will tend to be large (via the investment multiplier). But many Keynesians doubt that the interest rate affects investment very much and so they doubt that monetary policy has considerable *real* effects.[3]

11.2.2 Lags in the effect of macroeconomic policy

But since fiscal policy is not merely "tax cut and away we go" (and monetary policy is not always slow), economists have put some effort into

---

[2] Let us go into a little more detail for commercial banks (in a tight money period). Defining tight money as a restriction of the rate of growth of the money stock we recall that the "liability reaction" of banks depends on what other methods of raising funds they have, in the face of pressure on their reserves through M_1 and M_2. If they are able to acquire funds through repurchase agreements or CDs (the latter became noncompetitive because of the application of Regulation Q in the 1966 and 1969 tight money periods), they may well not have to ration their loans. But these sources of funds are better suited to large banks than small banks and so the latter suffer somewhat, comparatively. On the asset side of the balance sheet, one finds that banks do not, in general, take special advantage of tight security markets by shifting funds away from their regular loan customers. This fact, which implies that there are no special asset effects to consider, is probably the result of banks' wishing to keep their customers happy in the long run (by foregoing a short run opportunity). See David P. Eastburn and W. Lee Hoskins, "The Influence of Monetary Policy on Commercial Banking," *Business Review, Federal Reserve Bank of Philadelphia* (July/August 1979).

[3] We should note here, although we will return to it later in this chapter, that some Monetarists (e.g., Milton Friedman) believe that both fiscal and monetary policy are effective but that the effect is so *erratic* and *unpredictable* that we would be better off not using either, except in situations of emergency. We will also return, in Chapters 13 and 15, to the effect of monetary policy on the *credit available* to the mortgage market and to certain sectors (notably small firms). The real point, to anticipate, is that monetary policy may affect the economy in a very uneven way (we will look at some of this evidence later).

trying to estimate the lags that occur with the two types of policy. Before we generalize this topic, let us consider a typical tax cut, the "tax cut of 1964" as discussed by Herbert Stein in his book *Fiscal Revolution in America*. I can do no better than to quote the opening paragraph in his chapter 17:

> The tax reduction promised by President Kennedy on June 7, 1962, was signed into law by President Johnson on February 26, 1964. At no time was the enactment of a large tax cut seriously in doubt. The delay resulted from the need to resolve a number of other issues, especially about the tax reforms that would be included in the tax revision package and about the federal expenditure levels that would accompany the tax cut. The delay, the discussion that went on during it, and the outcome all reveal the complexity of the considerations that entered into the decision. These considerations were not only the "new economics" of full employment and the old Puritan ethic of balancing the budget, but also the old [Andrew] Mellon philosophy of reducing taxes to stimulate economic growth, the ageless divisions of opinion about the scale of government activity and expenditures, the desire of taxpayers for tax reduction, and the desire of politicians to obtain credit as donors of tax reductions.[4]

We should also point out that almost *two years* of discussion preceded the 1962 decision by President Kennedy to press ahead with the cut. More recently, there was a protracted discussion over President Carter's tax cut, in 1977–78 and, as well, the *substance* of the cut itself was often changed, as the economy shifted about.

In addition to the fact that fiscal policy may be slow in coming, it may be ineffective. You will recall that in Chapter 7 we briefly discussed the "permanent income" and "life-cycle" theories of consumption. Both of these theories emphasized *wealth* as the appropriate variable in the aggregate consumption function, but the former also emphasized that consumers would concentrate on *regular* (permanent) additions to their income and ignore *transitory* additions. The message of this theory is then clear: if the tax cut in 1964 were considered to be a *permanent* change in income, American consumers might respond positively (and quickly) in the way the law makers desired; if not—if they thought it might be reversed as soon as the economy heated up—they might not respond, preferring to save most of the "windfall" and merely to use the interest on it, in their current spending plans. If the wealth-oriented consumption theory is correct, and the evidence gathered so far on aggregate consumption behavior does tend to support it, then, fiscal policy is more of a one-way street: any aggressive use for fine tuning—on and then off again—will cause consumers to delay their spending until they have got the pattern of the policy

---

[4] Herbert Stein, *Fiscal Revolution in America* (Chicago: University of Chicago Press, 1969), p. 422. Reprinted by permission of the University of Chicago Press. © 1969 by The University of Chicago.

down. If they do not spend, then fiscal policy will not work.[5] So fiscal policy, too, has some subtleties of its own.

Monetary policy is also subject to lags especially after it is put into motion. In particular, it may well take some time for changes in financial variables to affect the economic system. Indeed, if we have to wait until interest rates have affected investment (as the Keynesians would say we do) it could be a very long wait. Of course, lags are endemic in any system in which decisions have a long-run influence and thus it is not just investment that is involved. Let us not be precise, just yet, as to the possible length of such lags in macroeconomic policy; but let us note that if the lags are very long, there is the possibility that a particular policy might make things worse. Suppose that an undesired rise in the price level induces the monetary authorities to reduce the quantity of money, but, for various reasons, the bulk of the effect of the reduction does not reach the economy for several years. Further, suppose the economy itself has reversed in the meantime, so that the effect of the reduction on the money supply comes when prices are already falling (for other reasons). The policy, then, would worsen things, when the effect hits, because it would tend to drive down the price level still further. This is an adequate justification for studying the problem.

The length of the lag, therefore, is a problem, but an even more serious matter, since one can quite possibly learn to live with a given lag, is that the lags seem to vary from period to period. In fact, at least one economist (Milton Friedman) seriously feels that the lag in effect in monetary policy for the United States has been as long as 18 months and as short as 6 months in recent years and has varied so much that it defies even careful prediction. This is a serious charge. Actually, a whole series of lags in the policy design should be considered, from the original idea (or the stimulus to the policy makers) down to the final effect on the goal variables. In the first place there is an *information lag,* often longer than three months, between the occurrence of an event and its measurement by the authorities. To a certain extent this lag can be reduced by finding economic variables that forecast economic events—an obvious example is to use planned business investment—but so far, such forecasts have not served us very well.[6] The next lag in the policy system is the so-called *inside lag,*

[5] In these circumstances a politically motivated tax cut—just before an election—may not work immediately (if at all) since elector-consumers may not expect such a cynical device to be kept up. The contrasting view is that "political business cycles" will be generated in this way (if, presumably, the permanent income hypothesis is not valid). The evidence, at this stage, is really nonexistent, but the idea is an interesting one.

[6] There is another problem with respect to information, and that is that "fresh" or "preliminary" information tends to be less accurate than revised information, so that decisions taken on the basis of the former tend to have a wider range of uncertainty. Our Gross National Product figures, for example, are continually being revised; and at any rate it is conceivable that the wrong direction could be given to monetary policy because of a sizable statistical error of this sort.

the lag between the appearance of the need for policy action and the taking of the action. The inside lag itself consists of a *recognition lag,* induced by the delay in recognizing that a change is needed, and an *action lag* (which will include any of the indecisiveness of the policy maker), representing the time it takes to get things moving. When the data change and are fed into the Federal Reserve's meetings, patterns must emerge—that is to say, events must repeat themselves—before a decision to act will be made. The best that can be done, if data are collected monthly with an information lag of three months, is to arrive at a decision to do something four months after the event. Here, it turns out, monetary policy has a special advantage over fiscal policy, for once the decision to conduct an open market operation is made, the system manager can begin to operate on the next day.[7] Thus, the potential action lag for the most important instruments of monetary policy—open market operations, changes in the rediscount rate, changes in reserve requirements, and changes in margin requirements—is essentially zero.

We have seen that each of these instruments works on the system in a slightly different way; and each, too, works with a lag. Actually, the lag-in-effect or, if you will, the *outside lag* is a very long series of future adjustments that can only be measured arbitrarily, for example, by picking some percentage of the total effect (say, 95 percent) that must be realized and measuring the time it takes to be realized (say, 32 years). When an instrument is changed—when reserves, for example, are altered by an open market operation—it takes time for the money stock to alter; then, perhaps six months later, the effect of the change in the stock of money will begin to dominate the price level. If the first part of this lag, perhaps caused by the slowness of banks to run off their excess reserves, is two months—refer to this as the *final lag*—the lag-in-effect, in our arbitrary example, would measure eight months. The total lag of the monetary policy would then measure 12 months in our (possibly understated) *example,* as drawn up in Table 11.1.

Table 11.1 hypothesizes lags for open market operations and changes in reserve requirements when money is already tight; in this case, the instruments would tend to attack the availability of funds directly. But 12 months may be the best one can expect, and the methods that attack the price of credit (for example, changes in the discount rate, which also operates fairly indirectly) may well take a longer time to work themselves out. In particular, if the main effect of a change in an interest rate is to stimulate or retard investment spending and if we have to wait around for the effect to work itself out, we might well have gone through a cycle or two

[7] There are some bits of fiscal policy in the hands of the Executive, but most major changes must go through Congress. This is an uncertain and time-consuming route; and, more seriously, the action lag has been very long in some instances.

Table 11.1: The lags in monetary policy (open market operations)

Lag		*Months*
Information lag		3
Inside lag	Recognition lag	1
	Action lag	0
Lag-in-effect	Instrument-effect lag	2
	Final lag	6
Total lag		12

before the main impact occurs, because some private investment plans have a very long horizon indeed in our economy. Thus we run the risk of having our particular effect materialize at a time when the situation calls for the opposite effect; monetary policy, if the lags are long enough, can be destabilizing, particularly in the event that the lags are *variable* (as they may well be) or in the case when we don't know the true length of the lag and make incorrect judgments about our policy effects.

11.3 "CROWDING OUT" AND THE INTERACTION BETWEEN FISCAL AND MONETARY POLICY

Up until now we have skirted a basic issue in macroeconomic policy analysis concerning our ability to conduct fiscal and monetary policies that are independent of each other. It is true, of course, that we have made a number of points regarding the interaction of these policies, as follows:

a. They share, to some extent, common objectives.

b. They both work through product and financial markets, although clearly in different ways.

c. They are both constrained, to some extent, by the realities of a modern large-scale government (which has to deal with the effects of persistent and variable deficits).

In addition, we have pointed out that there is a budgetary interaction, in the American system, in that earnings from the large portfolio of government securities held by the 12 Federal Reserve Banks are routinely transferred *back* to the Treasury after the expenses of operating the Federal Reserve System are deducted.

These sorts of interaction certainly imply that monetary policy cannot be conducted without reference to the fiscal situation, but there are additional aspects to consider that increase considerably our need to visualize the policy in a combined manner. To see this, let us set down again the simple *IS-LM* model of Chapter 7 and consider the traditional Keynesian multiplier analysis (which is generally worked through the *IS* sector). Let us use $C/P = a_1 + a_2(Y/P)$ for the consumption function, and $I/P = b_1 - b_3 i$ for the investment function and add an equation for government spending,

$$\frac{G}{P} = t_1, \tag{11.1}$$

where t_1 is a "control" variable measuring (for purposes of argument) discretionary fiscal policy.[8] Combined with the investment and consumption functions and with a clearing equation of $Y = C + I + G$, the *IS* curve that we earlier reported as Equation (7.12), in a slightly different arrangement, becomes

$$i = -\left(\frac{1 - a_2}{b_3}\right)\frac{Y}{P} + \left(\frac{a_1 + b_1 + t_1}{b_3}\right). \tag{11.2}$$

We can, immediately, graph a maximum fiscal policy for the case in which the interest rate is constant. Thus for a change, $\Delta(G/P)$, from t_1 to t_2 and for a fixed (unchanging) interest rate represented by a horizontal *LM* curve,[9] we get the situation shown in Figure 11.1. The horizontal distance $y_2 - y_1$ $(= \Delta y)$, recalling that $y = Y/P$, is given, algebraically, by the expression

$$\Delta y\left(\frac{1 - a_2}{b_3}\right) = \frac{\Delta G}{b_3},$$

which, if you work through the algebra, produces

$$\Delta y = \frac{1}{1 - a_2}\Delta G, \tag{11.3}$$

which is the traditional and simple Keynesian result; note that the slope of the *LM* curve is irrelevant in the event that we are in the liquidity trap (or when the interest rate is held constant as, for example, by an interest-stabilization type of monetary policy).

---

[8] We will be more realistic in a moment, when we introduce the revenue sources for this expenditure into the problem, but this simple device will get things going here.

[9] The horizontal section of the *LM* curve could be justified in terms of a liquidity trap, as was discussed in Chapter 6. Since such a result seems far removed from anything we have seen in recent years, we will not stay with it for very long here. Note that we are changing both y $(= Y/P)$ and t_1 and holding i constant; mathematically, we have solved

$$di = \frac{\partial i}{\partial y}\,dy + \frac{\partial i}{\partial t_1}\,dt_1$$

for $di = 0$.

Figure 11.1: A pure fiscal policy (in the "liquidity trap")

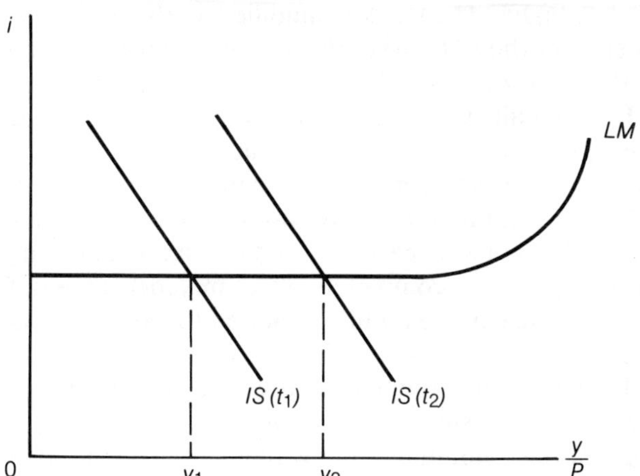

But Figure 11.1 and Equation (11.3) are clearly not very general, as we have noted, and the solution, which implies a strong (ultimate) effect on real income as a result of fiscal injection, is seriously overstated. Thus, in particular, let us draw in an upsloping *LM* curve, as in Figure 11.2, and represent it by Equation (7.17), here repeated for reasons of clarity, as

$$i = \frac{f_1 - \frac{g_1}{P}}{f_3 + \frac{g_3}{P}} + \frac{f_2}{f_3 + \frac{g_3}{P}} \left(\frac{Y}{P}\right) . \tag{11.4}$$

Figure 11.2: Fiscal policy in the *IS-LM* model, illustrating simple crowding-out

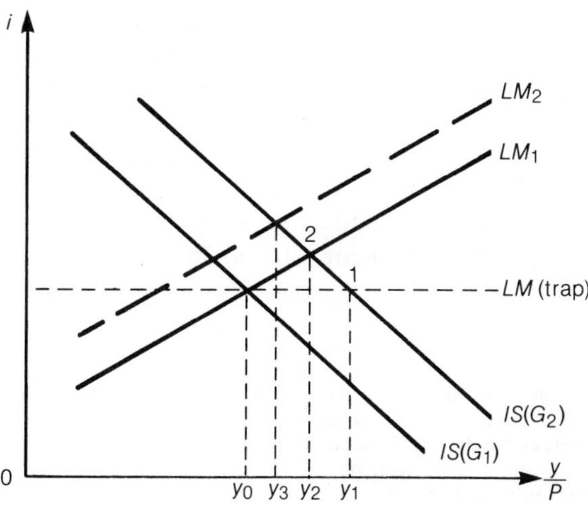

As the graph indicates, the full effect on income we obtained in the earlier case ($y_1 - y_0$ in Figure 11.2) is now modified so that only $y_2 - y_0$ results; indeed, the steeper the *LM* curve, the less of an effect we would get here. In the limit there would be no effect of fiscal policy, when *LM* is perfectly vertical.[10] This is called *crowding out* and it operates by means of the interest rate; it is called crowding out because the rise in the interest rate squeezes out some private consumption and investment (from point 1 to point 2 in Figure 11.2) as the money market returns to equilibrium. Indeed, when the *LM* curve is perfectly vertical, an increase in government spending from G_1 to G_2 is completely offset by a decrease in $C + I$ *of the same amount* (because of the requirement that the money market return to equilibrium).

The mechanics of crowding out involve the government's presence in bond markets (we are assuming a bond-financed deficit). In particular, if it enters these markets searching for new funds, it will tend to drive interest rates up, and the higher interest rates will then tend to produce lower investment and consumption. The important point to note, in any event, is that an interest-induced "crowding out" is capable of severely reducing the effectiveness of fiscal policy. Of course one immediately sees why a relatively constant interest rate policy might be of interest to the fiscal authorities (the interest rate tends to move against them in *two* ways: in the sense of crowding out and in the sense of creating future budgetary problems on account of the higher interest payments they must make).

Turning to monetary policy we also see that a similar type of effect occurs, although private expenditure is not crowded out. Looking back at our money supply function, we see that we can represent monetary policy by a shift of the function—in particular, if g_1 in $M_s = g_1 + g_3 i$ increases, the money supply curve shifts to the right. This effect, too, would be at a maximum if the *IS* curve were flat, although not much is made of this in the literature. At any rate, as Figure 11.3 demonstrates, monetary policy, too, has to live with less than a maximum result. Indeed, the interest rate effect here acts along the *LM* curve (from point 1 back to point 2) and represents the fact that real money balances are taken up in idle (possibly speculative?) balances rather than spent to generate real income as the interest rate falls (as it must to bring the spending (*IS*) market back into equilibrium). So both fiscal and monetary policy are potentially weakened by interest rate effects that are obviously hard to estimate (to say the least).

---

[10] This possibility is often called the extreme Classical or Monetarist case (with *some* justification) but as such it is as much a straw man as was the liquidity trap. The point is that the multiplier effect has to be modified (by $f_2/[f_3 + g_3/P]$) so that the money market *also reaches its equilibrium*. This will, of course, reverse some of the earlier effect since it involves a higher interest rate.

But this is not all, as you may have observed, because there is an additional variable in the problem—the price level—that we have been illegitimately holding constant throughout the analysis. This, as we will discuss directly, also affects both fiscal and monetary policy. Consider fiscal policy as described in Figure 11.2. Suppose that the pressure of fiscal policy, however financed, produces an upward movement in prices (on average); as we have constructed our system, this will produce a *leftward* shift of the *LM* curve (or an upward shift if it is flat) back beyond y_2 (perhaps, even, to y_0). Thus, this "price" crowding out, in which even more private expenditure ($C + I$) is eliminated as the fiscally induced inflation induces the private sector to curtail its operations, is an *addition* to the crowding out by means of the interest rate. It is illustrated in Figure 11.2 by LM_2 and the solution y_3 (which could theoretically represent *less* private spending in real terms than y_0). This effect clearly introduces further variability (and uncertainty, as well) into the effect of fiscal policy.[11]

Monetary policy, also, has a "price level" effect and in this case, at least, it is somewhat more obvious since most observers find it easier to link up changes in the quantity of money with the rate of inflation than to link up fiscal policy with inflation. In this case our reference is to Figure 11.3. Here the inflation that results from the "reallocation of monetary resources" shifts the *LM* curve back again; indeed, some may argue that it goes all the way back and, consequently, you cannot affect real variables

Figure 11.3: The interest-rate effect on monetary policy

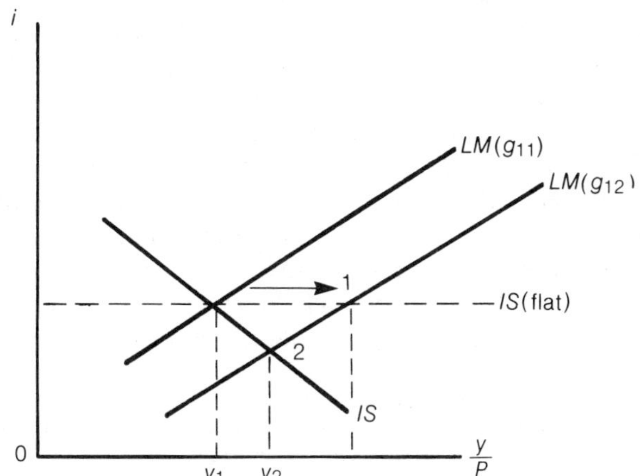

[11] Of course, we are also on the border of another sort of issue involving the possible tendency of fiscally aggressive governments to swallow up the private sector as they seek (innocently and perhaps ineffectively) to stabilize the economy.

(like y) by means of monetary policy.[12] Note that an effect of monetary policy is to stimulate the growth of the money-creating industry, *and little else*. This makes a nice point to carry back to our discussion in Chapter 2 on the influence of inflation on bank profits and in Chapter 3 on the rapid growth of the money industry in recent years.

So monetary and fiscal policy are not as simple a set of prescriptions as one might have thought, and there is a further complication that arises because of an explicit connection between the two. You may recall, from Table 5.13, that the Federal Reserve Banks hold a substantial portion of the national debt as the offsetting balance sheet item against both the currency they issue and the quantity of reserves of the member banks which they hold. In fact, the federal government, when it conducts a fiscal policy (such as a government expenditure) has three sources of revenues, broadly speaking, since it cannot spend out of thin air; these are:

a. Increased tax revenues.

b. Borrowing (an increased deficit, in effect).

c. Money creation (really high-powered money creation).

This can be expressed formally. Any government spending must be financed, so that an additional equation,

$$G = \Delta B + \Delta H + T,$$

must hold, and any *increased* expenditure *must* come from these sources. Let us see how this affects our analysis.

Let us, arbitrarily, rule out increased tax revenue as a method of finance of an unemployment-inspired fiscal policy since the increased tax revenues would have to come from the same public we are trying to stimulate; this leaves bond financing and high-powered money creation. If we finance by the latter, clearly, the effect of the fiscal policy will be the largest possible; indeed, we can *add* together the effects for fiscal and monetary policy, since the increase in H shifts the money supply curve to the right (by, it must be admitted, a multiplied amount). Of course, *both* price crowding out effects occur to move us back, but at any rate it is likely that an additional influence would bear upon a fiscal policy financed by money creation, however unpalatable these ideas may be.

---

[12] Both the Keynesians and the Monetarists (recently) associated with "rational expectations" seem to have had this view, although this model is not adapted to the latter problem (which we will discuss in Section 11.5). There is a difference in the two effects, because an additional price level term appears in the monetary policy version as the result of the fact that a curve (the money supply curve) with money illusion in it is itself shifting. Algebraically, the influence of this additional sum here is to reduce further the value of Δy as the price level increases. To work this out, you need merely note (from Chapter 7) that f_3 has a negative sign (which, for a positive change in g_1 and in prices, gives the result just stated). So there is some slight reason here to suppose that monetary policy is "less effective" on real incomes and, perforce, more effective on prices.

The more complicated case—and the one "normally" considered by the government—is the bond-financed fiscal policy; here the Treasury sells bonds to the public rather than to the banks and simply puts the cash back into the banking system in order to neutralize any effect on the Federal Reserve's balance sheet (and, accordingly, on the monetary base or on high-powered money). Let us look at the bond market, briefly, to see what is going on; Figure 11.4 is relevant. We have labeled the vertical

Figure 11.4: The bond market during a fiscal policy ($i_2 > i_1$)

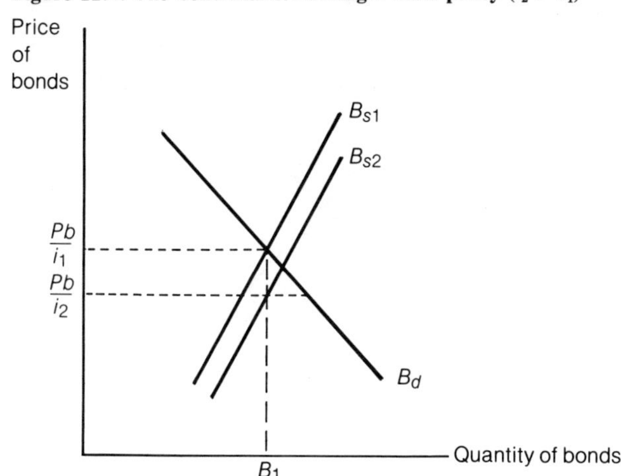

axis as the *price of bonds;* thus, we assume that at higher bond prices people demand fewer bonds and at lower prices they demand more. Similarly, a bond supply curve with a positive slope can be assumed. Now the price of bonds is related to the market rate of interest in an *inverse* way. In particular, recalling Equation (6.5) or the equation in Footnote 3 of Chapter 6, we see that when the opportunity cost of holding a particular bond goes up—that is, when *other* interest rates go up—the bond price goes down. This is because an opportunity that has a fixed payout trades at a lower price when other opportunities get better. Thus as we move down the vertical axis in Figure 11.4, the interest rate is *rising* (if this does not make sense it will, in a moment).

Now suppose that the federal government enters the bond market with a new issue—a new supply—in order to finance its stimulatory fiscal policy. This is a rightward shift of the bond supply curve, and it produces a fall in the price of bonds and, accordingly, a rise in the interest rate. To put it another way, if the federal government puts pressure on financial markets with a sizable bond issue, higher interest rates will surely result. Now in terms of our model, which has an interest rate but no bond market, there is no simple and direct way to represent this situation. One suspects, of course, that a *further* interest rate crowding out will occur and, in fact, that is the case; indeed, both the *IS* and *LM* curves will be involved. Let us arbitrarily assume that the money market has to bear the whole burden of additional adjustment; the situation there is depicted in Figure 11.5. Assuming that there is no feedback between the two markets

Figure 11.5: The money market adjustment to a bond-financed fiscal policy

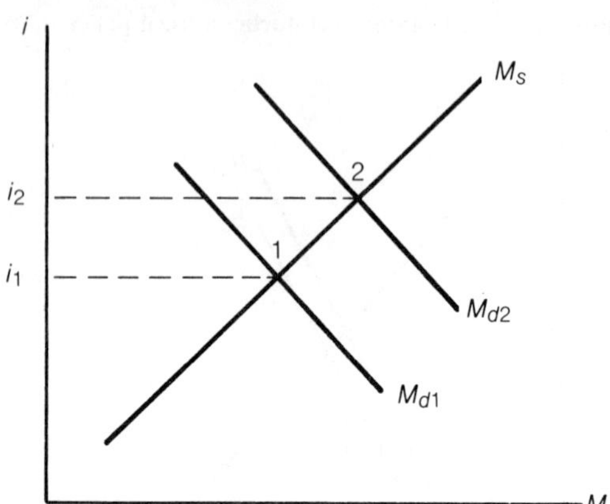

(feedback would suggest an interest rate somewhere between i_1 and i_2—we are merely simplifying), then the money market is not cleared at the new and higher interest rate. If we stick to the fixed money supply in nominal terms (Figure 11.5 is in nominal terms), then our movement here would be up the M_s curve to point 2—an increase in the stock of money accompanied by an inflation-induced shift of the demand for money to Md_2, as predicted by Equation (7.13). Looking, then, at Figure 11.6 we can show this as a leftward shift of the *LM* curve (as before)—one can analyze it in terms of the parameter f_1 in Equation (7.14)—that reduces or crowds out the fiscal action because of the bond financing. Consider, then, the total result in Figure 11.6. The fiscal policy shifts the *IS* curve to IS_2; this produces an initial crowding out, from point 2 to point 3, because the money market must clear at the higher interest rate. Both because of the increased money stock and the generalized pressure on resources, prices begin to rise; this shifts us to point 4. Now for the method of finance: pressure on the bond market, as we have *illustrated,* requires a yet higher interest rate; this, in turn, requires a further leftward shift of the *LM* curve (via inflation) to point 5.

The point should be obvious. Fiscal policy, unless financed by money expansion or, equivalently, unless accompanied by a policy to hold the interest rate constant (via a monetary expansion) is not necessarily going

Figure 11.6: Perfect crowding-out (the deficit approach to fiscal policy)

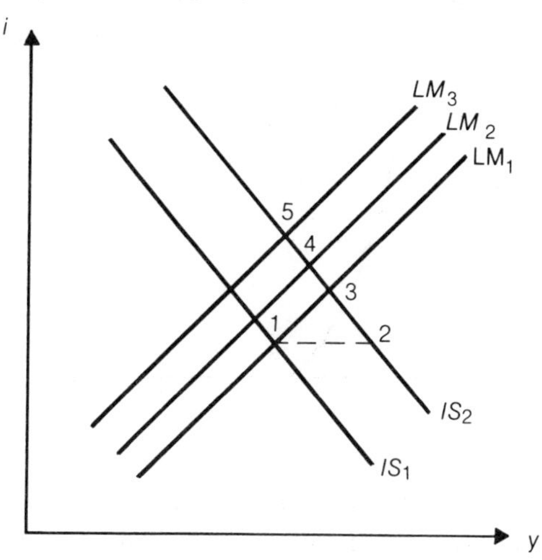

to produce a "full" or predictable effect on real income and employment. Indeed, it is very likely that an initial positive effect (some way along the line between point 1 and point 2) will be actually *reversed* quickly (consider the sequence of points 1, 2, 3, 4, 5, which may well correspond to the temporal pattern). Even if one cannot agree that a reversal is likely, one would have to agree that a policy problem exists here because these processes (*a*) are not fully understood and (*b*) require full knowledge of the system (of all the parameters in the model) if they are to be counteracted. The knowledge must be accurate, of course. But not just fiscal policy is subject to these problems; monetary policy also produces similar effects, with a greater role going to the price effect. Finally, we should note that there is a vigorous dispute over the actual extent of crowding out in the American economy, with the Keynesians, by and large, producing smaller estimates than the Monetarists (although both agree it exists).[13]

11.4 THE PHILLIPS CURVE

In the 1950s a British economist, William Phillips, first traced out and attempted to explain an empirical relationship that he observed between *changes* in money wages and unemployment (U). In subsequent versions this was refined to a relationship between inflation rates ($\Delta P/P$) and unemployment; indeed, something like Figure 11.7 apparently held for a

[13] See the discussion in Jerome Stein, ed., *Monetarism* (Amsterdam: North-Holland, 1976).

Figure 11.7: The Phillips curve

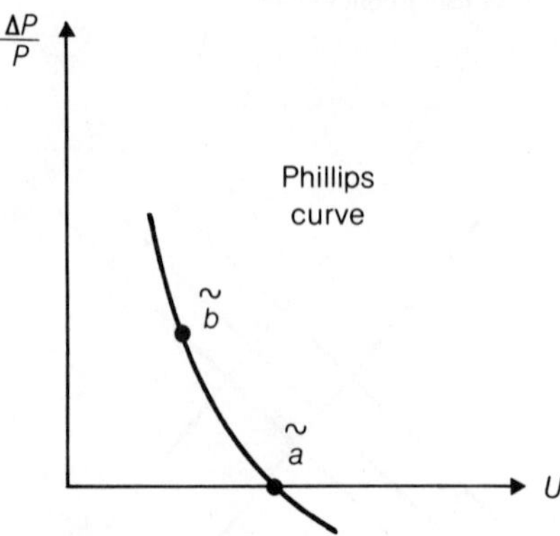

very long run of British data. The general idea is a simple one: as labor markets tighten (as demand expands), wages (and prices) would tend to rise. This rise in wage and price levels accelerates (it is argued) as the pressure on markets steps up (and unemployment falls) to such a degree that the rate of change of prices may also rise. Thus, while prices and not the inflation rate rise directly in the theory, the latter may also rise (especially if the "demand pressure" is stepped up) particularly near full employment (at values of unemployment to the left of point $\tilde{a}$). This, too, is not implausible, particularly as a short-run proposition.

The foregoing proposition is basically an empirical one, and this fact provides it with some strength (although it does not always show up), and it provides us with an interesting problem, since we should be able to link it to our basic macro theory in some way. The strength also has some very important implications, for if there actually is a stable Phillips curve, then the two *objective* variables involved—unemployment and inflation—are actually substitutes along a well-behaved path and we can reduce unemployment only if we are willing to have more inflation. A very clear policy choice would then seem to exist: we can have an unemployment of $\tilde{a}$ in Figure 11.7 (call it the *natural* rate of unemployment) or we can have less (by means of monetary and fiscal policy) but when we have less, we must pay for it with more inflation. Point $\tilde{b}$, though, is attainable and we may reach it, *if the curve is stable*.

Since the Phillips curve started its life as an empirical generalization, it is natural to look at some recent data to see whether the same generalization holds for the United States. In this case, let us look at a graph (Figure 11.8) drawn up by the Federal Reserve Bank of St. Louis. Here we see a circular time path (moving clockwise as it drifts to the right) for the inflation-unemployment trade-off. Within selected intervals, though, we can see several negatively sloped *short-run* Phillips curves superimposed

Figure 11.8: Inflation and unemployment, 1954–1978 (annual data)

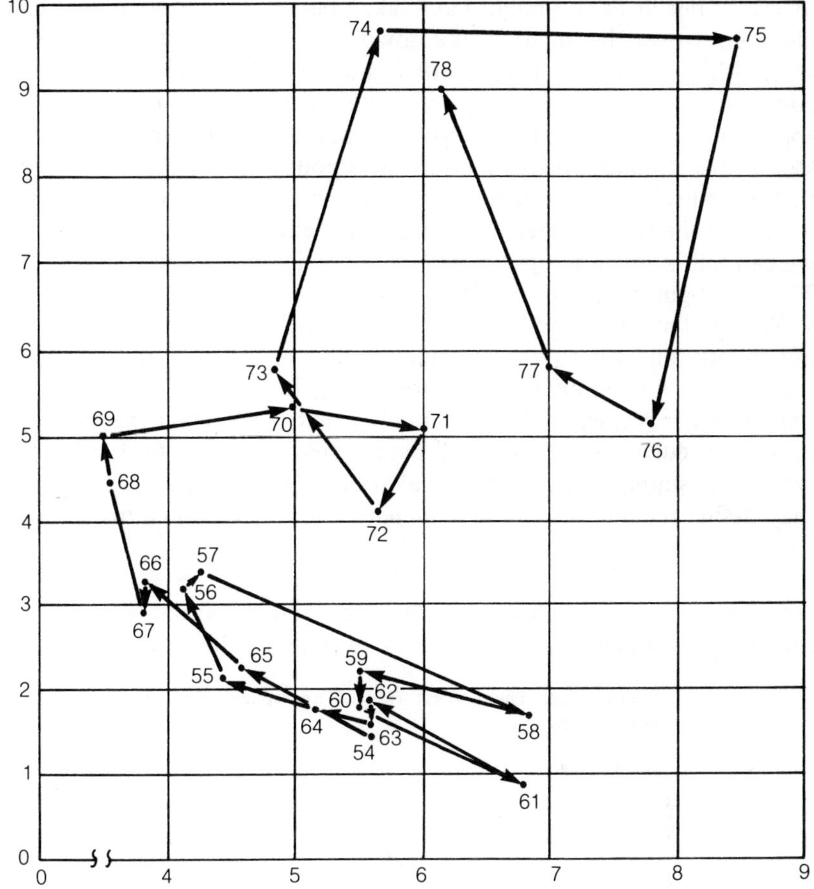

* Percentage change in the GNP implicit price deflator.
† Percent of civilian labor force.
Latest data plotted: 1977.
Source: John A. Tatom, "Does The Stage of the Business Cycle Affect the Inflation Rate?" *Review, Federal Reserve Bank of St. Louis* (September 1978), p. 9.

on a positively sloped (or even vertical) *long-run* Phillips curve.[14] It is *as if* we used our monetary policy to try to pick a point on the short-run curve with lower inflation and *higher* unemployment (in 1969 and 1973 particu-

---

[14] Most of the major industrialized countries with comparable inflation experiences (look back at Chapter 9) have found both inflation and unemployment worsening in recent years (have found, that is to say, a positively sloped Phillips curve).

larly) and saw *both* get worse as the curve suddenly shifted (look at 1970 and 1974–75). In 1969, if we could have gone back down the curve drawn, then a 1.8 percent inflation and 5 percent unemployment would seem to go together; but in 1970 it might have taken between 7 and 9 percent unemployment to get the inflation rate down to 2 percent (extending the lines along which 1970 and 1972 or 1970 and 1971 lie). This change in our circumstances is alarming and, as far as one can say, is not as widely appreciated as it ought to be. Note, in particular, that the monetary restraint, fiscal policy, prices-and-incomes policy, and a sharp recession in that period were all unable to put us back on the first curve (we continued to drift to the right). Indeed, if policy were effective in this period, for all we can tell, it made things worse (1969 was a tight-money year and 1972–73 was a tight-money interval).

We will have to again bring back our models of Chapters 7, 8 and 9 to appreciate fully what might be behind these results. Let us first suppose that there is a fixed number of workers (L_T) in the economy and that this fixed number is greater than the number that would clear the market (L); L, in particular, is the quantity determined in Footnote 4, Chapter 8, which had supply and demand equal in the labor market. In this event, we may define the *natural rate of unemployment*[15] to be equal to

$$U = L_T - L. \tag{11.7}$$

It is, let us say, the amount $\tilde{a}$, in Figure 11.7; the situation in the labor market itself appears in Figure 11.9. Now suppose the federal government

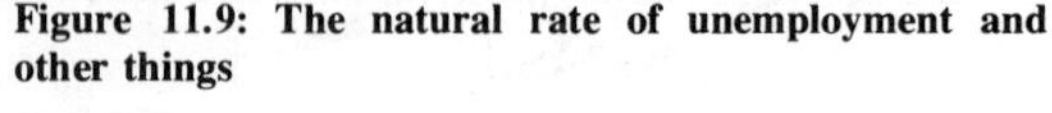
Figure 11.9: The natural rate of unemployment and other things

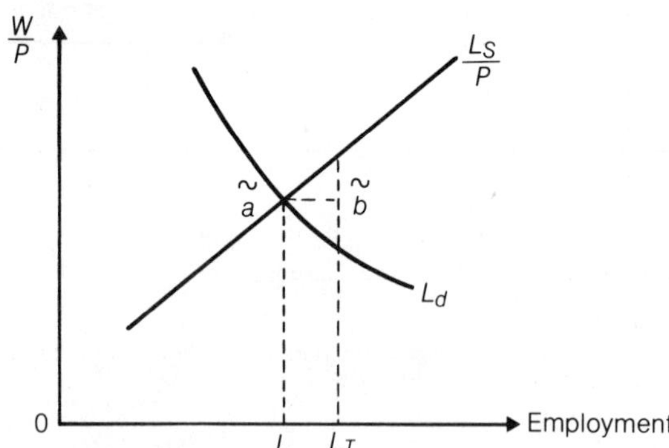

---

[15] This is "natural" only in the sense of market clearing. It is positive because it represents the current technology of the economy and the efficiency of labor markets, etc. The use of the word "natural" has offended some people but is, in any event, now widely employed; "equilibrium unemployment" or "short-run equilibrium unemployment" would have been better terms.

tries to reduce the quantity of unemployment by an appropriate fiscal and monetary policy, seeking to get to point $\tilde{b}$ in Figure 11.7; this increase in aggregate demand would have no effect on employment if there were no money illusion in the labor market, because the aggregate demand–aggregate supply relation would look like Figure 8.5, for the Classical case. In that case, there is no increase in real output to be carried back to the labor market, and so long as prices and wages move up together, nothing will happen. We would, in Figure 11.7 simply move up vertically from point $\tilde{a}$, in this extreme Classical case.

But suppose, instead, that there is money illusion in the labor market so that Figure 11.9 holds; then, the "more general" positively sloped aggregate supply curve of Figure 8.7 holds. This situation is one in which workers respond to a rise in money wages by offering more labor services, *regardless of what happens* to the price level (it is, of course, also rising). Workers are *tricked* by the monetary and fiscal policy into reducing unemployment; furthermore, the trick works (it takes us to point $\tilde{b}$ in Figure 11.7 and Figure 11.9, and it takes us up the aggregate supply curve in Figure 8.7).

Actually, both the employers and the workers are fooled in this way. The main reason they are fooled is that they accurately see the nominal rise because it is *their* nominal wage and *their* price, but, given the cost of acquiring information, they are much less well informed about the other wages and prices they need to form a general picture. To calculate their *real* wage (and price) accurately, they need this general price information. Whenever the inflation rate moves erratically, such effects can be expected.

But several problems emerge. To stay at $\tilde{b}$ in Figures 11.7 and 11.9—since it is not a market-clearing point, we must continue to inflate. Worse, workers will catch on to the fact that the *real* terms of their contracts have not changed, and will shift back to point $\tilde{a}$ in Figure 11.9; they will come to *expect* inflation (much as investors did in Chapter 9) and to build these expectations into their contracts. Thus, to keep unemployment at the new level, *once the workers catch on,* the government will have to step up its operations. In effect, in Figure 11.7 the Phillips curve will shift to the right (as, indeed it has). This is the line of reasoning behind the Monetarist-inspired "expectations-augmented Phillips curve": in the short run we can reduce unemployment below the natural level by fooling workers, but as they catch on, we must step up the pressure; this movement is slow or fast depending on how quickly price expectations catch on to the underlying causes of inflation (we call this failure to adjust "adaptive" expectations). The *long-run* Phillips curve, in this event, may well be a vertical line (look again in Figure 11.8) at the natural rate of unemployment. In this event, the long-run cost of an anti-unemployment monetary policy may well be more inflation with no change in unemployment; indeed, a pessimist might argue that we may even tend to have more of both, if the intercept of the Phillips curve shifts to the right.[16]

11.5 RATIONAL EXPECTATIONS

Recently, some Monetarists have proposed an even stronger version of this expectations-augmented Phillips curve that actually denies that monetary policy has any firm role to play at all (other than to "control" prices). This is known as the *rational expectations* theory and it contradicts the idea of adaptive expectations. To begin with, let us notice that in the Monetarist model just outlined, the expectations of future inflation rates were generally based on past inflation rates. Thus, in our previous analysis, we got a short-run Phillips curve because the monetary-inspired inflation tricked some economic agents to offer more services than they would have if they had known that their *real* conditions had not changed; thus, as they reacted to the news that prices in general were rising, they revised upward their expectation of inflation and revised downward their offer of services. We now call this, as just pointed out, the *adaptive expectations* hypothesis, and it is important because (*a*) it provides another explanation of why there are lags in the effect of monetary policy, (*b*) it shows why there are real effects of monetary policy, and (*c*) it explains the (sometimes) positive slope of the Phillips curve.

But suppose, instead, that economic agents are not tricked in this way. Suppose that they, too, have a model of how the economy functions and that it is the right model. Suppose, in particular, that they know that the principal long-run effect of a monetary increase, that is faster than the economy can absorb, will arise in the inflation rate; in this event, being "rational," they will monitor the available data on the money supply (which is, after all, made much of, on a weekly basis, in *The Wall Street Journal*) and in the case in which it is growing faster than it should, they will instantly (being "rational") revise their calculations. In this scenario no direct short-run real effects occur as a result of monetary policy (they appear to occur in Figure 11.8 for coincidental reasons), and monetary policy is powerless as a short-run stabilization tool.

Needless to say, this approach has drawn fire from both sides. First of all, we should note that it *is* a distinct possibility (or, even, a limiting case), and that it can provide an explanation of why monetary policy seems to get us into trouble. For example in terms of Figure 11.8 we moved up a short-run Phillips curve in 1967 and 1968 *for other reasons* and then, after the tight money policy of 1969 was finished, we stepped up the rate of

---

[16] Much of this is inspired by the discussion in Milton Friedman, "The Role of Monetary Policy," *American Economic Review* (March 1968); see also Thomas M. Humphrey, "Some Recent Developments in Phillips Curve Analysis," *Economic Review, Federal Reserve Bank of Richmond* (January/February 1978).

production of money too quickly (to try to mop up unemployment) only to produce nothing but inflation (we tricked no one). But the theory does not give much play to nonmonetary explanations of inflation (hence draws the fire of Keynesians) and, perhaps more tellingly, attributes to the private sector both too much knowledge (even the authorities, who have better analytical equipment, may have the wrong model) and too much ability to adjust. With regard to the latter, we note that whether or not you can trick economic agents, many of them are locked into long-term contracts (wage, mortgage, and the like) and will simply not be able to react to changes in current policy. So some potential effect of a monetary policy is already built into the economic system.

This is not the place to present an appraisal of who is winning this rapidly escalating debate (see the references cited at the end of this chapter), but one should note, at the least, that the mere existence of such basic *and unresolved* issues (as "Does monetary policy work at all?") ought to be fundamentally disconcerting to those who would merely pull the monetary lever on the basis of the blind faith of the recent past. This, perhaps, is a good note on which to leave the subject of the transmission mechanism and turn to the actual workings of (recent) policy.

11.6 STUDY QUESTIONS

Essay questions

1. What is the exact relation between unemployment and the inflation rate that causes the latter to rise as full employment is approached? Try to give both a microeconomic and macroeconomic interpretation. Are expectations involved in any way? In what way (if at all) is the money supply involved in your answer?

2. It has been argued by some economists that, following an open market operation, a considerable amount of time elapses before individuals get their portfolios realigned. What does the length of the lag depend on and what, do you think, is a reasonable portfolio-adjustment time period? Do interest rates and brokerage fees play any role in your answer?

3. Should one also emphasize the variability as well as the length of the lags in fiscal and monetary policy? Compare the expected variability for the two approaches, using income tax rates for your fiscal policy and an open market operation for your monetary policy. Try to be specific.

4. Discuss the effects of a tight money monetary policy on the distribution of real income. How would you expect the distribution of income to move over the business cycle in the absence of monetary policy? Try to find some recent data for the United States to support or contradict your conjectures.

True-false discussion questions

These statements are meant to be somewhat ambiguous, and to provoke discussion thereby.

1. The length of the lag-in-effect in monetary policy (an open market operation) is shorter if the policy is a more vigorous one.

2. If inflationary expectations are accurate, then the Phillips curve will shift erratically, whether or not the government tries an activist monetary policy.

3. Changes in interest rates will not affect investment spending much since interest is a small part of the total cost of business operations.

4. The longer the lag-in-effect of monetary policy, the more variable will the effect of the policy be, other things being equal.

5. The reduction of an expansionary monetary policy may well be less than that of a fiscal policy since the former has no interest-rate crowding-out while the latter does.

6. The failure of the Phillips curve is essentially good for macroeconomic policy since it implies that both unemployment and inflation can be improved; if the Phillips curve held, the authorities would have to make a choice.

7. If the *LM* curve were such that there is no interest-rate crowding-out, then fiscal policy, as financed by bond issue, would itself not be crowded out, even in the long run.

8. If expectations are "adaptive" rather than "rational," then shifts in the Phillips curve brought about by changes in the aggregate supply sector will tend to be self-defeating, but only in the long run.

11.7 FURTHER READING

Eastburn, David P., and W. Lee Hoskins. "The Influence of Monetary Policy on Commercial Banking." *Business Review, Federal Reserve Bank of Philadelphia* (July/August 1978).

Federal Reserve Bank of Boston. *Consumer Spending and Monetary Policy: The Linkages*. 1971.

Friedman, Milton. "Inflation and Unemployment" (The Nobel Lecture). *Journal of Political Economy* (May/June 1977). See also Friedman, Milton. "The Role of Monetary Policy." *American Economic Review* (March 1968).

Hamburger, Michael J. "The Lag in Effect of Monetary Policy: A Survey of Recent Literature." In *Monetary Aggregates and Monetary Policy*. Boston: Federal Reserve Bank of Boston, 1974.

Laidler, David. "Money and Money Income: An Essay on the Transmission Mechanism." *Journal of Monetary Economics* (April 1978).

"Rational Expectations—Fresh Ideas that Challenge Some Established Views of Policy Making." *Annual Report, Federal Reserve Bank of Minneapolis,* 1977.

12

The climate and conduct of American monetary policy: Some further problems and some lessons from recent experience

12.1 INTRODUCTION

In Chapters 6, 7, and 8 we discussed the elements of a basic macroeconomic model that, itself, contained the variables that we have come to consider as the major objective variables (as analyzed in Chapter 10). In Chapter 9 we focused attention on one of the variables—the rate of change of prices—mostly because it seems, by the previous arguments in this book if nothing else, to lie firmly in the domain of monetary policy. There we argued that the problem of inflation has a worldwide character, a fact that suggests that we may not be able to resolve it at the national level. Even so, in the last half of Chapter 10, we considered how monetary policy might be used to influence the inflation rate (and other variables) in the sense of setting some "instrument variables." There we pointed out that some important slippage in the policy itself seems to occur in the sense that a change in an instrument does not seem to lead uniquely to a change in the quantity of money.

If that were all one had to worry about, then there would still be plenty of scope for an active monetary policy; but as Chapter 11 has pointed out, the transmission of the monetary impulse (the change in M) is itself delayed and even possibly ambiguous in both the short- and long-run effects on the final variables. Indeed, as we pointed out, our knowledge of what we optimistically call "the transmission mechanism" is far from complete and in any event is not far enough along for us to feel totally confident that an active monetary policy will pay us a sufficiently rich dividend. But there are more problems, as we will see in the first part of Chapter 12, because the underlying model itself is still poorly understood (or, at least, not agreed upon), and it seems we must do the best we can in a kind of groping-along procedure. This procedure is described as one in which intermediate financial variables are so monitored (a "targets-indicators" approach) that an active monetary policy *could* be successful. But when we turn to the actual policies of recent years, the accumulation of potential problems—from data measurement to incorrectly designed policies—seems to have put us in the position of actually having relatively little success with our policies, *whatever* we seem to have been trying to do. Worse, at least to those who would accept some of the theoretical arguments up to this point in this book, many of the important problems in the design of a successful policy do not appear to be recognized by the monetary authorities, at least if we go by their published policies (and the data). Indeed, this chapter will conclude on this rather dismal note.

12.2 UNCERTAINTY AND FISCAL AND MONETARY POLICY

In the preceding chapters we have presented a number of reasons that the operation of fiscal and monetary policy may well not be successful; primarily, these problems have arisen because of lags in adjustment or because of our inability to capture expectations although we have also mentioned mistaken or contradictory policy choices. These are all relevant concerns, of course, but a matter of even more importance may well be the following: the basic *model* of the economy which we use to guide our choices may be (*a*) wrong, (*b*) incomplete, (*c*) badly estimated, or, more likely, all three at once. To see the possibilities just recall that Keynesians, arguing from a complete theoretical model, think money does not matter (much), while the Monetarists, also arguing from a firm theoretical standpoint, think pretty much the opposite. More seriously, neither position—even the extreme views—has been completely eliminated by a generation of careful empirical testing of the basic propositions.

The problem is basic, actually, and we need not confuse the issue by bringing up the Keynes-versus-the Monetarists debate; it arises, in truth, because we are trying to deal with our control problem by constructing a model (we have to, of course, and that is why it is a basic problem). Think back to the general model of Chapters 7 and 8. That model omitted financial markets and foreign markets; had a fixed stock of capital; had a very highly aggregated structure (it had only one kind of consumer good, in effect); was static; basically omitted the government (and, of course, the government's budget constraint); assumed, generally, perfect competition; was written in a linear form; and was totally deterministic in that all of the relations were assumed to hold without error (that is, to hold exactly). All models have such a list appended to them; formulation of a model with fewer constraints, in an attempt to achieve total generality, considerably raises the cost of using the model (for example, if we added another sector then, in certain cases, we could not use two-dimensional graphs). However, the last item, the totally *deterministic* nature of the model, is unacceptable (and, indeed, we generally do not take that approach), and we should, at least, generalize here beyond that level.

In fact, each equation of our model is subject to important qualifications and each is estimated, in practice, with "error." The errors arise, to repeat the point, at least partly because the model is untrue for every case and, indeed, the ratio of error to truth in the model is our usual index of the quality of the model.[1] Thus consider the scatter of points in Figure 12.1; these points, we might argue, represent the amount of business

Figure 12.1: Representative data on the investment function

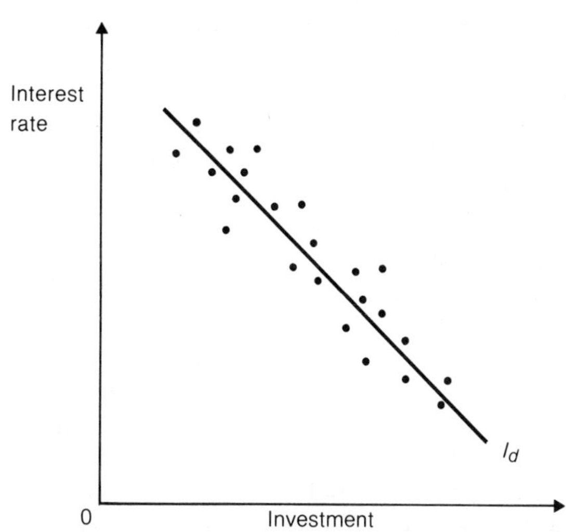

investment that we *actually* observed at various levels of the interest rate in recent years. This is the way the information on aggregate investment looks; it is a scatter of points relating the interest rate to investment, collected at different points in time. Now if we "model" these data—if we

[1] Errors also arise because of incorrect data; we call these "measurement errors."

try to draw a straight line consistent with the model of Chapter 7 through the scatter—the model (the line) will not touch all the points (and probably will not touch any of them exactly). The difference is the "error" or unexplained (by the model) component of the relation. Basically, then, each of the equations in our model—whatever the nature of the model—has some error attached to it, and as we combine equations we bring along (to the *IS* and *LM* curves, for example) this accumulated error. Naturally, we attempt to reduce this error by strengthening the model and improving our data, but an important error will always exist (particularly in the investment and foreign components of our standard macro models), so this is a continuing problem.

Clearly, then, one way to distinguish between the Keynesian and the Monetarist models is by their relative overall performance in the sense of explaining past economic behavior. We can report—indeed we have taken the position in this book—that both models have their moments (perhaps real cycles are best dealt with by Keynesian models and price level cycles by Monetarist models) but the issue is bound to remain in its present undecided state for some years. More positively, though, and this is the point of departure for this chapter, we are able to show which approach we ought to take—either controlling the interest rate or the money stock (assuming, of course, that we want to stabilize the economy)—if we know in advance which sector (the real or the monetary) is subject to the larger unpredictable change (that is, is subject to the greater error). Let us consider this problem.

Assume that the single objective of monetary policy is to stabilize the level of real national income (Y); assume, as well, that we can do this by either controlling the interest rate (in which case monetary quantities are free to vary) or controlling the quantity of money (in which case the interest rate is free to vary). These statements are made with a picture of the money market in mind similar to that in Chapter 7 or in Figure 12.3. Consider the simple *IS-LM* model in Figure 12.2. In a completely deterministic world—let us say one represented by *IS* and *LM*—it makes absolutely no difference whether one aims at an interest-rate or a money-stock target. It makes no difference because whether we fix the interest rate or fix the money stock, we can put the *LM* curve anywhere we like (via either of our monetary policies) and thus achieve any level of income (our objective) consistent with *IS*. But suppose the *IS* function is subject to such (unknown) disturbances in the underlying functions that its position can be anywhere between IS_1 and IS_2 in Figure 12.2; assume as well that the *LM* curve is fixed (i.e., known) at either LM_2 (the fixed interest rate case) or at LM_1 (the fixed money stock case). Suppose, as well, that our objective is y_f—for full employment—and that we will pick that approach (stabilize M or stabilize i) that gets us the *closest* to y_f in the sense of getting the narrowest *band* of potential variation around y_f. Now, as

Figure 12.2: Monetary policy with random errors in *IS* function

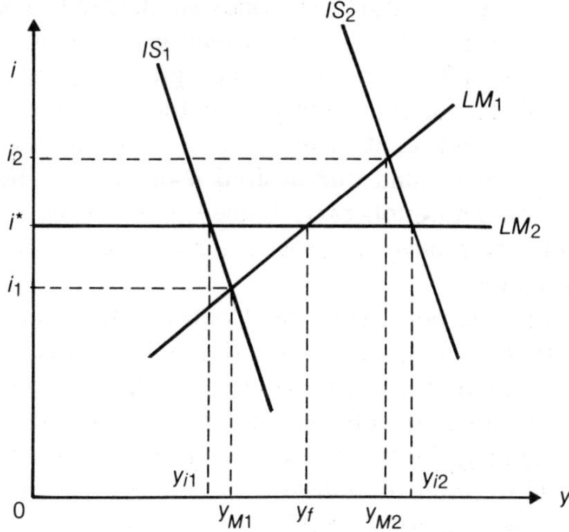

Figure 12.3: The money market for alternative monetary policy strategies

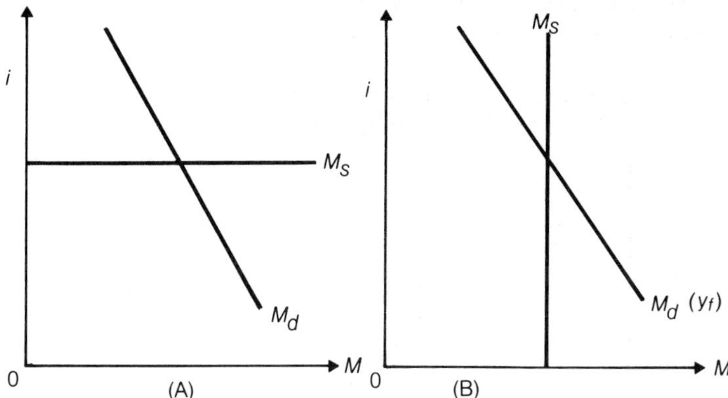

noted, if we fix the interest rate we will get the horizontal LM_2; this comes from the money market as pictured in Panel *A* of Figure 12.3. Alternatively, if we control the money stock, Panel *B* of Figure 12.3 is the situation; in this event the *LM* curve will have a positive slope in the (i, y) space; thus LM_1 is the result.[2]

Turning to our comparison, the *LM* curve is LM_2, the curve that results from the ''interest rate stabilization'' policy; in this event real income will

[2] The interested reader can refer back to the equations in Chapter 7 to work these effects out, more precisely.

lie anywhere between y_{i1} and y_{i2} *as the curves are drawn* in Figure 12.2. This range was calculated by taking the possible range for the *uncertain IS* curve. If, alternatively, we adopt the money stock stabilization approach, and LM_1 is the resulting *LM* curve, then real income will lie somewhere between y_{M1} and y_{M2}, so far as we can predict, given our uncertainty about the nature of the disturbances in the real sector (affecting the *IS* curve). *Clearly,* the money stock control policy is a better policy (in terms of getting a tighter band around our desired level of real income) if real "disturbances" dominate monetary. Indeed, one suspects this is how a Monetarist might recommend we proceed, in general, under the assumptions of this paragraph.[3]

But this approach is not inevitable. Consider, for example, the case when the *LM* curve is subject to a considerable fluctuation and the *IS* curve is not; this situation is one in which the money market is relatively chaotic (as Keynesians frequently assert). Again we will consider the two policy choices: holding the interest rate constant or holding the money stock constant. If we hold the interest rate constant, Panel *A* of Figure 12.3 is still the relevant picture; in this event we can bypass the unpredictability of the *LM* curve and produce any interest rate we wish (e.g., i^*) in order to produce y_f, the desired goal of full employment national income. Look at LM_3 in Figure 12.5. On the other hand, if we decide to hold the money stock constant, then if the disturbances in the *LM* curve are due

Figure 12.4: A money market with large random disturbances in the demand for money

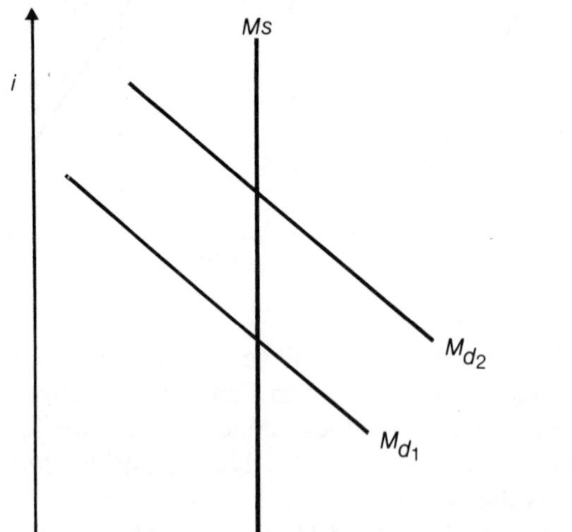

[3] Note, though, that we must be able to control the *LM* curve, and some Monetarists, at least, feel this is not necessarily possible.

Figure 12.5: Monetary policy random errors in the *LM* function

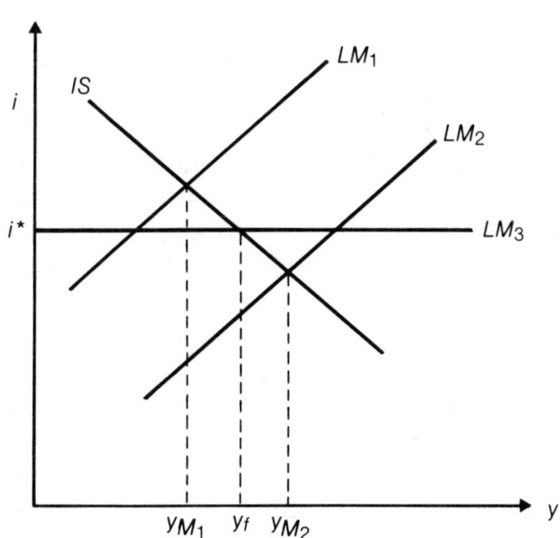

to our inability to pin down the demand for money (as shown in Figure 12.4) then the *LM* curve in Figure 12.5 can lie anywhere between LM_1 and LM_2; this produces, for the policy of stabilizing the money stock, a potential variation of real income between y_{M_1} and y_{M_2} that, clearly, is greater than that with an interest rate stabilization approach ($= y_f$). So the interest rate stabilization approach has some validity, at least in this simplified context.[4]

There are several important points one might carry away from a discussion of this sort. For one thing, it should be apparent that the *actual approach* to monetary policy will depend on the quality of our information in a more specific way than one might have expected. For another, even the "interest stabilization approach," which we were so negative about in Chapters 9 and 11, has its merits. Then, too, one finds a certain consistency in the Keynesian approach (on the one hand), which sometimes argues for interest rate stabilization as the best we can get our of monetary policy and often claims that the monetary sector is harder to pin down than the spending sector. The Monetarists (on the other hand) feel (*a*) that the demand for money is a stable function of a few key variables, (*b*) that the *IS* curve is relatively hard to predict, and (*c*) that much of the instability one observes in the *LM* curve comes from the pursuit of erroneous monetary policies (such as stabilizing interest rates). Indeed, they argue, all would fall into place (as in Figure 12.2) if a money stock determination policy were pursued.

[4] The principal shortcoming is omission of the effect of inflationary expectations on *i* (and on the underlying functions), as discussed in Chapters 9 and 11.

12.3 THE TARGETS AND INDICATORS OF MONETARY POLICY

The discussion so far has actually evaded what might be the central question in monetary policy itself: In a world in which the authorities have imperfect knowledge of the causation and the timing of causation with regard to the determination of the final variables in the system, what operating rules and provisional techniques should they employ to instruct and guide them? They need, in short, to know what effect on the final variables they are having as a result of past changes in instruments, and what the influence of other effects is (since, unless they disentangle these two sets of effects, they can never judge the adequacy of their policy). It is easily recognizable that what is involved here is basic to monetary policy, since it involves casting our problem in realistic terms; while there are other issues, involving improvements in the basic design of the theoretical models to include stochastic (uncertain) elements, here we will discuss the division of the intermediate financial variables through which monetary influences flow into two sets of variables: a set of *targets* that can be hit by the policy instruments and a set of *indicators* that measure the effect of the policy actions on the final variables.

To begin with, we should emphasize that the problem arises in the first instance because, as we have noted, the authorities possess only limited information about the structure and workings of the economy. In other words, they need to know about the general shape of the structure of the economy, the impact of exogenous (outside) forces, and the size, significance, and stability of the parameters of the economic system in order to allow them to follow the simple-minded approach implicit in the model presented in Chapters 7 and 8. In fact, the monetary authorities must make do with the information that they possess, and what they possess is a series of half-verified hypotheses (for example, that the demand for money is a stable function of a few key variables), some often inconsistent forecasts from econometric models and from other less formal sources, and a great deal of practical information on how financial markets function. Since their information on financial markets is likely to be the best of this lot, it is small wonder that an alternative to what we might now describe as a "full-information" monetary policy is adopted. This alternative takes the form of selecting certain financial variables to be targets and certain others to be indicators, as already suggested. The details of this choice depend on the information available, on certain logical restrictions, and, of course, on the authorities' perceptions of, and prejudices about, the economic system.

Before considering the basis for this choice, let us consider a definitional problem. In particular, let us note that the word *target* is defined here to mean the values of the intermediate financial variables that are under the direct and unambiguous influence of one or more of the instruments. This is emphasized now because there is a tendency to define words like target with considerable model-specificity; for example, one hears of interest-rate targets, money-stock targets, and even price-level or growth targets. In this book we are referring to the final variables that the authorities are instructed to aim at as "goal" or "objective" variables, rather than targets. We note, however, that one of the goals, the authorities' assumption of responsibility for maintaining orderly financial markets and, in particular, for seeing that Treasury operations are not accompanied by unduly large changes in interest rates or in private, corporate, and bank portfolios, should really be referred to as an "intermediate goal," since stability of financial markets is not usually thought of as an end in itself, at least by a large part of the electorate.

One might at first glance think, in view of the fact that the authorities possess full information about their own instrument settings, that they possess sufficient information to measure the influence of policy adjustments on the goal variables, but for a number of reasons, this is not so. One major difficulty we have noted is that all sorts of lags exist in the response of the system to various impulses; and the lags vary not only from cause to cause but also they vary from period to period, making it most difficult to disentangle the effects of known influences, let alone the effects of the unknown. Even more serious, perhaps, is the influence of the unknown: exogenous influences affect every aspect of a nation's economic life. In particular, exogenous factors are known to influence both the goal variables and the intermediate financial variables. Take two simple examples: it is a very large country indeed that can assert that world prices do not affect domestic prices (an objective variable) and, similarly, the dependence of domestic interest rates on world interest rates (an intermediate variable) is generally thought to be pervasive. Worse, there are many other exogenous influences to consider, for "exogenous" in the economist's language refers not only to influences from outside the economy but also to influences from outside his particular model. Thus, in the final analysis, the list of what is essentially exogenous—and therefore disturbing to the line of causation from instrument to goal variable—depends on how much the authorities know about the nature and workings of the economic system. That, *clearly,* is not enough to enable them to observe the effect of changes in their instruments on the final variables; in short, a policy of "groping along" is the only choice, if we are to have any policy at all.

Visualize, then, a policy instrument, such as an open market operation, as it works its way through to the price level. At the first stage, the authorities buy or sell government securities, *and interest rates react.* Later, as banks adjust their portfolios and call in or expand their loans, *bank deposits* (*money*) *change.* Finally, as the loan activity produces increases or decreases in purchases, quantities produced and prices (and the price level) begin to change, unevenly, of course, because of the diffuseness of the effect and because the various demand and supply elasticities throughout the economy dictate whether it is prices or quantities that adjust first (although in the long run much of the effect will be on money prices). The interest rate and the money stock, in this process, were *intermediate* financial variables that reacted first—before prices and quantities (and, therefore, before employment) and they (along with either high-powered money or the monetary base) are our candidates for either "target" or "indicator" status in our realistic policy design.

12.3.1 Indicators

To be an *indicator,* formally, of economic activity (GNP, the price level, or the level of employment) the variable in question ought to be *closely* related in an unambiguous way to the final variable it is supposed to predict; it should generally "indicate" what is to come. Generally, the money stock (but *not* M_1 recently) or the stock of high-powered money (or the monetary base) has worked well in the prediction of money national income (or the price level), although there has been enough slippage in the relation to warrant some caution in its acceptance. Generally, in spite of a lot of popular belief to the contrary, the interest rate has not worked particularly well as an *indicator* of monetary "tightness" or "ease." In particular, both empirical work and theoretical work have been pessimistic about the use of the interest rate in this way. With regard to the theoretical argument, as we have already seen in Chapter 9, one of the arguments against the interest rate is that a rise in the nominal interest rate (i) brought about by the expectation of an increase in the inflation rate should not be treated as if it were a move toward tighter money, because the appropriate policy—an increase in the quantity of money—would actually worsen the inflationary situation (and validate the expectation). In practice, thus, when a nominal interest rate changes you just cannot tell without further information, whether it is "indicating" tight money or loose money. If you cannot tell which of these it represents, then you cannot tell whether it will be followed by a price level increase or a price level decrease.

There is a second theoretical problem with the interest rate as an indicator, and that concerns the problem of lags in adjustment in the economy. Let us return to the *IS-LM* model, and suppose that the spending sector (represented by the *IS* curve) is slow to adjust, compared to the monetary sector. We can represent the "slow to adjust" hypothesis by drawing two *IS* curves—IS_{SR} and IS_{LR}—the first representing a relatively inflexible curve (in the short run) and the second representing the final position of the curve, as it (arbitrarily) rotates through point 1. A good reason for the short-run inflexibility, of course, is that many spending plans—especially investment plans or spending on consumer durables—take some time to formulate (and carry out). Then, in Figure 12.6, let us assume that—following an increase in the quantity of money (a shift of the *LM* curve from LM_1 to LM_2)—the adjustment is along the *short-run IS* curve initially.

Figure 12.6: Monetary policy with long spending lags

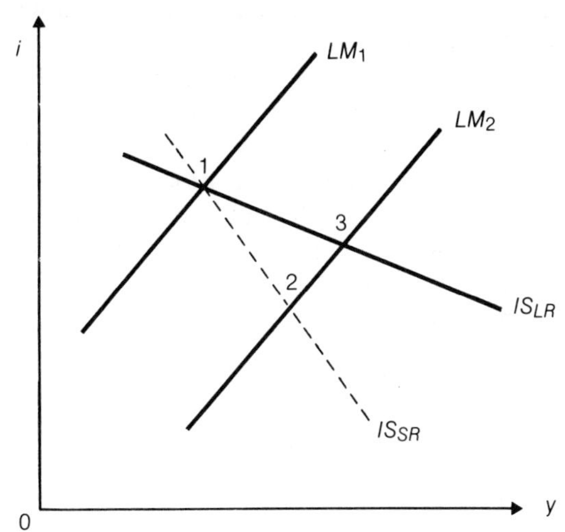

In Figure 12.6, then, we show an immediate adjustment along IS_{SR}—the short-run *IS* curve—and a final adjustment along IS_{LR}; the way this could be worked is that we can visualize the movement as down the IS_{SR} curve from point 1 to point 2 and then, as a second stage, the *IS* curve would gradually rotate until it reached its final resting place. The second part of the path of adjustment is from point 2 to point 3. Now the reason the interest rate is a bad indicator of the direction of movement of real income (the objective variable) in this case is that real income increases steadily as we go from points 1 to 2 to 3, *while the interest rate goes through a cycle,* first falling (1 to 2) and then rising (2 to 3). Clearly, this would be a totally ambiguous indicator since, in the real world, we usually do not have enough information to correct for this problem (we do not know for certain in which range we lie, and an interest rate rise, for example, can be associated with a rise or a fall of real income).[5] Thus, if the money market adjusts more rapidly than the goods market—and it almost certainly does—the interest rate will essentially "overreact" to monetary policy.

[5] To see the truth of this, work out what happens when the *LM* curve shifts leftward.

On net, then, there are *two* theoretical reasons that the authorities would be ill-advised to use the interest rate as an indicator of the effect of monetary policy—the expectations problem and the overreaction problem.

We have been using the word *indicator* in this section in a very particular way: the indicator is a variable that indicates the effect of monetary policy on the objective variables. As such it is going to be a financial variable pretty much (itself) under the control of the monetary authorities. The word *indicator* also appears in a popular concept known as the *leading indicators;* these are economic variables, not necessarily connected with monetary policy, that *predict* the goal variables (notably the rate of growth of national income). They do not, that is to say, concern themselves with the separation of policy influences from total influences; they simply predict, using, of course, any variable that works well in practice. Consider, as the best example, the Composite Index of Leading Indicators (CLI) published by the U.S. Department of Commerce. This indicator is really an index of 12 items as follows, a list that is designed to identify the turning points in the American business cycle *before* they occur.

Average workweek of production workers in manufacturing.
Index of net business formation.
Index of stock prices, 500 common stocks.
Index of new building permits, private housing units.
Layoff rate, manufacturing (inverted).
New orders, consumer goods and materials, 1967 dollars.
Contracts and order for plant and equipment, 1967 dollars.
Net change in inventories on hand and on order, 1967 dollars (smoothed).
Percentage change in sensitive prices, wholesale price index of crude materials excluding goods and feeds (smoothed).
Vendor performance, percentage of companies reporting slower deliveries.
Money balance (M_1), 1967 dollars.
Percentage change in total liquid assets (smoothed).

Note, first, that the last two items in the list are "monetary indicators" so that, clearly, money officially matters when a good prediction is needed.[6] This index has had a remarkably successful record in predicting the periodic recessions we have had in the United States since 1947. To see this,

[6] Over 300 candidates were screened (by seeing how well they "predicted" post–World War II cycles) in order to obtain the 12 listed here. One doubts, of course, that M_1 will be retained in the index (see Chapter 1).

Figure 12.7: Composite Index of Leading Indicators (1967 = 100)

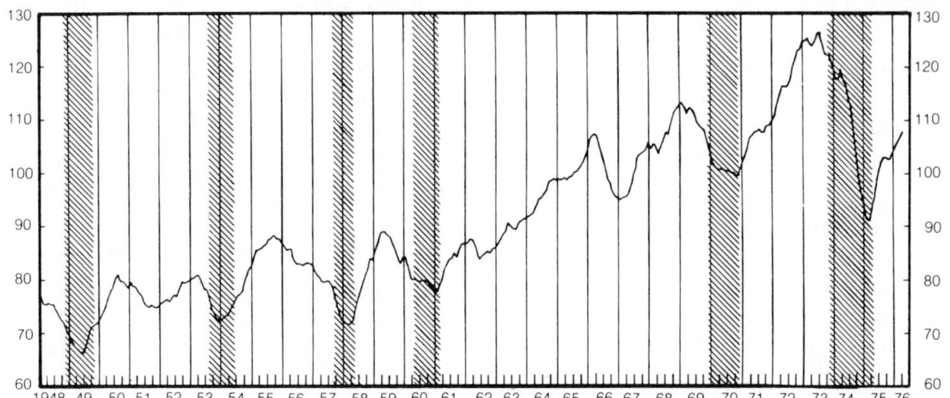

Note: Shaded areas represent periods of recession as defined by the National Bureau of Economic Research, except for the latest recession, which is tentatively judged to have ended in March 1975.

Source: Maury N. Harris and Deborah Jamroz, "Evaluating the Leading Indicators," *Monthly Review, Federal Reserve Bank of New York* (June 1976), p. 169. The list in the text also comes from this source.

consider Figure 12.7, which shows the recessions (shaded areas), and the CLI (as a jagged line). All of the recessions to 1976 were signaled well in advance (and the upturns at least slightly in advance), and the only serious blunder in the series came during the credit crunch of 1966, when an expected downturn did not materialize.

12.3.2 Targets

The criteria for a target variable in the targets-indicators design of monetary policy are that it be easily and quickly hit by the instruments and that it be easily calculated without too much of a lapse in time. Again, we will compare the money stock and the interest rate in terms of their effectiveness as targets. In Chapter 10 we considered some of the recent data on monetary policy actions in 1977 and observed that if the policy were one of controlling the money stock—if the money stock is the target—then it was a remarkably elusive target throughout much of the year, with an unmistakable effect only coming in the October–November pinch. This is a general comment, probably; the money stock is not always a good target. On the other hand, as we shall see in the remainder of this chapter, the interest rate can work well as a target and, whether or not it does, the Federal Reserve employs it in that capacity.

We should make an important point here about the *interaction* of targets and indicators. Unless the authorities can hit the target without error and unless the target is unambiguously linked to final activity, two *different* variables should be used, one as the target and one as the indicator. We have argued in effect that there are no such variables (even the monetary base is not always linked exactly to the money stock) so that this warning is of some considerable practical significance. The reason for this *caveat* is quite straightforward: if you choose a single variable to do the job—let us call it a "target-indicator"—and if at the same time there are other variables influencing the "target-indicator" variable, you would tend to attribute to *policy* influence what is, in fact, *outside* influence. That is, if the single variable is influenced *both* by outside forces and policy forces, and you assume that all effects are policy-induced (i.e., that the variable is a good target variable), then, when the variable predicts the goal variable accurately, you will claim policy success that is unjustified (and, in the future, make policy errors, if the magnitude of the outside force changes). The same sort of problem arises if one mistakenly reverses the two variables, aiming at an indicator (as if it were a target) and predicting the effect on the goal variables by using a target variable (rather than an indicator variable). In this case the authorities do not realize that *all* of the variation in the target is policy-induced since they think it is an *indicator* (which, by our definition, is partly outside-influenced). Thus, after the authorities partition the effects on the indicator into outside and policy-induced components, they move to negate (for example) the (assumed) outside effect, which, in fact, is just part of the policy effect. The lags in the effect of policy, which were discussed in Chapter 10, make all of this more plausible since what appear to be outside effects (with, for example, opposite signs) may just be the (long delayed) "fruits" of the policies.[7] Indeed the authorities may, in effect, spend much effort trying to smooth out the effect of their own policy on the intermediate variables, contributing in the process *more* rather than less stability to the objective variables. So the careful use of the intermediate variables is an important part of the monetary policy scenario.

12.4 RECENT MONETARY POLICY: SOME EXAMPLES

12.4.1 Monetary policy in the late 1960s

We have, since the beginning of Chapter 5, worked hard on the analytics of monetary policy, although we have, from time to time, sought relief in the reality of actual data and in historical incidents. Now we will look at the actual technique in two separate instances, one in the 1960s and one in 1977–78, in order to illustrate the techniques and to show the steady improvement in the policy approach of the Federal Reserve. We will also show that we are a long way from having an ideal policy design.

[7] Indeed, as we pointed out in Chapter 11, lags always have this undesirable potential in the policy design.

When the Federal Open Market Committee (FOMC) meets, all of the Federal Reserve bank presidents, including the five who are elected and therefore eligible to vote, participate in the discussion. Another representative at these meetings is the system open market account manager, a member of the staff of the New York Federal Reserve Bank, whose ultimate responsibility it is to translate the final resolutions into action. In general, the FOMC will review the evidence and, after deliberation, draft and vote on a resolution to be passed on to the manager and to be published a month later in the *Federal Reserve Bulletin.* A memo from 1968 is the following, quoted in full:

> Economic policy directive to the Federal Reserve Bank of New York adopted by FOMC on January 9, 1968:
>
> The information reviewed at this meeting indicates that over-all economic activity has been expanding vigorously, with both industrial and consumer prices continuing to rise at a substantial rate, and that prospects are for further rapid growth and persisting inflationary pressures in the period ahead. The imbalance in U.S. international transactions worsened further in late 1967, but the new program announced by the President should result in a considerable reduction in the deficit this year. Following announcement of the program, foreign purchases of gold slackened abruptly and the dollar strengthened in foreign exchange markets. Long-term bond yields have declined in recent weeks but some short-term interest rates have risen further. Bank credit has changed little on balance recently as banks have disposed of Government securities to accommodate strengthened loan demands. Growth in the money supply has slackened and flows into time and savings accounts at bank and nonbank financial intermediaries have continued to moderate. In this situation, it is the policy of the Federal Open Market Committee to foster financial conditions conducive to resistance of inflationary pressures and progress toward reasonable equilibrium in the country's balance of payments.
>
> To implement this policy, System open market operations until the next meeting of the Committee shall be conducted with a view to maintaining the somewhat firmer conditions that have developed in the money market in recent weeks, partly as a result of the increase in reserve requirements announced to become effective in mid-January; provided, however, that operations shall be modified as needed to moderate any apparently significant deviations of bank credit from current expectations.

Now in this statement we see that the Federal Reserve wishes to "restrain inflation" and will do so by "maintaining somewhat firmer conditions" in the money market. How on earth, we might ask, could they have judged their results at the end of the month? And, more urgently, what does "somewhat firmer conditions" mean in quantitative terms?

This style of management was not an isolated instance during that period; consider another example, the resolution passed on April 1, 1969.

The following current economic policy directive was issued to the Federal Reserve Bank of New York.

The information reviewed at this meeting suggests that, while expansion in real economic activity has moderated somewhat further, current and prospective activity now appears stronger than earlier projections had indicated. Substantial upward pressures on prices and costs are persisting. Most long-term interest rates have risen further on balance in recent weeks, but movements in short-term rates have been mixed. In the first quarter of the year bank credit changed little on average, as investments contracted while loans expanded further. In March the outstanding volume of large-denomination CD's continued to decline sharply; inflows of other time and savings deposits were moderate; and growth in the money supply remained at a sharply reduced rate. It appears that a sizable deficit re-emerged in the U.S. balance of payments on the liquidity basis in the first quarter but that the balance on the official settlements basis remained in surplus as a result of further large inflows of Euro-dollars. In this situation it is the policy of the Federal Open Market Committee to foster financial conditions conducive to the reduction of inflationary pressures, with a view to encouraging a more sustainable rate of economic growth and attaining reasonable equilibrium in the country's balance of payments.

To implement this policy, System open market operations until the next meeting of the Committee shall be conducted with a view to maintaining firm conditions in money and short-term credit markets, taking account of the effects of other possible monetary policy action; provided, however, that operations shall be modified if bank credit appears to be deviating significantly from current projections.

The language and tone, for a quite different experience, were astonishingly similar to those of the earlier directive, but now we find the instruction to "foster conditions conducive to the reduction of inflationary pressures." Significantly, however, given this much more positive objective, the instruction, again, is to "maintain firm conditions" in the money market.

What the Federal Reserve meant by "firm conditions" is not entirely obvious, but most observers feel that the intention was to stabilize interest rates in the sense of a *target* variable. Since the stated final objective was to stabilize prices, this seems to imply that the authorities then thought that a stable nominal interest rate implies a stable price level. The fact that this may not be the case (see Chapter 9) was certainly not mentioned in the directive. Another possible interpretation of these remarkably vague statements is that the choice to stabilize interest rates was generated by an informal arrangement between the Treasury and the Federal Reserve, and not by any particular view of the economic realities. We know that up until 1951, and particularly during the war financing periods from 1940 to the end of the Korean War, the Federal Reserve was put into the position of "making" the market for Treasury debt in the sense of keeping the interest rate low. The Treasury, that is to say, had massive new and refunding operations to undertake, which would have been very expensive to the taxpayer. These operations, if undertaken in a thin market, would tend to become expensive at times; that is so because in a relatively thin market the interest rate necessary to pay to lenders might shoot up around the issue date of a big government bond offering. An alternative, which must have made some considerable sense during the war period, is for the Federal Reserve to support the Treasury bill rate, a support that would take the form of actually buying securities in order to hold up the price of bonds in general (and therefore, to hold down interest rates). In effect, to this extent the Federal Reserve would finance a share of the war effort, ending up, at the end of the war, with a much larger portfolio of government securities than it might otherwise have had.

Since the buying of Treasury securities funnels reserves into the banking system, we can argue that under these conditions the quantity of money would really depend on the needs of the Treasury, or at least importantly so; clearly, then, the Federal Reserve would not have much scope for active monetary policy. In 1951, we are told, the Federal Reserve and the Treasury had it out and produced the well-known accord of that year. In the accord, it is argued, the Federal Reserve convinced the Treasury of the need for an independent monetary policy; and it is noticeable that from that point on, many interest rates began to fluctuate (mostly rise). Usually, this is where things are left: the Federal Reserve now has control over the money stock but generally chooses, instead, to smooth out fluctuations in the money market (Treasury bill market). In fact, in recent years, one of the functions of the Federal Reserve has obviously been to smooth out the effects of the large and numerous Treasury fiscal operations, a smoothing that must have the same general effect as during the period before 1951. The Federal Reserve still cannot simultaneously soften the impact of Treasury operations by holding the line on interest rates and control the money stock; thus a policy dilemma, which is still part of the scenario, impedes the success of American monetary policy, although in late 1979, the Federal Reserve did indicate that it was going to concentrate on money stock control in the future.

12.4.2 The runaway money stock of 1977–1978

The foregoing aspects of monetary policy are still part of the story of recent monetary policy, but the tone of policy has changed in the desirable direction of more precision, and in terms of at least the recognition that a policy of stricter monetary (quantity) control might be necessary. More importantly, we now have explicit target interest rates and several monetary indicators. In particular, the Federal Reserve picks an operating *target*—usually a range of values of the federal funds rate—and conducts an open market policy designed to pin the federal funds rate at the center point of that range. It then monitors the rates of growth of M_1, M_2, and M_3 to see whether these rates fall within a desired "operating range"; patently, some attempt to use the monetary variables as an *indicator* is part of this policy design. Finally, the Federal Reserve sets long-range (annual) goals (for M_1, M_2, M_3, and bank credit), which it reconsiders quarterly. During 1977 and 1978, as we saw in Chapter 9, the money stock occasionally seemed to get out of control and the authorities had to move pretty firmly to get it back down. The Federal Reserve still publishes its policy directives, but preceding these directions is a considerable amount of analysis of the current economic situation; the directive for July 9, 1977 is as follows.

The following domestic policy directive was issued to the Federal Reserve Bank of New York:

The information reviewed at this meeting suggests that real output of goods and services grew in the second quarter at about the rapid rate of the first quarter. In June industrial output continued to expand at a substantial pace. The rise in employment moderated, and the unemployment rate edged up from 6.9 to 7.1 percent. Total retail sales remained at about the level reached in March; for the second quarter as a whole, however, sales were moderately above the first-quarter level. The wholesale price index for all commodities declined in June, owing to sharp decreases among farm products and goods; as in May, average prices of industrial commodities rose appreciably less than in earlier months of 1977. The index of average hourly earnings rose over the first half of the year at about the same pace that it had on the average during 1976.

The average value of the dollar against leading foreign currencies had declined more than 1 percent over the past month; the declines were especially marked against the Japanese, German and Swiss currencies. In May the U.S. foreign trade deficit diminished somewhat from the high rate in the first 4 months of the year.

M-1, after rising at an exceptionally rapid rate in April, increased little in May and grew at a moderate pace in June. Growth in M-2 and M-3 also was moderate in June. Inflows to banks of time and savings deposits included in M-2 picked up somewhat, after having slackened for a number of months, and inflows to nonbank thrift institutions remained sizable. Business short-term borrowing expanded sharply in June. Market interest rates in general have changed little in recent weeks.

In light of the foregoing developments, it is the policy of the Federal Open Market Committee to foster bank reserve and other financial conditions that will encourage continued economic expansion and help resist inflationary pressures, while contributing to a sustainable pattern of international transactions.

Growth in M-1, M-2, and M-3 within ranges of 4 to 6½ percent, 7 to 9½ percent and 8½ to 11 percent, respectively, from the second quarter of 1977 to the second quarter of 1978 appears to be consistent with these objectives.

These ranges are subject to reconsideration at any time as conditions warrant.

The Committee seeks to encourage near-term rates of growth in M-1 and M-2 on a path believed to be reasonably consistent with the longer-run ranges for monetary aggregates cited in the preceding paragraph. Specifically, at present, it expects the annual growth rates over the July–August period to be within the ranges of 3½ to 7½ percent for M-1 and 6½ to 10½ percent for M-2. In the judgment of the Committee such growth rates are likely to be associated with a weekly-average Federal funds rate of about 5⅜ percent. If, giving approximately equal weight to M-1 and M-2, it appears that growth rates over the 2-month period will deviate significantly from the midpoints of the indicated ranges, the operational objective for the Federal funds rate shall be modified in an orderly fashion within a range of 5 to 5¾ percent.

If it appears during the period before the next meeting that the operating constraints specified above are proving to be significantly inconsistent, the Manager is promptly to notify the Chairman who will then decide whether the situation calls for supplementary instructions from the committee.

Votes for this action: Messrs. Burns, Volcker, Coldwell, Gardner, Guffey, Jackson, Lilley, Mayo, Morris, Partee, Roos, and Wallich. Votes against this action: None.

On August 4, subsequent to the next meeting, nearly final estimates indicated that in July M_1 had actually grown at an annual rate of about 18.5 percent and M_2 at a rate of about 16.5 percent. Indeed, the July–August period Federal Reserve projections suggested that the annual rates of growth for both aggregates would be well above the upper limits of the ranges specified by the Committee in the next-to-last paragraph of the domestic policy directive issued at the July meeting. The Federal funds rate had averaged 5.80 percent in the statement week ended August 3, up from 5.45 percent in the week ended July 27 and 5.35 percent in the preceding three weeks. The manager of the system open market account was then aiming at a funds rate of 5.75 percent, which was actually the upper limit of the inter-meeting range specified in the directive; thus he sought the advice of the chairman.

Against this background, Chairman Burns recommended on August 4 that the upper limit of the range for the federal funds rate be increased to 6 percent so that the manager might have some additional leeway for operations, while continuing to take account of the current Treasury financing and financial market developments. He further recommended that this additional leeway be used very gradually, and only in the event that the aggregates continued to register values far beyond the committee's objectives; the following appeared in the *Federal Reserve Bulletin:*

On August 5, 1977, the Committee modified the inter-meeting range for the Federal funds rate specified in the next-to-last paragraph of the domestic policy directive issued on July 19, 1977, by increasing the upper limit from 5¾ to 6 percent.

Overall, these instructions, which included an inter-period variation in the objectives on August 4, are much more precise both in setting ranges for M_1 and M_2 (the indicators) and in setting a federal funds interest rate target.

When we consider all of the decisions over the two years though, while the 1970s-style policy is much more precise than the 1960s version, there still appear to be problems. First consider a tabulation of the monetary policy targets for 1977 as collected by the Federal Reserve bank of St. Louis in Table 12.1. First of all one notes that federal funds rate targets seem to be hit pretty well; indeed, a policy-induced "tightening," in the sense of a considerable rise in this rate over the year, is visible. Such a usage—to indicate "tightness" in this way—is, in effect, using the federal funds rate as both a target and an indicator; this is unwise under present conditions, and an index of the lack of wisdom is the behavior of the money stock (either M_1 or M_2), which was erratic and, for some time, *loose,* in the sense of growing too rapidly for "monetary stability." That is, the behavior of the money stock in March, April, June, July and September, *indicated* that the interest rate *target* was set too low.

But there is more in Table 12.1 of policy interest. The Federal Reserve, in June, July, August, and September specified a wide range of M_1 that it never succeeded in hitting; that is, for four straight months the money stock grew faster than the upper limit the authorities would have liked. Further, and this is *most* curious, their reaction to the spurt in M_1 in June was to raise the "target" limit although, we should note, as we documented in Table 10.3, they did conduct a considerable open market operation in this period (apparently to no avail). Actually, there is another odd aspect of this period, which underscores (at the least) the problem of monetary management when the information is slow to arrive. Consider the following quotations from their published minutes of three meetings in the summer of 1977:

Meeting of June 21, 1977:
. . . throughout the inter-meeting period, incoming data suggested that over the May–June period M-1 and M-2 on the average would grow at rates well within the specified ranges. Accordingly, the Manager continued to aim for a weekly average funds rate of about 5⅜ percent, and the rate remained at close to that level during the period.

This was an accurate statement, as Table 11.1 shows.

Meeting of July 14, 1977:
. . . throughout the inter-meeting period, incoming data suggested that over the June–July period M-2 and M-1 would grow at rates within those (their) ranges. Accordingly, the Manager of the System Market Account sought to maintain the Federal Funds rate around 5⅜ percent.

Now this was not accurate, as both M_1 and M_2 were *well* above their range at that time.

One would think then, that at the next meeting there would be some alarm. There was, to be sure, a telephone meeting on August 5, and the federal funds target was pushed up to 5.75 percent and then to 6 percent at the regular meeting of August 16. But, even so, we got our third straight month of a money stock growing faster than the target (which was revised downward).

> *Meeting of September 20, 1977:*
> Data that become available in the weeks immediately following the August FOMC meeting suggested that over the August–September period M-1 was growing at a rate in the upper half and M-2 at a rate near the midpoint of their respective ranges. Accordingly, the Systems Account Manager continued to seek a Federal funds rate of around 6 percent.

This was, again, inaccurate (showing the weakness of a monetary target), and in the following month, this policy proved to be one of ease, as M_1 leaped ahead by almost 10 percent. Only in October (with the firm policy we discussed in Chapter 10) did the money stock come under control for the rest of the year. The problems, clearly, were that (*a*) the monetary data were not accurate, and (*b*) the authorities tended to employ the interest rate as an *indicator* in spite of its many ambiguities. Thus, some of the instability in 1977 was almost certainly policy-induced.

We might conclude this discussion of monetary policy in 1977 with a pictorial presentation of the policy record as drawn up by the Federal Reserve Bank of New York; it appears in Figure 12.8. There we see that only for one week did the federal funds rate slip outside its specified range, while for 5 of the 12 monthly M_1 ranges and for 3 of the 12 M_2 ranges, they were off-target.[8] Of the remaining seven money stock ranges (M_1), only three actual rates lay within the lower half of the targeted range. On net, then, 1977 was a year of monetary ease, as indicated by the actual rate of growth of the money stock. A Monetarist, who uses the money stock to predict (indicate) prices, would then assert, and many did, that late 1977 and 1978 would show more rapid inflation—and so they did.

Turning to an analysis of monetary policy in 1978, we find even more uncertainty and even inconsistency, although things end on a strong note. For one thing, there was considerable turmoil within the Board of Governors, which, by the end of the year, had lost four of its seven members in various ways, to be replaced by two new members (with two positions unfilled), one of whom was the new chairman (G. William Miller). The style of the Board's operation went from the partly Monetarist—but cer-

[8] Note, as well, that the April–May and December–January result was only contained in the range by moving the range *upward*, a result which is condonable in the December–January figure, *but not* in the April–May figure, considering the poor result in the March–April money stock.

Table 12.1: FOMC operating ranges, 1977

	Short-run ranges*						
				Ranges specified		Actual growth rates	
Date of meeting	Federal funds rate range	Initial federal funds rate target	Period to which M_1 and M_2 apply	M_1	M_2	M_1	M_2
January 17–18	4.25–5.00%	4.625–4.750%	Jan.–Feb.	3–7%	7–11%	3.1%	8.4%
February 15	4.25–5.00	4.625–4.750	Feb.–Mar.	3–7	6.5–10.5	3.1	7.9
March 15	4.25–5.25	4.625–4.750	Mar.–Apr.	4.5–8.5	7–11	12.4	11.1
April 19	4.50–5.25	4.750	Apr.–May	6–10	8–12	10.1	9.1
May 6†	4.50–5.50	5.250	—	—	—	—	—
May 17	5.25–5.75	5.375	May–June	0–4	3.5–7.5	2.6	6.4
June 21	5.25–5.75	5.375	June–July	2.5–6.5	6–10	11.4	12.4
July 19	5.25–5.75	5.375	July–Aug.	3.5–7.5	6.5–10.5	12.1	11.6
August 5†	5.25–6	5.750	—	—	—	—	—
August 16	5.75–6.25	6	Aug.–Sept.	0–5	3–8	6.6	7.2
September 20	6–6.50	6.250	Sept.–Oct.	2–7	4–8	9.7	9.1
October 17–18	6.25–6.75	6.500	Oct.–Nov.	3–8	5.5–9.5	5.3	7.4
November 15	6.25–6.75	6.500	Nov.–Dec.	1–7	5–9	3.1	5.2
December 19–20	6.25–6.75	6.500	Dec.–Jan.	2.5–8.5	6–10	7.4	7.0
January 9, 1978†	6.25–7	6.750	—	—	—	—	—

Date of meeting	Longer-run ranges‡				
	Target period	M_1	M_2	M_3	*Credit proxy*§
January 17–18	IV/76–IV/77	4.5–6.5%	7–10.0%	8.5–11.5%	7–10%
April 19	I/77–I/78	4.5–6.5	7–9.5	8.5–11	7–10
July 19	II/77–II/78	4–6.5	7–9.5	8.5–11	7–10§
October 17–18	III/77–III/78	4–6.5	6.5–9	8–10.5	7–10

* Short-run ranges were adopted at each of the FOMC's regularly scheduled meetings. The ranges for the monetary aggregates were specified in terms of two-month simple annual rates of change from the month prior to the meetings at which the ranges were established to the month following the meeting. The ranges for the federal funds rate were specified to cover the period from the meeting at which the ranges were adopted to the following regularly scheduled meeting. Short-run ranges were made available in the "Record of Policy Actions of the Federal Open Market Committee" approximately 30 days after each meeting.

† Telephone or telegram consultations were held between scheduled meetings for the purpose of modifying intermeeting ranges for the Federal funds rate.

‡ Chairman of the Federal Reserve Board Arthur F. Burns announced intended growth rates of monetary aggregates over the indicated one year periods in statements presented before Congressional Committees at intervals of approximately 90 days.

§ At the July 19 meeting the Committee decided to replace bank credit proxy with a broader measure of all commercial bank credit. This change was made in part because of the growth in importance of nonmember banks (credit proxy is based on data for member banks) and in part because the proxy does not include certain borrowings by banks from the nonbank public.

Source: *Review, Federal Reserve Bank of St. Louis* (March 1978), p. 3.

Figure 12.8: FOMC ranges for short-run monetary growth and for the federal funds rate, 1977

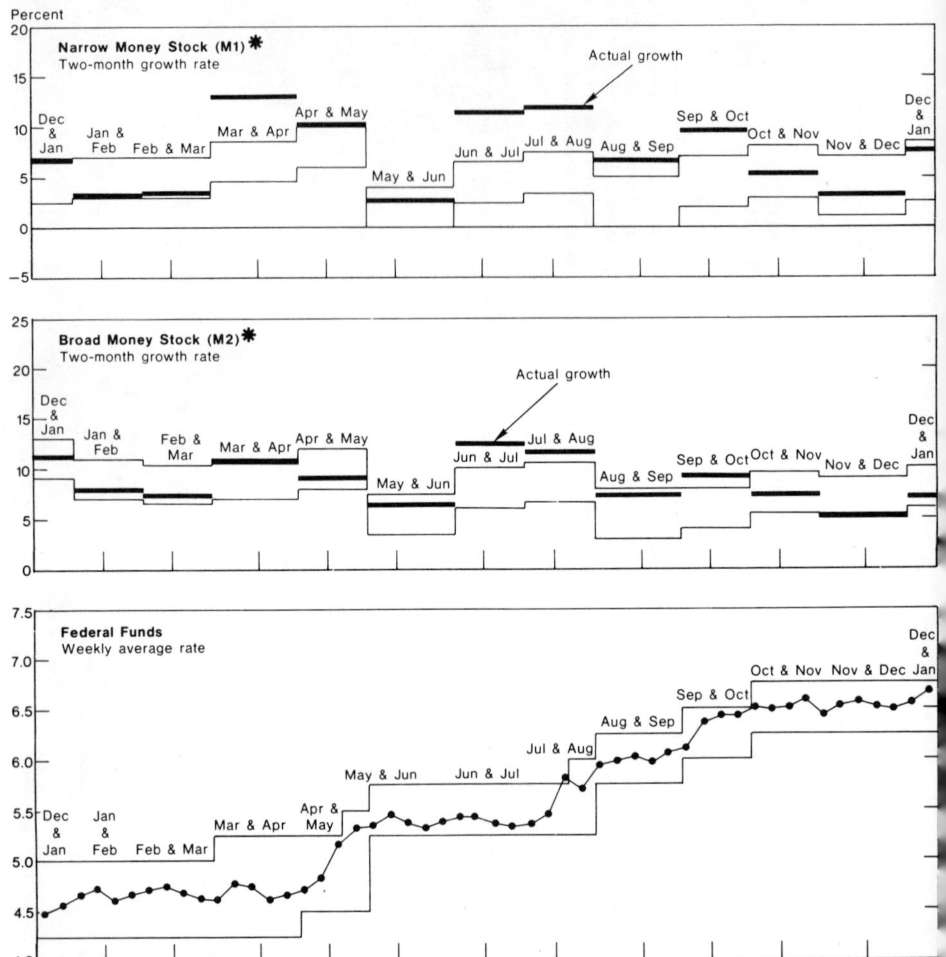

Note: Shaded bands in the upper two charts are the FOMC's specified ranges for money supply growth over the two-month periods indicated; in the bottom chart they are the specified ranges for federal funds rate variation. Actual growth rates in the upper two charts are based on data available at the time of the second FOMC meeting after the end of each period.

* Seasonally adjusted annual rates.

Source: *Quarterly Review, Federal Reserve Bank of New York* (Spring 1978), p. 47.

tainly independent—operation of Arthur Burns's chairmanship to Miller's essentially Keynesian-style policy, which seemed considerably more in harmony with the interests of the White House (and the Treasury?). Figure 12.9 documents much of the policy stance itself. During 1978 the discount rate was raised 7 times and the target range for the federal funds rate was raised 11 times from January through September. The money stock (however measured) grew faster than either the average of the

Figure 12.9: FOMC ranges for short-run monetary growth and for the federal funds rate, 1978

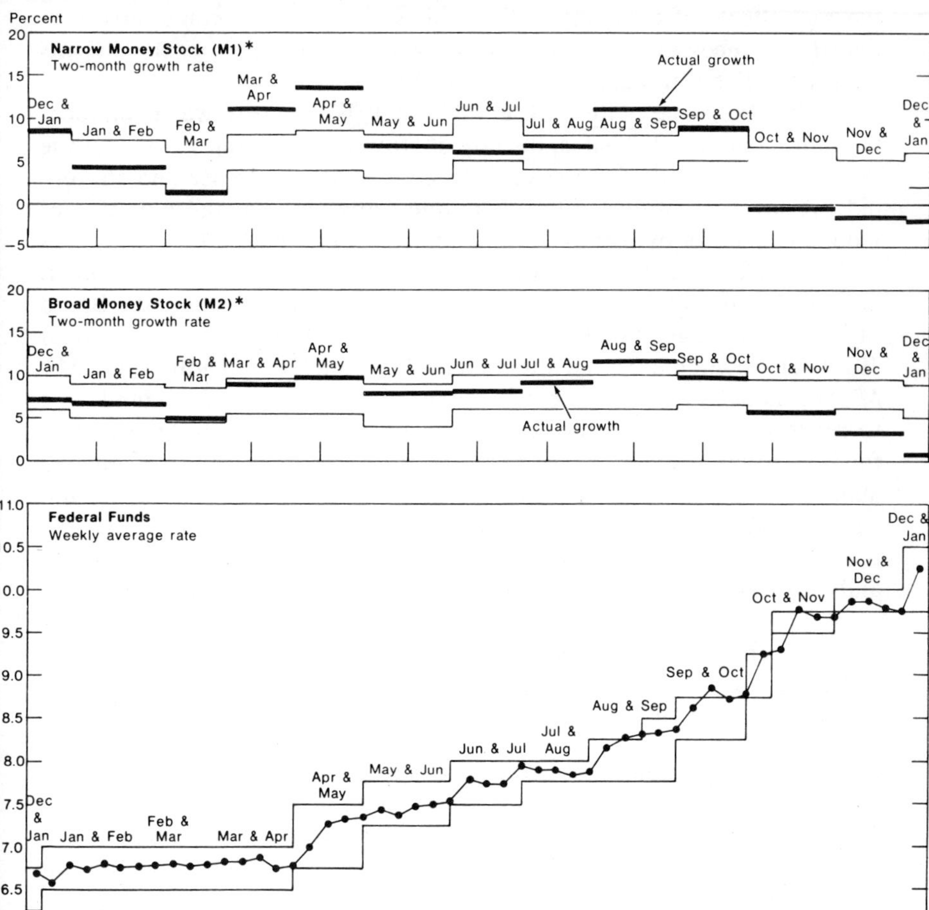

Note: Shaded bands in the upper two charts are the FOMC's specified ranges for money supply growth over the two-month periods indicated. No lower bound was established for M1 at the October and November meetings. In the bottom chart, the shaded bands are the specified ranges for federal funds rate variation. Actual growth rates in the upper two charts are based on data available at the time of the second FOMC meeting after the end of each period.
* Seasonally adjusted annual rates.
Source: *Quarterly Review, Federal Reserve Bank of New York* (Spring 1979).

short-run targets or the long-run targets (which were unchanged at 4–6.5 percent for M_1 and 6.5–9 percent for M_2 through September).[9] Toward the end of the year, though, particularly after November 1, monetary growth

[9] By October 11, 1978, M_1 had grown at the annual rate of 13.1 percent, and M_2 had grown at the annual rate of 12.4 percent. These are *outside* the long-run ranges so, on net, the interest rate "targets" must have been consistently *too* low during the preceding nine months. In the October meeting, when the quarterly review of the long-range targets was discussed, there was incomplete agreement as to what to do with M_1, because of the arrival of automatic transfer. The range for M_2 was unchanged.

came down *very rapidly*. Indeed, recalling our discussion in Chapter 11 on the real effects of monetary policy, this sudden change could have produced the recession (and, *eventually,* some easing of prices) that was widely predicted to begin sometime in 1979.

In 1979 the same pattern observable in 1977 and 1978 was continued, with the same result. That is, the rate of growth of the money stock (or the monetary base) and of the price level continued to increase and so, too, did the level of interest rates. It is quite obvious that the old style of monetary control by means of tight control of the federal funds rate was no longer effective, for many of the reasons given in Part II of this book, and this became even more obvious when the new Chairman of the Board of Governors, Paul Volcker, announced a switch of policy (in October 1979). This switch focussed attention on the monetary quantities (M_1, M_1^+, M_2, the monetary base, and bank loans) and allowed the federal funds rate to reach equilibrium. After the announcement of the switch the federal funds rate was up sharply and the prime rate of commercial banks reached almost 16 percent (up from around 13.50 percent). At this writing it is too early to evaluate the new policy fully, but it may well be fair to say that the Federal Reserve has switched to wider bands for the federal funds rate and, at the same time, to a policy of attempting a closer control over the monetary quantities. If this is so, and it may well not be, then it is a welcome change to the existing method of monetary "control."

Let us make several other observations about the Fed's policy until late 1979 by way of concluding this discussion of the real thing.

a. The Fed, apparently, sees no inconsistency in having short run objectives which, *in sum,* are inconsistent with their long run objectives. For example, for the first nine months of 1978 the upper limit of the month-to-month target for M_1 was *above* the 6.5 percent long-run range. This is not sensible.

b. Until possibly November 1978 (through 1977 *and* 1978) the Fed's discount rate and federal funds rate policies seem to have been *following* the prime rate rather than leading it. The moves in October and November, though, seem to have been more aggressive, as was the federal funds policy in late 1979.

c. Curiously, the Fed responded to rapid money stock figures (M_1) in a number of cases by *raising* the upper limit of the operating range of M_1 rather than by lowering it (see, for example, April, July, and October 1977 and the increases in the range in April and September 1978). This policy appears to be an explicitly destabilizing one. Indeed, after the 19 percent increase in M_1 in April 1978 became known to the Board, it was ignored on the grounds that it essentially represented a seasonal factor.

On net, then, one can at least conjecture that a slightly firmer approach in the spring and early summer of 1978—with regard to the federal funds rate *or* the rate of growth of M_1 and M_2—may well have pulled the economy back from *both* the monetary splurge in August–September *and* the sharp contraction in the monetary aggregates in the last three months. The same comment applies to 1979. One must not forget that if the Federal Reserve picks a federal funds target rate *below* the rate that clears the market—as it may well have done in many cases in the 1977 to 1979 period—it is essentially fueling the monetary expansion to the extent that it enforces the lower rate. The tight money policy of late 1978, that is to say, may well have been necessary because of the easy money policy of mid-1978, and so forth. Recall, as well, that a federal funds rate of 7.5 percent, when inflation is 7 percent, is a *real* federal funds rate of .5 percent. That would certainly be too low for monetary stability, in most cases.

12.5 STUDY QUESTIONS

Essay questions

1. No doubt, one reason the Federal Reserve used to have such vaguely worded policy directives (to the New York Federal Reserve Bank) was to avoid tying the hands of the manager of the System Open Market Account. Does the new system—with M_1, M_2, and the federal funds rate target—tie his hands any more? Which do you think is a better approach (vintage 1969 or vintage 1977–78) and why? You may want to consider how *effective* policy has been, in your answer.

2. Try to analyze what might happen to the effectiveness of American monetary policy if the Federal Reserve mixed up its targets and indicators, using a true target as if it were an indicator, and *vice versa.* What might go wrong if, in fact, the Fedejal Reserve uses the variables as if there were no targets-indicators distinction (e.g., both variables are indicator and target at the same time) when, in fact, a distinction should be made?

3. Look at some recent policy directives (in the *Federal Reserve Bulletin*) and try to evaluate recent monetary policy in terms of the targets-indicators approach. Does it help to have so many targets and indicators, or does policy appear to be somewhat ambiguous? You can also look for an interpretation in the annual survey of FOMC actions published in the monthly *Review* of the Federal Reserve Bank of St. Louis or the *Quarterly Review* of the New York Federal Reserve Bank.

True-false discussion questions

These statements are meant to be somewhat ambiguous, and to provoke discussion, thereby.

1. By the term "resistance to inflationary pressures" the Federal Reserve means that it will not let the money stock expand if the demand for money increases.

2. "Tightness" or "ease" of monetary policy can be judged either in terms of the behavior of the money stock or the behavior of the interest rate.

3. Velocity tends to fluctuate very little, in practice, because of the Federal Reserve's policy of stabilizing interest rates.

4. Control of the federal funds rate will not ensure stability of the money stock primarily because of the instability of the demand for money.

5. Using the interest rate as an indicator of the tightness or ease of monetary policy is perhaps the only thing we can do under the present conditions, when recent institutional changes in the banking sector have made the exact location of the *LM* curve hard to find.

6. If the authorities use the money stock as a target variable and the interest rate as an indicator, then they may well get worse results for monetary policy than they are currently achieving with the opposite approach.

7. The behavior of commercial bank excess reserves in recent bouts of tight money is partly the result of the fact that the Federal Reserve has not seen fit to keep its discount rate in line with other market rates.

8. Since our economic models cannot be estimated with perfect accuracy, we are better off using fiscal policy, since its effects are stronger and usually come in the desired direction (with a short lag).

9. If the Keynesian theory of the demand for money is not correct and the Monetarist is, then the correct stabilization policy is monetary and not fiscal.

12.6 FURTHER READING

Look again at the references to Chapter 10, especially the first two.

Brunner, Karl, ed. *Targets and Indicators of Monetary Policy*. San Francisco: Chandler Publishing Co., 1969.

Friedman, Benjamin M. "Targets, Instruments, and Indicators of Monetary Policy." *Journal of Monetary Economics* (October 1975).

Harris, Maury N., and Deborah Jamroz. "Evaluating the Leading Indicators." *Monthly Review, Federal Reserve Bank of New York* (June 1976).

Poole, William. "Optimal Choice of Monetary Policy Instruments in a Simple Stochastic Macro Model." *Quarterly Journal of Economics* (May 1970).

Saving, Thomas. "Monetary-Policy Targets and Indicators." *Journal of Political Economy* (August 1967).

Tanner, J. E. "Indicators of Monetary Policy: An Evaluation of Five." *Quarterly Review, Banca Nazionale del Lavoro* (December 1972).

Winningham, Scott. "Automatic Transfers and Monetary Policy." *Economic Review, Federal Reserve Bank of Kansas City* (November 1978).

Part III

The domestic financial markets

13

The financial intermediaries

13.1 INTRODUCTION

Chapter 13 is the introductory chapter for a set of four chapters (13–16) on the interactions among the financial institutions and how these interactions impinge on commercial banking and on monetary policy; in a fundamental sense it is the natural extension of Chapter 5 into a consideration of M_2 and M_3, although we will also refer to some of the policy issues of Chapters 6 to 12. In Chapter 13 we will discuss the nature of the business of the principal financial intermediaries before considering both how they affect policy and how they are affected by it. In Chapter 14 we will present a basic model of financial decision making—the mean variance model—and consider how it enriches our understanding of financial behavior. One of the by-products there will be an alternative derivation of the demand for financial assets (such as money) that will be somewhat more precise and considerably more general than those used to this point.

In Chapters 15 and 16 we will turn to two specific markets, the bond market and the stock market, in our effort to comprehend as wide a financial spectrum as possible in this book. In particular, in Chapter 15 we will consider the nature of bond holding in the economy, especially as it involves the holding of government bonds. In addition, we will tackle some of the questions that arise when two or more interest rates (we will consider a long-term rate and a short-term rate) are included in the problem; this is the analysis of the "term structure of interest rates," which is of recurring interest to policy makers, as we shall see. Then, in Chapter 16, we will take up the financial behavior of business firms. Here we will look at their *uses* of funds—and how they differ from those of individuals—and their *sources* of funds: stocks, bonds, and the "cash flow" from their business operations. Further, with regard to the common stocks themselves, we will consider how monetary policy impinges on the stock market and, finally, how even the average prices of common stocks may be of interest in the practice of monetary policy.

Since World War II the growth of nonbank financial institutions, taken collectively, has been spectacular. These institutions, the mutual savings banks, savings and loan associations, credit unions, and life insurance companies, also bring problems of regulation and control as they grow. On the problem of control, the main concern has been with the possibility that the hold that the Federal Reserve is presumed to have over the economy will somehow be weakened. One aspect of this is the following: if the authorities try to squeeze credit by putting pressure on the commercial banks, they could be frustrated if lending by financial intermediaries replaces lending by commercial banks. It can happen; and, we will see in this chapter, it did happen in several instances in recent years, although the policy influence is not clear. Another aspect of the control problem concerns the effect of "tight" money on the intermediaries themselves. A rise in market interest rates, whether or not induced by monetary policy, can cause a *runoff* of deposits from the "thrift banks" into, for example, Treasury bills, which affects the institutions, of course, and also their customers. These customers, we will see, are primarily people wanting mortgages, and the housing market can be, and probably has been, subject to undesirable fluctuations in demand in the circumstance just described.

This chapter, in addition to considering the monetary problem just introduced, will also undertake to describe to some extent the characteristics of the principal financial intermediaries. Partly because the task is critical to our understanding of monetary matters, we must be careful to define our terms—needed here are *intermediation* and *credit*—and the formal question we will consider is: Are commercial banks unique in some way (in comparison to financial intermediaries)? We begin with our definitional problems.

A financial intermediary has the following characteristics.[1] It will accept deposits (or issue "shares"), and it will make loans (or purchase investments), paying interest on the former and receiving interest on the latter. It will achieve profits from the services it renders in:

[1] We are defining an intermediary here by its characteristics; see Chapter 1 for a discussion of the problems involved in such an approach.

a. Spreading the risks of its small depositors.
b. Lending longer (or in different markets) than it borrows.
c. Helping to improve the overall allocation of financial resources.

Finally, it will tend to hold its cash reserves either in currency or as deposits in commercial banks. Aside from the last point, at least for members of the Federal Reserve System, a commercial bank is a financial intermediary in that it apparently carries out substantially the same activities. In fact, nonmember banks generally can hold a portion of their cash reserves at (other) commercial banks, as we have seen, so they would fit this definition exactly.

To take another tack, it might seem easy enough to distinguish intermediaries from banks—if we ignore the time deposit problem—by the fact that commercial banks issue the medium of exchange (deposits) while intermediaries do not. But these days (in some states) intermediaries can accept NOW accounts (negotiable order of withdrawal accounts) and these are "checkable" (and pay interest); even certain types of mutual funds (the "liquid asset" type) permit checks to be drawn, further blurring the lines. Nevertheless, a real distinction between the two does exist, particularly in that demand deposits pay no interest and in that intermediaries specialize in mortgage lending. Indeed, (deposit) bank money is a medium of exchange and consequently has a direct economic function to perform, while all other financial instruments serve primarily in indirect capacities, except for the NOW account, which we will discuss at the end of this chapter.

Paying interest is a sign of a credit arrangement, and it is probably more helpful to keep money and credit apart than to confuse them by equating the interest rate aspect of a credit arrangement with the medium-of-exchange function of money. Credit, of course, arises in a large variety of ways, many of which do not involve financial institutions at all. A bill of exchange might be drawn up, for example, when a business firm wishes to pay for some materials later than it receives them; it will want to do this because there will be a delay until it receives its funds, with the delay depending partly on how long it takes to manufacture the firm's product. The business firm that supplies the materials acquires the bill of exchange (which includes a provision for the interest cost of the operation), and it may take any of the following actions.

a. Hold it, being satisfied that the interest earned thereby is adequate.
b. Rediscount it at the local bank in exchange for the cash it needs.[2]

---

[2] When a security changes hands on a "discount" basis it does so with the interest rate built in, rather than explicitly stated. In particular, a 90-day Treasury Bill sold at $98 but redeemed at $100 carries an implicit interest rate of around 8 percent ($2 × 4 ÷ $98). A financial instrument can be rediscounted any number of times (bills of exchange are usually created on a discount basis).

c. Rediscount it at an accepting house (another type of intermediary), in which case a financial intermediary's depositor is the ultimate lender.
d. Sell it directly to a lender.
e. Exchange it directly with its own suppliers, in which case we might be tempted to call it money.

Money, in some ways, is easier to analyze than credit, as this complexity should demonstrate. But let us consider the extent of the intermediary sector before we return to the theoretical problems.

13.2 THE PRINCIPAL FINANCIAL INTERMEDIARIES

The principal "intermediaries" in most analyses of the problem are the savings and loan associations and the mutual savings banks; these, indeed, make up (along with the commercial banks and credit unions) the measure of moneyness M_3. Let us discuss the former, first. The original savings and loan associations date from the 1830s in the United States and are either corporate or mutual (depositor-owned) in structure. There are more than 5,000 S&Ls in the country with the proportion of state and federally chartered being in the ratio 3 : 2. They are supervised by either a state agency or the Federal Home Loan Bank Board, with the latter also supervising state institutions which have their deposits insured (up to $50,000) by the Federal Savings and Loan Insurance Corporation (FSLIC), as most do. The Bank Board also sets the interest ceilings (in consultation with the FDIC and the Federal Reserve) and the minimum amount of these savings accounts and short-term borrowings that the S&Ls must hold in certain liquid assets (set at 6 percent at the end of 1978).[3] The Bank Board also rules on the type of mortgage (and other activity) permitted by the S&Ls in its purview (it is currently permitting variable-interest-rate mortgages, which can be adjusted with market rates, and graduated-payment mortgages, which have payments that start low and rise over the life of the mortgage).[4] Finally, note that the S&Ls can borrow from the Federal Home Loan Banks (see Table 13.1) in the lender-of-last-resort sense.

[3] This reserve requirement is varied as circumstances dictate. Thus, in 1978, it was lowered from 7 percent to 6.5 percent effective May 1 and from 6.5 percent to 6 percent on December 12 (to be effective January 1, 1979). There is also a "short-term liquidity requirement" for savings accounts alone, which is currently at 2 percent (it was lowered from 3 percent in two steps—May 1st and January 1, 1979).

[4] The former are presently available only in California and the latter are designed to help younger households (in the face of high housing prices). In early 1979 the Bank Board opened up the question of permitting branching across state lines (in compact market areas such as New York or Washington), giving the impression that this will soon arrive in savings banking.

Table 13.1

A Balance Sheet for Savings and Loan Associations
Year-end 1968 and 1978
($ billions)

Assets	*1968*	*1978*	*Liabilities*	*1968*	*1978*
Mortgages	130.8	432.8	Savings capital	131.6	431.0
Cash and investing securities	12.5	44.8	Borrowed money	5.7	
			FHLB	—	32.0
Other	9.5	45.9	Other	—	11.0
			Loans in process	2.4	10.7
			Other	2.8	9.9
			Net worth*	10.3	29.0
Total assets	152.8	523.6	Total liabilities	152.8	523.6

* This item includes reserves and undistributed profits.
Source: *Federal Reserve Bulletin*.

At the end of 1978, the American savings and loan associations had the configuration of assets and liabilities given in Table 13.1, where it is compared to that of 1968. The average annual rate of growth of deposits in these institutions was 24.3 percent, a rapid growth, although commercial banks, too, have grown pretty rapidly (see M_2 in Table 1.1), at 12 percent overall, and at 17.8 percent per year in their time-deposit function. The mortgage lending of S&Ls, too, has expanded pretty much in the same proportion and is presently 82.6 percent of their total assets (it was 85.6 percent in 1968). Clearly, it is not much of an oversimplification to put it that a savings and loan association lends long and borrows short and makes its income on the spread in interest rates between the two items (see Table 2.6 for the current rate at which they "borrow" most of their funds).

The second major intermediary, and the second major additional part of M_3, itself the broadest concept of money actively used by the Federal Reserve for the measurement of the effect of its monetary control, is the *mutual savings bank* (MSB). The MSBs are, by definition, mutual institutions—that is, are depositor owned—and they are all state-chartered and regulated. They began in the United States just before 1820 and they now number around 500; they are concentrated in New York, Massachusetts, Connecticut, Pennsylvania, and New Jersey, where 90 percent of the total deposits in the industry are located (33 states have no MSBs). These banks have deposit insurance primarily from the FDIC although there is a state fund in Massachusetts; the FDIC, in turn, provides federal regulation *and* exerts the same control over interest ceilings (in consultation with the FSLIC and the Federal Reserve) as it does on the S&Ls. The liquidity and investment requirements of the MSBs are set by their respective chartering states.

The balance sheet of the MSBs at the end of 1977 is given as Table 13.2. Immediately, one sees that a simple sum of S&L and MSB assets and liabilities would not characterize these "savings banks." For one thing, the MSBs have not grown nearly as rapidly as the S&Ls; indeed, the average annual rate of growth in the total deposits of the MSBs (in Table 13.2) is only 12.2 percent, a rate not even as fast as the time deposits of the commercial banks (17.8 percent).[5] For another, while the main asset item

Table 13.2

A Balance Sheet for Mutual Savings Banks
Year-end 1968 and 1978
($ billions)

Assets	*1968*	*1978*	*Liabilities*	*1968*	*1978*
Mortgages	53.3	95.2	Total deposits	64.5	—
Other loans	1.4	7.2	Ordinary savings	—	71.7
U.S. government securities	3.8	5.0	Time and other deposits	—	69.4
State and local government securities	0.2	3.3	Other deposits	—	1.5
Corporate securities	10.2	39.8	Other liabilities	1.4	4.7
Cash	1.0	3.7			
Other assets	1.2	4.0	General reserve accounts	5.3	10.9
Total assets	71.2	158.2	Total liabilities	71.2	158.2

Source: *Federal Reserve Bulletin*.

of the MSB is the mortgage, it is but 60 percent of its total assets (down from 74.8 percent in 1968); similarly, *corporate* securities, an item not even separately included in the figures for S&Ls, make up 25 percent of the typical MSBs assets (up from 14.3 percent). Note that MSBs hold slightly higher "general reserves" (6.8 percent versus 5.5 percent) and have larger "time" deposits than do S&Ls. The time deposit, of course, is an indication of the preferences of the customers of the MSB; on the other, MSBs themselves choose to hold larger reserves, no doubt as extra insurance against fluctuations in the volume of their business (recall that they have suffered from runoffs, in the past).

There are two other major intermediaries that we should discuss here, one of them included in M_3—the credit unions—and one not—the life insurance companies. Credit unions, which are employee- (or employer-) sponsored institutions for mobilizing small amounts of capital (much of it directly out of paychecks) and engaging in small loans to their depositors, are growing steadily and had total assets of $62.6 billion at the end of

[5] The main reason for this, no doubt, is the fact that the MSBs are concentrated in the northeastern part of the United States; this area is not growing as rapidly as the rest of the country.

Table 13.3: Intermediaries in the American economy, 1970–1978 ($ billions)

	Commercial banks		*S&Ls*		*MSBs*		*Life insurance companies*		*Credit unions*	
	Savings and time deposits	*Percent change*	*Deposits*	*Percent change*	*Deposits*	*Percent change*	*Assets*	*Percent change*	*Deposits*	*Percent change*
1970	228.1	—	146.4	—	71.6	—	207.2	—	—	—
1971	269.8	18.3	174.2	19.0	81.4	13.7	222.1	7.2	—	—
1972	311.8	18.4	206.8	18.7	91.6	12.5	239.7	7.9	—	—
1973	362.2	13.9	227.0	9.8	96.5	5.3	252.4	5.3	—	—
1974	416.7	15.0	243.0	7.0	98.7	2.3	263.3	4.3	27.5	—
1975	449.6	7.9	285.7	17.6	109.9	11.3	289.3	7.9	33.0	20.0
1976	487.4	8.4	335.9	17.6	122.9	11.8	321.6	11.2	39.2	18.8
1977	542.5	11.3	387.0	15.2	133.9	9.0	350.5	9.0	46.8	19.4
1978	623.7	15.0	431.0	11.4	142.6	6.5	389.0	11.0	52.5	12.2

Note: Year-end figures.
Source: *Federal Reserve Bulletin*.

December 1978; in recent years these have grown at 23 percent per year. The life insurance companies are a little different; they are an intermediary to the extent that they deal in personal savings, but they also provide a direct service, and that arises in connection with the life insurance itself. That is, in accepting the bets that their customers make on their lives, they are unlike S&Ls and the MSBs: the life insurance company has a final product (insurance). Their business has grown pretty rapidly, too; thus, at the end of 1968 they had assets of $187.7 billion, while at the end of 1978 this was up to $389 billion (an average annual rate of growth of 10.7 percent). Their mortgage loans are sizable but are not their biggest asset; even so, they were up from $70.1 billion to $105.9 billion.

Finally, we consider some recent data that compare the rate of growth of the principal financial intermediaries over recent years; we include, for purposes of comparison, the time and savings balances of commercial banks. In Table 13.3 we see that all of these institutions have grown steadily but that there is some sign that funds shift back and forth between the institutions, shifts that are apparent even looking at the yearly percentage changes. In 1974, a year in which the American economy was in recession (and money was relatively "tight"), all of the intermediaries, *but not commercial banks,* continued a downslide in their rates of growth that had started in 1973. On the other hand, in 1975, as the recovery got under way, growth switched out of the commercial banks into the intermediaries. Indeed, 1977 and 1978 show the same pattern as 1974, suggesting that there are still strong switches of allegiance between the time and savings deposits of banks and those of the financial intermediaries, *in spite of* our firmly controlled interest rates across the entire sector. Clearly, an aggregation of this entire sector (to include time deposits) would show a much more stable pattern than do the individual components; indeed, this is the rationale for using the measure M_3. This finding of relative stability is of special interest for policy control, further, since the total of *credit* supplied by these institutions will also be reasonably stable; indeed, we may also wish to control the total of credit rather than the total of money, in our overall policy design.[6]

13.3 MONETARY INSTABILITY IN THE PRESENCE OF INTERMEDIATION

We should begin our discussion, which involves the possibility of destabilizing intermediation and disintermediation (runoffs) in financial mar-

[6] As we will see below, there is some runoff entirely out of the M_3 total, into such things as Treasury bills; the total savings sector seems to have suffered in this way in 1973, with the attendant effect on the customers of these institutions (mostly mortgage holders). In 1978, in contrast, the "money market instruments" tied to the Treasury bill rate may have helped a little, although the "liquid asset funds" of the major stock brokers were also growing very rapidly.

kets, with some further reference to the savings and time deposits of commercial banks. In our discussion in Chapter 5 we ignored these deposits, even though the savings account carries a substantially lower reserve requirement (3 percent); this left the analysis incomplete, since shifts do occur between the demand deposits and the savings and time deposits of banks, as the figures in Table 1.1 indicate. The point is actually a simple one, although the proof is somewhat tedious.

Suppose the monetary authorities attempt to enforce a tight money policy aimed at contracting bank loans. If customers can be induced (through a favorable interest rate) to shift their balances from demand to savings and time deposits, then commercial banks can frustrate this particular tight money policy. To analyze this possibility, we must first amend our formula for the determination of the money stock to deal with this complication. Thus, define

$$M_2 = C + D + T.$$

Let us redefine high-powered money as

$$H = C + R_D + R_T,$$

where we now distinguish two types of reserves (R_D and R_T) with different requirements. When we divide M_2 by H, we obtain

$$\frac{M_2}{H} = \frac{C + D + T}{C + R_D + R_T}; \qquad (13.1)$$

dividing through by D, we obtain

$$\frac{M_2}{H} = \left[\frac{\frac{C}{D} + 1 + \frac{T}{D}}{\frac{C}{D} + \frac{R_D}{D} + \frac{R_T}{D}}\right],$$

and further operating on R_T/D, using the fact that $R_T/D = (R_T/T)(T/D)$, we have

$$M_2 = H\left[\frac{\frac{C}{D} + \frac{T}{D} + 1}{\frac{C}{D} + \frac{R_D}{D} + \left(\frac{R_T}{T}\right)\left(\frac{T}{D}\right)}\right]. \qquad (13.2)$$

Here we have two ratios determined by the banks (or held at the legal minimum), R_D/D and R_T/T, and two ratios determined by the public (C/D and T/D); H is still under the control of the Federal Reserve (so, clearly, any change in these ratios could be offset by an open market operation of the Federal Reserve).[7] This formula is more general than the one used in the analysis of Chapter 5, which we are now extending, and it has the same potential (and problems) of that formula. But since it is not general—having only a portion of small savings (it does not have MSB and S&L deposits)—we will not further analyze it here.

The main question we have set ourselves in this section concerns the economic differences between commercial banks and financial intermediaries. This is not going to be easy because commercial banks and financial intermediaries (S&Ls for purposes of reference) *appear* to operate in pretty much the same way in that they lend in one market and borrow in another; of course, so do the Federal Reserve Banks. Now any definition of an intermediary that includes the 12 Federal Reserve Banks is not very operational; they are, after all, unique in that they exercise (collectively) discretionary control over the money stock by methods that take the form of open market operations, changes in reserve requirements, and changes in the discount rate at which commercial banks borrow from the Federal Reserve. Actually, what underlies the uniqueness of the Federal Reserve Banks is the simple fact that they hold the reserves of commercial banks. That is, whether or not the Federal Reserve can effectively use any of its instruments depends on its holding bank reserves, *reserves which commercial banks cannot create at their own discretion*. This is obvious enough with reserve requirements, so that is clear enough, but it is also true that if there were no reserve requirements—if (or rather, to the extent that) commercial banks held their reserves at *other* commercial banks—the consequence of a Federal Reserve sale of a bond from its portfolio would cease with the initial exchange. For example, if one buys a bond from the Federal Reserve and draws down his balance at a commercial bank, the Federal Reserve will own the deposit at the commercial bank; but the commercial bank will not care, so long as the Federal Reserve does not actually seek currency for its deposit. Thus, so long as the Federal Reserve keeps its deposit in the commercial banking system (and there is no way, in this example, to take it out, other than as cur-

[7] The intermediaries do not hold their reserves in the Federal Reserve, but if they did, we would have something like the following in place of M_2:

$$M_3 = H\left[\frac{\frac{C}{D}+\frac{T}{D}+\frac{S}{D}+1}{\frac{C}{D}+\frac{R_D}{D}+\left(\frac{R_T}{T}\right)\left(\frac{T}{D}\right)+\left(\frac{R_S}{S}\right)\left(\frac{S}{D}\right)}\right].$$

Here S is the savings deposit and R_S/S the reserve ratio. Shifts between C, T, and S by the public would still destabilize the money stock in this event but, as we shall see, such shifts are certainly easier to visualize in the event of such an approach to intermediary reserve requirements.

rency), then the Federal Reserve would not be able to operate as a central bank.[8]

The Federal Reserve, consequently, is unique in our trilogy of financial institutions because member commercial banks hold their reserves in it; are commercial banks unique because S&Ls hold their reserves in commercial banks? The answer is a modified yes—an analogy holds—even though commercial banks obviously lack the discretionary powers of the Federal Reserve. In fact, a pyramid of intermediary credit is built on the reserve held at the commercial bank such that

a. Changes of the public's allegiance *among* the intermediaries do not affect the total of credit.

b. Changes in the supply of S&L reserves by *commercial banks* have a greater influence on credit than similar changes by the financial intermediaries themselves.[9]

These aspects are formally identical to two other points we can make about the relationship between the Federal Reserve and commercial banks, which are that

c. Changes in the public's allegiance among commercial banks do not affect the money supply.

d. Changes in the supply of reserves by the Federal Reserve have a far greater influence on the money supply that do changes in the demand for reserves by the commercial banks.

Let us illustrate. The point made under (*a*) is obvious, so long as all financial intermediaries have roughly identical reserve requirements, which, in general, they do (generally we do not go beyond the S&Ls and MSBs in considering this topic); similarly, point (*c*) is reasonable enough, although the mixture of member and nonmember banks does offer some potential for variation here.[10] Similarly, point (*d*) has been, in effect, argued by the use of the multiplier equation in Chapter 5. But the establishment of point (*b*) requires a more general analysis; we will tackle this indirectly. To begin with, we may use our multipliers approach yet one more time to show how financial intermediaries—basically treated differ-

---

[8] Note, *apropos* of our discussion in Chapter 4, that the two Banks of the United States operated a kind of monetary policy in the early 19th century that was similar to that just described. When they wished to curtail monetary expansion they presented the notes of commercial banks (the equivalent of the deposit) for collection in gold or silver (the equivalent of currency in the example just considered). They did this rarely, though, and without the official approval of Congress.

[9] The commercial banks, we are saying, *demand* reserves at the Federal Reserve Banks; indeed, in various points of this book, we have seen this demand change (e.g., in 1932–39), as discussed in Chapter 5.

[10] Recall from Chapter 5 that the monetary base is adjusted for these shifts.

ently from banks—are involved in the creation of M_1. Recall, first, our definitions from Chapter 5, which had

$$M_1 = C + D_b$$
$$H = C + R$$

for money and high-powered money, respectively; here we designate D_b as the checking deposits of commercial banks.[11] Now D_b, when there are S&Ls, consists of the deposits of the public and the deposits (reserves) of the S&Ls; thus

$$D_b = D_P + D_{SL}. \tag{13.3}$$

This implies, when we divide M by H and substitute in Equation (12.1), that our money stock is determined by

$$M_1 = H\left(\frac{C + D_P + D_{SL}}{C + R}\right). \tag{13.4}$$

Now, *by definition,* $D_{SL} = D_{SLP}(D_{SL}/D_{SLP})$, where D_{SLP} is the deposits made by the public in the S&Ls; thus we may write

$$M_1 = H\left[\frac{C + D_P + D_{SLP}\left(\frac{D_{SL}}{D_{SLP}}\right)}{C + R}\right]. \tag{13.5}$$

Let us divide all terms in the brackets by D_{SLP}; this yields

$$M_1 = H\left[\frac{\frac{C}{D_{SLP}} + \frac{D_P}{D_{SLP}} + \frac{D_{SL}}{D_{SLP}}}{\frac{C}{D_{SLP}} + \frac{R}{D_{SLP}}}\right]. \tag{13.6}$$

Then, finally, since

$$\frac{R}{D_{SLP}} = \left(\frac{R}{D_b}\right)\left(\frac{D_b}{D_{SLP}}\right) \text{ and } \frac{D_b}{D_{SLP}} = \left(\frac{D_b}{C}\right)\left(\frac{C}{D_{SLP}}\right),$$

we may reorganize our expression to get:

$$M_1 = H\left[\frac{\frac{C}{D_{SLP}} + \frac{D_P}{D_{SLP}} + \frac{D_{SL}}{D_{SLP}}}{\frac{C}{D_{SLP}} + \left(\frac{R}{D_b}\right)\left(\frac{D_b}{D_{SLP}}\right)}\right]$$

$$= H\left[\frac{\frac{C}{D_{SLP}} + \frac{D_P}{D_{SLP}} + \frac{D_{SL}}{D_{SLP}}}{\frac{C}{D_{SLP}} + \left(\frac{R}{D_b}\right)\left(\frac{D_b}{C}\right)\left(\frac{C}{D_{SLP}}\right)}\right]. \tag{13.7}$$

---

[11] Note that we are not analyzing M_3 but M_1 in this discussion.

Note, in the final version on the right side of Equation (13.7), the presence of a residual term, D_b/C, which represents no particular "sectoral decision" in the following "sectoral" analysis.[12]

(*i.*) The ratio C/D_{SLP} is determined by the public—it expresses the public's preference for currency as a ratio of S&L deposits; an increase in this ratio will tend to *decrease* the money stock (try some numbers to work this one out); the converse also holds. Note, though, that when C/D_{SLP} changes—let us say, increases—D_b/C can hardly remain constant, since the currency in circulation is rising relatively (H is constant, so the central bank is accommodating the desire for currency by debiting bank reserve accounts); indeed, D_b/C would tend to fall, which would tend to moderate the reduction in the money supply caused by the increase in currency preferences.

(*ii.*) The ratio D_{SL}/D_{SLP} represents the reserve preferences of the S&Ls; if they decide to hold higher reserves as deposits at commercial banks, the formula implies that the money stock will increase. This may not seem sensible, since all they do, when they increase their reserve balance, is to call in loans from the public (which pays by running down *its* bank balances), but the implication of fixed ratios here is that the public will simultaneously adjust its other assets (to hold C/D_{SLP} and D_P/D_{SLP} constant). When it does this, and moves out of S&L deposits and currency, it will, on net, tend to increase the money supply. This is sensible, really, in that all we started with was an increased demand for bank deposits (by S&Ls). Note that D_b/C would tend to *rise* in this case, a result that tends to moderate the increase in the money supply caused by the rise in D_{SL}/D_{SLP}.

(*iii.*) The reserve ratio of banks is given by R/D_b; an increase in this will, as before (in Chapter 5) reduce the money stock. This effect is not necessarily going to cause much of an offsetting change in D_b/C, as both D_b and C will tend to fall as banks curtail operations (and since the Federal Reserve holds $H = C + R$ constant, *by assumption*).

(*iv.*) Interestingly, shifts in the public's taste for deposits between intermediaries and banks, as embodied in D_P/D_{SLP}, will tend to change the money stock; indeed, *ceteris paribus,* a shift toward S&Ls will tend to reduce the money supply, as a glance at the formula (Equation 13.7) shows. Note that if the deposits find their way back to the system (via S&L and reserve activity), D_b/C need not change in this case.

Finally, with regard to the last result (iv), we could argue that even if reserve requirements were the same between intermediaries and banks, so that $(D_{SL}/D_{SLP}) = (R/D_b)$, this runoff effect would still occur. Thus, we

[12] To convert to M_3 we just need to rewrite the numerator in Equation (13.7) as

$$\left(\frac{C}{D_{SLP}} + \frac{D_P}{D_{SLP}} + \frac{D_{SL}}{D_{SLP}} + 1\right).$$

have proved that *runoffs* among the financial institutions affect the money stock; the runoffs can be prevented to some extent by fixing all interest rates, at the risk of an even more serious runoff (as we shall see) out of both banks *and* intermediaries (into Treasury bills, stocks, and bonds); this actually works to the detriment of the intermediaries compared to the banks, since money (currency and demand deposits) tends to circulate back into the banks. The business of the banks, that is to say, is less affected by this sort of pressure, although they would lose time deposits; in this sense we see that banks differ in having the medium of exchange in addition to their intermediary function.

We may, at long last, attack proposition (*b*) directly. By point (*ii*) the effect of a change in S&L reserves is possibly only slightly negative on the money supply (at most). Thus the loss of credit to the system is the amount of credit extinguished in the first instance when the S&L called in its loan, and any net contraction of the total credit in the system is caused by a rather minimal reduction of the money supply (the cash, after all, is returned to the system). On the other hand, when the banks put an *equal* amount into their reserves, a multiplied contraction of bank credit results; furthermore, for fixed ratios, the S&Ls will lose deposits and they, too, will be forced to curtail credit. Clearly, the bank's reserve decision is "high-powered" compared to the reserve decision (of an equal amount) of the financial intermediary. So, it seems, a technical difference does exist.

The upshot of all this technical discussion is that financial intermediaries pose a threat to monetary control only insofar as there are shifts of funds between the various intermediaries, the commercial banks, and the public. In particular, the cases we have considered suggest that if monetary policy is vigorous enough to (*a*) change interest rates sharply, or (*b*) provide sharp supply-induced changes in the quantity of money, then *individuals* or even the intermediaries themselves may react in such a way as to destabilize partially the money stock. While this is worrisome, much of the effect, at least *within* the M_3 category, has been alleviated by imposing operating ceilings on the rates of interest that are involved. This, as we shall see in the next section, does not deal with all of the problems that arise, since the total intermediary sector (but usually not the banks) has been subject to a runoff problem as their competitors have gained the edge in any general liquidity scramble (by means of variable interest rates). This problem is not unknown to the authorities, and in a final section of the chapter we will consider some of the devices currently being used to deal with these problems.

13.4 THE EFFECTS OF MONETARY POLICY ON THE INTERMEDIARIES

What most intermediaries do, as it turns out, other than to hold the deposits of their customers, is to lend *mortgage* funds to individuals and corporations. That is, of fundamental importance to the smooth flow of funds to the housing market (to the purchasers of homes, primarily) is a smooth flow to the intermediaries themselves. Consider the figures in Table 13.4, first, on the annual amount of mortgage activity among all

Table 13.4: The supply of mortgage funds to the American economy, 1973–1978 ($ billions)

	1973	*1974*	*1975*	*1976*	*1977*	*1978*
All holders	*682.3*	*742.5*	*801.5*	*889.3*	*1,019.7*	*1,169.5*
1–4 Family	416.2	449.4	490.8	556.6	650.4	759.6
Multifamily	93.1	100.0	100.6	104.5	111.4	121.9
Commercial	131.7	146.9	159.3	171.2	192.1	211.8
Farm	41.2	46.3	50.9	57.0	65.7	76.2
Commercial banks	*119.1*	*132.1*	*136.2*	*151.3*	*176.7*	*213.8*
1–4 Family	68.0	74.8	77.0	86.2	101.4	126.9
Multifamily	6.9	7.6	5.9	8.1	8.7	10.9
Commercial	38.7	43.7	46.9	50.3	58.6	67.0
Farm	5.4	6.0	6.4	6.7	8.0	9.0
Mutual savings banks	*73.2*	*74.9*	*77.2*	*81.6*	*88.0*	*95.0*
1–4 Family	48.8	49.2	50.0	53.1	57.5	62.2
Multifamily	12.3	12.9	13.8	14.2	15.3	16.5
Commercial	12.0	12.7	13.4	14.3	15.1	16.3
Farm	.1	.1	.1	.1	.1	.1
Savings and loans	*231.7*	*249.3*	*278.6*	*323.1*	*381.2*	*432.9*
1–4 Family	187.1	201.0	223.9	260.9	308.4	355.3
Multifamily	22.8	23.8	25.5	28.4	33.4	36.4
Commercial	21.9	24.5	29.1	33.8	39.5	41.2
Life insurance companies	*81.4*	*86.2*	*89.2*	*91.6*	*95.7*	*105.0*
1–4 Family	20.4	19.0	17.6	16.1	14.7	14.6
Multifamily	18.4	19.6	19.6	19.2	18.9	19.3
Commercial	36.5	41.2	45.2	48.9	53.4	60.8
Farm	6.0	6.3	6.8	7.4	8.6	10.4
Federal and related agencies*	*46.7*	*58.3*	*66.9*	*66.8*	*70.2*	*82.1*
Mortgage pools or trusts†	*18.0*	*23.8*	*34.1*	*49.8*	*70.2*	*86.7*
Individuals and others‡	*112.2*	*117.8*	*119.3*	*125.1*	*137.8*	*153.9*

* These consist of the Government National Mortgage Association, the Farmer's Home Administration, the Federal Housing and Veterans Administration, the Federal National Mortgage Association (50 percent of the total), Federal Land Banks, and the Federal Home Loan Mortgage Corporation.

† These are mortgages backed or guaranteed by the Government National Mortgage Association, the Federal Home Loan Mortgage Corporation, or the Farmer's Home Administration.

‡ Others include real estate investment trusts, state and local credit agencies, state and local retirement funds, noninsured pension funds, credit unions, and miscellaneous U.S. government agencies.

Source: *Federal Reserve Bulletin*.

holders. In Table 13.4 one sees that, indeed, in recent years all of the major financial institutions (including the banks) have steadily increased their mortgage commitments, with S&Ls, though, accounting for a steadily increasing percentage of the total (33.9 to 37.0 percent) and of the small mortgage loans (44.9 to 46.8 percent). Life insurance companies, on the other hand, concentrate on commercial mortgages, in competition with the commercial banks. Note that life insurance companies have actually reduced the absolute quantity of their small mortgage loans in recent years. Finally, there is nothing in Table 13.4 to suggest that the supply of funds to the housing industry suffered at all during the monetary storms of 1973 to 1978, at least if annual data are employed. But this has not always been the case—and may not hold in the future—and it is instructive to go back to the *credit crunches of 1966 and 1969* to illustrate the problem.

The period immediately preceding 1966 was one of rapid expansion for the United States; as the figures in Table 13.5 illustrate, some sign of a

Table 13.5: Economic activity in the United States, 1965 and 1966

	Annual rate of growth (percent)				
Year and quarter	*Real income*	*Price level*	*Money stock*	*Velocity (residual)*	*Unemployment (percent)*
1965					
I	8.7	0.7	2.8	6.6	4.83
II	6.9	3.2	0.2	9.9	4.73
III	6.8	1.1	3.5	4.4	4.47
IV	8.4	2.2	9.7	0.9	4.20
1966					
I	5.9	3.6	6.6	2.9	3.83
II	1.8	4.2	0.4	5.6	3.83
III	4.0	3.2	0.2	7.0	3.80
IV	4.5	2.8	3.6	3.7	3.67

Source: *Federal Reserve Bulletin.*

"heated" economy had begun to appear in 1965, and historically low levels of unemployment were reached. This, of course, was the period of Vietnam escalation. The underlying causes of the situation were obviously connected with the Vietnam War, particularly in view of the attempt to divert resources from the private to the public sector when the economy as a whole was expanding rapidly anyway. At any rate, through the last three quarters of 1965, whether as a result of financing the needs of business or of cushioning the effect on capital markets of extensive fiscal operations, the money stock grew rapidly. Prices, too, began to shoot up, with about a one-quarter lag behind the money supply; the inflation figures can be compared with an average value of 1.1 percent for inflation from 1953 to 1961. After the first quarter of 1966, the brakes were put on, and the rate of growth of the money stock fell almost to zero; the velocity of money grew rapidly and, again with a one-quarter lag, the rate of inflation decreased markedly. These symptoms were in large part produced by a tight money policy, a policy that affected the intermediaries, the banks, and the customers of both types of institutions—particularly the housing market—perhaps even more than it affected the rest of the economy, which actually did not go into a recession on this occasion.

We may analyze these events by using a device that commonly has been neglected—the flow of funds—although its detail is of particular value for this sort of problem. The flow of funds measures the change in various financial stocks (of assets and of liabilities) for various arbitrary periods of time. Generally, in the flow-of-funds table, a distinction is made between the final users of the funds and the *intermediate* suppliers; the *ultimate* suppliers of funds, of course, are savers, primarily individuals and corporations.[13] We see, when examining Table 13.6, that the mortgage market was hard-hit in 1966 and that (no doubt) the most important reason for this was a drastic decline in funds available to MSBs and S&Ls, which together grew $5.8 billion less than they had in the previous year.

Table 13.6: Annual flow of funds, 1964–1967 ($ billions)

	1964	*1965*	*1966*	*1967*
Net uses				
Mortgages (public)	25.6	25.2	17.7	19.8
Corporate bonds	6.6	8.1	11.1	16.0
State and local securities	5.6	7.1	5.6	9.4
Foreign bonds	0.9	1.2	0.9	1.2
Other bank loans	13.6	19.8	13.0	12.9
Treasury debt (public)	2.6	−2.4	−1.9	3.4
Federal agency debt	0.6	2.9	4.8	4.0
Total	55.5	61.9	51.2	66.7
Net sources				
Mutual savings banks	4.1	3.6	2.5	5.0
Savings and loan associations	10.9	9.3	4.6	8.9
Life insurance companies	6.4	6.7	6.7	6.4
Fire and casualty insurance	0.8	1.0	1.5	1.2
Private, noninsured pension funds	2.1	2.1	1.9	0.7
State and local retirement funds	2.7	2.9	3.2	3.8
Open-end mutual funds	0.4	0.4	1.0	−0.3
Commercial banks	21.5	27.9	17.2	36.6
Others	6.6	8.0	12.6	4.4
Total	55.5	61.9	51.2	66.7

Source: Adapted from a table developed by the research department of Salomon Brothers and Hutzler, New York.

Commercial banks also show the effects of the scramble for funds in 1966; but they more than recovered in 1967, while the MSBs and S&Ls were, collectively, still short of their 1964 rate of increase; and, more significantly, so were the funds made available to the mortgage market.

[13] The term "flow" is a misnomer here, as we used it in Chapter 1. Frequently you will find *uses* referred to as the demand for funds and *sources* as the supply. This, too, is misleading, for the net change in any of the stocks in a flow-of-funds table is determined by both supply and demand.

Since everybody seems to have lost, we cannot conclude that tightness of money spreads itself unevenly around the financial sector—except for life insurance companies, who also sell a product—but we certainly see that *final* users (new home owners in this case) are affected unevenly, depending on where they get their funds. This lesson is clear from the table, for, in contrast, corporations—especially—and most arms of the government seem not to have had difficulty, at least with regard to obtaining funds in the bond markets.[14]

The credit crunch of 1966, then, while it quickly brought down the rate of inflation in the economy, had an uneven effect, being especially severe in its influence on the housing market; this process as it works through the intermediaries is often called *disintermediation* and is considered a fundamental problem by most Americans (to whom a vigorous housing sector is almost a macro-policy objective). Let us consider another period, three years removed from the last, which has been dubbed the *credit crunch of 1969*. The data appear in Table 13.7. Here we again had an accelerating inflation that produced a leveling off of the growth of the money stock, especially in the summer of 1969. In addition, the level of free reserves of commercial banks fell during much of the year (and was highest during the period May–August), itself indicating some monetary tightness.

What is curious about the credit crunch of 1969 is that a slow growth of the narrow money stock (even slower than 1966) does not seem to have produced much of an effect anywhere in the financial markets. Indeed, all categories increased steadily, with bank loans showing several slow periods, but rising rapidly over even the last part of the year. Now one thought that suggests itself is that intermediation has stepped in to confound American monetary policy; that, after all, is what our analysis in Section 12.3 suggests. This would be the case if higher S&L and MSB interest rates pulled funds out of the banks' time deposit accounts so that they were, in effect, "recycled" through the credit markets. Actually, this is clearly part of the explanation, since the time deposits of banks fell by $9.1 billion from January to December 1969. But this leaves a puzzle, because while banks were under two kinds of pressure—monetary policy was squeezing M_1 directly and time deposits (at a lower reserve requirement) were in effect being recycled into demand deposits (at a higher reserve requirement)—*bank loans somehow expanded rapidly*. On net, the

[14] There were several other events affecting the intermediaries and the banks in 1966. For one thing, the banks dipped into the Eurodollar market and borrowed from the Fed to ease part of the pressure on them; for another, in the summer, banks experienced a runoff of their large CDs, which had a ceiling rate of 5.5 percent under Regulation Q, when market interest rates went past 5.5 percent. The Federal Reserve, concerned about the effect on S&Ls actually *lowered* the ceiling rate to 5 percent; it also raised the reserve requirement on large time deposits (such as CDs) to 6 percent (from 4 percent). Regulation Q no longer applies to the large CDs of commercial banks.

Table 13.7: Money and credit in the 1969 "Squeeze" ($ billions)

Month	*Narrow money supply*	*Free reserves*	*Bank loans*	*Commercial and finance company paper, bankers' acceptances*	*Real estate loans by MSBs*	*Life insurance company mortgage loans*	*S&L mortgage loans*	*Business investment*
January	195.8	−0.480	261.1	21.8	53.6	70.2	131.4	—
February	196.3	−0.596	263.1	22.9	53.8	70.4	132.1	—
March	196.8	−0.701	265.0	23.7	54.0	70.5	133.0	(15.2)
April	198.1	−0.844	270.5	24.4	54.2	70.7	134.0	—
May	198.3	−1.102	272.7	25.3	54.4	70.8	135.0	—
June	199.0	−1.064	283.8	26.0	54.7	71.0	136.2	(17.7)
July	199.3	−1.074	283.2	28.3	54.9	71.7	137.1	—
August	199.0	−0.946	280.7	29.5	55.1	71.2	138.0	—
September	199.0	−0.831	284.3	29.7	55.2	71.4	138.6	(18.2)
October	199.1	−0.992	284.0	31.9	55.3	71.6	139.2	—
November	199.3	−0.988	286.2	33.6	55.5	71.7	139.7	—
December	199.6	−0.829	293.6	31.6	55.8	72.1	140.2	(20.1)
Change over 11 months								
Absolute	+3.8	−0.349	+32.5	+9.8	+2.2	+1.9	+8.8	+4.9
Percent	+1.9	—	+12.4	+45.0	+4.1	+2.7	+6.7	+32.2

Source: *Federal Reserve Bulletin.*

credit "crunch" does not seem to have existed, although the money stock was certainly curtailed sharply.

We must look more closely at the sectors involved before we jump to the conclusion that intermediation was responsible for all of the events in 1969. Let us first discuss the methods commercial banks employed to avoid the squeeze. There seem to have been three sources of funds during the period:

a. + $8.6 billion from selling government bonds.

b. + $0.4 billion from borrowing at the Federal Reserve.

c. + $18 billion from an increase in "cash assets."

The latter is not analyzed carefully in any published figures but seems to stem largely from a rise in "interbank" and "other" demand deposits. What seems to have happened is that certain funds, especially Eurodollars (dollar deposits in European banks, whether American or foreign-owned) were tapped in the emergency in the sense that liquid funds could be borrowed there, denominated in dollars. This is a type of intermediation, basically, but it seems to be more a technical flaw, since Eurodollars were simply ignored in most analyses of the system at the time. The intermediation produced by selling off government securities (but, significantly, not private securities) was helped, but not in the sense of an increase in the money stock, by the government's general support of the bond market.

Let us finish this discussion by examining the record of the MSBs and S&Ls to see if, in 1969, the intermediaries actually intermediated in frustration of monetary policy. In Table 13.8 we list the principal sources of

Table 13.8: Sources of funds for MSBs and S&Ls in 1969 ($ billions)

	MSBs	*S&Ls*
Deposits	+2.40	+3.96
Borrowings*	+0.08	+4.05
Net change in federal government securities held	−0.69	−1.39

* For MSBs, which did not borrow, this item represents "other liabilities."
Source: *Federal Reserve Bulletin*.

funds to these intermediaries in 1969. Clearly there is considerable intermediation shown in the first entry (deposits), and the third entry (the government-supported "intermediation") cannot be ignored. Even so, we also cannot ignore the $4.05 billion that was lent *directly* to the S&Ls by the government. We can conclude this discussion by suggesting that on the evidence here, destabilizing intermediation seems a factor, but that in 1969 it was only about as important a factor as direct government intervention, this intervention taking two forms:

a. Explicit lending, especially to the S&Ls.
b. Support of the government bond market.

Further, some institutional safety valves, notably the Euro-dollar market, also seem to be quite important.[15] But, on net, 1969 was a rather half-hearted credit "squeeze," perhaps so because of the movement of the economy into a recession that time around (it did not happen in 1966).[16]

More recently, to pick up once again the discussion of current monetary events, we have had a re-emergence of concern over the housing industry in the wake of the tight money policy of 1977 and 1978. Thus, as we observed in Chapter 10, the Federal Reserve put the clamps on the economy in October 1977 and again in November 1978. Table 13.9 recalls this

Table 13.9: Some financial flows from late 1977 to early 1979 ($ billions)

	Total savings funds committed to MSBs and S&Ls	*Borrowings of the S&Ls*	*Mortgages of the MSBs and S&Ls*	*Percent change in mortgages*
1977				
August	501.6	22.0	447.0	—
September	508.9	22.9	452.9	1.32
October	511.8	24.2	458.5	1.24
November	513.9	25.5	463.8	1.16
December	520.9	27.8	469.3	1.18
1978				
January	524.4	27.9	473.0	.79
February	527.1	28.7	476.8	.80
March	536.0	29.3	482.2	1.13
April	536.5	31.9	487.6	1.12
May	539.2	32.8	493.2	1.15
June	547.3	34.3	499.5	1.28
July	550.8	35.7	504.2	.94
August	553.3	37.2	509.5	1.05
September	561.2	38.6	514.4	.96
October	564.1	39.9	519.1	.91
November	566.4	41.0	523.9	.92
December	573.6	43.0	528.1	.80
1979				
January	578.6	42.4	531.0	.54
February	582.1	41.4	533.8	.53

Source: *Federal Reserve Bulletin.*

experience from our earlier tables and introduces some other figures appropriate to the broader financial climate we are dealing with in this chapter.

[15] We will continue the discussion of the Eurodollar market in Chapter 18.

[16] Recall, again, that the leading indicators were declining through *all* of 1969 (see Chapter 12).

As you will recall, tight money, in the sense of control of the money stock, was first instituted in October 1977; this did produce a decreased rate of increase of commercial bank mortgage commitments. In the third quarter these were up $7.6 billion, but in the first quarter of 1978, they were only up $4.5 billion. For the MSBs and S&Ls, deposit growth did slow down in October and November and again in April (sharply) and October 1978. It seems that savings flows were generally "on-and-off" during the 15 months covered in Table 12.9, but did manage to increase by 12.5 percent over the entire period. At the same time the mortgages of these institutions grew slowly in January and February 1978, and turned down again in September and October, although they actually increased 16.1 percent over the 15-month period. The reason that mortgages held up (the deposit growth is "below average") is probably related to two things:

a. The rapid growth of borrowings by the S&Ls at the Federal Home Loan Banks (*up 81 percent*).
b. The use of the new "money market instruments"—to be discussed in the next section—from June 1978 on, which enabled the savings banks to avoid the traditional runoff into Treasury bills.

Even so, as the record tight money policy took hold after November 1, 1978, one hears again of problems from the mortgage market, and the flow of funds into the savings banks again tapered off, with a resulting decline in mortgages.[17]

13.5 EXPERIMENTS WITH VARIABLE INTEREST RATES IN FINANCIAL MARKETS

As we have seen in this chapter, the runoff problem has several serious sides to it:

a. Monetary policy can be frustrated.
b. Financial institutions suffer fluctuations in the volume of their business.
c. The customers of financial institutions may have to suffer from the effects of credit rationing.

Both theoretical and empirical support for these possibilities has been given here; on the other hand, the evidence also suggests that the problem

[17] For one thing, state usury laws and legal ceilings on the mortgage rates of federally chartered S&Ls have caused savings banks themselves to shift funds away from mortgages (into CDs, for example). For another, "money market mutual funds" have proved to be able to offer attractive rates—and a certain amount of flexibility—and grew rapidly in this period. These last are mutual funds that invest in a variety of bonds and bills and charge a fee to the depositor. They offer competitive rates and two advantages: they will take smaller deposits (e.g., $2,500 compared to $10,000) and they are instantly liquid; indeed some permit check writing (e.g., in $500 amounts).

does not always emerge. The *regulatory approach* to the problem, clearly, has been to extend the authorities' control of interest rates and reserve requirements to a broader and broader spectrum of financial institutions. But this has not really brought the problem to an end, if only because a saving unit can always shift entirely out of the "short-term financial" sector, and so, recently, several experiments in the *other* direction—toward allowing flexible interest rates—have surfaced. These concern the NOW accounts of intermediaries, the money market instrument (for time deposits of six months in maturity) of both commercial banks and the savings institutions, and, most importantly, the *proposed* phasing out of interest rate ceilings.[18]

The NOW accounts—called, formally, negotiable order of withdrawal accounts—began in New England in the early 1970s as a device used by saving banks to attract customers. Technically, the NOW account of a savings bank permits a customer to draw checks on his interest-bearing savings deposit. Thus, it is an interest-bearing demand deposit (they are, at present, cleared through the commercial banking system). At present it is available at some commercial banks, and, along with the automatic transfer from savings to checking accounts, is a method of permitting commercial banks, if they wish, to pay interest on demand deposits.

The NOW account, clearly, has the general economic advantage that it puts some needed flexibility into the savings market at a point that has been regarded by many to be a particularly sensitive one. We should not, however, overstate the gain since banks (etc.) had already found ways to accommodate their customers' desire for flexibility:

a. Allowing phone transfers.
b. Automatically transferring funds each way in their checking and savings accounts.
c. Letting their customers use checks on their bank credit cards.

Thus, in a way, legislation is merely catching up with the times. Generally, though, commercial bankers are concerned about NOW accounts, at least if they do not get a slice of the action; if they do, though, they will be able to compete and, more particularly, they will be able to dispense with the "free" services they provide, which in some cases, no doubt, are more expensive to them than a small interest payment would be. As well, the economy would gain from having a flexible price here. On net, though, the NOW account promises little advantage to the runoff problem; indeed, if it is *partially* or gradually instituted, as it is at present—mostly in the

[18] During the summer of 1978 new eight-year, 8 percent accounts were also permitted of banks and eight-year, 8.25 percent accounts for savings institutions. This rate, for a change, *may* actually offer savers a real yield after inflation (for the next eight years) is deducted. Not all banks actually offered these at 8 percent at first (but at lower rates).

savings banks but not in the commercial banks—it may increase the runoff problem for a time.

The money market instrument is another matter, since it offers the small-savings sector as a whole a chance to compete with other, more flexible capital markets. This runoff, we saw, appeared in 1966 and may have again been in operation in late 1977 and early 1978, in the wake of the tight money policy at that time; indeed this instrument may have kept the mortgage market going in the second half of 1978. Technically, what these instruments did was to permit banks and intermediaries to offer the following terms to investors:

a. Denominations must be in the minimum amount of $10,000 for a period of six months.
b. The interest rate, when negotiated by commercial banks, will be equal to the six month Treasury bill rate.
c. The interest rate paid by savings banks is to be .25 percent higher than the commercial bank rate (this was eliminated in early 1979).

Thus, clearly, the runoffs between intermediaries are not affected, but the potential exists for commercial banks and savings banks to hold on to deposits which might otherwise run out of the system entirely.

Finally, we note the most important concession of all, the elimination of interest rate ceilings on banks and intermediaries entirely. At the time these words were written, both chambers of Congress were considering legislation to phase out interest rate ceilings, over a ten-year period. While this legislation will certainly not go through in exactly the way it was worded in late 1979 in the separate House and Senate bills, it is very likely that many of the interest rate ceilings will be dismantled by the mid-1980s. As we have pointed out in this chapter, this should help the runoff problem considerably, although, no doubt, there will be an attendant uncertainty as to how to measure the money stock exactly.

13.6 STUDY QUESTIONS

Essay questions

1. When this book was written the situation described in Section 12.5 with regard to the money market instruments was changing almost on a week-to-week basis. What is the current situation and how does it compare with that in the text? In particular, has greater flexibility brought more or less stability to the financial markets?

2. We have argued that life insurance companies have a product to sell and so they differ fundamentally from the other intermediaries. Yet in Chapter 2, we noted that commercial banks can also be thought of as manufacturing a product—demand deposits—which they agree to buy back at face value. Compare these two views, and then consider whether or not time deposits should also be taken as a product, too, in the senses just described. Look back to Question 3 in Section 2.6 for a reference.

3. Discuss the following statements about time and savings deposits and S&L and MSB deposits:

a. They are "money at rest" rather than "money on the wing," but money nevertheless.

b. They are interest-bearing and consequently are not money.

c. They are not a means of payment and are not money, while credit cards (when used) are money (a means of payment).

4. Carefully compare the MSBs and the S&Ls in terms of their portfolio behavior over the last several years (the data in the *Federal Reserve Bulletin* would suffice here). Do you see any problem with an aggregation of their deposits, then (to make up M_3) in this period?

True-false discussion questions

These statements are meant to be somewhat ambiguous, and to provoke discussion, thereby.

1. The presence of financial intermediaries tends to destabilize the money supply, especially when a tight money policy is followed.

2. A financial firm would be considered an intermediary if it lends for a longer term than it borrows.

3. If the Federal Reserve held the reserves of the intermediaries, then the formal distinction between intermediaries and commercial banks would break down.

4. A "heated" economy affects the profits of intermediaries in the same way it affects those of the commercial banks.

5. A financial intermediary can be distinguished from a commercial bank on the grounds that the former deals in credit and the latter in money.

6. The presence of financial intermediaries tends to frustrate monetary policy primarily on account of the actions of their depositors.

7. When the market for mortgage funds is adversely affected by tight money, it is generally the higher interest rates rather than the availability of funds that affects the housing market.

13.7 FURTHER READING

Burger, Albert E. ''An Historical Analysis of the Credit Crunch of 1966.'' *Review, Federal Reserve Bank of St. Louis* (September 1969).

Chandler, Lester V. *The Monetary-Financial System.* New York: Harper and Row, 1979.

Dougall, Herbert E., and Jack E. Gaumitz. *Capital Markets and Institutions.* Englewood Cliffs, N.J.: Prentice-Hall, Inc., 1975.

Goldsmith, Raymond. ''The Development of Financial Institutions During the Post-War Period.'' *Quarterly Review, Banca Nazionale del Lavoro* (June 1971).

Gup, Benton E. *Financial Intermediaries.* Boston: Houghton Mifflin Company, 1976.

Harless, Doris E. *Nonbank Financial Institutions.* Richmond, Va.: Federal Reserve Bank of Richmond, October 1975.

14

The mean-variance approach to financial behavior

14.1 INTRODUCTION

Following the relatively practical discussion of Chapter 13, which was designed to broaden the context of the discussion to include the financial intermediaries, it is necessary to spin out some more theory before we return again to specific cases involving the financial markets. What we need, in particular, is a more general approach to financial markets so that we can deal efficiently with the problems that are introduced when a very broad spectrum of assets—shortly to include bonds and equities in addition to money and intermediary deposits—are brought into the discussion. The two models that we propose to use in this task are the *mean-variance* (or *portfolio*) model and the *inventory* model; both of these provide insights into financial behavior, insights that range from an understanding of how financial behavior may be explained (or rationalized) to some interesting amendments to our general macroeconomic model (and to our policy discussions).

Roughly speaking, the mean-variance model that we will present in Section 14.2 enables us to tackle directly the problem of *risk,* which is inherent in any financial market. In particular, we will classify (in principle) the various market instruments—money, bonds, and equities—by their average (expected) returns and by the risk attached to them and show how an investor might choose a portfolio of these items, taking these characteristics into account. Then, because money is one of the items in the portfolio, and we are especially interested in how it can be approached in a portfolio context, we can move on to a formulation of the demand for money that has some satisfying implications for our understanding of why people hold money. In particular, as we will discuss, the *speculative demand* for money of the Keynesians will be considerably enriched by the adoption of this approach (since, after all, "speculation" is risk-taking behavior). We will be interested in this model for its own properties, but we also find that it has applications in bond markets (Chapter 15), equity markets (Chapter 16) and international financial markets (Chapters 17 and 18, especially), so this chapter is fundamental to much of the remainder of this book.

An alternative approach, the inventory model, which we will discuss in Chapter 16, approaches the subject more as if the money-holding unit were a business firm, with an *inventory* of liquid assets (including cash). Generally speaking, each of the assets has some use (for example, having a lot of cash around cuts down on trips to the bank) and, to balance against these benefits, has some costs, such as the interest foregone by holding non-interest-paying cash. The logical thing to do, if you have such an inventory problem, and you are trying to maximize either profits or utility, is to minimize the net costs of holding these inventories; this, as we will see, implies a demand for money inversely related to the interest rate for the money-holding unit that uses the inventory approach. While the analysis applies both to individuals and businesses, the discussion often tends to be worked in terms of the business demand for money; in this sense, as we shall see, the model does provide some insights into the differences between the business and the private demands for money. In addition, the model has some exact predictions about the magnitude of certain influences (especially income) on the demand for money, influences that may well be correct in an empirical sense. But we will defer the discussion of this alternative financial model until Chapter 16, at which point we will see what additional insights it offers.

14.2 THE MEAN-VARIANCE MODEL

We begin by defining the mean (or average value) of a series of n numbers, $X_1, X_2, \ldots X_n$,

$$\text{Mean} = \bar{X} = \frac{X_1 + X_2 + \cdots + X_n}{n} = \sum_{i=1}^{n} \frac{X_i}{n}. \tag{14.1}$$

We are interested in this chapter mostly in the mean (or average) values of a series of returns on securities; thus, consider the data in Table 14.1 for

Table 14.1: Representative yields (percent) for three common stocks

Year	*A* (*Bank*)	*B* (*Oil*)	*C* (*Steel*)
1	21.6	44.6	41.9
2	4.6	8.8	7.8
3	7.1	12.7	16.9
4	5.6	1.5	3.5
5	3.8	30.5	13.3
6	8.9	9.6	73.2
7	9.0	1.6	2.1
8	8.3	12.8	13.1
9	3.5	1.0	6.6
10	17.6	15.4	90.8
Average yield	9.0	13.8	26.9
Standard deviation of yield	5.7	13.2	29.8

three representative equities (*A, B, C*), which, for a ten-year period, we can assume had the average yield of 9.0 percent for Stock *A*, of 13.8 percent for Stock *B*, and 26.9 percent for Stock *C*.[1] The data in Table 14.1 are historical information on the stocks in question, available for all potential assets for which there is a sufficiently active market to generate realistic past data. Indeed, even money (M_1) has a ''yield'' in this sense, although all one can measure accurately is a negative component—the rate of inflation—as things stand (we have used an implicit rate of return in Chapter 1, though, which is close enough to what we intend here).

When one commits his wealth to a particular asset, he naturally has in mind *future* yields, since those are the ones he will obtain; thus Table 14.1, which has an average *past* yield for each of the three securities, might also be used as the basis of a projection to future periods: we might reasonably (but not necessarily accurately) *expect* Stock *A* to yield 9 percent in year 11 (the next period), for example, on the basis of the average of all past yields. From this point of view, Stock *C* looks the best, since it yields 26.9 percent, *other things being equal.* But other things are not equal in Table 14.1; indeed, the yield of Stock *C fluctuates* considerably more than the others in the table. Thus, if one had put his funds into Stock *C* at the beginning of year 10, he would almost have doubled his bet; neither of the other stocks did nearly as well. He may, though, not have done this if he used year 9 as his inspiration, since that year the stock made only 6.6 percent. Note, in that connection, that Stock *C* was beaten in five of the ten years, including two cases in which it was beaten by the relatively low-yielding Stock *A*. This is not an unusual result, although Table 14.1 is a contrived example.

[1] Note that the yield represents the rate of return on equity, where the calculated return is dividends plus capital gains, and the equity value is taken at the beginning of each year (as if it were an investment undertaken at that time).

The problem, in a nutshell, is that stock yields fluctuate differently and that fact is a source of concern to investors; indeed this fluctuation provides, essentially, the *risk* of an investment to the investor (the risk of the failure of the company aside). Suppose, for example, that one had \$100 to invest for three years, starting in year 7; if he had put it in Stock A, he would, with recompounding, have had \$122.18 by the end of year 9.[2] By the end of year 9, Stock B would have returned only \$115.75, while Stock C would have returned \$123.10. Thus a relatively safe stock (A) with a much lower *expected* yield (up to year 7) actually did almost as well as a stock (C) that fluctuates fairly wildly, and did better than another (moderately) fluctuating stock (B).

The additional factor that is needed here, to make a sensible choice, is the *expected* variation in the stock yields. To calculate this we may again argue that a series of historical data is our best guide, and look at the variance of past stock prices. We may define the *variance* of a series of returns as

$$\text{Variance} = \frac{\sum_{i=1}^{n} (X_i - \bar{X})^2}{n} = \text{Var}(X), \tag{14.2}$$

where we are averaging (dividing by n) the squared deviations of actual returns (X_i) from their mean value ($\bar{X}$). This concept may well measure the risk attached to each security, in the sense of capturing the variation one might *expect* to get in the future (on the basis of past information), assuming, again, that the past data are the best available guides to the future. The variances for the three stocks in Table 14.1 are 32.5, 174.2, and 888.0, respectively, and this suggests a basic consideration: more expected earnings ought to be associated with more expected risk, and they are in our example.[3] The reason, quite simply, is that risk is an undesirable quality (usually) and one requires more compensation—more yield—to persuade him to take up riskier securities.

We will work with the variance in what follows, but because the variance is a measure of the average *squared* deviations around the mean, it is actually more useful, especially for visual presentations, to work with the standard deviation (because it is measured in the same units (%) as the yield); these are also provided in Table 14.1 for our three sample stocks. The situation in Table 14.1 is also depicted in Figure 14.1. Here, as already noted, we find that in our example if you wish to earn more, you will also have to incur more risk; indeed, some investors will clearly tend to prefer

---

[2] By recompounding we mean that the original sum *plus dividends* are reinvested each year; that is how we arrive at \$122.18 for Stock A in this example.

[3] Note that we do not correct for degrees of freedom here, arbitrarily. If we had, we would have divided by n-1 instead of n in Equation (14.2), when we produced our sample estimates in Table 13.1.

Figure 14.1: Means and standard deviations for representative securities

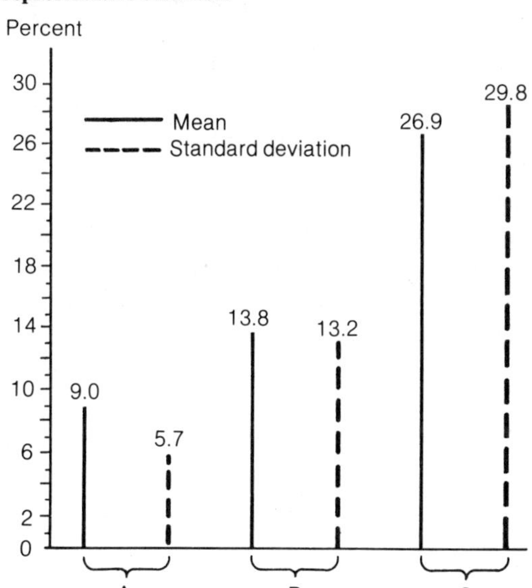

Stock A, with its relatively low risk (low standard deviation), suggesting a relatively *safe* return. But generally, as we shall see, individual investors have more than one security in their portfolios—are diversified, as we say—and, in terms of our example, actually tend to buy some combination of the three securities in order to get into exactly the position they desire in terms of the risk and return *from their entire portfolio*. Let us consider how this more general choice problem might be analyzed in this *uncertain* (i.e., risky) situation.

When events, such as the future yields on common stocks, are essentially uncertain, it is frequently possible to attach probabilities to the likelihood of their coming to pass. A *probability* is a kind of percentage, in effect, and it is a positive number with an upper limit of unity; that is,

$$1 \geq P \geq 0. \tag{14.3}$$

It is obvious that at least subjective probabilities can be assigned to future events, at least in some circumstances. Suppose, for example, one is picking a card from a deck of 52 cards. If it is a "fair" deck, then, you would give 1/52 (equal to a probability of 0.019) as your chance of getting the ace of spades on the first draw. Some events are certain to occur (the sun rises), and to them we would attach probabilities of 1; thus, if we picked all 52 cards, without putting any of them back, we would say that we had a 100 percent chance of getting the ace of spades. If under any circumstances, we list *all* of the outcomes possible, the sum of their probabilities will also be 1; this idea is expressed as

$$\sum_{i=1}^{n} P_i = 1. \tag{14.4}$$

It is here that the analogy with the percentage is the strongest. Statements (14.3) and (14.4) constitute the formal definition of probability, as we will refer to it in this text.

Let us consider an example. Suppose you had the information given in Table 14.2 on the chances of winning various sums of money, let us say in

Table 14.2: A chancy outcome

Situation	*Payoff*	*Probability of winning*	*Expected value*
X_1	\$100	0.25	\$ 25
X_2	200	0.25	50
X_3	300	0.40	120
X_4	400	0.10	40
			\$235

a lottery. We will not worry yet about how you got the information on the probabilities, but in many situations, such as for an honest roulette wheel, there are reasonably well-known chances attached to each possible outcome.[4] We can also construct a picture of the information, which is presented in Table 14.2; thus, in Figure 14.2 there is drawn a curve connecting the points so as to underscore one other point about probability distributions: they can be drawn as if they were continuous.

The sort of opportunity described to this point is not economically realistic in an important sense: there is no potential loss involved. Even so, we can make it into an economic problem by asking how much you would pay for the gamble described here. Your answer would depend on your taste for income, but we could find out something about you if we faced you with a price of \$235 for participating in the lottery; \$235 is the *expected* value of the gamble in Table 14.2. The formula for calculating the expected value in this case is given as Equation (14.5); the hat (^) over the X indicates that it is a random variable or, alternatively, describes an uncertain outcome.

[4] These could also be *subjective* probabilities that you attach to the outcomes based on your knowledge of the situation. Needless to say, when we broaden the framework to the subjective, we must allow that wild guesses (so long as they sum to 1) can also be described by the model we are presenting here.

$$\text{Expected value} = E(\hat{X}) = P_1X_1 + P_2X_2 + P_3X_3 + P_4X_4 = \sum_{i=1}^{4} P_iX_i \tag{14.5}$$

Recall, again, that the P's are probabilities.

Figure 14.2: A probability density function for the data of Table 14.2

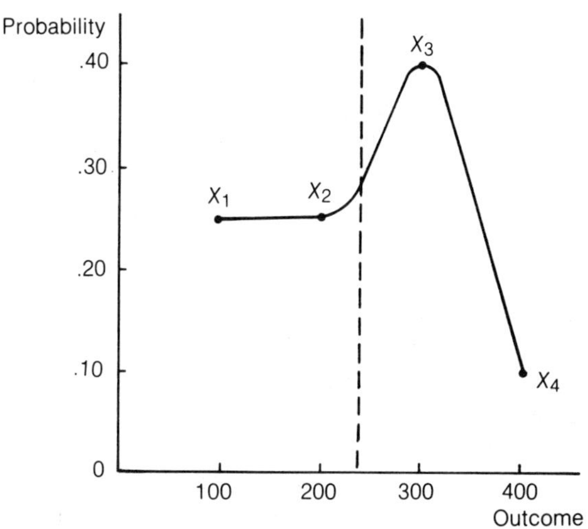

The general idea behind this formulation is quite straightforward: we *weight* the value of each outcome by the chance of getting that outcome. Then, *assuming* everyone judges risky situations solely in terms of the expected value of the outcome, if one attempted to sell the set of payoffs in the table for \$240, practically no one would buy; but if it were sold for \$230, there would be a considerable number of takers as things stand. If, in fact, the wheel were random, in the long run one would tend to pay out \$235 per spin and either go broke or break even; one could not make money as long as everybody judged things in this way and the market for these chances was a broad one.

It is sometimes argued that gambling is economically irrational (except for the fun of it); that is, it is sometimes argued that it is irrational to judge uncertain prospects in any way other than by their expected value. We know that gambling flourishes; even a life insurance policy is a kind of macabre bet with an insurance company—a bet you generally hope to lose in the short run. But even gambling is not an irrational practice, if only because a small chance at a very big pot—a pot big enough to change one's way of life—is very hard to resist. Consider Table 14.3, in which the

Table 14.3: A very chancy outcome

Situation	Payoff	Probability of winning	Expected value
X_1	$ 100	0.7999	$ 79.99
X_2	200	0.0500	10.00
X_3	300	0.1500	45.00
X_4	1,000,000	0.0001	100.00
			$234.99

overall expected value is approximately the same as in Table 14.2. Here we see that we might easily be willing to pay more than $235 for the gamble illustrated in Table 14.3, for the very small chance to become a millionaire is very tempting. In point of fact, people generally will not be indifferent between these two situations, and it certainly depends on what use you could make of the funds if you won them. Furthermore, a good deal of the psychology of the participants in the stock market is wrapped up in this example. But more importantly, gambling, in the sense of taking a speculative position in a risky venture, is here seen as a rational act that is guided by economic principles. In the same sense, the purchase of a stock is a gamble.

In Table 14.1, in which we listed three stocks (A, B, C), we illustrated the *past* behavior of the yields of a potential portfolio of three stocks. A portfolio, generally, is any collection of securities. Thus, with one-third of our funds in each of the stocks of Table 14.1 we would have one portfolio; with one-quarter in each of A and B and one-half in C we would have another. Investors will generally want to compare the characteristics of various *portfolios* rather than the characteristics of the individual stocks, except as to their contribution to the entire portfolio. We will consider two of the characteristics of a portfolio in the rest of this section; they are

a. The expected earnings of the portfolio as a whole.
b. The variance of the portfolio as a whole.

Suppose, for example, that we had $1 in each of the three securities (A, B, C). The expected earnings of this sum of securities is simply the sum of the individual earnings:

$$E(\hat{S}) = E(\hat{X}_1) + E(\hat{X}_2) + E(\hat{X}_3). \tag{14.6}$$

Thus, for $1 in each of the securities, the expected earnings are

$$\$0.090 + \$0.138 + \$0.269 = \$0.497, \tag{14.7}$$

if we use the means of past performance to guide our expectations about future earnings. In this case we *actually* assumed that one-third of our funds went into each stock; we will find it more convenient to use weighted averages (the three one-thirds are weights, summing to unity), and a reformulation of Equation (14.7) gives us Equation (14.8), the expected return of the portfolio that assigns funds equally to the three stocks:

$$\tfrac{1}{3}(0.090) + \tfrac{1}{3}(0.138) + \tfrac{1}{3}(0.269) = 0.166. \qquad (14.8)$$

In an even more general formulation, since the means are really *expected values,* we could write Equation (14.8) as Equation (14.9); here the W_i are weights, as just described.

$$E(S) = W_1E(\hat{X}_1) + \ldots + W_nE(\hat{X}_n) = \sum_{i=1}^{n} W_iE(\hat{X}_i) \qquad (14.9)$$

with

$$\sum_{i=1}^{n} W_i = 1.$$

In Equation (14.9), the $E(\hat{X}_i)$ terms are the expected returns (or, as it stands here, the average values of the past yields of the stocks, where all past yields have an equal probability); the weights in Equation (14.9) are the percentages of funds invested in each of the alternatives. These weights are actually what the investor chooses (we could also work in absolute dollar amounts, but things are somewhat easier to grasp in this way).

Now the second element in the choice problem we have set ourselves is the *risk*. We will assume that the typical investor will tend to dislike additional risk (is not a compulsive gambler). In these circumstances, since earnings imply positive utilities and risk implies disutilities, the typical investor will make his choice on the margin between risk and return; he will, for example, add riskier (and higher yielding) stocks to his portfolio until the extra earnings he gets exactly compensate him for the extra risk he expects to have to take. Clearly, what we are saying is that for each risk-averse individual one ought to be able to construct the ideal portfolio (of the set of stocks being considered).

The problem we must next consider is how to measure risk *for the portfolio as a whole*. Above we suggested that a reasonable measure of the expected risk for a single stock is its expected variance; indeed, we defined a variance in Equation (14.2). For a portfolio of two or more stocks a variance can also be calculated (for example from the past yield data) but a new complication arises because the variance of a sum (of, that is to say, a portfolio) is *not* simply the sum of the variances of the individual components. Indeed, for two stocks (X_1, X_2), the variance of the two together is given by

$$\text{Var}\ (\hat{X}_1 + \hat{X}_2) = \text{Var}\ (\hat{X}_1) + \text{Var}\ (\hat{X}_2) + 2\ \text{Cov}\ (\hat{X}_1\hat{X}_2), \qquad (14.10)$$

where a third element, the *covariance,* also has to be included in the calculation.[5] This covariance is formally equal to $\rho\sigma_{X_1}\sigma_{X_2}$ where ρ is the correlation coefficient and σ_{X_1}, σ_{X_2} are the standard deviations of the two variables X_1 and X_2. The standard deviation, of course, is the square root of the variance (of X_1 and X_2). What is important about this result is that the variance of the portfolio—of the sum of the two stocks, that is to say—consists of the sum of the individual variances *plus* an adjustment for the *correlation* between securities. In particular, since Var $(\hat{X}_1 + \hat{X}_2)$ is a measure of the *risk* of the overall portfolio, it is clear that for *given* X_1 and X_2, two securities with a positive correlation (which, that is to say, move together, like steel and autos) are riskier than two that move in opposite directions. This helps explain why people diversify their portfolios and is not an obvious fact until you have gone through this exercise. Finally, note that Equation (14.10) has a more general form,

$$\begin{aligned}\text{Var}\,(\hat{X}_1 + \hat{X}_2 + \cdots + \hat{X}_n) = {} & \text{Var}\,(\hat{X}_1) + \text{Var}\,(\hat{X}_2) + \cdots \\ & + \text{Var}\,(\hat{X}_n) + 2\,\text{Cov}\,(\widehat{X_1X_2}) + 2\,\text{Cov}\,(\widehat{X_1X_3}) \\ & + \cdots + 2\,\text{Cov}\,(\widehat{X_{n-1}X_n}),\end{aligned} \tag{14.11}$$

and a weighted form, which can also be written out more generally as

$$\text{Var}\,(W_1\hat{X}_1 + W_2\hat{X}_2) = W_1^2\,\text{Var}\,(\hat{X}_1) + W_2^2\,\text{Var}\,(\hat{X}_2) + 2W_1W_2\,\text{Cov}\,(\widehat{X_1X_2}). \tag{14.12}$$

The latter is of interest for our portfolio problem, where the weights are amounts (or percentages) invested in the two (or more) securities. Note that money (when we assign an explicit rate of return for it) could be an item in this general financial portfolio.[6]

To visualize how an individual might structure his actual portfolio choices among financial securities, consider the construction of *efficient*

[5] This formula is proved in the appendix to this chapter although it is, at any rate, a standard result in elementary statistics and is easily verified.

[6] To see how one might use this approach directly, return to the data in Table 14.1. There we had

	Yield	*Variance*
A	.090	.0032
B	.138	.0174
C	.269	.0888

The yield of a portfolio with one-third of the funds in each stock is .166, as we calculated in Equation (14.8); the yield on a portfolio with all of our funds in stock *C* would be .269. When we compare the variance of the two portfolios by use of Equation (14.12), we get .0769 for the first and .0888 for the second. So we get more risk, and considerably more return, for taking the second portfolio. Of course, whether or not one actually takes the second bet depends on his attitude toward risk; the text continues the discussion of this point.

portfolios. The problem with the apparatus we have built to this point is that there seems to be no clear way to get our portfolio into shape except by trial and error; and there are a lot of stocks in the world. However, in principle one can find a much smaller set of possible portfolios, which we will call a set of efficient portfolios, among which the individual investor can choose, after he decides what his personal trade-off is between risk and yield.[7] In fact, we will define an efficient portfolio as one for which any further gain in yield is associated with an increase in risk. To put the matter another way, an efficient portfolio is one for which an investor cannot adjust his holdings (of his currently held stocks) and get more yield without at the same time settling for more risk. If he can add more shares of a stock to his portfolio, and portfolio earnings rise while the portfolio variance stays the same, then he ought to make such an addition, assuming (as we are) that he is risk-averse. Indeed, we generally assume just that.

Let us return to the problem of the selection among three stocks, which we will now designate as Stock 1, Stock 2, and Stock 3, to distinguish them from our earlier specific example. Let us assume that the wealth holder has a fixed amount of money to invest; but to avoid the complexities of dealing in dollars, we will formulate his limits not in dollars but in the percentage of his (given) funds. Of course, what is being suggested here is that the investor has a *budget constraint* and that this budget constraint is in effect a set of weights, where the weights are the percentages of his funds in each of the three stocks. Equation (14.13) is this budget constraint, which, of course, adds to unity.

$$X_1 + X_2 + X_3 = 1. \tag{14.13}$$

We can graph his equation to gain a further perspective; in fact, in Figure 14.3 we use two stocks (X_1 and X_2) explicitly, and Equation (14.13) is represented as a straight-line budget constraint between these two points. Each point in Figure 14.3 gives us the percentage of our funds held in each of the three stocks; at $\tilde{P}_1$ we have 25 percent in Stock 1 and 50 percent in Stock 2; the 25 percent in Stock 3 is measured implicitly. At point $\tilde{P}_2$ we have split our funds equally between Stock 1 and Stock 2, and at $\tilde{P}_3$ we have all our funds in Stock 1.

We have already suggested that the expected return for the portfolio can be measured by

$$E = \text{Expected return} = X_1r_1 + X_2r_2 + X_3r_3. \tag{14.14}$$

[7] Recall that we are not showing exactly how an individual chooses between risk and earnings. That, we have said, is a matter of taste; and, in this text, we simply assume that people know their own minds and choose accordingly. Our purpose is to expose two important economic variables, risk and earnings, that generally enter into portfolio decisions.

Figure 14.3: Portfolio space

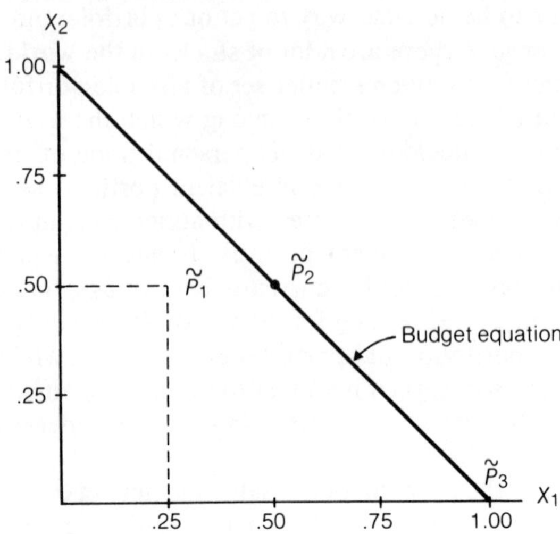

Thus, for $\tilde{P}_1$ of Figure 14.3 and the following arbitrary data on yields:

$$r_1 = 0.10,\ r_2 = 0.05,\ r_3 = 0.07,$$

we have

$$E = \tfrac{1}{4}(0.10) + \tfrac{1}{2}(0.05) + \tfrac{1}{4}(0.07) = 0.068,$$

for example.

Let us keep things as general as possible, and eliminate X_3 (which is "invisible" in the problem anyway) by substituting Equation (14.3) into Equation (14.14); the result is

$$E = X_1(r_1 - r_3) + X_2(r_2 - r_3) + r_3 \tag{14.15}$$

or numerically,

$$E = 0.03X_1 - 0.02X_2 + 0.07.$$

The next step is to draw "equal-earnings" lines, lines along which all portfolios provide the same earnings. First, we should recall that the unknowns in the problem are the percentages spent on each stock; then, if we wish our portfolio to earn 0.07—if we wish E to be equal to 0.07—we would write Equation (14.15) as

$$E = 0.07 = 0.03X_1 - 0.02X_2 + 0.07,$$

which is a straight line in the space of Figure 14.3, through the origin, with

Figure 14.4: Equal-earnings lines

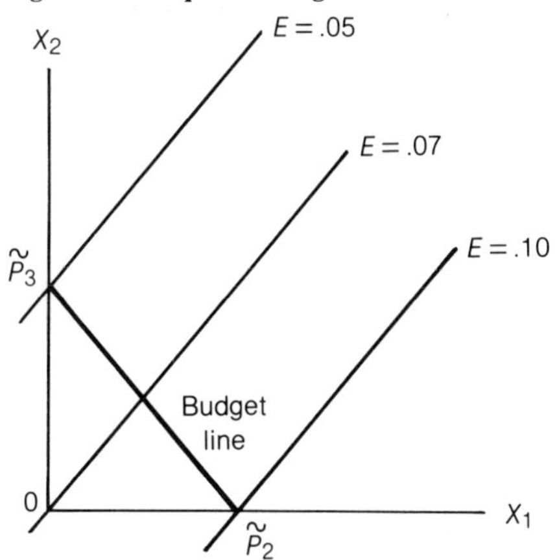

a positive slope of 3/2.[8] This is illustrated as $E = 0.07$ in Figure 14.4, and one of the combinations along which a portfolio of X_1, X_2, and X_3 returns 7 percent is seen to be the origin (O), the point at which all funds are in Stock 3 (and earnings are 0.07 per dollar invested). We see that $E = 0.10$ goes through $\tilde{P}_2$ and that $E = 0.05$ goes through $\tilde{P}_3$; we also see that these lines are parallel (because the slope is always 3/2) and that there are an infinite number of ways we can adjust our investor's portfolio to obtain the required earnings along each line (and there are an infinite number of lines, for that matter).

We are now well on the way to seeing the economic problem in all of this. If we aim at earnings of 0.07 (for example), then the point on the $E = 0.07$ line that represents the lowest variance possible is clearly the optimal point; it is also the "efficient" portfolio for that earnings figure, for the investor has thereby obtained the least variance for his desired earnings. Solving for the minimum variance is no easy matter, of course; and it does, in general, require mathematical skills beyond those required for this book. We will satisfy ourselves with a diagram illustrating the problem, but one that describes the principles involved, at any rate.

The variance-covariance formulas—for example, Equation (14.10)—are ellipses in two dimensions when we solve for equal-variance equations.[9] One way they might appear is shown in Figure 14.5. Since the equal variance curves are smooth ellipses, it is apparent that there are

[8] To see this, simply write the equation as $X_2 = (0.03/0.02)X_1$, which is equivalent to the version in the text. Note that the way we have set things up here, and drawn them in Figures 14.4 and 14.5, is arbitrary and depends on our numerical example (although the general points made do not).

[9] Or, alternately, they are "quadratic forms." An ellipse has the general form of $Ax^2 + By^2 = G$, which is also a quadratic.

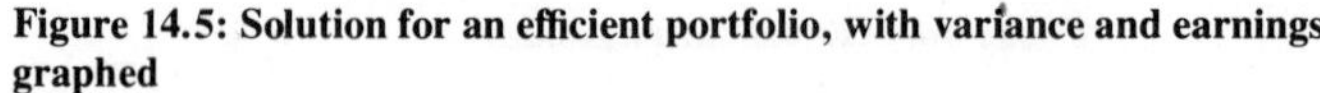

Figure 14.5: Solution for an efficient portfolio, with variance and earnings graphed

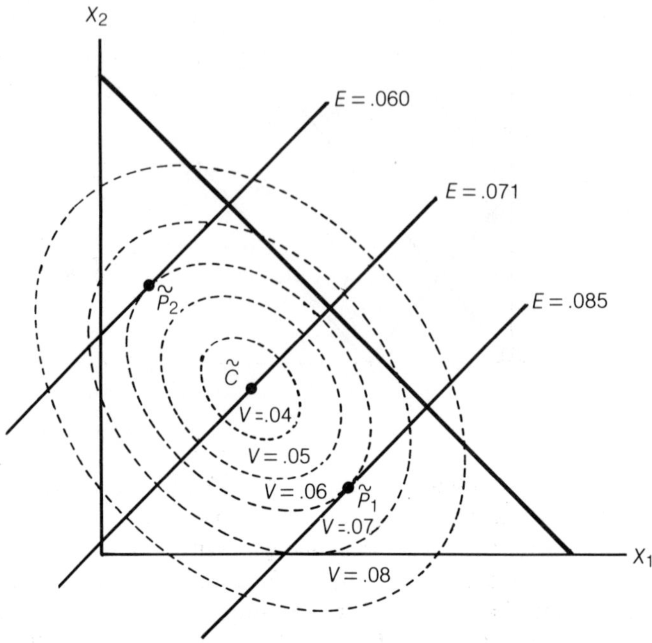

certain interior points that can be eliminated right away. In particular, we can scratch out $\tilde{P}_2$ because it has the same risk as $\tilde{P}_1$—that is, $\tilde{P}_1$ and $\tilde{P}_2$ are on the same equal-variance ellipse—but $\tilde{P}_2$ has lower earnings (.06) than $\tilde{P}_1$ (.085). It is not rational, under our assumptions, to pick $\tilde{P}_2$ when $\tilde{P}_1$ is available. The center ($\tilde{C}$) does not necessarily have zero risk (it might if cash were in the portfolio), but we can see that all earnings lines above $\tilde{C}$ are inferior to some of the lines below $\tilde{C}$ because of the shape of the ellipses (which is essentially arbitrary here). In particular, for each line above $\tilde{C}$ we can find a line below that has the same earnings but lower risk, as things are drawn. We can get all the possible "efficient" (i.e., superior) portfolios by drawing all the conceivable equal-earnings lines below $\tilde{C}$ and moving along those lines until we come to a tangency with an equal-variance line. This point of tangency, as one can readily see, will provide the lowest risk in each case. $\tilde{P}_1$ is one such efficient point, and for each possible equal-earnings line, as drawn, there is one best (least-risk) point; the locus of these points is drawn in Figure 14.6, for our arbitrary example. Thus, as one moves down the efficiency locus, the portfolio gets riskier and earnings get higher; all along that line risk must be traded for yield, and when one is off that line one can always find a point on the line that is better (in the sense of offering more return for no additional risk).

Figure 14.6: Efficiency locus

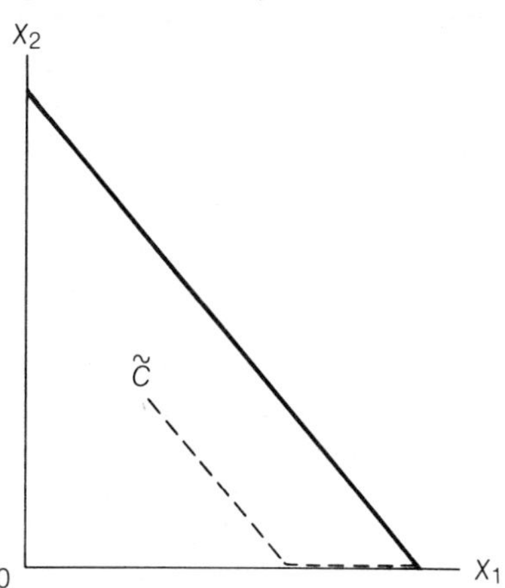

The problem is now reduced to picking a point on the efficiency locus; that depends on the tastes of the investor, that is, on his attitude toward risk compared to earnings, and cannot be solved by an outsider, like the market analyst. If, that is to say, the market analyst is provided with an *exact* desired risk, an *exact* desired earnings, or the trade-off between the two, he can find the best portfolio from among a set group of stocks (for a set amount to be invested), by employing the methods of this section, or the equivalent.[10]

14.3 APPLICATIONS OF MEAN-VARIANCE METHODS TO THE STUDY OF MONEY AND FINANCIAL INSTITUTIONS

The foregoing seems to tackle the problem of portfolio management from the point of view of an individual dealing primarily in securities with explicitly measurable yields. Yet, in fact, it is a perfectly general approach and can be extended to deal with money and other liquid forms of wealth so long as individuals perceive the flow of services from these entities in the form of yields; it can also deal directly with the portfolio behavior of financial institutions, as we shall see. Let us consider several results for the demand for money before turning briefly to the financial institutions.

The first thing to notice is that the portfolio model implies that individual wealth holders may well choose among a fairly broad spectrum of

[10] As the number of stocks goes up, the cost of producing the solution goes up. Thus one would have to balance this cost against the gain of using the information; for institutions, computer solutions might pay off, but individuals would probably not find computer systems sufficiently profitable. Nevertheless, individuals probably think along these lines, so the analysis has considerable intuitive appeal, if nothing else.

assets, comparing their yields and variances and picking the combination that provides the least risk for the earnings desired. We worked in terms of the portfolio as a whole in our earlier discussion, but the general implication of a diversified portfolio for the demand for money is actually something like Equation (14.16), where P now refers to the price level, and we use r for nominal interest rates:

$$M_d = f\left(r_b, r_e, \frac{\Delta P}{P}, Y\right). \tag{14.16}$$

Here we see that when we take money as an item in a portfolio, then the yields on other assets—equities (r_e) and bonds (r_b) in this case—may well also be relevant, along with income and the inflation rate. The variances would matter, of course, but we will ignore this aspect of portfolio choice for a moment and concentrate on the different yields. Now this equation is roughly consistent with what is called the Keynesian approach to the demand for money; thus it is interesting that something very much like this appears in Milton Friedman's famous paper "The Quantity Theory of Money—A Restatement" as a Neoclassical equation for the demand for money.[11] This is not a coincidence; both the Keynesians and the Monetarists seem to have settled on a standard demand for money which is very much like Equation (14.16), or, for that matter, very like the simpler equations used in Chapter 6, 7, and 8.

But Keynes—the originator of the liquidity trap—is actually not part of this general consensus because of his rather special theory of the speculative demand for money. Keynes's version of the demand for money, which we summarized in Chapter 6 and referred to in Chapter 1, was actually once thought to be founded on notions of uncertainty. You will recall that we argued earlier that individuals formed expectations about the course of future interest rates and then took a position (speculated) in bonds or money depending on what they expected to happen to the yield on bonds. Since "speculative" behavior usually implies uncertain returns, it would seem that this is an uncertainty problem, but it is not. In fact, the speculators of the Keynesian theory individually had absolute conviction (had no uncertainty) about what was going to happen to interest rates. The basic idea around which these "speculators" formed their predictions was that of a *normal* level of interest rates. For example, if the market interest rate were above an individual's normal interest rate, he would expect interest rates to fall (bond prices to rise) and thus hold bonds; he would do the converse if the market rate were below his expected normal rate. It is also important to recognize that this normal rate is an individual's view and not that of the market; there is no *market*

[11] Milton Friedman (ed.), *Studies in the Quantity Theory of Money* (Chicago: University of Chicago Press, 1956).

normal rate (of course, there is an average normal rate) because individuals will have different opinions about what is normal. Thus, since individual opinions will differ, at any high interest rate there is always someone still holding money (still believing that the normal interest rate is higher than that); but the higher the rate of interest, the smaller will be the number of individuals expecting (with certainty) a further rise in rates. This argument provides the explanation for the smooth downsloping relation between interest rates and money holding that we argued exists in the demand for money designed by Keynes.

This relation, as noted, is based on *certainty,* since individuals face uncertain events as if they knew perfectly well what was going to happen. But Keynes actually said:

> It is interesting that the stability of the system and its sensitiveness to changes in the quantity of money should be so dependent on the existence of a variety of opinions about what is uncertain. Best of all that we should know the future. But if not, then, if we are to control the activity of the system by changing the quantity of money, it is important that opinions should differ.[12]

Thus, clearly, Keynes actually meant to apply his method to the case of uncertainty; we can agree that this is an important issue, because it is important that the demand for money be defined logically, but it is certainly going one step too far to say that this is *actually* how expectations are formed. It seems more likely that individuals will discover, from sad experience, that their guesses are often incorrect and will become generally cautious as their experiences pile up;[13] when individuals react as if the future they expect has some chance of not coming about, one may well wish to deal with uncertainty pretty much along the lines of this chapter, rather than to rely on the differences-of-opinion rationale of Keynes. Let us undertake such a formulation for the demand for money.

Let us assume that an individual can hold either money or a quantity of a government bond, that the interest rate on the bond is r_b, and that the yield on money is zero ($r_m = 0$).[14] We will assume that the individual holds both money and bonds and that these relative quantities are the ones which we wish to determine, at each level of interest rates. Since money has a zero yield, the individual will expect the return of his portfolio to be r_bB, with B defined as the fraction of funds invested in bonds, as in Equation (14.17); M is the fraction invested in money:

$$r_bB = \text{Expected return} = \bar{X}. \tag{14.17}$$

[12] John Maynard Keynes, *The General Theory of Employment, Interest, and Money* (New York: Harcourt, Brace & World, 1963), p. 172.

[13] That is, at the least, they will surround their guesses about the future with probability distributions.

[14] Note that we are also implicitly assuming that there is some possibility that the individual will need his funds before the bond matures (or there would be no risk).

In our earlier analysis each of our securities had a variance and also a covariance; but because money has a zero rate of return, it is only the variance in the bond yield that matters in our estimation of the risk of the portfolio. That is, the general measure of the risk of the portfolio is

$$\text{Var}\,(r_b + r_m) = B^2\,\text{Var}\,(r_b) + M^2\,\text{Var}\,(r_m) + 2BM\,\text{Cov}\,(r_m, r_b),$$

but since the terms involving money are zero by virtue of our assumption of a zero yield for money, we may write the variance of the portfolio as

$$\text{Var}\,(r_b + r_m) = B^2\,\text{Var}\,(r_b).$$

Then, the standard deviation (σ) of the portfolio is simply the square root of this expression:

$$\sigma(r_b + r_m) = B\sigma(r_b). \tag{14.18}$$

To get the trade-off between risk and return that the factual information in Equations (14.17) and (14.18) implies, let us simply look for the slope (or relationship) between earnings and risk. That is, let us calculate the ratio $\bar{X}/\text{Var}\,(r_m + r_b)$ by dividing Equation (14.17) by Equation (14.18):

$$\frac{\bar{X}}{\text{Var}\,(r_m + r_b)} = \frac{r_b}{\sigma(r_b)}. \tag{14.19}$$

This, clearly, is a straight line in the risk (σ), return ($\bar{X}$) space, with $r_b/\sigma(r_b)$ representing the slope between $\bar{X}$ and Var $(r_m + r_b)$, as visualized in Figure 14.7; a line, there, is such as that denoted by r_{b1}. The individual, then, will pick a point on the line designated by r_{b1}, representing his portfolio (B_1, M_1), which satisfies his optimal tradeoff between risk and return, under the expected conditions.[15] To get from this formulation to the demand for money, all we need to do is to face the individual with a second interest rate. If the individual holds M_1 of money at r_{b1}, at r_{b2}—a higher rate of interest—he will hold more bonds and less money simply because he is getting a higher return without more risk. (This would follow if we postulate no interdependence between the level of bond yields and the standard deviation of bond yields.) That is, r_{b2} would have a steeper slope in the $\bar{X}$, Var $(r_m + r_b)$ space, as Equation (14.19) verifies directly.

This formulation of the Keynesian demand for money as a portfolio problem has several distinct advantages. For one thing, we can get two

[15] You may visualize consumer preferences by an indifference curve sloped as follows:

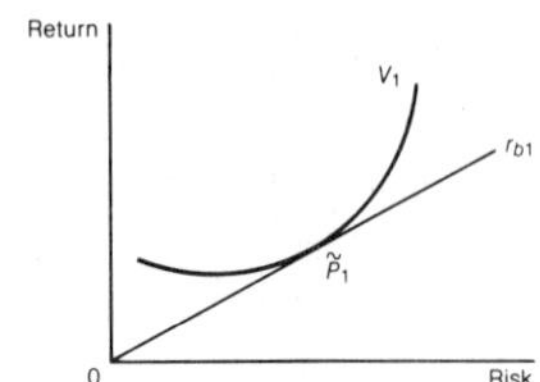

Figure 14.7: The risk-yield trade-off lines for various interest rates

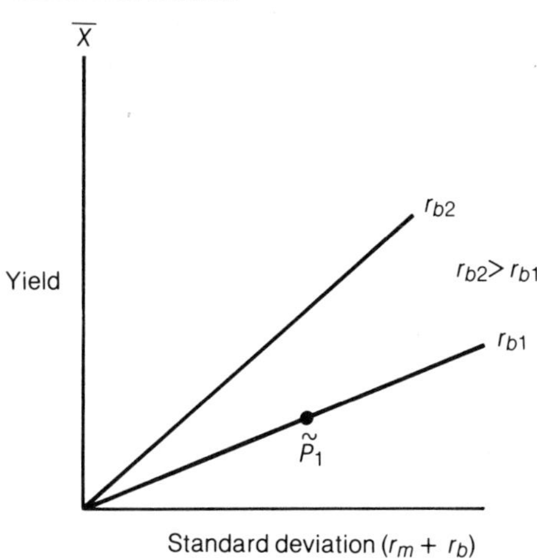

dimensions to the opportunity cost of holding idle cash: alternative earnings and alternative risk (if $\sigma(r_b)$ rises, the lines in Figure 14.7 rotate toward the standard deviation axis). Then, too, we have a negative relation between r_b and the speculative demand for money, given $\sigma(r_b)$, which depends on standard portfolio theory and not on such contrivances as "differences of opinion" or "normal interest rates." As well, uncertainty is formally introduced (in the form of the standard deviation), and this is clearly moving us one step closer to the real world. Finally, the framework employed here generalizes readily, both in the direction of being able to comprehend alternatives other than short-term bonds (such as long-term bonds and equities) and in providing us with an answer if cash actually pays an interest rate and that interest rate is also variable. This last is relevant if only because we are presently observing a strong trend in that direction in the American financial system, at least with regard to the payment of interest on checkable deposits.

For a second application of the portfolio method, consider the portfolio choices of commercial banks. Actually, because they are technically intermediaries, commercial banks have two portfolios to manage: a portfolio of assets and a portfolio of liabilities (as we pointed out in Chapter 2). Furthermore, the decisions of commercial banks on assets and liabilities are interrelated since the base of all of their activities includes both time and demand deposits, and these can fluctuate considerably (and independently) both seasonally and cyclically. Banks, and other intermediaries, we are saying, when they construct their portfolios of assets—that is, when they pick their optimal portfolios—have three types of risk to consider instead of two:

a. The risk they will need to liquidate to meet an unusual cash outflow.
b. The risk attendant with holding assets whose prices fluctuate (e.g., Treasury bills).
c. The risk of default either of the firms whose securities they hold or of the individuals to whom they have lent funds.

As well, of course, they are regulated in various ways, and regulations often change (and so do reserve requirements). In the face of this, it is small wonder that the financial institutions that deal in liquid savings and demand deposits tend to hold fairly liquid assets and tend to be fairly diversified, holding bonds, bills, loans of various sorts, mortgages, cash and, even, undistributed profits. Needless to say, financial institutions will prefer under these conditions to drive their customers into time deposits, since time deposit accounts turn over much more slowly and are therefore less risky, thereby enabling banks to switch their assets into higher yielding (and necessarily riskier) loans or investments. Of course time deposits also have lower reserve requirements. Indeed, as automated transfer between checking and savings accounts has spread since late 1978, we have not observed any real reluctance by banks to adopt the new system.

The point just made, that a reduction of risk on the liability side of a financial institution's balance sheet might actually lead to the assumption of riskier assets without increasing the overall risk taken up by the institution has an immediate application to commercial banks. In particular, we have recorded in Chapter 2 the popular argument that if commercial banks undertake to pay interest on demand deposits they will tend to undertake riskier loans and will be more likely to fail in this event; one important argument behind the Banking Act of 1933 is just this argument. What we are saying now is that *if* commercial banks start to pay interest on demand deposit and *if* this induces an increase in their demand deposit accounts relative to their time deposit accounts, then, assuming that their overall risk increases and that they are risk-averse so that the portfolio model applies literally, they may well undertake *less* risky rather than more risky investments in order to decrease total risk (*given* earnings).[16] This is the opposite of what many feel to be the fact, and it is inconsistent with our present policy stance, but it is, nevertheless, a logical deduction using the methods of this chapter.

The only important financial institution in our descriptive collection in Chapter 13 that does not fit neatly into the picture just painted is the life insurance company. Life insurance companies, as we have noted, are not typical intermediaries for they sell "savings" along with simple insur-

[16] Net earnings would hardly rise in this case, so this is a sensible statement; indeed, only if earnings rise (and it is hard to see how this change could cause that) would it be sensible to increase risk (if one adopts the portfolio model).

ance; as well, they are important in the mortgage market, especially for large mortgages. These companies intermediate in two senses: in the sense of spreading risk for savers and in the sense of absorbing some of the financial risk of mortality. These are two different matters, particularly since insurance per se is clearly a product in its own right (the product, if you will, is "protection"). As the manufacturers of a product, insurance companies need not pay the same heed to variations in their cash flows: the pure insurance in force is not a conventional liability, since one can only cancel *pure* insurance, one cannot "withdraw" it. But life insurance companies are also the holders of savings, which generally can be withdrawn (with penalty), or borrowed upon; in this case these companies are in somewhat the same position as the other intermediaries. In any event, of course, both sorts of activity by insurance companies involve the acquisition of a portfolio of securities as their funds (however acquired) are invested.

It is in the nature of the business of insurance companies that very long-term commitments can be undertaken. Insofar as they intermediate (in this case, borrow short and lend long), they are not unlike other intermediaries in function, although they can count on getting more long-term savings (in the sense of individuals' preferred holding periods for their funds) then can savings and loan associations. Also, insofar as insurance policies are a long-term commitment and big companies are able to predict fairly closely their future cash needs (since mortality tables are fairly stable), one might expect insurance companies to prefer long-term to short-term investments. Indeed, such seems to be the case. But there is another aspect of future risk, whether it is judged by an insurance company or by an individual, and that is that investors generally are more certain about the near future and quite hazy about the distant future and probably require a risk premium—some extra return—to compensate them for going long. That is, the risk of an adverse fluctuation in bond prices—assuming there is some possible need for the funds in the intervening period—is greater, the longer the bond has to go until it can be cashed in (to maturity). Insurance companies, possibly, are peculiar in this instance, though, since they may well be willing to go as long as the market can go. Indeed, the securities market does not manufacture a security with a maturity date far enough in the future for insurance companies, quite possibly, and so, consequently, they go into very long-term mortgage commitments. We will consider the implications of this in Chapter 15, after we have presented an analysis of the term structure of interest rates, which is the necessary theory to understand these considerations fully, but for now it should be clear that insurance companies, too, will have a portfolio of risky assets and, it should be clear, their portfolio will (and does) differ from that of commercial banks in having a higher percentage of long-term securities in it.

14.4 APPENDIX

To see more clearly how we obtained Equation (14.10), let us return to the formula for the variance, which we defined in Equation (14.2); that expression was for the variance of a single security. Suppose, though, we have two securities, X_1 and X_2, so that our variances are

$$V_1 = \frac{\sum_{i=1}^{n} (X_{1i} - \bar{X}_1)^2}{n} = \text{Var}(\hat{X}_1)$$

$$V_2 = \frac{\sum_{i=1}^{n} (X_{2i} - \bar{X}_2)^2}{n} = \text{Var}(\hat{X}_2).$$

Before we calculate the variance of the two securities taken together—that is, Var (S) = Var $(X_1 + X_2)$—let us pause to consider a notational device. We have called the *mean* of the series of returns an *expected* value (by analogy with our discussion of probability); it is the *average* of the series where every item in the series is expected to have an equal weight (= 1/10 in our example in Table 14.1) in the final average. Writing out one of the expressions in Equation (14.10) as (we drop the "hats" for the moment)

$$V_1 = \frac{\sum_{i=1}^{n} [X_{1i} - E(X_1)]^2}{n},$$

we can see that the process of measuring the variance is also clearly an averaging, where each squared item is again given equal weight. Thus we may write this expression as

$$V_1 = E[X_{1i} - E(X_1)]^2 = E(X_{1i} - \bar{X})^2,$$

where the inner expectation represents the calculation of the mean, and the outer, that of the variance.

Returning to our problem with the two securities, we had to calculate the value of Var $(\hat{X}_1 + \hat{X}_2)$ for the portfolio of two stocks. This would be written as

$$\text{Var}(\hat{X}_1 + \hat{X}_2) = E[(X_{1i} + X_{2i}) - (\bar{X}_1 + \bar{X}_2)]^2.$$

The next step involves squaring out the terms in the square brackets; this yields

$$E[(X_{1i} + X_{2i})^2 + (\bar{X}_1 + \bar{X}_2)^2 - 2(X_{1i} + X_{2i})(\bar{X}_1 + \bar{X}_2)].$$

Squaring and reorganizing, we have

$$\text{Var}(\hat{X}_1 + \hat{X}_2) = E(X_{1i} - \bar{X}_1)^2 + E(X_{2i} - \bar{X}_2)^2 - 2E(X_{1i}X_{2i} - X_{2i}\bar{X}_1 - X_{1i}\bar{X}_2 - \bar{X}_1\bar{X}_2). \quad (14A.1)$$

This, recalling Equation (19.10), is

$$\mathrm{Var}\ (\hat{X}_1 + \hat{X}_2) = \mathrm{Var}\ (\hat{X}_1) + \mathrm{Var}\ (\hat{X}_2) + 2\ \mathrm{Cov}\ (\hat{X}_1\hat{X}_2)$$

The expectation on the right of Equation (14A.1) is the *covariance* (which is equal to $\rho\sigma_{X_1}\sigma_{X_2}$, where ρ is the correlation between X_1 and X_2, and σ_{X_1} and σ_{X_2} are the standard deviations of the two securities).

14.5 STUDY QUESTIONS

Essay questions

1. The methods of this chapter treat upward fluctuations in stock prices in exactly the same way as they treat downward fluctuations. Is this in accordance with market practice? Why might a case be made for an asymmetrical approach? Do margin dealings in stocks enter into the discussion?

2. We did not emphasize in this chapter that one of the considerations an individual will bear in mind when he thinks about his portfolio of stocks is his expected uses of the funds in the future. Discuss some of the ways this might change our conclusions about portfolio behavior. How might this consideration make it more obviously "rational" to be a gambler?

3. Why did we emphasize that individuals must actually form opinions about risk before anyone can solve a portfolio problem? In what specific ways might this be done? You probably have a lifetime plan (which might be a bit fuzzy at the edges); what is your implicit trade-off pattern like? Is age likely to affect an investor's risk-return tradeoff? (Be specific.)

4. How might a common stock with a low interest yield be equivalent to one with a high interest yield? Why is it difficult to judge a company's prospects from the interest rate alone? How does the market influence the yield of a common stock?

5. It is sometimes argued that wealth holders (or money holders) are simply unable to estimate the probabilities needed to implement a mean-variance model—that they act as if they have "no idea" what is going to happen. Can you conceive how one might construct demand-for-money models under these conditions? See Paul Davidson, *Money and the Real World,* 2d ed. (London: Macmillan, 1977).

True-false discussion questions

These statements are meant to be somewhat ambiguous and to provoke discussion, thereby.

1. If a stock has both a higher yield and a lower variance than those already in one's portfolio, it should be added to the portfolio.

2. If two securities have the same expected yield and variance, then for all practical purposes it doesn't matter which one is held in one's portfolio.

3. We cannot assign probabilities to future events because such an assignment implies we know the chance that something will come to pass.

4. We cannot analyze two different types of money (e.g., currency and demand deposits) by a portfolio model since, for all practical purposes, both have the same yield.

5. If the variance of a particular stock goes up, then the mean-variance model would assert that a sensible investor would buy less of it.

6. The expected variance of a stock would not necessarily be used as a measure of the risk of the stock if the stock were expected to have a higher yield over the period in question.

7. The reason that many investors hold bonds, common stocks, and money simultaneously is that when they do, they get the benefit of different rates of return.

14.6 FURTHER READING

Markowitz, Harry. *Portfolio Selection.* New York: John Wiley & Sons, Inc., 1959, pp. 1–153.

Tobin, James. "The Theory of Portfolio Selection." In Hahn, Frank, and Frank Brechling, eds., *The Theory of Interest Rates.* London: Macmillan, 1965.

15

The bond markets

15.1 INTRODUCTION

Almost from the beginning of this book we have kept bonds somewhere in the background and never brought them directly into the picture. Even as early as Chapter 1, we talked about the interest rate as an opportunity cost for holding money (especially M_1), but we did not go further than the interest-bearing liabilities of the financial intermediaries in characterizing these alternatives; to this list, then, we must now add corporate and government bonds (and bills). Later, when we discussed commercial banks and the Federal Reserve, we noted the presence of treasury obligations (bills and bonds) among their assets, but we provided no explicit analysis of their portfolio decisions (although the portfolio analysis of Chapter 14 certainly applies directly). Finally, in our theoretical discussions of the demand for money, a bond was, in general, implicitly part of the problem; this was especially true in the case of the Keynesian "speculative demand for money," since this theory motivated money holding in terms of the wealth holder's expectations about the future direction of bond prices (or interest rates). Now, though, it is time to confront directly both the data and the analysis of the bond markets in order to generalize still further our analysis of the financial markets.

In the first section of this chapter we will look at the broad data for corporate and government bonds. Further, while we will measure and comment on the stock of bonds and its components, we will consider it to be the main task of this section to dig into the *supply* of bonds; we will be especially interested, here, in the supply of government bonds, since that is intimately bound up with the supply of money in the American banking system, as we have already pointed out, especially in Chapters 4, 5, 10, and 12. In Section 15.3 we turn to questions of the demand for bonds; here we will consider the major holders of corporate and government bonds, at least up to the point where the data let us down. Finally in the last section in the chapter, we consider another important difference in bonds that we have quite simply ignored to this point; they differ in term-to-maturity (i.e., in redemption date). Here we will look at the relation between long- and short-term interest rates (or long- and short-term bond prices). It will turn out that important policy questions arise; for example, we will discuss the possibility of using the now revived "operation twist" of the early 1960s. This involved having separate policies for short-term rates (high) and for long-term rates (low). In addition, some clarity can be given to certain theoretical issues raised but not resolved at earlier points in the book. These are, primarily, the concept of *liquidity* and an interesting difference between Keynes and the later Keynesians on the question of which interest rates belong in the demand for money (and, presumably, in the standard macroeconomic model).

15.2 THE STOCK OF BONDS: A DESCRIPTION

Let us, first, look at the *new* securities issues of state and local governments and corporations in recent years; we also include a breakdown on corporations' issues of stocks and bonds, on a broad industry-by-industry basis. In Table 15.1 we note a steady growth of new bond issues by state and local authorities, such that the total of new loans is up from $11.3 billion in 1965 to $48.6 billion in 1978, a 25.4 percent increase on an average annual basis—this is faster than the increases in the monetary totals (M_1–M_5) noted in other chapters. Furthermore and of some interest to our policy discussion of Chapter 13, the imprint of credit crunches and recessions is also apparent in these figures. Thus, in the 1966 credit crunch there seem to have been pretty generalized negative effects on corporate and local security issues, although manufacturing corporations, at least, showed no signs of having trouble obtaining borrowed funds. Indeed, the recession year of 1970 actually was a good year for bond finance. This result is actually not a surprising one, and neither is the fact that the previous year was a dismal one; it is not surprising because *a.* Interest rates would have been relatively favorable for borrowers in 1970.

b. Corporate borrowing will tend to decline when a recession is *expected,* as it may well have been in 1969 (look back to the index of leading economic indicators in Figure 12.7, which showed a marked decline by the end of the first quarter of 1969).

Indeed, one response to these data might be to point out the obvious: a slowdown in corporate investment activity will produce a decline in the demand for funds (i.e., stock and bond issues) and, by means of the investment multiplier, a decline in the economy. From this point of view, 1978 would have been expected to be a reasonably good year for the economy (and it clearly was), while the slowdown in new issues in the corporate sector in 1978 suggested trouble (in terms of actual investment expenditures) in 1979.

But probably the figures of most interest in the discussion of the supply of bonds—and certainly the most controversal—are those for the federal government; Table 15.2 contains a summary. There we find, as is the usual pattern, a steadily growing national debt, but one that is only up 145.9 percent over the 13 years reported in the table. Nevertheless, the federal government is a big supplier of debt, and it attracts a lot of attention since many believe in a balanced budget (which is clearly not achieved) and fear the growth of big government. To get another perspective on the growth of the national debt, consider some figures recently published in the *Economic Review* of the Federal Reserve Bank of Kansas City; they are collected in Table 15.3.

Table 15.3 contains information on several important points on the supply of bonds by the Treasury; these concern the growth and changing composition of the national debt. In particular, the first thing one notices is that the debt has grown rapidly, particularly in recent years, reaching a rate of growth of 10 percent per year in the 1966–76 decade; this is pretty evenly spread over nonmarketable and marketable issues. But, even so, this growth has not been excessively rapid by two standards: one is in comparison to state and local debt (which grew at an annual average rate of 19.6 percent in the same period) and the other is in relation to GNP, where the ratio of debt has fallen steadily (but, of course, this is *nominal* and not real GNP—it is rising faster than real GNP). It is pretty clear, since the total share of the federal government in GNP has been steady at just a little over 22 percent, that taxation has picked up the slack here. We can also see in the table that in the last ten years the relative interest burden of the debt has increased somewhat (at 1.2 percent per year on average); this has occurred, obviously, on account of the inflation-induced increase in interest rates and has not been stopped by the gradual shift toward tax finance

Table 15.1: Bond and stock issues (gross proceeds), 1965–1978 ($ billions)

	1965	*1966*	*1967*	*1968*	*1969*	*1970*	*1971*	*1972*	*1973*	*1974*	*1975*	*1976*	*1977*	*1978*
State and local (all issues)	11.3	11.4	14.8	16.6	11.9	18.2	25.0	23.7	24.0	24.3	30.6	35.3	46.8	48.6
Corporate (all issues)	16.0	18.1	24.8	22.0	26.7	38.9	45.1	40.8	33.4	37.8	53.6	53.5	54.2	45.3
Bonds	13.7	15.6	22.0	17.4	18.3	30.3	32.1	27.7	22.3	31.6	42.8	42.4	42.2	35.2
Stocks	2.3	2.5	2.8	4.6	8.4	8.6	13.0	13.1	11.1	6.2	10.9	11.1	12.0	10.1
Bond issues														
Manufacturing	4.7	5.9	9.9	5.7	4.4	9.2	9.4	4.8	4.3	9.9	17.0	13.3	12.5	8.8
Commercial and miscellaneous	1.2	1.2	2.0	1.8	1.9	2.0	2.3	2.7	1.3	1.8	2.8	4.4	5.9	4.7
Transportation	1.0	1.8	1.8	1.7	1.9	2.2	2.0	1.8	1.9	1.0	3.4	4.4	2.0	2.0
Public utility	2.3	3.1	4.2	4.4	5.4	8.0	7.6	6.4	5.6	8.9	9.6	8.3	8.3	7.1
Communication	.8	1.8	1.8	1.7	2.0	5.0	4.2	3.7	3.5	3.7	3.5	2.8	3.0	3.3
Real estate and financial	3.8	1.7	2.2	2.2	2.7	3.9	6.6	8.4	5.7	6.2	6.5	9.3	10.4	9.3
Stock issues														
Manufacturing	.7	1.2	1.2	1.3	1.9	1.3	2.2	1.8	.6	.5	1.7	2.2	1.3	1.2
Commercial and miscellaneous	.2	.2	.1	.1	3.0	2.5	2.4	2.9	1.6	1.0	1.5	1.2	1.8	1.8
Transportation	.1	.1	.5	1.6	.2	.0	.4	.2	.0	.0	.0	.0	.4	.3
Public utility	.6	.5	.7	.9	1.3	3.0	4.2	5.0	4.7	4.0	6.2	6.1	6.0	5.0
Communication	.8	1.8	1.8	1.7	2.0	5.0	4.2	1.1	1.4	.2	1.0	.8	1.4	.2
Real estate and financial	3.8	1.7	2.2	2.2	2.7	3.9	6.6	2.1	2.9	.6	.5	.8	1.0	1.6

Source: *Federal Reserve Bulletin*.

Table 15.2: The national debt (U. S. Treasury; $ billions)

	1965	*1966*	*1967*	*1968*	*1969*	*1970*	*1971*	*1972*	*1973*	*1974*	*1975*	*1976*	*1977*	*1978*
Total gross public debt*	320.9	329.3	344.7	358.0	368.2	389.2	424.1	449.3	469.1	492.7	576.6	653.5	718.9	789.2
Marketable	214.6	218.0	226.5	236.8	235.9	247.7	262.0	269.5	270.2	282.9	363.2	421.3	459.9	487.5
Bills	60.2	64.7	69.9	75.0	80.6	87.9	97.5	103.9	107.8	119.7	157.5	164.0	161.1	161.7
Notes	50.2	48.3	61.4	76.5	85.4	101.2	114.0	121.5	124.6	129.8	167.1	216.7	251.8	265.8
Bonds	104.2	99.2	95.2	85.3	69.9	58.6	50.6	44.1	37.8	33.4	38.6	40.6	47.0	60.0
Nonmarketable†	99.2	104.3	112.0	115.7	127.0	136.3	157.4	174.6	197.6	208.7	212.5	231.2	255.3	294.8
Savings bonds and notes	50.3	50.8	51.7	52.3	52.2	52.5	54.9	58.1	60.8	63.8	67.9	72.3	77.0	80.9
Government account series‡	46.3	52.0	57.2	59.1	71.0	78.1	85.7	95.9	108.0	119.1	119.4	129.7	139.8	157.5
Other (mostly foreign issues)§	—	—	3.1	4.3	3.8	5.7	16.8	20.6	28.8	25.8	25.2	29.2	38.5	56.4

* The total does not equal the sum of the parts because of small amounts of convertible bonds and non-interest-bearing debt.
† Before 1973 this is nonmarketable plus special issues.
‡ Held almost entirely by U.S. government agencies and trust funds; before 1973 this is "Special Issues" and included the holdings of Federal Home Loan Banks.
§ Before 1973 this is entirely foreign issues (26.0 in 1973).
Source: *Federal Reserve Bulletin*.

Table 15.3: The size and composition of the federal debt, 1956–1976

	1956	*1966*	*1976*	*Average annual change* *1956–66*	*1966–76*
Size					
Total interest-bearing debt (A)	$274.2*	$325.0*	$652.5*	1.9%	10.1%
Nonmarketable issues	113.8	107.0	231.2	−0.6	11.6
Marketable issues (B)	160.4	218.0	421.3	3.6	9.3
Interest outlays in U.S. budget (C)	6.3	11.3	34.6	7.9	20.6
Percentages					
A of GNP	65.2%	43.2%	38.2%	−3.4	−1.2
B of GNP	31.0	21.1	18.0	−3.2	−1.5
C of total budget outlays	8.9	8.4	9.4	−0.6	1.2
Composition (term to maturity)				*Change*	
Under 1 year	34.9%	42.1%	51.2%	7.2%	9.1%
1–5 years	30.6	30.3	33.7	−0.3	3.4
5–10 years	12.7	15.4	10.1	2.7	−5.3
Over 10 years	21.8	12.2	5.1	−9.6	−7.1

* Billions.
Source: V. Vance Roley, "Federal Debt Management Policy," *Economic Review, Federal Reserve Bank of Kansas City* (February 1978).

or by the rapid shortening of the average maturity of the debt. The latter—visible as a 7.1 percent *per year* fall in long-term debt (debt maturing in over ten years) and a 5.3 percent *per year* fall in debt of 5–10 years to maturity—helps reduce the interest burden in that long-term securities tend to require higher interest rates than do short-term securities.[1] Note, in Table 15.2, that the bonds issued by the Treasury have fallen, since 1965, from $104.2 billion to $60 billion; this implies that the long-term bond market (at least from this source) is becoming increasingly "thin," although an upsurge is noticeable in 1978 (continuing into 1979). One can readily surmise that the only important reason for this reduction in the average maturity of the debt is the interest saving to the Treasury. But we will return to questions of the term structure of interest rates in Section 15.4.

The last major issuer of debt in the economy is the institution that is either a federal agency (such as the Defense Department) or a federally-sponsored but privately owned agency (such as the Federal Home Loan Banks discussed in Chapter 13). These have provided a range of securities (primarily in the maturity range of one to ten years) that have increased

[1] This is the result, quite possibly, of the risk associated with waiting for one's funds.

from \$22.7 billion at the end of 1966 to \$50.7 billion at the end of 1971 and to \$152.6 billion by July 1979. This is, of course, a faster rate of growth than that experienced by the federal government (but not state governments) and reflects, primarily, the intrusion of the government into agricultural and mortgage lending markets (most of the \$152.6 billion is federally *sponsored* agencies). We are not planning to isolate the issues that arise on account of the rapid growth of these institutions (since they are roughly the same as those already mentioned for other arms of the government) but we should note, just for the record, that (*a*) the rate of growth seems to be slowing a little in the late 1970s (to 1977) and (*b*) the principal holders (in 1977) are the government itself (including the Federal Reserve) and commercial banks. Indeed, almost 30 percent is part of the liquid "backing" of the money supply (M_2) and this makes sense, since the agency securities are as safe as treasury issues, for all practical purposes.[2]

15.3 THE DEMAND FOR BONDS

The foregoing is essentially descriptive; it is now time to return to the theoretical and policy issues (although the institutional detail will certainly continue to flow). The most obvious thing we can say, thinking back to our discussion of Chapter 14 on the mean-variance framework, is that the bonds supplied by the major institutions—the corporations, the state and local governments, and the federal government—will be fitted into private portfolios (whether domestic or foreign) by the rules laid out there—that is, by their relative contributions to the risk and return of the investor's portfolio.[3] In this respect, bonds are a pretty safe asset in the sense of default risk (i.e., failure of the institution to meet an interest payment), with the federal government having virtually no chance of default, state and local governments having a somewhat greater chance of default,[4] and

[2] Mutual savings banks and savings and loan associations also hold substantial agency issues. For a further discussion of this market see "The Market for Agency Securities," *Quarterly Review, Federal Reserve Bank of New York* (Spring 1978).

[3] In recent years the variability of interest rates has increased considerably and, thus, so have average yields (as predicted in Chapter 14). The two sources of this change appear to be the general monetary disturbances of the 1965–78 period *and* monetary policy. The latter has affected the federal funds rate (the target rate of the Federal Reserve) initially—its variability has increased—and has spilled over into rates in general. See V. Vance Roley, "Interest Rate Variability, the Level of Interest Rates, and Monetary Policy, *Economic Review, Federal Reserve Bank of Kansas City* (October 1978).

[4] State and local governments have, of course, defaulted in the past (e.g., in the early 1840s) and, no doubt, they will in the future. Indeed, the rapid growth of state and local debt in recent years has not gone unnoticed by the taxpayers (who must fork out the funds for interest rate payments and are showing signs of revolt). To the extent that taxpayers pull the rug out from under local authorities—by simply lopping off their tax revenues—their bond issues (outstanding) will be perceived as increasingly risky, one suspects. The situation in New York City in the late 1970s (and in Cleveland in 1978–79) is, no doubt, part of this emerging pattern.

corporations having the most (although bonds normally have a prior claim on the company's assets and bond holders often escape with something even when a firm is wiped out). But governments and their agencies also hold a substantial portion of the stock of bonds and it is highly unlikely that the "optimal investment" strategy described in Chapter 14 will apply to them, since it is based on the assumption of rational microeconomic behavior. Thus, we will have to consider their reasons for constructing their portfolios in the way that they do in a separate analysis.

The data on bond holding are obviously not going to be totally revealing because it is very hard to track down the private (especially the foreign) holdings of corporate issues in any detail; nevertheless the picture and the trends are pretty clear, as the following tables demonstrate. First of all, let us look at some very recent summary data for "private domestic nonfinancial investors," in Table 15.4. These figures suggest, quite simply, that

Table 15.4: Direct lending in credit markets by private domestic nonfinancial investors ($ billions)

	1974	*1975*	*1976*	*1977*	*1978*
U.S. government securities	18.2	22.2	19.4	23.8	33.1
State and local obligations	10.0	6.3	4.7	5.6	8.8
Corporate and foreign bonds	4.7	8.2	4.0	.2	−.9
Commercial paper	4.8	3.1	4.0	16.6	27.8
Other	8.2	5.5	11.8	16.6	18.8
Total	45.9	45.3	43.8	62.9	87.7

Source: *Federal Reserve Bulletin.*

individuals and other nonfinancial investors (mainly corporations themselves) do take up a considerable portion of the U.S. debt, but these sectors are not big lenders to state and local governments or to the corporate sector. The large total for commercial paper represents primarily corporate activity. Note the sudden increase in U.S. government securities held by nonfinancial investors in 1978; this is evidence of the runoff problem (the funds were probably going mostly into Treasury bills): we saw, in Chapter 13, that funds were starting to drain out of the financial intermediaries as the treasury bill rose in 1978.

Table 15.4 provides a meager harvest, but when we come to consider the national debt, the issues involving our big central government emerge again. Let us, first, look at some broad measures of the activities of the suppliers of funds to the federal government, as provided in Table 15.5. Every one of these suppliers of funds (demanders of bonds) has taken an increasing quantity over the years, *but not at the same rate.* At the top of the percentage increase column (at the far right of the table) is the foreign

Table 15.5: Gross American national debt by owner ($ billions)

	1965	*1966*	*1967*	*1968*	*1969*	*1970*	*1971*	*1972*	*1973*	*1974*	*1975*	*1976*	*1977*	*1978*	*Percent change 1965–78*
U.S. government agencies and trust funds	59.7	65.9	73.1	76.6	89.0	97.1	106.0	116.9	123.4	138.2	145.3	149.6	154.8	170.0	184.8
Federal Reserve banks	40.8	44.3	49.1	52.9	57.2	62.1	70.2	69.9	75.0	80.5	84.7	94.4	102.5	109.6	168.6
Private investors	220.5	219.2	222.4	228.5	222.0	229.9	247.9	262.5	260.9	271.0	349.4	409.5	461.3	508.6	130.6
Commercial banks	60.7	57.4	63.8	66.0	56.8	62.7	65.3	67.7	60.3	55.6	85.1	103.8	102.4	93.4	53.9
Mutual savings banks	5.3	4.6	4.2	3.8	3.1	3.1	3.1	3.4	2.9	2.5	4.5	5.7	6.0	5.2	−1.8
Insurance companies	10.3	9.5	9.0	8.4	7.6	7.4	7.0	6.6	6.4	6.2	9.5	12.5	15.6	15.0	45.6
Other corporations	15.8	14.9	12.2	14.2	10.4	7.3	11.4	9.8	10.9	11.0	20.2	26.5	22.2	20.6	30.4
State and local governments	22.9	24.3	24.1	24.9	27.2	27.8	25.4	28.9	29.2	29.2	34.2	41.6	55.1	68.6	199.6
Individuals															
Savings bonds	49.7	50.3	51.2	51.9	51.8	52.1	54.4	57.7	60.3	63.4	67.3	72.0	76.7	80.7	62.4
Other securities	22.4	24.3	22.3	23.3	29.0	29.1	18.8	16.2	16.9	21.5	24.0	28.8	28.6	30.0	33.9
Foreign and international	16.7	14.5	15.8	14.3	11.2	20.6	46.9	55.3	54.7	58.8	66.5	78.1	109.6	137.8	725.1
Other (includes S&Ls)	16.7	19.4	19.9	21.9	25.0	19.9	15.6	17.0	19.3	22.8	38.0	40.5	45.0	57.4	243.7
Total gross debt	320.9	329.3	344.7	358.0	368.2	389.2	424.1	449.3	469.1	492.7	576.6	653.5	718.9	789.2	145.9

Source: *Federal Reserve Bulletin*.

and international holder, whose holdings are up an astonishing 725.1 percent in the 13 years covered, much of it in the last two years. This reflects, as we will discuss in Chapters 17 and 18, the breakdown of the IMF system and the substitution of an "IMF-convertible currency system" in which the dollar is the chief convertible currency. That is, the United States is the chief provider—by means of its large balance of payments deficit—of liquid funds for foreign reserve accounts, both official and unofficial. It is thus "convenient" for this large pool of reserves that the Treasury also runs a big deficit in its budgetary operations and finances it with the same short-term securities that foreign *official* holders seem to prefer, *at least for the present.* See Chapters 17 and 18 for a continuation of this discussion.

U.S. government agencies and trust funds have taken more than their share of the debt (up 184.8 percent) and so too have state and local governments (up 199.6 percent). For both, these securities provide steady incomes of a nontax variety; for the latter they are also a substantial reserve against any threats against their tax base. The private sectors other than the miscellaneous category (probably, in this group, the corporate pensions and the government-sponsored agencies are the largest) have all taken up the national debt at a lower than average pace, thrusting the burden of absorbing the growing debt on the above-mentioned governmental units *and the Federal Reserve.* The latter has increased its holdings by 168.6 percent in the 13 years. This is a policy issue because, as we saw in Chapter 5, this is the principal item behind the monetary base (or the stock of high-powered money).

Let us be clear about what is involved here: to the extent that the Treasury is unable to find private or other government buyers of the debt at satisfactory interest rates, it must either change the interest rate (thus increasing the burden of the debt) or persuade the Federal Reserve to take up the residual. Since the Treasury spends the proceeds in any event, commercial bank reserves must rise. Note that the final consequence is roughly the same whether the deal is a direct one or an indirect one; an indirect one, of course, is the case where the Federal Reserve stabilizes the interest rate—in the open market—whenever a sizable Treasury offering has come on the bond market, without actually arranging a direct purchase from the Treasury. The "burden of the debt," clearly, is a broader concept than merely the interest burden, since we are suggesting that the figures in Table 15.5 bear out the often-heard contention that we have also paid for the debt in a more subtle way than the interest payments—in, quite possibly, a too liquid financial system as the direct result of federal fiscal needs. Indeed, a further result, if we follow this line, has been an undesirably rapid inflation, although it would be risky to try to quantify these effects with the data at our command here. Note that having it as a visible interest payment rather than an increase in Federal Reserve holdings of Treasury offerings (see Table 15.3) makes the burden on the public more obvious, since a direct transfer must be made; the public, one could argue, should insist that the debt be marketed at equilibrium prices (i.e., at the higher interest rates) so that the real burden of the debt can be properly calculated (and voted on!).

One other set of data that bears on private (and government) portfolio behavior concerns the holdings of the government debt by its term-to-maturity. We noted, in Chapter 14, that commercial banks, because their liabilities are, in effect, short-term, may well tend to prefer short-term assets; similarly, life insurance companies, with very long-term commitments, may well prefer very long-term securities. At the same time, the supply of the long-term securities of the federal government has declined dramatically, as, apparently, the government has sought to reduce its interest burden. Under these pressures, how have the various holders responded? Table 15.6 has a summary. The top line in the table, one can argue, represents the *supply* of different maturities; clearly, the national debt is shortening quickly, in the sense that very-long-term securities (actually are those over ten years) have declined relatively in this period. Private wealth holders have accommodated themselves to this situation remarkably well. Banks, in particular, seem not to have altered their portfolios much, *in a percentage sense*. Insurance companies have made adjustments, in the sense of becoming more liquid, but they are still, as we predicted in Chapter 14, much less liquid than banks (but less so than in 1969). What is really interesting, here, aside from the confirmation of some earlier conjectives, is the behavior of the Federal Reserve Banks—they have actually gone longer, and have increased the weight of all securities over five years, as a percentage of their total holdings, from 14.3 to 23.3 percent; this has occurred in spite of the fact that the stock of long-term securities has become level at around 19 percent of the total. Indeed, they now have over 26 percent of the securities over 20 years in maturity (up from practically nothing). One guesses that there are four main reasons for this:

a. Any purchase of a long-term bond helps the Treasury avoid the bother of repeatedly turning over short-term debt (i.e., it is done as a service to the Treasury, at nonmarket prices).

b. It increases the flexibility of open market operations, in that the Federal Reserve may be able to operate at the long end.

c. It keeps the higher interest payments (on long-term bonds) within the Federal structure (recall that the Federal Reserve transfers back its excess profits to the Treasury).

d. It reflects attempts by the Federal Reserve to keep long-term rates down (in comparison with short rates) perhaps in conjunction with point (*a*) and perhaps because of a desire to stimulate long-term investment by putting downward pressure on long-term interest rates (compared to short) by buying long-term securities.

Table 15.6: The marketable national debt (holdings by maturity; $ billions)

	1969				*1978*			
	Total	*Under 1 year*	*5–10 years*	*Over 20 years*	*Total*	*Under 1 year*	*5–10 years*	*Over 20 years*
All holders	235.9	118.1	20.0	16.0	487.5	228.5	50.4	25.9
U.S. government agencies and trust funds	16.3	2.3	2.5	3.4	12.7	1.5	2.0	2.0
Federal Reserve banks	57.2	36.0	7.6	.4	109.6	52.8	14.8	8.6
Private investors	162.4	79.8	9.9	12.2	365.2	174.2	33.6	15.3
Commercial banks	45.2	15.1	4.4	.4	68.9	20.6	7.5	1.4
Mutual savings banks	2.9	.5	.3	.7	3.5	.8	.5	.1
Insurance companies	6.1	.9	.2	2.0	11.6	1.8	2.9	.8
Nonfinancial corporations	5.0	3.2	.1	.0	8.3	4.0	.4	.1
Savings and loan associations	3.8	.8	.4	.4	3.8	1.4	.1	.0
State and local governments	13.9	6.4	1.2	2.9	18.8	8.1	1.6	3.6
All others	85.4	52.9	4.0	5.7	250.3	137.3	20.7	9.2

Note: Year-end figures.
Source: *Federal Reserve Bulletin*.

This last is sometimes referred to as "operation twist" and will be discussed in more detail in the following section.

15.4 THE TERM STRUCTURE OF INTEREST RATES

In preceding sections we have edged toward a more general framework for the bond market in which bonds differ by class of issuer and by their maturity date. We have discussed the issuers as much as we are going to (except for the corporations, which we will return to in Chapter 16), but there are a considerable number of issues still ahead of us with regard to the term to maturity; on that topic we will arbitrarily restrict our discussion to U.S. government bonds because the data are the best available and because we can isolate "pure interest-rate" problems from problems that arise because of default risk. In our earlier chapters we generally discussed "the" interest rate; the step we are now going to take involves a discussion of multiple interest rates, arranged in a "structure," by term to maturity;

Figure 15.1: The U.S. Treasury term structure of interest rates, April 1978

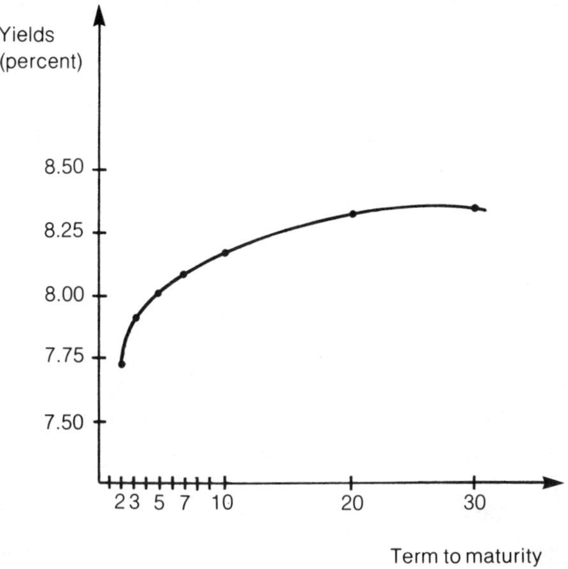

Figure 15.1 represents the term structure of yields on U.S. government securities at the end of April 1978. Notice how the curve in this case is steep in the first section and then flattens out as the term to maturity lengthens.

15.4.1 Some theoretical issues

In earlier chapters we skirted two issues that we now must confront. One of these concerns the definition of liquidity, and the other concerns a basic difference between the Keynesians and John Maynard Keynes over whether a long-term rate or a short-term rate is the appropriate one in monetary analysis. Let us take these up in that order.

In our discussion in Chapter 1, we referred to the concept of liquidity in passing; we preferred to concentrate there on the functions of money—especially as a medium of exchange and as a store of value—and argued that currency and demand deposits are the obvious possessors of these characteristics. We could, then, define liquidity as ''moneyness''—that is, as the ability to mediate in exchanges in all markets—whereas the system just described implies that only currency and demand deposits are perfectly liquid; this, however, competely eliminates liquidity as a separate idea. When we take the empirical approach, we might wish to define money empirically as the most liquid financial asset in the system; that is, we could rank financial assets by their ''liquidity'' and select in one way or another a set as ''money,'' a set as ''near-money,'' and a set as ''non-money.'' This approach, though, requires that we define liquidity itself.

One view of how *liquidity* might be approached is to consider as liquid all assets that are close substitutes for the medium of exchange; this is an economic approach and, further, to the extent that an item is a close substitute, to that extent it has ''moneyness.'' Now since all items possess ''moneyness'' in the sense of being exchangeable into money in a monetary economy, all things are partly money. If all the degrees of moneyness across the system at a moment of time could be added up, we would also end up with the stock of liquidity if we take this approach. Once again, though, we have both a difficult empirical problem and have totally merged the concept of money with the concept of liquidity.

To escape this semantic trap, we might look for explicit measures of liquidity, but to do that we need to be fairly specific. One approach, and certainly the most popular, is to use ''the ease with which an asset might be converted into cash when needed,'' as a measure of liquidity. This ease—and ease certainly includes the explicit expenses involved—depends on

a. The costs of converting the item into cash—the transfer and brokerage costs.

b. The chance that you will have to sell off the item at a loss (if it is marketable).

c. The ''thinness'' of the market in which you will have to sell in the sense of the number of buyers and sellers participating on any given day (houses are hard to sell quickly, usually).

d. The typical "holding period"—the average length of time until the money holder expects to have to use the funds.

This is essentially a technical explanation of liquidity; and, clearly, we can evaluate the liquidity of alternative assets readily in this way, although assets will still have these characteristics in different degrees.

Consider the savings deposit (the passbook account). Clearly, you can convert at a fixed price, although you may have to take an interest loss unless you happen to need the funds on the day your interest is credited to your account or unless there is daily compounding of your interest earnings. There is no market to worry about (so "bid" prices will equal "ask" prices), and you can hold the savings account for a day or for a lifetime, although if you do the latter deliberately (*with certainty*) you are not doing the sensible thing, since you could have earned a great deal more in a safe but less "liquid" asset. As an alternative, consider the liquidity of a 30-year government bond; this bond has an explicit brokerage cost or transfer fee, which, however, may well be *less* per dollar than the charge (the "substantial penalty for early withdrawal") for converting time deposits to cash. On the other hand, you may have to take a market loss if you sell the bond before maturity; then, too, the government-bond market, while thin in the sense that a seller of a *large* block of bonds may move prices himself, is certainly broad enough for small sellers, who could not do this. Finally, if you have a very long horizon (like an insurance company), you may well not regard a 30-year maturity as less liquid than a 1-year security (and you would certainly save on brokerage fees).

The foregoing scheme has a number of dimensions and does not really offer a unique ordering of the liquidity of financial assets, since (for example) some assets that had good markets were shown to have high transfer costs. An alternative scheme, worthwhile primarily for its simplicity, is simply to measure liquidity on the basis of term to maturity. Thus, all "demand" assets, whether they pay interest or not, are perfectly liquid; all 1-year assets are highly liquid; while all 30-year bonds are considerably less liquid. "Liquidity preference" by this measure would be the general tendency to hold cash unless some alternative return were offered. Notice that by the characteristic of perfect liquidity (available on demand), M_1 plus the passbook accounts of banks, MSBs, and S&Ls would be "money" but that *time* deposits (where an explicit maturity is arranged) would not.

Turning to the second of our theoretical issues, we consider the emergence (and resolution) of a debate over what Keynes actually said and how it contrasts with the views of those who followed him but perpetuated his ideas *as they* saw them (call them the Keynesians). The latter were responsible for the Keynesian Revolution, which dominated academic and policy-making circles from 1940 to the mid-1960s. Among the representative figures were Alvin Hansen of Harvard University, James Tobin of Yale, and Paul Samuelson of M.I.T. This, as we will see has some direct policy implications and it also involves the term structure of interest rates. Keynes's view of monetary policy—liquidity traps and other aberrations aside—was couched in terms of the government's control of short-term interest rates as a means to altering the long-term rate (and thereby altering investment spending). He felt that long-term rates would be slow to respond to such pressures, but that they would move in the desired direction if the policy were consistent enough and could be maintained for a sufficient length of time. In this scenario, when a vigorous monetary policy is conducted, the authorities are basically switching in and out of short-term securities in such a way that short-term debt is *monetized*. The consequence is that cash and short-term securities become very close substitutes in the eyes of market participants; indeed, Keynes favored a definition of money that was quite broad (possibly even beyond M_5). Finally, since all short-term assets are substantially alike, Keynes considered that the appropriate interest rate for the demand for money was the *long-term rate*. This, again, results because a change in the short-term rate caused merely a shift *within* the category he felt was truly money (for purposes of control), while the long-term rate represented an *alternative* (and hence the opportunity cost) to money holders.

Much of the subsequent Keynesian approach to the problem can be explained in terms of the portfolio model of Chapter 14; recall that "Keynesian" does not necessarily refer to Keynes himself (i.e., that there are on occasion different views among the Keynesian economists as to what is important). The idea is similar to that of Keynes himself, but here the notion of substitution is given greater prominence; if a specific asset is particularly close substitute for money, then it is on the relevant frontier between money and nonmoney. To put it another way, among the assets "money," short-term bonds, and long-term bonds (and equity) *the margin of decision* (in money holding) for the typical wealth holder is not between money and long-term bonds, but between money and short-term bonds. Few investors, that is to say, switch back and forth between long-term assets and money; instead, long-term assets are adjusted in relation to "not-quite-so-long-term" assets, and money holding is not involved directly. Therefore, referring to the demand for money, the short-term interest rate is the appropriate rate for the demand for money since it represents the yield on the main alternative asset; the long-term security is not in the picture when the decision is made (it is "dominated" by the other, shorter security).

Needless to say, such an interesting confrontation has brought forth quite a battery of tests; the results of actual tests, while still not conclusive (because they vary), favor the short-term rate, by about three to one.[5] But

[5] See David Laidler, *The Demand for Money* (New York: Dun-Donnelly, 1977).

we should note that it is also possible to approach the problem in a more direct way, without worrying about whether one is Keynesian or not, and ask a simpler question: How many interest rates are relevant to the demand for money? From this point of view a broad measure of money, such as M_3, which may well not show significant variation in its total (look at the Figures in Table 1.1) as interest rates move about, may well respond *positively* to short-term interest rates and *negatively* to long-term rates, with the former measuring the *direct* yield on the aggregate (being, in formal language, an "own rate") and the latter measuring the opportunity cost of holding the aggregate (being, in effect, a "cross rate"). Such an approach, with two or more interest rates, would seem to require a portfolio model, though. Milton Friedman, among others, has suggested that the entire term structure may be relevant for the demand for money.[6]

15.4.2 Theories of the term structure of interest rates

Let us, before we turn to some of the more policy-oriented aspects of our subject, return to the formal study of interest rates, which we first took up in Chapter 6. A bond is best conceived of as a loan for a specified period of time, from the issue date (lending date) to the maturity date (repayment date), with explicit conditions for both the repayment of the loan and the "rental" payment for the borrowed money. (This is a very broad definition and could even include the time deposit.) Most private bonds in the United States are issued in units of $1,000. We define the issue value of a bond as the *face value* (F) and most bonds are redeemed (at the redemption date) at or near their face value. The rental payments are paid over the life of the contract in the form of a coupon (C), which is stated in the original contract. In Chapter 6 we considered, in Equation (6.5), the present value of a stream of future payments; that formula applies literally to the use of a bond. Thus, assume a bond with n years to maturity, with a face value of F, and with a stream of equal coupons for each of these n years of ($C_1, C_2, \ldots, C_n$); that bond will, if yields in general for all other n-period bonds are (on average) R_n, tend to trade at the following price:

$$P_n = \frac{C_1}{1 + R_n} + \frac{C_2}{(1 + R_n)^2} + \cdots + \frac{C_n + F}{(1 + R_n)^n}. \qquad (15.1)$$

Equation (15.1) defines the present value of the stream of returns (including the repayment of the principal, F), where the discount rate is R_n, itself representing the *yield* of the relevant alternatives.

[6] Milton Friedman, "Time Perspective in Demand for Money," *Scandinavian Journal of Economics* (December 1977).

Equation (15.1) represents the yield on an n-period bond; similarly, simply by varying n, we can calculate a set of yields for bonds (if they exist) maturing after $n - 1, n - 2, \ldots, 1$ periods; such would represent a term structure of yields. Later we will return to these yields when we take up the policy issues, but in the meantime we will look into another concept—a *forward interest rate*—that can be derived from the same market data just described. Suppose, in supplement to Equation (15.1), we conceive of the same price as being determined not by a single yield (R_n) but by a series of one-year yields ($r_1, \ldots, r_n$) with the total of these one-year rates covering the same time period; the result is

$$P_n = \frac{C_1}{1 + r_1} + \frac{C_2}{(1 + r_1)(1 + r_2)} + \cdots + \frac{C_n + F}{(1 + r_1)(1 + r_2) \cdots (1 + r_n)} \qquad (15.2)$$

Since we are talking about the same bond in either case, we can equate these two expressions; further, let us assume (arbitrarily) that $C_i = 0$ and $F = 1$ so that we are, in effect, merely asking about the present value of a dollar received in n years' time. The result, clearly, is

$$(1 + R_n)^n = (1 + r_1)(1 + r_2) \cdots (1 + r_{n-1})(1 + r_n), \qquad (15.3)$$

which is to say that we are conceiving of the long-term rate as a geometric average of the relevant short-term rates up to that point.

To calculate those short rates—which we may fairly call *forward* rates—we can employ the following technique. Since, clearly, $(1 + R_{n-1})^{n-1} = (1 + r_1)(1 + r_2) \cdots (1 + r_{n-1})$, we can divide Equation (15.3) by this expression; the result, directly, is a formal and practical definition of a forward rate:

$$r_n = \frac{(1 + R_n)^n}{(1 + R_{n-1})^{n-1}} - 1. \qquad (15.4)$$

Note that R_n and R_{n-1} are, in principle, obtainable from newspaper quotations (one may have to interpolate if the exact data cannot be found).[7]

[7] Recently a new market—the futures market for U.S. Treasury bills—has arisen in the United States. It is now possible to deal in Treasury bill "futures," that is, buy and sell for *future* delivery, on the basis of regular market quotations. On July 7, 1978, the following were quoted yields on this market:

1978	Sept.	7.47
	Dec.	7.90
1979	Mar.	8.22
	June	8.45
	Sept.	8.66
	Dec.	8.86
1980	Mar.	9.07
	June	9.24

The Treasury bill rate ("spot" rate) on July 10, 1978, was 6.95 for Sept. 28 and 7.78 for the end of June 1979. Thus one could buy Treasury bills to be issued at the end of June 1979 at 91.55

Now if investors actually consider the relative properties of adjacent maturities—as we agreed was the case for the Keynesian demand for money—then we can argue that they will do so in response to these forward rates. Indeed, by a suitable adjustment of short and long sales one can actually arrange to lend for one year (say for the year 1990) at the 1980 forward rate that holds for 1990 (you can also do this in the Treasury Bill futures market as noted in Footnote 7). These are, that is to say, market rates (although they were derived in a somewhat less than general way). As such, they are of practical value.

But there are also theoretical and policy issues concerning the term structure of interest rates and the forward rates and these are of more interest. The main theoretical question concerns the determination of the shape of the yield curve itself (of either $R_1, \ldots, R_n$ or $r_1, \ldots, r_n$) and there are two main views:

a. Long-term rates are *expected* rates—perhaps even expected one-year rates for some future period—and as such are determined by speculators (as broadly defined).

b. Long-term rates are determined by investors who prefer to lend long, matched (or approximately matched) by borrowers who prefer to borrow long.

The first view is known as the *expectations hypothesis;* it implies that only if you alter the views of speculators as to what is to come will you affect the long-term rate. The expectations hypothesis is generally paraphrased by the statement that long-term bonds and short-term bonds are close substitutes. The second view just mentioned is also known as the hedging or *segmentation hypothesis;* the general idea is that each participant in the market has a preferred maturity. In particular, institutions (and possibly individual investors) will tend to match up the term to maturity of their assets to that of their liabilities. Indeed, we commented earlier that this might be the case both for commercial banks and life insurance companies. But let us define our terms more carefully before moving on.

We must ultimately define and illustrate the concepts of speculation and hedging, but we actually must begin with another concept, and that is *arbitrage*. We define an arbitrage operation as one in which a profit is obtained by buying a product in one market and simultaneously selling it in another at, presumably, prices that are further apart than the sum of the transactions and (where relevant) transportation costs. We are most familiar with this technique in international finance; but we need only note here

---

(100 − 8.45); when that date comes you are guaranteed 8.45 percent by the seller of that yet-to-be-issued bill. This is a gain if, at that date, Treasury bills are priced higher. I have not included transactions costs in these simple comparisons. One guesses that much of the difference between 8.45 percent and 7.78 percent is eaten up by the commissions to the futures dealers.

that in domestic bond markets such opportunities arise only rarely, if at all, and thus we can neglect arbitrage for now. This leaves us with "covered" operations (in which no gains or losses aside from those planned can be obtained) versus "uncovered" operations.

It is tempting to describe *speculation* in a psychological sense, but it is not wise to do this because of the ubiquity of speculation in most Western economies. Anyone who is uncovered (unhedged) against any potential chance of loss or gain is thereby a speculator with regard to that variable. If you happen to run your automobile over the president of a large oil company, you can be relatively certain that your hedge (your automobile insurance policy) will not be sufficient to cover the damages—you are speculating, in effect, against this rather unlikely risk. In financial markets one speculates when he or she is not insulated against the fluctuations of the prices of his or her assets and liabilities—thus, widows who own only American Telephone and Telegraph common stock are, essentially, wild-eyed speculators in that they are completely uncovered against changes in the fortunes of that particular company. One may well think that this is too broad a definition of speculation and, consequently, recommend the restriction of the term to a person who *consciously* speculates in some sense; but, on inspection, the latter definition is not very useful. The reason is that there is no way, except in certain narrow markets such as the foreign exchange market (where "amateur" speculators do not seem to dominate), to distinguish conscious speculators from the nonspeculators who are also nonhedgers. Both take a financial "position" and may even respond to roughly the same stimuli, at least for any empirical test we might invent.

Hedging, in this chapter, will mean the insulation against interest-rate (or bond-price) fluctutions by matching the maturity of financial assets with the maturity of financial liabilities. A practical example, if true, is that of the life insurance company, with liabilities (policies) actuarily of a very long term matched by holdings of long-term bonds and mortgages of an equally long term. To illustrate hedging (and speculation) consider the following illustration, involving our basic equation with forward rates. Suppose, for example, we bought a two-year bond while simultaneously selling a three-year bond. The following equations represent this arrangement:

$$\begin{aligned} \text{Buy Bond } A\text{: } P_2 &= \frac{C}{1 + r_1} + \frac{C + F}{(1 + r_1)(1 + r_2)}; \\ \text{Sell Bond } B\text{: } P_3 &= \frac{C}{1 + r_1} + \frac{C}{(1 + r_1)(1 + r_2)} + \frac{C + F}{(1 + r_1)(1 + r_2)(1 + r_3)}. \end{aligned} \tag{15.5}$$

Since we simultaneously bought and sold for two of the three years, we are insulated from changes in r_1 and r_2; what we gain on the one hand, we will lose on the other. Our net contribution to the money market is to borrow money for the third year—we will repay one year later when we pay off our three-year bond. Thus, if interest rates rise over the period, our asset (Bond A) will fall in value, while our liability (Bond B) will rise in value. If the change is in r_1 or r_2, we will not observe any change in our position; but if it is in r_3, we will have gained, since Bond A cannot be affected by the change, while the price of Bond B will fall. For the first two periods we are covered (hedging) against interest-rate fluctuations, but for the third we are uncovered (taking a position) until the end of the period. In fact, we can either borrow or lend at these rates; and anyone who is, perforce, uncovered for any of the forward interest rates, whether he is aware of it or not and whether he is "long" or "short," is *speculating* in bonds, at least as that term is broadly defined.

With these technical matters resolved, we are in a position to return to the theoretical issues described earlier. First we should note that yield curves, actually, are not all sloped like Figure 15.1; a representative sample, indeed, is given in Figure 15.2. Thus, while one often thinks of type I

Figure 15.2: Typical yield curves

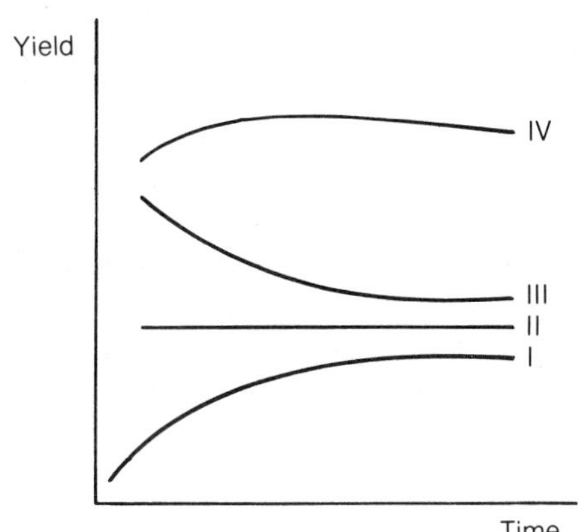

as the "normal" curve, type IV has been quite common in recent years (especially at higher interest rates), and all four types have been observed in the American capital market since 1971. If there are no biases of any sort in the market, we might expect type II to rule, *on average*. In this case, everyone might be assuming that the current interest rate (R_1), whatever it is, will rule forever; this is likely if opinions are diverse or conditions especially unsettled. Indeed, if this is the case, then Equations (15.1) and (15.2) are equivalent, and we can speak of "the" interest rate as we have done earlier in this book. What is really being suggested, though, is that the shape of these curves depends on expectations about the future course of interest rates. That is, the easiest, and in some ways the most plausible, explanation of each of the four curves in Figure 15.2 is that the shape is determined by the net judgment of the market as to what will happen to interest rates over the periods to come, in comparison with the current one-year interest rate (R_1). Thus, under the expectations hypothesis, curve type I represents a net effective judgment by the market that interest rates will rise; curve type III, that they will fall; curve type IV, that they will first rise and then fall; and curve type II, that they will remain constant. But, unfortunately, it is difficult to think of ways to test such a wide-sweeping hypothesis—wide-sweeping because it can explain everything.

To take a concrete example, suppose that one expects interest rates to fall (that is, he expects bond prices to rise) over the course of the next year. If his conviction is strong enough to cause him to take action, he will sell off some other asset (perhaps money) and buy, say, a one-year bond. What happens in the bond market, if this occurs, is that funds are now available for one-year loans; and if our individual represents net market opinion in some sense, the price of a one-year bond will be bid up, and r_1 will fall. In this way, the shape of the yield curve could be determined by speculative activity. This is the expectations hypothesis in its purest form—and the expectations tend to be self-confirming, at least in this case.

Hedging behavior, technically the perfect opposite of speculation, actually takes two forms in bond markets. Hedging arises because of "fear" of, or more accurately distaste for, risk and, in this particular market, distaste for interest-rate risk (or, if you prefer, bond-price risk). One way in which we would look for the influence of hedging is in what is generally termed the *risk premium* that might be levied on interest rates in proportion to the length of time until a bond matures. That is, runs one explanation, the further a bond is from its maturity date, at which time all risks of changes in the level of interest rates in general will have been passed, the more likely it is that the lender might have to recall his loan (sell his asset) on unfavorable terms. In terms of our *forward* interest rates in Equation (15.2), what we are saying is that each forward rate (r_1 to r_n) really consists of two components; one, a pure interest-rate part, and one, a liquidity-premium part; we would then write a series of forward rates as

$$r_{1E} + r_{1L}, r_{2E} + r_{2L}, \ldots, r_{nE} + r_{nL}. \tag{15.6}$$

This would be in contrast to the "pure" speculative view, in which the r_L terms are zero. Here we run into a particularly serious problem, because it turns out that this proposition is supported by the same data that supported our expectations theory. With reference to Figure 15.2 we pointed out that the most frequently occurring yield curve was curve type I, the upsloping version; indeed, this type is the average shape for any reasonably long period. If in Equation (15.6) there are no firm expectations or if expectations average to zero, then, as a matter of arithmetic, liquidity premiums, which pile up in the yield formula, will make the average curve slope upward. But if expectations are *also* biased toward rising rates, a bias which is possible even given the highest interest rates now common, the same result, curve type I, is consistent with both the hedging and nonhedging theories, at least as the former was just phrased.

The second form of the hedging theory concerns the balance-sheet evening-out already described at several points in this chapter. This is more straightforward and implies that individual submarket rates (for example, r_{10}) will be isolated from the rest of the structure, although, perhaps, linked by the inevitable overlapping that modern financial firms obviously provide. With regard to the last point, for example, we have seen that commercial banks, with most of their liabilities 'on demand,'' have assets spread all the way along the yield structure even through a large percentage are in a fairly short-term form. The implication of concentration of both assets and liabilities in the same maturity class is that such submarkets might tend to become isolated and reflect only the forces within the submarket rather than developments at other points along the interest-rate structure. Thus rates will depend on the relative supply and demand in each submarket; accordingly, any structure you can think of can then be explained (by supply and demand). But this is enough of the (as yet unresolved) theoretical puzzle; let us consider some policy issues.

15.4.3 Policy issues and the term structure of interest rates

We should summarize the results of Sections 15.4.1 and 15.4.2 before moving on, in case the complexity of the analysis has left some issues confused. With reference to the facts, we have argued, basically, that one can define a term structure of interest rates within which one can arrange deals and that this structure actually varies considerably over time. With reference to the theories, in turn, we have argued that two polar views are possible—either (*a*) expectations about future interest rates or (*b*) financial hedging—to explain the pattern. In particular, although a combination of the two is obviously preferable, it is possible to explain any particular structure in terms of either of the two theories, as we have seen. And, as we shall see, the theories imply different policy approaches (to, among other things, monetary policy).

Suppose, to begin with, that the hedging view is correct and that term-differentiated bond markets are relatively insulated from each other. Suppose, as well, that one accepts Keynes's view and feels that only by changing a long-term rate—and hence affecting business investment—would a policy have any sizable effects on the economy. Under these conditions one might well try to aim at long-term rates *directly* by conducting monetary policy in long-term securities and be relatively certain, since hedgers would not move away from their "preferred" maturities, that the desired interest-rate change would occur. Even if one is not a Keynesian, of course, and the market is actually dominated by hedgers, it would be possible to design separate policies for long and short rates. For example, one might deal out a tight money policy at the short end of the market—working in the Treasury bill market—and actually lower rates at the long end, to prevent a tight money policy from producing a recession. This policy, which, if it worked, might twist a curve like type I in Figure 15.2 into something more like type III, is known as "Operation Twist" and was part of the policy discussion (and maybe even a part of the actual policy framework) in the early 1960s. It may well be revived from time to time, since it is an appealing idea.

A policy somewhat related to Operation Twist, with, at least in one case, a similar historical pedigree, is that known as "Bills Only." The Federal Reserve, it is argued, would be better off to conduct open market operations in Treasury bills alone because that market is the only one that is broad enough to absorb the kind of change in the money stock we are likely to need if we depend on monetary policy for an effective push to the economy. One reason it might like to do that is that it usually wishes to bring about a change in the money stock without changing interest rates and, further, without upsetting the capital (especially the long-term securities) market. This policy of Bills Only is also based on there being some separation in the markets with respect to term to maturity, for broadness or narrowness of the market is not an issue if all rates move together because of speculative forces. This policy has not been mentioned by name in recent years but it is abundantly clear from our data in Table 15.3 that under the present conditions the Federal Reserve does deal primarily in short-term securities although, as we noted above, its leverage over long-term rates is increasing.

Actually, in the last paragraph, we mentioned speculative forces, and it is now time to consider a policy scenario in which the "expectations hypothesis" is confirmed. Basically, the argument is that long-term rates are averages of expected rates (or, alternatively, that forward rates as we calculated them are actually expected rates) and that only by altering expectations of interest rates would the authorities be able to influence long-term rates. Putting it another way, investors will not care where they are along the structure and if, for example, one attempts (by policy) to drive down the long rate by buying long-term securities, investors will simply switch from long to short securities (which are now relatively more attractive), driving down short rates as well. Thus, in this view, long and short securities are perfect substitutes, and long and short rates tend to move together. Quite clearly, under this view, neither of the policy wrinkles mentioned is sensible, since:

a. The policy of Bills Only is irrelevant if all securities move together.
b. The policy of Operation Twist would not work, again because all interest rates move together.

It would be nice if one could report that this important theoretical issue had been resolved, so that we could get on with our policy, but it has not. No doubt, the truth about the term structure is somewhere in between but quite possibly, it is closer to the expectations end than to the hedging end.[8] In a way, it would be convenient if the speculative view were correct, for then one could dig out, by means of our formula for forward rates, a set of interest rates that, we could legitimately argue, reflected market expectations of future interest rates. These would be of interest to investors, of course, and they could be used in the index of leading indicators (see Figure 11.1) although, at present, there are no interest rates in that series. On the other hand, it is certain that some investors do use the term structure in this way, if only as a rough guide to what the market might be expecting. So there is a policy problem here, as well as an interesting confrontation between the contrasting theoretical views, and no final resolution of the issues.

15.5 STUDY QUESTIONS

Essay questions

1. Which characteristics of a market contribute most to the liquidity of the item traded in the market? Are any of these measurable? Is there any overlap between the characteristics?

2. One reason for not conducting monetary policy in long-term bonds is that the long-term market is fairly thin, especially on a day-to-day basis. What would be the effect on the short-term interest rate, on expectations about interest rates, and on investment, of a sizable open market purchase of long-term debt?

3. We have likened a bond to a simple loan. Could we also link demand deposits into the structure of interest rates? How would we measure the return on demand deposits? How would we measure the term to maturity of, alternatively, demand deposits and time deposits? Where, then, does currency fit in?

4. Does the thinness of certain bond markets lead to an overly high price of "cover"? What economic interpretation would you give to the word "overly" in the last sentence? Should there be some government

[8] See the summary in Douglas Fisher, "The Term Structure of Interest Rates" in Richard Thorn (ed.), *Monetary Theory and Policy,* 2d ed. (New York: Praeger, 1976).

policy to encourage the production of cover in certain markets? What role do intermediaries play in this process?

5. Why is an upsloping yield curve not conclusive evidence that the market expects rates to rise? Can we, nevertheless, use this curve to guide our predictions even if we cannot justify our theory in this way? Would we, in any event, expect predictions and theory to mesh nicely in such cases? Explain.

6. What assumptions are necessary to justify an analysis in terms of *the* interest rate? If interest rates are determined by expectations, is a single interest rate more or less likely to rule? Why?

True-false discussion questions

These statements are meant to be somewhat ambiguous, and to provoke discussion thereby.

1. The increase in the U.S. inflation rate in recent years cannot be attributed to the federal government, since the federal government's share of GNP has been constant.

2. No one would hold a long-term bond instead of a short-term bond when the chance of a fluctuation in the price of the long bond is greater than that of the short and when the long bond yields less than the short.

3. When the yield curve slopes downward, we are more certain that expectations are for lower rates than we are in the converse case.

4. The perfect hedge against interest-rate fluctuations is to hold non-interest-bearing cash.

5. If expectations dominate the yield structure, then the presumption is that it does not matter whether open market operations are in short-term or in long-term bonds.

6. The growth of the federal debt has been accompanied by an increasing burden of relatively long-term debt on American financial markets. This is referred to as "crowding out."

15.6 FURTHER READING

Articles in *Quarterly Review, Federal Reserve Bank of New York*. "Noncompetitive Tenders in Treasury Auctions: How Much Do They Affect Savings Flows?" (Autumn 1978); "Electronic Funds Systems and the Market for Government Securities," (Summer 1978); and "The Market for Agency Securities," (Spring 1978).

Burger, Albert E., Richard W. Lang, and Robert H. Rasche. "The Treasury Bill Futures Market and Market Expectations of Interest Rates." *Review, Federal Reserve Bank of St. Louis* (June 1977).

Cagan, Phillip. "A Study of Liquidity Premiums on Federal and Municipal Government Securities." In Cagan, Phillip, and Jack Guttentag, eds., *Essays in Interest Rates.* New York: National Bureau of Economic Research, 1969.

Dodds, J., and J. L. Ford. *Expectations, Uncertainty and the Term Structure of Interest Rates.* London: Martin-Robertson, 1974.

Meiselman, David. *The Term Structure of Interest Rates.* (Englewood Cliffs, N.J.: Prentice-Hall, 1962.

Roley, V. Vance. "Federal Debt Management Policy: A Re-Examination of the Issues." *Economic Review, Federal Reserve Bank of Kansas City* (February 1978).

16

Business corporations and the financial markets

16.1 INTRODUCTION

American business firms, as we have noted in passing, are important participants in the financial markets. Just like final consuming units, they hold cash and deposit accounts and securities, and they issue bonds (an individual does so, in effect, by borrowing at the bank), but they can also go one step further: they can issue common or preferred stock (equities). We looked at the general considerations behind money holding in Chapter 6, when we discussed opportunity cost and income factors; in this respect business firms are no exception to the general rules laid down there, although, as we shall see, some interesting variations must be discussed. In addition, in Chapter 14 we considered why a wealth holder might diversify his portfolio to obtain an optimal trade-off between risk and return; here we can immediately see that the business firm will live by the same rules. But of unique interest with regard to the business firm is the fact that a special kind of portfolio problem faces them because, once they have decided to undertake a capital project, they can raise the funds needed by debt, by equity, or, of course, by retaining earnings. We are, in fact, interested in both of the securities just mentioned, because the external decision, which clearly will be based on some kind of economic considerations, involves the supply of two different financial entities to the financial markets, one fixed in payment and one fairly flexible (particularly its price).

When we turn to the policy issues involving the business firm, a number of factors emerge. For one thing, the business firm may well have a demand for money that differs substantially from the private demand. The difference could be in terms of either the interest rate or income and could imply, when different, that under certain conditions (when funds shift about between firms and individuals) the demand for money or the definition of money could vary in an unpredictable way. Consider, for example, what might happen if business firms respond to a short interest rate and individuals to a long rate and something like the Operation Twist of Chapter 15 is applied (that was a policy in which long rates were pushed down and short rates up). In this case, business firms may reduce their money balances (on account of the rise in the short rate) while individuals increase theirs; as a result, the total money stock may not change at all (so if the short rate policy was designed to reduce inflation, it probably would not succeed). There is another policy issue, in addition, because large-scale business firms are the source of much of the investment spending in the economy, and it is the volatility of investment spending—as magnified by the investment multiplier (see Chapter 11)—that many feel is the root cause of the rolling adjustments (recessions) we now experience in the American economy. In a nutshell, since firms will obviously pay attention to financial market conditions when they invest, there is potential here for either stabilizing or destabilizing investment when monetary policy is implemented, at least insofar as investment is sensitive to changes in market interest rates. Finally, we will consider some technical points in the relation between stock and bond prices with particular reference to the proposition that consumer stocks are a hedge against inflation; we will also comment on the cyclical behavior of some familiar stock averages since they may well embody expectations accurately. The expectations we have in mind are the expectation of inflation rates as well as those of general business conditions.

16.2 THE FIRM'S DEMAND FOR MONEY

The business firm can obviously be approached as if it were an individual (since it is owned, ultimately, by individuals), but there are alternative approaches that may be justified since the environment of the business firm is different from that of the individual. For one thing, a business firm may consider money to be a factor of production; for another, it may control the quantity of money it holds pretty much as it controls its stocks of (manufacturing) materials—by maintaining an *optimal inventory* of them. In either case, a clear difference exists in comparison with individual behavior (as described in Chapter 6) if only because decidedly more exact rules for optimal money holding can be devised for the business firm, as we shall see.

Consider, briefly, a "money as factor of production" argument. Formally, we could write a production function for the typical firm, as

$$X = \phi(K, L, m) = \phi_1 + \phi_2 K + \phi_3 L + \phi_4 m, \tag{16.1}$$

where m is real money balances. Note that we also include the linear version of the function. As before, we may assume that ϕ_1, ϕ_2, ϕ_3 are all positive; *similarly,* let us agree that ϕ_4 is positive, reflecting the positive contribution of money balances to the (aggregate) firm's output. This positive contribution could result from saving time in the hiring of labor or in purchasing materials (if we need a justification at this stage). In equilibrium, each factor of production is hired up to the point at which the cost, i_m (or opportunity cost), is equal to the additional contribution of the last unit ($\Delta X/\Delta m$) to the output.[1] This is the condition that

$$i_m = \Delta X/\Delta m. \tag{16.2}$$

We may transpose Equation (16.2) to $\Delta m = \Delta X/i_m$ and then convert it into nominal units by multiplying each side by P, the price level (it is appropriate for our aggregate firm); the result is

$$\Delta M = \frac{\Delta Y}{i_m}, \tag{16.3}$$

where $M = Pm$ and $Y = Px$, arbitrarily. In this form we see that changes in income will directly produce changes in money holding (as it did for individuals) and that an increase in the interest rate will cause a decrease in the rate of change of money holding (as it did for the individual, approximately).[2] The strict proportionality, of course, is the result of our overly restrictive approach. At any rate, when taken as a factor of production in a fashion roughly parallel to any capital good, the aggregate firm's money holding is seen (*a*) to respond to income and the interest rate in the usual way and (*b*) to depend on the technical coefficients of the production function (on, that is to say, the ability one has to substitute money for labor or capital in the optimal production plan). But we did not make anything of the latter, in Equations (16.2) and (16.3).

The preceding is basically an exercise, although it does suggest an easy way to explain business money holding as arising from the needs of the

[1] This, of course, is the "wage equals marginal physical product" condition for a competitive factor market. Note that we use $\Delta X/\Delta m$ rather than the correct partial derivative here.

[2] Real money balances here are being treated as a capital good (as is labor, for that matter) and so Equation (16.3) resembles an investment function in that the *change* in money holding is equated to the *change* in income. Look back at Equation (7.4) for a parallel discussion.

production process (they are needed to hire the inputs, for example). But many economists would argue that business firms do not actually convert money into final products in the same way that labor, materials, and capital are "converted"; instead, they suggest, money is held for purely financial purposes. To be sure, money can "produce" financial gain (facilitated payments, etc.) but this type of gain has nothing to do with the shop floor, as it were. This is clearly a sensible concern, although one certainly does not need to be dogmatic on this point; but as it turns out, there is an alternative model for the business firm—the *inventory model*—that gets us to about the same point as Equation (16.3) without the need to assume that money is a factor of production. In addition, the business firm can be treated in a different way from the individual, and that, too, accords with one's prejudices (although the inventory model *can* be applied to individuals, of course).

The point of departure for the inventory model is to frame the problem not as that of maximizing expected profits by holding an optimal amount of a productive resource, but as that of avoiding some costly or inconvenient occurrence by holding an optimal amount of money. The costly events occur, then, if one runs out of money; these costs can be quite definite (a penalty cost) or they can be indefinite (such as embarrassment) or, more usually, both. The individual, for example, who runs out of funds in his bank account and receives a notice from the bank will have to pay a penalty to the bank and usually to the person who cashed the check (and, in addition, will have to explain himself to the latter). A firm may face even more dire measures (consider what might happen if the workers are not paid).

A business firm, typically, has a cash inflow as well as a cash outflow and, typically, both are somewhat variable so that the net of the two may well be decidedly uncertain. The problem the firm has is straight-forward, though: suppose it decides to hold a stock of cash and a stock of time deposits, which it can redeem in a pinch, and it wishes to minimize the former because it is losing interest (on the time deposits) by holding cash. How does it construct its ideal portfolio? Of course, if one could switch out of an interest-bearing account—like a time deposit—with no explicit cost, cash would be held at the minimum, (zero), so that is one way of looking at it. But in fact, one usually has to pay a broker's fee (or possibly, lose a little interest in the form of a "substantial penalty for earlier withdrawal"); one also often has to travel to the bank, although these sorts of costs are currently diminishing through the establishment of electronic funds transfers, primarily. Let us suppose that each conversion of a time deposit into cash costs b (the brokerage fee or penalty), and that C is the amount of cash withdrawn. Let us suppose that the firm expects to have to convert T dollars per time period, so that T/C represents the number of times cash is restocked from the time deposit account per time period.

Each time we go to the bank to restore our cash balance (by switching from the savings account) we incur the cost b. Thus $b(T/C)$ represents the money cost of all the trips to the bank in a given time period.

Before we proceed we should consider an example. Suppose, on net, it costs $.05 to convert any amount of time deposits into cash, perhaps because it costs something to go to the bank; b is $.05. Suppose that our expected cash requirement for the entire period is $100 ($T$ = $100) and, assuming this is evenly spread out, we meet this with an average cash holding of $25 ($C$ = $25). Thus, the cost of this operation for all trips is $.05 (100/25) = $.20. It would be *lower* if we held a larger cash balance; thus if C = $33.33, we would only need three trips to the bank; expected total costs would then be $.15 for the three trips. When we hold as much as $25 in cash, though, we lose the interest earnings on the bank time deposit; indeed, if C is the cash we are holding, then $C/2$ is the average cash we hold in *each* of the other periods. That is, if we go and get $25, and gradually run it off, half of it will be run off in half the time (let us assume); if $25 is what we get each time, then $12.50 is our average cash balance. It is this average that is losing the time deposit interest payments (at the rate of interest of i).

Put the two together—that is, add the cost of all the trips to the bank which is $b(T/C)$, to the interest foregone, which is $iC/2$—and you have the total costs of keeping an inventory of cash; this is

$$\frac{bT}{C} + \frac{iC}{2} = \text{Total cost.} \tag{16.4}$$

The problem, then is to find the optimal holding of cash—the demand for money, C^*,—given the interest rate (i), brokerage fees (b), and the estimated overall cash needs for the period (T). T, itself, could be proportional to sales (or income, if the individual operated by these rules).

Since we are dealing with a business firm, the problem is to equate the marginal cost ($\Delta TC/\Delta C$) with the marginal revenue of the operation. Since the marginal revenues *of selling the product* are fixed here (by assumption), the effect on marginal revenue of varying cost *itself* is zero; thus, we need to find the optimal cash holding when $\Delta TC/\Delta C$ is equal to zero. The problem is to find the value of C such that the falling brokerage costs ($\Delta bT/\Delta C$) are exactly equal to the *additional* costs ($i\Delta C/2$) of holding idle cash; this is given by[3]

$$-\frac{bT}{(C^*)^2} + \frac{i}{2} = 0. \tag{16.5}$$

[3] You actually can see this two ways. One is to calculate $\Delta TC/\Delta C$ directly and set it equal to zero (if you have the calculus). The second is to graph the various functions as the text does, in Figure 16.1.

Figure 16.1: The optimal inventory of cash

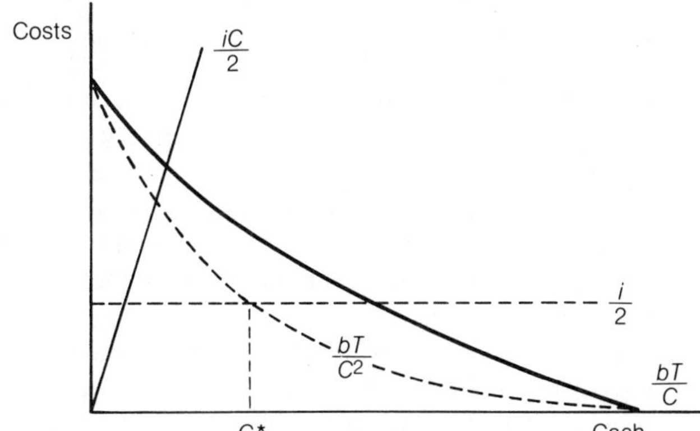

To see the solution graphically, consider Figure 16.1. There we show the function bT/C, which is a declining function (costs are on the vertical axis) for increases in C. Similarly, the function $iC/2$ is a positively sloped function. By analogy, we can treat the declining bT/C function as if it were a total revenue curve; therefore, it has a marginal curve with a steeper slope (bT/C^2).[4] Similarly, the $iC/2$ curve has a marginal curve with a flatter slope ($= i/2$), which we may treat as analogous to marginal cost. Thus, to pursue the analogy, the optimizing condition in Equation (16.5) is equivalent to a marginal cost = marginal revenue expression; an optimum is illustrated at C^*. To the right of C^*, any additional units of cash holding will add more to opportunity costs ($i/2$) than it saves in the expense of trips to the bank (bT/C^2); to the left of C^* there are unexploited savings in total cost that can be gained by holding a larger balance.

The inventory model is of special interest to economists because it gives a simple and exact solution for the (business firm's) demand for money. Since Equation (16.5) describes the optimal money holding for a cost minimizer, we can assume that this is the amount that is actually chosen; that is, we can treat C^* as the demand for money; rearranging, we get

$$(C^*)^2 = \frac{2bT}{i}, \qquad (16.6)$$

[4] Note that the slope is for Figure 16.1, which is graphed in the costs-cash space; the expressions here have to be rearranged somewhat to do that:

$$C^2 = \frac{bT}{\text{costs}} \text{ and } C = \sqrt{\frac{bT}{\text{costs}}}.$$

in which case

$$C^* = \left(\frac{2bT}{i}\right)^{\frac{1}{2}}. \tag{16.7}$$

This equation says that the demand for money is directly proportional to the *square root* of transactions (or income) and inversely proportional to the square root of the interest rate. The effect of an increase in sales (or income) would be to increase cash holdings, but not by the full amount; similarly, an increase in the opportunity cost (i) will tend to decrease cash holdings, as all of our previous models have argued, although this result is a pretty specific one.

We are not in a position to confirm whether or not business firms take a portfolio approach, an inventory approach, a factor-of-production approach, some other approach, or some combination of approaches, but we do have the results from a number of studies that indicate that businesses do react differently from individuals. In particular, *manufacturing* firms may well

a. Hold a lower percentage of their sales (or their transactions or their net income) in cash than do individuals (of their income).

b. Respond to a short-term interest rate while individuals respond to a long-term interest rate.

c. Hold cash and demand deposits rather than savings and time deposits in comparison with individuals.

These results suggest that the typical aggregations (e.g., M_1, M_2) may be ambiguous on this account, especially with regard to the interest rate (the total also varying with shifts of funds between businesses and individuals). Furthermore, approaches such as Operation Twist, which is designed to stimulate long-term investment while it taxes money holding, may actually hit business firms harder than appreciated, causing them to cut down on the size of their holdings of cash *and other items* (such as working capital). The other items, of course, are stocks of materials and the like; the upshot is that the Twist may well be perverse in effect in the short run, cutting inventory investment immediately and affecting long-term investment only after a long delay. See the discussion of Operation Twist in Chapter 15. Note that nothing we have said here precludes one from analyzing the individual money holder by means of the inventory model; the firm is used here as a good example of a case where the model seems *likely* to apply.

16.3 THE ECONOMICS OF STOCK PRICES

No explanation of capital markets would be complete without a discussion of the determination of common stock prices, both day-to-day and over longer periods of time; as well, the popular averages of stock prices have a number of uses of interest to our various policy problems. In the first place, we will look at an approach to the firm in which the value of the equity (ownership stock) of a corporation is a key economic variable. We will claim that under normal conditions all economic influences, both internal and external to the firm, will be reflected in changes in the value of the equity of the firm, that is, if they affect the firm at all. In the second place, we are interested in the determination of stock prices themselves; of course, stock prices are obviously determined by supply and demand, but actually pinning down the determinants of these influences is a little tricky on account of the dominance of speculative behavior in stock markets. We will resort to several approaches in our discussion—with particular emphasis on the "random walk" model—and these will help to clarify things considerably. Then, in our general discussion we will link up with our earlier material in two ways:

a. We will explain the supply and demand for corporate debt and equity.
b. We will see what consequences the existence of an equity market has for monetary economics.

There is, inevitably, a lot of myth about the determination of day-to-day stock prices; and we must acknowledge that some of it may well be correct, at least in particular cases. The real question, from either the amateur's or the professional economist's point of view, ultimately concerns whether any system of forecasting (other than prior knowledge of the future earnings of the firm) can actually work in an *a priori* sense. The interest of the stock trader in successful prediction is obvious, of course, while that of the economist is somewhat less so. In fact, the economist gets involved because of the general questions of economic efficiency and, of course, because he may wish to incorporate stock prices in his forecasting model. With regard to the former interest, let it be noted that a competitive and efficient stock market is a desirable institution in a capitalist nation, especially if it can absorb large and/or numerous transactions in either new or old securities. Then, to the extent that the "net earnings" of firms are the principal determinants of firms' stock prices, one may also argue, the market will be correctly conveying vital information about the state of the economy.

In contrast, it is known that the stock market is quite sensitive to what appear to be large and random shocks. One apparent reason for this sensitivity is the thinness of the day-to-day market in many issues. That is, on any day in New York—even a big turnover day—only a very small percentage of the holders of each of the stocks traded actually participate in the market. Thus, on a daily basis the market is thin, and, if you want to sell, you will have to deal with those who came that day. If bad economic news comes at the same time, it might be that certain buyers hold off, in anticipation of a fall; this would mean that sellers might face temporarily lower prices. If the bad news is judged especially significant, this may even push down the popular stock averages, particularly those, like the Dow-Jones Industrial Average, which is composed of only a few stocks. The market *may* also react to good news; at any rate, whether or not it does,

a. The news itself is fairly random.

b. The sudden changes in stock prices are not great (in percentage terms) and tend to reverse themselves readily.

c. Many more "causes" are identified in the popular press than are ever likely to be proved to be relevant.

Indeed, the day-to-day fluctuations may well be *totally random* in spite of a lot of popular opinion to the contrary.[5]

One way we might find out whether systematic methods work is simply to see how much mileage we can get from the opposite—that is, from random methods of explanation. It is surprisingly difficult—surprising in view of the firmness of the mythology of the stock market—to show that any particular method or any particular set of institutions can outdo the random method. The basic input to the *random walk hypothesis* is the idea that the principal component of tomorrow's stock price (P_{t+1}) is today's price (P_t); a minor component is a random number (U_t) to represent the unpredictable day-to-day fluctuation:[6]

$$P_{t+1} = P_t + U_t. \tag{16.8}$$

When we come to predict tomorrow's price (P_{t+1}), we would take the "expected value" of both sides of Equation (16.8), this would give us Equation (16.9), for we expect that the mean of a series of random numbers, whose values can be as large positively as negatively, would be zero (that is, $E(U_t) = 0$):

$$E(P_{t+1}) = P_t. \tag{16.9}$$

The late Paul H. Cootner once explained the forces behind these expressions thus:

While individual buyers or sellers may act in ignorance, taken as a whole, the prices set in the marketplace thoroughly reflect the best evaluation of

[5] It is actually not very easy to predict which way the market will react to a given event, although when we read about it afterwards, the commentators' rationalizations often express considerable certitude as to what the most important influence was.

[6] Actually, it might be better to write $P_{t+1} = aP_t$ in order to account for the fact that expectations in general might be biased upward or downward. That is, stock prices could be systematically expected to rise ($a > 1$), fall ($a < 1$), or remain unchanged ($a = 1$) if traders have such biases.

currently available knowledge. If any substantial group of buyers thought prices were too low, their buying would force up the prices. The reverse would be true for sellers. Except for appreciation due to earnings retention, the conditional expectation of tomorrow's price, given today's price, is today's price.

In such a world, the only price changes that would occur are those which result from new information. Since there is no reason to expect that information to be nonrandom in its appearance, the period-to-period price changes of a stock should be random movements, statistically independent of one another.[7]

It will pay us, in coming to grips with this proposition, to think about the empirical side of the problem; what, indeed, constitutes a refutation of Equation (16.9)? Actually, the best way to state our hypothesis is to note that the best you can do to forecast tomorrow's price is to employ past data on price changes. If you do, though, since today's price embodies the entire influence of the past, you will be no better or no worse than anyone else in the market. That is, all who can read the newspaper and find today's prices are on equal ground, at least insofar as the influence of the past is concerned. Indeed, so long as no one can predict U_t (the random component of the stock price) on average, no one can do better than monitor the past price data (if this hypothesis is correct). If there are systematic influences contained in U_t, then the model is untrue.

While day-to-day fluctuations in common stock prices are, probably, essentially random (so far as any evidence goes), it is also known that individual common stock prices tend to follow the earnings of the individual corporations *in the long run*. This result is not inconsistent with the foregoing and, indeed, actually comes about because speculators are operating—successfully—in the stock market. Again returning to a statement by Paul H. Cootner, we can summarize this connection as follows:

Assuming that no investor exercises monopoly power in the market for the stock, the price at any time will be the weighted average of investor expectations, where the weights are the wealth the investor has invested or is prepared to invest in the market. If any group of investors was consistently better than average in forecasting stock prices, they would accumulate wealth and give their forecasts greater and greater weight. In the process they would bring the present price closer to the true value. Conversely, investors who were worse than average in forecasting ability would carry less and less weight. If this process worked well enough, the present price would reflect the best information about the future in the sense that the present price, plus normal profits, would be the best estimate of the future

[7] Paul H. Cootner, "Stock Prices: Random versus Systematic Changes," *Industrial Management Review*, vol. 3, no. 1 (Spring 1962), p. 25.

price. The existence of randomness in stock price changes does not imply that stock prices have no relationship to the real world of events, but only that investors make no systematic errors in forecasting those events.[8]

This is not the place to consider the evidence for these views in any detail, but, one can generalize, most students of the subject have conceded that individual stock prices follow a random pattern in the short run and basically follow net earnings in the long run. The behavior of the *averages,* as we will see below, is another matter.

16.4 THE SUPPLY OF EQUITY AND DEBT BY PROFIT-MAXIMIZING CORPORATE ENTITIES

When the business firm approaches the capital market for funds (whether it is planning to use debt, equity, or its own retained earnings), it is generally considering an investment (i.e., an expansion of plant, equipment, or inventories). When it undertakes an investment (as we discussed in Chapter 7 for the aggregate firm), there are a number of factors to consider. These are, generally,

a. The cost of the new equipment.

b. The expected returns from the investment (or investments).

c. The cost of borrowed funds (or the opportunity cost of using retained earnings).

In setting up its decision framework, the business firm will estimate its expected net earnings ($R_1, R_2, \ldots R_n$) for each future period ($1, 2, \ldots, n$) from undertaking a particular new investment. The cost (C) of the investment will then be compared with the stream of returns ($R_1, \ldots, R_n$), with the whole project evaluated by Equation (16.10):

$$C = \frac{R_1}{1 + r} + \frac{R_2}{(1 + r)^2} + \cdots + \frac{R_n + \text{scrap value}}{(1 + r)^n}. \qquad (16.10)$$

This equation is clearly a discounting formula;[9] but in this case the rate of discount (r), which bears the alternative labels of an *internal rate of return* or the *marginal efficiency of investment* (MEI) so long as we are talking about a profit-maximizing firm in perfect competition, is not a market variable as such.

---

[8] Paul H. Cootner, "Refinement and Empirical Testing: Introduction," in Paul H. Cootner (ed.), *The Random Character of Stock Market Prices* (Cambridge, Mass.; M.I.T. Press, 1964), p. 80. Reprinted by permission of MIT Press.

[9] Note that r is the "solution" to Equation (16.10), calculated after the other information has been gathered. Note that its use is essentially the same as that of the yield of Chapter 15, although here it is referred to as an *internal rate of return*.

The typical firm, then, will consider a range of projects, each, let us say, designated by a particular cost of a machine ($C_1, \ldots, C_k$); this will be the actual investment expenditure. Each of these projects will also have a stream of expected returns ($R_{1k}, \ldots, R_{nk}$), and consequently, each will have a different internal rate of return ($r_1, \ldots, r_k$). On the other hand, assuming that it deals in competitive markets, each firm will face a given cost of borrowed funds—i.e., a given interest rate of i—which represents, in effect, its budget constraint. The situation is depicted in Figure 16.2. There, as the interest rate (i) declines, additional projects will be-

Figure 16.2: The investment decision of a typical firm

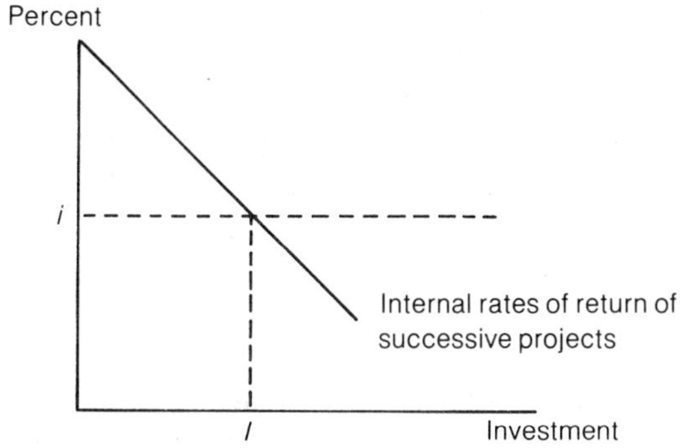

come profitable; this accounts for the negative slope of the "projects schedule" in Figure 16.2. For the market as a whole, as the cost of borrowed funds declines—other things being equal—firms will undertake more and more investment. The negatively sloped aggregate investment function of Chapter 7 evidently has pretty solid micro-foundations.

Turning to the data, we find that the typical business firm in the United States uses three main sources for its investment funds—retained earnings, bonds, and stocks—although all are, in principle (in a perfectly competitive environment) controlled by the rate of interest (i). As Table 16.1 suggests, however, the relative use of these components fluctuates considerably with general business conditions in the United States. As noted in Chapter 13, the credit crunches of 1966, 1969, and 1973 do not seem to have slowed down business investment in those years, although it is apparent that investment slowed down later (in 1967, 1971, and 1975, as indicated in the table), as the "accelerator principle" would suggest.[10]

[10] Alternatively, it is just that investment projects take some time to initiate, *and to stop*, so that (for example) the result for 1967 is simply the result of decisions made in 1966, during the high interest rate period. Note that this delayed effect of monetary policy (if that is what it is) is one of the reasons why some Monetarists argue that active monetary policy is dangerous.

Table 16.1: Sources of corporate funds, 1965–1978 ($ billions)

	New security issues				
	Bonds	*Stocks*	*Undistributed profits*	*Business expenditures on new plant and equipment*	*Ratio bonds to stocks*
1965	13.7	2.3	26.7	52.0	5.96
1966	15.6	2.5	29.1	60.6	6.24
1967	22.0	2.8	25.9	61.7	7.86
1968	17.4	4.6	24.2	64.1	3.78
1969	18.3	8.4	20.5	71.2	2.18
1970	30.3	8.6	14.6	79.7	3.52
1971	32.0	12.9	21.1	81.2	2.48
1972	27.7	13.1	30.3	88.4	2.11
1973	22.3	11.1	43.3	99.7	2.01
1974	32.1	6.2	52.4	112.4	5.18
1975	42.8	10.9	40.9	112.8	3.93
1976	42.4	11.1	56.4	120.1	3.82
1977	42.2	12.0	61.3	135.7	3.52
1978	35.2	10.1	68.9	153.6	3.48

Source: *Federal Reserve Bulletin*.

Note, too, that in 1969, corporations made more use of stock issues, probably because of the rapid decline in undistributed corporate profits. In 1970, during the recession, undistributed corporate profits fell further, drying up that source of funds, and corporations turned this time to debt issue; this pattern was repeated in 1975. Note that when corporate retained earnings (and profits) spurt ahead, as in 1971–73, outside sources (bonds and stocks) are typically avoided. So there is a strong cyclical pattern to the quantity of debt and equity used for corporate investment and this seems to come *not* from a cyclical pattern in investment demand itself, but from the cyclical behavior of corporate profits. Overall, the corporate investment figures themselves seem remarkably stable in this table (taken on an annual basis), although the method of finance changes rather dramatically. Note, finally, that 1978 found firms increasing their expenditures on plant and equipment, but shunning both bonds and stocks in favor of retained earnings and (other) liquid sources. It seems that a prerecession pattern of "tight" money may well influence the results for that year. "Tight" here means merely that firms may have judged the interest rates on bonds to be (temporarily) too high.

But not only is there a cyclical pattern in the total of new corporate debt and equity, there is a pattern in the ratio of the two; consider the last column in Table 16.1. Quite possibly, corporations prefer to use internal sources, but given their overall needs for investment funds, they also have to go to the market; when they do this on a large scale they will increase the supply of either debt of equity, depending on the circumstances. Thus in the recession of 1970 they shifted sharply toward debt finance; they also did this in the recession of 1974. But debt as a percentage of new funds has recently declined from the figures ruling in the mid-1960s, as we can see, by comparing 1965–67 with 1976–78.

The corporation, of course, is not indifferent to the composition of its capital structure, and will (in line with our earlier comments on portfolio behavior) consider both the relative cost and the relative risk associated with each method of finance. The costs will vary with market conditions, of course, but the risks, in general, will vary with the firm's overall debt-equity ratio. In particular, debt implies a fixed interest payment, and it is the ratio of the interest bill to corporate earnings that might measure the risk to the firm; the risk, in particular, is that corporate earnings will be inadequate to meet the interest payments (in a bad year) and that the firm will have to default on its interest payments (to fail, in effect). Clearly, indeed, the more variable the firm's earnings, the lower will be the desirable ratio of debt to equity; further, in industries with generally variable sales (and earnings), the debt-equity ratios will be low compared to, say, public utilities, whose earnings are very stable. Such, in fact, is what we tend to observe.

The central question behind all of this concerns whether or not a new variable—D/E for the debt-equity ratio—ought to be included in the investment function, of the firm, of the industry, and of the macroeconomic model. The following propositions can be deduced, under perfectly competitive (market) conditions.

a. The *market* value of the firm is independent of its debt-equity ratio.

b. The expected yield on a share of the firm's stock depends on the debt-equity ratio.

c. The quantity of investment does not depend on the method of finance (on the debt-equity ratio).

In illustration, suppose that a firm (Company A) has 100 shares of equity (stock) currently valued at \$8 per share in the market; the market value of equity would then be \$800. Suppose the firm has debt of \$200 and earnings of \$100 and suppose that the market interest rate is 0.05. The total "value of the firm" would then be \$1,000; its debt-equity ratio would be .25, and the rate of return on its equity can then be calculated simply as

$$r = \frac{\text{Profits}}{\text{Value of equity}} = \frac{\$90}{\$800} = 0.11.$$

Note that the only cost we are considering in this analysis is the interest expense (.05 × \$200 = \$10). This firm has more risk than a completely unlevered (debt-free) firm in the same industry, obviously; therefore, the rate of return on the common stock of this the firm should be higher in order to compensate for the greater risk (as we pointed out in Chapter 14). Let us assume that an unlevered firm, Company *B*, has the same earnings of $100 and has a market value of $1,000; its rate of return on equity will then be 10 percent ($100/$1000). Note that this figure is equal to debt plus equity for Company *A*.

Let us accept this as an equilibrium statement (we are referring to stock investor's equilibrium) and see what is likely to happen to the price of the first company's stock if it tries to increase its leverage (its *D/E*). Since it is the reaction of stockholders that determines what happens, let us take the viewpoint of a representative stockholder, let us say one who, to begin with, holds 10 shares of Company *A*, the levered firm, and no shares of Company *B*, the unlevered one. The data so far assumed are summarized in Table 16.2. The individual stockholder will have personal leverage of

Table 16.2: A levered versus an unlevered firm

	Company A	*Company B*
Earnings	$ 100	$ 100
Equity value	800	1,000
Debt value	200	—
Company value	1,000	1,000
r	0.112	0.100
Cost of capital	0.100	0.100

.25, which is equal to company leverage, since he is holding only Company *A*'s equity and, we assume, he is satisfied with this portfolio. Now suppose that Company *A* issues $200 more of debt and retires $200 of stock, thus raising its leverage coefficient to .67. If this deal is profitable, as it seems to be—since the rate of return for the firm is greater than the interest rate (.11 versus .05)—the price of the firm's common stock rises 25 percent, from $8 to $10 per share. Company *A* now has net earnings of $100 – 0.05 ($400) = $80; and its common stock, of which there are now 75 shares, is valued at $750.

The first thing we notice is that hypothesis (*a*) above—that the firm's value is unaffected by the debt-equity rate—is violated because Company *A* is now valued at $400 + $750 = $1,150, and the hypothesis asserts that it should be valued at $1,000. The second thing is that the individual stockholder who did not sell his shares of Company *A* now has a much higher debt-equity ratio (more default risk) than he originally seemed to be happy with and will want to rearrange his portfolio—in fact, he will want to sell some of this stock in Company *A*. The reason he will do this now can be seen clearly; the rate of return on equity is actually lower in the second case than in the first—it is now 0.107—and the stockholder has a much riskier security. The situation is depicted in Figure 16.3. We actually

Figure 16.3: Risk and return for the individual stockholder

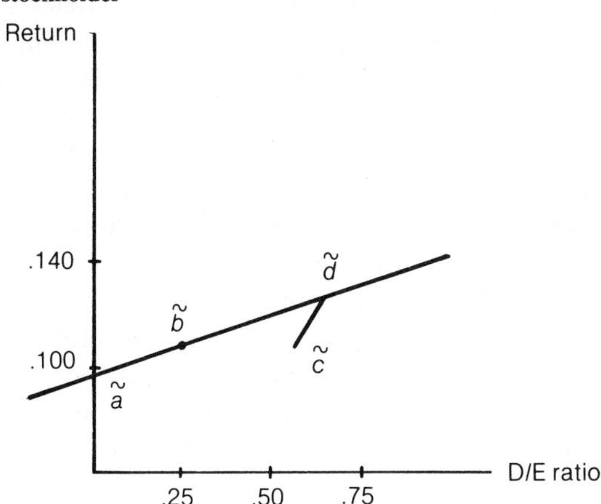

have stated only one point on the investor's risk-return profile—.25 debt-equity to .112 earnings (at point $\tilde{b}$)—but we may assume he was aware of the riskless alternative (point $\tilde{a}$) in which all of his funds are invested in Company *B*. For the new situation he is at point $\tilde{c}$, which is clearly inferior to $\tilde{b}$ (involving considerably more risk and *less* return).

The individual's reaction to being thrust into an inferior position by Company *A*'s financial policy will be to sell shares of Company *A*; he may do this until he reaches point $\tilde{d}$ on the original trade-off line between *A* and *B*. Point $\tilde{d}$ represents a market price for *A* of $600 and a rate of return of .133; at that point the market value of the firm is back to $600 + $400 = $1000, as proposition (*a*) asserts. The investor, of course, will not sit at point $\tilde{d}$, but will probably move back down to point $\tilde{b}$ by purchasing stock of Company *B*. This assumes that $\tilde{b}$ was the best point on the line in the first place. Thus, when it is all over, Company *A* has an unchanged value and higher rate of return on equity, in accord with proposition (*b*). Individual stock holders, rejecting the riskier method of finance, brought this result about by selling the stock of the company to get back into their desired risk-return position.

We will not undertake a formal proof of proposition (*c*), but we ought to consider its rationale, at least. Indeed, when one is considering a new investment project under the assumptions we have adopted, the method of finance will not affect the choice of project, and the critical factor will be the rate of return that is common in the industry. Thus, we may paraphrase all three propositions by saying that the overall hypothesis amounts to the argument that the critical elements considered by the firm before it undertakes an investment project (or changes its method of acquiring finance) is what effect the project will have on the market value of the firm's common stock. If the project is expected to raise the market value, the firm will go ahead, for the market is then being expected to judge the additional risk as more than compensated for by the higher earnings. When put this way, the argument is eminently sensible.

We should, before we turn to the behavior of the popular stock averages, consider some qualifications to the foregoing. We have assumed perfect competition (and, hence, full knowledge) and we have also assumed no "investor inertia" in the foregoing, and these are not entirely reasonable for all situations. In addition, we have said nothing about tax laws or about retained earnings. Suppose, for example, that Company *A* and Company *B* are both subject to a 50 percent corporate income tax on their net earnings. If the two firms are in equilibrium in Table 16.3, then introduction of the tax provision changes the situation, for Company *A* has a tax deduction in the form of interest payments of $10 that Company *B* does not have. Thus, the value of Company *A* is understated; and as the ratio of debt to equity grows, the value of Company *A* diverges from that of Company *B*. Since we actually have such a tax law in the United States, the capital structure of the firms in our economy depends on the debt-equity ratio; the basic economic forces are those described above, but they must be qualified to this extent. With regard to retained earnings, consider the figures of Table 16.1 again. There one can see that the retained earnings of corporations are generally the most important element in their generation of investment funds. One reason we might reasonably be surprised at this is that the *implicit* cost of using these funds is the same as the *explicit* cost of floating a bond issue; that is, the firm should charge itself the market rate of interest on its borrowings from itself. The usual direct answer to this is that by using its own funds the firm will be able to avoid dealing for funds in a highly variable market (and will avoid brokerage fees). One of the variable elements in that market is well known: monetary policy probably affects the availability of funds to corporate users, and this uneveness they would just as soon avoid. But of equal importance is the fact that when a firm retains its earnings rather than distribute them, the shareholders will—if the firm is as successful in its new ventures as it was in its old (i.e., does not reduce the profit rate)—be taxed at the capital gains rate rather than at the income tax rate. Thus, for individuals with higher marginal tax rates on income than on capital gains, it would pay to buy shares of a "growth stock"—i.e., a company that favored growth in the value of its common stock over increased dividends. A wide variety of such choices, even within particular industries, can be made. Again, a firm is seen to be able to affect the market value of its stock by adjusting its capital structure, so again the basic hypotheses of this section must be adjusted for this consideration.

There are other, more specialized, qualifications that have been raised concerning these cost-of-capital theorems. Most of these are objections to the competitiveness and frictionless nature of the assumed world, factors that we generally must consider in the final analysis. For example, there is surely some difference between borrowing rates for big firms and for small; and there are transactions costs that make personal arbitrage expensive and that vary depending on the size of the customer's account. Further, there is the limited liability feature of owning corporate stock, so that, for example, an individual may prefer to borrow through a levered corporation rather than on his own hook. We could go on like this indefinitely, but instead let us state our results somewhat more broadly than we have explained them as follows. The price of the equity of a private corporation will depend on:

a. The rate of return on its physical assets.
b. The debt-equity ratio of the corporation.
c. The dividend payout rate of the corporation.
d. The cost of borrowed funds.

It will further be constrained by

e. The availability of borrowed funds.
f. Tax laws.

These factors, presumably, will affect the relative supplies of debt and equity to the financial markets, and that, ultimately, is the point of this exercise.

16.5 MONEY AND STOCK PRICES

The general points about investors concerning common stocks and money have already been made; that is, common stocks, like money and bonds, are a distinct type of financial asset; and when an individual chooses among these broad categories, he will weigh return versus risk for each instrument. How you proceed in the further disaggregation of these categories depends on the problem in hand; for example, one might wish to have M_1 and M_3, or preferred and common stocks, but the general rules of the model of Chapter 14 are still relevant no matter what the degree of disaggregation. That leaves us with three main topics:

a. The behavior of stock averages.
b. The relation between stock prices and rates of inflation.
c. The relation between stocks (and the stock market) and monetary policy.

Let us take these up in turn.

There are two main stock indexes in general use—the popular Dow-Jones average of 30 industrial stocks and the Standard & Poor's index of the stock prices of 500 corporations—and both of these are usually available in daily newspapers. The broadly based Standard & Poor index is obviously more reliable as an index of overall trends in stocks and, further, has a place in the list of *leading* indicators in the Composite Leading Indicators Index discussed in Chapter 12. It has a place there because the stock market consistently signals the end of a boom period in the economy well in advance of the turning points in the general figures on employment, output, etc. Of course, this signal is not unambiguous and, indeed, (*a*) the length of the lead is quite variable, (*b*) it sometimes misses a cyclical turning point, and (*c*) it often signals a turning point when none arrives. But it is still a very popular (and useful) guide to investor expectations of the behavior of future corporate earnings.

Turning to concerns of more than financial interest, let us consider the relation between stock prices and rates of inflation. For one thing, we have noticed that corporate profits may be sensitive to inflation rates (we noted that banks often actually have increased profits when there is rapid inflation). That is, it is possible that there are "profit inflations" or "profit squeezes," and if there are, corporate stock prices should respond. Indeed, in Table 16.1 we could argue that 1975, in which inflation stayed high while the economy was moving out of the recession, showed up as a profit squeeze on corporations that were unable to pass on the "pushed costs" negotiated in 1973 and, especially, 1974 (the rate of inflation in 1974 was 11.0 percent in consumer prices and 18.8 percent in wholesale prices).

There is a second aspect to the inflation-stock price relationship and that concerns the hedge-against-inflation argument in favor of common stocks. Suppose that individuals expect business firms, whose product prices might reasonably be expected to be marked up in inflation, to have increased nominal earnings in exact proportion to the inflation. Presumably individuals will then tend to switch from bonds to common stocks, because nominal returns on bonds are fixed while the nominal earnings of corporations are expected to keep approximately in line with inflation. Under these conditions, the prices of the bonds sold will fall (and bond yields will rise) while the prices of common stocks will rise. Thus, we would expect the differences between the yields on the two instruments, calculated on an average, to be a reasonably good index of expected inflation. Furthermore, if expected inflation is closely related to actual inflation, we would expect this yield difference to widen with more rapid rises in prices and to narrow when prices rise more slowly. This has a unique value in our macro model, if correct, because this would give us a measure of $(\Delta P/P)_e$ for use in our real interest rate–nominal interest rate equations in Chapter 9, for instance.

The data, though, show us that even though there is a gap between the two yields and even though this gap widens with *actual* inflation rates, the

Table 16.3: Inflation and corporate bond and stock prices, 1962–1975

	Percent change in consumer prices	*Corporate bond yields (percent)*	*Corporate dividend-price ratio (percent)*	*Col. 2 minus col. 3*	*Corporate earnings-price ratio (percent)*
1962	1.15	4.62	3.37	1.25	6.06
1963	1.23	4.50	3.17	1.33	5.68
1964	1.31	4.57	3.01	1.56	5.54
1965	1.65	4.64	3.00	1.64	5.87
1966	2.91	5.34	3.40	1.94	6.72
1967	2.82	5.82	3.20	2.62	5.71
1968	4.21	6.51	3.07	3.44	5.84
1969	5.36	7.36	3.24	4.12	6.05
1970	5.92	8.51	3.83	4.68	6.46
1971	4.21	7.94	3.14	4.80	5.41
1972	3.38	7.63	2.84	4.79	5.50
1973	6.22	7.80	3.06	4.74	7.12
1974	10.97	8.98	4.47	4.51	11.60
1975	9.14	9.46	4.31	5.15	9.03

Source: *Federal Reserve Bulletin.*

relationship is not a particularly neat one; the data for some recent years are collected in Table 16.3. Actually, until 1972, a pretty close relation is observable, with the difference between the corporate bond yield and the corporate dividend-price ratio moving up with the rate of inflation; if this difference is the expected rate of inflation in $i_b = i_s + (\Delta P/P)_e$, then in 1972 expected inflation was (correctly) actually greater than actual inflation. But after 1972, and especially for 1974 and 1975, corporate bond rates did not seem to be responding to *actual* inflation (although, of course, they still could have been responding to *expected* inflation, although these "expectations" were clearly in error, after the fact). Indeed, the corporate earning-price ratio, which was relatively constant through 1972 (as one might expect by the stock-hedge argument) actually took off after 1972. In a nutshell, corporate earnings seem to have kept pace with inflation, but corporate stock prices did not. This, consequently, might suggest that investors found other hedges against inflation (such as real estate) and thus weakened the link between inflation and stock prices. Of course it is also possible that corporate profits, themselves, were not expected to keep pace with inflation (because of an expected profits squeeze).

There are, of course, more direct relations between money and stock prices having to do with general credit conditions—that is, with the quality and cost of credit—and with monetary policy. The most obvious relation occurs on account of the regulation of stock market margin requirements (see Table 10.7), which is under the control of the Board of Governors of the Federal Reserve. These requirements are not varied much (we went through the inflation of 1973–75 without a change), but when they are raised (as in November 1972, when they were pushed up from 55 to 65 percent) the stock market usually reacts sharply. The stock market also reacts (although not often by very much) to changes in the discount rate and even to the release of published figures on the money stock (when a large change occurs). These factors can be added to the long list of potential "causes" of the day-to-day fluctuations in stock prices.

In the case of the changes just mentioned there is actually some substance to the market response to money stock figures, although, of course, not on a day-to-day basis. Thus, consider the figures in Table 16.4, which

Table 16.4: Common stocks and money, 1960–1978

	Percent change in Standard & Poor's index	*Percent change in M_1*
1960	−3.5	0.6
1961	17.8	3.1
1962	−6.4	1.5
1963	12.0	3.7
1964	17.4	4.6
1965	8.4	4.6
1966	−2.6	2.6
1967	0.9	6.6
1968	7.4	8.0
1969	−0.9	3.3
1970	−14.9	5.2
1971	18.1	6.5
1972	11.1	9.2
1973	−1.6	6.0
1974	−22.9	4.6
1975	2.8	4.1
1976	19.8	5.9
1977	−3.8	7.4
1978	−2.1	7.8

Source: *Federal Reserve Bulletin.*

shows annual percentage changes in the Standard & Poor's index compared to percentage changes in the money stock since 1960. These figures suggest that tight and loose money, in the sense of the rate of growth of the money stock, did seem to be related to stock price behavior in the 1960s. Indeed, a pretty sharp inverse relation seems apparent there, although in the 1970s it is hard to pick up any strong relation. This latter result, no doubt, is because of factors, already discussed in this section, affecting corporate profits, as well as, of course, the confusion that inflation itself brings to nominal figures like those in Table 16.4. In that connection, we should note, the hypothesis is that tight money (or easy money) affects the stock market; this actually cannot be ascertained by inspection of the money stock data alone. Thus a 4.6 percent growth of the money stock in 1974, with inflation roaring along at 11 percent, probably reflects tight money, while in 1964, a similar growth rate is probably easy money (up from a growth rate of 3.7 percent) in view of an inflation rate of 1.3 percent.[11] And, finally, we should recall, both sets of figures respond to general business conditions, with the former, almost certainly, responding to *expected* business conditions.

16.6 STUDY QUESTIONS

Essay questions

1. How is it possible that day-to-day fluctuations in stock prices may be random and long-period ones systematic? Is not the long run the sum of the short runs? What, then, must be true about day-to-day fluctuations?

2. The stock market analyst usually referred to in newspapers is a shadowy figure indeed. It is noticeable, for example, that the analyst will use the same phenomenon—for example, an outbreak of war in the Middle East—for support of opposite movements in stock prices. Does it follow that the analyst is taking nonsense, or is there some economic reasoning behind all of this?

3. Does the thinness of the stock market have anything to do with the apparently large fluctuations in stock prices one observes? Are the fluctuations actually as large as they seem? Look at some recent data for a typical blue chip stock—using closing prices—and work out, for various margin requirements, the profits that could have been made if your foresight had been as good as your hindsight. Don't forget to include transactions costs.

4. Comment on the following news item: "The market yesterday was reasonably firm, with gains outnumbering advances by 4 to 3. The Dow-Jones Industrial Average was off .60 on rumors that the Boeing 767 was having engine trouble. Otherwise the market would have been marginally higher."

5. Why is the behavior of common stock prices dominated by expectations? Which expectations serve an economic function and which do not (if any do not)? How did you decide to define an economic function in your answer?

---

[11] An inflation of 11 percent requires an 11 percent increase in the quantity of money "to feed itself." To put it another way, to stay even, the demanders of money, in an 11 percent inflation, would need an 11 percent increase in the stock of money. In 1974 they were only provided 4.6 percent and, hence, money may well have been tight.

6. What connection is there between the cost of capital and the corporate supply of debt instruments? Do all debt-issuing organizations go through the same procedure to arrive at their optimal strategy? Do individuals? Explain.

7. We emphasized that the market value of a firm's equity is a key variable and, earlier, that banks are business firms. Could you work out the effect of monetary policy on the system by looking at the value of bank equity? What sorts of effects might turn up? Do expectations get in the way at all?

8. If common stocks are such a good hedge against inflation, why did the stock market drift downward from 1965 to 1970 at exactly the same time that the rate of inflation was rising? Give both a monetary and an expectations explanation of these events.

True-false discussion questions

These statements are meant to be somewhat ambiguous and to provoke discussion, thereby.

1. When the rate of change of the money stock increases, the easier money will affect stock market indexes primarily through the availability of stock market credit.

2. Firms that use retained earnings as a source of investment funds clearly save money (in the form of interest charges).

3. If common stock prices are determined entirely by speculative activity, then no hypothesis ever will beat the random walk hypothesis.

4. The stock market indexes could correctly predict future downturns in the economy, even though the individuals involved in stock ownership cannot.

5. While individual common stocks follow a random walk, the popular averages clearly do not, since the latter often correctly predict business cycle turning points.

16.7 FURTHER READING

Dougall, Herbert E., and Jack E. Gaumnitz. *Capital Markets and Institutions.* Englewood Cliffs, N.J.; Prentice-Hall, 1975.

Eiteman, Wilford J., Charles A. Dice, and David K. Eiteman. *The Stock Market.* New York: McGraw-Hill, 1969.

Solomon, Ezra, and John J. Pringle. *An Introduction to Financial Management.* Santa Monica, Calif.: Goodyear Publishing Co., 1976.

Sprinkel, Beryl. *Money and Stock Prices.* Homewood, Ill.: Richard D. Irwin, Inc., 1964.

Part IV

International financial markets

17

Exchange rates and the balance of payments

17.1 INTRODUCTION

In this chapter we begin our study of international financial markets with a description of how these markets work; this study is continued into Chapter 18, where we consider how fiscal and monetary policy can be conducted in a world that has substantial capital and goods transfers between nations. In addition, in Chapter 18, we will undertake a discussion of the recent "monetarist approach" to the balance of payments and will see how this approach fits into the general analytic and policy issues of Chapters 17 and 12).

What we will seek to do in Chapter 17, though, is to lay out the basic facts concerning the determination of exchange rates, on the one hand, and the nature of the balance of payments accounts (mainly of the United States) on the other. This is a somewhat technical chapter in some ways, but there is considerable relief here, nevertheless, in the form of illustrative material from recent history. Indeed, some amazing things have happened in international finance in recent years, and it is one of the tasks of this chapter to provide as much information as possible on these matters, especially as they impinge on the rapidly changing American situation. Indeed, toward the end of this chapter we will discuss the "international money muddle'' that has developed in the world since long before the Second World War, culminating in a system of variable exchange rates that has often been referred to as the dirty float (in the 1970s).

17.2 THE DETERMINATION OF EXCHANGE RATES

When an individual in the United States buys a British product, he usually does so after comparing the British price with the American price (assuming there is a comparable product in each country). Now there are actually three prices involved in this transaction, not two, for the American price is quoted in dollars and the British in pounds; indeed, in addition to the two separate prices, one must also know the *rate of exchange* (which is the third ''price'') between the two currencies before he knows whether the British pound price is lower in terms of dollars. The use of the exchange rate between two countries is actually quite straightforward, although the analysis is often quite cumbersome. If, for example, the British product cost £12 delivered to New York and the American equivalent cost $25 at the same delivery point, then, if the exchange rate is around $1.80 per pound (or, what is exactly the same thing, 56 pence per dollar), the British price translates into $21.60 at that exchange rate; the better buy is, accordingly, the British product.

The exchange rate between the dollar and the pound is currently a market-determined rate, although both governments (especially the British) attempt to stabilize it somewhat when it moves too rapidly for their respective tastes. Thus, a simple supply-and-demand analysis is appropriate. The American who wishes to buy the British product may either send the British dealer a check written in dollars or buy pounds at his local bank and send them in the form of a cashier's check or draft. In either event, as suggested in Figure 17.1, when we analyze the supply and demand for the British pound, in this deal, the American importer is a *demander* of pounds.[1] Similarly, a British importer is one of the ultimate suppliers of pounds (or, if you wish, demanders of dollars). That is, the American importer may (*a*) either supply dollars (demand pounds) directly, in which case the British exporter obtains the dollars and has them converted (by his bank) to pounds, or (*b*) deal with an American bank by buying pounds (a bank draft) and sending them to the British exporter. In the first case a British bank has a dollar-denominated check to clear through the exchange market while in the second, when the U.S. bank buys pounds (for the American importer), it will do so, in effect, in the

[1] If we were analyzing the supply and demand for dollars, we would visualize the American importer as the *supplier* of funds. It does not matter whether we analyze the market for dollars or the market for pounds, as they are perfect opposites in this example (assuming only two currencies).

foreign exchange market. Both ways of performing the operation go through the foreign exchange market that deals in pounds and dollars, and *both* imply a rightward shift of the demand schedule in Figure 17.1. There,

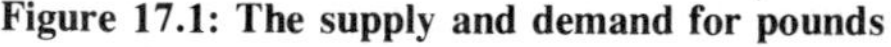

Figure 17.1: The supply and demand for pounds

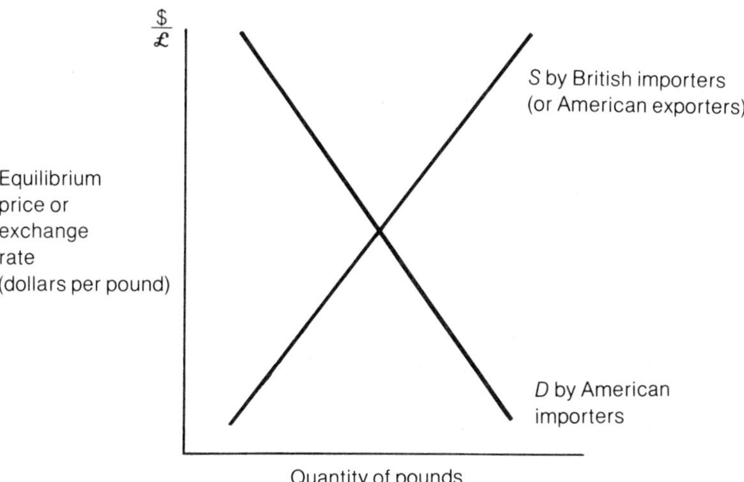

as well, we illustrate a supply-of-pounds schedule where the supply of pounds (or, if you wish, demand for dollars) arises from the import of American goods by (for example) British buyers. Note, finally, that these supply-and-demand schedules apply to all exchange-using transactions and thus involve all market-related transfers between the economic agents (or governments) of nations; these are, categorically,

a. Transfers of goods and services.
b. Private capital transfers.
c. Official capital transfers (when the market is used).

We will want to think of the exchange rates between national currencies as determined in this broader context.

In Figure 17.1 we labeled the horizontal axis "quantity of pounds"; this means, of course, the value of pounds exchanged measured *in British currency units*. The vertical axis was labeled the price of pounds; this price is the number of dollars each pound will fetch, and is denoted $/£1 or simply $/£. It is a ratio of prices—an exchange rate—and, as such, contains two different currency units, one in the numerator and one in the denominator; we may, though, refer to its unit as "dollars" (or better, "dollars per pound"). Thus, when the pound appreciates in value—when it fetches more dollars—we will find $/£ higher; this accords with common sense. To see this clearly, consider what happens when an American suddenly decides to purchase more British products (to import them). To do this the American must obtain British pounds in the foreign exchange market (since his bill will be in pounds). This directly produces a new demand for pounds and a rightward shift of the demand curve in Figure 17.1; in turn this tends to increase the $/£ exchange rate (the price of pounds).

Figure 17.2: A fixed payment system

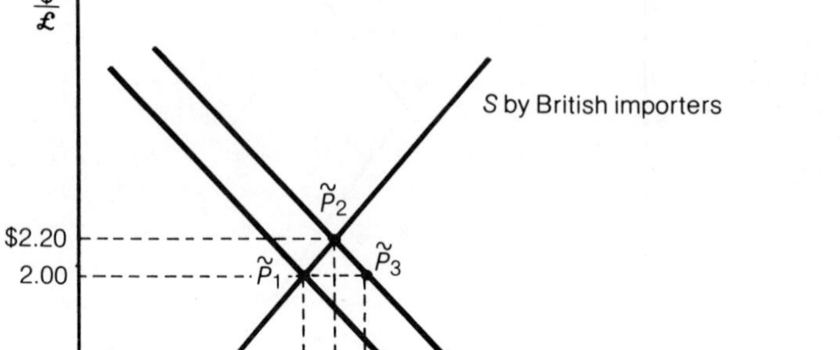

To see another way in which the market operates, consider a second diagram, in Figure 17.2, in which a system that no longer operates, the fixed-exchange-rate system, is depicted. Let us suppose, here, that we are in initial equilibrium at a quantity of pounds transferred in the exchange markets of £10 billion and a price of $2 for £1; equilibrium is at $\tilde{P}_1$. If we assume that Americans, perhaps because of a boom in the United States (which raises incomes and hence foreign spending) or because American prices are rising faster than British prices, increase their demands for British products or capital, then the demand for pounds will shift, to D_2. Now under the conditions of Figure 17.1 this would imply, as Figure 17.2 is drawn, an increase in the value of the pound to $2.20 per £ and a clearing at $\tilde{P}_2$ (where £11 billion are exchange for dollars).

But suppose instead, that the American government wished to keep the $/£ exchange rate at $2 per £ as part of its strategy of maintaining generally fixed exchange rates with all major currencies. If we are talking about market rates here, then what the U.S. government has to do, since the demand for pounds is greater than the supply of $2.20 per pound, is to provide £2 billion to the market, at least in the illustration in Figure 17.2.[2] If they actually have £2 billion in their coffers (in New York at the Federal Reserve Bank), then all is well (except, of course, that some of the U.S. reserves of British money have gone); note, in particular, since a supply of pounds is a demand for dollars, that the U.S. government gets (its own) dollars back. If the U.S. government does not have pounds, it can also get them by selling off gold (or using its IMF balance—see below); in this case it still ends up with dollars but its gold stock or its IMF credit balance has decreased. In any event, it should be clear, stabilization (or fixing) of exchange rates involves holding a quantity of acceptable international reserves of gold, International Monetary Fund (IMF) balances, and foreign currencies with active and stable markets; under present conditions, with a managed (or "dirty") float for the dollar against other currencies, this reserve is still used actively; at the end of 1978 it was $18.6 billion, valued in terms of an index of major-country exchange rates.[3]

Actually, the preceding analysis applies strictly to what are called *spot* (or current) *exchange rates;* the spot rate is the rate for immediate delivery of funds in the exchange markets. In Table 17.1 we illustrate a sample of spot exchange rates taken from the IMF publication *International Finan-*

Table 17.1: Spot exchange rates, March 1978 (currency units per U.S. dollar)

	March 1	*March 16*	*March 31*	*Direction of change*
Australian dollar	.878812	.879198	.874814	−
Austrian schilling	14.3975	14.6525	14.5650	+
Belgian franc	31.1100	31.6600	31.4800	+
British pound	.514060	.523505	.538706	+
Canadian dollar	1.1170	1.1235	1.1322	+
Danish krone	5.5210	5.5975	5.5640	+
French franc	4.70750	4.69300	4.58050	−
German mark	1.9920	2.0356	2.0230	+
Italian lira	849.30	857.05	852.50	+
Japanese yen	238.00	233.00	222.40	−
Netherlands guilder	2.1440	2.1730	2.1635	+
Norwegian krone	5.2400	5.3025	5.3080	+
South African rand*	.869565	.869565	.869565	None
Spanish peseta	79.738	79.802	80.023	+
Swedish krona	4.5690	4.6115	4.5888	+
SDR	.809547	.813432	.808621	−

* Stabilized.
Source: International Monetary Fund, *International Financial Statistics*.

[2] Note that in fact it is usually the British government that intervenes in the market to stabilize the rate, not the American government.

[3] At the end of 1970, when the United States was on the fixed rate system, the reserve stood at $14.5 billion, but that was before the great inflation in the world economy (which started in 1971, roughly).

cial Statistics for March 1978; they are in foreign currencies per U.S. dollar. These rates reflect market forces, as already noted; thus, in March 1978, the U.S. dollar improved against 11 of the 15 currencies in the table but actually fell against the SDR rate (a weighted average of the 16 currencies); this clearly, was because of the fall of 6.5 percent in the Japanese yen/U.S. dollar rate in that month (the fall continued for several months thereafter). Finally, note that these rates are often very volatile, even on a day-to-day basis.

But foreign exchange markets also exist in future exchange contracts; these are forward exchange markets—markets in which one can buy and sell currencies for future delivery (or future payment)—to deal with the needs of hedgers (and speculators) in different currencies. A *forward exchange rate* is simply the rate of exchange between two currencies defined at a particular future date; that is, you can buy or sell pounds *forward* in the currency futures market. On June 30, 1978, for example, the *spot* rate for pounds was $1.8530/£; the following futures rates (or forward rates) were also quoted that day:

30 days	$1.8400
90 days	$1.8400
180 days	$1.8260.

Now the most obvious user of this market is someone who wishes to protect himself (*hedge*) against exchange rate risk. If, for example, you are expecting to have to pay £100 in 90 days, and you do not want to bear the risk that the pound will be more expensive than $1.8530 in 90 days, you can buy pounds *for delivery in 90 days* at the rate of $1.8400; you "buy" them now, but you do not actually have to deliver the funds (dollars) until you get your British funds, in 90 days. This, actually, looks like a good deal, although you forego any gains you might have made if, in 90 days, the pound were cheaper than $1.84, because (transactions costs aside) the pound delivered in 90 days is cheaper than the pound delivered at present (*perhaps* because the pound was expected by the market to fall in value over the 90 days). On the other hand, if you had wanted German marks that day, you would have been faced with

Spot	$.4823
30 days	.4844
90 days	.4888
180 days	.4961,

perhaps because the market expected the mark to gain in value, compared to the dollar, over the 180 days after June 30, 1978.

This process is called *covering* against (or *hedging* against) exchange rate risk and describes what is generally thought to be the most important economic function of the futures market in currencies (at least to those dealing in commodities internationally). By this means anyone in the world expecting to pay pounds in 90 days has the chance of buying them now for future delivery and avoiding any exchange risk in pounds. Similarly, anyone in Britain (let us say) who has to have a foreign currency in 90 days can *buy* that foreign currency forward, *selling* pounds forward. Thus, both sides of the market will normally tend to exist and the forward exchange rate will clearly be determined at a level that clears the market of forward funds. On the other hand, hedgers are not alone in this market; there are those who are partly covered and many who are not covered at all. Indeed, most people are "long" (uncovered) in their own currency (although they do not contemplate any foreign exchange dealing, usually). To the extent that one is uncovered (unhedged), he is, by definition, a *speculator,* at least as we defined this term (broadly) in Chapter 16. But the most active speculators in this market—the gnomes of Switzerland by popular legend—are those who take up foreign exchange risk deliberately, in the expectation of speculative profits. Thus, if one actually expected the pound to rise, not fall, compared to the dollar in the 90 days after June 30, 1978, he may well have bought pounds (sold dollars) forward on the basis of this belief. That sort of speculation we might again term *active* speculation to distinguish it from the more casual sort undertaken (perhaps unwittingly) by, e.g., tourists (and, of course, by those who never dream of a foreign purchase directly).

The foregoing is written as if speculation occurs in actual currencies—i.e., in printed bank notes—but that is generally not the case. In fact, only quick profits tend to be taken in deposits (denominated in the relevant currency), and the more usual longer-term gains are generally taken in short-term securities. Indeed, a 90-day speculation could be engineered in Treasury bills, although when that is done, any difference in the respective Treasury bill rates becomes part of the problem. Thus, an American business firm that needs pounds in 90 days and has the cash now, could buy British 90-day Treasury bills (converting its dollars at the spot exchange rate); if it did so, it would get its pounds in 90 days *and earn* 9.13 percent (the British Treasury bill rate). If the funds were kept in the United States, and put into U.S. Treasury bills (at 7.00 percent), then pounds would have to be bought forward (at the rate of $1.8400); clearly, we can now see *one* reason that on June 30, 1978 the (dollar) forward rate for pounds was lower than the spot rate: the British Treasury bill rate was higher than the American Treasury bill rate. Of course, such differences—between interest rates internationally—are of interest to investors other than currency dealers, and the forward market actually provides the means whereby an investor in one country can safely move his funds between the Treasury bills of two different countries. The process, indeed, is one important reason that one can observe a tendency toward *parities* between interest rates, internationally (we say parities rather than equality since the forward exchange rate is also part of the calculation), as we have noted.

17.3 THE BALANCE OF PAYMENTS

Most nations take an interest in the value of the exchange rate between their currency and either a few key currencies or an index of foreign currencies in general. Some exchange rates are fixed (we saw in Table 17.1 that the South African rand was temporarily fixed in terms of the dollar) in terms of a key currency, and some are variable, but, it is probably safe to say, none is totally variable because the governments of most countries still intervene to smooth out some of the fluctuations in the exchange rate of their currencies. That being the case, a stock of international "wherewithal" (reserves)—gold, convertible currencies, IMF balances, and special drawing right (SDR) balances at the IMF—is needed to enable a nation to play the stabilization game. In particular, if one's currency is depreciating rapidly (and if this were deemed undesirable) one might *buy* it; you buy it with the international "wherewithal" and, consequently, you have to keep a stock of this on hand. When, on the other hand, your exchange rate is appreciating and other countries are buying their own currencies, your country will tend to acquire international reserves as a consequence. It is, clearly, an inventory problem very much like that suggested in Chapter 16 for a firm's cash balance, although a profit-maximizing framework would hardly be appropriate here, since governments are involved for reasons that are, in fact, not always easy to understand.

The fundamental approach to the description of the influences on the stock of international reserves employs the concept of *the balance of payments*. Let us examine this item for the United States; we will discuss the historical record, as we proceed, in a series of steps. For the years 1969 to 1978, the "current account" of the United States is shown in Table 17.2. The most striking thing about the figures there is the sudden appearance of large trade deficits in 1971, 1972, and 1974, which reappeared in 1976 and reached the astronomical total of $34 billion in 1978. This result on trade, in turn, affected the "balance on current account" (the summary number for the entire table), which reached a negative $15.3 billion for the year 1978.[4]

Let us not hastily conclude that the United States suddenly became noncompetitive through, let us say, excessively rapid inflation, because that view cannot really be maintained, at least on these figures; indeed, we note that U.S. exports have risen steadily (these are in nominal terms, of course). One important additional explanation behind the figures lies in the behavior of imports and, most especially, in oil imports, although this does not, by any means, account for all of the $34.1 billion for 1978 in

[4] The "balance on current account" is not a separate entry in Table 17.2, but only the sum of the other numbers. Table 17.2 is a "balance sheet" of sorts.

Table 17.2: The current account of the United States, 1969–1978 ($ millions)

	1969	*1970*	*1971*	*1972*	*1973*	*1974*	*1975*	*1976*	*1977*	*1978*
Merchandise exports	36,490	41,980	42,769	49,338	71,410	98,310	107,133	114,694	120,576	141,844
Merchandise imports	−35,830	−39,870	−45,648	−55,797	70,499	103,679	98,150	124,047	151,706	175,988
Balance of trade	660	2,110	−2,879	−6,409	911	−5,369	8,983	−9,353	−31,130	−34,144
Net military transactions	−3,341	−3,371	−2,854	−3,621	−2,287	−2,083	−833	312	1,334	531
Net investment income	5,975	6,242	7,950	4,321	5,178	10,227	6,007	15,933	17,507	19,915
Net other service transactions (travel, transportation)	497	588	728	2,803	102	812	2,163	2,469	1,705	2,814
Balance of goods and services	2,011	3,592	699	−5,930	3,905	3,586	16,269	9,361	−10,585	−10,885
Remittances, pensions, and other transfers	−1,266	−1,410	−1,459	−1,606	−1,945	−1,710	−1,727	−1,878	−1,932	−2,048
Balance on the above	745	2,182	−760	−7,537	1,960	1,876	14,542	7,483	−12,517	−12,933
U.S. government grants (not military)	−1,644	−1,739	−2,014	−2,173	−1,938	−5,475	−2,893	−3,145	−2,776	−3,028
Balance on current account	−899	444	−2,774	−9,710	22	−3,598	11,650	4,339	−15,292	−15,961

Source: *Federal Reserve Bulletin.*

Table 17.2. But inflation, as we have seen in earlier chapters such as Chapter 9, is a factor, too, and in the course of our discussion in this and the next chapter we will want to consider how the U.S. inflation rate (compared to foreign inflation rates) helps to explain the current account situation.

Turning to the individual items in Table 17.2, we can note a few other broad trends. For one thing, U.S. exports rose at an annual average rate of 32 percent (with much of it coming in 1973–74, a period in which imports also took off), which is clearly pretty rapid, even when adjusted for inflation. One also notices a rise, but not a steady rise, in the net investment income of the United States. This figure, of course, represents the net earnings from the vast American holdings of foreign securities and direct investments. Finally, we note the decline of a once controversial part of the deficit—the net military transaction—which, after the end of the Vietnam War, has gradually turned around until the United States actually shows a surplus here. This simply means that the United States provides military goods and services—and receives foreign exchange for them—in excess of the cost of goods and services bought from foreign governments plus the exchange cost of maintaining U.S. military operations abroad.

The situation for the current account is really very straightforward; indeed, the net figure represents, in effect, the net demand for dollars (at current exchange rates) arising out of the various categories in the table. When we go "below" the bottom line of the current account however, we enter the murky world of international monetary politics; as well, we will have to look at both private and official capital transfers between the United States and all foreign countries.[5] Beginning with the private sector, we look at American capital flows in Table 17.3 for the years 1975 through 1978. The idea behind Table 17.3 is that if Americans purchase securities abroad, in Section (1) in the table, they add to the U.S. deficit on the balance of payments. This, of course, is because such a transaction represents the demand for the relevant foreign currencies in which the securities (or plant and equipment) are denominated. This explains the minus sign in the top of Table 17.3 and the plus sign attached to the offsetting foreign capital transactions in the United States.

In Table 17.3 one notices that Americans purchase many more securities abroad than do foreigners in the U.S.; that is, comparing the last two rows of Section (1) of the table, with the last three rows of Section (2), we see for all years in the sample there is a big net *outflow* of capital. This, of course, helps explain the surplus item—net investment income—in the current account figures in Table 17.2; that is, the capital flows out and the interest and profits flow in. Indeed, the net interest flow is sometimes

[5] Note that the Balance on current account ≡ Capital transfers + Change in reserves.

Table 17.3: U.S. private capital flows, 1975–1978 ($ millions)

	1975	*1976*	*1977*	*1978*
Change in U.S. private assets abroad (increase is +)	−35,368	−43,865	−30,740	−54,963
Bank reported claims	−13,532	−21,368	−11,427	−33,957
Nonbank reported claims	−1,357	−2,030	−1,700	−2,256
U.S. purchase of foreign securities, net	−6,235	−8,852	−5,398	−3,389
U.S. direct investments abroad, net	−14,244	−11,614	−12,215	−15,361
Changes in foreign private assets in the U.S. (increase is +)	8,643	18,897	13,746	29,293
U.S. bank reported liabilities	628	10,990	6,719	16,860
U.S. nonbank reported liabilities	319	−507	257	1,676
Foreign private purchases of U.S. Treasury securities	2,590	2,783	563	2,248
Foreign purchases of other U.S. securities, net	2,503	1,284	2,869	2,899
Foreign direct investments in the U.S., net	2,603	4,347	3,338	5,611
Balance of 1 and 2 (net private capital flows)	−26,725	−24,968	−16,994	−25,670

Source: *Federal Reserve Bulletin.*

marginally larger than the net capital flow, reflecting the long history the United States has had as a mature creditor nation. The securities figures do fluctuate somewhat, but the really sharp volatility comes in the bank-reported items, most of which are short-term. This probably reflects relative interest rates in the U.S. and abroad and speculative activity in the dollar and other currencies, although we can hardly document these observations.

The net figure in Table 17.3 is generally negative, indicating that on balance, private capital flows have tended to contribute to the overall balance-of-payments outflows for the United States. When we take Table 17.2 with Table 17.3 we find that the private capital flows dominated the current-account total (which was actually positive in 1975 and 1976) and *both* were negative in 1977 and 1978; indeed, in 1978 the total of the two was −$41,631 million, a figure that compares with the trade deficit in 1978 of −$34,144 million (although capital flows are almost equally involved). The deficit of −$41,631 million in 1978, in any event, was a record for the United States.

Now a negative balance of payments in a world of flexible exchange rates is not a problem, but in the days when the IMF supervised the fixed-exchange-rate system, a nation could sustain a deficit (and a fixed exchange rate) only if it were able to draw on official international reserves. A serious balance of payments "problem" in those days meant that a nation's stock of reserves was declining to the point that it would run out (if it kept on trying to maintain the old exchange rate in the face of current plus capital account pressures). But when exchange rates are perfectly flexible, the market clears itself and a national government need not maintain a stock of reserves; indeed, the balance of payments itself is a somewhat outmoded concept if exchange rates are perfectly flexible, since no official action in capital markets is then required. Even so, a casual glance at U.S. newspapers reveals a considerable concern with *both* the balance of payments *and* the exchange rate. While this interest is certainly misguided, and any domestic policy undertaken to help control the exchange rate is equally misguided (remember November 1, 1978?)—as we shall see in Chapter 18—we will plow on down the official part of the balance of payments, in Table 17.4 to see how the deficit revealed in Table 17.3 was "financed," officially.

Table 17.4: Government transactions in the U.S. balance of payments, 1975–1978 ($ millions)

	1975	*1976*	*1977*	*1978*
1. Change in U.S. government assets, other than official reserve assets (− is increase)	−3,470	−4,213	−3,679	−4,657
2. Changes in foreign official assets in the United States (+ is increase)	6,907	18,073	37,124	33,967
(of which U.S. Treasury securities):	4,408	9,333	30,294	24,063
3. Change in U.S. official reserve assets (− is increase)	−607	−2,530	−231	872
Gold	—	—	−118	−65
Special Drawing Rights (SDRs)	−66	−78	−121	1,249
Reserve position in International Monetary Fund (IMF)	−466	−2,215	−294	4,231
Foreign currencies	−75	−240	302	−4,543
4. Net official offset to private balance of payments	2,830	11,330	33,214	30,182
5. Private sector balance of payments	−15,075	−20,629	−32,286	−41,631
6. Statistical discrepancy	+12,245	9,299	−928	11,449

Source: *Federal Reserve Bulletin.*

The table is divided into six main entries. In the first we include a non-policy-oriented component of government transactions that is of no special interest except in balancing the books. In the second part we record net *official* transactions by foreign governments in U.S. securities; these are voluntary (that is, basically negotiated) increases in *official* foreign holdings of U.S. government and private securities. Here we see the single most important fact in this story: foreign governments provide the offset to the growing U.S. private deficit by holding more and more U.S. Treasury securities. This item, indeed, was $30.3 billion in 1977 and $24.1 billion in 1978 and came close, *by itself,* to matching the private sector deficit, at least, in 1977. Note that these are additions to foreign security holdings, which totalled $68.1 billion for the four years covered in the table.

The point just made is worth emphasizing: the present system—the one being operated now by the world's central banks—so far as the United States is concerned, is one in which the U.S. current account and capital deficit are absorbed in a liquid form—U.S. Treasury bills—by foreign central governments. The "official reserves" (the third major section in the table), consisting of gold, Special Drawing Rights, IMF balances, and foreign currencies, are clearly *not* part of the story in the late 1970s. Indeed, these items have generally increased during the recent period (a minus sign in that part of the table is an increase). Clearly, then, the system we presently use is not based on reserves in the sense that the U.S. has to pay out reserves to meet a deficit.[6] We will, in the next section, sketch out the time pattern of reserves, for the United States and several other countries, to show a rather surprising fact: while the old system showed clear signs of applying deflationary pressures in the sense of slowing the growth of resources of the participating nations (except for the United States), the new one—the managed or dirty float—does not. Indeed, the new system actually shows increasing reserves for most countries, although the *nature* of the world's reserves has changed considerably. We will, in the remainder of this chapter and in Chapter 18 consider what lies behind these data, at least in terms of the basic economics involved.

17.4 WORLD RESERVES

The analysis of previous sections has stressed two points: we live in a world of relatively fluctuating exchange rates for most countries—a world that has evolved from one that had relatively fixed exchange rates—and in order to influence its exchange rate against market pressures, a country must either negotiate a deal with its creditors (as the U.S. has, in effect) or use its official liquid reserves in the open exchange markets. In this operation countries use the balance of payments as a kind of guide to the underlying causes of "reserve pressure." Of course, we should again point out, to the extent that exchange markets are allowed to clear themselves, official transactions will be unnecessary; that implies that we will also have to keep track of exchange rates in what follows.

[6] Actually, under the "perfectly" fixed-exchange-rate system the United States did not have to pay out reserves either; that is, the United States, even then, was the world's banker and, as such, did not have to settle up (*in practice*). This, incidentally, probably accounts for the *correct* omission of the balance of payments objective in the Federal Reserve's official list of objectives *until 1962,* as discussed in Chapter 10. As already noted, the present concern for both the balance on the current account *and* the exchange rate is *doubly* misguided, given the nature of the system. We will continue this discussion in Chapters 17 and 18, at various points.

For the United States, the situation since 1956 is presented in Table 17.5; we will explain the IMF Reserve position and the SDRs below, but for now they can be thought of as analogous to the reserves of commercial banks held at the Federal Reserve Banks. In a way, Table 17.5 tells much

Table 17.5: U.S. official reserves at end of year, 1956–1978 ($ millions)

	Total reserve assets	*Gold stock total*	*Convertible foreign currencies*	*Reserve position in IMF*	*SDRs*
1956	23,666	22,058	—	1,608	—
1957	24,832	22,857	—	1,975	—
1958	22,540	20,582	—	1,958	—
1959	21,504	19,507	—	1,997	—
1960	19,359	17,804	—	1,555	—
1961	18,753	16,947	116	1,690	—
1962	17,220	16,057	99	1,064	—
1963	16,843	15,596	212	1,035	—
1964	16,672	15,471	432	769	—
1965	15,450	13,806	781	863	—
1966	14,882	13,235	1,321	326	—
1967	14,830	12,065	2,345	420	—
1968	15,710	10,892	3,528	1,290	—
1969	16,964	11,859	2,781	2,324	—
1970	14,487	11,072	629	1,935	851
1971	12,167	10,206	276	585	1,100
1972	13,151	10,487	241	465	1,958
1973	14,378	11,652	8	552	2,166
1974	15,883	11,652	5	1,852	2,374
1975	16,226	11,599	80	2,212	2,335
1976	18,747	11,598	320	4,434	2,395
1977	19,317	11,719	18	4,951	2,629
1978	18,650	11,642	4,374	1,047	1,558

Source: *Federal Reserve Bulletin.*

of the story of the trials of the international payments system since the mid-1950s. Under the old fixed-exchange-rate system, when gold was $35 an ounce, the United States gradually lost gold reserves as it, along with the other IMF nations, sought to maintain the fixed parities between currencies (or between their currencies and gold). Gradually, convertible currencies—dollars, marks, yen, etc.—edged out gold in the official reserves of most countries (only in 1966–69 and 1978 did the United States hold much in the way of convertible currencies), but by the late 1960s it was apparent that the world's stock of reserves was not growing adequately; thus the SDR (for Special Drawing Right) was added to the IMF quota, becoming a new kind of reserve. The quantity involved in SDRs, though, was quite small, and the whole system collapsed in 1971, a year in which the total reserves available to the United States were only $14.5 billion (at the start of the year) and a year that saw a $30 billion deficit in the U.S. balance of payments. The deficit (or rather $28 billion of it) was taken up by foreign governments. The results since then, clearly, continue in this pattern, with 1977 and 1978 being years very comparable to 1971, although no attempt is currently made to fix exchange rates rigidly. In any event, much of the world was forced onto at least partly flexible exchange rates in 1971.

Even before 1971 the rest of the world had difficulties staying on the fixed-exchange-rate standard. Practically every currency was forced to devalue or (rarely) revalue at one time or another and balance-of-payments problems were routine items in the daily newspapers. One of the problems that was alleged to apply to the fixed-rate system was that total world reserves were not growing adequately, although when we look at Table 17.6 we note that the average annual increase in the period was 5.6 percent, a total that compares favorably with world money-supply figures. From 1970 to 1978, *quite remarkably,* while most of the period (and many countries) showed years of "flexible" exchange rates, when liquid assets accumulations of the sort reported in Table 17.6 were not absolutely necessary, the average annual percent increase in world reserves was actually 24.9 percent, much of it in U.S. dollars.

Looking at the totals for various areas, we note the declining role of the industrial countries, especially in comparison with the oil-exporting countries; the latter are, though, presently gaining securities rather than gold. Most other areas have expanded in rough proportion to their 1960 figures. The world payments system has evolved, it seems, into the dollar standard, with oil at the root of a strong general drift of reserves (in percentage terms) away from the industrial nations.[7] Note, though, that the industrial nations are adding to their holdings of convertible currencies, too; it is clear that by means of the U.S. deficit, reserves are manufactured for the growing needs of the major industrial powers, both for their own accounts and for the settlement of their overall deficit with the oil-producing countries.[8] This may not be a satisfactory system for all concerned, but it seems to be working, at least for the present; in any event, it is hard to think of a workable alternative at present. But before we continue with our analytical discussion in Chapter 18, we should pause to consider how

[7] The United States imports a substantial amount of oil, but it is only just over 2 percent of U.S. GNP, less than either Germany or Japan (at 2.9 percent and 3.4 percent of GNP in 1977). It is worth underscoring that this is *not* a problem to the United States, so long as the world is on a dollar exchange standard. Oil is, of course, only one item in the balance of payments, and it is paid for as we go along. The problem arises because we insist on defending a particular exchange rate, not because we use a product not in sufficient supply at home. See Douglas R. Mudd and Geoffrey E. Wood, "Oil Imports and the Fall of the Dollar," *Review, Federal Reserve Bank of St. Louis* (August 1978).

[8] From 1970 to 1977 the external liabilities of the United States grew from $46.96 billion to $192.28 billion, or by $145.32 billion. World reserves grew, in the same period, by $168.99 billion.

Table 17.6: World reserves ($ millions)

	1960					1970					1978				
	Gold	*IMF*	*SDR*	*C.Curr.§*	*Total*	*Gold*	*IMF*	*SDR*	*C.Curr.§*	*Total*	*Gold*	*IMF*	*SDR*	*C.Curr.§*	*Total*
World total	37,745	3,570	—	18,493	59,808	36,996	7,697	3,124	45,433	93,250	35,605	14,839	8,110	220,844	279,443
Industrial countries*	33,964	3,218	—	9,933	47,115	31,143	6,134	2,423	26,106	65,806	30,114	9,153	6,033	115,126	160,426
Oil exporting countries†	711	70	—	1,568	2,349	1,173	211	79	3,550	5,013	1,271	4,398	480	40,043	46,192
Other Western Hemisphere‡	972	89	—	1,134	2,195	727	415	225	3,088	4,454	656	502	563	20,591	22,312
Other Middle East	508	8	—	397	717	504	20	8	1,121	1,653	529	26	51	6,593	7,199
Other Asia	71	36	—	2,203	2,747	698	213	99	4,821	5,830	726	162	391	18,933	20,212
Other Africa	993	14	—	864	949	95	134	71	1,661	1,960	73	63	160	2,801	3,097
Other Europe		38	—	1,263	2,294	1,750	204	89	3,528	5,570	1,663	351	249	14,871	17,134
Australia, New Zealand, South Africa	213	98	—	988	1,299	906	368	130	1,558	2,962	618	184	184	1,886	2,872

* Industrial countries are the United States, Canada, Japan, Austria, Belgium, Denmark, France, West Germany, Italy, Netherlands, Norway, Sweden, Switzerland, and the United Kingdom.
† Oil exporting countries are the so-called Arab countries plus Indonesia, Nigeria, and Venezuela.
‡ Other Western Hemisphere are South and Central American countries.
§ C.Curr. = convertible currencies.
Source: *International Financial Statistics*.

the fixed payments system evolved over the course of the last 200 years into the present compromise. This discussion will help to show the inconsistencies that brought down the older systems.

17.5 THE GOLD STANDARD

In some ways it would be appropriate here to return to the fable of Chapter 1, in which we left our mythical country with a conglomerate monetary system—with commodities and paper money circulating side by side—and consider how *nations* might organize their monetary relations with each other. The most obvious way, of course, is to base domestic trade on both currency and precious metals and international trade on precious metals alone. In fact, though, international trade generally did better when it was based on a national unit—whether it be Greek, Roman, Italian, Spanish, Dutch, British, or American, to run through 2,500 years of history—as well as on precious metals. Thus even the old *gold standard,* the relevant method of operation in the 19th century, was really a gold-and-convertible-currency standard, in which only international clearings had to be effected in gold and silver, at least if required.

In the 19th century, to begin at a suitable point, the British were in charge of a gold bullion standard, a system in which the British pound (the currency) was kept exchangeable in terms of gold. The British were not always able to maintain a fixed price (they were "off" gold from 1797 to 1821, for example), but their problems were small compared to those of the United States, where financial crises, the hard money movement of the 1830s, the Civil War, and the pressure toward bimetallism all presented problems to control of the value of the dollar in terms of gold. Basically, what was done during this period was that the United States (Treasury) attempted to keep the dollar in line with the pound while permitting full convertibility internally. The government was, in effect, wedded to the idea of the gold standard, although, as we shall see, its record of maintaining this was not especially outstanding.

We have discussed, in earlier chapters, the numerous bank supensions during the pre–Civil War period; as well, we considered the effect of Andrew Jackson's hard money policy of the 1830s, which produced, perhaps incidentally (in view of the parallel collapse of the cotton market), a series of financial crises and a rapid shrinkage of the American banking system (to 1844). In effect, the U.S. went on specie (gold and silver) internally, and, no doubt helped by the gold discoveries in California in the 1840s, managed to keep the value of the dollar in line with that of the pound, even though the U.S. financial system was chaotic at times, until the Civil War. At the start of the Civil War, the federal government, in need of large quantities of funds, first sought to raise them in gold; this, as well as an unfavorable balance of trade, immediately put such a strain on the quantity of gold available for the monetary circulation that first the banks (December 1861) and then the Treasury (early 1862) went off gold. What that meant for the former was inconvertibility of notes and deposits into gold (except at the market rate), and what it meant for the latter was abandonment of the fixed exchange rate (of $4.86 to the pound), which until that time had been maintained by the U.S. Treasury by means of dealings in gold.[9]

During the Civil War American prices rose sharply, of course; as well, the United States moved steadily toward a uniform currency, composed of Greenbacks (Treasury obligations) and National Bank Notes. As a result of the war and its method of finance, American prices rose more steeply than did British in this period and so a healthy *premium* built up on gold (or, on what is the same, the pound, since Britain maintained the convertibility of the pound) compared to the dollar (i.e., the Greenback). This premium was market-determined, and, in effect, reflected the flexible exchange rate that the United States was employing (by not being on the gold bullion standard). After the Civil War the United States government set about legislating a return to the gold standard; in April 1866 Congress agreed to retire the Greenbacks, an act designed to make it possible to resume gold payments by removing a basic inflationary pressure. But an immediate recession thereafter prompted a suspension of the retirement of the Greenbacks in February 1868; $44 million had been returned by then. In March 1869 Congress declared that the national debt would be repaid in specie at the old exchange rate with the dollar; this was followed, in January 1875, with the Resumption Act, which declared that the United States would aim for resumption of the gold standard on January 1, 1879, at the old parity of $4.86, and instructed the secretary of the treasury to use surplus revenue for this purpose (to buy dollars) and even to sell bonds to accumulate a reserve of gold to be used upon resumption.

During this period, curiously enough, prices were falling around the world, so in order for the relatively overinflated U.S. economy to achieve a successful resumption, American prices had to fall that much more. The United States grew rapidly in real terms over this period, perhaps at an annual rate somewhere between 4.5 and 6 percent; the money stock, however (1867 to 1879), grew only 1.3 percent a year, while prices actually *fell* by 5.4 percent per year. Indeed, this "contractionary" monetary policy succeeded in bringing about the resumption, in effect, which occurred on January 1, 1879, without incident. But the price decline continued, though at an abated pace, and another monetary storm—in some ways more serious because it involved certain "populist" issues—arose over the coinage of silver.

---

[9] We are referring, of course, not to an exact fix at $4.86/£ but to narrow bands around that number. As well, the Bank of England helped stabilize the dollar, in effect, by reacting whenever gold flowed toward the United States.

From the 1790s until 1853, the United States was on a bimetallic standard (gold and silver). The two major pressures in this period operated in the 1830s when the Jacksonians raised the mint ratio (of their prices) from 15 : 1 to 16 : 1 (gold to silver) and in the late 1840s, when the gold discoveries brought Gresham's law to work and drove silver out of circulation. The latter brought about the Coinage Act of February 1853, in which silver was reduced to a subsidiary role (as minor coins with a coin value greater than the market value of silver). The act was needed since the medium of exchange (silver coin) was disappearing and private note issues were multiplying.[10] It was the first and probably major step on the way to the Gold Standard Act of 1900.[11] Thus, prior to 1873, the United States had been legally empowered to coin both gold and silver and was, in effect on a kind of bimetallic standard. But in 1873 Congress passed another Coinage Act, which demonetized silver. This little-noticed legislation was made known in 1875 by the silver agitators as the "Crime of 1873," when the market price of silver fell below the old mint parity for the first time in 39 years. The cause was a rapid increase in silver production. At the same time, as already noted, the United States had a steadily falling price level (which continued to fall until the gold discoveries of the 1890s); this brought out considerable agitation for resumption of the silver coinage and for the expansion of the issue of the Greenbacks (a political party was formed for that purpose in 1875). The silver mining groups were joined by debtors (who were paying in appreciated funds) and by farmers (whose prices were also falling *and* who were in debt), a political combination that was powerful enough to get the Bland-Allison Act passed, over President Rutherford B. Hayes's veto, in February 1878. This act provided for government purchases of between $2 and $4 million of silver per month; in fact, nearly $400 million of silver coin or silver-backed currency came into circulation by 1890. At that time, these purchases were actually stepped up, although they were suspended in 1893, when the silver purchase clause in the act was repealed.

Silver never made it to bimetallic status, though, although in the 1890s in the United States, the combination of agrarian and labor involvement and silver agitation produced a popular champion in William Jennings Bryan, a defeated candidate for president in 1896 and 1900. What defeated

[10] Being on a bimetallic standard implies fixed ratios between the two metals and between the metals and the currency. By Gresham's Law, which in effect, says there can only be one price for a product in a given market, a country on a bimetallic standard will be "on" either one or the other, depending on which is less valuable in the open market. (Bad money drives out good.) Thus, by 1853, the market price of silver was higher than the mint price and no silver was brought to the Treasury—it was more valuable in the open market and was kept out of monetary circulation. Sir Thomas Gresham was an Elizabethan financier who died in 1579.

[11] David A. Martin, "1853: The End of Bimetallism in the United States," *Journal of Economic History* (December 1973).

these various elements of discontent was not a repressive government, although there was some official reaction to the agitation, but the return of world-wide inflation following the Klondike and South African gold discoveries. The price rise, from 1897 to 1914, was about 2 percent per year and the economy continued to grow, in real terms, at around 4 percent per year. One of the consequences of this prosperity, then, was the decline of the silver agitation and the passing into law of the Gold Standard Act in March 1900, an event that finally brought the gold standard to the United States in the legal sense.[12]

From 1900 until 1933, the United States was on gold *internally* at 23.22 grains of pure gold per dollar (i.e., individuals could buy and sell gold on those terms); *externally* it went off only during the First World War, from September 1917 to June 1919. In 1931, during the Great Depression, Britain went off gold; the United States held on until March 1933, but then was itself forced off.[13] When the United States returned to gold it did so under the Gold Reserve Act of 1934, which reduced the dollar to 13.714 grains of gold (or to $35 per ounce of gold); this act also severely limited private dealings in gold while emphasizing both the obligation to maintain the price of gold at $35 per ounce (this lasted until 1968) and the link between gold and the money supply (this started to erode in the 1950s, when the United States began to lose its large gold stock).[14] Finally, the adoption of a flexible exchange rate in 1973 (after a short float in 1971), which was preceded by a short period of a dual gold exchange standard in which official and private markets for gold existed side by side, meant the end of the gold standard for the United States, for the foreseeable future.

17.6 THE INTERNATIONAL MONETARY FUND

The 1930s, as we have seen, were associated with considerable domestic economic disharmony, which (for purposes of our discussion in this chapter) was associated with a variety of price level (and domestic money supply) problems; as well, they preceded (and helped produce) the political disorder of the Second World War. One of the outcomes of that was was a greater emphasis on international cooperation in a variety of areas, one of which was that of exchange rate control. The general idea underly-

[12] The market price of silver stayed below the mint price until the 1960s, when Gresham's Law again went into operation. Then, as the market price of silver rose, both the U.S. silver-based coins and silver certificates disappeared from circulation, to be melted down or redeemed.

[13] During World Wars I and II most countries were forced off the gold standard; in what follows we will ignore those gaps in the record.

[14] This act had two controversial features: (1) individuals were required to turn in their gold to the government at $20 an ounce (so the Treasury made a large capital gain) and (2) all contracts that had a gold clause (as a protection against inflation) had that feature cancelled. The gold clause is again legal (since 1978) in the United States.

ing most of the payments plans put forward since the 1930s had been to build a self-correcting mechanism similar to that attributed to domestic economies with a central bank. The idea was to have final payments between nations made in a medium that countries could not directly create; the hope was that there would then be a natural discipline to the system insofar as the quantity of the medium itself did not readily respond to political pressure. Gold, which is most often thought to serve best in this role, is a commodity, unfortunately, and in relatively diminishing supply as things stand. Thus, systems relying on gold alone tend to be faced with an annoying scarcity; this scarcity implies, if the price is fixed (as it was, at $35 an ounce), that unless some subsidiary reserve is made available, domestic money supplies (and price levels) would tend to fall; recognition of this problem (but not recognition that the main idea was not a sensible one) led to a number of proposals to expand the world's stock of reserves while at the same time keeping a rein on its total quantity.[15] This has been the rationale of the IMF system, which sought to introduce a managed *supplement* to the old gold exchange approach.

When a country pegs itself to a fixed-exchange-rate system, it pledges itself to deal with depreciations of its currency by using its reserves—gold plus convertible (into gold or dollars) currencies—to buy the currency. When it runs out of reserves, a country can always devalue, if it cannot make a deal with one of the other nations (which must be gaining); in addition, it can undertake some sort of domestic contraction, or pursue a tight money policy (to attract foreign funds drawn by a higher interest rate). An alternative approach, partly justified because domestic contraction may seem too drastic a measure in many cases, was the movement during the early 1940s to create an International Monetary Fund. The IMF arose out of the discussions begun during World War II, and its final charter reflects two quite different views of what was needed at the time: a British view and an American.

Let us begin with the consensus. It was generally agreed, partly on account of the experiences of the 1930s, that

a. Exchange rate changes ought to be rare.

b. The IMF ought to have the power to examine the policies of the deficit nations (i.e., those losing reserves).

c. The IMF ought to provide an efficient clearing mechanism for international payments.

However, when it actually came to making over the mechanism itself, and in particular to defining the extent of the lending power of the IMF, the

[15] As we will see in Chapter 18 it is as if there were a "world stock of money" and a "world stock of high-powered money reserves" at which the "world price level" remains stable. This seems (roughly) to be how the system was thought of there, although one does not find it analyzed in these terms.

dispute became intense. The British put forward a proposal engineered largely by John Maynard Keynes. The Keynes plan called for an international currency, called Bancor, which was to be valued in gold but not to be tied to any particular central bank. The world central bank would clear payments and compare deficits and surpluses with the quotas assigned to each nation. Countries would still have their own gold and convertible currency balances but could channel short-run problems to the IMF. The latter, in turn, would always be "solvent," since one country's deficit is another's surplus: the IMF would lend to deficit countries from the surplus of other countries. In the Keynes plan, countries would have automatic access to their credit lines (up to 25 percent in a year), and this feature was especially attractive to countries that expected (at least in the short run) to run deficits.

The liberal-access provision of the Keynes plan was not emulated in the White plan (which was named for the American Harry Dexter White); in that version, there was no mention of an international currency, and only simple quotas were envisioned, with much more closely controlled and limited access to fund balances by the member nations. In a way, the White plan was modelled on the idea of the American Federal Reserve; the reserves were to be locked up and countries which were forced to *borrow* persistently from the IMF—their lender of last resort—might be required to undertake domestic contraction on the assumption that the underlying problem was *structural* in some sense (and, quite possibly, located somewhere in the domestic economy).[16] At any rate, out of these conflicting views grew an institution that monitored international payments and stored a growing quantity of international reserves; it evolved to the point where (*a*) it disapproved of persistent borrowing, and (*b*) it disapproved of frequent exchange-rate changes. The IMF grew rather slowly, considering the rapid growth of the volume of international trade.

The IMF itself grew out of meetings held at Bretton Woods, New Hampshire, in 1944. While many of the disagreements aired during the early years of World War II had been ironed out by that time, the questions of the size of the quotas and the method of administering them had still to be solved. The system adopted set rather low limits upon these quotas, and modest revisions have been made subsequently; the American figure, originally set at $2,750 million, had slowly risen to $5,160 million by the end of 1969; in March 1978 it was $6,700 million.[17] To see the mechanics of the fund, consider the U.S. quota (in $ millions) in 1969

[16] This was the idea of a "fundamental disequilibrium" in the balance of payments (although the problem was probably the system itself). There could, of course, be an "external fundamental disequilibrium" for a country that suddenly lost its export market to a new product (such as synthetic versus natural rubber); presumably a devaluation would be sensible in that case.

[17] These are valued in SDR units; see below.

and in 1978; we take the former date because it was before the SDR was used.

	1969	*1978*
Gold subscription	1,290	1,675
Currency subscription	3,870	5,025
Quota	5,160	6,700

These figures give the sums of gold and dollars that the U.S. had supplied to the IMF. In 1969, the fund *actually held* $3,196 of U.S. currency—the rest had been used to clear U.S. deficits—leaving the United States with a net fund position of $4,486 million; at the same time (1969) the United Kingdom, with a quota of $2,440 million, found the fund holding $4,507 million in British pounds, so that the British were in deficit to the fund in the amount of $2,067 million). These figures were fairly typical for the time.[18]

As we have already mentioned, the IMF grew rather slowly in the years prior to 1969; this was due to the rather conservative outlook imprinted on it by the Americans after World War II, although the Americans were not alone in favoring a low rate of growth of international reserves. One way this American view came to dominate in the fund was through the dominance of the American economy and the size of the American gold stock. As well, the United States was expected to maintain a balance of payments surplus for a long time after the war. A more practical reason for the U.S. dominance concerns the voting procedures. The Americans wanted, and got, a system of voting weights proportional to the size of the quota subscribed. This gave the United States an effective veto power over most structural matters, for which an 80 to 85 percent vote is necessary, and it is one reason that many people feel the system was American rather than international. Other blocks of countries (not Communist, though), particularly the later European Common Market, also have come to have veto power, but usually the members of the potential blocs do not vote alike. Perhaps this objection to the American monopoly was overrated, but it is just as well to point out that the IMF has still not lived up to what many consider its potential. Indeed, one suspects, a drastic rewriting of its basic charter will probably be undertaken in any revival of the influence of the fund in the future.

The pressures on the IMF, from the start, were particularly great. The system started out with a dollar shortage brought about by the choice of a set of exchange rates (the previous rates, generally) that were inappropriate; then, after the outbreak of the Korean War in 1950 and the ensuing world-wide inflation, country after country succumbed to the device of an occasional devaluation in order to try to reconcile the needs of external

[18] After the save-the-dollar tight money policy of November 1978, on December 31, 1978, the IMF held $7,601.5 of U.S. dollars, which was 90 percent of a revised quota.

balance with the internal objectives of maximum growth and minimum unemployment. World reserves grew slowly, although the United States gradually disgorged its huge gold stock and a dollar glut—again reflecting a disequilibrium set of exchange rates—began to surface. As well, during this period, an anomaly of the IMF system—the nonparallel treatment of surplus countries (which in terms of the IMF dogma, it seems, have a "fundamental disequilibrium" because they were doing something "right")—produced further resentment among the less fortunate nations (that is, those with persistent deficits).[19]

The system, then, by late 1967 was one of an insufficient quantity of reserves to defend an outmoded set of exchange rates. The U.S. deficit was providing some reserves, but this was not adequate and was the source of an additional paradox in the system: the U.S. deficit made the dollar seem "weak" while the quantity of dollars was not large enough to save the system (then—but see below). At any event, in September 1967, the member countries of the IMF agreed to create a new type of automatic reserve, the special drawing right (SDR). These rights, allocated to countries on the basis of their fund allocation, were adopted somewhat slowly (they were first used in 1970, on the eve of the collapse of the IMF system), although they clearly gave the system what it seemed to need, in that they were a more flexible form of reserves. Indeed, the SDR resembles the Bancor of the Keynes plan, in having the general properties of being (*a*) generally acceptable within limits by all participating countries, and (*b*) not contingent on any structural reforms in the deficit country. Thus SDRs can be used as a matter of right and are clearly a permanent addition to international reserves. SDRs, that is to say, are kind of international money, useful insofar as they are acceptable in exchange by governments. Indeed, SDRs are not a liability of any government, since no firm provision for the repayment of the "loan" is made; they are, technically, liabilities of the IMF and are backed by agreement but they are not convertible into anything at the fund.[20]

To gather some idea of the limited extent of both the IMF and the SDR at the present time we can look back at Table 17.6; as well, we list in Table 17.7 the situation in March 1978 for the member nations of the IMF. In Table 17.7 we see, clearly, that the total SDR allocation has risen to

[19] Both the Keynes and the White plans were not restrictive with regard to surplus countries. The White plan did permit the IMF to declare a country with a persistent surplus to have a "scarce" currency, and, then, to permit member countries to discriminate against it. It was never invoked and the most persistent surplus country—West Germany—was requested to revalue on occasion, although this does not seem to have had any permanent effect on its tendency to generate a balance-of-payments surplus.

[20] The term *Special Drawing Right* was a concession to those countries—notably France—that were firmly opposed to an international money. While we have such an international money now—for the SDR is a new form of money—it is not called money, nor is it referred to by any of the usual synonyms for money.

Table 17.7: IMF positions, March 31, 1978 (SDRs millions)

	Quota	*Gold subscription*	*Currency subscription*	*Fund holding of currency*	*SDR allocation*	*Net acquisition (+) or net use (−) of SDRs*
All countries	29,219.8	6,596.9	22,609.3	32,858.8	9,314.8	−1,238.8
Industrial countries	18,365.0	4,401.3	13,963.7	15,087.3	6,177.7	62.7
United States	6,700.0	1,675.0	5,025.0	3,474.3	2,294.0	−116.6
Japan	1,200.0	300.0	900.0	278.3	377.4	116.8
West Germany	1,600.0	350.5	1,249.5	573.1	542.4	407.5
Italy	1,000.0	250.0	750.0	2,238.7	318.0	−107.6
United Kingdom	2,800.0	611.3	2,188.7	6,139.8	1,006.3	−538.2
Other Europe	1,548.0	353.2	1,194.8	3,599.8	405.1	−153.8
Australia, New Zealand, South Africa	1,187.0	255.2	931.9	2,032.8	384.0	−195.5
Oil exporting countries	1,421.0	289.9	1,131.1	736.2	374.2	14.6
Other Western Hemisphere	2,270.0	542.9	1,727.1	3,308.6	766.8	−275.0
All others	4,428.8	754.4	3,660.7	8,094.1	1,207.0	−691.8

Source: *International Financial Statistics* (IMF).

$9,314.8, which puts it at one-quarter of the total IMF contribution to international liquidity. On the other hand, the largest user, the United Kingdom, has drawn on it only to one-tenth the extent it has permitted the IMF to hold its currency. Net uses of the SDR, that is to say, are still quite small. Note that the IMF is now holding currency in excess of the total allocation of gold and currency (is acting like an international central bank, in effect) with Italy, the United Kingdom, and a large number of underdeveloped countries being the chief users in this sense. This possibility was not envisaged in the original charter, and represents a departure from the practice prior to 1971; this may become even more common in the future, especially if the world tries to move away from the dollar system it is presently living with. Looking back at Table 17.6, we see that in 1970 the SDR was 3.3 percent of world liquidity, while at the end of 1977, it was down to 3.1 percent; thus, whatever its promise as a new device, it has failed to keep pace with the dollar. Neither, for that matter, has the IMF quota.

In 1969 the United States had its credit crunch and in 1970 entered a recession, the first in almost a decade.[21] In the decade prior to the recession, the United States had followed a generally expansionary monetary policy at home (as judged by the rate of growth of the monetary base) compared to the policy ruling in the 15 years 1946–60. Officially, the United States, in this period, seems to have thought that it could have less unemployment permanently at the cost of only a moderate inflation. In the fixed-exchange-rate system then prevailing under the IMF direction, this meant that instead of insisting on a devaluation of the dollar (which would have been self-correcting) or the conversion of dollars to gold, foreign countries actually accumulated dollars and thus absorbed the inflationary pressures in their monetary bases. After the recession of 1970, in 1971 a record world inflation and a record U.S. deficit meant that the U.S. had to abandon its current relation with gold (then at $42.22 per ounce); at first the United States tried for a new rate, in August 1971, but it was forced to float in 1973. The present system, the government-managed or "dirty" float, then simply happened.[22] Discussion has continued, and the main

[21] We are here borrowing a bit from Chapter 18 in order to complete the story of this section. See also Jürg Niehans, "How to Fill an Empty Shell," *American Economic Review* (May 1976).

[22] The system actually went down in stages. In the autumn of 1969 the West Germans were forced to revalue; they did so by floating upward to a new par value. In May 1970, the Canadian dollar was again floated (it had floated from 1950 to 1962); thus, the U.S. float after August 15, 1971 (the United States was searching for the new equilibrium rate) was really the third major currency to float in this period (the mark was floated a second time, just after the Canadian dollar floated). From summer 1971, to France's floating freely in January 1974, countries tried to stabilize their currencies but generally failed. The French float was really the last straw for the old system, since the French were generally the strongest opponents of flexible exchange rates. (They favored a return to gold.)

industrial nations continue to hold meetings, but, so far, only minor alterations have been adopted. These include the following actions.

a. They created an IMF "oil facility" for recycling the *petrodollars* of the oil-exporting countries to the oil-importing countries (this amounts to only 5 percent of the petrodollar surplus).

b. Industrial countries agreed to try to limit the fluctuations in their exchange rates.

c. The official price of gold was abolished in the revised constitution of the IMF (in the Kingston Agreement of January 1976).

d. The fund has begun to disburse its gold stock, with some returned and some sold auction-style on world markets, the proceeds to go to underdeveloped countries (Kingston, 1976).

e. IMF quotas were increased by one-third as of summer 1977 (Kingston, 1976).

We can expect further developments of this sort as efforts continue to try to revive the IMF, perhaps modified to deal solely in the exchange rate stabilization problems of the member nations.

17.7 STUDY QUESTIONS

Essay questions

1. How do you account for the significant change of the American merchandise balance to a negative figure in 1977–78? Dig up some figures for inflation in some of our big competitors and discuss whether or not inflation seems to be involved. What has been happening to capital flows? Is there some direct relation?

2. The rhetoric of international finance suggests that deficit countries are to blame, but the analysis does not. Is it possible that it is easier to cure a deficit than to cure a surplus (gifts aside)? Is this because of rigidities in the system? Do your answers to these questions have political implications? If so, spell them out.

3. Why, do you suppose, do so many business firms (and banks) let themselves go uncovered in their foreign exchange dealings? Is there an optimal level of exchange rate insurance, then? Would it make sense to have a government agency help build up the forward market in order to reduce transactions costs here? Which costs, specifically, could it help to lower?

True-false discussion questions

These statements are meant to be somewhat ambiguous and to provoke discussion, thereby.

1. It makes no sense to talk about the exchange rate as a price determined by supply and demand when the prices actually determined are those of products, in the first instance.

2. The balance-of-trade figures are the determining elements in a country's balance of payments, while the capital flows are passive, moving to complete the *balance* of payments.

3. One important reason world gold production lagged between the 1930s and the early 1970s is related to the fixed-exchange-rate system used during this period.

4. The purchasing power of gold would be the "world" price level if all countries were firmly tied to the United States dollar.

5. The American preference for minimal changes in exchange rates cannot be reconciled with the American preference for freer trade.

6. Since the market price of gold is permitted to fluctuate, one cannot also operate a system of world-wide *fixed* exchange rates.

7. Additions to the American balance-of-payments deficit rather than to the stock of gold is a cheaper way to create international reserves.

8. The American balance-of-payments deficit and the American federal budgetary deficit arise from the same cause: excessive federal spending.

9. Generally speaking, world reserves should expand as rapidly as world trade.

17.8 FURTHER READING

Clark, Peter B., Dennis E. Logue, and Richard James Sweeney. *The Effects of Exchange Rate Adjustments.* Oasia Research Memorandum, Department of the Treasury, 1974.

Friedman, Milton. "The Case for Flexible Exchange Rates." In Friedman, Milton, eds., *Essays on Positive Economics.* Chicago: University of Chicago Press, 1955.

Friedman, Milton, and Anna J. Schwartz. *A Monetary History of the United States.* Princeton, N.J.: Princeton University Press, 1963.

Humphrey, Thomas M., and Thomas A. Lawler. "Factors Determining Exchange Rates: A Simple Model and Empirical Tests." *Economic Review, Federal Reserve Bank of Richmond* (May/June 1977).

Niehans, Jürg. "How to Fill an Empty Shell." *American Economic Review* (May 1976).

Scammell, W. M. *International Monetary Policy, Bretton Woods and After.* London: Macmillan, 1975.

18

The monetary approach to the balance of payments

18.1 INTRODUCTION

This chapter moves the discussion of Chapter 17 into an area in which the controversy is decidedly more difficult to avoid, although the issues are, underneath, still the same practical ones. What we have to consider here are the economic relations between nations with particular reference to spending flows and to the monetary linkages. This will, when completed, enable us to present results concerning the efficiency of monetary and fiscal policy in either fixed or flexible exchange-rate systems and to appraise the characteristics of our present system, which is a mixture. We will then be able to show how factor (especially capital) mobility can affect a domestic macroeconomic policy in either of the two exchange-rate regimes (fixed or flexible).

We will actually begin in Section 18.2 with a discussion of a major dispute that has existed over fixed versus flexible exchange-rate systems; this enables us to set the stage for our policy material. Then we consider, in Section 18.3, a popular approach to the balance of payments (or the exchange rate). This begins with a discussion of the *purchasing power parity* theory, which links the exchange rate between two countries to the relative price levels in those countries; this done, we will consider the broader monetary approach, which links the purchasing power parity theory to the general macroeconomic model and to the balance of payments. These tasks done, we can consider the broader-ranging debate over the effectiveness of monetary and fiscal policy, before looking into the Monetarist prescriptions (and into the problem of the present world inflation). We will conclude on a practical note with some observations on actual capital flows in recent years, emphasizing bond markets and the international spread of banking. Here we will also consider some of the provisions of the International Banking Act of 1978, especially as it affects foreign banks doing business in the United States.

18.2 THE FLEXIBLE-EXCHANGE-RATE CONTROVERSY

As we have noted, during the period of IMF supervision of the international payments mechanism, exchange rates were not perfectly rigid in a number of ways:

a. Some countries abandoned the system from time to time (e.g., Canada, from 1950–1962), in favor of a flexible rate.
b. Some countries were on a fixed rate only for a short period (England, for example, for about half the period from 1945 to 1971).
c. Some countries used a series of multiple exchange rates to attempt to control the situation (notably South American countries).
d. Many countries made unilateral changes (mostly devaluations) when they thought it would be to their advantage.

To all of these changes the IMF was officially hostile, although usually circumstances and the excessive inflexibility of the system left the deviant countries with little choice in any event. Let us consider, briefly, the devaluation approach to flexibility, since it is relevant to our present system of the managed (or dirty) float, before we turn to a preliminary discussion of the mechanics of full flexibility.

Let us assume that the British are contemplating changing the $/£ rate and wish to estimate the effect on the balance of payments (on, that is to say, their official reserves). Thus, suppose that the $/£ rate is presently $1.80 per pound and they are thinking of lowering it to $1.62. When they do, (*a*) British importers will face higher pound prices for foreign products (and reduce their demands accordingly); (*b*) British exporters, who will receive more pounds, will be stimulated to try to sell more abroad (if they can); (*c*) American importers will find British products 10 percent cheaper in dollars and buy more; and (*d*) American exporters will tend to want to supply less to the British, now that the dollar price has fallen. The layperson would assert, immediately, that the British stand to gain on all four counts, on their balance of payments, but this is not so. The reason, simply, is that the balance of trade is calculated in terms of total expenditures—i.e., total revenues—and the behavior of these depends on the relative elasticities of demand and supply. Thus, for example, if the American demand for British products were inelastic, a fall in the dollar price would actually *reduce* American expenditure on British products. This, then, would be a negative contribution to the balance of payments, and it could be sufficient to outweigh the positive effect generated by the reluctance of the British to spend abroad.

Other factors also could intervene to make devaluation a risky business. For one thing, speculators might get the idea that further devaluations are coming and move against the pound in the spot market; this would tend to push the total balance of payments more negative. For another, it is likely that British costs would rise directly (the British import many of the raw materials they use); this could be involved with a validated cost-push inflation, which could undermine the new exchange rate (see Chapter 9). In the long run, as well, even if there were an increase in official reserves, an addition to the monetary base might occur, which would also generate inflation, although we are for the moment abstracting from that problem. On net, there are enough worries to explain why the effect of managed devaluations and revaluations, *solely to make a gain on the balance of payments,* may not be easy to predict. This is not to say that currencies have not been over- or undervalued in the past, but merely to suggest that once you decide to manage the exchange rate it may actually be hard to tell which way to jump, even assuming that the goal of an increased official reserve is a reasonable one. One way to decide, of course, is to let the rate "float" periodically, to find its new level; indeed, this is a currently popular approach. This, in turn, raises the fundamental question of this section: Why not let the exchange rate float all the time? Let us consider the technical arguments put forward on both sides of this somewhat emotional issue.

The most obvious reason for preferring a fluctuating exchange rate system is the free-market one: the fluctuating price (exchange rate) will clear the market and therefore not require that official payments flow in order to effect the clearing. In addition, there is the free-market argument that the resources tied up—gold, the IMF, the domestic exchange authorities, etc.—will be free to find their best (better?) alternative uses. These arguments are clear enough, although the second is perhaps minor, but there are three further advantages to the system of flexible exchange rates that are clearly important, if true:

a. The macro policy instruments used to stabilize the exchange markets will be free to concentrate on domestic policy problems.

b. A system that clears itself will also tend to be a more stable one (we shall define stability in a moment).
c. Trade barriers are not needed for balance-of-payments reasons.

These positions are more hotly debated than the free-market arguments.

With regard to the second point, the argument concerns the effects of a changing market rate on speculators and the managers of domestic economies. Under the partly rigid rates of the IMF regime, when exchange-rate changes were made, the pressure was usually so intense that both the timing and extent were fairly obvious to everyone, at least given the usual view of what governments were trying to do. Under these conditions, speculators could hardly lose and, it could be argued, the pool of international *hot money* (short-term speculative balances) built up steadily during the 26 years of living under the IMF. With a perfectly flexible system, however, an equilibrium exchange rate will occur, at which speculators are evenly matched with hedgers, arbitrageurs, and intervening governments. Furthermore, if speculators come to expect that the actual rate will tend to fluctuate around an equilibrium (or normal) rate, then speculation *itself* will tend to be stabilizing: speculators, when the dollar is too high, will tend to drive it back to equilibrium by selling dollars in expectation of a fall in its price. Indeed, by selling the dollar in these circumstances they will actually drive its price down.[1] Actually, governments operating in this arena will also tend to act in a stabilizing fashion, unless, of course, other policies (domestic) actually make the situation worse.

But, we should be aware, speculators may well not adopt this view. If not—if, for example, speculators anticipate a fundamental change in the exchange rate—their actions will drive the rate toward the new, anticipated level. Indeed, under any system, any rate the speculators pick will be achieved if they are strong enough. Further, if speculators simply throw out the past in their calculations and operate as if exchange rates are a "random walk" (see Chapter 16), then what they will do is widen the swings in exchange rates as they hop onto a moving rate, betting that it will continue to move in the same direction. Aside from the possibility that exchange rates will be driven all over the place by speculators, a possibility that clearly has not come to pass, this part of the rebuttal to the floating-rate view does emphasize an important change in the new regime: exchange rates now do fluctuate more, *whatever the cause* (price levels

---

[1] It has been argued that if speculators try to fight against an equilibrium rate they will tend to lose money and thus be eliminated as an important destabilizing factor in exchange markets. This may well be true, of course, but in fact (*a*) governments still interfere in exchange markets (losing money too), setting up the possibility of nonrandom movements (as before), and (*b*) new speculative money is always appearing, stimulated by the huge gains that can be made if you win (even though the *expected* payoff may be negative). See the argument in Chapter 14 for an example of this situation in the domestic stock market.

also fluctuate more), and the costs of transactions in foreign currencies have definitely gone up in recent (floating) years.

On net, then, the technical advantages of a flexible system have been sufficient that it has not been possibile to convince a sufficient number of the major countries to return to a perfectly fixed system. But some groups of countries—notably the European Common Market (EEC)—have sought to attempt to form *currency unions* (or common floats) in which the members of the union have exchange rates that are fixed (or fluctuating only within fairly narrow bands) with each other.[2] As it stands, the success of such ventures has not been considerable; some of the reasons can be found in a literature on *optimum currency areas*. The fundamental questions are the following: Should the entire world be one currency area (i.e., bound together by fixed exchange rates)? Should each country be a currency area in itself, as is the case under the flexible rate system? Is there some other system, such as the present set of customs unions, that would be better? The answer would be found by weighing the costs and benefits both on a per-nation and on a world-wide basis (although the viewpoint of the latter would not be easy to establish); at any event, this answer would give meaning to the word *optimum* in the context of the concept of the currency area.

If a country joins a currency union, then it surrenders autonomy in terms of its money supply. Thus, if the country has the macro-policy objectives of maximum employment, minimum inflation, and a rapid rate of growth, then the decision to join (or to revive the IMF) would have to be based on the overall gain it would expect to make in achieving these objectives. Note that in this view "balance-of-payments stability" becomes a goal of policy only after a nation joins the currency union and then (rationally) only because it is intermediate to achieving the other objectives. An optimal currency area is traditionally drawn on the basis of the factor mobility (especially the capital mobility) between nations; if two nations have perfect factor mobility, then the two ought to be part of the same currency area. Quite simply, this is because demand shifts within the economy will be dealt with by factor shifts without generating regional unemployment and inflation. Consider first, two countries, *A* and *B*, both of which have maximum *internal* factor mobility but none with each other. Suppose, then, that demand shifts from *B* to *A*. Under flexible rates, *A*'s currency will rise in value relative to *B*'s; this will tend to bring *B* more

[2] At the end of 1977, of a total of 69 major countries studied, 11 were floaters; 6 were in the European Common Market); 27, mostly South American and African, were pegged to the U.S. dollar (and were floating *with* the dollar); 4 were pegged to the British pound (and hence floating with the pound); and 27 were "basket peggers," tying their currency to the value of a "market basket" of foreign currencies. The latter are mostly (but not entirely) underdeveloped countries. See Leroy O. Laney," A Diminished Role for the Dollar as a Reserve Currency?" *Voice, Federal Reserve Bank of Dallas* (December 1978).

business at the expense of A and will tend to relieve the unemployment in B. Furthermore, if factors are mobile in B, the adjustment is quick, in terms of shifting to whatever goods are now demanded from abroad.

On the other hand, suppose that A and B each consist of two regions, A_1, A_2, B_1, B_2, and that A_1 and B_1 have great factor mobility with each other and so do A_2 and B_2, but that there is no factor mobility between A_1 and A_2 (or B_1 and B_2). Now suppose that demand shifts from Region 1 to Region 2. Region 1 (A_1 and B_1) will suffer unemployment and Region 2 will have prosperity (and maybe inflation). No change is required in the exchange rate between the two countries A and B as things stand, but neither country can solve the unemployment problem in Region 1 (by increasing the money supply) without at the same time increasing the inflation problem in Region 2 (or vice versa, in case of a money-supply decrease). Thus, in this case, whether or not A and B became a currency union, unless there were mobility between Region 1 and Region 2, there would be no gain to be had. Region 1 and Region 2, on the other hand, would make effective separate currency unions, other things being equal.

The real point of all this is that optimal currency areas can exist where the factor mobility between the members of both labor and capital is great *and relatively costless,* but that one must be careful in drawing the lines. In particular, it is not obvious that the *national* unit should form the basis of a currency area in view of the possibility that nations may themselves be composed of inhomogeneous and poorly connected regions. For example,

a. While the United States may presently be a homogeneous area, it was not always so; indeed, substantial regional differences in wage rates and interest rates existed at least until 1914 in the United States.

b. Canada may consist of two separate areas, as recent political events have also suggested, with the area west of Quebec being enough like the western United States to suggest that a fixed exchange rate with the United States might improve the allocation of resources across the two areas. On the other hand, Quebec and the rest of eastern Canada might well have more options in its employment and inflation policy if it floated its exchange rate with western Canada and the United States.

c. The EEC has tried repeatedly to bring about a currency union or a common float, but the dissimilarity of the economies, coupled with lower-than-required mobility of capital and labor, has made it impossible to maintain any fixed internal rate so far. Indeed, both France and Italy may well themselves be presently sufficiently inhomogeneous to suggest that a regional reorientation of national boundaries in Europe might produce a better macroeconomic policy record, taking the EEC as a whole.

Of course, none of these conjectures makes any sense politically; what is suggested, though, is that a policy such as that of the EEC to try to introduce a common currency must be accompanied by a policy toward regions, in the sense of either explicitly moving resources or at least encouraging the movement of resources in order to put the currency area on a solid economic basis.

18.3 THE MONETARY MODEL OF INTERNATIONAL ADJUSTMENT

Let us assume a country called A, small enough that, like a competitive firm, it has no significant control over either the prices of commodities or the interest rate in the world as a whole. Assume, as well, that all goods are traded internationally. Under these conditions, says the *purchasing power parity* theory, the exchange rate between this nation and all other nations ($E_{W/A}$) will depend on the relative price levels in country A and the rest of the world; the relation quite simply is

$$E_{W/A} = f\left(\frac{P_W}{P_A}\right), \tag{18.1}$$

where W refers to the rest of the world. The exchange rate is expressed in a market basket of foreign currency units per unit of A's currency. The functional form is used in Equation (18.1) simply because we do not observe an equality in practice. Even if one accepts the purchasing power parity theory it is conceivable that transport costs, trade restrictions, and the like could prevent equality. Note, for later reference, that if the relation held exactly we could write

$$P_W = (E_{W/A})P_A, \tag{18.2}$$

where the world price level is seen as a weighted average of domestic prices, with the exchange rate terms providing the weights (we would sum separately over the P_A's and P_W's). This expression, then, defines the world price level (in a purchasing power parity system); its rate of change, consequently, is the *world rate of inflation*. This concept, which is a main prop in the recent monetary approach to the balance of payments links that newer theory to the older (Neoclassical) purchasing power parity theory. To see how Equation (18.1) might be determined suppose that for some reason (let us say a monetary expansion), the price level in the domestic economy (P_A) rises. In this event, A's goods are more expensive than W's; this, in turn, since by assumption the same products are available elsewhere at a lower price, will cause a reduction in the demand for A's currency (in foreign exchange markets) and a decrease in the exchange rate, as Figure 18.1 illustrates. In this event, the exchange rate is

Figure 18.1: The effect of inflation in country *A* on its exchange rate

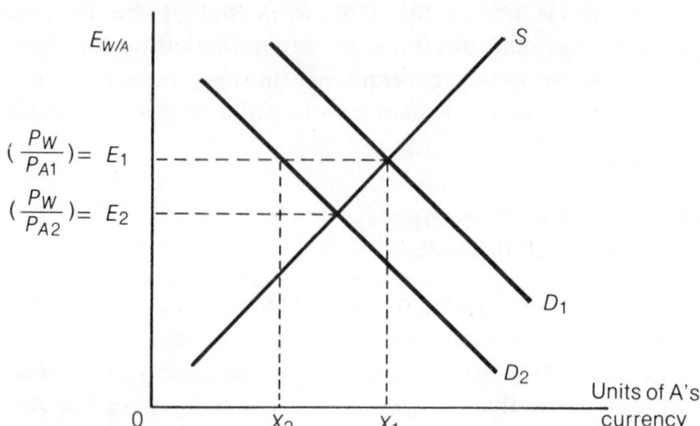

adjusted by international traders in a process we may legitimately call *arbitrage* (under our assumptions) since the traders are able to buy the goods wherever they are the cheapest. Indeed, the exchange rate moves until the prices of all internationally traded goods are the same across the world.[3] Note that country *A* can pursue any monetary policy it wants (can have any rate of inflation) but it will not sell any more (if it is a small country) since the exchange rate will move to insure that external purchasing power is unaffected. In this event, foreigners will not purchase any changed quantities of *A*'s goods, nor will *A*'s citizens (unless they are confused by the inflation rate in some way—that is, unless there is some money illusion); therefore, there are no obvious real effects of the inflationary policy (for example, no employment effects), except those that might occur in the transition period.[4]

The result just presented referred to a flexible-rate system; in a fixed-rate system we may assume the same causal sequence, but suppose in Figure 18.1 that instead of E_2 clearing the foreign exchange market, we have

[3] There is a debate about whether, in fact, this micro-economic proposition is valid. Irving B. Kravis and Robert E. Lipsey, in "Export Prices and the Transmission of Inflation," *American Economic Review* (February 1977) claim not. That is, they feel that internationally traded goods, after adjusting for the usual factors (tariffs, transport costs) do not meet this "law of one price". Of course, whether this is because purchasing power parity has failed or because the so-called world goods are really very specific to each country, would have to be verified before the theory would be considered damaged in any way. *Furthermore,* the statement in Equation (18.1) is a macro-concept and *could* stand without any proved micro-foundations, simply as a matter of (macro) adjustment to (macro) monetary pressures.

[4] Note the similarity between this argument and the *domestic* version described in Chapter 11. There we said that changes in the exogenous money supply had short-run (transitional) real effects but only price-level effects in the long run. The proposition here, of course, is really the same.

E_1, because of the desire of the exchange authorities of the world to stabilize their exchange rates. That is, let us assume that each of the other countries in the world, noticing its exchange rate appreciating, sells its currency (i.e., buys *A*'s currency) to private traders in order to keep their exchange rates at the old par value. To hold down the price of their currencies and to hold up the price of *A*'s currency, in this case, the authorities will have to buy $X_1 - X_2$ in country *A*'s currency units. Note that if all other countries make this adjustment, then *A* will not need to do anything to stabilize (this "*n*th country assumption" was used in Chapter 17 in our discussion of the balance of payments). Each of the rest-of-the-world economies, since it is buying *A*'s currency from (let us say) domestic sources, must put its own currency into circulation. The net effect is an expansion in monetary bases everywhere as the citizens of other countries acquire the *W* currency units that arose from the deficit of country *A*. These additions to foreign monetary bases will stimulate growth in foreign money stocks and in foreign price levels, unless an offsetting open market operation in the domestic money market occurs. Carrying out such an operation, of course, subordinates domestic monetary policy, in effect, to an external objective (exchange rate stabilization). If the monetary managers in all other countries do maintain their exchange rates with *A*, without domestic monetary restraint, then Equation (18.1) will be restored, in the only way it can be, with a rise of P_W. Thus, world reserves rise and inflation is exported from country *A* to the rest of the world since the international arbitrage over commodity prices must continue until Equation (18.1) holds.

We might, at this point, consider several reasons that the purchasing power parity theory might not always work perfectly as an explanation of exchange rates, even though the underlying theory is clearly a sensible one. One of these is that nonmarket price determination in certain industries subject to price discrimination might prevent prices from responding easily. Call this an international version of the "administered prices" doctrine we discussed in Chapter 9. Another is that monetary (exchange) authorities may pursue other internal policies, such as an unemployment policy, so that a short-run divergence from the purchasing power parity norm is observed; then, too, there may be restrictions on trade flows, such as tariffs or quotas, so that goods do not move quickly enough to effect a rapid arbitrage. Furthermore, not all goods are traded internationally (most services, for example, are not) and, one should add, domestic prices are sometimes slow to react because they are (possibly) "administered." Indeed, if all goods are traded internationally, then the purchasing power parity theory is essentially made into a tautology by the actions of arbitraging traders. Finally, we should point out, we have also abstracted from information costs and transactions costs and these, too, could prevent or delay the total equalization of exchange rates and relative price levels.

Our description so far has emphasized arbitrage-type goods flows; this, in turn, is considered by its opponents to be an uninteresting theory, since it seems to require that all goods be exchanged internationally and assumes away all frictions. Indeed, quite often the theory seems to have been put forward with no formal causal mechanism; what could be used to complete it, at least as the Neoclassical economists conceived of the theory, is reference to the behavior of the money stock. In particular, if two countries, *A* and *B*, are in an equilibrium trade position, then an increase in the quantity of money in *A* will (by the quantity theory of money) increase prices and, by the mechanism described above, produce the devaluation of *A*'s currency. Similarly, a decrease will produce the opposite effect.

The process just mentioned considered a devaluation in the exchange rate, which was itself produced by an inflation; the inflation, in turn, was created by a monetary injection. This seems a simple enough case, and it certainly has some direct policy implications, but it also raises another interesting question: How does a devaluation itself affect the balance of *payments* (and the price level)? To begin with, we clearly should look at a broader context than just the balance of trade; thus, consider the following definition of the balance of payments:

$$(X_g - M_g) + (X_s - M_s) + (X_m - M_m) \equiv 0. \qquad (18.3)$$

This relation argues that the sum of the balance of trade $(X_g - M_g)$, the balance of capital flows $(X_s - M_s)$, and the *flow* of money internationally $(X_m - M_m)$ must add up to zero in a correctly constructed balance of payments. *M*, more conventionally, would be the net flow of international reserves (called "money" here arbitrarily); if positive, then outflow exceeds inflow and a deficit in the balance of payments would be said to exist. Equation (18.3) is an identity, and so it appears to contain a redundant element (that is, if $X_g = M_g$ and $X_s = M_s$, then X_m must equal M_m). But Equation (18.3) is also a *flow* equation, in which the changes in a stock (the stock of money) are included. Thus, even if economic agents are satisfied with their goods flows and their capital flows and hence the balance of payments adds up, economic agents may not be satisfied with the *stock* of money they hold. To be in full equilibrium, both stock and flow equilibrium conditions must be met. Equation (18.3), in other words, is the correct equation; it is also the point of departure for the "monetary approach."

Let us reconsider the devaluation problem we tackled a few pages back. If the devaluation produces a trade surplus (without, for the moment, considering how the security flow will react), then, for Equation (18.3) to hold, $(X_m - M_m)$ must have a negative value—a negative value here corresponding to a money inflow. Then, *if the demand for money is stable* (that is, if it does not shift under these conditions to absorb the new funds), an excess supply of money will be induced by the devaluation.[5] This will, inevitably, lead to lower domestic interest rates (in the first instance) and higher prices, as the money works through the system (that is, through the credit and commodity markets). Note, especially, that by operation of purchasing power parity the positive effect of the devaluation on the trade balance (if, indeed, there were such) would tend to be reversed ("crowded out") as domestic prices rise. Of course, if the authorities "sterilized" the money inflow by selling securities in the domestic market, they could avoid these pressures, at the cost of higher interest rates, although in this case the capital flows ($X_s - M_s$) would tend to react in Equation (18.3). A small country, of course, faced with inexorable pressure and with some reluctance to issue new securities, may well run out of securities to sell. In the converse case, when a country has a persistent balance-of-payments deficit, it will eventually run out of reserves (unless, like the United States, it can find willing holders of its currency, at higher interest rates).

At this point, before expanding the Monetarist approach to its full potential, we should consider some problems that have been raised in connection with the simple model just described. For the first, we must note that the argument rests on the existence of a stable demand for money (i.e., a nonshifting demand for money), which should be taken, following our discussion in Part II, to include expectations of inflation since as long as the expectations are themselves correctly founded on the past behavior of the money stock, there is no reason for the demand for money itself to be unstable. The stability, though, is at least a partially open issue at present since evidence gathered from 1974 onward, even accounting for expectations, has produced some damaging evidence for the stability argument, in the sense of relatively large shifts of the function. For the second, we should note that the argument also links the monetary base to the money supply and then with prices in a direct (and no doubt Monetarist) way. This last, while useful in many ways, is not essential so long as the general pressure is in the direction indicated, as it probably is.

Let us, following the late Harry G. Johnson, summarize the main policy conclusions of the monetary approach to the balance of payments before turning to the case of the related world inflation rate and world money supply.[6] First, let us note that the users of the monetary approach are not interested in which goods are traded (if they are), since to a Monetarist, inflation is not described in terms of the specific goods for which a surplus occurs after the devaluation, but in terms of the quantity of money com-

[5] That is, ($X_m - M_m$) must be negative: money must be imported (into the monetary base).

[6] Harry G. Johnson, "The Monetary Approach to Balance of Payments Theory and Policy: Explanations and Policy Implications," *Economica* (August 1977).

pared to its demand. Second, we should note that the Monetarists are not interested in exports or imports, alone, but in the movement of goods and services *and* in capital flows. These points made, then, the Monetarist arguments imply the following (according to Johnson).

a. All balance-of-payments disequilibria are essentially monetary in origin in that money flows will tend to restore equilibrium unless the authorities use monetary policy to sterilize the impact of the underlying causal factor (and prolong the disequilibrium). The oil crisis, for example, need not produce a balance-of-payments deficit for oil-importing nations unless the countries involved use monetary flows (and the domestic money stock) to resist the monetary contraction. If this approach is taken, a devaluation will occur that will tend to restore the balance of payments equilibrium.

b. Balance-of-payments disequilibria are necessarily transitory, since a small country with a surplus will probably run out of domestic assets (as it sterilizes an inflow) and a country with a deficit will run out of foreign reserves, so that (at least in the latter case) a devaluation will have to occur to restore balance in the foreign payments accounts.

c. More provocatively, but logically enough, all balance-of-payments disequilibria could be handled (if so desired) by means of domestic monetary policy, *without requiring exchange rate changes*. This follows if one accepts point (1), since if the cause is monetary, then so, too, can the cure be. Furthermore, and this is why the terms are italicized above, it implies that the analysis applies for either a fixed-exchange-rate or a flexible-exchange-rate system.

d. The argument for preferring to use devaluation instead of domestic credit expansion to increase real income and employment, since both amount to the same thing as far as their external effects (and price-level effects) are concerned, is that one is easier to bring about than the other. This choice relies on political insights (such as those discussed in Chapter 11) as well as on the relative strength of price rigidity and money illusion in domestic markets as opposed to that in foreign (and foreign exchange) markets.

e. Again provocatively, import quotas, exchange controls, and the like—devices that are often used to attempt to influence the balance of payments—will improve the balance of payments only if they *increase* the demand for money. That is, if domestic prices are raised by such controls, some spending will be diverted to foreign goods; if the public holds larger cash balances, the spending will not happen. Put this way, it seems an unlikely scenario.

f. Finally, the Monetarists argue that a faster growth of real income may actually tend to improve a country's balance of payments (*given* the money stock) by increasing the demand for money. It is often thought that the money stock actually grows too rapidly to be absorbed (even though, in all probability, money is used by consumers more than in proportion to growth), so domestic inflation results. Recent examples of an increase in the demand for money may have occurred in Japan, Germany, and Switzerland (particularly Japan).

The foregoing is strong stuff for some and it has been met with less than full enthusiasm by non-Monetarists. Clearly many assumptions underlie this analysis (such as lack of price ridigity and lack of money illusion) and these certainly create one problem to consider. In addition, of course, we should recall the possibility that speculation in currencies could be destabilizing. Then, too, we have the problem that there are many trade restrictions and the like, possibly even frustrating the law of one price. Finally, and this is not a criticism of the approach, we should underscore the point that while a situation of balance-of-payments disequilibrium has a monetary *interpretation,* it need not have a monetary cause (except, perhaps, in the long run). We mentioned, indeed, that the energy crisis was a sufficient cause. The careful reader will note the formal analogy with the two stages of the *validation* argument for nonmonetary causes of inflation in a closed economy. In that case, the money market reacted immediately (to clear), and only if a constant (sterilized?) nominal interest rate was aimed at by the authorities did the situation get worse instead of better. But let us expand the argument to cover both monetary and fiscal policy and both domestic and international objectives before we close the cover on these policy issues.

18.4 MONETARY AND FISCAL POLICY IN THE WORLD ECONOMY

This section will end the discussion of monetary (and fiscal) policy by taking it up in the international context. There are two basic hypotheses. One, somewhat the more intriguing, is that the business cycle (and especially the cycle of prices) is really an international problem rather than a national one. We have already considered, in passing, the Monetarist argument that the dominant world power, the United States, has, because it decided to let the money stock grow too rapidly after the early 1960s, steadily exported inflation to the rest of the world. Given the fixed exchange-rate system until 1971, with gold and the dollar linked at an unrealistic price, other countries apparently preferred to accept the inflation, rather than allow their exchange rates to appreciate, although their abilities and desires to cope with the pressures clearly varied somewhat. Of course, the fixed system came under increasing pressure thereby, and ultimately it broke down; the ensuing period of semi-flexible rates, far from giving the world a chance to recover from inflation by means of sensible domestic policies (shielded by the market-determined exchange rate) actually saw a more rapid inflation. Basically, it has been argued, the world agricultural crisis, the emergence of the OPEC cartel, a decrease in general productivity, and a rise in unemployment (a politically sensitive issue) have led to the rise of aggressively expansionary domestic monetary policy, which has produced new records in peacetime inflation (in spite of the potential to do better because of the flexible exchange rates). We will look at some of the evidence, as we spin out the story in an international context, below.

The second major hypothesis of this section, and the last major theoretical topic of the book, concerns, basically, the effect of capital flows under fixed or flexible exchange-rate systems and the design of monetary and fiscal policy under these two exchange-rate regimes. If capital flows are considerable, we will see, then under a fixed-rate system, monetary policy is likely to be most useful in helping to stabilize the quantities in the exchange market (by means of its effect on domestic interest rates and thereby on capital flows). Fiscal policy (tax rate policy) would then work better on internal objectives. In a flexible-rate system, under these conditions, the situation is reversed, as we will see. These are preliminary conclusions in a way, and the real policy choice is a much more complicated one; indeed, much of the complication comes from expanding the theoretical design (and we will discuss this briefly), but some comes from the nature of the capital flows themselves. We will, accordingly, look at some data on financial capital flows with special reference to the Eurodollar market and to the arrival of international banks in the United States. We pick these aspects of capital movements, rather than the broader concept of the balance of payments, primarily because this is a book on money and banking and these are the main items of interest in that domain.

18.4.1 World prices, world interest rates, the recent world business cycle, and the world money stock

Let us first look at some data on the extent of the "real" business cycle in some recent years, in a number of major industrial countries; the data are in Table 18.1. We see, quite clearly, that 1974 was a worse year for all countries than was 1973 (let us call this evidence of existence of a world cycle) although not all countries went into recession (and Italy was close to its average for the period). Even so, one can notice considerable variation among the countries in earlier fast or slow years; for example in 1967 four of the seven countries slowed down (with West Germany having a recession), but three did not. Similarly, in 1964 six of the seven countries speeded up, but Italy slowed down. More recently (not in the table)

Canada did not recover from the 1974–75 recession nearly as rapidly as did the United States, and thus seems to have lost, for the time being, its coincident pattern with U.S. cycles. One might conclude that there appear to be world cyclical *pressures,* and even that these may be more likely to produce coincident cycles in a fixed-rate system (for reasons we have already given), but that single economies, *even in the fixed-rate system,* often went their own way. And, although we will not tabulate them here, the data on cycles are much more diverse if one moves away from the seven highly industrialized countries listed in Table 18.1

Table 18.1: Yearly percent change in real GNP in selected countries, 1961–1974

Year	*Canada*	*France*	*West Germany*	*Italy*	*Japan*	*United Kingdom*	*United States*
1961	2.8	5.6	5.4	8.3	14.4	3.5	1.9
1962	6.8	6.7	4.2	6.3	7.0	1.3	6.6
1963	5.2	5.4	3.4	5.4	10.4	4.3	4.0
1964	6.7	6.5	6.7	2.9	13.2	5.3	5.5
1965	6.7	4.5	5.6	3.6	5.1	2.4	6.3
1966	6.9	5.6	2.9	5.9	9.8	2.0	6.5
1967	3.3	4.9	−0.2	6.8	12.9	2.0	2.6
1968	5.8	4.6	7.3	6.4	13.4	3.2	4.7
1969	5.3	7.3	8.3	5.7	10.8	1.5	2.7
1970	2.5	5.8	5.8	4.8	10.9	2.0	−0.4
1971	5.8	5.3	3.0	1.6	7.3	2.1	3.3
1972	6.0	5.7	3.4	3.1	8.7	3.4	6.2
1973	6.9	5.8	5.3	5.9	10.2	6.0	5.9
1974	2.8	3.8	0.4	3.5	−1.8	−0.2	−2.1

Source: Norman S. Fieleke, "The Worldwide Inflation," *New England Economic Review* (May/June 1976), p. 7.

Turning to prices, we consider a more detailed breakdown of the recession of the 1970s for the same seven industrialized countries in Table 18.2; these data cover the period 1973–76 (you may also look back to Table 9.1 to see how the eight-year inflation rates (1953–77) coincided). The peak in the (unweighted) average for the seven countries came in the second quarter of 1974; this was, as well, a quarter in which three countries were in recession (the United States, Canada, and West Germany); indeed, by the end of the year all seven countries were in recession (the annual data in Table 18.1 do not pick this up),[7] although the rate of inflation had not abated much (and actually reached its peak in two cases). Again we note a strong similarity in inflation experience, with all of these countries experiencing sharp increases in their inflation rates, although the timing and,

[7] The real GNP figures (compounded annual rates of growth of GNP, as percentages) were −1.7, −12.9, −6.5, −9.4, +0.9, −5.9, and −6.8 for the same countries (in the same order as Table 18.1) in the fourth quarter of 1974.

Table 18.2: Inflation rates in seven industrialized countries, 1973–1976 (annual rates of change—2-quarter moving averages)

Year and quarter	*Canada*	*France*	*West Germany*	*Italy*	*Japan*	*United Kingdom*	*United States*	*(average)*
1973								
I	5.8	6.2	7.7	11.1	8.5	7.6	4.9	7.4
II	8.6	5.9	7.9	12.2	17.1	7.6	7.5	9.5
III................	10.6	9.2	5.8	10.7	17.7	9.2	8.7	10.3
IV................	9.6	10.8	6.0	10.0	15.6	10.9	9.2	10.3
1974								
I	8.8	13.5	9.1*	16.9	32.0	15.5	11.2	15.3
II	12.0	16.6*	8.2	22.5	32.8*	21.6*	12.0*	18.0
III................	13.3*	15.6	5.2	26.8	18.1	18.8	11.8	15.7
IV................	12.0	13.5	4.6	29.1*	17.1	15.5	12.3*	14.9
1975								
I	10.2	12.3	6.7	20.5	12.4	22.9	10.3	13.6
II	8.9	10.8	7.9	12.0	10.6	34.2*	7.2	13.1
III................	11.6	9.6	5.4	9.9	9.1	30.4	7.3	11.9
IV................	11.4	9.1	3.3	10.7	6.7	16.7	7.5	9.3
1976								
I	7.0	9.6	5.3	14.3	9.3	13.4	5.6	9.2
II	5.8	9.8	6.5	21.9	11.7	13.4	4.6	10.5

* Peaks in the rate of inflation (see text).

Source: Donald S. Kemp, "Economic Activity in Ten Major Industrial Countries: Late 1973 through Mid-1976," *Review, Federal Reserve Bank of St. Louis* (October 1976).

more noticeably, the extent varies considerably (not, however, on account of the real cycle itself, though), as a comparison with Table 18.1 reveals.

There are actually two Monetarist-oriented explanations for this pattern. One, already alluded to, refers to the policy spillover from the purely fixed rate system (which was finally abandoned in 1973). This view is that although the flexible system shielded countries from *automatic* monetary spillovers (letting exchange rates instead of balance-of-payments quantities do the adjusting) individual countries chose to deal with the slowing down of the world economy in real terms (following the energy and agricultural crises of the 1971–73 period) by aggressive monetary—and sometimes monetary-backed fiscal—policy. This produced the desired effect on real growth and employment, but also produced inflation (which intensified when the same economies actually did slow down in 1974.)[8] To see how this proposition might be justified, consider Table 18.3 on the behavior of the narrow money stock in these same seven countries. These data show peaks in the rate of growth of the money stock (marked with an asterisk), which invariably came earlier (by as much as seven quarters) than the peaks in the inflation rate (also marked with an asterisk in Table 18.2). Even the differences in timing in the various inflation rates can be explained to some extent in this fashion.

The second Monetarist hypothesis concentrates not on the individual country data—which rarely show such a clear pattern as we have just seen anyway and could be expected to show even less under flexible exchange rates when countries are free to follow divergent monetary policies—but on *world* prices and the *world* money stock (and *world* foreign exchange reserves). The process begins with the monetary base of an individual country, which would expand for a country gaining international reserves (whatever the exchange rate regime). Under the old fixed-rate system, before 1971–73, the demand for international reserves expanded steadily, while the supply apparently rose more slowly. The demand consisted of a private-sector component (used in the same way money is) and a public-sector component (with the latter used to insulate the domestic economy from foreign pressures). As the U.S. balance of payments gradually drifted into deficit, the United States found itself, in effect, filling the gap between the official demand and supply of convertible currencies. In 1971, then, the world woke up to an apparent "glut" of these dollar reserves, which forced the United States to attempt a devaluation; since then world reserves have continued to grow with the demand for them, with the United States (so far) standing ready with an elastic supply of dollars.

---

[8] Since $MV = Py$. Note that countries had more ability to do this after 1973, since, to the extent they did not pursue a fixed exchange rate, their domestic monetary policy was free to help stabilize domestic employment. The reason policy produced domestic inflation, of course, can be interpreted in terms of the expectations-augmented Phillips curve of Chapter 11.

Table 18.3: Rates of change of the money supply in seven industrialized countries, 1971–1976 (2-quarter moving averages)

Year and quarter	*Canada*	*France*	*West Germany*	*Italy*	*Japan*	*United Kingdom*	*United States*
1971							
III	17.3%	10.6%	16.2%	19.4%	34.6%	8.7%	8.7%
IV	16.6	10.7	11.6	19.0	30.2	18.0	4.7
1972							
I	14.2	11.8	11.2	17.4	18.7	19.7*	5.0
II.........	9.4	13.8	13.9	19.7	17.8	16.5	7.9
II.........	13.1	17.2*	16.7*	17.0	15.5	11.1	8.5
4	18.5*	16.4	15.0	19.8	30.2	12.6	8.9*
1973							
I	16.6	8.4	9.1	19.1	38.2*	9.2	8.4
II.........	13.7	9.6	2.9	20.7	28.6	12.0	7.1
III	13.8	9.2	−5.1	26.9*	21.5	5.5	6.1
IV	10.0	7.3	−1.1	21.1	11.9	3.1	5.4
1974							
I	9.4	14.6	7.2	16.5	11.7	3.5	5.7
II.........	15.8	18.5	8.5	14.3	15.1	−1.4	5.9
III	6.8	4.4	10.8	10.7	12.3	13.8	5.0
IV	−0.6	9.4	12.9	8.5	7.4	25.9	4.2
1975							
I	14.2	16.1	12.3	11.7	9.2	20.9	2.3
II.........	18.5	4.3	14.2	3.2	10.1	19.5	4.1
III	16.2	14.0	16.7	8.6	12.4	28.3	7.4
IV	25.3	22.6	18.9	20.0	11.9	19.4	4.8
1976							
I	12.5	21.4	13.3	—	16.1	13.1	2.5
II.........	−3.0	15.0	6.0	—	17.0	14.2	5.6

* Peaks in rate of growth of money stock (see text).
Source: Donald S. Kemp, "Economic Activity in Ten Major Industrial Countries: Late 1973 through Mid-1976," *Review, Federal Reserve Bank of St. Louis* (October 1976).

From this point of view individual countries have experienced their share of the world rate of inflation as world high-powered money has expanded.

To see some evidence in favor of this scenario, consider the picture in Figure 18.2 for world prices, the world money stock, and world reserves, from 1961 to 1974 (quarterly data to 1958 are also available in the same source). Here one sees a clear relation between the world money stock (a geometric average of national figures) and international reserves, especially under the fixed-rate system, until 1969. After 1969, world reserves take off for two years (perhaps making up for lost time) while the world money stock rose quite a bit less sharply. World consumer prices were pretty insensitive to these early developments, but they certainly shot up after 1972 (in response, the Monetarists would argue, to the increase in the world money stock).[9] The sequence is clearest when one looks at the

[9] Note the steady increase in the world money stock from 1969 to 1972.

Figure 18.2: The world inflation problem

Source: H. Robert Heller, "International Reserves and World-Wide Inflation," *International Monetary Fund Staff Papers* (March 1976), p. 86.

turning points; in particular, the peak in the rate of change in international reserves preceded the peak in the changes in the world money stock, which, in turn, preceded the peak in world inflation rates (which is, arbitrarily, at the end of the period).

We are not trying, here, to be fair to the various nonmonetary theories of these events, but we should note that the Keynesians have also produced explanations of them. We have mentioned the oil and grain crises of the early 1970s; these took the form of price rises in basic industries (what could be more basic than food and energy?), which were transmitted to prices in general by accommodating monetary changes. The behavior of exchange rates and international liquidity in this view are just further pressures that tended to be validated in this period.[10] Then, too, one could argue that a world-wide combination of rising union pressure, pressure on governments to employ macroeconomic policy to solve microeconomic employment problems, and political pressure on most major governments to redistribute income more evenly by means of tax and fiscal policy (and,

[10] The only problem is that most of the non–Monetarist causes are one-shot affairs that would tend to reverse themselves without a monetary validation *and that* would not be sustained unless a further (unnecessary) validation occurred. The price effect observed in Figure 18.2 is a sustained one.

as it turns out, by inflation) has tended to raise costs, reduce employment and, thereby, to turn on the validation mechanism, no doubt unwittingly. Some of these factors—particularly those that are "one shot" in nature, or the union pressure—do not seem to fit the experiences of the period very well, but, in any event, the total package certainly represents the view of a large part of the American population. The fact that it is held without a theory of monetary validation and the fact that the role of the explicit monetary policy we have seen—over and over again, in this book—is simply ignored, are certainly its chief problems. It may also, since we are speaking of the electorate, continue to dominate the "politically feasible" view of things for some time to come.[11]

Before we leave the area of "world this" and "world that" we ought to pause for a moment and draw out a little further an implication of the Monetarist–purchasing power parity approach with regard to the determination of exchange rates. Frequently, one hears concern expressed for the behavior of (e.g.) the exchange value of the U.S. dollar as if it were purely a trade-flow problem and could be dealt with by pumping up our exports or paring our imports (especially of oil). It is true, of course, that one can temporarily affect the situation by forcing up the prices of foreign goods (at the expense of a worsened allocation of resources). However, if the cause of the undesired change in the exchange rate is a relatively rapid domestic inflation, then the cure ought to be related to the cause of the inflation, and the exchange rate (which is, after all, merely a price reacting in the direction that clears the exchange market) should be left to its own devices. *If,* further, the monetary inflation hypothesis is correct, then the way to stop the decline of the dollar is to stop the relatively excessive inflation and not to prop up the dollar by policy means, unless that means either slowing down the domestic monetary expansion or speeding up foreign monetary expansion.

We should present some data on this issue, just to illustrate the potential of this monetary interpretation. Since 1971, the dollar/SDR rate has gradually turned "against" the United States, with a total rise of over 20 percent in the number of dollars an SDR unit could buy (it was $1.086 in 1971). The story since 1974 is told in the first column of Table 18.4. There we see that the United States did get a decrease in the $/SDR exchange rate in 1975 (note that decreases are "improvements" in the language of the exchange control authorities) out of the combination of a slowed inflation and a sharp recession (which helped the trade and current account balance) and a further increase in 1976 as the U.S. inflation rate fell even more than did the rates in other industrial countries. In 1977

[11] We should point out that the governments of some countries (notably the United Kingdom and Canada) seem convinced of the appropriateness of nonmonetary explanations. See the individual country papers in the volume edited by Lawrence B. Krause and Walter S. Salant (cited at the end of the chapter). The British changed their approach in 1979, as the result of Mrs. Thatcher's election.

Table 18.4: The dollar and inflation, 1974–1978

	U.S. exchange rates				*Inflation rates (percent per year)*					
	IMF (*$/SDR*)	*W. Germany* (*$/mark*)	*Switzerland* ($/franc)	*Japan* (*$/yen*)	*World*	*Indust. countries*	*U.S.*	*W. Germany*	*Switz.*	*Japan*
1974	1.224	.415	.394	.332	15.3	13.1	10.9	7.0	9.7	24.3
1975	1.171	.381	.382	.328	13.6	10.8	9.2	5.9	6.7	11.9
1976	1.162	.423	.408	.341	11.5	7.8	5.8	4.5	1.7	9.3
1977	1.215	.475	.500	.417	11.5	7.8	6.5	3.9	1.3	8.1
1978	1.303	.547	.617	.514	9.9	6.8	9.0	2.6	1.1	3.8

Source: *International Financial Statistics.*

and especially in 1978, when there was considerable concern about the "problem", the dollar declined again, *as the U.S. inflation rate started up again.* Indeed, in the first "year of disaster" (1978), the U.S. inflation rate was actually *above* that of the major industrial countries and going sharply in the opposite direction to that of its major trading partners. Of course, as the individual country figures in Table 18.4 indicate, the inflation-rate disparity—and, of course, the exchange-rate disparity—with the three countries most discussed in the newspapers was also in the direction that the "monetary approach" predicts. The combined policies of November 1, 1978 (discussed in Chapters 10 and 12), we might conclude, since they appear to have drastically affected the rate of growth of the money stock, may well produce the desired effect on the exchange rate (the *impact* effect was pronounced).[12] Of course, to a Monetarist this latter is merely incidental, and the real problem is to bring the rate of growth of the quantity of money into line with the (real) rate of growth of the economy, in which case the exchange rate will take care of itself, generally.

18.4.2 International capital flows and monetary (and fiscal) policy

Capital (both financial and real) has always flowed internationally—sometimes abundantly—and so has population, both, no doubt, primarily in pursuit of economic objectives. With regard to capital, of course, it is the lure of higher interest rates (or profit rates) that draws it abroad; indeed, if capital were perfectly mobile between industries and between nations, then any differences that would appear in national or regional interest rates, other than those associated with unique aspects of the local economy (such as the risk of default due to government policy), would tend to be eroded as capital sought out the highest return. This movement is presently a matter of degree, of course, and *nominal* interest rates differ markedly from country to country, and it is also a matter of some considerable policy importance. In particular, capital inflows can influence the effectiveness of domestic macroeconomic policy under some pretty general conditions. Let us begin with the policy debate before we turn briefly to some actual data.

Consider, first, the *fixed-rate system* (or, for that matter, the dirty float). Let us suppose that a country wishes to stabilize the domestic price level and the balance of payments (two objectives), and that to achieve these objectives it has two policy instruments, a monetary one and a fiscal one,

[12] The $/SDR rate was $1.281 in September and $1.349 in October. After the policy was laid on, in November, the rate was back to $1.272 (the August rate was $1.271). In January 1979 the rate was $1.285. All the policy did, then, was wipe out the 5.3 percent devaluation of the dollar in October. There was, as we have pointed out elsewhere, no immediate effect on inflation.

as well as a stock of foreign liquid reserves. Let us assume that its balance-of-payments objective is to protect its fixed exchange rate. For its monetary policy instrument, let us suppose the country attempts to control (or influence) the interest rate (by a suitable monetary injection) and for its fiscal policy, let us assume that it can generate a budgetary deficit or surplus (by a suitable tax rate change). Then, argues Robert A. Mundell,[13] under fixed exchange rates monetary policy ought to be aimed at the external objective (when a transitory deficit appears) and fiscal policy at the internal objective; indeed, he comments, fiscal policy would be impotent in attempting to reach the external objective, while monetary policy could not reach the internal objective. Consider the *IS-LM* diagram of Figure 18.3, in which we have the usual domestic *LM* curve; in addition,

Figure 18.3: *IS-LM* in the international case

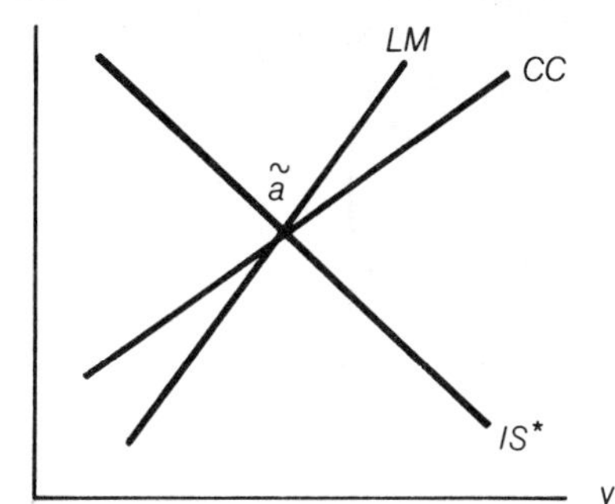

we have a foreign-trade-augmented *IS* curve—we have added $(X - M_I)$—designated *IS**, and a foreign exchange market equilibrium curve, here designated *CC*.

The new curve, *CC*, represents equilibrium in the balance of payments in that any imbalance in the current account (see Chapter 17) is offset by a corresponding movement of capital in the capital account, along this curve, so that no outflow of official liquid reserves is needed.[14] At higher levels of domestic income (y), the gap between exports and imports grows greater (let us assume we start with a negative gap), since the imports (the propensity to import being positive) will increase as income increases while exports do not (we hold foreign income constant, of course). To match the growing deficit on the trade account, capital must be drawn in by raising the interest rate; given imperfect capital mobility, this implies an upsloping *CC* schedule. We will assume the existence of an overall

[13] Robert A. Mundell, *International Economics* (New York: Macmillan, 1968).

[14] That is, the balance in the capital account is equal to, but of the opposite sign to, the balance in the current account.

equilibrium so that all three curves intersect at point $\tilde{a}$. This is the usual assumption.

To see what might happen to monetary policy in this case, consider Figure 18.4. Here let us suppose that the *LM* curve is shifted to the right

Figure 18.4: Monetary policy in a fixed-exchange-rate system

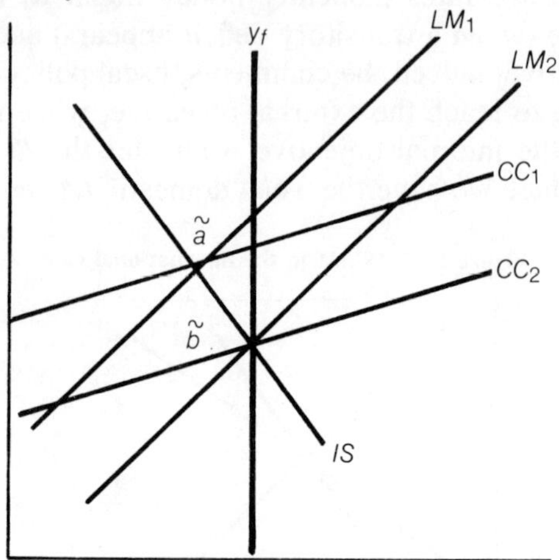

(by an increase in the domestic money supply), in order to lower the interest rate and produce a larger real income (let us say at y_f). We start at point $\tilde{a}$. At point $\tilde{b}$, the interest rate is well below the rate that would provide capital-account equilibrium; we can simplify by arguing that a balance-of-payments deficit (of a capital-account origin) ensues and reserves flow out of the country. This outflow, in turn, reduces the foreign component of the monetary base and shifts the *LM* curve back in the direction of point $\tilde{a}$. Indeed, the run-down of reserves and the simultaneous reduction of the money stock will continue until we reach point $\tilde{a}$, again. Thus, we have seen, monetary policy will not reach the internal objective; on the other hand, it can reach an external objective directly. To see this, just start with the *CC* curve at CC_2 and shift it to CC_1 (producing a balance-of-payments deficit at point $\tilde{b}$). In this instance, a policy-induced monetary contraction would quickly get us to point $\tilde{a}$. In any event, the persistent use of monetary policy to cure a domestic depression (in real income) can succeed only so long as adequate foreign reserves are available to meet the demand for them that results from pushing the domestic interest rate out of line with foreign interest rates.

Fiscal policy in the same context is a shift in the *IS* schedule to the right, as illustrated in Figure 18.5. Here, though, we will take up two

Figure 18.5: Fiscal policy in a fixed-exchange-rate system (Case I)

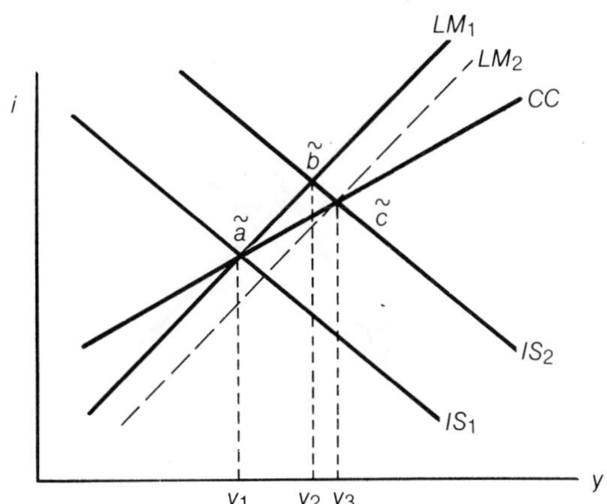

separate cases. For the first let us suppose that the *CC* curve is as drawn in Figure 18.5—that is, flatter than the *LM* curve. Let us suppose that the increased budget deficit (somehow) takes us to point $\tilde{b}$; at that point the interest rate is too high for external equilibrium (we are above the external payments equilibrium curve), and a capital inflow will result (attracted by the higher interest rate). This inflow will increase the monetary base and cause the *LM* curve to shift to the right; full equilibrium occurs at point $\tilde{c}$. Note, especially, that fiscal policy is even more effective than may have originally been intended (if we had considered only the internal objective of y_2) since we got a further injection of money via the capital account surplus. This is, incidentally, a counteraction to the simple interest-rate "crowding-out" involved in moving up the *LM* curve, although what might happen to price-level crowding-out here, as a result of the *further* monetary injection, should also be considered.

There is another possibility, though, and that is that the *CC* curve is more steeply sloped than the *LM* curve (actually, our monetary policy example could also have been reworked from this point of view). In this case refer to Figure 18.6. Here we can visualize the same fiscal policy, producing a disequilibrium at point $\tilde{b}$, in the foreign exchange market. But in this case, since we are below the *CC* curve, the interest rate is too low for external equilibrium and a capital *outflow* will result. This outflow will decrease the monetary base and hence the money supply, shifting the *LM* curve to the left and crowding out the fiscal policy. Between the two cases, then, the issue is clearly an empirical one: Does capital move relatively smoothly between nations, so that Figure 18.5 is the correct one (and fiscal policy is augmented by, in effect, adding a foreign sector to our

Figure 18.6: Fiscal policy in a fixed-exchange-rate system (Case II)

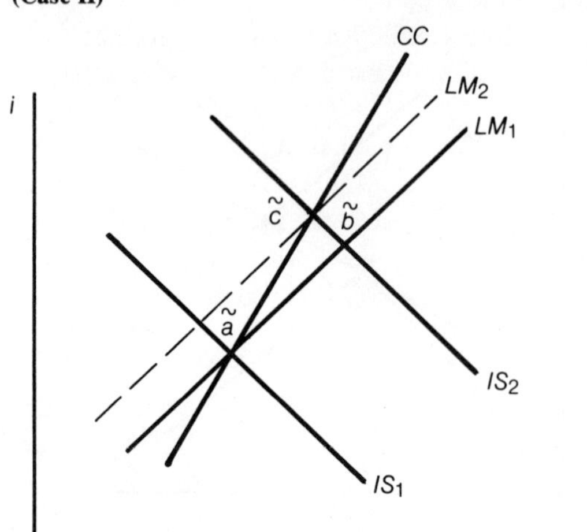

standard macro model), or is it sluggish, so that an additional crowding-out occurs to frustrate domestic fiscal policy? *Clearly,* these issues can be important, particularly to a country that is substantially "open". But the empirical issues have not been resolved (although the policies themselves are sometimes aggressively employed), so we will have to leave things at that.

The results with a *floating-rate regime* are broadly opposite to those just stated, although the external objective requires a new definition in view of the flexible exchange rate (indeed, why have any external objective at all?). Under the dirty float, of course, we still have an analysis similar to the fixed-rate system; with imperfect capital movements both fiscal and monetary policy then may have a role to play on domestic objectives. If a country does not attempt any sort of intervention and thus has no interest in the balance of payments, then the effects on the domestic economy make themselves felt through the exchange rate. Let us consider the case of perfect capital mobility first. For the fixed-exchange-rate system, to go backwards for a moment (in Figure 18.4), the balance of payments equilibrium curve (the *CC* curve) becomes perfectly horizontal if there is perfect capital mobility; in this case a balance-of-payments deficit probably can be immediately corrected by monetary policy, but because interest rates cannot move up at all, there is not even the temporary stimulus to the domestic economy shown in Figure 18.4. Indeed, a trade imbalance is corrected by a capital flow (or a monetary policy induces a trade imbalance, which in turn stimulates a capital flow), and this happens automatically. Domestic fiscal policy, though, is more effective in this case, as a glance at Figure 18.5, with a flat *CC* curve, would indicate, because the shift of the *IS* curve induced a shift in the *LM* curve (in effect), so that a *combined* monetary-fiscal policy was produced. The point is, of course, that interest-rate crowding-out will not occur if capital flows readily from abroad.

When we turn to the flexible system, though, monetary policy would be more effective domestically, in the event that interest rates cannot move. In particular, as Figure 18.7 demonstrates, a monetary expansion moves

Figure 18.7: Monetary policy under flexible exchange rates

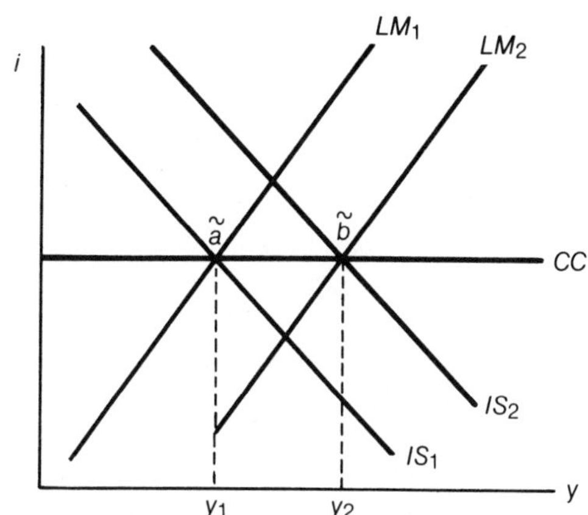

the *LM* curve to the right, and, when the fall in the exchange rate occurs, because of inflation for example, the *IS* curve also shifts to the right (if a trade surplus is stimulated by the fall in the exchange rate).[15] The reason, clearly, is that there is a trade account surplus generated by the fall in the exchange rate. Full equilibrium occurs at point $\tilde{b}$ in Figure 18.5, where monetary policy is shown to have its maximum impact on real income.[16] Note that there is no leftward shift of the *LM* curve to cancel this effect out, since the authorities do not deal in foreign exchange if a clean float rules (so that the monetary base is unchanged). Of course, foreigners now probably own more of the domestic money stock, but for the calculation of the monetary base it is irrelevant who owns the funds.

Fiscal policy, in the event of a flexible exchange rate, could be further hampered by an "exchange-rate crowding-out" effect. Consider, for ex-

[15] We should note that this is a long-run result. In the short run, if commodity demands do not respond quickly to the exchange-rate change, then the *IS* curve will not shift as much, and the effectiveness of monetary policy is less.

[16] This, too, is a domestic policy that has been augmented by the "anti–crowding-out" effect emanating in the foreign sector.

Figure 18.8: Fiscal policy under a flexible exchange rate

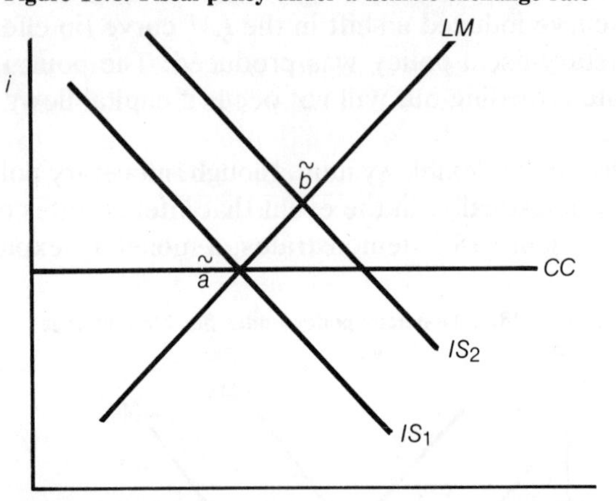

ample, the scenario in Figure 18.8, in which fiscal policy shifts the *IS* curve from IS_1 to IS_2; again we assume perfect capital mobility. With interest-rate crowding-out, we might go to point $\tilde{b}$, if domestic equilibrium were all that we had to consider. But at point $\tilde{b}$ we are above the *CC* curve, a position that is synonymous with a balance-of-payments surplus (the interest rate is too high for equilibrium, so funds will move toward the domestic economy). This will produce a rise in the exchange rate, which will, in turn, create a trade account deficit (X-M_I); this, in turn, will shift the *IS* curve downward, back toward IS_1.[17] Indeed, so long as we are above the *CC* curve, the exchange rate will rise and the *IS* curve will shift down; it must end up at point $\tilde{a}$, a position in which fiscal policy is seen to have had no effect. As before, this result occurs for any degree of capital mobility so long as the *CC* curve lies to the right of the *LM* curve.[18] Note that the steeper the *CC* curve, the less effective is monetary policy in the case of the flexible exchange rate.

18.4.3 Financial capital flows in practice: Some matters of interest to money and banking

All of these policy conclusions focus attention on actual international capital flows, and it would be interesting to see whether (and where) capital does flow freely enough to suggest that the United States ought to

[17] Again, this is a long-run result. In the short run the *IS* curve may not shift. In this event fiscal policy has a short-run effect that is crowded out in the long run. Note that the *LM* curve does not shift here because by freeing the exchange rate we make it unnecessary to consider any adjustment in the monetary base.

[18] If the *CC* curve coincides with the *LM* curve, though, then point $\tilde{b}$ is an equilibrium point and fiscal policy works. Furthermore, if the *CC* curve is perfectly vertical, and no capital flows across borders at all, then an expansionary fiscal policy will be associated with a trade deficit, the exchange rate will fall, and the *IS* curve will shift to the right further (increasing the deficit). This is an unstable result, though, and would have to break down somehow.

stick solely to monetary policy (and domestic objectives) in the new regime of floating exchange rates (that is to say, if we ever fully adopt that regime). To begin with, we should emphasize that the most interesting topic is the flow of short-term capital; we note, for example, that these flows (no doubt) brought down the fixed-rate system in the 1971–73 period. More generally, we have pointed out that in the face of contrasting capital flows, stimulated by monetary and fiscal policy, the GNP of a country could be expanded easily (if other countries cooperated) and a monetary-induced expansion could go on for a long time, but not forever, of course; furthermore, ever-improving capital flows (a flatter and flatter *CC* curve) will make it more and more difficult to use domestic monetary policy to control the domestic level of employment (in a fixed-rate system). We mentioned one piece of evidence in connection with the 1969 credit crunch in Chapter 13: Eurodollars flowed back to the United States, so commercial banks were able to avoid (at a cost) curtailing loans even though their total deposits fell. This Eurodollar market is a sign of the times and Euro-funds are presently a large and fluid source of capital, and, in addition, are probably an interest-sensitive one.

A Eurodollar is a short-term security (e.g., a time deposit) or checking account in a European (or overseas American) bank that is denominated in dollars rather than in the local currency. They arose, in the 1960s, primarily as a way to hedge against devaluation of the local currency, but they now exist for a large variety of purposes, one of which is their ready availability for currency speculation and another, of course, is that they fit nicely into diversified international portfolios (the three-month Eurodollar rate is consistently above the three-month Treasury bill rate). The chief suppliers are any business firms (chiefly multinational) or banks that wish to hold dollars (and, generally have acquired them in their ordinary business operations abroad). There are other popular Euro-currencies than the dollar (the yen and the mark). Note that to the extent a multinational firm holds a Eurodollar deposit, it would not need to hold a dollar deposit in an American bank (*in* the United States). Thus growth of the Euro-currency system is to some extent a *substitute* for the domestic demand for money. There may come a day, indeed, when we will need to include Eurodollars in an expanded measure of the money stock (M_{37}?).

Trying to get an accurate estimate of the size of the Eurodollar market is not easy, although certain data are published by the Bank of England. Thus, in Table 18.5 we show a summary of *all* the foreign-currency liabilities of as many of the banks in the world as possible, as collected by the Bank for International Settlements (BIS). Here it is clear that the market, at a reported \$686 billion,[19] is truly enormous, with the United

[19] We should point out that there is quite possibly a serious amount of double-counting in these figures. It has been said that as much as 50 percent of this total is merely "inter-bank" deposits that arise because of the needs of *clearing* the financial flows in international markets and are, consequently, not *held* for the reasons mentioned above.

Table 18.5: Euro-currency liabilities of the BIS countries and certain other U.S. banks, March 31, 1978 ($ billions)

BIS countries			
Austria	6,996	BIS countries	416,453
Belgium/Luxembourg	29,335	Other Western Europe	27,198
Canada	13,479	Other developed	2,905
Denmark	3,294	Eastern Europe	8,028
France	36,580	Caribbean area	54,015
Italy	11,180	Latin America	36,578
Japan	8,766	Middle East	76,754
Netherlands	24,819	Other Africa	10,820
Ireland	1,895	Other Asia	39,867
Sweden	2,998	International institutions	6,845
Switzerland	80,492	Unallocated	6,455
United Kingdom	86,200		
United States	85,063		
West Germany	25,356		
Total	416,453	World total	685,918

Source: *Quarterly Bulletin,* Bank of England.

States, United Kingdom, Switzerland, and the OPEC countries (Middle East) being dominant users and, clearly, having the potential to undermine any monetary policy that produces a higher interest rate. Note, too, that this market has grown very rapidly in recent years.

This is not the place to go into a full-scale investigation of the extent of capital flows, but we underscore one fundamental fact, that investment and portfolios have gone increasingly international in recent years, so that differences in world interest rates have come steadily down, at least in the main financial centers. In December 1969, for example, when we had a fixed-rate system, the following interest rates could be observed (these rates were at their closest, probably, for that year):

Eurodollars, London	10.06%
Treasury bills, New York	8.30%

In November 1977, one noticed,[20]

Eurodollar deposits in London	7.00%
U.S. Treasury bill rate	6.21%
Euro sterling deposits	7.37%

This is very impressionistic evidence, of course, and a lot more of this sort could be gathered, but the general impression one gets—and one sees no real dispute in the literature on this point—is that capital flows are steadily increasing and that world interest rates are very gradually drawing together, with the only major exceptions seeming to be provided by the

[20] All quotations are taken from the Bank of England's *Quarterly Bulletin.*

rather uneven application of monetary policy in certain countries, such as the United States.

These currency matters aside, let us turn to one final aspect of the international financial markets, the spread of international banking, particularly as it affects the United States (and American monetary policy). The first thing we should note is that American banks, especially the "top 20" have long been aggressive internationally and have operated virtually everywhere in the world, often under conditions very unlike those in the United States. This is another rapidly growing aspect of American banking, and Table 18.6 shows the situation through 1978. We see, indeed,

Table 18.6: Foreign branches of U.S. banks, 1975–1978 ($ billions)

	1975	*1976*	*1977*	*1978*
World total liabilities	176.5	219.4	258.9	305.8
United Kingdom	74.9	81.5	90.9	106.6
Bahamas and Caymans	45.2	66.8	79.0	91.1
Others	56.4	71.2	89.0	108.1

Source: *Federal Reserve Bulletin.*

nearly a 25 percent yearly growth rate, which is well above the growth rate for these (or any other) banks in the United States. The effect on the mobility of funds is obvious (as is the potential for undermining monetary policy in foreign countries).

But for some reason Americans are more interested in the "encroachments" of foreign banks in the United States than in our encroachments abroad. Here we run into an interesting problem, because while these banks operate in all of the traditional areas of American banking, data for them have not been available (until recently). The main reason, of course—and this is the source of much of the concern, obviously—is that these banks are not members of the Federal Reserve System *nor are they insured* by the FDIC. Nevertheless, some numbers are available, and they indicate that the total assets of foreign banks reached $100 billion by mid-1978, up from less than $20 billion in 1970. The concerns expressed, mostly from official sources, have covered regulation (mostly), safety, and (even) monetary control, and the result was the International Banking Act (IBA) of September 17, 1978.

Prior to the IBA foreign banks operated only under state charters and managed, sometimes, to sidestep regulations prohibiting branching across state lines. The IBA requires, in contrast, that they establish a "home state" and do no branching (although they may operate other types of financial services) across state lines; in return, foreign banks may now acquire federal charters (and Federal Reserve membership), although one does not expect a rush in this direction.[21] On the regulatory front, the Federal Reserve now sets reserve requirements for foreign banks whose parent organization has more than $1 billion in total world assets, and most do. Furthermore, examination is conducted by the same agencies that investigate U.S. banks—the Federal Reserve, the comptroller of the currency, the FDIC, and state banking agencies—depending on the foreign bank's charter, but with one other wrinkle: the Federal Reserve can examine *any* foreign bank. On the question of the activities of foreign banks, such as the acquisition of "investment banking" interests (which are prohibited to U.S. banks) and the use of the holding company to control a market or to expand into nonbanking activities, the new legislation puts the foreign banks on the same footing as American banks. Finally, the act makes FDIC insurance voluntary for foreign banks unless they have retail deposits (deposits less than $100,000). If they do, they must join the FDIC scheme.

In a nutshell, foreign banks, at one stroke of the presidential pen, have become, if anything, more strictly regulated than domestic banks, at least in principle. While most of these regulations are designed to increase safety rather than to frustrate the workings of the competitive system, one has to wonder why these banks grew so rapidly in the first place. At least one thought is that they were able to offer more competitive terms to their customers since they were unencumbered by the complex American regulations. Finally, at least as it now stands, American banks with branches abroad are considerably less regulated by the agencies of foreign governments than the converse. This lack of reciprocity was directly debated by Congress in the course of the discussions on the IBA but was rejected in favor of safety and the national interest. As we have pointed out in Chapter 3 with regard to domestic banks the trade-off between safety and what we might call the "competitive edge" was once again resolved in favor of the former, as one might have expected.

18.5 STUDY QUESTIONS

Essay questions

1. Try, once again, to answer Essay question 3 in Section 9.6.

2. If capital movements are instantaneous, in response to changes in interest rates, could a country maintain its identity in terms of fiscal and monetary policy? Explain carefully. Does this imply that it is friction in the economic process that keeps countries apart? Explain the nature of the frictions that currently operate. Is it sensible to keep the frictions alive

---

[21] The law now requires that a *majority* of the board of directors of a federally chartered bank be U.S. citizens. The previous law required that all directors be U.S. citizens.

in order to help the effectiveness of monetary policy domestically, or is this doing things the wrong way around?

True-false discussion questions

These statements are meant to be somewhat ambiguous, and to provoke discussion thereby.

1. If the fixed-rate system were actually to work as it is supposed to, no monetary instruments would be used up in defending exchange rates.

2. The greater the importance of goods that are not traded internationally, the less the validity of the purchasing power parity doctrine.

3. When a country facing a balance of payments deficit raises its domestic interest rates at full employment, it will experience cost inflation as the main economic pressure to restore equilibrium to its balance of payments.

4. If accelerated inflation goes along with a balance of payments surplus in a particular country, then the causes of the inflation are probably nonmonetary.

5. The faster a country grows, the less likely it is to have a balance of payments deficit, since it is able to meet domestic demands by its rapidly expanding domestic output.

6. In 1978, the rate of growth of the money stock in much of Western Europe increased dramatically. Since this was caused by an increased demand for money fueled by sharply faster growth, it could not be expected to affect these countries' exchange rates with the United States.

7. A doubling of the world's stock of gold overnight would tend to lead to doubled world prices, under present international arrangements.

8. Recent evidence suggests quite strongly that countries with relatively rapid inflation tend to have unemployment and balance-of-payments problems at the same time.

18.6 FURTHER READING

Coppock, D. J. "Some Thoughts on the Monetary Approach to Balance of Payments Theory." *Manchester School* (September 1978).

Frenkel, Jacob A., and Harry G. Johnson, eds. *The Economics of Exchange Rates.* Reading, Mass: Addison-Wesley Publishing Company, 1978.

Humphrey, Thomas M. "The Monetary Approach to Exchange Rates: Its Historical Evolution and Role in Policy Debates." *Economic Review, Federal Reserve Bank of Richmond* (July/August 1978).

Johnson, Harry G. "The Monetary Approach to Balance of Payments Theory and Policy: Explanations and Policy Implications." *Economica* (August 1977).

Krause, Lawrence B., and Walter S. Salant, eds. *Worldwide Inflation*. Washington: The Brookings Institution, 1977.

McKenzie, George W. *The Economics of the Euro-Currency System*. New York: Halstead Press, 1976.

Segula, John P. "A Summary of the International Banking Act of 1978." *Economic Review, Federal Reserve Bank of Richmond* (January/February 1979).

Index

N

This book has been set VIP in 10 and 9 point Times Roman, leaded 2 points. Part numbers and titles are 36 point Times Roman Bold. Chapter numbers are 64 point Times Roman and chapter titles are 20 point Times Roman Bold. The size of the type page is 27 by 46 picas.